FAMILIES IN MOTION

Dedicated to our teachers of the past,
our students of the present,
and the family scientists of the future.

FAMILIES IN MOTION

DYNAMICS IN DIVERSE CONTEXTS

CLARA GERHARDT

Samford University

Los Angeles | London | New Delhi
Singapore | Washington DC | Melbourne

FOR INFORMATION:

SAGE Publications, Inc.
2455 Teller Road
Thousand Oaks, California 91320
E-mail: order@sagepub.com

SAGE Publications Ltd.
1 Oliver's Yard
55 City Road
London EC1Y 1SP
United Kingdom

SAGE Publications India Pvt. Ltd.
B 1/I 1 Mohan Cooperative Industrial Area
Mathura Road, New Delhi 110 044
India

SAGE Publications Asia-Pacific Pte. Ltd.
18 Cross Street #10-10/11/12
China Square Central
Singapore 048423

Acquisitions Editor: Joshua Perigo
Production Editor: Laureen Gleason
Copy Editor: Karen E. Taylor
Typesetter: C&M Digitals (P) Ltd.
Proofreader: Theresa Kay
Indexer: Karen Wiley
Interior Illustrator and Cover Concept: Claire Gottschalk
Cover Designer: Gail Buschman
Marketing Manager: Zina Craft

Printed in the United States of America

Library of Congress Cataloging-in-Publication Data

Names: Gerhardt, Clara, author.

Title: Families in motion: dynamics in diverse contexts / Clara Gerhardt, Samford University.

Description: Thousand Oaks: SAGE, [2020] | Includes bibliographical references and index. | Summary: "Dynamics of the family is a complex set of interrelated cogs; like the dials and wheels within a sophisticated timepiece. Families in Motion is a comprehensive and contextual view into how all of the dials and wheels of that complex set work together. Ultimately, it explores the complexities of the family regarding roles, functions, development, and issues that occur. Grounded in theory, author Clara Gerhardt examines the ever-changing movement, communication and conditions on both the family as a system and on each individual member within the system. This text is also aligned with the requirements of the Certified Family Life Educator (CFLE) set of standards. Covering approaches from the theoretical to the therapeutic, Families in Motion will support students in extending their cultural competence while understanding families and the members within those families with greater confidence."— Provided by publisher.

Identifiers: LCCN 2019028905 | ISBN 9781544329208 (paperback) | ISBN 9781544329185 (epub) | ISBN 9781544329215 (PDF)

Subjects: LCSH: Families.

Classification: LCC HQ503 .G456 2020 | DDC 306.85—dc23
LC record available at https://lccn.loc.gov/2019028905

This book is printed on acid-free paper.

SFI label applies to text stock

19 20 21 22 23 10 9 8 7 6 5 4 3 2 1

Brief Contents

Detailed Contents

15 Dynamics of Happiness 335

Preface

FROM THE HEAD AND FROM THE HEART

Families in Motion was written from the head and from the heart. It targets the inner workings of the family: those cognitive technicalities encased in a pulsing heart. Day-to-day life demands the reverse; we tend to reveal our somewhat technical and restrained casing first, while inside our heart makes us uniquely us.

In this book on dynamics, I tried to go to the sacred space we co-visit as therapists. It includes a poetic narrative, threaded throughout the text in the form of authentic insights. These reflections are gifts of trust that allow us a glimpse behind the veil.

The theories are dropped like breadcrumbs at the end of each chapter. They provide structure to the maze, a reminder of how to find our way home. They represent how things have been explained by others. We will find theories that align with us, while others do not speak our language.

There was method in the layout:

- Part I sets the loom, provides the structure to weave the story.
- Part II looks at how we communicate to tell that story.
- Part III leads us past some of the landmarks of the human journey, including pain and joy.

All family journeys are travels to unknown destinations. Because we are embedded within our families, this family journey also becomes our personal journey. In circular fashion, we influence the dynamic of our families, and we in turn will be shaped by our families.

And it will address both our heads and our hearts.

Acknowledgments

Books are born in quiet places. During the creation of this manuscript, I lived at the corner of Hope and Despair, that strange intersection of confidence and vulnerability. My deepest gratitude goes to my family, friends, and colleagues who sheltered me during the vulnerable stages, and who boosted my confidence when I needed hope.

This book is in response to my students, who asked for readable, real-life textbooks, where the knowledge is accessible and understandable. That also leads us close to the hybrid ground where scholarly and popular approaches intersect. I have tried to honor both by providing a relatively formal framework but embellishing it with real-life stories. To all the brave authors of authentic insights, you have my deep-felt appreciation for your courage and your willingness to let us eavesdrop on your conversations. You provided the congruent narrative.

Those closest and dearest to me: thank you for creating the space and facilitating the solitude to transform thousands of words into keystrokes. I value your attention as I bounced ideas off you, and am grateful for endless cups of tea and emotional sustenance. Specific acknowledgment goes to Claire Gottschalk for your artistic eye and renderings, including the concept of the technical heart featured on the book cover. You translate my ideas into visuals in a way only you can. I also thank Emmett Burton for exploring exciting cover concepts and typography—your creativity is much appreciated; Anton Bosch and Makiwa Mutomba for generously sharing their artwork, which was used in several chapters; Edward Gottschalk, for introducing me to the wizardry of the dictated word; and both Edward and Paul Gerhardt for various acts of computer genius. Nicole Smith was the research assistant and counselor everyone covets, with wisdom beyond her years. Thank you for tipping the scales toward Hope again and again. Jo King, my cherished colleague and friend since my student years, dissolved my writer's block in Kununurra, Western Australia. Thanks also go to my oldest friend and loyal buddy Kurt Buss, for a second generation friendship spanning an entire lifespan; to Deborah Burks, Irva Hayward, and Christina Ochsenbauer, inspiring role models and friends; and my colleagues, especially Kristie Chandler, Jonathan Davis, Celeste Hill, Rachel Fitzpatrick, and David Shipley. The book is also in memory of Dan Sandifer-Stech, with gratitude. My fellow therapists Dale Wisely, Bart Grooms, Matt Bunt, Steve Sweatt, and others not identified by name remind me why we chose this profession.

A delegation representing academic expertise at its best guided me with wisdom, compassion, and experience. I thank the following colleagues for their professional reviews, which steered me away from the cliffs, and toward the safer pastures of creativity. They include

Kerry Arnold, *Community College of Philadelphia*

Harriet Bachner, *Pittsburg State University*

Rhonda R. Buckley, *Texas Woman's University*

Jennifer George, *University of Georgia*

Brian Gillis, *Auburn University*

Nicholas Koberstein, *Keuka College*

Julie Ann Liefeld, *Southern Connecticut State University*

Laura Nathans, *Penn State Scranton*

Teresa Sabourin, *University of Cincinnati*

Margaret Vaughan, *University of Massachusetts, Boston*

Meeshay Williams-Wheeler, *North Carolina Agricultural and Technical State University*

My family of origin contributed to the impetus to reflect about family dynamics; after all, these are the places where we love deeply but are also privy to a spectrum of other emotions, not all of them comfortable. My siblings Hanna, Frans, and Martin know where and why some of this material was conceived. I write in loving memory of my mother Anna Alida and my younger brother Willem. Other family members to single out are Erika, Andrew and Christi, David and Tatum, Claire and Edward, Paul and Jenine, Clara W. and Otto W., and the inspiring next generation, residing all across the globe.

My gratitude goes also to the SAGE dream-team of editors and editorial assistants, especially Laureen Gleason, Karen Taylor, and others not mentioned by name, who turn ideas into real books. I am especially grateful to Joshua Perigo for his vision, and for making that first phone call that got us talking.

Last, I thank my inner circle: my husband Michael, our children, their spouses, and our grandchildren. You are the ones who have allowed me to be within this intricate web of our personal family dynamic—the only place I can and want to be.

About the Author

Clara Gerhardt, MBA, PhD, is a licensed clinical psychologist and a licensed marriage and family therapist. She received extensive international training as a systemic family therapist. From the early 1980s onward, she sat in the front rows as the great family therapy movement was unfolding. She attended workshops by many of the pioneers in the field, a veritable who's who of family therapy that is slowly receding into history as these pioneers are passing on. This provided her with a unique and personal perspective of the early and by now historic days of family therapy.

Her many publications include *Parent-Child Relations: An Introduction to Parenting* (2019), now in its 10th edition. She contributed a number of entries to the *Encyclopedia of Family Studies* (2016) and the *Encyclopedia of Marriage* (2020). She is contributing editor to a publication of the National Council on Family Relations (NCFR) and writes a regular column, *Perspectives*. She published over a hundred articles related to popular psychology. Her academic home is at Samford University, where she is professor and past chair in Human Development and Family Science. Her favorite courses to teach are "Counseling Foundations," "Parenting," and "Multicultural Perspectives." Dr. G.—as her students call her—has presented at about 200 conferences on six continents. She is the product of three continents and speaks five languages fluently. She is exceptionally well traveled, but the best journeys are those leading home to her family.

PART

I

The Dynamic Family System

Families are the sheltered place where we seek comfort, support, and renewal and where we anchor our hopes, dreams, and disappointments. Families are in a constant state of flux; they have a life of their own, like the ebb and flow of the ocean. It is this changing nature that provides them with their uniqueness. Families are dynamic in that they have their own energy, which propels them toward constant evolvement. As individuals, we contribute to the larger truth of the family, and families in turn elaborate the story of our personal lives.

The dynamic of the family explains why the whole is greater than the sum of its parts. If a core family consists of half a dozen or so members and we add up those individual life stories, that family's story will be so much greater and more complex than the tales of those separate lives. The narratives of family members intertwine to create a greater entity: the dynamic family. Those families combined add to the fabric of a society; in fact, families are the building blocks of a society.

The family that contains these stories adds its own dimensions and influences. Our families can propel us to greater heights, or lure us to the dark. Families influence our future by providing a model on which we base our own families of making. Families have a history, and the customs and traditions that come with that past provide continuity for its members.

There is no escaping the dynamics of our families; typically we are born or welcomed into a specific family, and this unit provides the background music for our lives. Families continue across time. They existed before we joined them, and they will continue long after we have departed. They provide that thread of continuity around which we can weave the stories of our lives.

> "In each family a story is playing itself out, and each family's story embodies its hope and despair."
>
> **Augustus Napier (b. 1938),**
> family therapist, from *The Fragile Bond*

CHAPTER 1

Family Dynamics

SETTING FAMILIES IN MOTION

Learning Outcomes

After studying this chapter, you should be able to

1. Define *family dynamics* and describe the implications of dynamics.
2. Illustrate the interrelationship between human *lifespan development* and family dynamics.
3. Justify the relevance of studying family dynamics. Explain the scope of the *family sciences* in various professional contexts.
4. Analyze the different ways of defining *family*.
5. Compare and contrast the definitions of *family* and *family households* by the United States Census with how the family is generally defined in the family sciences.
6. Consider the *diverse* expressions of families in terms of form and function.
7. Describe the *characteristics* of a well-functioning family.
8. Explain how and why a family functions as a *system*.
9. Describe the *functions* of the family.
10. Summarize how *theories*, *psychoanalysis*, and *psychodynamics* relate in a familial context.

Setting Families in Motion

Family dynamics concern the highly personal workings within families. These can be expressed in direct and indirect ways, in an overt or a covert manner. Dynamics are about the effects and outcomes of behavior: what it sets in motion. Family dynamics have to do with the inner mechanisms of a family group. Families can have their own language, their unique ways of communicating. Families contain guidelines and expectations.

Family dynamics represent an extra dimension pertaining to the family. It is like a collection of force fields, whose influences wash over us to become noticeable in our daily lives.

The dynamics of families are about the processes that make families the way they are: what makes them tick. Families follow their own rules, while also complying with certain external demands. They are embedded in a larger society and in a culture. They are influenced by their members, but in turn they influence all those individuals claiming that particular family as their own.

Families are also the place to shelter, celebrate, mourn, grow, and renew. The family unit can provide security and a sense of belonging, but if it fails in its tasks, it leaves individuals stranded. By and large, well functioning families exert their own magic and hold uncountable rewards for those privileged enough to be a part of them.

> **"If the family were fruit, it would be an orange, a circle of sections,**
>
> **Held together but separable—each segment distinct."**
>
> Letty Cottin Pogrebin (b. 1939),
> American journalist and writer, from *Family Politics*

Family Dynamics: Meaning

Dynamics is about *motion*. It is the opposite of being static or still. Most formal definitions include references to "forces" or "changes," including those properties within a system or process that *initiate change*, that *stimulate growth* and development. The definitions allude to patterns and processes that herald change, allow for growth, and signal activity and movement. Al Ubaidi (2017) offers the following definition and implications:

> A family dynamic is the scheme of family members' relations and interactions including many prerequisite elements (family arrangements, hierarchies, rules, and patterns of family interactions). Each family is unique in its characteristics; having several helpful and unhelpful dynamics. Family dynamics will ultimately influence the way young people view themselves/others and the world. It will also impact their relationships/behaviors and their future wellbeing.

The everyday use of the word *dynamic* calls up lively and vital associations. For instance, if we refer to a *dynamic personality*, it tends to imply someone who radiates life and energy; we can expect somebody who is interesting, enthusiastic, maybe excitable, and possibly a little unpredictable. If music is described as being dynamic, it tells us that it will be the opposite of soothing; it will probably contain volume changes and be upbeat and energizing.

Dynamics represent the forces that can shape interactions within a family; usually a specific dynamic may underlie a series of transactions (Britton, 2016). The word *psychodynamic* contains two components, namely, *psyche*, pertaining to the soul or spirit, or the inner workings of the mind as the meaning has evolved in the context of psychology, as well as the word *dynamic*, implying a vital and changing nature. In its Greek origins, the word *dynamic* implies strong, powerful, and energetic attributes. It could then imply that forces combine, "sometimes smoothly but sometimes in opposition, to create *continual motion* and change" (Forsyth, 2019, p. 18; italics added).

In a psychodynamic context, as it is generally understood, the term *dynamics* can imply a searching for the hidden meaning of the behavior and thus an explanation of the behavior. It is an attempt at explaining the underlying motivation or reason for behavior. It can presume that actions may have a repetitive component, if a similar underlying dynamic persists. Hence, searching for the patterns that might be occurring within individuals and families may facilitate an understanding of the reasons underlying certain behaviors and interactions. The word *psychodynamic* was originally used in a psychoanalytic context, but it has taken on a more general and relaxed meaning (Gabbard, 2017, p. 2). Often, it is replaced with the more abbreviated concept of "dynamics."

In social contexts such as family systems, *family dynamics* is used to denote those aspects that change or progress, those places where movement and growth occur. It can imply a sense of transformation or motion. Additionally, as implied by the concept of psychodynamics, investigating family dynamics can be the process of searching for and uncovering the emotional motivations and possible hidden psychological reasons for behavior.

Change is also involved if we consider the bidirectional influence between families and individual family members. Our self-concept is supported by our family; its members are the people close to us, involved in the formation of the complexity of our identity. What we think about ourselves is, in part, the product of the reflection we see in our family's eyes. Our families turn us into the people we become, and we in turn influence and shape our families. It truly is a bidirectional achievement: "We create our families just as we are created by these families" (Galvin, Braithwaite, & Bylund, 2014, p. 2).

The title of this book highlights the movement and motivation implied in the term *dynamics*: *Families in Motion: Dynamics in Diverse Contexts*.

FOCUS POINT

Families are units in constant motion—growing and changing as demands inside and outside the system influence the whole. Family dynamics deal with the inner workings and behavior of the family, the ways culture and society affect it, and how its members influence each other. Family dynamics represent the movement and growth that occurs as family systems adapt and change, both in relation to the larger system around them and to the intimate system within the family itself.

Definition: In social contexts such as family systems, the word *dynamics* is used to denote those aspects that change or progress, those places where movement and growth occur.

The word *psychodynamics* can mean the process of searching for and uncovering the emotional motivations and possible psychological reasons for behavior. Psychodynamics can imply the emotional motivations and psychological reasons for behavior.

Authentic Insight

Family Dynamics: All Work Is Family Work

"How did you do that?" is a common refrain for me in a family therapy session, as I try to understand the interactions families are sharing with me. To me, the question speaks to the core of family dynamics. Family dynamics is about *how* things happen in families, not necessarily why they happen, which separates the focus of family dynamics from the main emphasis in psychology. Family dynamics (from a family systems perspective) emphasizes a sequence of behaviors—what happened first, then what happened, and then what followed. . . .

Family dynamics is the complement to the static or structural component of a family.

When I think of family dynamics, I remember a pair of engineering courses I took at Georgia Tech. The first course was Statics, describing the ways that forces interact in objects at rest. We practiced understanding the forces inherent in bridges, walls, and other objects that aren't supposed to move. Then, and only then, could we understand the next course: Dynamics, where those objects were moving and the force equations become more complex.

For much of human history, family dynamics were the context of human development, because all work was family work.

Jonathan Davis, PhD, is a professor of human development and family science and a licensed marriage and family therapist.

Lifespan Development and Family Dynamics

Human lifespan development is about how individuals change over the course of their *individual* lives, their journey from conception to death. **Family dynamics** is also about constant change—that of the family within which individual lives are embedded. They are inextricably linked; they complement each other like dancers in a well-choreographed routine. The changes that occur within the family over the lifespan of that family unit are also referred to as **family life course development** (White, Klein, & Todd, 2014).

This book closely references human lifespan development by placing it within the context of family dynamics.

Looking Back and Looking Forward

Families hold up the mirror to what happens in a society and in turn they are a reflection of that society's hopes and aspirations. The children of a society may seem voiceless, but their fate typically speaks loudest. What happens to the youngest ones is the report card reflecting the grades we, as a society, can hope to earn in terms of family welfare, public policy, and family life education. Families are central to communities, and to societies. They influence the culture, as well as the larger context within which they are embedded (Bigner & Gerhardt, 2019).

Families reflect the values, strengths, and shortcomings of that society. When societies are under attack, that destruction enters the family and affects all the members, all the way down to the youngest and most vulnerable ones. On the other hand, when families thrive, they create productive, rewarding, and nurturing communities.

If we can find the *how* and *why* of these dynamic interactions, it leads us down the path of understanding, explaining, and possibly therapeutically intervening in the course that families take. What adds to the complexity is that participants of any dynamic system are often unaware of the reasons for their actions and sometimes even of the presence of these actions. A mother may be unaware that she is being overcontrolling toward her teenage daughter, yet this dynamic interaction tells us about the relationship and the potential challenges of the relationship. The pattern evolving between them may, in turn, guide us toward a suggested intervention to facilitate more positive outcomes.

Dynamic Interrelationships

The dynamic interplay between various changing factors in a family system is like a chain of domino blocks. Bump over the first one and it exerts a consecutive motion. This rippling that extends ever outward has also been compared to the effects of a pebble hitting water; the ripples extend in ever-growing circles long after the stone penetrated the surface. For a family member caught in the middle, the forces may seem overwhelming.

Dynamic interactions are interrelated. If one person in the system has outbursts of rage or has anger control issues, it will cause the others to walk on eggshells, trying to avoid setting off the ripple effect that occurs when the angry behavior is triggered, even inadvertently. Anticipating, managing, and controlling emotions through appropriate emotional regulation can be addressed with a cognitive behavioral approach (Meichenbaum, 2017).

In short, dynamics are concerned with what makes the system *tick*; what effects these unique workings elicit; and, if we are helping professionals and family scientists, how we can examine these complex interactions so that family members can use the insight and understanding to their own best advantage.

FOCUS POINT

Human lifespan development and family dynamics have an intricate link: both describe constant change. Human lifespan development looks at how individuals grow and change over time from conception to death. Family dynamics deal with the continuous movement (or dynamics) of the family. Individual lives are embedded in the context of their families.

Why Study Family Dynamics?

Dynamic transitions. Family dynamics as a field of study has the power to highlight the constructive, neutral, or even destructive forces in the lives of families and their members. For professionals working with families, an understanding of family dynamics holds a key toward explaining and understanding certain behaviors, which in turn can be important in guiding families toward optimal outcomes. Family dynamics also addresses the transitions that occur between persons and within the systems in which they are embedded.

The study of family dynamics is rewarded by gaining better insight into the mechanics of a particular family system or of many family systems in general. This perception in turn allows for information concerning what we can expect in typical family life and what constitutes family efficacy (Kao & Caldwell, 2017). It also enhances interventions such as family and related therapy, and it can aid better outcomes for the future, by informing public policy decisions, for example. Undoubtedly there are a host of other applications, but in essence the ethical study of families is to gain understanding and to support optimal outcomes. This can be achieved through a variety of professions in numerous contexts and applications.

Ancestry and identity. Because all of us can claim some family and ancestral background through our genetic makeup, it may be safe to say that no person is an island. The current interest in ancestry and DNA testing speaks to the connections we may seek out with our own past, as it can influence our present identity (Bennett, 2015; Bottero, 2015). Ancestral and family connections can be found somewhere, even if the direct connections were severed. In our histories, biological parents made it possible for our births to occur, despite the variations on the theme of parenthood that are possible.

Family scientists. The helping professionals directly concerned with the family and family well-being are often collectively called **family scientists**. As a group, these professionals can include family life educators, social workers, psychologists, counselors, marriage and family therapists, members of multi-professional medical teams, clergy, and experts providing spiritual counsel (We Are Family Science, n.d.). Indirectly a host of professions can be influenced by the needs and functions of families; architects and town planners focus on housing developments with the needs of families in mind, industrial designers may try to meet the needs of various family members through the design of products, social policy makers try to improve legal outcomes affecting families. Economists and those marketing products also benefit from insight into what families need to support optimal functioning. Legal professionals focusing on family law can become the mouthpiece for legal rights. These mentioned professions represent the tip of the iceberg.

FOCUS POINT

Family scientists and helping professionals concerned with the well-being of families come from many disciplines. Focusing on families, these professionals have the power to support optimal outcomes. Being well versed in family dynamics is valuable to those working with individual families or trying to influence public policy decisions.

Defining Families

The extent to which a society commits to supporting individual families as well as parenthood reflects the investment that group is willing to make toward the next generation and toward family resilience. Changing gender roles has meant discussions about equal pay for equal work, parental leave for both parents (not only the mother), free and compulsory schooling for all, support for families who are raising a child with special needs, and more. In short, appropriate public policy can provide the safety net that strengthens families and guides them toward greater resilience. The entire society benefits from these investments, as they strengthen the very fiber that makes up a given society; this support strengthens families and their futures.

Objective and subjective definitions. Families can be defined and described in objective as well as subjective ways.

- *Objective* definitions may focus on blood and marital connections or on the sharing of resources and domiciles.
- *Subjective* definitions may allow for how a person feels about someone being part of the family. For instance, in an amicable divorce, the two spouses may continue to refer to each other as family, especially if children are involved. If the separation was painful with many negative consequences, either partner may deny being a family member of someone with whom they no longer want to associate (Amato, 2014). This also explains why those persons to whom we feel exceptionally close may become "families of choice."

In the older objective definitions, the focus was on biological ties through kinship or marriage, legal connections, and persons living together in a consistent manner, while probably also supporting each other (Galvin, Braithwaite, & Bylund, 2014, p. 4). These same authors comment:

> Today, the family may be viewed more broadly as a group of people with a past history, a present reality, and a future expectation of interconnected mutually influencing relationships. Members often, but not necessarily, are bound together by heredity, legal marital ties, adoption, or committed voluntary ties. (Galvin, Braithwaite, & Bylund, 2014, p. 4)

Other subjective dimensions of family ties may be represented by who is in contact with whom, who talks to whom, who provides support or help, or who is available as a potential backup (Amato, 2014).

FOCUS POINT

The extent to which a society commits to supporting individual families as well as parenthood reflects the investment that group is willing to make toward the next generation and toward family resilience. Families can be defined and described in objective as well as subjective ways. *Objective* definitions may focus on blood and marital connections or on the sharing of resources and domiciles. *Subjective* definitions may allow for how a person feels about someone being part of the family. Other subjective dimensions of family ties may be represented by who is in contact with whom, who talks to whom, or who provides support.

"Family dynamics is the complement to the static or structural component of a family."

Jonathan Davis, PhD, LMFT

Census Definitions

One of the purposes of the U.S. Census is to capture population numbers and various demographics at a given point in time; in the United States, that time is typically once per decade. The Census is a mechanism to count or record all the persons in the United States and gain greater insight into selected demographics. These goals influence how units such as families, family groups, and family households are defined. Importantly, the census application of the term *family* can have wider and different applications, affecting how the family is defined in everyday, legal, and other scholarly contexts. As a census term, it is intended to capture the numbers of and related information about groups of people as they typically reside in one dwelling place at the time the information is captured. The intent is to count or record each person only once and to avoid duplication. The current definitions provided by the United States Census Bureau (2019) and applicable to the 2020 Census are as follows:

> **Family.** A family is a group of two people or more (one of whom is the householder) related by birth, marriage, or adoption and residing together; all such people (including related subfamily members) are considered as members of one family.
>
> **Family group.** A family group is any two or more people (not necessarily including a householder) residing together, and related by birth, marriage, or adoption. A household may be composed of one such group, more than one, or none at all. The count of family groups includes family households, related subfamilies, and unrelated subfamilies.
>
> **Family household.** A family household is a household maintained by a householder who is in a family . . . and includes any unrelated people . . . who may be residing there. The number of family households is equal to the number of families. The count of family household members differs from the count of family members, however, in that the family household members include all people living in the household, whereas family members include only the householder and his/her relatives.

The geography of housing. The census instructions between 1860 and 1940 showed gradual shifts. The Industrial Revolution caused families to move and reconfigure. World War I fell into that period and had far-reaching effects on family composition in tragic as well as unforeseen ways. There was an emphasis on space, on the geography of housing. In 1860, the important theme was largely who was under the same roof. The example was of the widow looking after herself versus a large group living together with one lead provider. In both instances, they were counted in the Census as one family (Pemberton, 2015).

By 1870, the overriding concern was who shared meals, who sat at the same table. Similarly, the phrase "separation from bed and board" gained popularity as divorce represented social stigma. This variation represents a legal separation, but technically the couple remained married to accommodate religious persuasions.

Location. Interestingly, the 1920 census definition of the family had a different emphasis, namely more on the *location* where a group of people shared living quarters. In the future, this location-based definition of the family would inform our understanding of the family household. At the time, it expanded the definition of the family to include those persons living together in a hotel or institution; for census recording purposes, they were counted as a family. In 1930, the census instructions distinguished between a *household* and *family* and clarified that they were interested in documenting the details of groups of people sharing living arrangements at the given time of the census record. For the purposes of the 1930 Census persons living together need not be related by blood or marriage. What allowed them to be counted as a family unit was the fact that they shared a household in the same living quarters. This distinction between a household and a family became even more pronounced in the 1960 Census in which a household is described as those persons who share sleeping and meal arrangements. These persons could also represent several generations living under the same roof (Pemberton, 2015).

Similarities. The aspects that have remained the same across the decades are that families are defined by who should be included in a household and the manner in which they are related. The shifts in emphasis fluctuated over the years but interestingly seem to have gone almost full circle. The views prior to 1930 are more in line with our current definitions of what comprises a household. In short, then, the current definition focuses on all those persons related to the householder, whether by birth, marriage, or adoption (Pemberton, 2015).

FOCUS POINT

One of the purposes of the U.S. Census is to capture population numbers and various demographics at a given point in time. It is a mechanism to count or record persons and gain greater insight into selected demographics. These goals influence how units such as families, family groups, and family households are defined. Importantly, the census application of the term *family* can have wider and different applications, affecting how the family is defined in everyday, legal, and other scholarly contexts. According to the U.S. Census, the definition of the family has been fairly consistent since 1930: a family consists of members of a household related by blood, marriage, or adoption.

SCHEDULE I.—Free Inhabitants in District No. 2 in the County of Fayette of Kentucky enumerated by me, on the 7th day of Augt 1850. Jno. M. Monroe Ass't Marshal.

Dwelling-houses numbered in the order of visitation.	Families numbered in the order of visitation.	The Name of every Person whose usual place of abode on the first day of June, 1850, was in this family.	Age.	Sex.	Color, (White, black, or mulatto.)	Profession, Occupation, or Trade of each Male Person over 15 years of age.	Value of Real Estate owned.	Place of Birth. Naming the State, Territory, or Country.	Married within the year.	Attended School within the year.	Persons over 20 y'rs of age who cannot read & write.	Whether deaf and dumb, blind, insane, idiotic, pauper, or convict.
1	2	3	4	5	6	7	8	9	10	11	12	13
		Nancy Wheatley	59	F				Maryland				
		Walter S. Wheatley	17	M		Printer		Kentucky				
408	429	John McCracken	41	M		Farmer	8,000	Ireland				
		Emily McCracken	54	F				Ireland				
		Frederic Myers	35	M		Gardener		Germany				
409	430	C. McFarland	44	M		None		Massachusetts				
		T. J. Moore	29	M		None		Maryland				
411	431	Augustus Mosebach	24	M		Baker		Germany				
		Charles Kanz	35	M		Baker		Germany				
		James Hanna	40	M		None		Ireland				
411	432	Henry Clay	73	M		Statesman	50,000	Virginia				

This image from the 1850 Census reveals diversity concerning countries of origin. Families have been consistently defined by persons included in a household and by the manner in which they are related. The last entry shown here, referring to Henry Clay, is of interest, as he was an eminent statesman and the size of his property was significant.

Source: United States Census Bureau, 2018.

Finally, here is a definition of the family by Galvin, Braithwaite, and Bylund (2014), which is relevant to family scientists and which differs from the typical census definitions:

> [Families are . . .] networks of people who share their lives over long periods of time bound by ties of marriage, blood, law, or commitment, legal or otherwise, who consider themselves as family and who share a significant history and anticipated future of functioning as a family. (p. 8)

Diverse Families

Diversity. Families display diversity in form and in function. In post-traditional societies, persons can join families through various avenues, most importantly by having relationships with someone already in a family. Families through marriage, adoption, by choice: a number of diverse alternatives lead to membership (Garbarino, 2017). As families have evolved and changed in form and function, there is more flexibility concerning what denotes a family and who can claim membership. In older literature and books focusing on the sociocultural history of families, these units were typically defined by focusing on the conjugal and nuclear aspects of the family (Akamatsu, Crowther, Hobfoll, & Stephens, 1992/2016; Hareven, 1999).

> History provides no support for the notion that all families are created equal in any specific time and place. Rather, history highlights the social construction of family forms and the privileges that particular kinds of families confer. (Coontz, 2000, p. 286)

Flexible configurations. In the United States, the traditional nuclear family has been in flux. Families no longer necessarily consist of a father and mother and their offspring. Households could be headed by single parents, same sex parents, or grandparents, who can step in to fulfill intergenerational parenting roles. Families can shape themselves into as many guises as are comfortable and desirable for the participants. Additionally, we can have a **family of choice**; for instance, in domestic unions we may treat a certain group of very close friends as if they were family, and, for all practical reasons, they may take on the function of traditional family members. Geographic location, bloodlines, marital status: all these things that were important identifiers of traditional families have morphed to allow for more flexible configurations. Two developments that have contributed considerably to this flexibility and that have far-reaching effects are shifting and evolving gender roles and same sex marital unions and related partnership rights.

Family responsibilities. Defining families by their responsibilities may also bring concerns, as not all families meet the same expectations in terms of roles and responsibilities. Single parents may raise their children in a family environment, but this may exclude the other biological parent. Families can be blended, and children can be welcomed through fostering as well as adoption. Some families adopt grown up members so that they can legally express their sense of familial responsibility, and because with legal adoptions come legal rights and responsibilities.

Location. Families do not all live in one place, even though they describe themselves as a family. The breadwinner spouse may be traveling many days of the year; the college-aged kids may have left the home for a distant campus. Some couples choose to be in long-distance relationships with the hope of a reunion when the economics and the logistics of their partnership allow this. In more recent times, the variations for marriage partnerships have expanded.

> The concept of family is imbued with symbolic meaning and lived experiences. And whatever its form, families provide the earliest types of nurturance, protection, and socialization for its members. Families provide the initial foundation for entering into community and societal relations, and they reflect meanings, trends, and conflicts in specific cultures. (Trask, 2010, p. 22)

Partnerships and commitments. According to the Pew Research Center (2015) concerning social and demographic trends, cohabiting parents and single parents are frequently occurring family forms (see also Geiger & Livingston, 2019). When various configurations collaborate to parent children, some of the parties involved may be coparenting. The family may go through transitions and change its composition during various stages of the family lifespan.

Divorce, remarriage, and cohabitation have added considerable diversity to family forms. Even in those families headed by two parents, a number of changes are apparent. In many of these families, both parents work outside the home, and children are participating in a variety of caretaking options. According to the Pew Research Center, almost a third of children under the age of 18 are living in single-parent households, while one in five children live with single moms (Livingston, 2018, April). These living arrangements can add a variety of stressors in that the lead parent does not have easily accessible backup. This, in turn, can make caregiving responsibilities very challenging, occasionally leading to burnout and despair for the parent in charge. If grandparents are available, they may absorb some of these stresses. In some circumstances, partnership insecurity and partnership interruptions can contribute to the dynamics of the family as experienced by the children in that household. With the feminization of poverty, single mothers are more likely to suffer financial hardship as opposed to their male counterparts (Abercrombie & Hastings, 2016).

Children. The research on families also indicates that the current norm of children per family unit is smaller, and this phenomenon is sometimes referred to as "shrinking family size." Having fewer children can be attributed to women's increased educational attainment and related labor force participation. The age of entering marriage has also increased with partners being older at the time of their first marriages (United States Census, 2017). Researchers have found that parents are often older and in possession of more education by the time they welcome their first child. Mothers, in particular, have greater access to higher education than in previous decades, and this is especially so in westernized countries.

Vocation. The better educated the mother is, the more likely she has a vocational skill set that is desirable and will beckon her into the labor force. Mothers have become lead breadwinners, and fathers, in turn, have been open to the prospect of being the lead parent or the more accessible parent when it comes to rearing children. As women's roles have changed, men's roles have also changed. In post-millennial relationships, greater sharing of all tasks is occurring, be they related to paid work or to the home (Lewis & Sussman, 1986). The financial realities of dual-income parents are distinct. When both parents are gainfully employed, the median income for the family tends to be almost double that of families with a single breadwinner.

In a summary report on some of the major demographic trends shaping the United States and the world, several pertain to families (Geiger & Livingston, 2019):

- Millennials are currently the largest segment of the adult population in the United States and outnumber the baby boomers.
- The changing American family means that children per household are becoming fewer with almost a third of childless adults stating that they are unlikely to have offspring. The trend for being older when a first child is born is continuing. The number of stay-at-home parents today is similar to what it was 25 years ago, namely close to 1:5 (Livingston, 2018, September).
- The immigrant share of the U.S. population is the highest in over a century, accompanied by cultural diversity.

Contemporary families. Plurality in family forms means that there is great variety, influenced by numerous factors including culture, geographical location, and environmental resources, to mention a few. In short, then, to quote family scientist Bahira Sherif Trask (2010),

> Around the globe, virtually, every Western and non-Western society identifies some form of family as part of its basic foundation. Cross-culturally, members of contemporary families are engaged with each other in various forms of material, economic, emotional, and ideational exchange. (p. 21)

When families function well, they are impressive, with almost magical qualities and capabilities. They nurture and sustain us; they are the core of humankind.

Characteristics of Families

A number of important characteristics and functions of families are summed up by Galvin, Braithwaite, and Bylund (2014, pp. 3–4). Loosely, these consist of the following:

- *Unique and individual.* There is no one way of seeing the family and no one way of being a family. Families are unique and individual, just like the family members who make up that particular family.
- *Reflect culture.* Because families are unique, they form their own identities, rules, rituals, ways of communicating, family culture, and more. Families also reflect the greater culture within which they are embedded.
- *Shared values.* Because the family functions as a unit, it creates its own family culture and shared worldviews. Importantly, families tend to share values. It is one of the parenting functions within the family context to impart those values, guidelines, and ethics to the children in that family.
- *Intergenerational and bidirectional.* Families can consist of several generations that exert bidirectional influences.
- *Investment.* Families invest in their unit and in the individuals within that unit by spending time, allocating resources, and displaying loyalty.
- *Developmental challenges.* Families respond to developmental challenges, which also prevent them from becoming static.
- *Individuality and identity.* Families can find very individual ways of communicating, and this process is bidirectional in that the communication contributes to the identity of the family. In turn, that family identity rubs off on the family members.
- *Communication.* Communication serves to construct as well as reflect family relationships (Galvin, Braithwaite, & Bylund, 2014, p. 3). Because family members spend so much time with each other, they use and understand communication shortcuts and idiosyncrasies that may elude an outsider.
- *Ever changing and vital.* Families are an ever-changing work of art, vital to society.

FOCUS POINT

Families can be defined in several ways. As society and social policies shift, so does the definition of the family. Traditionally, families have been identified by bloodline and marital connections. The forms and functions of families have morphed to include more flexible configurations, including intimate and personalized definitions. Defining families by their responsibilities may bring concerns, as not all families meet the same expectations in terms of roles and responsibilities. Divorce, remarriage, and cohabitation have added considerable diversity to family forms. Plurality in family forms means that there is great variety, influenced by numerous factors including culture, geographical location, and environmental resources, to mention a few.

GLOBAL GLIMPSE

THE FATHER OF A NATION: NELSON MANDELA

Interrelated dynamic forces. Consider the childhood and upbringing of the world leader and Nobel recipient Nelson Mandela (1918–2013). So many factors in his early childhood were influential during his formative years, including his cultural context and the nature of his immediate and extended family structure. As a person, he was grounded, unpretentious, and humble. This was his philosophy concerning leadership:

> It is better to lead from behind and to put others in front, especially when you celebrate victory when nice things occur. You take the front line when there is danger. Then people will appreciate your leadership. (Kruse, 2012)

When Nelson Mandela (1918–2013) reminisced about his own childhood in the hills of Qunu in the Transkei, he mentioned the role of the extended family; his cousins were as close to him as siblings.

Source: Kishyr Ramdial via Flickr, Creative Commons Attribution 2.0 Generic.

His social context influenced the person he became. When Mandela reminisced about his early years in the hills of Qunu in the Transkei, he described a childhood close to nature, with opportunities to explore and build skills:

> We lived in a less grand style in Qunu, but it was in that village near Umtata that I spent some of the happiest years of my boyhood. . . . It was in the fields that learned how to knock birds out of the sky with a slingshot, to gather wild honey and fruits and edible roots, to drink warm, sweet milk straight from the udder of a cow, to swim in the cold, clear streams, and to catch fish with twine and sharpened bits of wire. (Mandela, 1994, pp. 7–9)

His family represented the customs of a close-knit rural community. He mentioned his family of origin and the role of the extended family, which had duties like immediate family. For instance, his cousins were as close to him as siblings. In his autobiography *The Long Walk to Freedom* (1994) he describes this family arrangement, which may be hard to replicate in present times:

> My mother presided over three huts at Qunu which, as I remember, were always filled with babies and children of my relations. In fact, I hardly recall any occasion as a child when I was alone. In African culture, the sons and daughters of one's aunts and uncles are considered brothers and sisters, not cousins. (Mandela, 1994, p. 8)

Nelson Mandela left an enormous legacy, and he is credited for the peaceful transition in South Africa. His upbringing provided him with a deep understanding of his people, who lovingly called him the father of a nation.

The Family as a System

Families function as if they have their own identity, and in many ways they do. Families are characterized by unique ways of doing things. They can have their own secret codes, their own expectations, their own way of communicating; and the family members usually know these rules and expectations. Families do not demand an entrance fee to join them; there is no qualification, no hidden password. Typically, we enter a family rather serendipitously; we are born or welcomed into a family and the commitment is supposed to be for life.

Interrelatedness. When a family functions as a system, the members of that system influence and feel for each other. If one family member faces difficulties, the others may react in support and sympathize. If a child faces serious illness and requires extended treatments, the rest of the family is affected by that situation, and effects extend to the marital relationship of the parents and how the siblings interact, for example. Who plays what role can be part of the unwritten dynamic of that family system. In short, when we think of individual family members, we have to include the various circles of influence within which each person is embedded in the context of a family system.

Intergenerational composition. The beauty of families is that they are intergenerational, and typically there is great solidarity among members. Different age groups are represented, belonging to various lifespan stages. The young can learn from the older members, who in turn can be inspired by their more youthful counterparts. There is a constant give and take, which enriches the entire system.

Solidarity. A family can be defined by the bonds between its members, and these are diverse, ranging from the conventional to the unconventional. Members depend on each other; they are interdependent. Families are also described by what their function is intended to be. Traditionally, family members are loyal to each other and provide the ideal place to have and to raise offspring (Hareven, 1999). A family provides the commitment and the protection that is necessary for this lifelong commitment. It is the shelter of choice for all the lifespan changes members anticipate, a place that accommodates the frailties of the young, the old, and the infirm. It is also the venue that celebrates lifespan passages and provides the cultural rituals to do so. In these many ways, the family can impart resilience to its members (Walsh, 2016).

Family lifespan. The family as a unit or a system can follow its own predictable stages in family life. If the family is seen as an independently functioning unit whose members are interdependent, then it follows that the family can progress through predictable stages and may be confronted with challenges faced by families everywhere. There is a universality about families, even though each unit is unique. The lifespan stages of a family can denote the typical challenges faced by families at certain points in their development. For instance, a young family may be wrapped up in the demands of childcare for very young children, while the lead breadwinners of that family are also trying to establish careers and their own home base. A family in its midlife may have to deal with launching teenagers, while worrying about the health and care of elderly parents.

One of the prime roles of the well-functioning family is to nurture its members, sheltering them within the structure of that particular family unit. This protection and care will, in turn, give the members resilience to deal with obstacles. The family of origin will also provide us with an example of how we would like our own families to look, or what we would *not* like to perpetuate in our own homes.

"It has been a long road for us . . . to reach an understanding of just this phenomenon—the sense of the whole, the family system."

Augustus Napier (b. 1938), family therapist, from *The Family Crucible*

FOCUS POINT

A well-functioning family nurtures and shelters its members. When a family functions as a system, the members of that system influence and feel for each other; there is interrelatedness. The family has numerous unique characteristics that contribute to its identity. It functions as an independent system characterized by diversity in form and function. Membership is intergenerational. Members display solidarity and interdependence. Numerous interacting factors influence family dynamics.

Authentic Insight

The Gravity of Family Interactions

I grew up in rural Arkansas and, as a child, I had a conversation with the father of one of my friends. Ray was a plumber. I was fascinated by his work. All the pipes and tubes and blowtorches! One day, I said to Ray, "You have to be really smart to be a plumber." I will have to paraphrase Ray's response. "You don't have to be that smart," he said and went on to tell me that you mostly just have to know that waste products run downhill.

As metaphors go, this is not a bad one to represent a key aspect of family psychology, one that is so often present in the work of counselors and therapists and that has informed my work as a child and adolescent psychologist. In families, toxic material can flow from parents, who are at a higher level, down to the children, who are at a lower level.

Adults tower above children literally and figuratively. They have power over their children, a power that is too often abused, up to and including being a kind of child abuse. We should also be mindful that children often naturally blame themselves for things that go wrong in their families. For example, children are prone to blame themselves for their parents' divorces. Children tend to idealize their parents. So I have learned that children often employ this logic: *My mother is good. My father is good. Something is terribly wrong here, so it must be* my *fault. If I had only been a better boy or girl, this would not be happening.* This sad scenario is often made worse by parents who fail to take responsibility for putting their differences aside to work constructively together to take care of their children's emotional needs. Many serious marital battles and many divorces are fought on the backs of children. Few things weigh heavier on the hearts of children.

Parents have a duty—often neglected—to avoid allowing adult problems to flow down to their children. This requires self-care and the courage to confront our own behavior and to get the help we need as adults. I will not claim this is easy, only that the failure to protect our children from our individual difficulties, or our marital difficulties, can be destructive to the health and well-being of children. It can be as destructive as anything I have encountered in my work.

Dale Wisely, PhD, is a clinical psychologist specializing in children and adults. He has been in practice for over three decades.

Functions of the Family

Families have various roles. They provide support and create a network that can sustain the members and function as a stable emotional and economic unit. A family also has many work-related roles. In a sense, a family is like a company and its investors. The investors in that company are the family members. If they participate and pool their resources that family becomes stronger and more resilient. We can be individual investors, just as we are individual family members. But when we function as a family unit, we need also to bear the interests of the family at heart.

The family may go through transitions and changes in its composition during various stages of the family lifespan.

Source: © iStock .com/kate_sept2004.

Because families consist of humans and because humans are temperamental, changing, and sometimes erratic beings, families cannot be perfect. Families face their own challenges, but if a family can maintain appropriate cohesiveness and stability to support constructive outcomes for individual members, as well as for the family as a whole, then it is well on its way to fulfilling its task as a family successfully.

Rights of the child. Families have very special obligations toward their youngest and most vulnerable members, the children. According to the United Nations' ***Declaration of the Rights of the Child***, which was ratified in 1959, children have numerous rights that should be respected and enforced by nations universally. In practice, this ideal has had superficial buy-in, but the harsh and unsavory reality is that children continue to be victimized and exploited by adults, despite the best intentions expressed in such a declaration. Among some of the rights of the child are the following (United Nations General Assembly, 1989):

- *Belonging.* The child has the right to belong to and to identify with a family and to be nurtured by parents or by persons who will best care for the child entrusted to them.
- *Meeting needs.* Children have the right to have their basic needs for food, shelter, and safety met. Additionally, they have a right to education, to form their own opinions, to freedom of religious choice, and to speak their native language.
- *Child's play.* Children have the right to play and must not be forced into child labor, sexual activity, or warfare.
- *Peace and tolerance.* Ultimately, we as the adults should teach the next generation about peace and tolerance.

A child-friendly version of the UN Convention on the Rights of the Child can be accessed online (https://www.unicef.org/rightsite/files/uncrcchilld friendlylanguage.pdf).

Here are some of the rights of the child as explained to children by that document:

- All adults should do what is best for you. When adults make decisions, they should think about how their decisions will affect children.
- Your family has the responsibility to help you learn to exercise your rights, and to ensure that your rights are protected.
- You have the right to live with your parent(s), unless it is bad for you. You

have the right to live with a family who cares for you.

- You have the right to food, clothing, a safe place to live and to have your basic needs met. You should not be disadvantaged so that you can't do many of the things other kids can do.
- Your education should help you use and develop your talents and abilities. It should also help you learn to live peacefully, protect the environment and respect other people.
- No one is allowed to punish you in a cruel or harmful way.
- You have the right to know your rights! Adults should know about these rights and help you learn about them, too.

FOCUS POINT

Families have various roles. They exist to provide support and create a network that can sustain family members and function as a stable emotional and economic unit. Healthy families display a number of interacting and related characteristics that support both the individual family member as well as the family group comprised of multiple members.

SPOTLIGHT ON THEORIES

Introduction: Theories, Psychoanalysis, and Family Dynamics

Information and knowledge about the family and human psychological dimensions can be contextualized into a framework to guide our understanding. Generally, this is what we understand by a **theory** as it pertains to the family. Theories help us create a system that contributes to putting various pieces of information about families into a greater context. A well-structured theory facilitates our understanding and explanation of the dynamics occurring within families. Theories can enhance our insight by incorporating what has been observed in previous research on families, and this, in turn, can guide interventions and approaches to family therapy. Theories are the products of their time, of social and cultural contexts as well as of existing knowledge and research. In this manner, they can reflect as well as guide some of the leading and most prevalent thinking of the day.

Our knowledge base is extended by combining various insights, research outcomes, hypotheses, and general thinking about a specific field such as family therapy. Theories are not static, and they change in response to the research culture and findings of the day. Theories do not exist in watertight compartments. There is interdisciplinary influence, as scholars and family scientists explore all the contexts in which families function. Families are the inspiration but not the end goal. Theories can be combined, and they can change over time. For instance, what Sigmund Freud, Carl Rogers, or Murray Bowen thought at the beginning of their professional journeys was not necessarily the same as what they thought when they exited their careers. As they worked with individuals and families, their thinking matured and was influenced by their life's work.

There is no single theory that best connects the dots of our knowledge and our questions concerning the dynamics of families. Instead, if we have access to various theories, we have the option of a number of explanations. Different theories allow us to look at the subject matter from different angles.

(Continued)

(Continued)

Some of the theories will catch the light in just such a way that they enhance our insight concerning a given topic. In turn, that insight can guide our practice and our interventions with families.

More recent theories are often built on the insights of earlier theories. In combination, theories form a virtual staircase leading toward greater understanding and explanations of family-related concerns. Our current perspectives on families, especially on the dynamics within families, have been influenced by the thoughts and skills of numerous family-related professionals.

At the turn of the twentieth century, the time was ripe for the field of psychology to emerge. We tend to associate Freud (1856–1939) with the early beginnings of **psychotherapy**. He had definitely been subjected to numerous influences, which converged at this time. Freud was also surrounded by a group of colleagues who probably inspired, elaborated, and strengthened some of the brainwaves that culminated in his psychoanalytic theory. In reality, Freud's psychoanalytic theory did not emerge from "out of nowhere," although Freud was not shy of claiming it as his own—sometimes taking some liberties with the intellectual property of his colleagues. However that may be, there is still an ongoing place to acknowledge the relevance of the psychoanalytic and related psychodynamic approaches (Whitebook, 2017).

Psychoanalysis, as a term, is generally used to describe so-called *talk-therapy*, in which the therapeutic process is facilitated by increased insight and, importantly, based on the theoretical concepts of the psychoanalytic movement. In essence that meant attributing much of the behavior to especially unconscious motives. As a treatment model, it is labor intensive and takes months if not years; this path is often too arduous in our fast-paced society that demands instant gratification when at all feasible. **Psychodynamics** refers to the attempted explanation of how and why the psyche does what it does; it tries to provide the *why* for the behavior. In its context within psychoanalysis, psychodynamics considers the conscious as well as unconscious forces that can motivate and determine behavior. Psychodynamics as used in its Freudian psychoanalytic context seeks to explain the dynamics of behavior according to psychoanalytic principles.

In many therapeutic approaches, one of the central ideas concerns holding up the proverbial mirror for clients to see themselves. In a more classical psychotherapeutic approach, the thought was to make that which is unconscious (and hence not "known" to the individual) more conscious (Perry, 2016). In this way, one reveals the motivations and emotional forces that lead to specific behaviors. The aim is to bring this unconscious material into the field of consciousness, where it can be explored and examined. Sigmund Freud was on to something important when he presumed that we can reveal our unconscious through our dreams, the jokes we make, the slips of the tongue, and even by our free associations (Berger, 2018). Perry (2016) describes this phenomenon of revealing the unconscious in relation to the defense mechanisms we adopt:

> Sigmund Freud chose simple words to describe the function of each defense [mechanism] identified, noting that they kept uncomfortable things out of awareness, while keeping them symbolically on one's mind.

There are whole areas concerning our motivations for behavior that we do not examine, as we do not really know why we do certain things. Freud (1936/1992) hypothesized that we keep certain material out of our consciousness because it might be too threatening; it might upset the applecart if we looked it straight in the face. It might elicit anxiety. For that reason, it was thought that we disguise some of our actions: we use **defense mechanisms** (Cramer, 2015). In that way we could dress up the wolf in sheep's clothing: we could make the scary material less anxiety provoking by making it look a little different, by disguising it. Defense mechanisms were thought to help us manage anxiety; by distorting the world in various ways, we could make reality more palatable. From the point of view of **neuroscience**, we may achieve a similar outcome, namely, dealing with anxiety, through **emotional regulation** (also known as the self-regulation of emotions). The implication is that there may be an interface between psychodynamics and the findings of contemporary neuroscience (Rice & Hoffman, 2014).

In more recent contexts, the word *dynamics* stands in for the more formal *psychodynamics*. This is of particular relevance to the field of dynamics as it pertains to the family. Dropping the prefix also tends to drop the Freudian and psychoanalytic connotations. So the word *dynamics* can be used more loosely and can refer to a wider range of theoretical reference points.

In a Nutshell

- The way we view and think about families undergoes a morphing process in sync with greater cultural and societal developments. This developmental process becomes visible in theories about families and their dynamics, which can be described as the many reasons and explanations for what makes families do the things they do.
- Theories help us create a system that contributes to putting various pieces of information into a greater context. A well-structured theory pertaining to families facilitates our understanding and explanation of the dynamics occurring within the family context.
- In more recent contexts, the word *dynamics* stands in for the more formal *psychodynamics*. Dropping the prefix also tends to drop the Freudian and psychoanalytic connotations, so the term can be used more loosely and can refer to a wider range of theoretical reference points.

FOCUS POINT

Theories are the products of time, social and cultural contexts, and existing knowledge and research. Psychoanalysis describes insight-based interventions referencing the theoretical concepts of the psychoanalytic movement. Psychodynamics refers to how and why the psyche influences behavior. Within psychoanalysis and related psychodynamic approaches, conscious as well as subconscious forces are thought to motivate and determine behavior.

CHAPTER FOCUS POINTS

Family Dynamics: Meaning

- Families are units in constant motion, growing and changing as demands inside and outside the system influence the whole.
- Family dynamics deal with the inner workings and behavior of the family, the ways culture and society affect it, and how its members influence each other.
- Family dynamics represent the movement and growth that occurs as family systems adapt and change, both in relation to the larger system around them and to the intimate system within the family itself.
- *Definition:* In social contexts such as family systems, the word *dynamics* is used to denote those aspects that change or progress, those places where movement and growth occur.
- The word *psychodynamics* can mean the process of searching for and uncovering the emotional motivations and possible psychological reasons for behavior. Psychodynamics can imply the emotional motivations and psychological reasons for behavior.

Lifespan Development and Family Dynamics

- Human lifespan development and family dynamics have an intricate link: both describe constant change. Human lifespan development looks at how individuals grow and change over time from conception to death.

- Family dynamics deal with the continuous movement (or dynamics) of the family. Individual lives are embedded in the context of their families.

Why Study Family Dynamics?

- Family scientists and helping professionals concerned with the well-being of families come from many disciplines. Focusing on families, these professionals have the power to support optimal outcomes.
- Being well versed in family dynamics is valuable to those working with individual families or trying to influence public policy decisions.

Defining Families

- Families can be defined in several ways. As society and social policies shift, so does the definition of the family.
- Traditionally, families have been identified by bloodlines and marital connections.
- The form and function of families has morphed to include more flexible configurations, including intimate and personalized definitions.

Census Definitions

- One of the purposes of the U.S. Census is to capture population numbers and various demographics at a given point in time. It is a mechanism to count or record persons and gain greater insight into selected demographics.
- These goals influence how units such as families, family groups, and family households are defined.
- Importantly, the census application of the term *family* can have wider and different applications, affecting how the family is defined in everyday, legal, and other scholarly contexts.
- According to the U.S. Census, the definition of the family has been fairly consistent since 1930: a family consists of members of a household related by blood, marriage, or adoption.

Diverse Families

- Defining families by their responsibilities may bring concerns, as not all families meet the same expectations in terms of roles and responsibilities.
- Divorce, remarriage, and cohabitation have added considerable diversity to family forms.
- Plurality in family forms means that there is great variety influenced by numerous factors, including culture, geographical location, and environmental resources, to mention a few.

The Family as a System

- When a family functions as a system, the members of that system influence and feel for each other; there is interrelatedness.
- A well-functioning family nurtures and shelters its members. The family has numerous unique characteristics that contribute to its identity, including the following:
  - It functions as an independent system.
  - It is diverse in form and function.
  - It has diverse membership.
  - It has intergenerational members.
  - Its members display solidarity and interdependence.

Family dynamics are influenced by numerous interacting factors.

Functions of the Family

- Healthy families display a number of interacting and related characteristics that support both the individual family member as well as the family group comprised of multiple members.
- Families have various roles. They exist to provide support and create a network that can sustain family members and function as a stable emotional and economic unit.
- Healthy families display a number of interacting and related characteristics that support both the individual family members as well as the family group comprised of multiple members.

Spotlight on Theories: Introduction—Theories, Psychoanalysis, and Family Dynamics

- Theories help us create a system that contributes to putting various pieces of information into a greater context. A well-structured theory pertaining to families facilitates our understanding and explanation of the dynamics occurring within the family context.
- Theories are the products of time, social and cultural contexts, and existing knowledge and research. Psychoanalysis describes insight-based interventions and references the theoretical concepts of the psychoanalytic movement.
- Psychodynamics refers to how and why the psyche influences behavior. Within psychoanalysis and related psychodynamic approaches, conscious as well as subconscious forces are thought to motivate and determine behavior.
- In more recent contexts, the word *dynamics* (as opposed to *psychodynamics*) can be used more loosely and can refer to a wider range of theoretical reference points.

CHAPTER

2

Dimensions That Influence Dynamics

Learning Outcomes

After studying this chapter, you should be able to

1. Identify the connection between families and societies by referencing *tasks*, *structure*, and *context*.
2. Explain the different types of power an individual can assert on other family members as considered within the context of *influences in family dynamics*.
3. Summarize the different *dimensions* that contribute to family dynamics.
4. Discuss the impact of *family estrangement*.
5. Define *ecological systems theory* and explain the relationship between the individual and the various nested systems in that individual's environment.

Tasks, Structure, and Context

The dynamics of the family can be seen as a complex set of interrelated cogs, like the dials and wheels within a sophisticated timepiece. As one item turns, it sets something else in motion, and together they fulfill an important function. A family is a mini machine of sorts: it works because each part of that unit knows its role and fulfills it, and together they create the magical outcomes characterizing well-functioning families.

Tasks

One of the foremost tasks of families is to provide emotional and physical shelter for family members. Just like any other shelter, the family offers protection, membership, safety. It is the place where we can stop to rest and refuel, much like ships docking in a harbor to be replenished. Additionally, well-functioning families provide opportunities and support and allow for the pooling of resources. The family is the place where the young can spend their fragile years until they are sufficiently strong emotionally and physically to be launched into more independent lives. While nurturing and raising those younger family members, the parents have to help the youngsters unfold and utilize their potential. Parenting is a science in its own right, devoted to how best we can achieve the task of raising kids optimally.

There is something primeval about our shelters, the places we go to unwind and recover. For starters, they are intimate; ideally, our shelter is the one place we can appear without wearing masks, be congruent as a person (meaning to be as we appear to be, to be real), and still be accepted and loved for who we are. Family homes are intimate venues, we tend not to invite strangers into our homes, but we welcome our family, friends, and acquaintances, as the home is also the setting in which we are most likely to be seen and recognized for who we truly are.

Families change their tasks according to the developmental lifespan. Although the primary function in the early years of raising a family may have been predominantly linked to providing a safe and nurturing environment, offspring will launch and create their own family spaces, leaving the older generations with slightly different tasks.

Structure

The **extended family** comprises those individuals related through blood or marriage. This definition widens the pool considerably and typically makes the extended family unit intergenerational and probably diverse. Extended families cannot all live in one household, at least not in the typical Western household. Because of their size, extended families can be heterogeneous, meaning they can differ widely. If the group is large, the members have varying relationships with a wide range of emotional as well as physical proximity; we do not feel equally close or distant to all the family members that make up our clan. The very real genetic or marriage bond may be the glue that binds us. Additionally, many extended families use the same last name, a visible signal of connectedness.

Before the Industrial Revolution, starting in the mid-1700s in Europe, extended families had to pool their resources and labor for survival as a group (Stearns, 2013). As family groups, they additionally represented and functioned as economic units. Typically, they existed predominantly in semirural contexts, farming with livestock or agriculture. With the advent of the Industrial Revolution, men looked for work in the cities, and their nuclear families followed. It became harder to find social support. In an extended family, the grandparents could contribute to raising the youngest members of the extended family unit. In the urban contexts into which industrial jobs took families, that benefit was often lost as grandparents were too far for support, and the extended family fragmented into smaller units (Mokyr, 2011).

Families in their nuclear form are typically the smallest family unit and consist of a parental subunit and children—called the **immediate family**. This family form is also referred to as the **nuclear family**. Especially if the children are young, this group of people lives together in close-knit form and shares a physical and an emotional space. In this type of intimate environment, there are plenty of opportunities for sharing ideas, supporting each other, and traveling the path of life in tandem.

Authentic Insight

Family Tasks

It seems that families are foundational to so much of our lives and identities, so fundamental that it is hard to overstate their importance. Yet, in the United States, we have an individualism that obscures the importance of families. For example, health concerns are viewed as individual problems when really they are family stresses. Many acts of violence in the United States take place in relationships, and parenting is more challenging than ever because we don't have a context that supports family life very well. So there is a lot of work to be done to strengthen families, which are our natural support networks, given to us to help with challenges that life brings us.

Jonathan Davis, PhD, is a professor of human development and family science and a licensed marriage and family therapist.

Structure can be represented in several dimensions. Because the social conventions of what should or should not define a family have relaxed, families now come in all shapes and sizes. The **parental unit** is typically comprised of one or two adults who take most of the responsibility for that family. They are the providers, they garner an income, and they make major decisions and carry the burden of responsibilities. In a legal context, they are adults, with corresponding adult responsibilities. The parental unit can consist of several variations: both parental figures residing in the same household, a single parent alone as household head, or a single parent with possibly a second adult parenting from a distance or from another household. The parenting can also come from intergenerational settings, such as grandparents, or from coparents. Often the parents had the children together, but families and relationships are in flux as the many variations of family life have shown all too clearly.

The manner in which the children joined the family system might have followed a variety of avenues. Children could have been the biological offspring of the parents; as in the family's basic form, it is the parents who produce children. Children can also join the family through the support of ART (artificial reproductive techniques) or be welcomed initially in the context of foster care. Adoption is a significant and important way in which to grow a family (Child Welfare Information Gateway, n.d.). During the postmillennial period, it has been estimated that, in the United States, about 130,000 children per year have been welcomed into loving homes because somewhere birth parents made the difficult decision of giving their child a chance to experience the kind of family life that they could not offer at that time (Child Welfare Information Gateway, 2011, 2016).

Family composition colors the family scenario in yet another hue. The number and genders of the children as well as their unique personalities can combine to alter and influence the family dynamic. Families with one-child configurations will have a different dynamic interplay from that of a very large family with children spaced over multiple years.

Families represent a complicated formula, consisting of several elements, such as how many members are involved and their personalities, genders, and attributes, all of which will determine the emotional climate of that particular family. Additionally, the parenting occurring within that family will have different faces depending on the number of persons allocated to parenting roles. Several parties can be on the parenting team including coparents, grandparents, and other well-meaning adults (Bigner & Gerhardt, 2019, pp. 307–308).

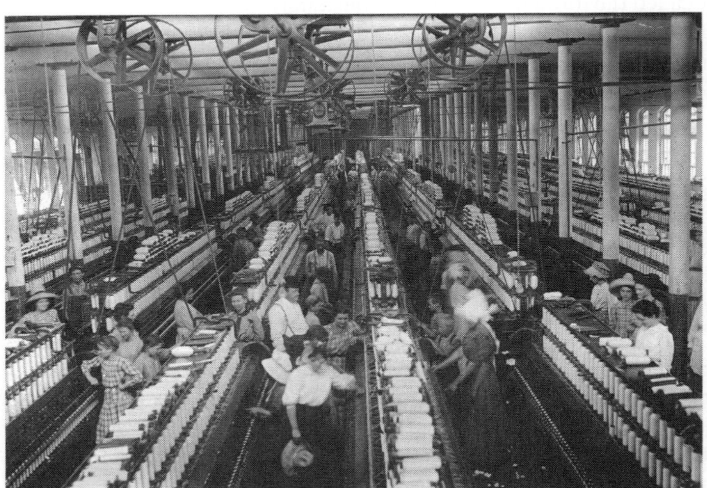

Women's work experience and the influences of the Industrial Revolution: Women at work spinning textiles at the Magnolia Cotton Mill's spinning room in Alabama, USA, presumably in the early 1900s. Note the children in the image; they may have been working themselves, or they may have accompanied their mothers to work as there was no childcare.

Source: Public domain.

Sibling ratios play a determining role as well in that siblings can provide a protective and a distractive function. The more siblings one has, the more likelihood that brothers and sisters will provide comfort and support during one's lifetime. The larger the family, the more divided the resources. This can be one of the challenges facing families in developing countries; the family size could exceed the resources required to give each child an optimal opportunity for education, skill development, and a more hopeful future. On the other hand, single-child family systems face unique circumstances as well. All the attention of four grandparents is focused on one grandchild, and, in return, that one grandchild may end up being sandwiched with responsibilities pertaining to the support of four aging grandparents. No mathematical expertise is required to calculate that the sheer inequality of the ratios indicates looming stress points.

Context

Families exist in many contexts. These can be defined by culture, geographical region, ethnicity, socioeconomic status, access to resources, civic engagement, public policy, resilience, and so much more.

Individuals are embedded within families. Families in turn are nested in societies. There is a bidirectional responsibility between societies and the families they encompass. Societies should ideally provide the greater backup that allows families to function optimally, and these aspirations can be anchored in public policy. Societies with their specific cultural and societal characteristics can differ radically, and these variations are imparted to the families within that society. Families in turn echo their cultural values back to that society.

For societies, families are very valuable components. Combined, families *are* the society; remove the element of the family and the fabric of a society disintegrates. For that reason, there is a co-responsibility between families and society. Families need to be civic minded and promote the best interests of the society at large. Family members must have a willingness to contribute meaningfully to the fabric of society through goal-directed labor and participation. Societies in turn need to shelter families through public policy that addresses aspects relevant to families. Safety, health care, education, and employment possibilities are high on the wish list of most families and become a reality if supported by public policy.

The era in which a family is growing and living will mark it in definite ways. For instance, consider the families of our great grandparents, those families who experienced a major war, refugee families, families in societies where education is inaccessible and poverty is the norm, or families with children who have special needs. In each of those scenarios, the family dynamic plays out differently. For that reason, it can be a challenge for a family to be responsible for its own well-being. In some dimensions, the family contributes significantly to its own well-being, and in other ways, the family can be the product of its larger system or context, such as its hosting nation's geopolitics, culture, or economy.

Families are also embedded in cultural contexts, and much of the communication and the subtleties of daily life are colored by cultural traditions. The particular culture of a region and a family can be very powerful in providing the nuances of communication. How open versus how guarded we are in our discourse can be a byproduct of how we were enculturated. Cultures that lean toward the individualistic side of the continuum tend to support open expression of personal opinions. In contrast, people in cultures leaning toward the collectivistic end of the continuum may be more reticent in expressing their points of view.

Additionally, all the members of the family group may not be at the same point of cultural immersion. Generally, the older generations, such as the grandparents, may be more conservative in their interpretation of cultural values. Younger generations exposed to a multitude of influences via travel, education, the Internet, and greater global mobility may be more flexible in what cultural heritage they decide to keep as part of their repertoire. Additionally, the younger generation

FOCUS POINT

Individuals are embedded within families, which, in turn, are nested in societies. There is a bidirectional responsibility and influence. Societies and the public policy enacted by them can provide greater backup for families, facilitating their optimal functioning. Specific cultural and societal characteristics can differ widely. For societies, families are very valuable components. Combined, families *are* the society; remove the family unit, and the fabric of a society disintegrates.

may have grown up in a different cultural context to that of the parents, especially if the older family members are immigrants or refugees.

Many invisible threads combine to weave the web within which each family is contained. Families vary greatly in access to both opportunities and those conditions that support family life. Accordingly, although universally families are connected by their familial bonds, they can also live very different family lives facing a great variety of family rewards as well as challenges.

The Influences on Dynamics

Power inequities. In any family unit, those who have access to resources, knowledge, skill, or other valuable assets may hold the seat of power. In ideal family contexts, the strengths of the family should be pooled so that the entire family can benefit from the attributes and benefits of constructive opportunities. If we think of resources available, then the person who has control over these likely holds the power.

There are other forms of social and emotional power that can be exerted inside the family. These power dynamics do not all revolve around resources. For instance, if one member of the family is bedridden or needs to use a wheelchair, then that family member may demand resources in terms of care and support. Members who do not have control of family resources but who need more attention or care on a daily basis can strongly influence the power dynamic of the family, both advertently and inadvertently.

Secondary gain. Not for nothing do people like the attention, or secondary gain, that can be received when they are ill. Sometimes, family members indicate they have symptoms for the sake of attention, and no sincere medical conditions are present. For instance, the so-called *help-rejecting complainer* describes a person who seeks help while simultaneously rejecting it (Berger & Rosenbaum, 1967/2015, p. 357). This complaint is more about the process of gaining attention rather than seeing a difficult situation resolved. The dynamic underlying the behavior is a cycle of complaining, gaining attention, rejecting the solution, and returning back to the complaint as no solution was found to be acceptable.

Families are not constant. Instead, families are in flux and respond to their environments. The context of any given situation may determine who holds the greatest power at any given moment. Think of a newborn infant joining the family unit. When that baby cries to communicate her need to be held or to be fed, she exerts considerable power over her caretakers, who will probably have to respond to this signal immediately and offer the baby whatever comfort she needs.

Abuse of power. It is not unknown for family members to abuse their power. Typical ways in which this can be done include the classic *guilt trip*. In this instance, a key family member, say the eldest brother, can induce guilt in others as a ploy to get attention or to get his way. It is not a fair way of doing things, but then we know from studying families that dynamics are not always a fair way of negotiation. It often occurs on an emotional level that has very little to do with the rational execution of plans. Another way could be by *belittling* and even *bullying*: seeking out the vulnerabilities of the other and relentlessly shaming or honing in on that person. Deprecating or intimidating others represents the misuse of power by someone who holds up a mask of strength to hide cowardice and insecurity.

Constructive or destructive power. Power can be found in different guises. When it comes to family dynamics, the distinguishing factor is probably whether the power is used in a constructive or a destructive manner. Constructive power can be found in the parent taking responsibility for providing for a family. Examples of destructive power plays could involve constant attention-seeking behavior, which can be very disruptive. By being disruptive it has the ability to manipulate family members. Another power ploy could be acting helpless. This approach would require help-giving behavior by family members, irrespective of whether it is genuinely required or not.

Power allocation. Power can also be allocated by influencing how family members feel about themselves. Ideally, one of the roles of parents is to support their child in forming a healthy and strong self-concept, which increases that child's power over time. The dysfunctional parent, however, could find power in humiliating and belittling a child and, in that moment, feel strong, without realizing the long-term damage this behavior is causing in a defenseless young person. By the same token, intimate partner violence can be a form of power allocation, however dysfunctional this behavior may be. Using threats, belittling the partner, doubting that partner's reality, or forcing that person to live in constant fear of setting off an irrational emotional outburst—all these behaviors can be dysfunctional and destructive forms of exerting power and maintaining control.

Hierarchical Power Inequities

Power dynamics in the family are virtually impossible to avoid. The nature of our parental roles means that we take responsibilities, that we provide, and that we also have authority within the context of the family unit. There can be hierarchical differences, and there can be power inequities. Both imply that the parties concerned come from different points of strength and vulnerability. These differences and inequities in turn influence the particular dynamic of interactions within that system.

Family hierarchies. A hierarchical structure is constructive if it is used to enable family members to develop and flourish in an atmosphere where their needs are respectfully met. The family therapist Salvador Minuchin (1999) familiarized us with the concept of **hierarchies** within the family. The parental unit should fulfill certain obligations and responsibilities toward the family. By the same token, certain things should remain at the parental level and not become the worries of children who are too young to be exposed to some of this information. For instance, sexual matters between parents belong in the parental hierarchy, and they have no place spilling over into the world of the children. Using children as a sounding board for parental disputes would also amount to an abuse of power. Grown-up problems should be solved by the parental generation within that family unit; these problems should not taint the world of children by robbing them of their carefree existence. It is part of a parent's role to shoulder those burdens that belong in the grown-up world and to leave young children their innocence and their faith in the knowledge that parents will provide and protect.

Family hierarchies are also associated with intergenerational contexts. It may be that the elders of a community are highly respected, as is typical in many African cultural contexts. In terms of societal respect, their wisdom places them in a more powerful societal position. Another example: an elderly grandfather may be quite powerless when it comes to making family decisions, but because he requires around the clock care, it may feel as if he is the center of the household, demanding all attention. In this manner, he can be powerful.

Coercion. One of the side effects of power is that it can set up an emotional playing field. The person exerting the power may be very finely attuned to the effects of that power. Wielding that power for the wrong reasons elicits emotions in incorrect contexts and can be seen as incongruent behavior. Regrettably, not all is fair in the world of family dynamics. Unscrupulous players can hijack emotions for their own ulterior motives. Part of the power model implies that we coerce other people to do what we want them to do irrespective of whether the bigger picture is ethical or healthy (Forsyth, 2019). We see this behavior especially in persons with limited emotional repertoires and in those who are very needy emotionally. Think of a man with narcissistic personality disorder, which has to do with excessive self-centeredness and self-aggrandizement. He will use power not only to achieve a concrete goal but also to make himself feel powerful. This abuse of power contributes to an unstable family dynamic in which actual circumstances and stated aims have little to do with behavior.

Neediness. Anxiety-driven needs may be so great and all consuming that they become a force in their own right; and the needs can fracture from the original context, gaining a life of their own. An example would be anxiety-driven or *neurotic neediness*. In this context, the person displaying the need seems like a *bottomless pit*. No amount of love or attention seems to fulfill that individual's needs; the person has an insatiable need for even more attention and acknowledgment. Those who have to provide this form of emotional stroking may soon burn out, as doing so is unsustainable. *Phobias* are another example of the effort involved in avoiding anxiety-eliciting situations. The person becomes trapped in an endless cycle of avoidant behaviors.

Strengths and vulnerabilities. Systemic differences in power highlight strengths as well as vulnerabilities. The inequities cannot be avoided and are virtually built into any system. Whether a relationship is between the mentor and mentee, the therapist and client, the doctor and patient, the teacher and student, the employer and employee, the older sibling and the younger sibling, the grandparent and grandchild, or the father and mother, it can benefit from an ongoing

FOCUS POINT

In any family unit, those who have access to resources, knowledge, skill, or other valuable assets may hold the seat of power. In ideal family contexts, the strengths of the family are pooled so that the entire family can benefit from constructive opportunities. There are other forms of social and emotional power that can be exerted inside the family and other structures supporting power distinctions, such as hierarchical differences and power inequities. Both imply that the parties concerned come from different points of strength and vulnerability. These hierarchies and inequities, in turn, influence the particular dynamic of interactions within that system.

Authentic Insight

Out of Control: When Dynamics Take on Lives of Their Own . . .

In a dynamic context, people sometimes invoke an emotional process that seems to take on a life of its own. An example is anxiety-driven or neurotic *neediness* for which no amount of input seems to fill the seemingly *bottomless pit of need*. The demands may seem insatiable for ever-greater acknowledgment. *Phobias* are another example of the effort involved in avoiding an anxiety-evoking situation. By doing so, the person is rerouted onto an endless detour of avoidant behaviors. Eventually, the secondary gain of the emotional enactment supersedes the original intent. This same folk wisdom is personified in the tale of the sorcerer's apprentice, in which things get out of control exponentially.

The poem about the sorcerer's apprentice, written in 1797 by the German poet Johann Wolfgang von Goethe, is believed to be based on an ancient Greek myth. In Goethe's poem, the apprentice is tasked with cleaning up while the sorcerer is out. The apprentice has limited knowledge of magic invocations, and is very pleased with himself when he can command the broom to fill a pail of water. This progresses well until the apprentice would like to end the task. None of his magical incantations do the trick; bucket after bucket floods the workroom. In a moment of inspiration, the apprentice hacks the broom in half hoping to end the cycle. Instead, he has now created two brooms, which can both carry water. In the happy ending, the sorcerer, not the apprentice, restores order with a magical command.

The lesson to be learned is not to evoke forces beyond our capabilities. When we deal with behaviors and their hidden emotional meanings, we may become as helpless as the sorcerer's assistant.

Some patterns of behavior seem to take on a life of their own, as they fracture from their original intent and meaning. Anxiety-driven needs may become so great and all consuming that they become a force in their own right. Think of all the avoidance behaviors displayed when one has a phobia. These behaviors, too, become difficult to control.

give and take, an exchange and mutually beneficial dynamic flow between the participating parties.

The Choreography of the Family Dance

Families participate in a complicated interpersonal dance that is choreographed by family dynamics. It is staged and performed by participating family members. Additionally, much of this happens unrehearsed, even randomly. For family-related professionals, there can be discernible patterns and reasons for this dynamic dance. If we view the different dimensions or facets that contribute to family dynamics, we can gain a clearer understanding of the complexity of the family dance.

Shared investments. For families to interact meaningfully, they need to prioritize time together. They need to invest in their family unit by sharing, trusting, celebrating, participating, and engaging in all the other rituals of daily family life. One piece of folk wisdom states that quality time also requires quantity time. There is no shortcut to quality parenting by reading the bedtime story extra dramatically on the few nights when one happens to remember; young children need time with their parents. This time is part of the ongoing bonding and commitment that strengthens family bonds and sets the stage for later family relationships.

Families, whatever the ages of the participants, need investments in terms of confidences, shared experiences, and the creation of new memories. Of course,

Family members participate in an intricate and dynamic dance.

Source: Jose Luis Pelaez Inc/ DigitalVision/Getty.

as the family lifespan progresses, the quality of family relationships will change as well, but in essence the investment remains. Gottman, the psychologist best known for studying marital communication, stated that little moments of shared experiences had the ability to strengthen relationships and keep them vital. Sharing the ordinary and the tiny unsung moments of daily life can strengthen the weave of the marital fabric (Gottman & Silver, 1999).

Even with this togetherness and sharing, family members have spaces within the family context that are intensely private. Some of the family tasks are carried out by certain individuals; we can empathize, but in essence it is their life story. We may share grief, and we may share joy, but of some things we cannot take ownership. In his writing, Bowen (1976) referred to these autonomous aspects of family life as a process of individuation during which one becomes appropriately separate—one has to differentiate from the family (pp. 65–66).

Spatial Dimension

One dimension of family dynamics can be described in terms of structure in space: the *spatial dimension*. Families occupy a distinct emotional space. It has to do with where the family is situated in time and also relates to the family's own lifespan position.

The members of that family contribute in terms of their unique personalities. We can have a whole blend of different and unique character traits found in different family members. We may find dominating personalities, the person who is always ready with a joke, members who are pleasing, the givers who contribute, and the takers who tend to demand more than they invest. It becomes a delicate balance between givers and takers; and these roles are not necessarily performed by the same persons in the same way and exhibiting the same qualities in all familial circumstances. Depending on the context, we can be takers in some instances and givers in others. This serves to illustrate that dynamics truly are part of an intricate dynamic dance.

Families are not static. They respond to whatever is happening between the family members and within the environment in which the family is impeded.

Boundaries and Individuation

If we describe families in terms of structure and distance, it brings us to elements such as **boundaries** between members of the family. Boundaries are those natural demarcations that indicate the level of privacy and space a family member demands—the emotional area each occupies. Murray Bowen (1976) talks about **individuation** as a function of appropriate and healthy family development, as well as individual development (p. 67). Individuation has to do with finding one's own unique personality as a separate person or as an individual. It is thought that once we have individuated and we know who we are, namely unique individuals standing on our own two legs, then we are in a better position to reach out to others and form relationships. Part of the task of adulthood is to individuate and figure out who we are. Armed with this knowledge, we enter relationships from a better vantage point.

Authentic Insight

Avner Barcai: Making the Abstract Visible

During the seventies, in my early training as a clinical psychologist, I observed a therapy session by the eminent Israeli child psychiatrist Avner Barcai. Barcai, born in Haifa in 1934, unexpectedly died of a heart attack when he was 46. His profound insight and novel approaches were a great loss to the family therapy community. The Barcai Institute, a family therapy training center in Tel Aviv, is named in his honor.

The family in this particular session had consented that therapists in training could observe through a one-way mirror. In this family with three adult daughters, the presenting problem was the eldest daughter who struggled with individuation. She did not want to leave the home to go to college. She felt safest in the familiarity of her own four walls and was failing to launch.

Barcai set the stage for the family members to relate patterns in their daily lives. One revealing aspect was that the daughters, as well as their mother, were very competitive while also overly close. These family members were so enmeshed, or close, that they constantly wore each other's clothes without asking permission of the true owners of said garments, always went out in a group, and did very little individually. No wonder it was daunting for the daughter to leave the comfort of her siblings and mother, who formed her most important social group.

Just before a break in the therapy session, Barcai whispered instructions to the family. After the break, the three girls as well as the mom came back. They were no longer dressed in the same outfits in which they had started the session. They looked like a motley crew, one was missing shoes, another wrapped in a coat, and a third clearly uncomfortable in a combination of mismatched items. Generally, it looked as if a big rearrangement of their wardrobes had occurred.

What the therapist had asked them to do during the interval was to return each item of clothing to its original owner. The idea was that each family member would be wearing only her own clothes—no borrowing! The ill-suited and incomplete clothing of the individual members after this swap became a very powerful metaphor for both the family and the therapist, showing, as it did, that these family members seemed to achieve congruence only as part a group and not as individuals. Then began the reality of slowly teasing out what belonged to whom, while encouraging a gradual move toward greater individuation.

Barcai had used a seemingly paradoxical yet also concrete and visible gesture to give meaning to the more abstract process that had been playing out within this particular family, and that had become part of the driving force inducing emotional stagnation and failure to move forward (Barcai & Rabkin, 1972).

Source: Based on Gerhardt (2016a).

Proximity and Distance

When we consider proximity and distance, it has to do with the interplay that links into intimacy between various family members. Just as with boundaries, proximity and distance can vary depending on context. When a family is going through a particularly stressful or difficult time, family members tend to seek out closeness, and their proximity increases. Being supported and surrounded by family members comforts us and gives us the strength to cope with demanding and difficult situations. Times of great difficulty and need, such as the crises of illness and death, lend themselves to greater closeness. We also tend to gather and rally around the people we love at times of great joy. When family members are getting married or celebrating births and life transitions of a joyful nature, family teams gather to lend their support and share the celebratory joy. Well-functioning families are partly characterized by these expressions of support and sharing.

Overt and covert communication. Different families have their own unique family rules, which can be expressed in an **overt** or **covert** manner. It can be very obvious to outsiders what the expected behavior for that family should be, but there are subtleties that are harder to detect, and these would be hidden, masked, or covert. The openness of behaviors is what is meant by overt. If we refer to covert or reserved communication, it can denote that it is reserved for a select few listeners or reserved for those persons who can decipher and interpret it. Covert communication is not clearly visible.

Similarly, families can subscribe to overt and covert rules. The overt rules are obvious and spoken about: "Please be home by midnight." The covert or hidden rules may be implied and not directly communicated: "If you betray my trust, I will not forgive you" or, a trickier one, "In our house, we do not talk about sex." When a family member breaks a covert or unspoken rule, the punishment may be more severe than when he or she breaks an overt rule, and the confusion arising out of misunderstanding and presumptions can be all the greater, too. In essence, whether the rules are overt or covert is also directly linked to the family's communication style. Some families cannot bring themselves to talk about certain things: these may include family feuds and family secrets. Some examples of silent ghosts in the family circle can be topics such as children born out of wedlock, extramarital affairs, or teenage pregnancies. Typically, these "unspeakable" topics are shrouded in shame, and family members know better than to disrupt the silence surrounding them.

Families have their own rules and traditions, and these may be expressed by individual family members. The unspoken rules may pertain to minor things:

- *This is where I usually sit at the dinner table.*
- *Do not move the paperwork on my desk.*

These are predictable boundaries and regular occurrences to improve harmonious family functioning. The rules can be spoken and clearly communicated (overt or open), or they can be implied (covert or hidden). Outsiders joining a family system may not be able to recognize these without an insider's help. Another example is an insider's joke. It implies that members within that specific group understand what is meant, but an outsider would find the meaning obscure. These forms of communication can add to group cohesion (Forsyth, 2019).

How openly we communicate can be an outcome of several contributing factors. Some individuals are naturally more extroverted and find it easy to communicate interpersonally. They may appear to be very open in their communication style. But openness by itself does not tell the entire story. We would also have to examine the level of trust, self-revelation, self-disclosure or even vulnerability that is occurring in this interchange.

A person working in the hospitality industry may come across as very approachable and open. That individual could facilitate a pleasant exchange that will contribute to a better atmosphere or delivery of customer-requested services. In certain professions, it is a great asset to be able to interact spontaneously in a friendly manner that puts customers and clients at ease. This person may have an open style of communication, but having this style does not necessarily tell us about the depth of that individual's interchanges or interactions.

Being reserved (or covert) means that we do not have our hearts on our sleeves, and we may be a little more difficult to read. In some professions, appropriate professional reserve is a great asset. An example would be the therapeutic relationship in a counseling situation. In this case, being reserved helps prevent boundary violations, which are instances when inappropriate intimacy or social exchange is occurring. These boundary violations can be detrimental to the trusting relationship that is being formed.

Counselors should not engage in simultaneous personal and professional relationships with their clients (ACA, 2014). One reason is that this type of inappropriate dual relationship could take advantage of client-therapist trust. Appropriate boundaries and appropriate confidentiality are cornerstones of professional helping relationships. These relationships have their own dynamic, which is based on seeking out professional help in well-defined contexts in which the help-giving professional is highly trained and accountable to an extensive set of ethical guidelines. The fact that boundaries are in place means that therapists can extend empathy in a professional manner and be shielded from professional burnout and from becoming overly involved, which can be detrimental to the therapeutic relationship.

When we exchange communication on a personal or professional level, a human dimension of *depth* is added. It serves a function in that we can change or modify our responses, as well as how we interpret the input we receive, in accordance with all that has previously occurred within this relationship, or its depth. For that reason, the interactions are not scripted; instead communication is a spontaneous and responsive game in which every new bit of dialogue is linked to what happened previously. We can think of this as a circular pattern of communication. For instance, if we feel resentful toward someone because we think that individual has done something we dislike, then our interaction with that person will be colored by that previous knowledge. Each new interaction is based on, and also responds to, what has gone before.

Enmeshed versus disengaged. The continuum from overly close (enmeshed) to overly far (disengaged) plays out in different formats at different times in a family's life. Additionally, there are cultural nuances to be considered, and what may seem overly close in one cultural context may take on a different connotation in another. Generally in this discussion, the proximity-distance component is seen against the backdrop of what constitutes constructive and positive functioning within that particular family context.

When families are too close for comfort and family members live inside each other's pockets, we described that as being **enmeshed**. The amount of distance between family members can tell us about the dynamics within that family. Distance and proximity have to do with levels of intimacy and sharing. As with the other dimensions, these can vary depending on the context. Because families are dynamic, these qualities reflect the nature of relationships between family members and are not static. They respond to various dimensions, including the intrinsic relationship between key members and the context within which emotional exchange occurs.

Disengagement can be a symptom of the rest of the relationship. It tells us about what is happening between spouses. It tells us whether they respect each other's opinion, whether they value sharing important information in their lives, and whether they jointly tackle tasks that are significant. Parents can be **disengaged** toward their children when they display minimal interest, cannot express warmth or care, and generally withdraw from their parenting role.

Here is an example of communication in a disengaged relationship. A husband looks out of the window and comments to his wife, "I wonder whose car is parked in our driveway." The wife answers, "Oh, didn't I tell you that I bought a new car?" If this couple had been communicating in an ongoing and transparent manner, the wife would have told the husband of her intention to buy a car and possibly asked for his opinion concerning the matter. But because there was a disengaged or distant relationship between this pair, it did not seem to occur to her to involve him in the decision making or to inform him concerning her actions.

FOCUS POINT

If we describe families in terms of structure and distance, it brings us to elements such as boundaries between members of the family. Boundaries are those natural demarcations that indicate the level of privacy and space a family member demands—the emotional area each family member occupies. The appropriate individual space that each family member acquires is part of the individuation process. Different families have their own unique family rules, which can be expressed in an overt or covert manner. The openness of behaviors is what is meant by overt, whereas the hidden dimensions are covert.

Patterns of Family Interaction

Family Cutoffs: Rifts and Feuds

In some instances, the family rifts have a well-grounded history or antecedent. The person being ostracized may have committed a heinous crime, embezzled family funds, or lied and been untrustworthy. That family member may have crossed sacred boundaries and transgressed to the point where reconciliation seems to violate basic values and principles. When this ongoing disrespectful behavior reaches a tipping point, the family may choose to cut off that individual to protect itself against a person now perceived to be a major disruptive influence, with the potential of causing great and even permanent harm.

Sharing and caring. Family members can express their feelings to each other by how involved they are with the highs and the lows in the lives of other members. Some families are separated through circumstances such as deployment, international jobs, and the like. Other families are separated by choice.

On a macrosystemic level, we find cutoffs of national scale. Originally built as a defense against invaders, the Great Wall of China can be seen from space and is a formidable structure denoting a barrier or boundary of this scale.

Source: duncan1890/DigitalVision Vectors/Getty.

As sad as it may seem, family estrangements, rifts, and feuds are far more prevalent than one thinks. In fact, "Scratch the surface of almost any family and you will find a significant cutoff. For those who have not had the pleasure, trust us that there are few more gut-wrenching experiences than being summarily dismissed by a close relative or friend" (Bruun & Michael, 2014, p. i). Literature, folklore, and mythology, as well as the major world religions, contain examples of and admonitions against what happens when parties quarrel and conflict tears families apart. The Shakespearean tragedy of *Romeo and Juliet* is agonizing in how the rift between the Montagues and the Capulets overshadows the potential future of this couple.

On a macrosystemic level, we find cutoffs of national scale. Consider, for instance, the former East and West Germany, Northern and Southern Ireland, North and South Korea, and Bosnia and Croatia, to mention but a few (Bruun & Michael, 2014, p. 1). The Great Wall of China can be seen from space and is a formidable structure denoting a barrier or boundary of this scale.

Family disruption and estrangement. A disruption in the family can be extreme, as in complete cutoffs and breaking off all communication. Disinheriting a person, treating that individual as if she or he did not exist or were dead, is a loss not only for the intended target but also for the person initiating the cutoff. It is very hurtful and probably this is one of its major motivators—to hurt and offend the other party. For any family that has experienced a feud or a cutoff, understanding the context—the background and the underpinnings that may have led up to this rift—is crucial. Mediators may have to be drawn into a potential resolution, but regardless of whether a cutoff is resolved, its price in terms of emotional loss, anger, resentment, and especially missed opportunities is almost always too high.

When disruption or estrangement occurs, it can be as damaging as an acrimonious divorce. In some cases, when the cutoff is extreme and hateful, it may feel like the emotional death of a family member. A definition is provided by Conti (2015):

> Family estrangement, the communication cut-off between family members, constitutes one of the family transitions, along with separation, divorce, remarriage, and adoption. Like the other transitions families undergo, estrangement might become a temporary or permanent condition. (Conti, 2015, p. 28)

A description of what a cutoff can mean in practical terms is provided by Bruun and Michael (2014, p. 5):

> A purposeful, painful, often abrupt rupture, resulting in the loss of a close or important relationship that in most cases existed for a significant period of time. The cutoff usually occurs when one or both parties are emotionally upset over an incident, a decision, a changed behavior or circumstance. In some instances the impetus may be less anger and a need for self-protection. The cutoff parties are . . . [no longer in] direct oral or written communication . . . or their interaction is seriously limited or curtailed.

If families are seen as systems with a great deal of symbiosis or togetherness, then an adversarial rift will create psychological disharmony not only for the feuding parties but also indirectly for all the other family members in that system. It is especially painful when an acrimonious distancing is one-sided; the victim of this emotional barrage can do little to mend the rift. Sometimes cutoffs are as permanent as divorces; at other times, they are clearly reconcilable. In some relationships, brief and temporary cutoffs may be used to facilitate the forgiveness and closeness that can follow during the making-up phase. In her book *Family Estrangement*, Agllias (2016) gives the following definition:

> Family estrangement is larger than conflict and more complicated than betrayal. It is entwined in contradictory beliefs, values, behaviours and goals and is the result of at least one member of the family considering reconciliation impossible and/or undesirable. The cessation of familial relations, whether that involves rejection or deciding to leave, can be an inordinately traumatising experience. (p. i)

Family estrangements are more common than anticipated. In a study by Conti (2015) with university students, over 40 percent of the questioned participants had experienced an estrangement. As one would like to expect intuitively, they were more prevalent in the extended family, especially if contact between family members was intermittent. While mentioning the topic to colleagues and friends, I found that almost everyone had a story to tell directly related to this topic, and cutoffs are indeed more common than we like to think.

Family estrangement is characterized by several components (Conti & Ryan, 2013):

- The communication cutoff is usually complete and persistent, in that intentional and direct communication between the family and the party cut off is averted and avoided. Communication can occur indirectly when designated family members, lawyers, or mediators act as go-betweens.
- One of the parties is usually more determined to maintain the cutoff and therefore also more resistant to intervention and mediation.
- A true emotional cutoff is typically instigated in order to exert some form of interpersonal power. This can include the intention to be hurtful by creating distance.
- If family members lose touch with each other but know how to contact each other and there are no ill feelings, then that situation is not regarded as a formal family estrangement.
- Maintaining a sense of injustice concerning injuries incurred in a relationship provides justification to persevere with the feud.

Some family feuds are inherited and gather strength and volume in avalanche-like manner over time. Agillias (2016) distinguishes between the following estrangements:

- *Inherited*: family loyalties are involved and persons may be forced to take sides.
- *Secondary*: for example, in-laws may get drawn into a feud not of their own choosing.
- *Absent*: the person who is cut off may not be present, as in an acrimonious divorce. Other absent estrangements are the consequence of addiction disorders, abuse, and other circumstances.

As the snowball rolls, it picks up more matter. The generation in which the emotional cutoff became most palpable and painful made it more difficult for subsequent generations to repair the damage. Clearly, these rifts build up and crescendo by layering misunderstandings, hurt feelings, resentments, and more. But they importantly also tell us about how these families communicate, how they resolve misunderstandings and deal with pain. Cutoffs and feuds cannot be simplified and reduced to a simple linear cause-and-effect pattern. As an anonymous client poetically remarked during a therapy session,

> I feel as if I am wearing a very heavy coat. But I don't remember putting it on. It must have settled on me fiber by fiber to reach its current weight . . . by now it's so heavy I can't take it off by myself. Plus I am scared of taking it off. It may leave me vulnerable. . . . I realize I will need professional help . . . especially to learn to live without this ongoing weight on my shoulders.

Authentic Insight

Origins and Outcomes of Pain

Bea came from a large family and had left home and been independent for quite some time. She had completed her studies and was successful in her profession. For all practical purposes, Bea was functioning like a grown up, facing her responsibilities and living her life. Along the way, she met a life partner, and they shared a home for about two years. She introduced her partner to the family and made no secret about their relationship. When she moved cities and states for a new job, the committed partner uprooted and accompanied her, providing all the support a dedicated partner would. All was good.

One day, Bea casually mentioned to her family that she had married. Reactions from the family were very mixed. Those family members who loved her were positive and supportive. She explained to them that big and public celebrations made her uncomfortable, and she simply did not know how to break the news to them without precipitating an avalanche of wedding preparations, which she wanted to avoid at all costs. But granddad was particularly upset and unforgiving. He felt it was a personal betrayal that he had not been told first, and he fussed endlessly within the family (and also to all his friends) and strongly and vocally disagreed with his granddaughter's decisions. What are the lessons in family dynamics to be learned?

Even though Bea was part of an extended family, it was her and her partner's right to celebrate their nuptials the way they did, privately and very low key. When the grandfather fusses and feels deeply hurt, we may have to look at where his pain originates. Is it disappointment in what he thought was a trusting relationship with his granddaughter? Why wouldn't she have shared her good news with him? Or is it her choice of partner? Why is he so disgruntled, and why is he so vocal about his disappointment? Is it about his granddaughter's needs or about his own needs? It would appear that this is about the grandfather's world, how he feels—it is about him.

In difficult family situations, we have to ask who has true ownership of the challenge or situation under discussion. This determination can be influenced by cultural context as well as by the particular family members we identify as our closest kin. Bea, being an emancipated, educated Western woman in the workforce, felt that the choice to marry and decisions about how that marriage would occur belonged to her and her partner alone. They saw themselves as the rightful owners of that decision, although clearly, in another context, that decision might have involved not only the couple but also those who are emotionally close to them: the people who love and support them. Why she chose to exclude her family and their support can tell us about the context of her position within that family, her level of trust, and her investment in the family, or perhaps about other emotions that might have prevented her from sharing her joy with family members.

The decision could also have been a very focused statement and communication to the family about the state of family affairs; her true emotional kinship and alliance might lie with the new partner, and she may have disinvested from her family of origin.

We can learn from the following principles of family functioning:

- What affects one person in the family, affects all the others to varying degrees because a family is also a system.
- Noncommunication is yet another way of communicating. By not making a major family-related event public to the family, a family member can send a very strong message. It is a clear statement of autonomy when it comes to this choice.
- This and similar decisions may exacerbate potential rifts in the family and can fuel feuds and disagreements.
- The family can use this event to find a reconnection to the daughter by showing its support and acceptance of the marriage and the new in-law.
- There can be many other nuances to explore, all unique to that particular family, its history, and its hopes for the future.

Why people do the things they do is a complex question. So it is naive to think in terms of simple answers when considering why they inflict pain or make the major decisions that affect their families and their futures.

In Conti's research (2015, p. 28), the average feud was surprisingly long, ranging from 4 to 5 years. This researcher also mentioned that, in nuclear family contexts, estrangement from biological fathers was the most frequently occurring form. Explanations seem to lie in the inability of former partners to maintain a civil working relationship, for whatever reason. Presumably, many of these relationships fail because of major differences and perceptions of disloyalty and unfulfilled responsibilities. These rifts are especially damaging to the children in the nuclear family, who lose access to a parent. They lose a parent through no fault of their own, and with it, they lose the emotional and other support that can accompany these relationships. The closer the relationship is, as in immediate (nuclear) versus extended families, the more hurtful and damaging the rift (Conti, 2015).

Ending Family Quarrels: The Journey to Reconciliation

Homeostasis or balance. A family seeks balance; its goal is to maintain homeostasis. Inserting destructive destabilizing forces such as family feuds into this fragile web is seldom worth the emotional harm they cause. The damage they do to the integrity of the entire family system is far reaching, and often the most innocent family members (i.e., the children) make the greatest sacrifices. Families can be fragile at best; they become strong through their unity and their loyalty toward members. Ongoing repairable rifts sap the resources of that system.

Undoubtedly, there is suffering for all participating parties when rifts occur. Sometimes, family members have reached an impasse, and it is too uncomfortable to change that particular homeostasis, however dysfunctional it may be. Reconciliation may require revisiting and revising preconceptions, past hurts and anger, the shadows and resentments from the past, and facing many unpleasant memories.

Reconciliation. To facilitate the mending process, the party initiating the feud and the parties maintaining the feud need to come to a place where they lay down their metaphorical weapons. Any family war is complex and destructive, and it has an excessive price tag in terms of diminishing the emotional health and resilience of the entire family. It may be one of the best investments in terms of family functioning and dynamics to initiate cautiously the forgiveness and healing process, and possibly this can be facilitated with professional intervention (Kelley, Waldron, & Kloeber, 2018).

Depending on the reasons and the types of estrangement, the reconciliation can be hopeful or hopeless. The bottom line is that estrangement is a complicated and damaging process that does harm to a family system. It blocks constructive communication and is an extreme form of stonewalling. Gottman has described stonewalling as one of the most dangerous interpersonal weapons, as it blocks avenues for communication and negotiation (Gottman & Silver, 1999, pp. 33–34).

As in bereavement therapy, a dual process model can be helpful in reconciliation to address grief, loss, and trauma recovery. Here are the two prongs of this model, based on its description by Agillias (2016, p. 141):

- Coping with the pain and loss that the feud, cutoff, or estrangement has elicited up to this point and, importantly, the pain and loss that contributed to the foundation of the estrangement process.
- Restoration-oriented grieving focusing on tasks that need to be undertaken in order to fill the voids created by the missing connections, to shape a new identity, and to reorganize life, bearing new realities in mind.

Specific techniques can be utilized to gradually reveal the underpinnings of estrangements, and this can be part of the healing process. *Genograms* are useful in documenting the emotional relationships as well as rifts between family members.

To maintain functional and constructive family relationships is an art in itself. Cutting off members of the family will systematically involve the entire family, and there is a steep price to pay in terms of shared family grief (Kelley, Waldron, & Kloeber, 2018). When both the estranger and estrangee hurt, it signals that a change could be beneficial. The more influential members of a family can use their hierarchical power to try to intervene and facilitate cautious reconciliations, even if a therapist or mediator needs to be involved to find a way out of this painful and mostly destructive maze.

FOCUS POINT

Family estrangement can be as damaging as an acrimonious divorce. Cases of extreme and hateful cutoff may feel like an emotional death of the family member. If families are seen as systems with a great deal of symbiosis or togetherness, then an adversarial rift will create psychological disharmony not only for the feuding parties but also indirectly for all the other family members in that system.

Authentic Insight

The Painful Price of Family Cutoffs

My father was old school when it came to parenting; he was super authoritarian and at times presumed the worst of us kids. He would aim words like poisoned arrows, hitting vulnerable targets. At various points in our lives, my siblings and I were told that we would amount to nothing, that we were untrustworthy, and more. Later in life, I learned that there was a term for what he occasionally showered on us when he lost it; it was verbal abuse. In all fairness, he had a kinder and more compassionate side as well.

My mom shielded us from him. She encouraged us, protected us, indulged us, and, in the end, neutralized the sting. My dad would wage a cold war against my mom. Days would go by that he would not speak to any of us. We tiptoed around him in fear of setting off an imaginary landmine; we never knew what would trigger the next outburst.

Sometimes I have wondered what I would say to him if I could speak to him as a grown up. Would I have better weapons to defend myself if he were my opponent now? But that is a futile question. I faced him as a child. When I was young, my dad's emotional hold stretched far into my life, like feared tentacles. Who knows the influences that a parent can exert on a child, ones that can follow him into adulthood and influence the direction of his dreams. Sometimes a shadow of him crosses my mind; those moments when I struggle with self-doubt, when I think I probably have done something wrong yet again, not that I would know what the misdeed might be. The pervasive sense of dread and guilt. I used to think of it as guilt because I'm alive.

To be expected, each one of my siblings remembers our father in a different way. One of my brothers sees him as a hero; another has deep compassion for him. But then he parented us differently. We weren't all doused with the same pent-up anger. He had his moments of wisdom, and I believe ultimately his intentions were good.

As an adult, one of my siblings used the art of the cutoff as his main defense when things got tough. In turn, each one of us siblings was cut off by him, sometimes for months, sometimes for years. Importantly he always instigated the feud; he was the one in control. I was the most recent victim of the cutoffs. It is almost as if I were playing musical chairs; I am looking for a chair as the music stops, and there is none. I am the one left standing. The brother who had been my childhood friend, my buddy, my confidante was the same person who blocked me from his phone, his email, his life.

My brother lashed out in the same way our father used to snarl at us. It was the example he had been exposed to in his tender years, so he modeled what he had experienced. When he felt hurt and defenseless, he looked for weapons, any weapons.

(Continued)

(Continued)

The price of the emotional cutoff is always too high; nothing good comes of it. It is paid not only by the person who has been blocked; it affects the entire family. My brother died one sunny Saturday. We had not reconciled. In my heart, I know that I had never been truly excommunicated from his world. I had called his bluff. In my mind, we are the same best buddies who supported each other in childhood and adulthood, who were abandoned in boarding school together, who bailed each other out of difficulty—always.

The deep love we shared continues and transcends any misunderstandings or inexplicable behavior. That is the miracle of an authentic heart connection. Nothing has truly come between us as siblings. Some bonds are forever, and nothing (not even a pretend cutoff) can sever them.

Anonymous

GLOBAL GLIMPSE

CULTURAL HUMILITY AND THE DIVERSITY OF FAMILIES

In a complex world where family forms and functions can be very diverse, helping professionals do well to have an open mind about contexts and cultures other than their own. The word **cultural humility** is frequently used to denote a variation of this sort of "unconditional positive regard," which is a phrase coined by Carl Rogers to describe a therapist's warm acceptance of a client's self-reported experiences, attitudes, beliefs, and emotions. This positive regard can also be applied in relation to customs and cultural contexts other than one's own. Bronfenbrenner made us aware of overarching influences such as culture. The following explains cultural humility, as the concept has been frequently used in current literature:

> Cultural humility was used in a variety of contexts from individuals having ethnic and racial differences, to differences in sexual preference, social status, interprofessional roles, to health care provider/patient relationships. The attributes were openness, self-awareness, egoless, supportive interactions, and self-reflection and critique. The antecedents were diversity and power imbalance. The consequences were mutual empowerment, partnerships, respect, optimal care, and lifelong learning. Cultural humility was described as a lifelong process. With a firm understanding of the term, individuals and communities will be better equipped to understand and accomplish an inclusive environment with mutual benefit and optimal care. (Foronda, Baptiste, Reinholdt, & Ousman, 2015, p. 210)

Definitions of cultural humility as well as cultural competence can vary greatly and are influenced by the discipline and practice context. The positive aspects pertaining to cultural humility are that it relies on a strong sense of empathy, or placing oneself in the other person's shoes. It is a professional way of trying to understand how the other may be feeling, while also keeping professional boundaries in place. Ideally, it should also foster awareness of inequalities within the relationship. These in turn can come from or be exaggerated by cultural fluidity.

One need not be an expert at the others' cultural contexts to practice cultural humility, but the prerequisites are that one has an open ear to learn from and be guided and educated by the other and that one withholds judgment of contexts that one might not fully understand from one's own cultural vantage point. Fisher-Borne, Cain, and Martin (2014, p. 165) add this perspective:

> Cultural humility . . . acknowledges power differentials between provider and client and challenges institutional-level barriers.

Personal accountability in the helping professions would require a willingness and commitment to work toward a greater understanding of a framework other than one's own.

Sources: Foronda, Baptiste, Reinholdt, and Ousman (2015); Fisher-Borne, Cain, and Martin (2014).

SPOTLIGHT ON THEORIES

Family Dynamics and Ecological Systems Theory

One of the significant theorists in family systems thinking is Urie Bronfenbrenner (1979). Bronfenbrenner was born in Moscow, Russia, in 1917 and immigrated to the United States at age six. He had a professional career as a developmental psychologist at Cornell University in Ithaca, New York. He died in 2005, leaving behind a considerable intellectual legacy. His personal life was inspiring and influenced the conceptualization of his theoretical model. He gained eminence as an expert on developmental psychology and made major contributions to the field of child rearing and human ecology.

Besides his theory, he is also known as one of the founders of Head Start, an initiative to provide appropriate preschool enrichment and education to children, especially in low-income contexts. He felt strongly that various systems in the child's life could be influential in promoting the best outcome (Bigner & Gerhardt, 2019, p. 117). Here is a tribute by Lerner (2005) to Bronfenbrenner and his significant contributions:

> For more than 60 years, Urie Bronfenbrenner has been both the standard of excellence and the professional conscience of the field of human development, a field that—because of the scope and synthetic power of his vision—has become productively multidisciplinary and multiprofessional. (p. x)

Bronfenbrenner named his original model **ecological systems theory**. Because Bronfenbrenner himself, as well as other researchers, reinterpreted aspects of this theory and expanded on it, it was later also referred to as the bioecological theory or model of development. Bronfenbrenner's theory explains how individuals and families are affected by a variety of interacting environments in a bidirectional manner. An individual's family, by being part of the total environment, is also influenced by other systems at work in that environment (Bigner & Gerhardt, 2019, p. 119). The systems envelop each other almost like Russian Matryoshka dolls, a set of dolls in which each doll contains a smaller version similar to itself.

Bronfenbrenner was particularly interested in these layers of influence that encapsulate and affect children and their families. In the model he conceived, he described the world of a child in terms of interrelated and nested layers, almost like the layers of an onion. With each next layer, another set of influences from the big wide world could influence the child. Closest to the child's world, in the inner circles, are the significant caregivers. Parents and those persons with whom the child has an ongoing and trusted relationship form the most intimate interactions in the child's world.

Microsystem. Bronfenbrenner describes these influences from close caretakers and the like as the **microsystem**, which metaphorically wraps around the core, the individual (in this case, the child). This layer of influence can be acquaintances, extended family members, teachers, and friends at school and other civic contexts.

Mesosystem. The **mesosystem** consists of connections or interactions between microsystems. Bronfenbrenner labeled this dimension to refer to the *connections* children make *between* their close environments, typically family, community, and school. It can include what occurs in the home and in the preschool playgroup with peers. Importantly, this layer can represent the linkages or connections between two or more microsystems.

Exosystem. An **exosystem** may be comprised of government agencies, community programs, the employment settings of parents, and other elements of the environment that a child does not participate in directly but that have an effect on the child nonetheless. This level represents an indirect environment, and the influences tend to occur in a more distanced or indirect manner, especially while the child is young.

Macrosystem. The large system is represented by a **macrosystem**, and this contains all the influences that play a direct and also an indirect role in the child's life. These aspects can include the culture at large, the ideologies of the country in which the child lives, the values and public policies of that country, and other related dimensions.

(Continued)

(Continued)

DIAGRAM 2.1

Bronfenbrenner emphasizes interactions between the individual and the many societal layers in which that individual is nested. On a macrosystemic level, the way in which families and societies locally and throughout the world influence one another can also be considered: what happens in one environmental aspect influences what occurs in others.

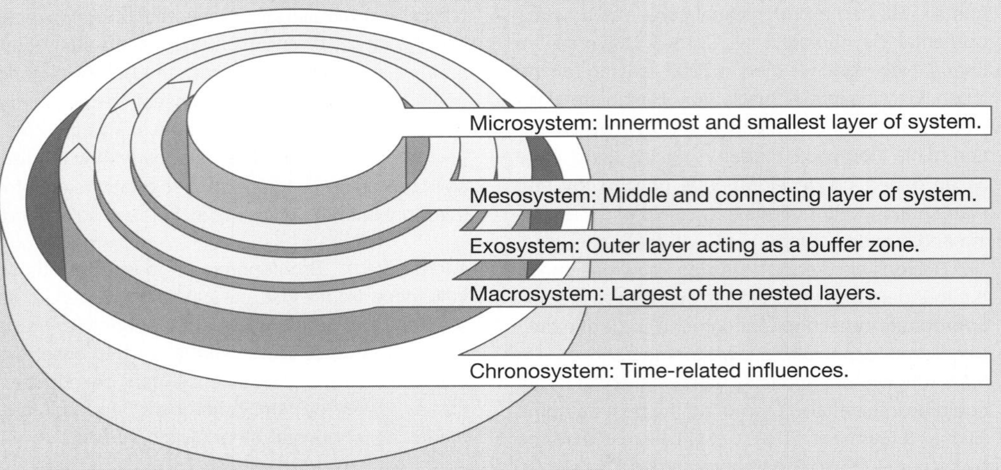
Microsystem: Innermost and smallest layer of system.
Mesosystem: Middle and connecting layer of system.
Exosystem: Outer layer acting as a buffer zone.
Macrosystem: Largest of the nested layers.
Chronosystem: Time-related influences.

Chronosystem. All these layers are embedded in the dimension of time, which Bronfenbrenner chose to call the **chronosystem**. If we think of a chronometer as a very accurate timepiece, we can deduct that the chronosystem has to do with time and related influences. Life transitions and sociohistorical events can occur in the chronosystem. For instance, many of our grandparents or our great grandparents may have experienced the Great Depression. The shared hardship may have influenced them in similar ways. It could have encouraged them to be more frugal, it could have taught them to be careful with their possessions and be aware that hardship can occur at unanticipated moments, or it could have encouraged them to be more community-minded.

As a more current example, we can turn to the events of 9/11. There was a worldview that was fairly trusting and possibly even innocent until the traumatic events of 9/11 played out. These events changed our worldview if we were Americans. Placing this experience into Bronfenbrenner's model, we see that, as one cohort in time was exposed to similar traumatic events, its members were shaped by the memories and fears that these events elicited.

According to Bronfenbrenner's model, we live in nested layers of influence (see Diagram 2.1). Importantly, this influence is **bidirectional**, meaning that power is exerted in two directions. For instance an individual can be influenced by cultural components in her macrosystem. In turn, she influences the culture, as do other individuals who contribute to that culture. In this way, the influences move backward and forward; they are bidirectional.

Large-scale interpretation. Society as a whole can be viewed as an immense collection of families. Just as one family can reflect its cultural context, exert an influence on the greater culture, and be influenced by that culture, a large grouping of families, that is, society, can create a similar interaction on the macrosystemic level. The ecological systems perspective outlined by Bronfenbrenner emphasizes the dual influence between families and societies locally and throughout the world. Essentially, what happens in one environmental aspect influences what occurs in others.

Because families make up society, they affect the various environments in which they live. The family ecology view leads to an examination of the ways that various sociocultural environments influence family and functioning. Bronfenbrenner used the concept of a *process-person-context-time* model to emphasize the common complexity and interrelated influences at different levels of the system (Bigner & Gerhardt, 2019, p. 118).

Bioecological Theory: Process-Person-Context-Time Model

The four interrelated pillars or concepts of this model are process, person, context, and time (PPCT); and it forms the basis of the expanded bioecological model elaborating Bronfenbrenner's more mature version of his theory during the mid-1990s.

- *Process* refers to processes (occurrences, proceedings) allowing for development, as in human development.
- *Person* refers to personal (individual) characteristics and how these play a role in social interactions.
- *Context* refers to the circumstances and relationships (events, surroundings) in the five interconnected systems described in the original ecological systems theory.
- *Time* refers to the dimension (sequencing) affecting factors in the micro–, meso–, and macrosystems.

Subsequent developments. As with many theories, Bronfenbrenner's theory evolved over time as he elaborated it with growing insights. It has also, on occasion, been misinterpreted by enthusiastic scholars, and some conceptual confusion has been known to occur. Nevertheless, he has made a major contribution by emphasizing concepts such as the interrelatedness and bidirectional nature of influence. Concerning the work of Bronfenbrenner, authors Tudge et al. (2016) used this phrase in a title: "Still misused after all these years."

Background. Bronfenbrenner's own life contributed to these insights. Because he was an immigrant, he was acutely aware of the influences of culture and changing social contexts. He believed that these influences were sufficiently pronounced to deserve formal acknowledgment. In the context of family dynamics, the influences can originate in as well as target all these described layers. Remember too that the mutual influence between the systems and between the systems and the family is neither clear-cut nor watertight. It is more like a pebble falling into water, causing a ripple effect whose movement can be bidirectional.

> [Bronfenbrenner] has himself been the foremost theoretician of human development over the past half-century. . . . His ideas have been the ones that stood the test of time to represent fundamental concepts used in all the developmental systems theories that constitute the cutting-edge models of human development. (Damon & Lerner, 1998 as cited in Bronfenbrenner, 2005, p. xii)

Tribute. The tribute to Bronfenbrenner published by Cornell University at the time of his death stated the following:

> He spent many of his later years warning that the process that makes human beings human is breaking down as disruptive trends in American society produce ever more chaos in the lives of America's children. "The hectic pace of modern life poses a threat to our children second only to poverty and unemployment," he said. "We are depriving millions of children—and thereby our country—of their birthright . . . virtues, such as honesty, responsibility, integrity and compassion." (Lang, 2005)

This psychologist's deep conviction about what it takes to support developing children was one of the major motivating factors in conceptualizing and initiating Head Start, which he accomplished with a dedicated team of like-minded professionals and the support of the U.S. Department of Health and Human Services (www.acf.hhs.gov/ohs).

"We now know what it takes to enable families to work the magic that only they can perform. The question is, are we willing to make the sacrifices and the investment necessary to enable them to do so?"

Urie Bronfenbrenner (1917– 2005),
developmental psychologist

FOCUS POINT

Bronfenbrenner's ecological systems theory explains how individuals and families are affected by and affect a variety of interacting environments; influence is bidirectional. An individual's family, by being part of the total environment, is also influenced by these other systems. The systems are nested within each other.

GLOBAL GLIMPSE

OUR SOCIAL FABRIC OF INTERCONNECTEDNESS

Born over a century ago, Urie Bronfenbrenner (1917–2005) was acutely aware of our interconnectedness on many levels. None of us can truly claim to be isolated and totally autonomous islands. Strand after strand, we are woven into a social fabric, and we become integrated on so many levels. Bronfenbrenner was greatly respected by his colleagues for his original and insightful worldview. The following quotations by this developmental psychologist give us a glimpse into how he saw the world of children, their families, and societal contexts.

- "If we can stand on our own two feet, it is because others have raised us up. If, as adults, we can lay claim to competence and compassion, it only means that other human beings have been willing and enabled to commit their competence and compassion to us—through infancy, childhood, and adolescence, right up to this very moment" (Bronfenbrenner, 1978).
- "In order to develop normally, a child requires progressively more complex joint activity with one or more adults who have an irrational emotional relationship with the child. Somebody's got to be crazy about that kid. That's number one. First, last and always" (Bronfenbrenner, 1994).
- "Children need people in order to become human. . . . It is primarily through observing, playing, and working with others older and younger than himself that a child discovers both what he can do and who he can become—that he develops both his ability and his identity. . . . Hence to relegate children to a world of their own is to deprive them of their humanity, and ourselves as well" (Bronfenbrenner, 1973, p. xvii).
- "If the children and youth of a nation are afforded opportunity to develop their capacities to the fullest, if they are given the knowledge to understand the world and the wisdom to change it, then the prospects for the future are bright. In contrast, a society which neglects its children, however well it may function in other respects, risks eventual disorganization and demise" (Bronfenbrenner, 1973, p. 1).

Source: Quotations are from Urie Bronfenbrenner (1917–2005), a Russian-born, American developmental psychologist.

In a Nutshell

Family Dynamics and Ecological Systems Theory

- Increasingly, the family is viewed as part of a larger system. We cannot work with children in isolation, as they are the products of their interactions with many interrelated systems.
- Ecological systems theory is attributed to Urie Bronfenbrenner. He is a developmental psychologist, born over a century ago. He was one of the forces initiating the "Head Start" movement.
- Ecological systems theory acknowledges the systemic influences on the family or individual, as

well as the *bidirectionality* and *interrelatedness* of these systems, hence the reference to ecology.

- *Ecology*, as defined in biology, refers to the relationships as well as the interactions between an organism and its surroundings. In ecological systems theory, the focus is on the child and her multilayered and complex relations.
- The theory envisions several layers of bidirectional influence, circling outward. These range from the influences closest to the child (microsystem) through several other layers to the largest system of influence (macrosystem).
- Factors related to time, such as experiencing major cultural and societal upheavals, are addressed by a time dimension (chronosystem).
- Every child is nested in interrelated layers of influence, and for that reason, no child can be approached in isolation. If we wish to support the child constructively, we have to address these responsibilities at several points, ranging from input by families, educators, and social policies through to culture and the community at large.
- To understand family dynamics fully, we need to be aware of the many layers of bidirectional influence in which these dynamics function.

CHAPTER FOCUS POINTS

Task, Structure, and Context

- Individuals are embedded within families, which, in turn, are nested in societies. There is bidirectional responsibility and influence. Societies and the public policy enacted by them can provide greater backup for families, facilitating their optimal functioning.
- Specific cultural and societal characteristics can differ widely. For societies, families are very valuable components. Combined, families *are* the society; remove the family unit, and the fabric of a society disintegrates.

The Influences on Dynamics

- In any family unit, those who have access to resources, knowledge, skill, or other valuable assets may hold the seat of power. In ideal family contexts, the strengths of the family are pooled so that the entire family can benefit from constructive opportunities.
- There are other forms of social and emotional power that can be exerted inside the family and other structures supporting power distinctions, such as hierarchical differences and power inequities. Both imply that the parties concerned come from different points of strength and vulnerability. These hierarchies and inequities, in turn, influence the particular dynamic of interactions within that system.

The Choreography of the Family Dance

- If we describe families in terms of structure and distance, it brings us to elements such as boundaries between members of the family.
- Boundaries are those natural demarcations that indicate the level of privacy and space a family member demands—the emotional area each family member occupies. The appropriate individual space that each family member acquires is part of the individuation process.
- Different families have their own unique family rules, which can be expressed in an overt or covert manner. The openness of behaviors is what is meant by overt, whereas the hidden dimensions are covert.

Patterns of Family Interaction

- Family estrangement can be as damaging as an acrimonious divorce. Cases of extreme and hateful cutoff may feel like an emotional death of the family member.
- If families are seen as systems with a great deal of symbiosis or togetherness, then an adversarial rift will create psychological disharmony not only for the feuding parties but also indirectly for all the other family members in that system.

Spotlight on Theories: Family Dynamics and Ecological Systems Theory

- Bronfenbrenner's ecological systems theory explains how individuals and families are affected by and affect a variety of interacting environments; influence is bidirectional.
- An individual's family, by being part of the total environment, is also influenced by these other systems. The systems are nested within each other.

CHAPTER

3 Dynamic Family Commitments

Learning Objectives

After completing this chapter, you should be able to

1. Examine the importance of a *circle of safety* for an individual.
2. Explain the obligations of individual family members toward the family unit.
3. Identify the different types of *engagement*.
4. Analyze the relationship between the childhood experiences of parents and their subsequent parenting skills.
5. Specify the patterns of dysfunctional families.
6. Summarize *family systems theory* and discuss its explication of family interactions.

The Circle of Safety

As humans, we seek out our fellow travelers on the path of life. Generally, we like being networked within a social group. Bessel Van der Kolk (2014) says, "We are profoundly social creatures; our lives consist of finding our place within a community of human beings" (p. 112). We do better when we can rely on a wider safety net, when we can specialize our tasks according to our strengths and talents and collaborate toward a common goal: survival. Preferably, our survival is characterized by a good quality of life.

Archaeologists have revealed many types of human shelter. In the very northern areas of Scotland, we find low cave-like home structures, the roofs covered with soil and grass for insulation. They remind us how our ancestors might have tried to escape from wind and weather. To enter, one has to crouch and shuffle in on one's knees. We speculate that the low entrance had several functions. Besides minimizing the exposed areas where the cold and damp could enter, it also protected the family within in a more complex manner. If hostile persons were to try and enter the home, the architecture forced them to crouch. That made them vulnerable and, in turn, strengthened the position of the family within. Accessing one of these shelters on my Scotland visit literally brought me to my knees and gave me a moment to reflect on the meaning of shelter in an emotional context.

It is impossible to be vigilant at all times. Constant vigilance would exhaust us and deprive us of the sheer joy of the moment. Being embedded in the family context, we are within a circle of safety. The circle allows the helpless baby to be cared for, nurtured, and strengthened toward independence. It allows the elderly to adjust to diminishing strengths. It allows each member to make age- and

FOCUS POINT

Individuals network and widen their social groups to create a safety net. By collaborating and sharing strengths and talents, they are able to establish an inner circle that supports collaboration and survival. Because it is impossible to be on guard and alert at all times, a person finds it important to be a part of a larger group. Being embedded in a safe family unit allows an individual to deal with everyday challenges successfully.

lifespan-appropriate contributions. It is a place where we can focus our energies on becoming and developing, while the greater group shelters, guides, and nurtures.

The family is an ideal point at which to enter and also depart from the world, as it is a group deeply vested in our well-being. Family members make it their calling and life goal to be our guides and companions. In Christian scriptures, the metaphor of the shepherd and his flock is frequently used to denote the qualities of protection and guidance, which are vested in a leader for the greater good of the group. The word "pastor" is derived from the Latin word for "shepherd." In the ancient Mesopotamian religion, a deity named Tammuz was honored as being the patron god of shepherds (Black & Green, 1992, p. 72). The metaphor of the shepherd also occurs in Islam and in Sikhism.

Launching and Landing: The Dynamic Tasks of the Family

Families have lifelong tasks that evolve with the life cycle of the family. Because an extended family is comprised of members from various age groups, the tasks cover most aspects of human existence. There are numerous subtle interactions and contributions the family will make to ensure best outcomes for all of its members.

Ensuring survival and being able to fend off threats are lead family tasks. In 1996, psychologist Mary Pipher wrote a widely acclaimed book titled, *The Shelter of Each Other* (Pipher, 1996). This phrase captures the essence of what families represent: our family is the place from which we *launch*, and it is the place to which we return—where we *land*. Families are our shelter. In families that fulfill these functions well, the launching and the landing are accompanied by positive regard, by imparting all those emotions and actions that make us feel welcome, loved, and accepted.

When we experience the love and acceptance of our family, it envelops us with virtually magical strengths. It sets in motion the gentle crystal-like growth of self-esteem, the sense that we are intact. This emotional intactness is one of the key factors in negotiating interpersonal relationships and most of the challenges in our later lives.

The Dynamic Tasks of the Family

Families nurture, guide, educate, and do so much more. These behaviors are interwoven and shape the lives of all the family members. Belonging to a healthy, well-functioning family has many benefits and provides an excellent point of departure toward optimal outcomes. A family, as a group, has numerous responsibilities, but family members, as individuals, also have specific tasks and responsibilities. They each have obligations toward that family.

- *Commitment.* This important obligation means being willing and wanting to serve the family's causes by contributing to the greater good of the family, even if at times, no personal benefits come to you because of this commitment.
- *Nurture.* Families provide the warmth and caring of loving relationships.
- *Guidance.* Experienced family members share their wisdom and provide a shortcut to best practices.
- *Education.* Providing this formal form of guidance is often a family responsibility shared with specialists who make it their life task to educate.
- *Attachment.* It is like an invisible glue. Family members bond with one another and trust their sense that this is a "forever" relationship. Attachment allows us to link to something or somebody. It is reaching out to another human being for survival itself. The infant learns trust through a primary caretaker's response to her needs. Because of this ongoing interchange, she can attach with a sense of security, affecting future relationships.
- *Acceptance.* Importantly, in a well-functioning family, members are accepted and never relinquish the core thread of their commitment to one another, even when a family member strays from the straight and narrow.
- *Communication.* The family is a safe place to speak the concerns of one's heart and to be congruent (or real) without playing excessive games of diplomacy, sugarcoating the facts, or using other ways to soften the truth.
- *Democracy.* Additionally, families should incorporate a sense of democracy, so that all family members are heard and can have access to family resources, be they emotional or more concrete.
- *Respect.* Family members should all feel respected and supported. They should feel that the validity of who they are is affirmed and reconfirmed.
- *Loyalty.* Identifying with the family requires that we actively show our support, through thick and thin. We are loyal to the unit that shelters us, even and maybe especially when we face adversity. Families keep a united front toward the outside world. Loyalty means that the commitment is firm and trustworthy, especially when the road is rocky.

Ideally a well-functioning family should promote a sense of trust and safety. The family is not a place where we need to be on guard. It should not be a battlefield for family members. In short, families provide sanctuary—the place that allows us to feel safe and sheltered.

FOCUS POINT

The family launches an individual into the world and provides sanctuary to that individual when he or she returns to it. The family as a whole has responsibilities toward its individual members. In turn, family members have individual responsibilities and obligations to the family. The family as a well-functioning unit provides its members with commitment, nurture, education, attachment, acceptance, sanctuary, loyalty, and respect. When individual members are active in fulfilling their responsibilities toward the family, the unit functions successfully.

The Family Orchestra

Most of us have a strong individualistic streak within us, and this can be strengthened or downplayed by cultural contexts. Generally, Americans are thought to be individualists, whereas people from Asia are said to be more collectivist. Within this generalization is considerable room for variation, and a family's position on the individualistic-collectivistic scale will depend on individual family dynamics, the dominant culture, social customs, and more. No two people are totally alike, not even identical twins.

In a family, we form an orchestra of sorts, where we each contribute and blend our musical voices. Having a unique and expressive voice is a birthright, but for the family orchestra to be able to produce harmonious sequences of music, players need to time themselves, collaborate, and have respect, tolerance, and sensitivity toward fellow players.

The Von Trapp family singers, photographed in 1939. They were the inspiration for the movie *The Sound of Music*. The daughters were named Agathe, Johanna, Eleonore, Maria, Rosemarie, Hedwig, and Martina. A family has depth and complexity; there are a number of interacting elements that influence each other to affect family members' social lives and behaviors and so much more.

Source: Public domain.

Being in the orchestra means that we can sometimes play a solo tune while the other players are silent or provide the background music. But, in general, there is a coordinated cohesiveness that allows us to progress from ordinary to extraordinary. Indeed, when we add all these voices, a greater creative product is born. In psychology, we talk about the sum being greater than the parts. It forms a greater whole or *Gestalt*: the German term denoting form or shape (von Ehrenfels, 1890; Wertheimer, 1912).

In describing the typical family, we could ask specific questions. What are its main characteristics? But how can we best describe something as unique as a family? We could try to capture family members in a painting or photograph. We could try to describe each member of that family. Even doing so might not be enough to truly tell us about the core that sets that family apart, that makes it unique. That is because a family is more than a collection of related people. Even by grouping all the siblings, the parents, and the extended family members together, we still do not succeed in capturing the dynamic of that particular family system. In order to understand what that family and its members are really about, we have to look at other dimensions as well. We need to pay attention to the way in which they communicate with each other, how they influence each other, the importance of the roles they play in each other's lives, and the developmental aspect—namely, how that family changes over time. A family has depth and complexity; there are a number of interacting elements that influence each other to affect the social lives and behaviors of family members, as well as many other aspects of the family.

In short, if we belong to a healthy family, that membership will allow us to fly a little higher and reach a little farther—it will generally extend us in multifaceted ways, and we will achieve more than we could have on a solitary, isolated path.

GLOBAL GLIMPSE

CONNECTEDNESS

Ubuntu: I Am Because We Are . . .

Families are an important social institution. Part of their power is derived from the cohesiveness within the family system, and that in turn influences the dynamic. This same cohesiveness contributes to resilience, both of individual members and of the family as a whole.

An example of the power of group connectedness is expressed by the Xhosa people of Southern Africa. The word *ubuntu* in the Nguni language generally refers to our shared humanity. Some translations point toward the essence of our interconnectedness and a universal bond.

Therapeutically, it can imply the connectedness between the caregiver and the one receiving the care. It recognizes that healing is facilitated by acknowledging a common humanity sharing a common destiny. Ubuntu philosophy refers to a humanistic ethic and ideology: Ubuntuism.

In the context of the Truth and Reconciliation Commission, initiated by Archbishop Desmond Tutu (Nobel Laureate for Peace) in the post-apartheid years, the term has taken on a special meaning with implications of hope and healing. Tutu (1999) described the word *ubuntu* as meaning something along the lines of a person is a person through other people.

Ubuntu has been used to describe a human quality, African humanism, a philosophy, and a worldview (Gade, 2011). In the interim Constitution of the Republic of South Africa, Act 200 of 1993, the epilogue makes reference to this concept in the following sentence:

> . . . there is a need for understanding but not for vengeance, a need for reparation but not for retaliation, a need for ubuntu but not for victimisation.

Interestingly, in the world of computers, an open-sourced Linux operating system developed in South Africa is distributed and marketed under the name Ubuntu.

Sources: Gade (2011) and Tutu (1999).

Engagement

The word ***engage*** has several subtle variations of meaning, but in essence it refers to becoming a participant or taking part in an interaction. We can engage in a conversation, as in entering the dialogue. We can disengage when we leave the back and forth of the interaction. As a noun, *engagement* can mean a social event in which we participate. It can also be several steps more serious, as in being engaged or committed to being in an ongoing relationship. In whatever form we use the word, for example, the verb (*to engage*) or the noun (*engagement*), it implies a mutual participation. In family, friendship, business, and other variations of social relationships, there is a responsibility exerted by all who participate in that particular interaction.

We can draw people out and bring them into the orbit of an interaction by engaging them and including them. There is the engaging relationship, as in being committed to that particular social exchange. An engaging conversation can mean that it draws us in because it is sufficiently interesting, entertaining, or informative that we are motivated to participate. It contains its own magnetism. An engaging personality is someone with the skill of drawing us into participation. Engaging people can elicit responses or activate commitment because they seem to have a persuasive skill that makes us want to be included in their communications.

Appropriate and mindful engagement is a demand of the well-functioning family. If we are active members of the family, it is part of our role within that particular family unit to engage in rituals pertaining to this group of close relatives. We dialogue, we give our input, and we react to the cues provided by others in this group. In this way, family membership comes with the responsibility to participate. If the depressed mother, for instance, constantly withdraws into her room, she cannot be available to her children. She cannot actively meet their needs either emotionally or physically, and she may find it very challenging to care for them.

Disengagement

The act of withdrawing and pulling back from interactions can contain powerful messages of its own. For instance, by *not* replying to a letter or an invitation, we can imply or "send" a message that is even stronger than an active answer would be. Depending on context, a non-reply can be seen as a snub or a withdrawal. It changes the back-and-forth pattern of that particular relationship.

Availability and emotional investment. In the online dating context, the word *ghosting* has a very specific meaning. It implies that we are no longer available to electronic messages in whatever form. We do not respond, and it may seem as if we have gone up in smoke (or become ghostly). Once one party withdraws in this manner, it sends a very clear signal that a relationship is being broken off. At times, these messages are sent inadvertently. Being out of cell-phone range or not having access to Wi-Fi may remove us from communication loops. If the other party does not know the reason for the silence, it can send an unintended message.

Dialogue of the family. In families, there is a commitment to participate in the unique dialogue of the family. One of the most toxic ways of not communicating is **stonewalling**. This is when a metaphorical barrier is erected that stops and prevents dialogue. If members of a couple use stonewalling in their interpersonal warfare, they risk destroying the very fabric that binds them. Gottman (1994) described stonewalling as one of the "Four Horsemen of the Apocalypse," used predominantly by couples as a dysfunctional noncommunication strategy. It blocks any opportunity for negotiation that could pave the way toward resolving a difficult or conflicted situation (Gottman & Silver, 1999).

Of all the parenting approaches, stonewalling and a few others are outright harmful as they trigger a range of emotions that include feeling rejected or abandoned. The parent who consistently ignores a child sends a message that at least that child is not important or valued. For the child, being ignored by a parent translates to feeling rejected and having unmet needs. Stonewalling between parents and their offspring is a dangerous path.

Remember that family members are in engaged positions of communication and interaction with each other. When they choose to stonewall, to ignore, and to icily break the threads that bind the parties, no good will result.

FOCUS POINT

A family functions optimally when it is a cohesive unit. Engagement in a family implies that we become a participant or take part in interaction. If this occurs within the family unit, it establishes mutual commitment and participation that strengthens the family as a whole. Not being available or invested in the family (being disengaged) sends a message of withdrawal and contributes to dysfunction.

Shaping the Dynamics of the System

Relationship Responsibilities

When we commit to a familial relationship, be it as a parent or as a significant caregiver, we have a duty to respond to the emotional needs of the family's children. This, in turn, will allow each child to attach firmly and appropriately, providing the foundation for much of what is to follow. Being an engaged family member, parent, friend, or significant other means that we respond. We try to meet those basic needs for attachment that allow for trust to develop. The dynamic within the parent-child relationship will largely determine whether the child reaches the goal of living life as fully as possible, and how the child attempts to achieve that goal. These early relationships may color much of what follows. Parents are powerful in the relationship game because they can model behavior; they can be the example. As Bessel van der Kolk (2014), author of *The Body Keeps the Score*, writes,

> Our interactions with our caregivers convey what is safe and what is dangerous: whom we can count on and who will let us down; what we need to do to get our needs met. (p. 131)

The parents who respond to the needs of a child show by doing so that they are noticing him or her and modifying their own behaviors to meet that child at the point of need. The very young child expresses needs through crying, babbling, or other body language. Ignoring these expressions by not reacting creates a child who anticipates that her or his needs will remain unmet, creating yet further stress. Stress causes our bodies to release more than normal amounts of cortisol: the stress hormone (American Psychological Association, n.d.). This hormone, in turn, can affect other aspects of the child's physiology.

Responsive parenting implies that the parent reacts to the needs the child displays. This responsive interaction is also implied in the phrase *serve and return.* The child communicates in some form needing something from the parent. The child *serves* a message to the parent, much like a tennis player would serve the ball. The parent, in turn, *returns* that serve by responding, by being responsive (Center on the Developing Child, n.d.).

Responsible parenting implies that the parent is informed of commonly accepted childcare practices. The parent is able to *read* and understand the messages the child is communicating. Of course, parents can learn what works by trial and error. But by knowing the range of best practices appropriate for the developmental level of the child, parents learn preferred practices quickly and responsibly. Being aware of which best practices achieve the best outcomes for their child allows parents to use the insights gained from research without having to reinvent the wheel.

Barren Childhoods

We tend to take it for granted that responsible parents will be appropriately responsive. But there are situations in which parents are not able to be the best parents they might like to be. Among the many possible scenarios, one is particularly troublesome. Parents who themselves have grown up in emotionally deprived circumstances may not have had their own emotional needs fulfilled and are consequently less capable of taking on nurturing roles. When a child experiences trauma in the early years, it can curtail or limit her or his options for attachment.

Children ideally form a close and trusting bond with primary caregivers. If these caregivers are reliable and trustworthy, the child grows up with the sense that needs will be met, creating a zone of safety and security. This secure attachment allows children to cultivate agency: as they discover that their actions can change how they feel and how others respond, they learn that they can play an active role when faced with difficult situations (Van der Kolk, 2014).

On the other hand, when a parent cannot provide this optimal environment for a child, the child may withdraw, become disorganized in its attachment, or display a lack of emotional regulation. The child who is being parented by an unpredictable, possibly violent, or emotionally absent caretaker will learn not to make demands for nurture and comfort. In a sense, these children are being conditioned to give up when faced with challenges later in life (Van der Kolk, 2014). This conditioning leads the child to a place of deficit where it lacks some of the essential care it requires. The parent who is erratic, unpredictable, and prone to emotional outbursts helps create a hyper-vigilant child. The youngster has to be on guard for the next storm and cannot predict from which angle it will hit. In essence, this child cannot trust caretakers and will respond in equally unpredictable ways, lashing out or withdrawing in a disorganized manner.

The way we as adults relate to the various significant factors in our lives can often be traced back to the patterns we learned in our families of origin. The **microclimate** of our family of origin, our first family home, will revisit us in our future relationships. Through our parents, we create and build an inner landscape, also called an inner world (Schofield, 1998; McVittie & McKinlay, 2017). This inner world contains values, the perceptions we have of ourselves based on the feedback we receive from others, the things that motivate us, the things that are important to us, and so much more. Parents help children populate this inner world, to color it in and elaborate on it. This slow, almost organic process counteracts the barrenness that is created when children have no role models, no motivators, no cheerleaders. The responsibility of good parenting is great. With our parenting, we set the tone for much that is to follow.

Cultural Context

"Ghosts in the Nursery"

The frequently quoted phrase in developmental psychology contexts—"Ghosts in the nursery"—is attributed to Selma Fraiberg and her colleagues Edna Adelson and Vivian Shapiro, and it appeared in their research published in 1975. The metaphor they referenced is based on the fairy tale "Sleeping Beauty," in which a curse at birth determines the future of the fair princess. Ultimately, it requires the magic of a prince's kiss (and its implied promise of eternal love) to break the spell.

The phrase has since been used in various contexts to describe the fears of parents concerning the well-being of their children, for example, the fear of sudden infant death syndrome (SIDS). But its use by Fraiberg, Adelson, and Shapiro (1975) referred to the emotional burdens of the parents, unintentionally placed on children. The full title of their article was "Ghosts in the Nursery: A Psychoanalytic Approach to the Problems of Impaired Infant-Mother Relationships." Fraiberg was a social worker and psychoanalyst, and her two coauthors also had psychoanalytic training. Fraiberg has been likened to Anna Freud.

They argue that the way in which the past revisits us in the present influences our future. If newborns are not welcomed into a loving environment that provides the opportunities for firm, stable, and unconditional attachment, because of the ghosts in their parents' lives, the risk is great that the circle of safety that the child needs for optimal development cannot be established fully. Here is the concept in the original words of these authors:

(Continued)

(Continued)

> In every nursery there are ghosts. They are the visitors from the unremembered past of the parents; the uninvited guests at the christening. Under all favorable circumstances the unfriendly and unbidden spirits are banished from the nursery and return to their subterranean dwelling place. The baby makes his own imperative claim on parental love and, in strict analogy with the fairy tales, the bonds of love protect the child and his parents against the intruders, the malevolent ghosts.
>
> This is not to say that ghosts cannot invent mischief from their burial places. Even among families where the love bonds are stable and strong, the intruders from the parental past may break through the magic circle in an unguarded moment. (Fraiberg et al., 1975, p. 387)

The ghosts-in-the-nursery cycle can be interrupted and even discontinued. According to these authors, there is hope, and it is indeed possible to lay the past to rest successfully. Appropriate therapy, according to the psychoanalytic perspective held by Fraiberg et al., suggests interventions and therapy for parents, with the goal of encouraging their personal *ghosts* to depart (p. 420).

In the **psychoanalytic approach**, childhood trauma is thought to have far-reaching effects on the child and to negatively influence later outcomes. At a time when children were only just recognized as a demographic that needed developmentally appropriate child-centered interventions, the psychoanalytic approach was welcome, as it enabled social policy to respond accordingly. The necessity for approaches that acknowledged the unique needs and developmental qualities of children influenced a variety of disciplines and endeavors, including parenting practices, judicial rights and privileges, education, and medicine (pediatrics).

Alfred Adler, a contemporary of Freud's, is particularly remembered for his work with children and for his thoughts about the birth order of children in families. He encouraged the establishment of counseling centers, where families could seek professional help. He found that by involving the family in the treatment of children, he gained better insight into the total family context that could support that particular child. Additionally, he witnessed some of the outcomes for children of World War II, including separation from or the loss of a parent for vulnerable children, so he and his colleagues addressed topics related to attachment and loss, basic trust, and bonding behaviors (Erford & Bardhoshi, 2018).

Many parents realize that some of their own trauma should not be passed forward, and they try to shield children from this burden. This aim can be approached by initially acknowledging the trauma, possibly reliving it under therapeutic conditions, and ultimately undergoing therapy and establishing new and rewarding relationships, insight, life experience, and wisdom; this combination gradually allows a parent to move to a new emotional place.

In the work of Fraiberg et al. (1975), the suggested approach is this: parents are therapeutically guided to reexperience and remember their own childhood anxiety, to understanding it with refreshed insight, and, in this manner, to guard against a repetition of their own past experiences related to bonding, attachment, and relationship formation. Additionally, Al Ubaidi (2017) comments that victimized children emerging from dysfunctional families should be respected for their innocence in the situation. They did not initiate it; they inherited the toxicity from their parents. The trauma inflicted by their parents' harsh words and actions can cause emotional scarring that can accompany them for years to come. The hope we extend is to offer interventions that can put the past into a different light, and set the child free to face a less encumbered future.

"The past can revisit us in the present, to color our future."

Clara Gerhardt, 2018

Source: Fraiberg, Adelson, and Shapiro (1975).

Breaking the spell. Fast forward to when the traumatized child becomes a parent herself. She may not have been exposed to constructive parenting so will have no example on which to base her own behavior. Additionally, the memories of angry and disengaged parents may be so painful that it is easier not to parent than to let the memories from her own early life resurface. It is possible for these parents to break the spell of damaging patterns. In her research, Caroline Leaf, a communication pathologist and audiologist who works in the area of cognitive neuroscience, has found that the way we think about and choose to respond to life situations and circumstances becomes the signal that activates or deactivates the generational problems in our lives (2013, p. 58). Research further shows that if these parents engage in behavioral and mental interventions, their brains will experience distinct and focused changes (p. 69).

Children who are subjected to the pathological parenting of an older generation anticipate that their adult lives will contain the same abusive qualities. This anticipation may set the stage to repeat the harmful acts to which they have become accustomed. Victimized adults may try to blank out their childhood trauma by succumbing to addiction disorders and avoiding investment in close friendships and relationships. As they struggle to trust others, they may return to behavior that was learned while they were fending off attacks during their tender years.

Therapeutic interventions are the most effective ways to *interrupt* and *break* the circle of serious harm. Parents who were traumatized as children need to be released from the spell of harmful parenting before they can create their own healthy parent-child relationship, one that displays their courage in choosing a different avenue than the one they themselves were forced to tread in their tender years.

Healthy families. The differences between dysfunctional and healthy families include the length of episodes of dysfunctional behavior and the ways of recovery. The families who struggle may find it difficult to move beyond the negative patterns that dominate their lives. Healthy families have the ability to regain their balance and to resume constructive behavior patterns after brief spells of dysfunction. Importantly, healthy families should not be mistaken for *perfect* families. Healthy families will also face challenges that may feel insurmountable (Al Ubaidi, 2017). But healthy families will display resilience, will access extended support systems, will reflect about the situation, will communicate clearly, and will explore actively ways of interrupting and ending the negative spell.

Healthy families display a number of qualities that are associated with clear and emotionally supportive communication. Al Ubaidi (2017) highlights several of these qualities associated with optimal outcomes:

- Being respectful of the individual differences and emotional needs of family members
- Honoring the overt and ongoing rules within the family
- Being respectful of boundaries and privacy, without being secretive or distrustful
- Displaying flexibility to meet the needs of each family member
- Providing safe and secure environments free of physical and emotional abuse
- Allowing for second chances and self-correction, and extending forgiveness

Despite his many well-founded recommendations for supportive and nurturing family environments, Al Ubaidi (2017) reminds us of the realities of everyday families:

> **Perfection [in families] is unattainable, unrealistic, besides potentially dull and sterile.**

FOCUS POINT

The ability to form secure attachments shapes all our relationships and begins with the parent-child bond. If children do not come from situations of appropriate care or engagement, they will most likely become parents who are unable to care and engage appropriately with their own children. When responsible parenting is modeled and a vulnerable child's safety and security are ensured, a platform of trusting attachment is created from which other relationships can be negotiated. For children growing up without these trusting and nurturing elements, extensive intervention may be required.

Authentic Insight

Family Reunions

The loom of my family of origin was set before I entered it. Somewhere, my ancestors had worked out family patterns that worked for them. And we, the children, carved out our own patterns within the family's boundaries, until we could eventually launch and set up anew. Fast forward to the family reunion. I had not seen my siblings in almost a decade; I remember each one with unique traits, dislikes and likes, demons and dreams.

Childlike, I thought that I could reenter the system with old grievances resolved. My sibs told me they had changed. I thought I had changed. We each had new environments, new relationships, new challenges. It must be possible to go back and unwrinkle the fabric of the past—waft a steam wand to release the crinkles. Not so. A family of origin is virtually carved in stone. It's a tribute to what once was. It's past tense.

It's the family of creation we can change. Maybe we siblings had updated some external characteristics, but as we reentered the old system something disconcerting happened. Despite the family bonds, some old hurts still rubbed in wrong places. The boulder between some of us was still unmoved, and unwritten system rules resurfaced and pushed us back to a somewhat dysfunctional equilibrium. We just learned to tiptoe more carefully on the lily pads.

It is best to concentrate on the positive components that often save the day: the threads of genes and blood, the core loyalties that remained true and rekindled their essence. We looked at each others' older selves. Like an automatic camera lens adjusts with a click and a rotation, our view of the world was suddenly refocused, and we could not remember a time before now. I rediscovered what I loved in my family of origin and took up the threads of relationships where I had dropped them. Only my sibs have access to my childhood.

Families are oh so complicated. Entry is best reserved for those who know the unwritten codes and how to avoid setting off the trapdoors of past pains, and for those who know how to tap into the secret resources of support. Mostly, I am grateful that I can leave the "excess" family baggage within the context of one generation—the generation I share with my siblings, who also shared my tender years—while still being able to hang on to that which I cherish.

The developmentally appropriate way to achieve this position was for each one of us to have moved on and out, while maintaining the powerful foundations of family ties—to become autonomous, while remaining loosely connected to our family pasts. We left behind the unwanted; yet we cherished the select emotional heirlooms we needed for our own family connectedness, the ones we want to pass on to the next generation, thereby creating our own families with the promise of renewal.

And the result is this: A next generation that will dance the family tango all over again, but in its own way, and on its own terms.

Clara Gerhardt, December 2010, on the occasion of a major family reunion.

Dysfunctional Families

The most effective family patterns and rules can be overturned when a family is, or becomes, dysfunctional. All those patterns that were established to ensure good functioning can be hijacked to serve different needs. The communications that should facilitate understanding become the weapons of duplicity. Common signs of a dysfunctional family include the following (Al Ubaidi, 2017):

- Having chronic conflict and destabilization
- Being low on structure and high on chaos
- Saying one thing and meaning another
- Spreading untrue rumors, which demonstrates low respect
- Displaying reversal and confusion concerning roles
- Making accusations and being revengeful
- Ignoring personal boundaries and privacy; breaking confidentiality
- Attaching conditions to love, respect, and support

A **dysfunctional family** maintains its system of relating by exerting direct and indirect pressure on the members. The outcome is a continuation of ineffective behaviors (Sorrels & Myers, 1983). This pressure also explains why some families prefer to maintain the dysfunctional setup with which they are familiar, as opposed to making the changes that would lead to improved functioning. Family members may be maintaining a balance or equilibrium, even though it is at the expense of improved outcomes. There are many variations on the theme when it comes to the behavior displayed by dysfunctional families. In essence, these dysfunctional behaviors can be described as family processes that do not contribute to the greater good of the family.

Each one of these actions becomes an arrow to hurt an opponent. And like arrows with poisoned tips, they deliver much damage. For instance, in a family system where blaming is in the order of the day, members become defensive. If family members fear further attack, the most direct response may be to cease what they are doing. In this way, blaming can bring things to a halt. Blaming behavior can immobilize the targets, just like a poisoned arrow can stop an animal in its tracks. If one parent in a family constantly blames the spouse and the children, it precipitates a circle of events. The blaming behavior can be a symptom of dysfunction. It's a chicken-and-egg problem. Which came first? The one perpetuates the other. Diagram 3.1 illustrates this circularity.

Family Reunion, by Frédéric Bazille, 1867. Family reunions allow us to cherish the select emotional heirlooms we need for our own family connectedness, the ones we want to pass on to the next generation.

Source: Public domain.

DIAGRAM 3.1

In family contexts, a circular pattern of influence can occur. An event can feed on its precursor, or that which occurred previously, and also influence the next sequence, or what follows.

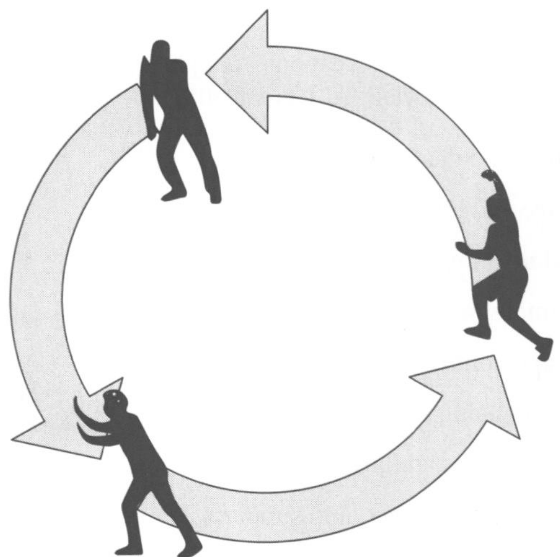

Families create the dynamic space in which relationship formation, self-regulation, and individuation should be able to occur. Even so, there can be an unwitting, intergenerational continuity of destructive behavior patterns, referenced in Bowen's family systems theory as the intergenerational transmission process.

We can try to sidestep obvious dysfunction by not engaging in it. We have memories and early experiences. In creating and maintaining our own families, we can stop to ask why we do what we do, or whether a behavior is negative. The explanations vary depending on the theoretical model we access. Importantly, with added insight, support, and information, we can choose to act in ways that will probably lead to positive outcomes.

There are numerous examples of parents from dysfunctional homes who make a concerted effort to break the vicious circle, to offer their own children a life script different from the one with which they themselves were raised. If we have been parented in unpredictable, harsh ways that make us feel unsafe and unheard, it is quite possible that this is the only model we know. When it comes to raising our own children, it is the path of least resistance to repeat that which was done unto us. Frequently, it may take considerable effort and professional intervention to change the preprogrammed patterns within us.

Changing the Intergenerational Script

It is possible to rewrite the intergenerational script, and countless parents have emerged from difficult childhoods to create nurturing homes. For instance, the boy who had been abandoned by his father during his own teen years may consciously decide to do better with his own children. Support systems may be the catalysts to precipitate altered behavior. Support may be found in an understanding partner or spouse who does not bring the same childhood baggage into the family system. Parents join insightful parenting groups, or sometimes they call in the help of a counselor. The bottom line is that it is possible to change the intergenerational script, even if doing so requires intensive professional guidance and support. What occurs in these circumstances can also reference Murray Bowen's *intergenerational transmission* process.

We transition through the stages of the family lifespan dealing with many dimensions: physical, social, emotional, and cognitive. All the fibers of our being have to change to accommodate each new lifespan stage and the many avenues that lead to a life well lived. As we partner with others, we enlarge our world to reach out. Perhaps we let another person enter, initially, just as a possibility, but as we progress in our relationship, that person might become an extension of ourselves. We have opened the door to a partnership and to the potential of a family of creation. Family members will reach into the corners of our hearts and draw out our hidden resources to give selflessly and endlessly. Being woven into the fabric of the family gives us hope and a sense of a meaningful future: it changes us as nothing else will. Through a constructive and mature partnership, we may be fortunate enough to turn into better versions of ourselves. Being embedded in a family can be the best educational experience, as we can learn about empathy, selflessness, and caring.

Family stories have many endings. We take the happy ones in our stride, but the heart-wrenching tragedies should also catch our attention. We know only too well that being part of the family in a constructive and engaged manner is an obstacle course like no other. There are disharmonious and quarrelsome families, socioeconomic hardships, processes of emotional impoverishment, and incompatible and irresponsible couples. Unstable partnerships and union disruptions are all too common. On the bigger platforms, the macrosystem and exosystem, there are even greater demons to contend with, such as food insecurity, dire poverty, lack of opportunity, and limited educational access. One of the cruelest and most dysfunctional of family behaviors is family violence, which builds walls within homes and between people.

Within the luxury of a stable two-parent family system, one parent need not fulfill all roles or meet all challenges. We are emboldened by our strengths; our partner helps us carry our weaknesses. In well-functioning families, the resources can be pooled. Ultimately, the family is the place where, through our fellow family members, we gain greater insight into ourselves. Well-functioning families provide an anchor and the space to build our lives among a web of possibilities. It's like a coral reef, a living, growing entity that shelters life. It is the platform from which we can launch children, but the family is also the place of safety where we can rest and rejuvenate.

Family inheritance or family baggage? As we create our own, well-functioning families, we may choose to emphasize those dimensions that are supportive and constructive while downplaying the less harmonious and dysfunctional components. We may be separated from family members, change partners, live on different continents, break communication. These may be temporary attempts at pushing our family memories aside. We are born in and from families. Our families launch us, and, ultimately, we return to those we call family, whether because of the genetic links or the emotional support and harmony a family offers.

Ideally, families create those dynamic spaces where we can be truest to ourselves. The reality is more sober: different families will form their own sets of values, rules, traditions, and behaviors. These can range from being supportive to being outright burdensome and limiting. Families create and live in a microclimate that they themselves produce and maintain: the family system.

Families are a lifelong commitment. Families are forever.

> **"Happy families are all alike; every unhappy family is unhappy in its own way."**
>
> Leo Tolstoy (1828–1910), from *Anna Karenina*

FOCUS POINT

Well-adjusted families create the dynamic space in which relationship formation, self-regulation, and individuation can occur. Dysfunctional families, on the other hand, can create toxic environments in which children fail to thrive. Dysfunctional families can be described as experiencing chronic conflict and destabilization; being low on structure and high on chaos; saying one thing and meaning another; spreading untrue rumors, which creates low respect; exhibiting reversal and confusion concerning roles; making accusations and being revengeful; ignoring personal boundaries and privacy and breaking confidentiality; and attaching conditions to love, respect, and support. Destructive intergenerational behavior patterns can persist unless there is serious intent to discontinue the vicious cycle. Parents from dysfunctional homes can make concerted efforts (possibly requiring therapeutic interventions) to offer their own children a life script different from the one they experienced in their families of origin.

Well-adjusted families create the dynamic space in which relationship formation, self-regulation, and individuation can occur.

Source: © iStock.com/Tanom.

SPOTLIGHT ON THEORIES

Family Systems Theory

A significant shift in thinking occurred once persons were seen within the context of their families and, more than that, once the powerful dynamics of that particular family as a unit were recognized. The early therapeutic approaches focused on the individual. By contrast, the family systems approach focuses on family relationships, seeing these as powerful contributors to both family and individual health.

Family systems theory has had numerous contributors, in terms of schools and theorists. Each has added a little twist to the general approach, adding diverse techniques in working with the family. What unites all these different angles of attack is their agreement that the family should be the entry point to the therapeutic process (Nichols & Davis, 2017, p. 54). The general principles of family systems theory have been applied in numerous contexts, ranging from industrial psychology and human resource management (Patton & McMahon, 2006) to more traditional family-oriented therapeutic techniques. The early roots of the movement are varied as well. There are some influences from the biological and natural sciences and from cybernetics, and precursors include couple and hence family therapy in the marriage counseling and child guidance contexts (Carr, 2012, p. 54). The latter date back to the early twentieth century. Initially, there were influences from the psychoanalytic movement as well, but as the therapeutic focus shifted from the individual alone to the individual within the context of a system, family systems theory gained momentum and acquired its uniquely systemic identity.

By the time all the voices in the choir of family systems thinking learned to sing in greater unison, the approach was already mainstream. In the 1970s, the demarcations between different schools and approaches within family systems theory softened, as all participants agreed to disagree and to adopt what at that time was referred to as eclectic approaches, while general family systems thinking was often the accepted default. *Eclectic,* as a term, had a somewhat random meaning, and it has been replaced by the more intentional *integrative*, as a descriptor for the meeting and melding of different approaches. For example, two angles in family therapy that are at times integrated are structural and strategic family therapy. In structural family therapy, the emphasis is on the interactions between family members. In strategic family therapy, there is an interest in finding solutions and changing outcomes.

Training and expertise within a given treatment approach are factors that often determine why some therapists prefer certain approaches above others. Even so, not all theoretical approaches meet all requirements in terms of framework, treatment models, and expected outcomes. Generally, the intent is to focus on what is best for the clients in a specific context, while tangentially considering the expertise of the therapist, irrespective of the niche from which the particular approach was developed (Erford & Vernon, 2018).

Thinking in a systemic manner also enriches multicultural, intercultural, and integrative dimensions. Once the context and the interrelatedness of factors are acknowledged, the complexity of these varied influences adds a meaningful multidimensional perspective.

The **wholeness** of a family implies that it amounts to more than the sum of the individuals acting independently. Some of the principles of Gestalt psychology, namely that the whole is greater than the sum of its parts, are acknowledged in family systems theory. The family as a unit takes on its own meaning and dynamic, and these go beyond the individual stories of family members. Other influences can be traced to biological or ecological systems occurring in nature. Families tend to function in ways similar to systems found in nature (Becvar & Becvar, 2013, pp. 62–67). Families are also described as being **social systems**. The complex interactions of the family influence and regulate its members' behavior, the way it performs as an integrated unit. Families display unique characteristics when they function in systemic contexts.

Additionally, families can be broken into **subsystems**; for instance, the parents can be one subsystem while the kids are another. The family systems approach has taken on such momentum that it is almost inconceivable to think of the family as a group of separate individuals or to think of families as isolated entities outside of their context within other wider societal systems. The general ideas and premises that are the foundation of family therapy, namely that the family functions as its own unit with far-reaching implications, has entered mainstream psychotherapy. Of all the approaches therapists can use, the top two are cognitive behavioral therapy and the family systems approach (Gurman & Kniskern, 1981/2014).

When a family functions as a system, it displays unique characteristics:

Homeostasis or equilibrium. Families tend to seek a place of balance, one that is relatively tension free. Families will try to maintain this condition of homeostasis and also work actively toward creating it (Becvar & Becvar, 2013, p. 66). It may sound counterintuitive, but sometimes families maintain dysfunctional behavior at the expense of more appropriate ways of adjusting in order to preserve homeostasis. Families may perpetuate somewhat dysfunctional behavior if that is the only behavior they know and it allows them to function within their familiar comfort zones. The process of changing a family's behavior or dynamic, even if it is for an improved outcome, may contain its own stressors, which families try to avoid.

Dynamic equilibrium. A dynamic process of change may contribute to a regrouping so that equilibrium can be re-attained and thereby contribute to stability.

Interdependence. Just like the players of a well-trained football team, family members may each have particular roles, duties, and functions that they perform within that family system. Each player in a team may have a specific role and personal

(Continued)

(Continued)

strengths that are contributed to the overall functioning of the team. Similarly the pooled emotional and physical resources of the family exceed the contributions of each individual member.

The functioning family has been compared to a decorative mobile in that the parts are interconnected, and they exert a bidirectional influence on one another. If we pull at the triangle hanging from one end of the mobile, we may disrupt the balance of the whole, as not only the part that we pull is being displaced—there is a ripple effect that influences all the other parts as well (see Diagram 3.2).

Circularity. In the family systems model, behavior is not explained as being linear—it cannot be traced to one point of origin. Instead there is a circularity: one event can feed the next, and it may not be easily discernible where processes start or end as they blend into greater systemic contexts.

Equifinality. The general meaning of this term is that, in an open system, a particular outcome may be reached through many different means. In family systems theory, this concept means that a family may share common rules and goals, but family members may differ concerning how standards are applied or goals are reached. As the saying goes, "Many paths lead to Rome"; there can be various ways of reaching a destination in family contexts as well, where that destination may be reaching a point of homeostasis or balance (Becvar & Becvar, 2013, p. 68).

DIAGRAM 3.2 **A mobile can illustrate the interdependence occurring within a family system. As one subsection within the mobile is moved, all the other pieces will have to shift in response to find a new balance point.**

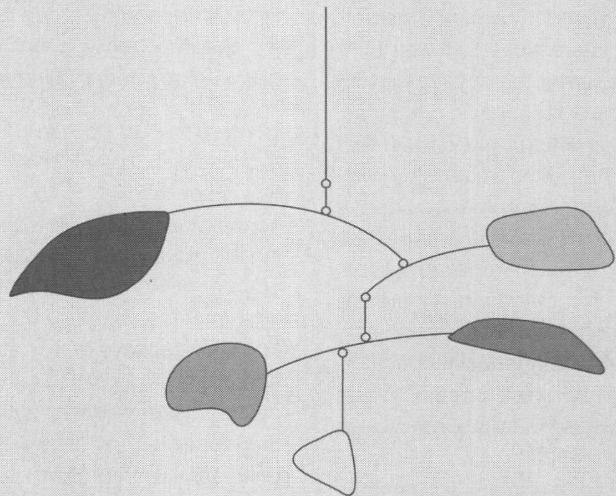

FOCUS POINT

Family systems theory explains the complex interactions of the family group. It addresses the unique ways that the group reaches decisions, negotiates, forms alliances, achieves goals, and seeks equilibrium or homeostasis. Group stability is a key outcome and can be achieved in a variety of ways, also referred to as equifinality. Family groups can contain subsystems, for instance, the parental dyad or the subsystem of the children. Family systems thinking encompasses numerous interpretations by individual therapists and schools. Currently, greater mutual acceptance and eclecticism within the general field of family systems therapy seem to be the norm.

Authentic Insight

The Dynamics of Systems Theory and Research

Systems theory informs qualitative inquiry, asking the fundamental question of how the system as a whole functions as it does. Though systems theory has not taken an obvious role in the controversies about the philosophy and methodology underpinning qualitative research, a systemic understanding is fundamental. The principle of holistic thinking, for example, asserts the interdependence of personal experience and context, of all the parts of a system, and of the interaction between the researcher and the participant. Another crucial tenet of systems theory is that causality is circular, or recursive; this principle is reflected in the process of qualitative research.

The advantages of systems theory include its rich vocabulary for process description. Systemic structures include boundaries, which define the system and regulate how matter and energy are inducted and expelled from the system. In addition, cybernetic feedback loops are channels of influence between elements of the system. Also, numerous specific processes are important to systems theory, such as positive and negative feedback, inputs and outputs, equifinality, and morphogenesis [the idea of formation and differentiation]. Isomorphism, or the similarity between processes at all levels of analysis, is a central tenet from which systems theory derives much of its explanatory power.

Systems theory motivates questions that surround the researcher's experiences with observations. For this reason, remaining informed by systems theory is a way to hear the participants' experiences as they define them.

Systems theory has influenced me greatly through my training as a family therapist. I continually ask the fundamental question that systems theory asks in qualitative research: How does this system function as it does? What are the component parts, and what are the ways in which the system may be influenced to strengthen this process? Since the researcher is the most important instrument of qualitative research, it seems wise to include systemic principles overtly in the study design.

Jonathan Davis, PhD, is a professor of human development and family science, as well as a licensed marriage and family therapist. This excerpt was adapted from his doctoral dissertation (Davis, 2004).

In a Nutshell

Family Systems Theory

- The family functions as a social system, and the family members make up that system.
- A family system takes on an identity of its own.
- There is bidirectional influence; what affects one individual family member will also affect the entire family and vice versa.
- Therapeutic interventions address the family as a system and as a whole.
- As opposed to being viewed as linear, behavior is seen in the context of circularity.
- The two most frequently favored therapeutic approaches in family contexts are the family systems approach and cognitive behavioral therapy.

CHAPTER FOCUS POINTS

The Circle of Safety

- Individuals network and widen their social groups to create a safety net. By collaborating and sharing strengths and talents, they are able to establish an inner circle that supports collaboration and survival.
- Because it is impossible to be on guard and alert at all times, a person finds it

important to be a part of a larger group. Being embedded in a safe family unit allows an individual to deal with everyday challenges successfully.

Launching and Landing: The Dynamic Tasks of the Family

- The family launches an individual into the world and provides sanctuary to that individual when he or she returns to it. The family as a whole has responsibilities toward its individual members. In turn, family members have individual responsibilities and obligations to the family. The family as a well-functioning unit provides its members with
    - commitment,
    - nurture,
    - education,
    - attachment,
    - acceptance,
    - sanctuary,
    - loyalty, and
    - respect.
- When individual members are active in fulfilling their responsibilities toward the family, the unit functions successfully.

The Family Orchestra

- A family functions optimally when it is a cohesive unit. Engagement in a family implies that we become a participant or take part in interaction. If this occurs within the family unit, it establishes mutual commitment and participation that strengthens the family as a whole.
- Not being available or invested in the family (being disengaged) sends a message of withdrawal and contributes to dysfunction.

Shaping the Dynamics of the System

- The ability to form secure attachments shapes all our relationships and begins with the parent-child bond. If children do not come from situations of appropriate care or engagement, they will most likely become parents who are unable to care and engage appropriately with their own children.
- When responsible parenting is modeled and a vulnerable child's safety and security are ensured, a platform of trusting attachment is created from which other relationships can be negotiated. For children growing up without these trusting and nurturing elements, extensive intervention may be required.

Dysfunctional Families

- Well-adjusted families create the dynamic space in which relationship formation, self-regulation, and individuation can occur. Dysfunctional families, on the other hand, can create toxic environments in which children fail to thrive. Dysfunctional families can be described as
    - Experiencing chronic conflict and destabilization;
    - Being low on structure and high on chaos;
    - Saying one thing and meaning another;
    - Spreading untrue rumors, which creates low respect;
    - Exhibiting reversal and confusion concerning roles;
    - Making accusations and being revengeful;
    - Ignoring personal boundaries and privacy and breaking confidentiality; and
    - Attaching conditions to love, respect, and support.
- Destructive intergenerational behavior patterns can persist unless there is serious intent to discontinue the vicious cycle. Parents from dysfunctional homes can make concerted efforts (possibly requiring therapeutic interventions) to offer their own children a life script that is different from the one they experienced in their families of origin.

Spotlight on Theories: Family Systems Theory

- Family systems theory explains the complex interactions of the family group. It addresses the unique ways that the group reaches decisions, negotiates, forms alliances, achieves goals, and seeks equilibrium or homeostasis. Group stability is a key outcome and can be achieved in a variety of ways, also referred to as equifinality.
- Family groups can contain subsystems, for instance, the parental dyad or the subsystem of the children. Family systems thinking encompasses numerous interpretations by individual therapists and schools. Currently, greater mutual acceptance and eclecticism within the general field of family systems therapy seem to be the norm.

CHAPTER

4 Observing Family Dynamics

Learning Outcomes

After studying this chapter, you should be able to

1. Define *observer effect*, and analyze its impact when we try to observe dynamic interactions.
2. Identify various approaches that make family dynamics somewhat visible or overt.
3. Explain some of the cultural constructions pertaining to family units.
4. Summarize some of the interventions developed to improve family functioning.
5. Identify some of the responsibilities professionals have when working with families.
6. Describe the eight concepts of *natural systems theory* (also called *Bowen theory*).

Observing Families

When we examine the dynamics of an individual in the context of a family system, we are looking at the interrelatedness of events; we are examining the movement or life of that system. Physicians use a stethoscope to listen to a patient's breathing or heartbeat, and to the skilled professional ear, the device tells a story of related and underlying conditions.

Breathing and heartbeat are manifestations of life. In a similar way, if we extend the metaphor, we can use an imaginary stethoscope to listen to the vital signs (dynamics) of a family system. It is this dynamic that sets in motion the intricacies of that particular family's functioning. Because of family dynamics, families function the way they do, with both the positive and negative aspects that can be the outcomes of a family's behavior. Family dynamics are central in that they represent the engine that drives the motion. Life itself is defined and characterized by the inherent quality of motion. Being permanently motionless may imply death, if we are referring to an organic life form. For families, it is this motion that shows us they are alive; they are progressing and changing.

When therapists work with a family, they try to elicit and capture several moments of that family's authentic functioning. They may do that in several ways, but most often it involves joining the family as an observer or even as a participant during a family ritual, such as a family dinner, and then leading a formal therapeutic session. One eminent Argentinian-American therapist, Salvador Minuchin (1921–2017), worked extensively with families who identified one of their members as dealing with an eating disorder. Before Minuchin commenced therapy, he typically met the family over a meal. He liked to observe them in their natural surroundings. In a formal therapy room, families might feel out of place. He found that this type of observation of families in their own surroundings revealed so much more (Rosman, Minuchin, & Liebman, 1975).

Whenever an additional person joins a system, that person also alters that system. An observer, however well meaning and unobtrusive, will still alter the system. When a therapist works with a family, the mere act of initiating family therapy changes that particular family. In formal theoretical terms, this change is called the **observer effect**. If a family knows it is being watched or if an outsider joins a family system, there is a strong likelihood that this in itself will cause subtle changes in behavior. Sometimes it even amplifies a behavior. Clients may bring all kinds of expectations and anxieties into the therapy space, even if that space is the clients' home, and the experienced therapist can anticipate and alleviate some of these emotions (Patterson, Williams, Edwards, Charmov, & Gauf-Grounds, 2018).

An observer subtly changes what is being observed by the mere act of joining the family system or observing the family with its permission. Ethics demand that therapy is instituted as a voluntary arrangement between the parties reflecting mutual consent, unless therapy is court mandated. The family may seek the help and intervention of a therapist because it realizes that its way of functioning as a family is no longer working for family members. As a system, the family may have become dysfunctional, or one of the family's members may be behaving in a way that alerts everybody else in the group that a change is indicated. This is also the point at which we encounter one of the paradoxes of family therapy.

A family may be dysfunctional, but despite the limitations of this abnormal functioning, it is what is familiar; family members think they know the rules. In its own strange way, this family has found a balance or equilibrium, even if it is at the expense of the wellness outcomes for each of its members. For the same reason, some families may resist intervention, as the known is preferable to the unknown or because change can be intimidating. While being in the transitional process, a family can be unclear about what the new balance or equilibrium might look like. The term *transitional anxiety* has been used to describe the discomfort associated with changing from one familiar situation to another less familiar one.

The process of change that has to occur in a family system in order for a family to move to a preferred way of functioning also opens up possibilities. These possibilities may represent uncharted territories, and for that reason members of the system may be hesitant to embark on such an exploration.

At times, therapists walk a tightrope between pushing for change and maintaining sameness or stability. A therapists' experience and particular therapeutic technique or style will largely dictate the process he or she follows. But regardless of the therapeutic approach chosen, therapists commonly have ongoing questions about their abilities:

> Paradoxically, the more one learns about how to do therapy, the more one realizes how much one doesn't know. This paradox can feed an individual's insecurity about being a therapist. In fact, it is not uncommon for students to question whether they have what it takes to be a therapist. (Patterson, Williams, Edwards, Charmow, & Grauf-Grounds, 2018, p. 4)

These same authors remind us that becoming skilled takes patience and time; it does not happen overnight. It is helpful to revisit those same talents and strengths

FOCUS POINT

An observer who joins a system alters that system. When a therapist works with a family, the act of initiating family therapy changes that particular family. This is called the *observer effect*. Paradoxically, families may resist changes to their family systems, as they are trying to maintain homeostasis or equilibrium. The known and familiar may be preferable to the unknown, even if the known represents a dysfunctional situation.

that first attracted us to the helping professions, be they intuition, the desire to provide support and help, or the need to make a difference. The road to becoming a therapist is paved with self-doubt, and for that reason, it is prudent to implement all the self-care and professional boundaries that will contribute to improved outcomes while also reducing the likelihood of burnout (Patterson et al., 2018, p. 11).

Making Dynamics Visible

Documenting Family Dynamics

Observing the dynamics of a family group is exponentially more complex than trying to understand individuals one at a time. Describing a family can be like stitching together numerous photographs or drawings to achieve animation. In this way, the sequence depicts motion, like a film clip. The many descriptions of families often seem to have the quality of a series of glossy photographs. Attractive and engaging, telling us a fair amount about the subjects, they document a mere sliver in time.

Most of us have seen photographs of our great-grandparents or earlier ancestors. Usually, they were formally posed in the studio. The earliest known surviving photograph, taken in 1826 by Joseph-Nicéphore Niépce, required an eight-hour exposure (National Geographic's, n.d.). Although technological advances reduced exposure time, early photographs still required their subjects to be still for up to fifteen minutes! To facilitate this, photographers devised a frame that supported standing subjects. The Victorian family and wedding photographs have a stilted and unspontaneous quality, which is not surprising considering how long subjects in these early photographs had to maintain a pose. Contrast this still photography with early movies, usually taken by an amateur and capturing shaky moments in motion. Charlie Chaplin and Laurel and Hardy come to mind, in rather jumpy black and white.

Importantly, these movies stitch together numerous individual photos so that we can see actual movement and the dynamics of the actors in these mini-dramas. Investigating family dynamics, then, means considering interaction and movement through time—people relating to one another and to their environment over many moments. The moving picture rather than the posed still-life photograph is the best analogy when it comes to documenting family dynamics.

Family Assessment

Therapists need samples of behavior, and because these samples are moments in the life of the family, they help therapists to see those still photographs we referred to earlier. But therapists also need samples that contain movement, sequences of motion. Many attempts have been made to capture some of these moments of movement in the lives of families.

In the world of music, it is important to document or notate using a set of symbols representing the music to be played. Musicians have perfected various notation systems. The experienced musician can read these notations fluently and play the music they represent. In the antique manuscripts by great composers such as Bach or Beethoven, we can see from their notation when they changed their minds or when they rewrote certain sections. The beauty of these notation systems is that, centuries later, an audience can access those same melodies the composers wanted us to hear.

Serious football fans watch the analysis of an important game on their TV screens and see how the commentator draws lines, arrows, and other symbols to mark the movement of players. This in itself may not be a complete notation system of a game, but it helps in explaining the tactics and the dynamics of a particular match. With digital photography, we can easily capture moments to relive them at a more convenient time.

In family therapy training, similar methods are used. With the clients' permission, therapy sessions can be recorded and subsequently analyzed. The intent is that trainee therapists can replay the moment, slowly examine what occurred, and learn from that situation.

Interrelatedness of interactions. Theorists have devised various methods of describing dynamics in family systems. All attempt to point out the interrelatedness of these family interactions—how the one affects the other in a nonlinear manner.

Fast forward a few decades and we find the interrelatedness idea recurring in relation to creative activities such as concept mapping. Creative endeavors encourage us to withhold our critical self-talk while allowing us to make unconventional connections. This linking and connecting process becomes a most important tool, helping us go beyond the conventional to create new combinations, as do the kaleidoscopic images that reinvent themselves with each twist. Improvisation, as employed by actors and comedians, also relies on the fresh connections that are made under extreme time constraints and that can be very funny if unanticipated and pushing the edges.

Two methods that attempt to give us a better idea of the relationships between members of a family group are mapping *family genograms* and *family sculpting*.

Family Genograms

Genograms allow us a glimpse into the development of relationships between family members. Mapping family genograms is also regarded as a way of conceptualizing that family's development (Dykeman, 2016). The genogram can place an individual within her or his generation of the family, or within an intergenerational family system. A **genogram** is a form of family notation that has similarities with the traditional family tree, which documents ancestors. The genogram gives us the added ability to indicate bonds between relationships, such as emotional qualities. Also, genograms can be used to document matters such as the incidence of hereditary diseases or other health conditions.

Using various symbols and annotations, we can document a family's relational aspects (see Figure 4.1). Genograms can be works in progress, becoming more intricate as families evolve (Bigner & Gerhardt, 2019, p. 122). The concept of the genogram is based on the work of McGoldrick and Gerson (1985) and has been expanded by several contributors. It is frequently used in family therapy, and students who study families find this form of family notation insightful (Ballard, Fazio-Griffith, & Marino, 2016).

FIGURE 4.1 ***Common symbols used in genograms to denote family relationships.*** **Genograms access a series of symbols and other information, e.g., age and gender, which adds to the depth of the genogram. Relationships can also be represented. Here is a selection of symbols that denote how family relationships can be expressed in genograms. A set of symbols for the emotional quality of the connections is also available.**

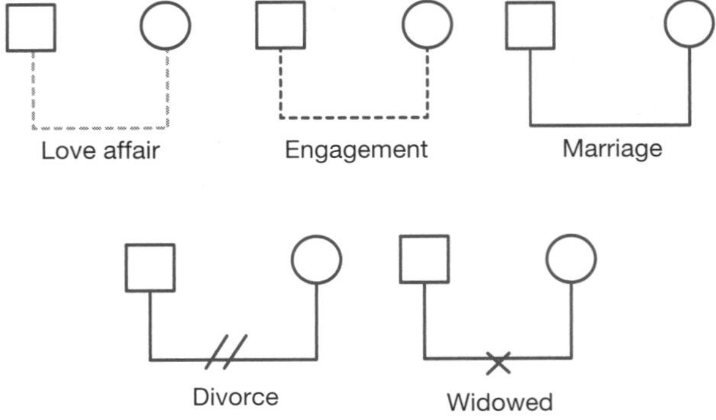

Source: Based on the work of McGoldrick and Gerson (1985).

For our example of an intergenerational genogram (see Figures 4.2 and 4.3), we meet an imaginary multigenerational family. Family members' names for this example were chosen from the most popular baby names recorded by Social Security in 2017 (Social Security Administration, n.d.). The last names of these families are also among the most frequently occurring names in the United States, according to the U.S. Census of 2010 (United States Census, 2016).

The first genogram depicts a family with young children and is straightforward (Figure 4.2). The second genogram shows the same family about 25 years later, after it has experienced various life-cycle events. Two of the grandparents have died, divorce has occurred, and a new blended family has formed. This progression in lifespan is depicted in the greater complexity of the second genogram (Figure 4.3).

Systemic family development theory allows us to understand the complexity and diversity of families. By examining the family at a particular point in its developmental time, it is possible to see that families share common stressors that challenge each generation. This model has significant practical applications. For instance, it may help us discover how family members fit together; it provides us with a way of connecting to our own ancestry. Are there recurring challenges of which we should be aware? A genogram could, for instance, trace hereditary diseases. It could also depict the emotional proximity or distance between various family members. Thus it could reveal long-standing feuds and alliances. The possibilities are endless. A family genogram extends the purpose of a family tree as used in ancestry. It superimposes qualities of interest by adding another layer on top of that particular family tree. In this manner, it can be informative concerning the functioning of that particular family system.

FIGURE 4.2 ***A genogram of a family with young children.*** **These genograms depict three generations. Men are depicted with squares and women with circles. Genograms can document a number of circumstances or events that take place within family systems.**

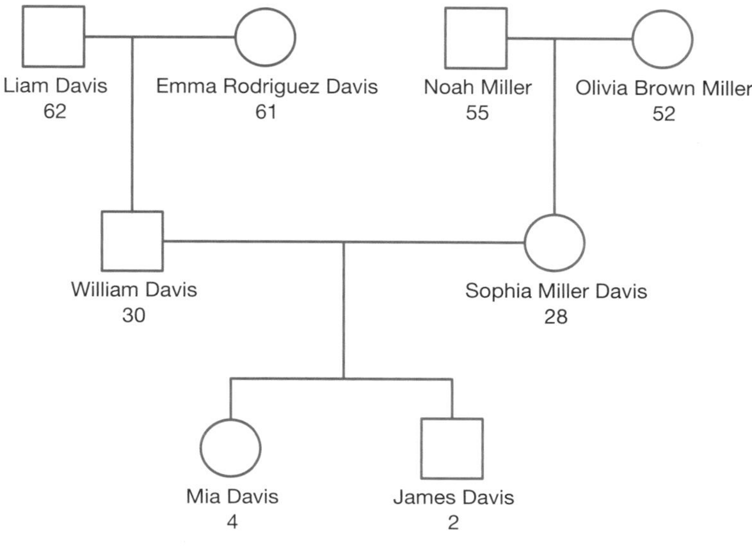

FIGURE 4.3 ***A genogram of the same family 25 years later.*** **Benjamin has been adopted by William, making Charlotte and William and children Benjamin, Ava, Mia, and James the blended core family. Benjamin and Ava are half-siblings while Mia and James are their stepsiblings. Mia and James are biological siblings.**

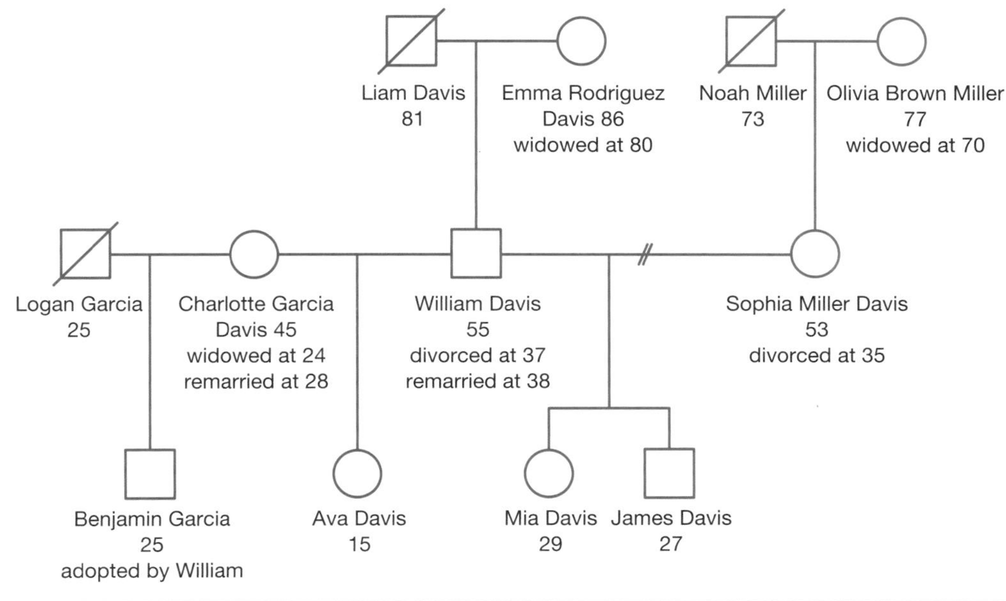

Authentic Insight

The Gift of a Genogram

One of my first experiences in a doctoral seminar was an introduction to a genogram. I had never heard of this tool. Now, I won't offer pastoral or premarital counseling without it. Essentially, a genogram is an annotated family tree. Instead of mere names and dates, a genogram offers an overview of the family system. Think of beginning with a family tree and then overlaying that skeletal framework with vital information about your family. The more work we are willing to invest concerning the dynamics of our families of origin, the more we can learn about ourselves. We can create a layer of information about emotional health and relationships. Where is the conflict or estrangement? Where is the enmeshment or dependency? Another key element is significant events. Theses may include relocations, employment transitions, divorces, suicides, accidents, or other life-changing events.

There is a reason these dynamics exist. As children, we aren't able to understand our family history completely. Things just happen; often children are left out of the painful conversations about what is triggering family conflict. We can create another layer, one examining the system's spirituality and religiosity, for example. We can examine everyone's vocation or education. In the process of creating a genogram, we begin to discern the gifts or challenges we inherited from our maternal and paternal families. How useful would it be, as we age, to understand our parents', siblings', and grandparents' medical histories? Likewise, we need to understand where abuse or addiction is present in our family system. I find it advantageous to record all this on one page, which provides a quick overview of the family's narrative.

Creating a genogram is a great gift because it helps us gain perspective on why our family is the way it is. This documented research will be a uniquely wonderful gift to pass on to our future generations. Of course, we know we aren't destined to repeat our family's mistakes, but we certainly ought to try to learn from them.

Blake Dempsey, MDiv, DMin, is the executive pastor at a church in Birmingham, Alabama.

Family Sculpting

Historic roots. During the 1960s and 1970s, while family therapy and systems thinking were relatively novel, researchers explored ways of documenting relationships within those systems. They were particularly interested in exploring concepts such as who was close to whom, the alliances within the family, and the potential breaks in communication. Doing so enabled researchers to look at hierarchy within family systems. This hierarchy was influenced by the flow of information and by which members belonged to particular subsystems, that is, by membership. Other areas of interest included how members adapted to the larger system as well as the personal influences individuals added to a particular system (Wedemeyer & Grotevant, 1982). Genograms and family sculpting were adapted to suit current needs in exploring and documenting family relationships.

But what is **family sculpting**? Here is a formal definition of "sculpting":

> Sculpting is a kind of non-verbal role-play in which participants are given a certain character and create a "sculpture" by arranging family members, social circles and professionals in ways which reflect the quality of the relationships of the people involved. (Andersen & Larsen, 2015, p. 556)

Family sculpting, then, is a therapeutic technique that asks a family member or two to place other members of the family in a scene, or sculpture, that demonstrates each person's position, attitude, and role in relation to those of other family members. Therapists might discover that clients and families find this type of concrete placement and visualization of relationships emotionally challenging. They may be reluctant to participate because the unspoken alliances become visible to everyone involved in the sculpting project.

On the other hand, this practical experience can be an eye-opener in that it can identify the complexity and the dynamics of emotionally laden situations (Andersen & Larsen, 2015). Family sculpting has also been used in training helping professionals, for instance, nurses. The technique can raise awareness and empathy in the team working with a specific family. Andersen and Larsen (2015) describe using this experiential learning technique with a group of students being trained in providing palliative care. By putting themselves into the shoes of the families to whom they are providing services, these caregivers develop greater empathy for the challenges a family may be experiencing while dealing with a family member's critical illness and impending death, for example.

Piha and Schmitt (2016) describe a nonverbal and nonlinear variation of family sculpting that they call "Blind and Mute." Here are the three cornerstones of this approach:

1. The sculptor doesn't tell anything about the situation to be sculpted;
2. The leader of the process chooses the actors for the roles which are unknown to everyone [else];
3. During the actual creation of the sculpture no words are used. (Piha & Schmitt, 2016, p. 169)

Related techniques. Family sculpting techniques have been adapted in several ways. Some use clay models and require that family members build a replica of their family with sculpting materials. Another variation uses paper cutouts of the lead figures in a family system, which can then be placed showing the relative proximity or distance between members.

Family boards. Another adaptation of the technique of placing family members in relationship to each other uses a **family board**. As a child growing up in pre-computer days, I remember teachers using similar felt boards onto which they would attach Velcro images of people. This sort of board was especially popular to illustrate stories to younger children. The storyteller had a range of cutout figures, animals, and other images and, as the story progressed, would stick the relevant figures on the felt board. In a family board, we use images of family members, for example, photos, to tell about family interactions.

The family board has been adapted for use with the visually impaired by making the figures three-dimensional. According to Schmidt and Kunnig (2015), this technique is especially useful as a nonverbal medium of communication, and children relate to it. A nonverbal approach also has the potential of being useful in cross-cultural contexts.

Family-of-origin concerns. Therapists in training should be aware that techniques such as family sculpting can be very valuable in making both clients and therapists aware of family-of-origin concerns, such as abuse, substance abuse, poverty, or other factors related to experiencing a difficult upbringing. These techniques can also be used during clinical supervision to clarify the relationships of the families being treated by trainee therapists. The family therapeutic system is clarified by depicting the family system in a nonverbal yet highly visual form. Piha and Schmitt (2016) also state that the actors who are portraying specific family members can improvise according to both how they feel and the sensational feedback they experience by being embedded in this type of system.

Authentic Insight

A Family Planetary System: Sculpting With People

My first introduction to family sculpting (or sculpting with people) was in the early seventies, under the supervision of Jessie Turberg, PhD, who was affiliated with the Ackerman Institute for the Family in New York. (Sadly, she passed away in 2001.) I attended two graduate training sessions that she presented in Johannesburg. We were starved for what she had to offer; it was fresh and novel in a field where little formal training was locally available. She introduced us to genograms and family sculpting. I remember the sense of connectedness she created among us; slowly we were aligning ourselves with the therapeutic approach that had its own identity, different from the models we had been exposed to in our earlier university training (Gerhardt, 2003, pp. 163–164).

Life-sized chess pieces. When Turberg demonstrated the technique, she used us, members of the audience, as life-sized chess pieces in the game of representing the family. She started with the core members of the family. In this instance, the family could be envisaged from the vantage point of one individual. For instance, if I placed myself in the center of the sculpture, I could arrange significant family members around me. Importantly, the literal distance at which chess pieces were placed represented the metaphorical distance in the relationship. The closer people stood to the leading individual, the greater their significance and role in that person's life. If a person felt further away in terms of emotions (rather than significance), the actual distance between that person and the lead actor would be greater as well.

Creating a planetary system. This exercise feels like creating a planetary system in which the leading person takes on the role of being at the center of that particular universe. From that central point, different actors in the family drama will be positioned further off or closer in, depending on their real-life roles and emotional proximity. Additionally, if members of this larger family colluded or formed alliances, they could be placed closer together. The spaces between the actors told an important story in terms of emotional closeness or distance. If the closeness was excessive, with a person being enmeshed, for example, this could be depicted by having that person at really close quarters—possibly uncomfortably close.

The first time I took part in one of these family enactments it shed a lot of light in terms of who belonged to which subsystem. It dramatized the inner workings of the family in a way that became tangible and visible. Children in a family seem to have an intuitive understanding of what these representations are all about, reminding me of another therapeutic truth: if we want to know what is happening in a family, ask the children. They are often more forthcoming than the adults.

Clara Gerhardt

FOCUS POINT

A number of family-related techniques and assessments were developed, including family genograms, family sculpting, and certain techniques within play therapy for children. Family researchers document relationships within family systems. They are interested in the hierarchy and subsystems within a family system, investigating who is close to whom, the alliances, and the potential strengths as well as breaks in communication. A family genogram can document a family at a particular point in time. It can highlight various dimensions, as it superimposes qualities of interest on top of that family tree. It is informative concerning the functioning of that particular family system. A number of other techniques serve to highlight the interrelated dimensions within family systems, for example, family sculpting.

Moving toward change. Family sculpting also helps move family members toward positive change. The supervisor of a session could ask, "What would make this situation feel more comfortable?" And, subsequently, the actors are free to adjust the system so it would feel comfortable.

This shift from how the family's reality is perceived to how it could become provides valuable feedback and training material for aspiring therapists.

Cultural Constructions of the Family

Symbols and identity. This subsection explores the ways in which we can represent our families socially and culturally and examines the clues we leave for later generations. Some of these clues can be found in the family album or in formal painted portraits. Other links to our past might be found in a family crest (if we happen to be able to trace one) or the family metaphor or symbol we create for ourselves.

The origins and meanings of our names may also link us to our ancestry. Last names often indicate a profession; think of Gardiner, Miller, Baker, and the like. Other names are meaningful in terms of places, for example, home villages. I can trace my first name back six or seven generations, as several great-grandmothers and earlier ancestors share the name. What an inspiration to know that my personal identifier, the name my parents gifted me, also connects me with many strong women in my past, with all those ancestors who went before and who serve as a foundation for the current family.

Family Group, by British sculptor Henry Moore (1898–1986). In family dynamics, we can explore concepts such as who is close to whom, the alliances within the system, and the potential breaks in communication. How we are positioned in space relative to other family members may give clues concerning relationships.

Source: Wmpearl.

Family photographs and the family album. Families can perform important detective work concerning their own heritage by looking at old family albums. Admittedly, some of the pictures can appear to be posed and stilted, but even so they can be one of the few links that tell us about the generations before us (Weiser, 2018). Annette Kuhn (2002), in her book *Family Secrets: Acts of Memory and Imagination*, makes the following statement concerning family photograph albums:

> Family photographs . . . get displayed one after another, their selection and ordering as meaningful as the pictures themselves. The whole, the series, constructs a family story in some respects like a classical narrative: linear, chronological; though its cyclical repetitions of climactic moments—births, christenings, weddings, holidays . . . —is more characteristic of the open ended narrative form of the soap opera than of the closure of classical narrative. In the process of using—producing, selecting, ordering, displaying—photographs, *the family is actually in the process of making itself.*

> The family album is one moment in the cultural construction of family. (pp. 19–20, italics added)

When we look at family photographs from the distance of being separated two or more generations, we try to read into the detail; we consider who is standing next to whom, what the nonverbal gestures are that tell us more about the authentic lives of these people who can no longer personally share their stories with us.

The landscape of the face. Do we recognize aspects of the landscape of our faces in any of these distant relatives? We might recognize the faint genetic clues of shared physiognomy; do we look just a little like our grandparents? Is that where the distinctive curly red hair makes an appearance in our ancestral line? Inherited physical characteristics can provide us with a sense of allegiance; somewhere we are sharing commonalities. We probably feel the same fascination for searching out these shared traits as we display for tracking our genetic ancestry. Does this commonality bond us in some mysterious manner?

I own the handwritten cookbook (1850) of my great-great-grandmother, the romance novelist. I peer at the finely written disciplined cursive and I wonder: Did her love of words translate to my passion for wordsmithery? Did these writing genes play hide and seek through various generations, to reappear here and now as an expression on these pages?

We are anchored to our past in many mystical and mysterious ways . . .

> **"The family album is one moment in the cultural construction of family."**
>
> Kuhn (2002)

Family metaphors. If photographs are the tangible and specific building blocks of family construction, then family metaphors are their more imaginative and interpretive counterpart. These metaphors will be highly individual, as they represent the personal images associated with a particular family. Historically, the family crest had precisely this function. It was a symbol representing a unique family while also showing that family's ancestry and its link to greater family systems, such as clans. In my maternal line, the last name Piper recurs. No need to guess the main symbol depicted on that family's crest; it is a flute player.

One brilliant and courageous former student of mine and her family chose an anchor as their personal symbol. They extended it further to represent the charity they founded. *Hope Heals* provides (among other things) summer camp experiences for families affected by disabilities (www.hopeheals.com/camp).

In a therapeutic situation, family metaphors can be created and explored for meaning. Important are the various associations attached to the metaphor. It can express our hopes and expectations regarding what that family should mean to us, and, typically, it contains an idealized component—that which we hope our own families can fulfill (Galvin, Braithwaite, & Bylund, 2014, p. 39). The seeking of a metaphor is also a way in which we create a family identity and a process whereby we can explore our place within that larger entity.

At summer vacation camps, we campers were asked to do something in order to promote and facilitate group bonding and cohesion. We were asked to find a name for our group and subsequently to create a banner with a symbol that would be associated with us. I remember as a teenager that the common symbols included various animals—the eagle and the horse were particularly popular choices. Some other symbols were the sun, a constellation of stars, a lion, a dragon; these are fairly stereotypical symbols that we also find in heraldry. Finding a metaphor to describe your own family may be harder to do. A recent symbol I came across was the family as a large shady tree, under which all the members could find shelter and protection. Another metaphor was the family as a harbor where various ships could drop anchor and feel safe.

As we establish our individual identities, we do so alongside our collective family identity; the one references the other (Handel & Whitchurch, 1994, cited by Galvin, Braithwaite, & Bylund, 2014, p. 55).

Dynamics and Children

Play therapy. Children have their own concepts of families. Some of this information can be accessed through play-related situations. For example, children could play with figures representative of family members. The concept of placing the figures in relationship to each other and using them in the context of **play therapy** has similarities with the sculpting process, which uses real people. In play therapy in general, practitioners have used intergenerational dolls, dollhouses, and other props to support children in play that can express aspects of family and social functioning. The scope is endless, and a wide variety of tasks and challenges can be addressed (Kottman, 2011).

GLOBAL GLIMPSE

TOY STORIES*

A number of cultural issues are pertinent in play therapy, requiring both cultural sensitivity as well as cultural competence. If play can project aspects of our inner lives, it also incorporates cultural components. Cultural contexts influence the choice of toys (Gil & Drewes, 2004).

Matryoshka dolls are culturally recognizable as originating from Russia. These nested dolls range from large to very small, and each doll contains a smaller version of itself. Marbles seem to be universally popular, but in Brazil, mud balls and even cashew nuts can replace the traditional glass balls, and the game of marbles, called búrica, búlica, papão, peteca, or gude, is often played according to local rules.

In Southern African cultural contexts, children often make their own clay oxen from the available materials in their surroundings. The tradition of making clay animals is long standing, and these are culturally important representational objects. Cattle in general have an important meaning; they represent wealth and hope. Cattle are given as *lobola*, or wedding gifts, before an impending marriage, and the number of cattle may relate to the perceived importance of the union (*lobola* means wedding gift or marriage price in Zulu and Xhosa). Increasingly, urbanization and the influences of Western cultural practices are eroding this custom.

Different cultural contexts vary in how much actual time is dedicated to play, and many versions of leisure time are variations of adult roles. Even in very diverse cultural contexts, play activities and toys may be gender specific: for example, young boys may be given bow and arrow sets whereas girls may be encouraged to play with dolls. The children may learn about adult responsibilities and aspects of socialization through these activities. As authors Gooso and Carvalho (2013) state,

> The psychological literature depicts the child as an active agent of his/her development since an early age; this conception seems to be often mistranslated in cultural practices and attitudes regarding the availability of time, space, choice of play partners and of play activities by the children.

Various cultural contexts may not fully employ the developmental learning opportunities contained within play. The pressures and realities of daily life could intrude into the world of play.

Source: Gooso and Carvalho (2013).

*A touching series, photographed by Italian photographer Gabriele Galimberti, depicting children from around the world with their most prized toys, can be found at the photographer's website and is titled *Toy Stories*: http://www.gabrielegalimberti.com/toy-stories.

In this image by Zimbabwean–South African artist Makiwa Mutomba, children are exploring their world. Current play therapy settings address a variety of scenarios and can include sand and water for fantasy play, as well as other carefully chosen toy scenarios.

Source: The Little Explorers/Makiwa Mutomba.

Historic roots. One structured approach to play therapy, dating from the 1960s, was the Scenotest, conceptualized by Gerhild von Staabs. Based on a psychodynamic model, it was especially suited in assessing the social relations of children (Humpolicek, 2013). The theory underpinning this approach was that it probably represented a form of guided projection, during which the child could act out the leading concerns in her life (Biermann & Biermann, 1998).

Boxed in a large container, the Scenotest includes figures and a lid that can be used as the space where the figures interact. The figures represent the entire extended family and include a number of random figures, such as a set of twins, a fairy, an authority figure, a nurse, a doctor, and figures representing at least three generations ranging from young to old. Additional props are provided and include food items, pets, and various structures representing the school, hospital, place of worship, and other significant settings. The test could be expanded to include a number of fences allowing a child to demarcate spaces.

A variation of this test was the World Test, which emphasized demarcation of spaces and provided various fences, walls, and barriers. It has fallen into disuse, as well-stocked play therapy rooms provide similar alternatives with building blocks and other construction materials.

FOCUS POINT

Metaphorically speaking, early psychology presented us with still-life photos of the family, but family *dynamics* represents the stitching together of those photos. It provides the fourth dimension that represents movement, the psychological motion that occurs within family systems. Families form images of themselves, which in turn can tell us something about those groups of people. Photographs and family albums may provide clues to previous generations. Other metaphors can be found in family symbols, names, and family crests. Family researchers and therapists explore ways of documenting relationships within family systems. They are interested in the hierarchy within a family system, for example, who was close to whom, the alliances, and the potential breaks in communication. This hierarchy is influenced by the flow of information and by membership in particular subsystems. Adaptation to the larger system and personal influences are also of interest. Children may share some of their constructions of family through the medium of play. A number of family-related techniques and assessments have been developed, including family genograms, family sculpting, and certain techniques within play therapy for children.

Family Interventions

Promoting transformation. The toolbox of the well-trained therapist may contain many techniques to reach the desired goal of improving the psychological health and functioning of a given family. Depending on the theoretical approach, these specific techniques may be tailored to support the basic premises of a theoretical angle.

A few of the frequently used tools are discussed in the following section. This brief list of tools is by no means exhaustive, but the section touches on how the therapist relies on basic interpersonal connections through listening, engaging, exploring, and finding understanding.

In a discussion of how mental health professionals apply their craft, Bűtz, Chamberlain, and McGown (1997) state that family therapy contains elements of chaos and complexity. Here are their own poetic words:

> Mental health professionals arrive at a more profound understanding of the dynamics of one of the most complicated nonlinear systems—the family . . . [Families] grow and change in complicated ways. Unlike a machine, which is a closed system, a family is open-ended, and its survival depends on its ability to weather periods of extreme turbulence and chaos en route to calmer oases. The job of the family therapist is to identify the strange attractors that promote transformation.

Promoting transformation can be seen as the leitmotif of the therapist's calling. It is finding the opportunities, the words, the gateway into the family system, the stimuli to facilitate constructive and appropriate transformation. But before anything can happen, there needs to be a relationship. There needs to be a connection and rapport.

Active Listening

> **"In the beginning was Freud. He was the founder of talking therapies—and in particular of listening therapies.**
>
> **He, more than anyone, taught therapists how to listen."**
>
> Clark and Layard (2014, p. 131)

Any talk of a toolbox of techniques would be one-sided if it were not complemented by the essential process of receiving the message: the listening. Without the open ear, no amount of communication can reach its goal. The well-spoken syllables come crashing down onto the concrete floor in front of the unhearing party. In developmental psychology, there is a lot of talk about *serve and return* (Center on the Developing Child, n.d.). The concept conveys the two-sided process of any communication: the giving and the receiving components.

Listening seems misleadingly simple. We might think of it as a passive process, one that requires little activity and input. This is where **active listening** comes in. Words are not poured into the ear of the recipient; the recipient has to decode them—to listen for the message behind the message, the tone, the intonation. So many shades of communication can be hiding behind the front line of words. Like waves coming ashore, the front row of waves may seem to be carrying the obvious meaning, but behind them are the other messengers, the ones conveying all the subtleties. The skilled therapist needs to have an open ear, an active ear, so the many notes of this orchestra are heard and not just the loudest and most persistent ones. It can be the whisper in the background, the afterthought, the hesitancy, the lowering of the voice that provides us with the path of crumbs to follow. Just as in the fairy tale Hansel and Gretel marked their way home by dropping breadcrumbs, a client may scatter subtle nuances in a conversation, and these can form the path leading us to the core.

Active listening has a lot to do with our own needs and anxieties. If we have a great urgency to make ourselves heard, we can interrupt, change the direction of the conversation, or turn down and even tune out the volume of our conversation partner. Active listening is about creating a space—a space that has room for new thoughts, that is welcoming enough to allow uncensored thoughts to flutter in, and that exudes an atmosphere of acceptance and warmth. The classic and frequently quoted comments by Carl Rogers (1962) state that therapeutic approaches can differ and can be altered to match the personality of both the therapist and the client, as well as to achieve the required outcomes. Even so, three essentials remain at the core, like the three muses of inspiration in antiquity: warmth, empathy, and congruence (Patterson, 1984; Shapiro, 1969).

Warmth, empathy, and congruence. The climate of family communication can give us many clues concerning the effectiveness of that communication. Climate refers to the emotional warmth present in that family and its interactions. The excellent therapeutic qualities described by Carl Rogers, namely, warmth, empathy, and congruence, are also displayed by well-functioning families.

- *Warmth* denotes the emotional feeling of being welcomed and appreciated and feeling comfortable in the family space. This aspect conveys the welcoming component. It has to do with creating the setting that exudes welcome, that enables one to become part of a group or relationship in which one feels safe.
- *Empathy* denotes understanding, the ability of family members to put themselves into another's shoes, so they can understand how that family member may be feeling even if the feelings are unlike their own. Empathy fosters safety, which in turn permits self-disclosure. It also involves the act of trying to understand the realities, including the subjective realities, of what another family member may be feeling or experiencing. Empathy recognizes *personal* boundaries; the empathetic person understands another's feelings while not necessarily sharing them. This is unlike sympathy, which can be a more informal variation on the theme.
- *Congruence* refers to genuineness or realness—knowing that what one experiences in the relationship is authentic. In family contexts, we would like to rely on the authenticity of those relationships. The family is the one place where we are loved and accepted, despite our shortcomings. We hope that a family tolerates minimal manipulative game playing or falseness. It is a comforting feeling that we do not have to wear a mask of perfection to impress those closest to us. Congruence can foster a sense of trust.

Combative communication. Research into clients who sue their helping professionals indicates that the anger directed at the physician is higher if they feel unheard, misunderstood, and neglected. Initiating legal action can happen without any instance of real or perceived negligence or malpractice. Aspects that can contribute to the decision to litigate include not only poor standards of care or the suffering of actual losses but also, importantly, emotional dimensions. Patients demanded greater transparency and an awareness of their suffering (Vincent, Phillips, & Young, 1994). They wanted reassurance that there was empathy for their condition. Denial and minimization of the patient's situation typically did not enhance the quality of the professional interaction. If the patient felt neglected, misunderstood, and unheard, a lawsuit was more likely. By suing care providers, the client makes doubly sure of not being ignored. This, in itself, is another way of communicating, albeit in a combative manner.

Questioning

One of the simplest ways to elicit information is to ask. It is the way we fill in the blanks, the way we create clarity and disperse nebulousness. In social interactions, it is acceptable to ask. There are some hidden boundaries though. In Western societies, it would be impolite to ask acquaintances what they earn, and it could be a transgression of boundaries to query political and religious beliefs. In most constructive work environments, these topics are regarded as too personal for the watercooler conversation; it is better to focus on work-related challenges.

Questioning is a basic form of human interaction. In a constructive therapeutic context, the dialogue should be respectful and focused on the client. Focusing the attention on the client (as opposed to the therapist) facilitates feelings of safety and respect.

As trainee therapists, we were taught to limit our use of closed-ended questions, which can be answered by a mere *yes* or *no*. These are the kinds of questions that find their way into an interrogation or a court of law. Those involved in a court hearing may be encouraged to answer succinctly—to offer no nebulous

HISTORICAL GLIMPSE

MICHAEL BALINT

Michael Balint (1896–1970) was a Hungarian-born physician who was deeply influenced by the works of Freud. He became a practicing psychoanalyst who focused on the art and skill of conversations in medical contexts. He was tremendously productive, publishing extensively while also fulfilling leadership roles in the British Psychoanalytic Society and acting as a consultant for the Tavistock Clinic in London.

Balint based his early work on observations of mother-infant relationships, but he also acknowledged that these relationships were often imperfect, creating what he called "the basic fault." Imperfection was bound to rear its head especially if these early relationships had to be expanded to include third parties. With this backdrop in mind, he extended his thinking to the imperfections in the patient-doctor relationship and focused on the obstacles and expectations locked within it. Ultimately, his theory proposed ways of improving these crucial relationships. If the relationship between the doctor and the patient could reveal less of "the basic fault" or fewer shortcomings, then it followed that the relationship in its improved form contained greater power for healing. He set up "Balint groups" in which the discussions focused on the psychodynamic factors of the doctor-patient relationship. His work is continued through the Balint Society.

In short, Balint was of the opinion that if patients felt that they were being listened to, truly heard and understood, the quality of the relationship would add significantly to the helping and healing process occurring between the caregiver and the care recipient (Johnson, Brock, & Zacarias, 2014).

If cultural misunderstandings are added to the mix, an even stronger relationship between the caregiver and the care recipient is needed, which speaks to the importance of cultural competence within this relationship (Chiu, 2010). As Nieuwboer, Perry, Sande, Maassen, Rikkert, and Marck (2017) state, "It all comes down to trust" and to minimizing the factors contributing to miscommunication in health care. They advise equality and trust to improve communication and emphasize that trustful relationships form the foundation and prerequisite for communication that occurs with integrity.

digressions as these can obscure attempts to reveal the truth. In the therapeutic relationship, our goal is to create good rapport in a conversation with a client. Our hope is to make that client feel sufficiently at ease to speak freely and randomly, even though the direction of this back-and-forth talk is subtly guided by the therapist in response to what is discovered in the seemingly meandering conversation.

Open-ended questions tend to elicit more detailed responses and lead to a more conversational tone (Graesser & Black, 1985/2017). The therapist is trained to listen actively for those topics that may need to be pursued further. A simple exercise that anyone can do from home is to observe a TV host interviewing a guest. Skilled hosts weave their questions into the conversation in an imperceptible manner, which has the effect of creating a spontaneous free-flowing conversation. For the audience, this is the most natural way of eavesdropping on an interaction. If a number of questions are fired at the interviewee, it closes avenues to natural communication. Additionally, the skilled therapist will hear which topics carry greater weight and need to be pursued further.

Authentic Insight

Athena's Family Leadership

Athena has been working with me for many years, traveling from a town in another part of our state where she has a staff position in a department with plenty of emotional reactivity. That was what brought us together initially, but soon we were exploring her family of origin and the challenge of dealing with her mentally ill mother. As Athena practiced managing her own emotional self in the midst of her department's intense emotional triangling, competitive pettiness, and sabotages, she not only got better at this, she also began being able to deal with her family of origin in a more constructive way.

A number of years into our work, she came in and said that she had been in a particularly anxious departmental meeting and had noticed something remarkably different in herself. Not only was she not experiencing her typical emotional reactivity to these people, she wasn't even having to work at it. Her changes had become so well integrated that they were now closer to being automatic. This was something to celebrate, but there were more challenges to come.

As her mother's functioning declined over the years, Athena assumed more of the leadership role in her family, for example, by working with her brother and some consultants on getting her mother's finances structured. More recently, her mother's condition deteriorated and she could no longer maintain her home. This was very upsetting to the family, but Athena was able to stay in touch with her older brother as they worked through the care options for her mother. She did this in a way in which she was calm, but stayed connected to others, voicing her ideas as she listened to the thinking of others.

This kind of leadership, as Bowen theory describes it, is not about telling other people what to do. Rather, it is a more organic way of being present and accounted for. Thus, Athena is more of a resource for her family than ever before, at a time when they need her the most. In the midst of what is still an uncomfortable situation, she states, "It's kind of like I have a Teflon coating—I see and feel the heat but don't get burned." Athena has commented on how in various ways she has been preparing for this period for many years. Her present level of functioning has not come quickly or without considerable sustained effort: "You gotta work for the Teflon." Yet she sees significant changes in these interrelated areas of her life, a real payoff for her courageous work.

Bart Grooms, MDiv, MEd, diplomate of the American Association of Pastoral Counselors, licensed professional counselor and supervisor, and licensed marriage and family therapist and supervisor

Circular questioning. The art of questioning may be harnessed to suit the ends of a particular therapist or therapeutic style. In one such approach, **circular questioning** is used to expand on the client's own insight into a situation (Brown, 1997). The therapist may feign not understanding in order to explore a topic with question after question. Depending on training, professional background, wisdom, and experience, the therapist may access insights and strengths from participants that will guide them toward constructive outcomes.

> Circular questions are used within systemic family therapy as a tool to generate multiple explanations and stories from a family situation and as a means to stimulate the curiosity of the therapist while avoiding the temptation to seek one definitive explanation. (Evans & Whitcombe, 2016, p. 28)

Circular questioning, in an expanded form, was a favored approach of the Milan therapeutic team. It was felt that the circularity of the questioning allowed for an evolutionary process to occur within the family. This in turn facilitated change, and the therapist could respond in real time during the family session (Penn, 1982). Besides, family systems thinking often incorporates a circular feedback model of causality in which events tend to be described within the context of what preceded them in a cycle. Circular questioning can enhance these insights and become an essential part of the therapeutic process. This is contrasted to a linear approach, which tends to focus on cause and effect. The complexity of families in the context of their systems lends itself to this circularity. Circular questioning can be a means of generating various narratives and explanations. It can be a means of seeing things in a fresh way by creating new stories (Evans & Whitcombe, 2015). With each renewed question, another variation of an answer is provided that may expand or alter the narrative.

In the older, objective definitions of the family, the emphasis was on biological ties through kinship or marriage, legal connections, and persons living together in a consistent manner, while probably also supporting each other (Galvin, Braithwaite, & Bylund, 2014, p. 4). These same authors comment:

> Today, the family may be viewed more broadly as a group of people with a past history, a present reality, and a future expectation of interconnected mutually influencing relationships. Members often, but not necessarily, are bound together by heredity, legal marital ties, adoption, or committed voluntary ties. (Galvin, Braithwaite, & Bylund, 2014, p. 4)

Healthy family relationships support all participants, so healing these relationships is a major therapeutic goal in working toward psychological health. The actual questioning process becomes a tool in shaping the family's insights and facilitating appropriate change.

Narratives. The emphasis here is on the narrative or the story that clients tell. Early therapists who emphasized this angle were Michael White and David Epston (1990) from Australia. Importantly, a narrative does not have to represent the family's entire objective reality. Instead, it can represent a key story as family members subjectively think it plays out in their family. It is their personal reality, influenced by how they experience events. **Narrative approaches** acknowledge both the objective and subjective dimensions of what families believe about themselves. The families are the experts in that they know their own stories best.

The stories can have a leading motif or theme, which can be either positive or negative. For instance, a family who feels that its life script or story is about being a victim will find it hard to change this narrative unless family members develop greater insight into where these stories originated. It can be that the family of origin promoted and modeled similar themes. The narrative that families believe about themselves, or that a couple believes about their shared partnership, can be a powerful influencer. This approach is also a meaningful entry into the world of children and has been used successfully in pediatric contexts (Marsten, Epston, & Markham, 2016).

Circular questioning can open the door to eliciting the extended narrative. Each time the story is retold, it may alter a little or change its angle. Narrative approaches, as used in grief support, allow the client to retell the story of loss. With each retelling, the client can catch new glimpses of fresh detail—even potential possibilities may appear. These are the pivotal points at which the beginnings of change can occur.

Suggestions. Many of these techniques cut across theoretical approaches and are not purely anchored in family systems theory. **Positive suggestions** have a lot to do with reinforcement, a method used by behaviorists in any number of cognitive behavioral approaches.

Another interventional variation that doesn't require catching someone doing something right, as in positive reinforcement, is to provide subtle suggestions that are positive but that are about something that has not yet occurred. For instance, an underachieving scholar can be encouraged with these comments: "I have a sense that you would really love to do this work. . . . I think you would be good at it." A carefully placed suggestion should not be confused with advice giving. The intent of the suggestion is to open the door just a tiny crack, to allow for new options.

The opposite of positive suggestions are negative ones. If we warn the child about to receive an injection with these words: "Don't worry this will not hurt!" We are probably defeating the object of providing support. By using the word *hurt*, which has associations with pain, we have already made a negative suggestion and basically set up the child to anticipate something unpleasant. This in turn heightens anxiety and reduces collaboration during the intervention. Obviously, both positive and **negative suggestions** are related to conditioning through reinforcement; we recognize principles of behaviorism in these approaches.

Advice giving, on the other hand, contains the risk of displacing the responsibility from the client to the therapist. This can reduce the client's autonomy; appropriate decision making is part of ownership, responsibility, and growth.

Psychoeducation. The premise of educational strategies is to expand the knowledge base and therefore to change some of the thinking about a topic. Insufficient information and ignorance can be powerful in creating anxiety, perpetuating stereotypes, and generally destabilizing a system. With appropriate education, especially **psychoeducation**, people can create a greater knowledge base that can serve a very therapeutic function. Commonly, psychoeducation is used with great outcomes in sex and relationship education, premarital counseling, career counseling, and genetic counseling, as well as in treating multiple disorders, such as depressive illness, bipolar disorder, and the like (Brady, Kangas, & McGill, 2016). In each of these examples of the application of psychoeducation, the process of providing facts and furthering insight contributes to the educational process.

In psychotherapy, the various facets of a conversation or a therapeutic session are so closely interwoven that it may be difficult to identify where the educational process begins or ends. Facilitating insight may be regarded as a subtle way of educating, depending on how one looks at it.

Psychoeducation is useful when the lack of factual information can create anxiety or tension. The premise is that, as we add to the knowledge base, we are displacing with more solid information the vague feelings of anxiety caused by lack of insight or access to the facts. The typical medical consultation contains significant amounts of information concerning treatments and procedures. Importantly, this information is to be provided in a manner that is understandable for the patient and considers a laypersons' level of education and general understanding of medical matters. The mere process of sharing information respectfully also creates a bond between the person providing the information and the recipient.

Paradoxical interventions. This approach is tricky and best reserved for therapists with advanced training; in other words, do not attempt it without supervision. Alfred Adler initially explored it in the 1920s (Bitter & Carlson, 2017). It is an interventional approach that uses an indirect, subtle message that seems, to the outsider, to be opposite of the therapeutic goal, in order to bring about change (Bjornestad & Mims, 2017, p. 1191). It can include prescribing the symptom and encouraging the family members to take part in acting out the specific behavior that is to be diminished. In lay language, we might call it *reverse psychology*. If we tell children not to touch an object, they might hardly be able to resist the urge to touch it, as their interest is now heightened by the request.

In a similar vein, a family may be asked not to communicate about the elephant in the room. In practice, that family may then find this subject irresistible. Having been given instructions not to do something, one feels a heightened urge to explore doing it cautiously, or at least one thinks repeatedly about doing it. Harnessing this

Authentic Insight

Connections

In a reflection describing her work as a physician, Emily Martin (2019) notes that there is a professional responsibility to deal respectfully with the pain and suffering of her patients:

> [F]ormative experiences helped establish an appreciation for the power of, and beauty in, confronting suffering. Facing it. Naming it. Identifying where it starts and stops and whether it's mine or yours. Learning how to find meaning in its faces and its folds. How to manage it, treat it, and eventually, let it go. (p. 1052)

For the person designated to accompany a person in pain emotionally and physically (such is the calling of helping professionals), there needs to be respect for the authenticity of the other, as well as the professionalism of being available to provide that support appropriately—not flinching back because the experience is exactly as expected, namely, painful. She continues to describe the privilege of being present in the hour of need, of not shying away but witnessing and assigning meaning.

> I have the privilege of sitting with patients and their families during what is often among the most challenging times in their lives. . . . I may struggle to navigate complex family dynamics, to be at ease with prolonged silence, to respond to anger with compassion, to know when to push and when to pause, to know what questions to ask and when to ask them. But, importantly, I [remain] wholeheartedly engaged with those who have invited me to be part of their medical care. Because that's where I find meaning: in the connection, in the vulnerability, in the partnership. In the story. (p. 1052)

There is a valuable narrative contained in these moments, and those persons who accompany patients on these journeys are important witnesses, adding to the meaning and relevance of the events.

Source: E. J. Martin (2019).

GLOBAL GLIMPSE

LANGUAGE FROM THE HEART: ONCE UPON A TIME . . .

In different cultural contexts, the iconic opening line "Once upon a time . . ." may not be present. Openings vary to mirror the cultural context of the storyteller. How a story opener reads in Canada will not be the same as in Namibia. Lyons (2019) quotes research by Chitra Soundar, an Indian-British author and storyteller, in her discussion of how fairytales are told in various tongues. In the Indian language of Telugu, the story would start with "Having been said and said and said . . ."; whereas in Tamil, another Indian language, the opening would be "In that only place. . ." When a Korean parent reads to a child, the first line might well be "Once, in the old days, when tigers smoked. . ." The equivalent in Catalan (a language spoken in northeast Spain) is "Once upon a time in a corner of the world where everybody had a nose . . ." or "Once upon a time, when the beasts spoke and people were silent. . ."

The following story, using culturally appropriate metaphors, was written by students from KwaZulu, South Africa. It addresses overcoming challenges and the value of group collaboration and support. They found the exact words and story that would be meaningful in their unique cultural context.

> One day Noktula discovered Bhubessi washing clothes down at the Umzumbe River bank. They started to talk to each other. Mbekezelie played on the other side of the Umzumbe River bank, throwing stones into the water and amusing himself. That day Mbekezelie spotted Noktula and Bhubessi hanging their clothes over the bushes next to the banks of the Umzumbe River. They waded into the river to swim, laugh and play. While they were swimming Mbekezelie and some other children hid the girls' clothes.
>
> When Noktula and Bhubessi needed to return home, they were dismayed. They looked and looked but could not find their clothes. Nomfundo heard their cries and was on her way down to the Umzumbe River to collect water. She placed her pitcher down and started to help the two little girls. . . . On the other side of the river bank they saw Mbekezelie. They shouted across the river and asked: "Have you seen our washing?" "Yes" he answered, "it's on this side of the river."
>
> As the two little girls wanted to wade across to fetch the clothes, they saw a leopard on the banks of the river. "We can't get to you; the leopard is there." Suddenly Nomfundo took off her shoe and threw it at the leopard to distract him. The leopard crept into the bush. Mbekezelie swam across the river and gave the clothes back to Noktula and Bhubessi. He apologized for playing such a prank on them. All was forgiven and the children started to play a game of rejoicing. This was a day the children would never forget. (Gerhardt, 2018, p. 189)

Children's stories and books can be powerful vehicles to convey meaning while also helping readers and listeners process emotions. The books are susceptible to cultural content, which makes each story unique and poignant. Each story's one-of-a-kind narrative frames a particular experience. The *narrative* can be used to explain an abstract concept or a lesson to be learned. The power of the story in interactions with children and youth is well documented. The story can be meaningful to the narrator, as it can tell about hardship, ambitions, dreams, and challenges. Storytelling and other acts of narration have been used in therapeutic work and family therapy contexts (narrative therapy).

Sources: This story was first published as a longer version in Gerhardt, C. (2018). South Africa: Family life as the mirror of a society. In M. Robila & A. C. Taylor (Eds.), *Global perspectives in family life education* (pp. 179–194). Cham, Switzerland: Springer; see also Lyons (2019).

particular approach in a therapeutic context may mean that families can be encouraged to approach a taboo subject they would not otherwise have the courage to deal with. The paradoxical request—to not think about it—might just give family members a sense of permission to think about and reflect on it. In skilled hands, this can be a powerful tool. Practitioners of the Milan school in Italy favored this approach and refined its application.

Humor

In this image by Zimbabwean–South African artist Makiwa Mutomba, children are immersed in play. Children's play and stories can be powerful vehicles to convey meaning while also enabling the processing of emotions. Their authentic narrative is the way in which they frame their experiences.

Source: The Skateboards/Makiwa Mutomba.

My grandfather taught me a life lesson that stayed with me: *If you make a joke, do so at your own expense.* If you don't, he maintained, a joke moves from the arena of mirth to where we cause embarrassment, shame, or pain. The joke is not a good joke if it hurts someone else, if it is cringe-worthy for the recipient.

In a documentary on the life and work of the scriptwriter Nora Ephron (1941–2012), she described that every challenging event in her family of origin was translated by her mother (also a scriptwriter) into *copy*. If a situation could be transformed into a joke or become part of a script in a humorous way, family members could laugh and disarm it (Dance, 2015). Taking the sting out of the painful event by seeing the light-hearted moment contained therein led to some of Ephron's strongest work, displaying her signature comedic voice. The film script *Sleepless in Seattle* (1993) puts a very human but also comical face on loneliness. Yet among the only things Ephron never regarded as copy-worthy was her own imminent death, which she kept secret from her closest family and friends. This was one situation that could not be disarmed in any way, and she built a barrier of intense privacy around it.

Appropriate **humor**, or adding an element of fun, allows us to step away from difficulty to find the lighter moment contained within that same troubling experience. It can be the pivotal point where we drop our emotional defenses and allow the truth to enter. In the hands of skilled professionals, humor becomes a trusted technique. When we add fun to a teaching or learning activity, the atmosphere becomes light-hearted and the task relatively easy.

In our classes in the family sciences, we use humor and fun to gain access to potentially difficult material or to accomplish curricular tasks students find daunting. An activity that is always accompanied by great mirth is substituting the words of popular love songs with texts that support a specific theory or approach. If platonic love is compared to erotic love, the newly coined words in the song clearly point out the differences. Recognizing works in the popular media that support a certain theory or approach can be used fruitfully to illustrate complex themes.

As family therapy professionals, we know that we have to find optimal ways of facilitating the educational process in families. We are united in that we prefer a little fun when it comes to dealing with challenges; at least we can try to find the light-hearted moment in the process. We can introduce fun and humor in our attitude to our clients, an upbeat and appropriate cheerfulness that conveys that we want to be here at this time in this moment with these people. Conveying that emotion appropriately can convey a sense of value and respect.

We care about what we do as professionals, and we care about our clients. Appropriately sharing the sunnier side of things can be infectious. Sometimes humor may just be the tool that allows us to find a teachable minute, that instant when some intervention will make a difference, the moment we are willing to try a more

HISTORICAL GLIMPSE

CARL WHITAKER

The Facilitating Charms of Humor

As a young marriage and family therapist, I was privileged to witness some training sessions by Carl Whitaker (1912–1995), who was regarded as one of the pioneers in this field. Whitaker was especially renowned for using some unorthodox yet effective approaches. The therapeutic situation I was observing seemed to be at an impasse: defensiveness and blaming trapped the family in a circular holding pattern. As a silent observer, I wondered how this master of masters would find or create a crack in the solid emotional wall that was blocking all progress.

Whitaker started fumbling. He fished a large white handkerchief from his pocket. As the family drones on in ways that seem to lead nowhere, Whitaker is slowly knotting the corners of the hanky. Ah, even the greatest of therapists experiences moments of boredom in a session, we as observers thought. How human! We can totally identify with this—he is one of us. And then he did what only Whitaker could have done. He put the knotted handkerchief on his head, like an ill-fitting bandana (Gerhardt, 2003, p. 166). It made him laughable and vulnerable at the same time. For a little while nobody in the family said anything: after all, this was the world-renowned expert.

Then one of the children in the family group started giggling and another commented on it. The elephant in the room had been named. The impasse had been broken by humor. It was a powerful yet simple maneuver, but what I remembered most distinctly was that Whitaker took the risk of making himself the object of mirth. The joke was on him, and that is why it hit the target so perfectly. Within a split second the therapy session had moved to an entirely different place, a point where the participants could be vulnerable in a safe environment—setting the tone for the constructive change that was to follow.

Carl Whitaker, personal observation by Clara Gerhardt, during a training session in Durban, South Africa, 1981.

Sources: First published in Gerhardt, C. (2016). The facilitating charms of humor. *Network: CFLE Perspectives*. National Council on Family Relations. Summer edition; see also Gerhardt (2003).

GLOBAL GLIMPSE

TOWARD A TRANSCULTURAL APPROACH

With the gradual birth of psychology around the late 1800s and early 1900s, the value of talking and of a therapeutic relationship becomes increasingly mainstream. Importantly, psychotherapy has neither one birthplace nor one midwife bringing it into the world. Many histories intertwine, and in different cultural contexts, a variety of supportive interventions existed and continue to do so. These practices (which may be psychotherapeutic in nature) also have a reciprocal effect on the culture; there is a bidirectional influence.

In response to or maybe because of the synchronicity of these events, individuals in a variety of cultural contexts find new ways of describing their suffering:

> In the twentieth century, the therapeutic encounter became a site where individuals were not only cured, or not, as the case might be; but also learnt to articulate their suffering in new idioms, reconceive their lives (and those of others around them) according to particular narrative templates, and to take on conceptions concerning the nature of the mind and reality. (Shamdasani, 2018, pp. 4–9)

Mental health or illness is moving out of the realms of secrecy and shame. The World Health Organization estimates that, in developed countries, about 40 percent of illnesses pertain to mental health, with anxiety and depression topping the list (Clark & Layard, 2014, p. 5). Given this prevalence, patients can talk about their vulnerabilities, particularly about mental health concerns.

Importantly, they can also conceive of wellness in a proactive manner, creating *wellness narratives* that validate the goals and outcomes of psychotherapy. Increasingly, we understand that the early psychotherapeutic models, which were stereotypical and borne out of Western contexts, need to be expanded to address transcultural needs. For instance, China has recently experienced a major growth in demand for therapists, a phenomenon that has been labeled psychotherapy "fever" (Branigan, 2014).

> Psychotherapy is a set of historically situated practices, which both embody and produce specific cultural values. Consequently, transcultural histories of psychotherapies would at the same time chart how psychotherapeutic practices have come to transform cultures. (Shamdasani, 2018, pp. 4–9)

As the world becomes more interconnected and cultural exchanges occur, psychotherapy may have to find new labels, ones that are not identified only with Western contexts. Culture and what it means to suffer and deal with mental challenges will continue to morph and change to accommodate the particular idioms from various cultural contexts (Martin, 2018).

FOCUS POINT

The toolbox of the well-trained therapist may contain many techniques to reach the desired goal of improving the psychological health and functioning of a given family. Depending on the theoretical approach, these specific techniques may be tailored to support the basic premises of a theoretical angle. Some of the frequently used tools include questioning (and circular questioning), paradoxical interventions, suggestions, narratives, humor, active listening, and psychoeducation. This brief list is by no means comprehensive.

constructive approach. Maybe humor even helps us to the sliver in time when we allow some of life's truths to make a difference for the better (Gerhardt, 2016a, pp. 14–15).

Working With Families

All the members of a family are also participants of the inner workings of that particular family. When things go well, there is little need for outside help. The difficulties arise when things become challenging. It is hard to seek help from fellow family members, as the relationships already contain elements of alliance, being vested, having a history, and anticipating a future. All those things are excellent for cohesion, but they can turn into obstacles when interventions are required.

This final subsection on our ethical responsibilities as therapists and helping professionals is by no means comprehensive. It is included here as a reminder. When we seek detailed content guiding us in our work with families, we have to cast our nets wider. In essence, this book examines and focuses on family dynamics, so other books focusing on the ethics and practice of family therapy will give more guidance.

Ethics. To work with families ethically requires deep respect for the family; one must be able to meet a family and see its vulnerabilities while also realizing its strengths. In traditional contexts, the typical task is to strengthen that family. This may mean different things. It could mean that the family is encouraged to stay together, to bond and invest. But for a family in trouble, it may mean helping that family transform its structure, guiding it to adopt another family form that is helpful and sustaining to all family members at the particular moment of the family lifespan. For instance, when parents divorce or separate, a rethinking of the configuration of that family is needed. The old rules have to be modified to allow for new family formations.

And when one parent dies, a family has to reestablish its entire world as a family. The challenge of losing any family member is that the remaining family members have to create and inhabit a new inner world. They have to slowly build a world that looks different because one member is no longer physically part of that world. They may miss him or honor her memory, but slowly they have to build an inner landscape with new reference points (Schonfeld & Quackenbush, 2009). Grief is not something people can get over, as in a finish line we can cross. The grieving process is the gradual growth toward becoming another person, a person who has to live without the beloved as a living presence encountered daily.

Professional obligations. Each helping profession will have a particular code of ethics. Generally, such codes will cover aspirational guidelines and enforceable rules. If one studies the ethical guidelines of the major groups of helping professionals such as counselors, social workers, psychologists, and others working with families, one can see that the ethical guidelines are grouped around themes. Here are a few of these central guidelines (National Organization for Human Services, 2015, Responsibility to Clients):

- Respect the dignity, privacy, and well-being of the client.
- Respect professional and interpersonal boundaries.
- Protect client confidentiality and privacy.
- Do not engage in dual relationships.
- Respect diversity and display multicultural competence.

First of all, do no harm. Working with families requires and implicates the two cornerstones of ethics: **non-maleficence** and **beneficence** (American Counseling Association [ACA], 2014). Non-maleficence, the action of avoiding that which causes harm, is the pillar helping professionals use as they work with families. To cause no harm is to be cognizant of the lenses clients use to filter what is around them and to know how far a client can be challenged without shattering his or her beliefs. Causing no harm is recognizing what mechanisms clients use to remain functional and not removing those until something better is found to replace them.

Beneficence is being aware of all these things and acting in a way that is for the good of the individual, family, and society. Helping professionals display beneficence when they keep in mind the best interest of the family and use that to influence how they interact with the family unit.

Process and content. By **process**, we mean the broad boundaries within which the content can be contained. Process is like the riverbed. Within it can flow the water consisting of specific content. **Content** refers to the facts, the details that color in the larger picture.

In family therapy, we can regard the general family systems approach as the process. The specific techniques and details that are filled in by each therapeutic approach or specific theoretical method can be regarded as the content.

Content can be ever changing. This fluidity is useful as the content illustrates the process. But sometimes, if we get too caught up in the content, we may miss seeing the bigger picture or the process. Selecting specific techniques to address various processes provides a mere glimpse into how certain theoretical approaches are applied, or into how some therapists may work. It references the tools at their disposal. But know that there are many more techniques and approaches out there; it is not possible to cover them all in detail in an introductory text.

In essence, we need to know that therapists have numerous techniques at their disposal. They will choose them according to their theoretical preferences, their own training and backgrounds, and their personal strengths and affinities, but all these factors are secondary to their consideration of what is best for the family they are serving. No listing of techniques and approaches can be exhaustive, but studying a few select examples may broaden our vision of how family therapists work to support the psychological health of families.

FOCUS POINT

All helping professionals have ethical guidelines that inform them concerning how to interact with their clients. These ethical obligations ensure that individuals and families are met with respect and consideration, especially in times when they are most vulnerable. The cornerstones of ethical behavior related to working with families are doing no harm and acting for the good of the family. By process, we mean the broad boundaries within which the content or details of the family system can be contained. Process is like the riverbed. Within it can flow specific content. Content refers to the facts, the details that color the larger picture. Specific examples of content can provide clues as to the process. Ultimately, it is the process occurring within families that has to be addressed, as the content can be varied and ever changing.

SPOTLIGHT ON THEORIES

Natural Systems Theory (Bowen Theory)

Natural systems theory, also known as **Bowen theory**, is based on the work of Murray Bowen (1913–1990). It has gained a significant following among family-related professionals because the theory provides a therapeutic model, which in turn identifies clear anchor points for the therapist. One of Murray's concerns was that the therapist's own personality and family experiences could get in the way of therapeutic work. By adhering to clear theoretical guidelines, a therapist can minimize this risk (Becvar & Becvar, 2013, p. 145).

The field of family therapy has evolved since the Bowen days, and some of his concepts have been absorbed into mainstream thinking about families. Bowen, too, was influenced by various sources. It is the nature of theory formation that inspiration comes from various angles, which are consolidated into a system by the theorist, who tries to create a mental map out of all the diverging strands. Bowen's theory represents a bridge between earlier psychodynamic theory and family therapy (Becvar & Becvar, 2013, p. 144). Natural systems theory has been applied in numerous specific family therapy endeavors, especially in clinical contexts, and with a wide variety of populations (Titelman, 1998). Hence, it is appropriate to discuss it in a chapter dealing with interventions in family therapy.

Murray Bowen graduated with an MD from the University of Tennessee, continued his training as a psychiatrist, and actively served in the U.S. Army during World War II. He was a small-town boy, growing up in a town with fewer than 1,000 inhabitants. His family of origin consisted of five children; he was the oldest. He became the first president of the American Family Therapy Association. He gained eminence for his work as a family therapist, and his theory, Bowen theory, has contributed greatly to the family-related therapeutic field.

Bowen anchored his theory in a systems approach to the family, which emphasizes the greater whole or system that is created by family members, while also acknowledging some psychodynamic strands. There is reciprocal interaction, in which various family members can try to balance out the emotional outcomes of that family system. For instance, if one member is overly anxious, then another member may react by becoming overly protective.

Legend has it that Bowen was inspired by occurrences at his extended family's Thanksgiving

(Continued)

(Continued)

dinner, which took place in his home state of Tennessee. He watched the various interactions between his family members and had a moment of revelation in which he began formulating the outlines of his theory. Over subsequent months and years, he continued to flesh out the details of what came to be known as Bowen theory. About that theory, Murray Bowen is credited with stating, "I finally knew one way through the impenetrable thicket which is the family emotional system" (as cited in Kerr & Bowen, 1988, p. 380). In a last interview, recorded in the hospital three days before his death, Dr. Bowen ended the conversation with a last message to his colleagues:

> You have inherited a lifetime of tribulation. Everybody has inherited it. Take it over, make the most of it. And when you have decided you know the right way, do the best you can with it. (Doherty, 1990; also cited in Boyd, 2007)

In essence, Bowen supported and elaborated concepts in family systems theory. He was convinced that families interact in a **multigenerational** manner and that we are influenced by the patterns in our families of origin, where we also learn the intricacies of particular family-specific interactions. According to Bowen, we all have family of origin issues, and we need to learn to deal with these constructively. In therapy, it is important to involve the key players in a particular system, as they are capable of influencing other members of the family, be it directly or indirectly. Bowen emphasized the individuation process. For individuals to form meaningful relationships, including relationships within their own families of creation, they first have to find and develop a sense of self and autonomy by individuating and differentiating themselves from their family of origin system. Being overly involved with other family members could hinder individuation and become unhealthy. He referred to this excessive closeness as **emotional fusion**. On the other hand, reducing or completely eliminating emotional contact with other family members can also be unhealthy. Bowen described this process of running away from or denying the importance of family, calling this important concept **emotional cutoff** (Titelman, 1998).

If one gets caught up in the eight core concepts of the theory, it can seem difficult to master, especially as Bowen tends to add his own angle to some of the phrases, requiring insight into the specific terminology used in this approach. At the risk of being overly reductionist and simplistic, I see this theory as focusing on alliances within the context of a system, as well as on the finding and strengthening of personal identity (individuation). Think of a newcomer joining an established high-school class. That newbie has to figure out a number of things while trying to find a social place in the class. Some of the newbie's concerns can be posed as questions: who associates with whom, which kids are cool, which are bullies, who ignores whom, which kids can I befriend, can I be strong and be me, how do I want to come across? And if that isn't enough to negotiate, the newbie will bring into the new situation all the memories and experiences of the past: Will it be like my previous school?

A family system contains similar dramatic patterns. There is history, there are alliances, some members won't speak to others (cutoffs), and some form power blocks for control. Others become the victims of the dominant ones. It is an intricate and complex social dance, which brings with it the history of intergenerational influences.

The core of Bowen theory describes eight interlocking concepts (Kerr, 2000):

- *Triangles.* These are three-person relationship systems in which power can shift, for instance through increased or reduced focus on one person in that configuration.
- *Differentiation of self.* This is the process of individuation. Becoming well-differentiated is a desired outcome of appropriate lifespan development.
- *Nuclear family emotional process.* Bowen identifies four basic relationship patterns that can become problematic: marital conflict, dysfunction in one spouse, impairment of at least one child, and emotional distance.
- *Family projection process.* These are the ways in which parents can pass on emotional problems to children.
- *Multigenerational transmission process.* This is the process by which influences can stretch across generations.

- *Emotional cutoff.* This is the result of unresolved emotional concerns that are handled (or rather not addressed) by avoidance and feuds.
- *Sibling position.* Birth order can be of relevance as it also affects position in the family system.
- *Societal emotional process.* Society may reflect and parallel the consolidated emotional processes of many individuals.

Bowen theory counts among the more detailed theoretical approaches in the family field, and the theory has driven practical therapeutic approaches. It certainly has a significant following and is taught in family therapy courses as one of several significant approaches (Becvar & Becvar, 2013, pp. 144–145). The complexity of the theory is challenging. Therapists wishing to use Bowen theory as their guiding light require additional training to master its concepts and to acquire the specific Bowenian vocabulary. In that respect, it is similar to a therapist acquiring, for instance, a psychoanalytic vocabulary before venturing into therapeutic contexts using that particular approach as a point of reference.

The contributions of Murray Bowen, the family therapist, gain in relevance if they are viewed in the context of his time. He was a true pioneer, and he succeeded in providing both theory and practical tools at a time when there was relatively little inspiration and few choices for family-related professionals.

> **"That which is created in a relationship can be fixed in a relationship."**
>
> Murray Bowen

In a Nutshell

Natural Systems Theory (Bowen Theory)

- Natural systems theory (Bowen theory) is attributed to Murray Bowen, an American psychiatrist and family therapist.
- The theory and its related therapeutic approach are anchored in family systems thinking while also referencing aspects of psychodynamic theory.
- Differentiation of the self (or individuation) is a central tenet.
- Bowen attributes far-reaching effects to multigenerational influences.
- Bowen describes the process of the emotional cutoff, a concept that has become mainstream.
- The theory postulates that eight interlocking concepts explain many behavior patterns. These eight concepts guide therapeutic interventions.
- Both the theory and the therapeutic principles are complex.

CHAPTER FOCUS POINTS

Observing Families

- An observer who joins a system alters that system. When a therapist works with a family, the act of initiating family therapy changes that particular family. This is called the *observer effect*.
- Paradoxically, families may resist positive changes to their family system, as they are trying to maintain homeostasis or equilibrium. The known and familiar may be preferable to the unknown, even if the known represents a dysfunctional situation.

Making Dynamics Visible

- A number of family-related techniques and assessments were developed, including family genograms, family sculpting, and certain techniques within play therapy for children.
- Family researchers document relationships within family systems. They are interested in

the hierarchy and subsystems within a family system; who is close to whom, the alliances, and the potential strengths as well as breaks in communication.

- A family genogram can document a family at a particular point in time. It can highlight various dimensions, as it superimposes qualities of interest on top of a family tree. It is informative concerning the functioning of a particular family system.
- A number of other techniques serve to highlight the interrelated dimensions within family systems, for example, family sculpting.

Cultural Constructions of the Family

- Metaphorically speaking, early psychology presented us with still-life photos of the family, but family *dynamics* represents the stitching together of those photos. It provides the fourth dimension that represents movement, the psychological motion that occurs within family systems.
- Families form images of themselves, which in turn can tell us something about those groups of people. Photographs and family albums may provide clues to previous generations. Other metaphors can be found in family symbols, names, and family crests.
- Family researchers and therapists explore ways of documenting relationships within family systems. They are interested in the hierarchy within a family system, for example, who was close to whom, the alliances, and the potential breaks in communication. This hierarchy is influenced by the flow of information and by membership in particular subsystems. Adaptation to the larger system and personal influences are also of interest.
- Children may share some of their constructions of family through the medium of play. A number of family-related techniques and assessments have been developed, including family genograms, family sculpting, and certain techniques within play therapy for children.

Family Interventions

- The toolbox of the well-trained therapist may contain many techniques to reach the desired goal of improving the psychological health and functioning of a given family.
- Depending on the theoretical approach, these specific techniques may be tailored to support the basic premises of a theoretical angle.
- Some of the frequently used tools include questioning (and circular questioning), paradoxical interventions, suggestions, narratives, humor, active listening, and psychoeducation. This brief list is by no means comprehensive.

Working With Families

- All helping professionals have ethical guidelines that inform them concerning how to interact with their clients. These ethical obligations ensure that individuals and families are met with respect and consideration, especially in times when they are most vulnerable.
- The cornerstones of ethical behavior related to working with families are doing no harm and acting for the good of the family.
- By process, we mean the broad boundaries within which the content can be contained. Process is like the riverbed. Within it can flow the specific content.
- Content refers to the facts, the details that color the larger picture.
- Specific examples of content can provide clues as to the process. Ultimately, it is the process that has to be addressed, as the content can be varied and ever changing.

Spotlight on Theories: Natural Systems Theory (Bowen Theory)

- Natural systems theory (Bowen theory) is the brainchild of Murray Bowen, an American psychiatrist and family therapist. The theory and its related therapeutic approaches are anchored in family systems thinking while also referencing aspects of psychodynamic theory.
- Differentiation of the self (or individuation) is a central tenet.
- Bowen attributes far-reaching effects to multigenerational influences.
- Bowen describes the process of the emotional cutoff, a concept that has become mainstream.
- The theory postulates that eight interlocking concepts explain many of the behavior patterns observed in families. These eight concepts guide therapeutic interventions.
- Both the theory and the therapeutic principles are complex.

CHAPTER 5

Explaining Dynamics With Theories

Learning Objectives

After completing this chapter, you should be able to

1. Explain the use and relevance of theories pertaining to the family.
2. Reflect on the factors contributing to the birth of the family therapy movement.
3. Consider the role of paradigm shifts in the understanding of families.
4. Define *ecology* and explain how it can be applied to family dynamics.
5. Discuss the five major shifts in an evolutionary approach to theories.

Theories: Seeking Connection and Meaning

A vine is best supported by a trellis. In practice, that means that vines can grow into an arbor if provided with a structure or lattice or other form of scaffolding. We can equate the vine to the knowledge available to us from our observations and research. In order to put this knowledge into a systematic format that will make it more accessible to other researchers, we anchor it in theory. This theoretical framework has the same function as a trellis. It is a structural support system.

Extending the same metaphor, the wide choice in trellises represents variability as provided by theories. The vine can grow on a rectangular design, on a very artistic construction, or we may like the usefulness of a V-shaped support system. In reality, grape vines are usually grown on structures that allow most of the grapes to be exposed to the sun. Here, the choice of the trellis has to do with functionality and what would work best in a given situation.

Neimeyer (2009, p. 1) eloquently illustrates how new theories and approaches are born, how they arise from and are inspired by that which has preceded them:

> No intellectual development arrives on the scene as a result of the "immaculate conception" of its founder. Instead, each inevitably arises from the co-mingling of concepts from previous generations, representing the fertile marriage of ideas having different intellectual pedigrees. Extending this "marriage" metaphor, we might even say that every nascent theory represents "something old, something new, something borrowed, and something "true."

A theory is a way of organizing information and knowledge. Theories in themselves do not represent or form the core of that knowledge base. Instead, theories are a way of creating the order that will help us explain or understand various situations. They are a way of connecting the dots, of facilitating meaning. Theories are not permanently solidified; they are not carved in stone. They develop and change as our knowledge base expands. They can also be influenced by macrosystemic events, such as the many cultural shifts that occur dramatically versus almost imperceptibly.

What Is a Theory?

How do we then describe a theory? A succinct definition of a theory is provided by Smith and Hamon (2017, p. 1):

> A theory is a tool to understand and describe the world. More specifically, a theory is a general framework of ideas and how they relate to each other. Theories can be used to ask and answer questions about particular phenomena.

Concerning the characteristics of a theory, these same authors state the following:

> A theory should also be flexible enough to grow and change, so that new information can be fed back into the theory, causing it to adapt and change . . . but a theory also needs to be general enough to apply to a wide variety of specific cases. In short, the usefulness of a theory is determined by its ability to describe more, rather than less, detail; to predict with more, rather than less, accuracy; and to apply to a broader, rather than a narrower, range of specific cases. (Smith & Hamon, 2017, p. 12)

Here are some of the characteristics of a theory.

- *Meaning.* A theory should contribute greater meaning to observations.
- *Generalizability.* A theory should be able to be applied to various contexts.
- *Descriptive ability.* A theory should be able to describe what is observed.
- *Flexibility.* Theories should be able to grow and change, to adapt to the current knowledge base.

Constructing Theories

Over the past century, marriage and family therapy has followed an intense developmental path. This journey is reflected in the theories that try to systematize and add meaning to the vast knowledge base that has been acquired. In short, then, "Theories provide a general framework for understanding data in an organized way and show us how to intervene" (Burr, 1995, quoted by Smith & Hamon, 2017, p. 2).

Smith and Hamon (2017) propose that a theory is composed of several building blocks. In forming a theory, the theorist starts off with *assumptions* or ideas about how to explain what is observed. These assumptions provide us with the foundation on which the theory can be built. The bricks that we use for this building consist of *concepts*, or specific ideas. The theorist then tries to find the interrelationship between the concepts. What is their value and meaning in relation to each other? These authors describe this process as the *glue* holding the theory together. It can also be likened to building the bricks with cement, so they can form a structure.

For a theory to be useful, it initially needs to be able to *describe* the observations. As these descriptions are linked together, the theorist may be looking for a

FOCUS POINT

Marriage and family therapy has followed an intense developmental path. This journey is reflected in the theories that try to systematize and add meaning to the vast knowledge base that has been acquired. Theories organize data to find relevance and meaning. This framework can influence research and therapeutic applications. Sustainable theories need to meet several criteria, including being descriptive, organizing concepts into a meaningful framework, pointing out the interconnectedness between events and observations, recognizing patterns from these observations, and providing a platform from which a hypothesis can be formulated.

recurring pattern. If a pattern appears, it lets us make cautious predictions. Some of these tentative predictions can be encapsulated in a research hypothesis. The actual research will then try to confirm or support the validity of the hypothesis or, alternatively, not support or reject the hypothesis.

Let us recap what we have learned about theory formation:

- *Assumptions.* These form the foundation on which a theory can be built.
- *Concepts.* These are the building blocks of a theory.
- *Description.* This consists of documenting observations to provide content and structure for a theory, while also testing applicability.
- *Interrelationships.* These can be considered the cement that binds the building blocks.
- *Patterns.* These are the recognizable and recurring sequences.
- *Hypothesis.* This tentative prediction is to be supported or not supported by research.

Birth of the Family Therapy Movement

The Growth of Psychology

The beginnings of the detailed study of the psyche, which occurred in both philosophical and therapeutic contexts, can be viewed as a screen gradually coming into focus, as opposed to one light-bulb moment in time. There is no clear birth date of psychology; several movements and theorists influenced each other. At the cusp of the nineteenth and into the twentieth century, psychology was in its infancy and without a distinct identity.

Between the two major world wars, the development and expansion of psychology took a dramatic turn. The world wars had precipitated a series of interrelated challenges that cut across all domains and included debilitating physical disabilities as a result of combat-related injuries, economic deprivation, physical displacement, the destruction of homes and workplaces, widowed adults, and orphaned children.

As a result of the orphaned and displaced children, therapists examined the concept of attachment, and variations of the *attachment theory* were born (Reese, 2018). The challenges were immense, and the price of war in terms of human suffering was incalculable.

Every war claims at least three generations as its victims. We have the actively deployed generation in the middle—sandwiched between the older generation, their parents, and the younger generation, their children. The price of war in terms of family life is always tragically and catastrophically high.

Reaching Out to Families in Need

The underpinnings of marriage and family therapy can be found in social work, and to this day there is a close affinity (and collaboration) between these two professions. Social workers were often privy to the personal home environment of a particular family, getting an insider's view into the usually private world of domestic toil and trouble. Hence, the social work movements of the nineteenth century did the groundwork for what was to become a profession focusing on the family.

In the twentieth century, more progress was made toward formalizing the help-giving professions that focused on family well-being. A number of related helping professionals carried the well-being of the family at heart, and the therapy teams were typically multi-professional. These teams operated in addition to those whose interventions focused on the individual.

Marriage therapy required both partners to be involved in the therapeutic interventions. Approaching the family as a unit seemed a logical progression.

From Individual to Family Contexts

The shift from individual to family contexts had begun as early as the 1940s. The first association for marriage counselors in the United States was founded in 1942, and this organization eventually became the current American Association of Marriage and Family Therapy (AAMFT). This organization initiated the formal intervention in and support of what had until then been regarded as a very personal and private matter, namely marriage. Child advocacy groups also saw the relevance of working with families. And religious organizations, too, realized that support for families was an important service to the community. Stabilizing families meant lower divorce rates and better outcomes for the children.

In Scotland, in the post–World War II years, social workers, counselors, and pastoral care practitioners shared expertise and collaborated to benefit families, working toward maintaining intact families as opposed to breaking them up (Willis, Bondi, Burgess, Miller, & Fergusson, 2014). One of the first counseling clinics was opened in Scotland in the 1940s, and, as was typical, it was located on church premises and had church support (Bondi, 2013). A concern of these clinics was to address the scars caused by war.

Parallel movements were stirring elsewhere, and many had an even earlier beginning. After all, Freud and his colleagues had been considering familial relations and psychosexual development in turn-of-the-century Vienna, Austria. Even earlier, French neurologist Jean-Martin Charcot (1825–1893) had been interested in the presentation of hysteria. Hungarian developments were reflected in the more relational and intersubjective theories of the "Budapest School" of psychoanalysis.

In short, awareness of and interest in psychology was spreading. The sociopolitical climates in various countries further fueled the new insights, indicating that the context of psychology was more widespread and international than is often acknowledged (Szokolszky, 2016). An intellectual paradigm shift was occuring in academic and related contexts, and it spilled over to influence the arts in general and literature and the visual arts in particular.

Once set in motion, this renewed and altered perspective of the family took on a momentum of its own.

Formalizing Family Therapy

Development of the family therapy movement was rapid and occurred simultaneously on several continents. Although the family therapy movement had earlier underpinnings, the more formal focus on the family as a system started in the early 1960s and steadily gained momentum throughout the rest of that century (Rasheed, Rasheed, & Marley, 2010). By the 1970s and 1980s, there were major movements and distinct schools of family therapy not only in the United States and Europe but further afield in Commonwealth countries such as Australia, New Zealand, and Canada. The leading family therapists appeared at conferences all over the world, presented numerous workshops, and, in so doing, spread the word concerning this relatively young profession (Gerhardt, 2003).

Two major theoretical schools of the sixties and seventies were (1) the family therapists collaborating in Palo Alto in the United States and (2) those identifying themselves as the Milan group in Italy. The Palo Alto Mental Research Institute (founded in 1958) offered the first formal training program in family therapy. The Milan school offered a systemic and constructivist approach to family therapy. But other countries yielded other approaches. In a book on global perspectives on family therapy (Ng, 2003), this specialization is described in Asia, Europe, Africa, and further afield. Specific countries also developed distinct family therapy movements, including Japan, Malaysia, Singapore, India, Russia, Nigeria, South Africa, Israel, and Brazil. There were many other initiatives, and combined they amplified the voice of the marriage and family therapy movement.

GLOBAL GLIMPSE

UMUZI, UMNDENI, NDYANGU, LELAPA LAKA, MUTA*

I experienced first hand one example of how family therapy spread worldwide, as I participated in the tender beginnings of the family therapy movement in South Africa. I was one of the original student members of the first organization focusing on the family. During the 1960s and 1970s, several important international therapists had come to visit, usually by invitation of universities or smaller study groups. One of the early conferences was titled "Psychopathology and the Mental Health of the *Family*" (italics added), hinting that the formal family therapy movement was getting ready to take off.

Early visitors included Donald Bloch and Jessie Turberg from the Ackerman Institute in New York, who visited in 1974, and Avner Barcai of the Philadelphia Child Guidance Clinic and Haifa University. I remember the sense of connectedness this created among us; slowly, we were aligning ourselves with the therapeutic approaches that had their own family-focused identity, different from the models we had been exposed to in our earlier professional training.

Florence Kaslow (1981) encouraged formal affiliation with the International Family Therapy Association. Her suggestion gave South Africans a sense of hope and belonging at a difficult historical time. In 1981, family therapists founded the South African Institute of Marital and Family Therapy (SAIMFT), and the organization became a mouthpiece for interdisciplinary professionals within the field and an organizing body that invited family-related experts to national and international conferences (Gerhardt, 2003, pp. 163–164).

As the nucleus of family-focused therapists began to emerge, an extended "family" formed around them and strengthened the discipline. It was in this context of international exchange that I was privileged to attend multiple workshops by Maurizio Andolfi, Edgar Auerswald, Donald Bloch, Luigi Boscolo, Gianfranco Cecchin, Mony Elkaim, Brad Keeney, Cloe Madanes, Salvador Minuchin, Virginia Satir, Mara Selvini-Palazzoli, Carlos Sluzki, Carl Whitaker, Michael White, and others. These legendary therapists trained the next generation, and I, for one, am deeply grateful for these unique and historical opportunities.

*The word "family" in various African languages, including Zulu and Sotho

FOCUS POINT

Social policy reform paved the way to address the needs of families and to ensure more hopeful futures for their children. The underpinnings of marriage and family therapy can be found in social work and related professions, and, to this day, there is a close relationship (and excellent collaboration) between professionals focusing on the family. Development of the family therapy movement was rapid and occurred simultaneously on several continents. Currently, theory referencing marriage and family systems is the second most utilized approach in therapeutic intervention.

Slowly but surely, family therapy became mainstream. Currently, cognitive behavioral approaches and marriage and family systems approaches rank among those most frequently utilized in therapeutic contexts.

Major Theoretical Paradigm Shifts

Theories and approaches build on each other, extending the knowledge base. The major theoretical shifts in psychology and related fields affect how we view family relations. In multimodal and integrative approaches relevant parts from several theories are combined. Newer approaches do not necessarily exclude or invalidate previous theories and approaches. Theories can evolve over time (Bigner & Gerhardt, 2019, p. 99).

Numerous theories have influenced our current perspectives on families, and especially on the dynamics within families. Each one builds on the insights of previous theories contextualized within a given time. Typically, as the thinking and the general societal values and approaches within cultural contexts change, theories adapt and alter to reflect these changes within societies and especially within families. The way we view families and how we think about families undergoes subtle shifts to reflect greater cultural and societal changes.

One very clear example of such a major shift is the movement toward greater gender equality. Changing gender roles affect not only women but also men—and, of

A historic example of a major paradigm shift occurred when the philosopher scientist Copernicus (1473–1543) expressed the dramatic view that the sun was the center of the universe and that the planets, including planet Earth, were orbiting around the sun. The artist of this engraving is unknown. It was published in 1888 in a book by Camille Flammarion and described as "A missionary of the Middle Ages tells that he had found the point where the sky and the Earth touch."

Source: Public domain.

course, the family. Greater understanding and acceptance of persons self-identifying on the LGBT spectrum has necessitated a reframing of how families are represented. The cookie-cutter stereotype of a mother, father, and two picture-perfect children, preferably one boy and one girl, does not represent the reality of authentic families in a living and breathing world. Add to this the tremendous variation in cultural influences, accounting for even greater diversity.

This image is recreated in the surrealist style. Freud and the psychoanalytic movement influenced the surrealist movement in art by emphasizing dreams, the imagination, and the subconscious. Salvador Dalí, a surrealist artist who painted *Persistence of Memory*, was interested in Freud's work and finally met him in 1938.

Source: © iStock.com/bestdesigns.

Paradigm Shifts

As our concept of the family reconfigures, it causes a ripple effect. Because family therapy theories are about the family and its functioning, these theories and approaches will change as ideas about the family change. When these shifts in thinking are sufficiently dramatic, they affect the notions we have about other things, and, almost like a wildfire, they push previously long-standing beliefs toward an entirely new perspective. When this occurs, we call it a *paradigm shift*.

One historic example of a major paradigm shift occurred when the philosopher-scientist Copernicus (1473–1543) expressed the dramatic view that the sun was the center of the universe and that the planets (including planet Earth) were orbiting around the sun. Copernicus's view was ahead of its time and did not align with the views held by most people, so it was resisted. Today, Copernicus's once radical view is seen as tested scientific fact.

Although we tend to associate theories with the scientific world, they fulfill an equally important role in the social sciences and in the context of studying the dynamics of the family. Indeed, a paradigm shift helped to create the social sciences. The psychoanalytic theory constructed by Freud and his contemporaries near the beginning of the twentieth century represents a shift in thinking—the development of a new perspective. This particular perspective had a domino effect, influencing literature and the arts, and leaving its mark on the thinking (*Zeitgeist*) of the day.

Once such a radical shift in thinking or perspective has occurred, it is virtually impossible to return unaffected to the worldview that preceded it. It is impossible to "un-think" an idea.

Within and Between People

Within people. Our thinking concerning family dynamics has undergone dramatic shifts. In essence, the early view of the family took a psychological approach, which viewed the drama of human life as being centered on the individual, on what occurred *within* the person. It focused on what was happening inside the heads and hearts of people. Therapeutic sessions were spent analyzing individual thoughts, fears, free associations, and dreams.

Freud, especially, thought that our unconscious mental processes were of critical importance, and he compared the subconscious to the larger, submerged part of an iceberg. The one-tenth of the iceberg that is above the water would represent the conscious processes. Freud proposed various techniques that could be used to access subconscious material, including analyzing dreams, free association, and slips of the tongue. Freud thought that dreams were the *royal road to the unconscious* (Freud, 1900). These various approaches focusing predominantly on the inner lives of individuals were labeled **intrapsychic approaches**. In the early twentieth century and onward, the major psychoanalytic and psychosocial approaches were exceptionally important in putting the study of the mind or psyche on the map.

Between people. To pin down the major shifts in thinking that have occurred in the field of therapy, specifically in psychological therapy, we could ask when and how the entire family, including the dynamic functioning of the family, entered center stage. The answer is when the therapeutic approach moved from being regarded as primarily intrapsychic (or within the person) to include what happens between people—in other words, with the advent of **interpsychic approaches**.

Historic underpinnings: Interactional emphasis. Harry Stack Sullivan (1892–1949), an American neo-Freudian psychiatrist and analyst, was an important spokesperson for opening up this larger interpersonal context. He is credited with the "interpersonal theory of psychiatry" (Sullivan, 1955/2011). He repeatedly emphasized that the personality of the individual lives within a network of

Authentic Insight

The Realness of Our Perceived Worlds

Phenomenology acknowledges the subjective reality of our perceived worlds—how real it feels to us, we who are living those experiences.

Family scientists and family therapists have used phenomenological methods to investigate the meanings of death in families, caring for children in high-risk neighborhoods, and perceptions of living with Alzheimer's disease, to name a few topics. In addition, family therapists often focus on meaning in their therapeutic work, and this kind of broadly defined phenomenological research over years has led to new understandings of how therapists can work more productively and ethically. In this sense, the establishment of family therapy as a profession was supported by a phenomenological exploration of the meaning of mental illness in the 1950s and 1960s, as pioneers in family therapy asserted that diagnosable behaviors have meanings in the context of family interactions (Boss, Dahl, & Kaplan, 1996).

The focus on participants' experiences, the meanings ascribed to these experiences, and the capacity for broad, exploratory inquiry make phenomenology well suited to endeavors involving [metacognition]. This allows us to focus on a particular experience and explore what this experience means to the client by examining her or his beliefs, convictions, thoughts, and feelings about the experience. We ask the client to create a metaphor to elicit subtle understandings of the experience.

Phenomenology's focus on experience and meaning is inextricably entwined with the description of the context that evoked it, and this interdependence of experience and context is particularly important in therapeutic explorations. We have some indication that the interaction between context and experience may be significant for the therapeutic relationship as well as the larger context of experience.

Jonathan Davis, PhD, is a professor of human development and family science, as well as a licensed marriage and family therapist. This excerpt was adapted from his doctoral dissertation.

Source: Davis (2004).

FOCUS POINT

Numerous theories have influenced our current perspectives on families, and especially on the dynamics within families. Each one builds on the insights of previous theories, and theories adapt and alter to reflect changes within societies. The way we view families and how we think about families reflect greater cultural and societal changes. When these shifts in thinking are sufficiently dramatic, they affect related areas, including social policy. New ideas and approaches have the ability to push previously long-standing beliefs toward an entirely new perspective, called a *paradigm shift*. Once such a somewhat radical shift in thinking or perspective has occurred, it is virtually impossible to return to the thinking that preceded it.

interpersonal relationships. We are embedded in interactions with others. He is one of the earliest neo-Freudians to speak out against a solely "intrapsychic" perspective. He emphasized the word *interactional* instead.

He is credited with having developed a psychiatric approach focusing on interpersonal relationships. He explored how different conditions, such as schizophrenia, may be implicated through the relationship dimension. Because he was so focused on the value and necessity of relationships, he thought that loneliness must be one of the most excruciating states of the human condition.

The seeds of systemic thinking. Dramatically, therapists began to place individual family members (or clients) into a playing field that contained other individuals or players, often the family. Individuals became part of a greater interpersonal connectedness.

A conception of the larger context was moving into the frame; the seeds of systemic thinking were germinating.

The Context of Systemic Thinking

The Family as a Team

Let us consider the shift from intrapsychic to interpsychic approaches using the metaphor of the team. In the early days of psychology, we focused almost exclusively on an *individual player*. Then we started paying significant attention to the *entire team*. That means that those strategies a team employs come into focus. Any serious fan of football or similar games knows that the coach is concerned not only about each individual player but also about the cohesion and team dynamic of that particular group of players. How the team functions is of utmost importance. Similarly, families are made up of individuals, and as family scientists, we are very interested in how those individuals interact to give life to the dynamic games that families play.

"The team is more than its players."

Folk wisdom

Dynamics and Systemic Thinking

Systemic thinking is bookended by several other important approaches to human functioning. Some of the earlier ideas concerning the psyche are anchored in psychoanalytic and psychosocial roots. The counterpart to these is represented by behaviorist and cognitive behavioral approaches. Humanistic ways of seeing the person represented an important turning point for the therapeutic process—and greatly influenced counseling techniques. Currently, there is renewed and extended interest in neurology and neuroscience, and these have become important sources for understanding some of the intricacies of the human mind.

Shifts. These shifts in thinking can be represented in visual form, making it clear that each preceding movement or approach put important foundational constructs in place that the next theories used as points of departure or inspiration. In this manner, we built on what had gone before, and, as folklore states, we stood on the shoulders of giants in order to extend our view.

Context. Similarly, everything that has preceded and followed the systemic approaches has value in its own right. The choice as to which theory or approach

Authentic Insight

My Journey: Applying Family Dynamics to Clinical Practice

Growing up, I attended over 20 schools in a variety of locations across the southern and Midwestern United States. My father's employment drove this high level of mobility. Despite the many geographical upheavals, my family offered stability and predictability in socially diverse contexts. These early life experiences were the foundation allowing me to grasp family dynamics in context. Understanding the abstract is grounded in the lived experience of the concrete.

My academic training in sociology provided me with a theoretical and conceptual framework that enhanced my understanding of family process and structure in social contexts. There is a nonlinear connection between biographical experience and society, one that is filtered through family and other social groups such as peers, coworkers, and the like. My first professional publication integrated systemic concepts developed by early family therapists with sociological premises to better understand an individual's experience of mental illness.

With my PhD dating back to 1970, I was sitting in the front row seats to observe the developing and expanding family therapy movement. I was involved in the establishment of the Clinical Sociology Association in 1978. Later I acquired clinical and supervision status through the American Association of Marriage and Family Therapy. One of my early research and practice efforts was in the area of cardiac rehabilitation and looked at noncompliance from a family systems perspective. This work further expanded my understanding of family dynamics as a primary consideration in the lives of persons coping with health concerns. I continue to focus most of my work on teaching and research in family, the sociology of children and youth, and illness and health.

There is a large body of literature that emphasizes the importance of social support in healing, with family being the front line for rendering that support. It has been a longstanding observation in research and clinical practice that enmeshed or disengaged families can render symptomatic behavior for family members other than the index patient, or the person medically diagnosed. This was an observation made in the early 1950s by Donald Jackson (1920—1968), a pioneer of family therapy. These insights positioned him and his group (including Gregory Bateson, John Weakland, Jay Haley, and William Fry) to become leading voices in family therapy, research, and training. The Mental Research Institute in Palo Alto, California, was founded by him, and he was its first director.

Family dynamic influences are powerful; they can lift us up or drag us down. Remaining cognizant of the greater sociological realities in which we find ourselves adds to our insight into all those dimensions that exert influences and the complexities that play out within those families.

Hugh Floyd, PhD, is professor and past chair of sociology and a licensed marriage and family therapist and supervisor.

is relevant in a given situation is largely determined by **context**. We need to have access to the bigger picture, and multiple angles provide greater clarity. Think of the old adage of describing an elephant from various angles. What we really need is the ability to put together the various angles for a detailed "bigger picture" that will enable us to increase and expand understanding.

Dynamics. What makes systemic thinking particularly relevant for family dynamics is that it looks at this this "bigger picture." An individual is seen and described bearing the family or the system in mind. As nobody functions as an isolated island, the connections between persons tell an entire story. In systemic thinking, we are interested in the multidimensional connections *between* various systems, which holds the key to much of our understanding of the dynamics of families.

A Dynamic Sample of Behavior

A family therapist or any other professional working with families can find it useful to get a glimpse of that family's behavior. These samples of family life document how the family changes from moment to moment. They display a dynamic and sequenced example of a family's behavior, emphasizing the movement or motion that occurs over *time* within that family.

This motion related to time *is* the dynamic of the family. As family-life professionals, we are interested in understanding what this movement or dynamic within the family represents.

The view from different angles. Different approaches focus on different aspects of the family system. For instance, the numerous approaches to family therapeutic models and theories reveal that particular theorists like to highlight those aspects of the family on which they focus in therapeutic interventions. They may look at several of the following characteristics:

- The *structure* of a particular family in terms of composition and how that structure affects the functioning of that family and its members.
- The *function* of the dynamic patterns, how and why they play a role in the family's functioning.
- The *boundaries* as created by family members and entire families. This can include subsystems formed within the family.
- The *language* used by the family, how family members communicate with each other, what are the stories or *narratives* they tell about themselves and their relationships.
- The *interrelatedness* of the family with other systems and their place in the constellation of the family.
- The *lifespan* of the family and how each specific point in *human development* affects individual as well as group dynamics.
- The *meaning* of what the family is communicating. In this case, the family may use *symbols* to support their interactions.
- The *difficulties* or challenges the family experiences, as represented by areas of disagreement. Challenges can elicit negative outcomes, including *conflict*.
- The *benefits* each family member experiences from interactions with other family members. This influences the *social exchanges* taking place between members.

- How *gender* of family members can implicate that family's structure and behavior.
- The *integration* of family characteristics, or putting together several of the mentioned dimensions.

Disco balls and varying reflections. Sometimes I think of all the different approaches as a disco ball with mirrored glass. Each little mirrored mosaic will reflect the light somewhat differently, but combined they infuse life into the light.

The sheer variety of approaches can seem overwhelming. I have been involved in this field for my entire career, which has spanned several decades. I still do a double take when I see these long lists of approaches. There are many different theories and angles from which to look at the family. But there is a meeting point somewhere; they can be integrated in a meaningful manner.

Photographic angles. I also like to think of the various approaches to the family as if I were a moviemaker trying to find novel photographic angles to tell its story. Sometimes the filmmaker will use a drone and show a scene from above or from a distance. The filmmaker can pan in or out, getting closer or stepping away from the action. At other times, close-ups or odd angles tell the most.

In the same way, the story of the family can be told from many angles. Perspectives can alternate or be combined. Each one can highlight a different facet of the family's complexity. As in any good and dramatic movie, various angles should serve to convey the plot—to tell the story of that particular family. More important, the story needs to be told in a dynamic fashion that acknowledges the occurring movement—the fact that families change.

The predominant approach we pick can be determined by our own skills, strengths, and preferences as a therapist. For instance, if I have a great sense of humor, it's likely that I will find a way to introduce humor into my therapeutic interactions. The eminent family therapist Carl Whitaker (1912–1995) was a master at doing precisely this. He used a self-deprecating form of humor to address difficult topics.

Different perspectives. Family-related theories and therapies can cover extensive ground and be a little baffling to the newcomer. It is helpful to first get a solid feeling for what the field in general looks like, including the overarching rules that allowed it to differentiate from other mainstream approaches and theories. It seems as if every time a major therapist or theorist changes the angle somewhat or emphasizes a specific technique, another name or approach is added. Consequently, a fledgling family scientist can feel pulled in all directions at once. If the list of a dozen therapeutic angles is puzzling, remember that, in essence, different facets of *one* whole are being emphasized.

The leading approaches in family systems theory have these key characteristics:

- The sum is greater than the parts (Corey, 2012, p. 397).
- Subsections of a system are interrelated and form an integral part of the greater system.
- The context adds meaning to individual and family behavior (Goldenberg & Goldenberg, 2013).
- Families display unique ways of communicating.
- The family responds and is influenced by its own feedback loops.

- The family is a system that can regulate itself.
- A family displays unique goals and will find its own unique ways of reaching these goals.
- A family can create and function according to its own set of rules.
- The family system tends to seek homeostasis or equilibrium.

This work, titled *Dreaming*, is by South African ceramic artist Anton Bosch. The many elements that can present in our dreams and thoughts are depicted. Bosch states that each viewer will find a personal meaning in an artwork, that meaning is open to individual interpretation.

Source: Dreamtime/Anton Bosch.

Select Approaches

Ecology emphasizes the interrelatedness of systems and considers how one aspect or subsystem can influence another. The term *ecology* is attributed to Ernst Haeckel who used it in 1866 to explain aspects of nature (Odum & Barrett, 2005). Applying the principles of ecology to the study of human behavior lets us look at our behavior in context, namely, in the context of our social, environmental, natural, and biological milieus, for example. Inspiration for this approach was naturally drawn from these fields as well, and we can find aspects from related and seemingly unrelated disciplines, such as physics, zoology, psychology, public health, and home economics, contributing to the greater understanding of the system and the influences exerted on and by the particular system.

Structural and structural functionalism. This approach could be used to consider how the *structure* of the family affects the functioning of that family and its members. This approach is based on a model of the biological body in which systems are interrelated and all systems have a function. The function of the family is far-reaching. Families can provide a context for procreation and the socialization of children.

Cognitive behavioral family therapy. The basic principles of cognitive behavioral therapy as applied in a group or systems context form the central tenet. People feel and behave in a way that is influenced by how they perceive and structure their experience (Corey, 2012, p. 279). It is in integrative approach in that it merges two other major approaches: cognitive behavioral therapy and a systems approach.

Social exchange theory. This perspective on the family incorporates insights from both psychology and sociology that propose that participating parties can enter a process of negotiation, so each gets what is desired and offers something of relevance to the other party. Family members experience benefits from interactions and *social exchanges* with other family members. In the classic spring-fall relationship, a younger partner may enter a romantic relationship for the benefits of material gain, stability, and social power. The older party may desire the benefits of youth, physical attractiveness, and health, as offered by the younger participant in the relationship.

Symbolic interaction theory. This approach helps therapists look at the *meaning* of what the family is communicating and at the *symbols* family members use to support their interactions. The general idea is that communication can be enhanced by understanding the symbolic attributions added to words. If we are on the same page, we can understand, for instance, the cultural context of language or subtle variations such as humor. The work of the American philosopher George Herbert Mead (1863–1931) is relevant. He was of the opinion that this understanding would enhance the interpretation of social interactions and, importantly for systemic thinking, that we are not isolated beings—that we interact. The term he coined for this was "intersubjectivity" (Simpson, 2014, p. 279). Participating persons can create a symbolic world between them, and these creations can, in turn, influence the nuances of the interaction. Mead acknowledged that these social realities contributed to how we as persons were shaped in our individuality; we were influenced by and we reference others.

Conflict theory. In relationships we find power differentials. This unequal distribution of strength, power to influence, resources, and the like can add to the vulnerability of one of the participating parties, and operate to the advantage of the more dominant party. Especially on a microsystemic level, as in therapeutic relationships, we need to be aware of this power differential, as it can color the way in which participants of the therapeutic interaction relate to each other. The ethical guidelines for the professions address many of these concerns by drawing our attention to the risks of dual relationships, boundary transgressions, and the like. On a macrosystemic level, the power differences between, for instance, upper and lower socioeconomic groups could affect individual families.

Feminist approaches. These approaches consider the *gender* implications of family roles and power dynamics.

Awareness has been raised concerning power differentials between the genders, which can include aspects such as communication, cultural and gender attributes and stereotypes, employment and remuneration, sick leave, medical treatment, and educational options (Corey, 2012, p. 331). In select contexts, gender-related roles are being redefined.

Narrative therapy. The core of this approach lies in the narrative, or the story, as told by participants. This approach examines the *language* used by the family, how family members communicate with each other, and what stories or *narratives* they tell about themselves and their relationships.

Therapeutic conversations can be the key tools used to promote greater understanding as well as healing (Freedman & Combs, 1996). On a macrosystemic level, we can look at the story a community tells about itself or the stories told by others in the form of oral history, descriptions of cultural attributes, or even jokes about national stereotypes. The leading exponents of this approach were Michael White (1948–2008), a social worker from Australia, and David Epston (b. 1944) from New Zealand.

Palo Alto group. In this instance, a group of colleagues who were all interested in family systems theory and therapy were working in the same geographical location (you have guessed it, in Palo Alto, California). I once visited the location and had a look at the unobtrusive quarters where this movement started. It seemed similarly humble as the garage where Bill Gates and his young fellow computer enthusiasts built their first computers and tried out the basics of their software. In essence, this approach focused on *solutions* and outcomes (also called outcomes-based therapy). Consequently, the focus of therapy was shifted away from the past somewhat and directed more toward the way solutions could be reached. This group also explored brief therapy approaches. As their primary intervention methods, group members used questions as well as techniques that strengthened positive aspects (reframing). The questions could have different intentions or goals, depending on the outcome in mind.

Milan school. This group of therapists worked in Milan, Italy. Their approach was essentially systemic, and they were in touch with the Palo Alto group. Similar to other systemic thinkers, they moved away from a linear approach to explaining events and maintained that causation was more complex in nature because behavior was influenced on many fronts. The antecedents of any behavior could not be judged solely on the face of things. They were also influenced by the work of Gregory Bateson (1904–1980), who was married to Margaret Mead (1901–1978); both were anthropologists. They highlighted the influence of the observer on a system (hence a therapist would change the system). The fuzziness between objective and subjective realities was also of relevance, especially in therapeutic contexts.

Integrative models. An **integrative therapeutic approach** draws together the best and most useful components from the available knowledge base to further the goals of therapy in a systematic and organized manner. The choices are largely determined by context, as well as outcomes-based research.

To Recap . . .

The family therapy movement did not occur suddenly; neither can it be attributed to one person. It came into focus because, on many fronts, therapists were exploring ways to do better in understanding and supporting families. Clusters of therapists explored these ideas, but they also influenced each other, and, importantly, they themselves were influenced by ideas in related fields. The movement steadily gained in recognition, starting in the 1960s, but there are earlier antecedents, depending on how narrowly we define the influences.

Systemic family approaches, almost paradoxically, were most critically influenced by the *systemic* changes in the thinking of the time. These early proponents recognized the interrelatedness of subsystems and that all systems—whether on a smaller or larger scale—had certain characteristics and "rules."

As a group, these theories gained momentum. They were cross-fertilized and inspired by one another. Probably the time was ripe for these ideas to surface, and so the system that encompasses therapeutic family interventions was born. The systemic approach to families has consistently gained ground, and currently it is regarded as the dominant way of understanding and dealing with that most unique system of all: the family. The world, including family scientists, was ready for this new way of seeing.

> **"If you heal the family, you will heal the nation."**
>
> Virginia Satir (1916–1988)

FOCUS POINT

The numerous approaches to theories of the family reveal that particular family scientists like to highlight those aspects on which they focus in therapeutic interventions. They may examine characteristics such as structure, boundaries, communication, or individuation. Ecology emphasizes the interrelatedness of systems and considers how one aspect or subsystem can influence another. Applying the principles of ecology to the study of human behavior allows us to look at behavior within a greater context, namely, the context of our social, environmental, natural, biological, and other milieus.

SPOTLIGHT ON THEORIES

The Evolutionary Path of Major Theoretical Approaches

Theories evolve over time. Various theories and related therapeutic interventions did not develop in isolation. The major theoretical shifts in psychological theories affect how we think about human relationships, including family relationships, and how we explain and understand behavior. In multimodal and integrative approaches, relevant parts from several theories are combined. Newer approaches do not necessarily exclude or invalidate previous theories. As family science professionals, we have a wide range of theoretical approaches to access. Each theory builds on the insights from previous theories and is also influenced by the scientific and other thinking of the time (Bigner & Gerhardt, 2019, pp. 95–99).

There are many different ways of creating a representation of the major theoretical approaches. The approach modeled in this chapter is to highlight major paradigm shifts in thinking, irrespective of the specific time in which they occur. Diagram 5.1 gives an illustration of these paradigm shifts, which are depicted in a progressive manner, looking a bit like a staircase, to reflect how major groups of theoretical constructs grew from previous insights and influenced future developments. In this model, five major shifts are shown (Bigner & Gerhardt, 2019, p. 99):

- **Psychoanalytic and psychosocial approaches** focus on the intrapsychic and the individual. Intrapsychic refers to the processes that occur within the psyche of an individual. Freud, Jung, and Adler are among the prominent names in this group.
- **Behaviorist and cognitive behavioral approaches** focus on behavior and those factors that can encourage or discourage

DIAGRAM 5.1 Theories and approaches build on each other, extending the knowledge base. The major paradigm shifts in thinking explain facets of family functioning. Newer approaches may incorporate aspects of previous theories. An integrative approach combines aspects from several theories and approaches.

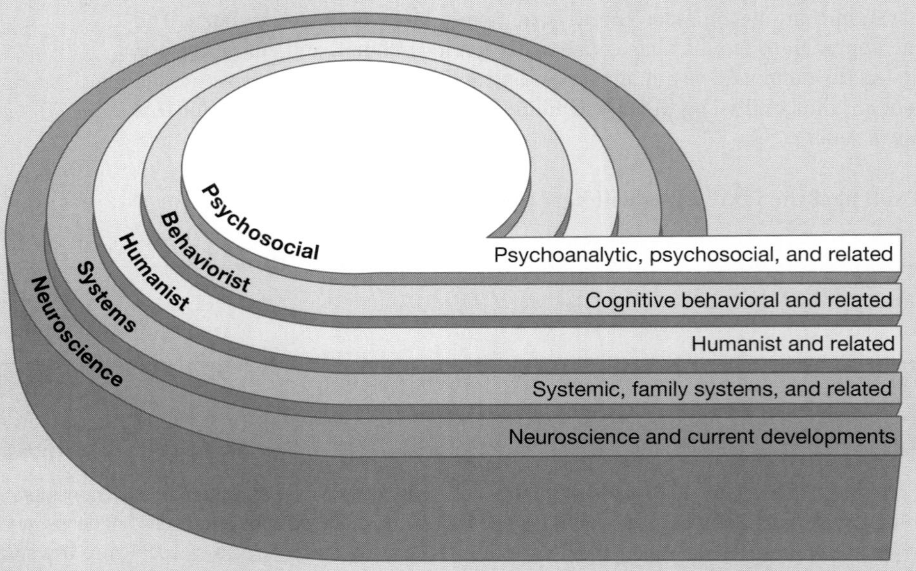

certain behaviors. In the cognitive behavioral approach, both behavior and the thinking about the behavior are relevant. Social aspects can be included, such as social learning and learning within a social context. Watson, Bandura, and Skinner are among the prominent names in this group.

- **Humanist approaches** focus on aspects that contribute to and define our humanness, including spiritual components. Therapy goals include self-actualization and becoming a fully functioning person. Rogers, Maslow, and Allport are among the prominent names in this group.
- **Systemic and family systems approaches** expand the focus to include the family and an emphasis on the interrelatedness of systems. The family systems approach acknowledges the family as a system with its own rules and outcomes. Prominent names are too numerous to list.
- **Neuroscience and related approaches** include insights discovered and expanded by scientific research and supported by computer science, imaging techniques, and other technological developments. Neuroscience has expanded our understanding of cognitive psychology and related fields. It provides insight into the functioning of the brain within various contexts. Prominent names are too numerous to list.

FOCUS POINT

Theories are partly a product of their context. As psychoanalytic, psychosocial, and family-related disciplines evolved, the context within which the family was described expanded and became multidimensional. Initially, the individual was viewed as the central focus of the therapeutic process. This focus on individuals was complemented by behaviorist as well as humanist approaches, each highlighting a particular dimension. A systemic approach to the family gained momentum once the greater context of societal systems was acknowledged. Over the past few decades, neuroscience has brought greater insights into neuropsychological functioning. This field is growing rapidly and is expected to provide continued insights.

In a Nutshell

- Theories help us create a greater context and they evolve over time. Various theories and related therapeutic interventions develop in an interrelated manner.
- Five major theoretical shifts can be noted. They are, in order of first appearance, (1) psychoanalytic and psychosocial approaches, (2) behaviorist and cognitive behavioral approaches, (3) humanist approaches, (4) systemic and family systems approaches, and (5) neuroscience and related approaches.
- The major theoretical shifts in psychological theories affect how we think about human relationships, including family relationships, and how we explain and understand behavior.
- In multimodal and integrative approaches, relevant parts from several theories are combined.

CHAPTER FOCUS POINTS

Theories: Seeking Connection and Meaning

- Marriage and family therapy has followed an intense developmental path. This journey is reflected in the theories that try to systematize and add meaning to the vast knowledge base that has been acquired.
- Theories organize data to find relevance and meaning. This framework can influence research and therapeutic applications.
- Sustainable theories need to meet several criteria, including being descriptive, organizing concepts into a meaningful framework, pointing out the interconnectedness between events and observations, recognizing patterns from these observations, and providing a platform from which a hypothesis can be formulated.

Birth of the Family Therapy Movement

- Social policy reform paved the way to address the needs of families and ensure more hopeful futures for their children.
- The underpinnings of marriage and family therapy can be found in social work and related professions, and, to this day, there is a close affinity (and excellent collaboration) between professionals focusing on the family (family scientists).
- Development of the family therapy movement was rapid and occurred simultaneously on several continents.
- Currently, theory referencing marriage and family systems is the second most utilized approach in therapeutic intervention.

Major Theoretical Paradigm Shifts

- Numerous theories have influenced our current perspectives on families and especially on the dynamics within families. Each one builds on the insights of previous theories, and theories adapt and alter to reflect changes within societies.
- The way we view families and how we think about families reflect greater cultural and societal changes. When these shifts in thinking are sufficiently dramatic, they affect related areas, including social policy.
- New ideas and approaches have the ability to push previously long-standing beliefs toward an entirely new perspective, called a *paradigm shift*. Once such a somewhat radical shift in thinking or perspective has occurred, it is virtually impossible to return to the thinking that preceded it.

The Context of Systemic Thinking

- The numerous approaches to theories of the family reveal that particular family scientists like to highlight those aspects on which they focus in therapeutic interventions.
- These may examine characteristics such as structure, boundaries, communication, and individuation.
- Ecology emphasizes the interrelatedness of systems and how one aspect of a system or subsystem can influence another.
- Applying the principles of ecology to the study of human behavior allows us to look at behavior in a greater context, namely, in the context of our social, environmental, natural, biological, and other milieus.

Spotlight on Theories: The Evolutionary Path of Major Theoretical Approaches

- Theories are partly a product of their context. As psychoanalytic, psychosocial, and family-related disciplines evolved, the context within which the family was described expanded and became multidimensional.
- Initially, the individual was viewed as the central focus of the therapeutic process.
- This focus on individuals was complemented by behaviorist as well as humanist approaches, each highlighting a particular dimension.
- A systemic approach to the family gained momentum once the greater context of societal systems was acknowledged.
- Over the past few decades, neuroscience has brought greater insights into neuropsychological functioning. This field is growing rapidly and is expected to provide continued insights.

The Dynamic Language of the Family

PART

II

We form attachments and we form families. We parent children and vest our hopes in their well-being and their future. What truly connects us is the set of fine web-like filigreed threads of communication that envelop us. They allow us to reach out and to receive, to give shape and meaning to our dreams. We can share our hopes with our neighbors. Our language allows us to express the turmoil and the ecstasy of our souls, and so much more.

How we communicate allows us to build thousands of imaginary bridges, crossing the divides between us. If it were not for our ability to find the words, to display the gestures, to raise the eyebrow, to buckle with pain, and to dance with joy, we would be trapped in solitary confinement. Communication is like an arterial system, a complex network of tiny capillaries transporting ideas and feelings to and fro—a system that is also capable of either alienating or bonding humankind.

Words and language are not mere verbal tags that we attach to things so that we can talk and write about them. By naming them, we are giving them an abstract life of sorts; we allow them to be born so that they can take their place among other concepts. Together, combined, and rearranged, all these words create something so infinitely larger than the original labeling system; they create a world with multidimensional meaning, with depth. Words allow us to move into the future, or to show that something happened in the past. We can capture those diverse threads of thought, a blend of fact and emotion, and pin them down for others to explore, enjoy, and revisit.

Communication becomes the vehicle with which we express our darkest secrets, our innermost pain and fragility, our moments of bliss; in short, it is our window to the world. It is simultaneously complex and confident. It is frustrating and elating. It is colored by who we are and by whom we befriend. It can be a weapon and a peace offering. It can be poison and it can be healing balm. It is somewhat like the air that we breathe, the water that we drink. It is the profound expression of who we are. It is communication, and it is language.

Families beget families.

A saying from folklore

CHAPTER

6

Communication and Family Relationships

Learning Outcomes

After studying this chapter, you should be able to

1. Identify different aspects of *communication* and of the early theories exploring communication within *family units*.
2. Explore various *emotional interactions* occurring within family communication.
3. Analyze the way *power* influences relationships and decision making within families.
4. Discuss some of the family challenges in the context of *multilingual* communication.
5. Describe *cultural echoes* as they occur in communication.
6. Summarize *communication accommodation theory (CAT)* and explain the key characteristics.

Reaching Out and Connecting

We reach out and connect in many ways. Mathematicians do it with numbers and formulae, musicians with sounds, visual artists tell the story in colors and shapes. Binary code can reduce communication to zeros and ones. We can communicate with emoticons; we certainly do that while interspersing texts with tiny visual cues, adding meaning to the brief texted message. Language counts as one of the most sophisticated ways of communicating, but it is certainly not the only way.

All these vehicles for communication are intricate, complex, and sophisticated. When a group is in agreement about what certain symbols and sounds represent, its members can exchange meaning and reach out. Language is an abstract set of symbols that allows us to connect, to share innermost thoughts and feelings, and to take our place in an intricate web of social relationships.

One of the things that is supposed to differentiate us from the animal world is our ability to reflect on the inner landscape of our feelings. This is also called **metacognition**. As humans, we are aware of ourselves, and we have inner dialogues with ourselves. We have a language of the mind. We self-talk. We roll ideas over in our minds, we have imaginary conversations, and we think of punch lines long after the appropriate moment has passed. Whatever dialogue occurred, it can replay in our minds while we formulate mental responses.

Communication is intended as a way for us to reach out, to be understood, to make our wishes known, but, importantly, it also enables us to react appropriately to the various communication cues we receive from those around us (Littlejohn, Foss, & Oetzel, 2017, p. 55). The receiving component of this interaction is equally important; we need to listen, understand, acknowledge, react, respond. Together, these communications form an intricate web, a backward and forward, a constant exchange or feedback loop of information. Another layer of complexity is added—by communicating, we can also add value. We can express our pleasure or our disdain. We can reach out or we can ward off.

Communication occurs within the context of communication partners. Communication is similar to a tennis game; when we serve the ball, we expect a return. In developmental psychology, the current emphasis is largely on this idea of *serve and return* as it occurs in interactions with infants and children (Center on the Developing Child, n.d.). The child or the caretaker reaches out and communicates, and the other party reciprocates or returns that communication. We know from the developmental research that the serve and return process is crucial for the healthy development of children because it reflects active involvement. It is a response to the cue and provides stimulation to the child.

Also, studies on the acquisition of language in infants and toddlers indicate that mimicking and copying occurs. More recent research has pointed toward the presence of mirror neurons, especially in the frontal lobes of the brain, that facilitate the process of imitating or copying behavior (Alford, 2016; Ferrari & Rizzolatti, 2015). We presume that language acquisition is facilitated by these mirror neurons. The mirror mechanism transforms various external inputs into behavior that becomes integrated into the repertoire of the perceiver. According to Rizzolatti and Sinigaglia (2016), "Mirror-based understanding has been defined as an 'understanding from the inside' because it provides a route to knowledge of others" (p. 757). This type of mirror-based understanding may facilitate the development of empathy (Lamm & Majdandžić, 2015).

By studying human behavior in cross-cultural contexts, we can see which patterns are universal and which are culture specific. Both biosocial factors and brain development contribute to the urge to communicate. The universality of the human capacity for language is important in human communication in general (Gibson & Petersen, 1991/2017, p. 11). It is possible that the accommodation process that occurs in communication is extended to other areas of learning.

> The most commonplace activities of our lives—the things we take for granted—can become quite puzzling when we try to understand them systematically. Communication is one of those everyday activities intertwined with all of human life so completely that we sometimes overlook its pervasiveness, importance, and complexity. . . . We treat communication as central to human life. Every aspect of our daily lives is affected by our communication with others, as well as by messages from people we don't even know—people near and far, living and dead. (Littlejohn & Foss, 2011, p. 3)

Different theories define communication from a variety of angles. As Littlejohn and Foss (2011, p. 7) succinctly state,

> **"Communication is so broad that it cannot be reduced or confined to any single paradigm."**

Focus on Family Communication

The formal discipline of family communication has been around for about half a century or longer. Family therapy scholars approached the family from a systemic point of view, and this included how families communicated within a group context. The Palo Alto therapists' early interaction studies, as well as the work by Virginia Satir, who came from the social work profession, verified that families could display their unique patterns of communication and that this deserved in-depth study. This research has since been elaborated by numerous other family therapists, including Paul Watzlavick, Jay Haley, Salvador Minuchin, Donald Jackson, Froma Walsh, and the Italian Milan group.

Communication is intended as a way for us to reach out, to be understood, to make our wishes known. We also need to listen, understand, acknowledge, react, respond. Together, these aspects of communication form an intricate web, a constant exchange of information.

Source: © iStock.com/Paul_Cooper.

Initially, the focus was on marital communication, but this soon broadened to include the entire family, the family across its lifespan, and multigenerational family communication patterns. The field was further expanded to include diverse family forms in a variety of contexts. Psychologists and family therapists are focused extensively on the dynamics of and the interventions for families. Communication scholars have focused on what has been labeled *the talking family*, a term attributed to Baxter (2004). When families communicate, they do so to exchange information, to manage, to relate, to negotiate, to define hierarchies, to delineate power, to control, and to perform many other functions (Galvin, Braithwaite, & Bylund, 2014, p. 59). The way in which a family communicates fleshes out that family's identity and defines and legitimizes family members as a unit. Relationships are expressed and defined through communication practices. Once the field of self-help exploded, the understanding of family communication patterns became an important piece of the bigger puzzle.

The communication sciences and related disciplines have made significant contributions to family dynamics, offering theories that have been invaluable in organizing research findings, creating theoretical models, and providing guidelines for the greater understanding of general as well as related and applied contexts, such as human resources, the worlds of work and business, negotiation skills, and conflict resolution.

Family communication science and other family-related professions cover overlapping areas of interest. What they have in common is that both focus on the family and how family members relate to each other. In family communication sciences, the primary emphasis appears to be on the *how* and the *what* of

FOCUS POINT

Communication within family relationships is an intricate, complex, and sophisticated process. Communication is intended as a way for us to reach out, to be understood, to make our wishes known, and to add value. The receiving component of this interaction is equally important; we need to listen, understand, acknowledge, react, and respond. Together, these aspects of communication form an intricate web, a backward and forward, a constant exchange of information between parties. Different theories define communication from a variety of angles. Family therapy scholars approached the family from a systemic point of view, which included investigating how families communicated within a group context.

communication as it pertains to the family and its subsystems. When the family is studied in the context of family therapy, there is an attempt to understand the *why* of both communication and behavior. This approach is directly tied to dynamics. Dynamics, in turn, guides us toward understanding behavior, which facilitates therapeutic interventions.

The Power of Language

Effects of Social Support on Family Dynamics

Communication scholars argue that the ability to communicate verbally is what distinguishes us from other living beings. It is what makes us uniquely human. The argument is also strong that language is powerful. Through language, we have the capacity to regulate interactions, create meaning, and act on our world. Verbal communication among families is powerful in many ways, especially as it relates to interpersonal relationships among family dyads. One such impactful use of language is social support. Though there are countless examples in the human experience of negative language use within families, the use of language to provide support is thought to be highly effective in maintaining positive family dynamics if enacted successfully.

Social support is quantified as emotional, informational, or tangible resources that we provide to others, especially in times of need or distress. Specifically, emotional, informational, and esteem support are set apart in their use of language to communicate care and concern. Communicating an available listening ear, giving well-informed advice, and/or validating someone's worth and contributions (to the family, to society, to other relationships, etc.) are all methods of support that can be thought of as positive forms of verbal communication. The stability of family relationships and bonds is heavily reliant on this view of one's family as a source of available support, and when performed well, social support behaviors can be one of the most effective communicative resources of relational maintenance among family groups.

Moreover, when an individual perceives that familial support is available, even if it is not sought, there is a considerable impact on that person's ability to cope in times of stress. Further, the impact on one's relational satisfaction is immediately positive. Thus, the family as a support network is a critical framework of examination. The support structure among family dyads has significant impact on the dyads' relational health, and further, the consideration of the entire family unit as a supportive network to individuals can be a measurement of family solidarity and the health of a family as a whole.

Ashley J. George, PhD, is an assistant professor of communication studies.

GLOBAL GLIMPSE

LINGUISTIC TANGOS

Politeness bias. Consider the terms we use to address our conversation partner in a one-on-one conversation. Here is David Shariatmadari (2019) on the topic of when we use first-person pronouns such as "I" and "we" versus the second person "you":

> According to linguistic theory, being addressed directly, while it improves clarity, is often perceived as a *face-threatening act*—something that imposes on the addressee and may feel too much like a barked order.

Face-negotiation theory (FNT) considers tokens and expressions of respect, honor, social status and connections, alignment or loyalty, and other characteristics that define aspects of the relationship. "*Face* refers to one's self-image in the presence of others" (Littlejohn, Foss, & Oetzel, 2017, p. 412).

In many languages there are strategies that avoid this type of directness and respect "face," sometimes even "saving face." It would be deemed impolite to address a person of higher social rank directly with a pronoun like "you." In English, there is the somewhat anonymous "one" that can stand in and create greater distance: "*One* could consider it impolite to be too direct in confronting the issue. . . ." An example of polite address from Afrikaans, a language related to Dutch, follows. It is more polite to avoid using the pronoun "you":

> Less polite: "Mother, could *you* do this for me, please?"
>
> More polite: "Mother, could *mother* please do this for me, please?"

Repeating the noun *mother* (not to mention the word *please*) is a respectful way of maintaining a certain linguistic distance or deference. This "politeness bias" occurs in other languages and cultural contexts as well. In German, there are two versions of the word *you*, namely, the informal *Du* and the formal *Sie*. In French, there are the parallel forms of *tu* and *vous*, the latter conveying the meaning of "you" with greater formality. The closest English translation would be *you* and *thou*, although the more respectful *thou* has fallen into disuse in modern English. We may still come across it in older biblical contexts or in plays by Shakespeare.

Shariatmadari (2019) provides two further examples:

> In Farsi, for example, a polite alternative to "you" (*shoma*) is the rather more indirect "your presence" (*hozuretan*). In Japanese, the bare pronoun is usually avoided, and a person's name or title plus an honorific suffix is used instead.

A minefield of cultural idiosyncrasies. How we address our conversation partner can definitely convey so much more about the relationship than the literal words might lead us to believe. Consider, too, the linguistic challenges faced by English-as-a-second-language (ESL) speakers; they may inadvertently stumble into a minefield of cultural idiosyncrasies.

Source: Shariatmadari (2019).

Any conversation contains the potential for a power dynamic to occur. In a friendship relationship, the power should ideally be equally distributed. Power inequality can also reflect cultural content and context.

Source: © iStock.com/matdesign2.

Emotional Interactions

Investment and Intimacy

Emotional intimacy. Emotional intimacy is not a one-off event. We do not create it, just to tick it off on our to-do list. **Emotional intimacy** requires topping up—it requires investment; partners need to take and make time to keep each other up to date. When friends no longer share new experiences, it can be difficult to sustain the relationship because they have to rely on past shared events. To maintain a vital quality continued investment has to occur. Having conversations in which we tell each other what is currently happening in our lives, including our joys and our woes, means that we continue to invest.

Because emotional intimacy is a form of investment, it requires ongoing renewal. Just like a checking account will become useless if we do not deposit new funds into it, we cannot withdraw benefits from a relationship without replenishing it. Once a relationship becomes acrimonious, it is very difficult to put the pieces back together unless both parties are willing to do so (Littlejohn, Foss, & Oetzel, 2017, p. 255). One of the biggest risks is the temptation to engage in unfair fighting. Imagine a marriage in which one person has been unfaithful. If the injured party continues to backtrack at moments of stress and keeps on using the affair as an accusation, it will be exceptionally difficult to move beyond the sense of betrayal (Carnes, 2018). Couples who seriously want to commit to saving their relationship will have to end outside relationships with third parties, as these distract from the primary relationship and destroy the sense of trust and intimacy.

Additionally, a couple may need to commit to not backtracking into the emotional territory associated with the betrayal. After the initial grief work is done and reconciliation has occurred, a couple may need to commit to moving forward. Some couples have been known to renew their vows, even buying new wedding rings, as a symbol that their relationship is now in a different place and they are committed to working on its stability and permanence. When a couple is basically compatible and partners have a shared history as well as a future, it may be worth the work to save that relationship. It is possible that the same difficulties that caused the breakup will be dragged into the next relationship. Changing partners is not a guarantee of greater happiness. Instead, it may be a good investment to seek professional help and explore what contributed to the breakup. The qualities involved in sustaining long-term relationships are complex, but if the relationship is emotionally sustaining, the effort to maintain it will be repaid over and over again.

Part of the creation of intimacy is the knowledge by both participants that shared information is private and privileged. The investment metaphor crops up again; trusting someone with very personal and private information creates both vulnerability and intimacy. Any self-disclosure is accompanied by potential vulnerability. For this exchange to work, both parties have to honor their mutual code concerning how to handle privileged and exclusive information (Settersten, 2018a, 2018b).

Self-disclosure. Families may define their own rules in terms of boundaries and opportunities for **self-disclosure** (Tardy & Smithson, 2018, p. 42). Some families tend to regard family matters as very personal, and their motto may well be "What occurs in the family stays in the family." This rule may be an attempt to protect family members from outside judgment and criticism. At the same time, it can create an insularity that cuts off potential support systems. Disclosure is also a means of forming emotional intimacy, and it typically rests on foundations of trust.

As both parties become more familiar with each other and share interests, they will be able to access details of each other's lives. This mutual investment in the friendship creates the climate that allows for emotional intimacy. For the latter to occur, there needs to be mutual acceptance, positive regard, and possibly a little admiration. These qualities set the tone for the exchange and explain why we are willing to disclose negative aspects of ourselves within the safety of a good friendship (Galvin, Braithwaite, & Bylund, 2014). It is said that good friends invest in each other despite knowing each other's darker sides. In an enduring relationship, we need not be perfect, but we do need enough in common to sustain mutual interests and maintain the relationship.

The process of friendship. Good friendships can be maintained over many decades; they can be lifelong. If there is mutual regard and respect, a friendship will resume at exactly the same point where we left it off, even if several years have lapsed. When good friends meet after many years, there may be an instant of adjustment. Like the autofocus lens of a good camera, the friends adapt their perspectives; there is a figurative twist and turn, as the lens adjusts—then the focus is crisp. It feels as if no time has lapsed at all. We continue as if no pause or interruption had occurred.

The prerequisite for this type of interaction is the ongoing core of the *process of friendship*. It truly contains a timeless quality. An aspect that feeds the mutual sense of positive regard within satisfying friendship is emotional support. Friends will say things that are affirming and complimentary. They overlook our faults, not because they cannot see them but because they are concentrating on the positive dimensions instead. These positive strokes are like reaching out; they are a positive way of touching, similar to positive expressions in body language.

Disinvestment

At times, the ideal interpersonal interaction does not occur. Prime examples are marriages or partnerships during the process of disintegration. It is possible that the partner who wants out of the relationship pursues this goal secretively, by means of steady and ongoing disinvestment. This withdrawing of emotional property from the partner may be facilitated because there is a new love interest, which might also be kept secret from the individual the disinvesting partner wants to desert. The disinvesting partner will cease to invest in the primary relationship; it's almost like letting a bank account go into the red. The one who wants out will no longer self-disclose and will slowly drift away. The partner being abandoned is unsuspecting and may not be aware that the balance of this marriage or partnership has been disrupted, possibly because this fact has been kept secret.

Indeed, the disinvesting partner may do so secretively for fear of upsetting the homeostasis or balance of that relationship. When the outside affair has taken on sufficient momentum that it threatens to become the primary relationship, the time may be ripe for the original partner, the one in the first relationship, to be confronted with the fact that there are now three people in this liaison. At that point, the partner who is being deserted may try everything in her or his power to regain the other's investment in the relationship, to recreate the relationship as it used to be. Usually it is too late because the horse has already bolted from the stable.

Emotional disinvestment. **Emotional disinvestment** usually occurs before the final break. In fact, emotional disinvestment in one relationship combined with a reinvestment in another typically facilitates and fuels the breakup. The person being deserted is often the last person to find out what game is being played. It may seem as if the destruction snuck up on the relationship without warning. But if one looks closely at the interaction patterns, it is apparent that the ghost of divorce had been hovering in that partnership for a long time but wasn't recognized by the partner being abandoned.

Metacommunication

This form of communication occurs when there is a second layer hidden behind the verbal communication. The second layer need not be expressed formally or in words. It is implied contextually. For instance, the request "Feel like having some coffee?" can mean anything from setting up a business meeting to testing the level of potential intimacy between the communicators. It is the context in which this phrase is used that will determine the meaning, and the communication can occur at different levels. Succinctly, metacommunication has been called "communication about communication" (Craig, 2016).

When **metacommunication** is unsolicited or unwelcomed or contains unwelcome metadata or information (Craig, 2016), an appropriate strategy would be to ignore it and focus on the literal meaning of the words communicated. For example, if a man asks a woman whether she feels like getting a coffee in order to test her level of interest in him and she is not at all interested, she could pretend to ignore the metacommunicative aspects of the question and answer, "Thanks, but I don't drink coffee." In that way, the metacommunication is stonewalled; it doesn't reach its target and falls on deaf ears. In other instances, it may be important to point out the metacommunication; for instance, in family therapy it may be appropriate to make sure that the communicator is aware that some of the phrases being used could be interpreted as guilt inducing.

Many of our facial expressions, the nature and length of eye contact, body language, and other nonverbal communication clues can amplify or soften the message we are sending. For instance, if a communication is intended as a joke, our facial expression can make it clear that we intend it to be humorous. These extra layers of communication can be lost in activities such as texting or sending emails, and communicators can get into trouble as only the literal aspect of the message is visible. This should serve as a warning for us to be extra careful and to consider the context of such texts. It is very tempting to misinterpret a complex message because only one layer of it is visible.

Congruence versus undercurrents. The term *congruence* is also used in the context of metacommunication. Congruence means authenticity or realness. Is the verbal message real in as much as it *does* inform the receiver of what it superficially seems to be conveying? Or is there contextual information that alters its meaning? This other meaning can be like an *undercurrent*, an additional dimension that may not be obvious initially if one sees only the calmness of the surface water.

In the context of family dynamics, these undercurrents make the communications between family members untrustworthy, incongruent, and sometimes unresolvable. "Did she just say what I think she said?" is an example of how trust can be undermined, as participating parties have to second guess what should be communication in one of the most trusted and supportive environments, namely that of the family. But then the reality is that families are imperfect, and games with varying stakes are played.

Bateson and the double bind. Gregory Bateson (1904–1980), a British anthropologist and pioneer in systems therapy whose first marriage was to fellow anthropologist Margaret Mead, made us aware of the paradoxes that can be contained in metacommunication (Craig, 2016). He described the "double bind," a situation in which the implied meanings can be so contradictory that there is no possibility of a "correct" response and no escape from the situation; you are

FOCUS POINT

Communication allows us to convey our meanings, feelings, and desires but also, importantly, to participate in and react appropriately to various communication patterns. These communications represent a constant exchange of information, some of which relates to how invested or disinvested family members are in relationships. Emotional intimacy and self-disclosure require trust and a sense of safety, which come with emotional investment. Emotional disinvestment can signal distance and a potential fracture in a relationship. Our nonverbal communication can amplify or soften the message we are sending. Metacommunication occurs when there is a second layer hidden behind the first layer of communication. The communication sciences and related disciplines have contributed many theories relevant to family dynamics; these have been invaluable in organizing research findings, creating theoretical models, and enhancing understanding.

doomed if you do, and doomed if you don't, as the situation cannot be resolved. This form of communication can be confusing and bewildering, and one of its motives is to exhibit covert control, even aggression.

At one time in history, it was thought that double binds could contribute to mental illness (Willison, 1969). With our current insight, the double bind may not be regarded as causing mental health problems, but it can certainly do much interpersonal harm and be symptomatic of extremely unhealthy relationships. Double binds are unresolvable.

A sophisticated example of a double bind would be the punishing father saying to the daughter, "It's not worth attending your graduation as you are only receiving a bachelor's degree, and not even *cum laude*." So the daughter cancels her attendance to please the father. Once the event is over the father says, "All my colleagues asked why you weren't at your graduation? I was so ashamed that you didn't go." In this double bind, the daughter can never please the father, as the targets and agreements keep on shifting. It does not take great insight to see that this is toxic behavior and that the daughter can only resolve the situation by exiting the communication field or disengaging from the relationship.

Power and Patterns of Decision Making

In essence, our communication serves to build relationships within the family. How we communicate, what we communicate, and the people involved will make an entire network of intricate family connections visible. The words we use serve to create a specific family culture, one that is most easily accessed and decoded by insiders.

Because families are very unique, their communication patterns will carry that individual stamp as well. As Segrin and Flora (2011, p. 87) succinctly state,

> Family processes involving power, decision making, and conflict are like fingerprints. No one decision or conflict is the same.

These same authors state that power is an interactional process; it cannot occur in isolation. For one person or party to come across as powerful and able to exert power, an opposite party is necessary, one who is vulnerable and willing or forced to relinquish his or her own power and act in a submissive manner. In power dynamics, it takes at least two to tango. One is the lead dancer who sets up the dance and the steps—the parameters of the power dynamic; the other is the person following the lead by being willing to submit.

Power dynamic. Any conversation contains the potential for a power dynamic to occur. In practice, one of the communicators usually has more power due to her or his position in the relationship and the quality of the relationship. Power can also be allocated indirectly because one of the parties is vulnerable and, in this way, less powerful. Power inequities require cognizance so that they can be acknowledged in a manner that is constructive for the interaction.

In a friendship, the power should be equally distributed, ideally. Sometimes turn taking may occur, but generally, friendships are characterized by mutual benefits that are gained from the interaction. When the power dynamic is *balanced*, it also sets the scene for trust and a sense of safety. Within these parameters, it is possible to self-disclose and to exchange confidences with the friend. By self-disclosing, we are taking risks in that we are making ourselves vulnerable; but we do so hoping that this vulnerability will be respected and protected.

Power inequality. Power inequality can also reflect cultural content. In some cultures, power inequity is accepted, and this acceptance is factored into the emotional distance between the parties. Whoever is deemed to be higher in the hierarchy of power will be treated with appropriate respect. The generalization is that Asian cultural contexts require this reverence to a greater extent than American cultural contexts (see the Global Glimpse titled "Linguistic Tangos").

Power can be acquired in unethical ways, as well, through threats, power displays, complex social interchanges, or even outright bullying (Arnold & Basden, 2008). It is a complicated dance, and when the stakes are high, the strategies can become increasingly devious. As much as we would like to think that power interactions are respectful and carry both parties' interests at heart, the reality can be sobering, reminding us that a lot of wheeling and dealing occurs behind the scenes.

Family Decision Making

Family power is complex because it extends beyond individual roles and the collective unit of the family. It can also be influenced by social position and resources, which in turn can implicate complex social meanings, for example, those outlined in social and research exchange theory as well as in the examination of gender and relational hierarchies (Littlejohn, Foss, & Oetzel, 2017, p. 241). A considerable amount of backward and forward occurs among family members; complicated and intricate negotiations take place to acquire and maintain the power.

In the context of the family, we expect parents to have the best interests of children at heart. In this type of scenario, it would be pathological and abusive to misdirect power in a manner that victimizes defenseless children who should, by all rights, be protected and guided by their parents.

Family decision making is closely linked to where the seats of power are located. In an authoritarian family system, decisions are likely to trickle from the top down, with little or no bidirectional feedback or input. The same type of process can be found in authoritarian work environments, where higher management expects workers lower on the hierarchy to follow orders unquestioningly. The fields of human resources and industrial psychology have spent much time and expertise analyzing and suggesting preferred relationships that maintain good morale as well as productivity.

Because power and family structure affect family decision making so substantially, all aspects must be considered as dynamic forces, changing over time. Members of families are constantly involved in a great communal building project, that is, the construction of their own family. They may build, and occasionally they may tear down; they can contribute, they may have a vision, and they can also alter the outcome. The family is a constantly evolving work of art, with family members providing the creative input.

Negotiation and family decisions. In negotiation, we have yet another example of the give and take between parties. In a negotiation, we try to offer something we have in return for something the other party has. There is quite a lot of politics involved because good negotiators try to get more than they give. What is being negotiated is also important. It is easy to give up something that is not very precious to the one party in exchange for something more desirable. Underlying this truth is the understanding that not all things are of equal value to all parties. For instance, a person buying a house may attach great value to moving in immediately and might be prepared to pay a higher price for this privilege. If the seller has a backup plan in place, for instance, a vacation home into which the seller can move, then it is easy to strike a deal. Both parties will be getting what they want, but for the seller, the sacrifice attached to this particular negotiation may be lower than for the buyer.

In family contexts, considerable negotiation takes place (Hess & Handel, 2016). Well-functioning couples know that it is important to pick one's battles; it is senseless to pick a fight over a minor variance of opinion. We can agree to disagree. This mature and sensible way of approaching relationships acknowledges that each party is autonomous and individuated and that we do not all have to subscribe to exactly the same opinions.

This principle of mutual respect, demonstrated by a willingness to listen to opinions and values other than one's own, is also the quality underlying cultural competence. In intercultural communication, the culturally competent individual would not expect participating parties to have the same cultural knowledge and insight. Instead, there would be a willingness to learn and to be open to what the other party could teach about that party's cultural way of life. Children also negotiate, perfecting the art of knowing which parent can be swayed more easily and playing parents off against each other—as if parents did not know that already.

Decisions can have an instrumental and an affective dimension. But these dimensions tend to overlap, so even though we think that a decision is purely instrumental rather than purely affective, both dimensions are usually present and exert mutual influence (Segrin & Flora, 2011, p. 74).

Instrumental decision. Instrumental decisions tend to be more concrete and not overruled by any emotional component. These decisions can have to do with factual situations in which an option has to be chosen. Shall we pay off our car loan now, or shall we pay it off later? Even that decision probably contains an emotional component.

Affective decisions. Affective decisions, on the other hand, may draw in our emotions, which in turn can be linked to family dynamics. For instance, affective decisions can involve choices, values, conflict resolution, feelings, roles within the family system, and family dynamics, which can be intergenerational. The family that has experienced the hardship of a major economic downturn may be hesitant to make a seemingly instrumental decision concerning a mortgage because of a number of associated emotions, for instance, the threat of financial insecurity.

Parenting styles. When a family functions in a very laissez-faire manner—let's say the parents are very permissive—that family may be ruled by the preferences and choices of the children. We know that, in practice, this parenting style does not lead to favorable outcomes because it is low on structure, accountability, and responsibility. For instance, if decisions concerning the meals being served are left to children, there may be a tendency toward junk food with low nutritional value. That could also be a metaphor for the dynamic of that particular family. If we place the responsibility for family decisions on the youngest members, we are tasking children beyond their developmental capabilities, and the outcomes may not meet the needs of the rest of the family members.

Parental styles influence parental decision making, which in turn affects the children in that relationship. The by-now historic work of Baumrind and her colleagues initially described three and later four major parenting styles that influence parent-child interactions (Baumrind, 1966, 1967). Ranging from the most to the least controlling, these include (1) the very authoritarian or controlling style, (2) the authoritative (appropriately balanced) parenting style, (3) the laissez-faire or permissive parenting style, and (4) the disengaged or withdrawn parent. Clearly, these parenting styles also influence decision making and hence family dynamics.

A number of social, familial, environmental, and individual dynamics can influence decision making.

Source: © iStock.com/fizkes.

Additionally, a number of other social, familial, environmental, and individual dynamics influence decision making. The nature of the relationships within the family also plays a major role, as these may range on a continuum from connected closeness to disconnected distance, that is, from enmeshed to disengaged (Olson, 2000). These variations have the ability to precipitate alliances in subgroups of family members. For instance, like-minded dyads can form when two people or two pairs within the family unit form an alliance. Ideally, the parents should represent a well-functioning dyad.

Triangulations have the ability to either strengthen or threaten the balance of the system, depending on the context. An example of a constructive triangulation could be the two parents interacting with their child: there are three participants in this subsystem. On the other hand, the domineering grandfather living in a multigenerational home environment can upset the balance by siding with his biological child against the spouse of his child. In this triangulation (the grandfather, his child, and his child's spouse), the grandparent can serve to drive a wedge between the dyad of the married couple.

Historic research. Segrin and Flora (2011, p. 87) reference the historic work of Turner (1970) who stated that decision making in families was predominantly influenced by three styles:

- *Consensus.* Family members try to be in agreement concerning the decision.
- *Accommodation.* Family members adjust to facilitate decision making.
- *De facto.* Whatever seems right for that situation determines the decision. In other words, the situation makes the decision. It could also mean that no decision is made, and the status quo is maintained, even if it is dysfunctional. Procrastination concerning decision making could be a decision in itself.

FOCUS POINT

Any conversation contains the potential for a power dynamic to occur. One of the communicators can have more power due to his or her position and the quality of the relationship. Power can also be allocated indirectly because one of the parties is vulnerable and, in this way, less powerful. Power inequality can reflect cultural content; and it can be constructive or destructive for the interaction, depending on the context. Power inequalities must be acknowledged in a manner that is constructive for the interaction. Family decision making is closely linked to the location of the seat of power. In an authoritarian family system, decisions are likely to trickle from the top down, with little or no bidirectional feedback. Parenting styles and decision making are interrelated. Decisions can have an instrumental and an affective dimension. These dimensions tend to overlap, and there can be mutual influence. In family contexts, considerable negotiation takes place to reach decisions. These decisions can result in aligned or nonaligned family communications.

This approach was a good beginning point from which to unravel the complexity of family decisions in the early days of the discipline, but, with time, it was regarded as a little simplistic. Family therapists then began to consider the family as a system and consequently factored in the idea that groupthink (the striving for consensus to maintain group conformity) influenced the decision-making process. So the question became how a family as a whole system reached decisions, which would give us clues about the dynamic of that particular family. If we consider the process of accommodation, for instance, family members are likely to adjust their decision making according to complex overt and covert rules, to power and submission dynamics, and on the basis of pleasing behavior and other factors.

Aligned versus nonaligned. There are endless variations in which family members can be aligned or nonaligned, shifting the power and hence the subtle and not so subtle dynamics of the family system. Conflict can become the lead character in the family drama and can influence the system in far-reaching ways.

Communication in Multicultural Contexts

Growing up in bicultural, bilingual homes, children instinctively seem to unravel what kind of communication belongs to which parent. This scenario plays out uncountable times each day in families across the world. With each language comes a **cultural echo**, as it were, and children in these families learn to juggle languages and cultural inputs and eventually blend them into a new and unique fusion.

In immigrant families, the home language may differ from the language of the host nation, and, importantly, different emotional qualities can be assigned to each. When multilingual parents want to say something in front of the kids that should not be understood, they switch to a language their children do not know. The effect sensitizes those children to nonverbal cues to unravel the details and find meaning.

Cultural Translators

The children of immigrants become literal as well as cultural translators and negotiators. They have access to the language of their heritage culture, but they are also being assimilated into the new host culture. Unlike their parents, they may have fluency in both these linguistic and cultural domains. This gives them very

Generalization, not always the case

unique and valued skill sets, which become highly prized in international work environments. These children frequently help their parents navigate the complex social structures of their new cultural home, and are described as cultural brokers. This process is known as *cultural brokering* (Lazarevic, 2017).

The extent to which immigrant children have to help their parents, and the context in which this help is provided, can add to or subtract from family cohesion. There appear to be distinct patterns associated with the intensity and frequency with which brokering has to occur—whether in a negative context it will elicit resentment or in a positive context add to family cohesion (Lazarevic, 2017).

A language is alive and vital. It also accesses emotions, and we have emotional associations with each language we know. A language has to be used almost daily to have complete and direct access to it. When a language is not used for a couple of years, speakers will say that they can understand everything but they struggle to find words. Finding the right word at the right moment means that we can access our intricate mental filing cabinet of language and retrieve what we are looking for instantaneously. This immediacy slows down when we do not use a language regularly.

We see this happening when an immigrant partners with someone from another cultural group and adopts that spouse's language. These choices can mean that the first language is not exercised. Language is like working out. Use it or lose it. Find friends in each of the languages you speak; those conversations are mental workouts to keep you fluent. Immigrants also tend to find a few friends with similar cultural and linguistic backgrounds in the host country, precisely to keep these linguistic and cultural connections alive. The children in these families benefit from the rich cultural contexts of their homes, although their own enculturation will be different from that of their parents; they are being shaped by a cultural landscape unlike the one to which their parents were exposed.

Lost in Translation

Another example of cultural brokering is reading translated literature. Once you have become familiar with a text in its original language, especially if that language is your own mother tongue, then translations lose immediacy and intimacy; hence the phrase "lost in translation" (also the title of a movie). Good translators who know their craft focus on the authentic idiom of speech in each language. Translators try to translate the exact meaning, but the vehicle has to be culturally appropriate and capture the nuances of the language into which they are translating.

Computer translations help us gain the gist in terms of meaning, but as yet they lose the nuances of idiom and tone. Compare this kind of cultural interpretation to interpreting a song. Some singers will add a personal and unique quality in the way they make the song their own. It has to do with phrasing, when they pause, which vowels they elongate, and, above all, having a unique voice. That would also explain why we like certain songs as interpreted by our favorite artists. If the same song is reproduced by a cover band, it falls flat. Superficially, the music may sound similar, but the subtleties, variations, and unique identifiers are absent. This process of immigrants feeling lost in a language that is not their own can partially represent a loss that also robs them of part of their identity.

Emotional Qualities

Languages contain unique emotional qualities, even if they are describing the same thing. In my early working days, I shared a carpool with university professors who taught in various global language departments. On one of our journeys, we discussed how compliments were given in different languages. Each language has its own angles and nuances that have to do with the cultural context of what it means to give a compliment. In some languages, a compliment was a statement of how an object made one feel, whether it was pleasing. In another language, the compliment took on a congratulatory tone, and in yet another, the compliment seemed to verbally stroke the recipient, as in flattery.

At the turn of the previous century in the United States, immigration was intended to create a melting pot of cultures, and different groups were expected to assimilate quickly and to encourage their children to speak only English and ignore the language of their ancestors. Current thinking has done a 180-degree turn, as we now like to preserve our cultural roots and heritage while also assimilating into the larger context of a diverse America.

Sorry business. For a monolingual person, this world of many languages can remain hidden. The closest way of experiencing it could be by acknowledging dialects and accents. We can observe differences in idiom depending on where a language is used.

For instance, when using English, the Aboriginal people in Australia have a touching expression: they refer to a sad occasion, such as a funeral, as *sorry business*. A place where much grief and mourning occurred may be called a *sorry place*. There is a musicality in the expression, and it says everything we need it to say.

FOCUS POINT

Children in bicultural families learn to juggle languages and cultural inputs and blend them into a unique fusion. The children of immigrants often have access to the language of their heritage culture, but they are also being assimilated into the culture of their host nation. Unlike their parents, they may have fluency in both these linguistic and cultural domains. Different languages contain unique emotional and cultural qualities, even if they appear to be describing the same thing.

GLOBAL GLIMPSE

TRAPPED IN AN UNINHABITABLE LANGUAGE

In a touching short story called *The German Refugee* (1963, as cited in Brown & Ling, 2002), author Bernard Malamud describes a displaced man who came to America after World War II. He had been an eminent and brilliant scientist, yet in his new homeland he could not fulfill his profession. His major obstacles were the insurmountable difficulties posed by this new language, English.

> To many of these people, articulate as they were, the great loss was the loss of language—that they could not say what was in them to say. You have some subtle thought and it comes out like a piece of broken bottle. They could, of course, manage to communicate, but just to communicate was frustrating. . . . There was a terrible sense of useless tongue, and I think the reason for his trouble . . . was that to keep from drowning in things unsaid, he wanted to swallow the ocean in a gulp: today he would learn English and tomorrow

(Continued)

(Continued)

> wow them with an impeccable . . . speech, followed by a successful lecture. (Malamud, 1963, as cited in Brown & Ling, 2002, p. 38)

The story continues to describe the mounting frustrations. The protagonist's mind was willing to learn, but in later adulthood, his German accent is rich and overpowering. English feels uninhabitable, and as brilliant as he is, his thoughts are locked in his mind because he cannot find the vehicle to utter them and communicate them in his new world. Eventually, he gets so disheartened that he stops taking language lessons:

> . . . each day [passed] in frenzy and growing despair. After writing more than a hundred opening pages he furiously flung his pen against the wall, shouting he could no longer write in that filthy tongue. He cursed the German language. . . . After that, what was bad became worse. When he gave up attempting to write the lecture, he stopped making progress in English. He seemed to forget what he already knew. His tongue thickened and the accent returned in all its fruitiness. *The little he had to say was in handcuffed and tortured English*. (Malamud, 1963, as cited in Brown & Ling, 2002, p. 39; italics added)

What makes the story so poignant is the disclosure in the final paragraphs that he is a Jewish refugee who lost his family in the Holocaust. His only language, German, has become contaminated by tragedy, by being associated with unspeakable loss. He feels trapped by his inability to communicate. The story reaches a tragic finale.

Another example of a second-language speaker trying to tiptoe from word to word is by Japanese-American author Hisaye Yamamoto (1921–2011), whose short story "Seventeen Syllables" is regarded as a defining work by this author. The story is about Rosie, from a Japanese-American immigrant family, who struggles to connect with her Japanese heritage and her Japanese-speaking mother.

> English lay ready on the tongue but Japanese had to be searched for and examined, and even put forth tentatively (probably to meet with laughter). It was so much easier to say yes, yes, yes, even when one meant no, no, no.

Because we live and breathe inside a language, it is easy to forget that this verbal freedom cannot consistently be taken for granted.

Sources: Malamud (1963/2002); Yamamoto (1988/1998).

Authentic Insight

Juggling Worlds While Juggling Words

I grew up in a bicultural home, so it was standard to hear two languages. Being exposed to various languages created a sense of normalcy; my siblings and I thought everybody's family was like that. My international education gifted me with a third and a fourth language. The fifth language became my major at university. I have wondered why my relationship to this fifth language is not as intimate as my connection to the other four. It has to do with social immersion, I think, with how necessary each language was to the social worlds I inhabited. Also, I have different associations with the context of the fifth language, and I began learning it at mid-adolescence—already a touch too late to absorb it by osmosis.

Even though I love being multilingual, I have a preferred language, and I have distinct emotions and cultural perspectives attached to each language. When I meet a new friend, the language in which we first communicated when we met tends to persist. The closeness of the relationship also varies depending on whether I speak to people in their mother tongue or not. The moment we share what is the first language for our language partner, we add a sense of cultural familiarity, and the sharing of the language assumes a familiarity and trust, because we are sharing something very powerful.

As an undergraduate student, I worked as a translator, and if I had not chosen my current career path, I might have continued as a linguist and translator. Instead, I am a hobby linguist, enjoying the fun of switching languages and connecting with people in one of the various communication systems anchored in my mind.

When I spend an extended time in a country with a language I know, I feel my brain switching operating systems. My mind starts thinking in the language I use most often; my self-talk and my inner conversations are in that language. When I do mental calculations, it is in the language that I am using most frequently at the time. But by using a language *frequently*, I don't mean having the occasional or daily conversation. Almost all the surrounding input has to be in that language. Owning a language requires total immersion—not borrowing a language, even if that borrowing is regular. Any well-loved language is a friend, a beloved language is a best friend, and the others are just acquaintances.

To claim fluency in a language, one should not have to think about how to use it. It is an automatic process. I experienced this first hand when I became a simultaneous translator for major events. You hear one language and without consciously thinking, you translate into another. In my mind, it feels as if I am picking up something with my left hand, handing it over to my right hand, and passing it on. The left hand would be one language, the right hand the other language. And something magical happens in between. The brain does a little tango step and connects one abstract symbol to another and adds meaning. This mental handing-over motion is where the translation happens.

When I do simultaneous translations, I cannot think too much about the cognitive content of the material, as this conscious thinking interferes with the translation process. Simultaneous translation occurs almost at preconscious level; it works better if one does it in a trancelike manner—the same way a typist's fingers automatically find the keys and create the words. Or it may be similar to tightrope walking—you can balance as long as you are relaxed and do not focus on the actual art of balancing. By observing what is happening, one loses spontaneity, and the brain gets distracted—very detrimental to fluency.

This process reminds me of the exponential complexity of cognitive mechanisms that allow us to use and manipulate something as magical as language. We share the language in which we communicate. We connect.

Clara Gerhardt

Cultural Echoes: Nuances in Communication

Using the language of therapy, we are trying to understand completely what the client is communicating by understanding the meaning behind the words, the emotion. The counterpart to this is active listening, not only for the meaning of the words but also for the cultural idioms.

Working across cultures can present its own problems. If we use a translator, we do not know if we truly hear what was intended. In the short story "The Interpreter of Maladies" by Jhumpa Lahiri (1999), she describes a Gujarati translator who assists the local Hindi-speaking doctor. He unwittingly adds his own interpretations to what he is translating, as he facilitates diagnoses and inserts cultural footnotes. When he tells someone about his job as a medical translator, that person responds:

> "So these patients are totally dependent on you . . . In a way, more dependent on you than the doctor . . . Well, for example, you could tell the doctor that the pain felt like a burning, not straw. The patient would never know what you had told the doctor, the doctor wouldn't know that you had told the wrong thing. It's a big responsibility."
>
> . . .
>
> Mr. Kapasi had never thought of his job in such complimentary terms. To him it was a thankless occupation. He found nothing noble in interpreting people's maladies, assiduously translating the symptoms of so many swollen bones, countless cramps of bellies and bowels . . . (Lahiri, 1999, p. 51)

Cultural Shorthand

Culture has to do with shorthand, the shortcuts to meaning in communication. Culture is, among other things, a set of symbols, values, and beliefs that can be understood by persons sharing that same culture. We can use these shared cultural artifacts as shortcuts to meaning. These shared cultural signs can make communication predictable because all the members of a particular group subscribe to them. Think of how the burglary at the Watergate building has made its way into our language; we now use the word *Watergate* as a short form for a scandal involving abuses of office, and the suffix *-gate* is added to words to connote a similar meaning: e.g., Bridgegate, Bendgate, Ebola-gate, or GaberGate. Changing cultural context may mean that subtle differences are misunderstood. Moving from one culture to another can be disempowering as a number of symbols, nuances, and especially humor from the new cultural context may elude us. This in turn makes cultural outsiders vulnerable and puts them at a disadvantage. Their communication cannot be as direct and confident as in their mother tongue. Even so, not knowing the cultural shorthand is the fate of millions of relocated people across the world, be they refugees, legal immigrants, expats, or part of an ever-growing international workforce.

Family Language

Family language, or the how and the what of communication within the family, influences parenting practices, assimilation into new cultural contexts, work opportunities, social contexts, and more. It has the distinct power to influence how that family dynamic will play out in a variety of contexts. King and Fogle (2013) are of the opinion that greater insight into how families manage multiple languages has the potential of influencing educational policies, starting with practices surrounding English as a second language (ESL). Family language addresses language use within the home and within the family. It influences language acquisition and leaves its imprints on the family as a dynamic system.

"The Silent Language"

Intercultural communication was not a topic of interest until the publication of a book with the title *The Silent Language*, by Edward T. Hall, in 1959. Since that time, the field of intercultural communication has exploded with a plethora of research articles and a number of well-founded theories. There is an overlap between cross-cultural communication and cross-cultural psychology, as psychological processes such as perception and cognition are a part of, as well as influential in, communication (Gudykunst, 2003, p. 1).

Cross-cultural communication theories highlight several aspects of the relationship between culture and communication (Gudykunst & Lee, 2003, p. 8):

- Because culture is intricately linked to communication, they have mutual influence. Communication influences cultural expression, and that expression is again a product of its cultural context.
- Communication can contribute to the formation and extension of culture.
- Theories conceived within the context of one culture can find some application in other cultures; there is a degree of transferability.

Theories can explain many facets of intercultural communication, and, importantly, how communication varies in different cultural contexts. Culture has been defined in many ways, but one facet that rings especially true is the following phrase: "[Culture creates] internal models of reality" (Keesing, 1974, as cited in Gudykunst & Lee, 2003, p. 8). One interpretation of this statement is that culture imparts a frame of reference, an internal structure and organization, which members of that cultural group can access, interpret, and apply. Cultural insiders with direct access to this frame of reference quickly understand unique cultural variations in communication. The same holds true for the insiders of a family's microculture. Even our view of self, how we express our self-concept, is affected by the internal structure provided by the culture of our society and our family, and by how this structure organizes communication.

"Ways of Seeing"

Our many selves are interdependent, and we adjust and readjust them in an ongoing manner based on the feedback loops we receive from the persons with whom we interact. John Berger (1972), the art critic, commented in his book *Ways of Seeing* that a woman has two ways of seeing herself. The first is the direct and objective reflection she perceives in her mirror.

The second is the trickier one; this view is determined by how she thinks other people see her, and it contains an evaluative thread. Where this insight links to the dynamics of the family is that the family plays a distinct and powerful role in the formation of this second image. One of the tasks of parents is to support positive self-concept formation in the children they parent. To fulfill this task optimally, one has to be cognizant of family dynamics because that can be the factor that facilitates or obstructs this process.

FOCUS POINT

Cultural echoes are the cultural threads woven into communication. Each language has a *cultural echo*, as words convey not only meaning but also cultural context. Communicating means understanding the cultural connotation behind words, the emotion, and hearing not only literal meanings but also cultural idioms. Culture facilitates the shorthand that occurs within communication. Culture is, among other things, a set of symbols, values, and beliefs that can be understood by persons sharing that same culture. The endless intricacies and subtler details of meaning and intent that constitute communication may be more apparent to cultural insiders. How we think about ourselves as entities, as persons linked to other persons, as part of communities—all these influence our cultural expressions.

SPOTLIGHT ON THEORIES

Communication Accommodation Theory (CAT)

Communication accommodation theory (CAT) emphasizes the interpersonal dimension of the communication process, which can occur in one-on-one conversations and in group and intergroup contexts. Communication is not only about words or verbal content; it can include the nonverbal dimensions of microgestures and facial expressions that are virtually imperceptible to an outsider but that can convey a message of interest or disinterest.

According to the communication accommodation theory, we do more than just send messages backward and forward between people. To facilitate communication, we try to get on the same page as our communication partner. There are two concerns:

(Continued)

(Continued)

- People choose how they communicate to match their communication partner. To do that they will make subtle behavioral changes, and this can occur in a feedback loop.
- We may or may not be aware of whether or how our communication partner is attuned to us.

Howard Giles (b. 1946) is a British-American sociolinguist who formulated a theory that focuses on the context within which communication occurs. Language and communication intersect with the greater field, or context, in which the exchange takes place. For family therapists, this is of special importance, as the context of the family may set up reciprocal communication patterns. We influence how persons respond to our comments, but we also frame our own comments because we have been subtly influenced by what went before; there is a circularity contained in communication. Another example would be refugees or immigrants trying to assimilate to a context that may be bewilderingly new and in which the old idioms cannot serve them.

A number of factors can contribute to why we make these adjustments. Among them are the power differential between the communicators and the micro and macro contexts, which could certainly affect the act of communication.

Convergence and divergence. Theorists supporting this approach look at two important patterns, namely, the convergence and divergence of communication behaviors. **Convergence** implies that a communicator tries to get closer to the communication partner by adapting to that person and, to an extent, modeling her or him. **Divergence** implies that a communicator moves away from the communication partner for various reasons.

When we converge or accommodate, we can overdo it and seem to be very overly pleasing. Alternatively, we could come across as patronizing or even condescending. In other words, the extent to which we identify with and try to be on the same page as our communication partners can influence the success of communication.

There is an additional factor: we may be seeking approval, and we most often want to be accepted, even liked. One way of achieving these goals is to mimic some of the verbal cues in our communication contexts. An example of this kind of behavior is the use of slang or specific words by members of a clique or group. Adolescents in particular may overuse certain words because they are fashionable or desirable in the context of their peer group.

The communication accommodation theory focuses specifically on how communication partners attempt to become more like the person with whom they are communicating, if they are seeking that person's approval. They may subtly adjust their communication patterns to align with those of the other person sharing the conversation.

In popular contexts, persons in sales and marketing are aware of subtle communication cues, and they try to align themselves with the customer to win that individual's approval and probably make a sale. For that reason, a salesperson in a clothing store is hardly likely to point out to a customer that a garment is unflattering. Salespeople stereotypically amplify customer communication cues, agreeing with the choice of the customer with the intent of making the potential buyer feel good about a prospective purchase. Using a metaphor from tennis, I might say it is as if both players play from the same side of the net. This alliance aims to create positive outcomes. Another example comes from customer support. If a customer complains about a product or service, the opening response will likely be, "I can understand your frustration." The person receiving the complaint is trying to defuse the difficult situation by displaying alliance with the complainer. This is the process of convergence.

In the process called divergence, the opposite occurs. The communicator wishes to achieve distance from his or her audience, for whatever psychological reason. Divergence can be attained by speaking in a way that neither mimics nor aligns with a communication partner. For instance, to display power and create distance, a person could use difficult terminology that the recipient of the message cannot completely understand. One example would be flawed communication between a doctor and a patient. Ideally, the doctor would attempt to speak at the level that the patient understands, explaining and possibly avoiding overly technical terms. Another example of an attempt to display power through divergence is the lawyer questioning a "hostile witness" in court. The legal professional could scale up language to intimidate that person, or to impress the jury.

In any given communication process inequities can occur. Ideally, the power balance between communicating parties should be equal or in balance. In that way, they can communicate more openly and less defensively. When there is a power imbalance in the communication pattern, it may emphasize the vulnerability of the person who is perceived to have less power. By the same token, the person who has greater social impact and influence may be perceived as controlling the situation. This perception in itself adds to that individual's power. Depending on the situation and the context, power imbalances can be detrimental to good communication.

In a number of unique situations, inequity in the communication process is desirable. A power imbalance can be valuable when having power represents authority and being in control. Extensive research has been done concerning the communication patterns of cockpit crews in aircraft. Accidents have occurred both when the most powerful member of the crew did not exert power and when that person's power went unquestioned—when communication was ambiguous and when an erroneous order by the high-ranking captain could not be questioned by an officer of lower rank. In their training, pilots and other cockpit crew members are made aware that communication extends beyond the exchange of information. Sending a message is one thing; how the message is received is another.

Social identity. Social identity is important in the communication process. If one of the parties is perceived as being very powerful or is revered, then the other person might be submissive. A simple example would be meeting somebody of exceptionally high rank or who is famous or financially powerful. We can use communication as a positive tool, and it can improve our image and strengthen how we are perceived by others. For instance, the lead speaker at a formal event may act with decorum and formality, which in itself adds to the perceived importance of the occasion. We may also add some deception to color the interpersonal actions in our favor, a technique perfected by confidence tricksters (Littlejohn, 2017, p. 255).

Social identity theory plays a strong role within communication accommodation theory. Social identity theory is rooted in social psychology and draws much inspiration from the following theories:

- Similarity-attraction theory
- Social exchange process theory
- Intergroup distinctiveness theory
- Causal attribution theory

Here are brief summaries of the key qualities of these theories:

Similarity-attraction theory. We are likely to be attracted to those people who hold similar attitudes and beliefs. For instance, if we are fans of the same football team, we may think that we have more in common with fellow enthusiasts than with supporters of the rival team.

Social exchange process theory. Persons exchange rewards to meet their own goals. They may even do a mental calculation of whether the cost of the choice is worth the reward. People try to achieve at least a balance between cost and reward. We can make a decision about whether a friendship is worthwhile based on the cost of the emotional demands it makes on us. If the rewards are high, for example, financial or social benefits, a person may retain a difficult friendship because the social outcomes are highly rewarding (Littlejohn et al., 2017, p. 253). An example is befriending a famous or rich person and thinking that, by association, some of that person's attributes will rub off on you and put you in a better social position (halo effect). Another classical example is the spring-autumn partnership—a young beautiful person marrying an older richer person with considerable social influence. Clearly, exchanges are taking place in this relationship and both parties think that the rewards are higher than the costs—or else it would not be sustainable.

This example links to **intergroup distinctiveness theory**. This theory proposes that members of a group compare their group's valued characteristics to those exhibited by other groups and seek to make themselves distinct from the "out-groups." Important for family dynamics is the idea that, if a person would like to belong to a group, that person will adjust her or his behavior and speech to facilitate group membership and group identity.

Causal attribution theory. How we explain someone's behavior will be more positive if the motive for that behavior is perceived as positive. Our evaluations of other people can be colored and influenced by what we presume their motives to be (Littlejohn et al., 2017, p. 57).

(Continued)

(Continued)

Attribution bias relates to this theory in that we tend to favor what pertains to ourselves and be more critical of others. For example, if we do well on a test we attribute it to our own intelligence and insight into the subject matter. If we do poorly, it is more comfortable to blame an outside force, for example, the professor who set an unfair test, thereby causing the bad grade (Shiraev & Levy, 2016, pp. 52–53, p. 294).

There is an added twist to this scenario in that we tend to be stingy with compliments toward others. So if my opponent plays an excellent match, I'll ascribe it to luck rather than acknowledging that person's superior technique. And if the opponent plays poorly? Well then, of course, it can be attributed to the opponent's intrinsic deficits (Manusov, 2018, p. 53). Needless to say, nothing is fair in the game of attribution, as long as we come out looking best.

FOCUS POINT

Communication accommodation theory (CAT) emphasizes the interpersonal dimensions of the communication process, which can occur in one-on-one conversations, in group conversations, and in intergroup contexts. Communication is not only about words or verbal content; it can include nonverbal dimensions, such as micro-gestures and facial expressions that are virtually imperceptible to an outsider but that can convey a message of interest or disinterest. Depending on the social situation, we can strive for convergence or divergence in relation to a communication partner: for similarity and closeness or for dissimilarity and distance, respectively. Communication can contain values and elicit judgments. We adjust our speech, and hence our communication, to fulfill the expectations in a given situation.

In a Nutshell

Communication Accommodation Theory (CAT)

- When we communicate, we can be similar to or dissimilar from our communication partners.
- We evaluate the conversation—the contents and the speaker—based on how we perceive that individual's speech and behavior.
- Communication can provide an indication of our group identity as well as our social status, for example, level of education or professional experience.
- Depending on the social situation, we can strive for convergence or divergence in relation to a communication partner: for similarity and closeness or for dissimilarity and distance, respectively.
- Communication can contain values and elicit judgments; and in such situations, communication is seldom completely neutral.
- We adjust our speech, and hence our communication, to fulfill the expectations in a given situation.

CHAPTER FOCUS POINTS

Reaching Out and Connecting

- Communication within family relationships is an intricate, complex, and sophisticated process. Communication is intended as a way for us to reach out, to be understood, to make our wishes known, and to add value.
- The receiving component of this interaction is equally important; we need to listen,

understand, acknowledge, react, and respond.

- Together, these aspects of communication form an intricate web, a constant backward and forward exchange of information between parties. Different theories define communication from a variety of angles.
- Family therapy scholars came to approach the family from a systemic point of view, which included investigating how families communicated within a group context.

Emotional Interactions

- Communication allows us to convey our meanings, feelings, and desires but also, importantly, to participate in and react appropriately to various communication patterns.
- These communications represent a constant exchange of information, some of which relates to how invested or disinvested family members are in relationships. Emotional intimacy and self-disclosure require trust and a sense of safety, which come with emotional investment. Emotional disinvestment can signal distance and a potential fracture in a relationship.
- Our nonverbal communication can amplify or soften the message we are sending.
- Metacommunication occurs when there is a second layer hidden behind the first layer of communication.
- The communication sciences and related disciplines have contributed many theories relevant to family dynamics; these have been invaluable in organizing research findings, creating theoretical models, and enhancing understanding.

Power and Patterns of Decision Making

- Any conversation contains the potential for a power dynamic to occur. One of the communicators can have more power due to his or her position and the quality of the relationship.
- Power can also be allocated indirectly because one of the parties is vulnerable and, in this way, less powerful.
- Power inequality can reflect cultural content; and it can be constructive or destructive for the interaction, depending on the context. Power inequalities must be acknowledged in a manner that is constructive for the interaction.
- Family decision making is closely linked to the location of the seat of power. In an authoritarian family system, decisions are likely to trickle from the top down, with little or no bidirectional feedback.
- Parenting styles and decision making are interrelated.
- Decisions can have an instrumental and an affective dimension. These dimensions tend to overlap, and there can be mutual influence.
- In family contexts, considerable negotiation takes place to reach decisions. These decisions can result in aligned or nonaligned family communications.

Communication in Multicultural Contexts

- Children in bicultural families learn to juggle languages and cultural inputs and blend them into a unique fusion. The children of immigrants become literal as well as cultural translators and negotiators.
- The children of immigrants often have access to the language of their heritage culture, but they are also being assimilated into the culture of their host nation. Unlike their parents, they may have fluency in both these linguistic and cultural domains.
- Different languages contain unique emotional and cultural qualities, even if they appear to be describing the same thing.

Cultural Echoes: Nuances in Communication

- Cultural echoes are the cultural threads woven into communication. Each language has a *cultural echo*, as words convey not only meaning but also cultural context.
- Communicating means understanding the cultural connotation behind words, the emotion, and hearing not only literal meanings but also cultural idioms.
- Culture facilitates the shorthand that occurs within communication. Culture is, among other things, a set of symbols, values, and beliefs

that can be understood by persons sharing that same culture.

- The endless intricacies and subtler details of meaning and intent that constitute communication may be more apparent to cultural insiders.
- How we think about ourselves as entities, as persons linked to other persons, as part of communities—all these influence our cultural expressions.

Spotlight on Theories: Communication Accommodation Theory (CAT)

- *Communication accommodation theory* (CAT) emphasizes the interpersonal dimensions of the communication process, which can occur in one-on-one conversations, in group conversations, and in intergroup contexts.
- Communication is not only about words or verbal content; it can include nonverbal dimensions, such as the microgestures and facial expressions that are virtually imperceptible to an outsider but that can convey a message of interest or disinterest.
- Depending on the social situation, we can strive for convergence or divergence in relation to a communication partner: for similarity and closeness or for dissimilarity and distance, respectively.
- Communication can contain values and elicit judgments. We adjust our speech, and hence our communication, to fulfill the expectations in a given situation.

CHAPTER 7

Communication and Control

Learning Outcomes

After studying this chapter, you should be able to

1. Analyze the ways *family scripts* influence individual family members.
2. Explain the different *negative* communication types that can exist in family units.
3. Summarize the unique functions *secrets* play in family dynamics.
4. Discuss how *privacy* and secrecy intersect in professional and workforce communication.
5. Summarize *communication privacy management (CPM) theory,* and explain its key characterizing descriptors.

Privileged information and even secrets can strengthen an interpersonal bond and support emotional intimacy within that relationship. On the flipside, privileged information can be deployed as weapons for self-defense or as a means of attack. Folk wisdom states that a secret is safe between the following: a living and a dead person. The fact that only one of those two parties is able to communicate with the rest of the world indicates what is generally thought of the viability of a true secret; secrets have a tendency to be revealed. They spill out advertently and inadvertently. In the revelation, they can empower or disempower, depending on who pays the greater price for that knowledge becoming public.

Family Scripts

Families find their own preferred patterns of communication. They also find the level at which they are comfortable in terms of expressing not only thoughts, feelings, dreams, and hopes but also anger, resentment, frustration, and more. The **family script** may define the unique way a family manages content and information. But what exactly is a family script? Family scripts are sets of expectations and histories and norms about a family that have developed into patterns guiding behavior, attitudes, and the details of interaction and speech. They also convey what cannot be expressed or done.

Some families have cues that act as codes to other members. Misread a cue and one can risk setting off a metaphorical land mine. Family scripts can contain information as well as being barometers concerning the emotional climate within that family group. The family script will reveal boundaries for communication and members will know within which delineated area they can communicate freely.

Scripts in the family of origin can influence the children from that family into adulthood and set the tone for their own families of creation. If one of our family scripts involves never openly expressing our feelings, it may be difficult to create a group whose members are sensitive to feelings and can talk about their emotional lives. Family scripts are powerful examples for the younger generation to follow. For instance, a particular family may use guilt as a way of controlling members. In practice, that means that family members are not truly free to do as they want. In contentious situations, there will be strings attached in the form of guilt. This powerful family script can rob children of choices and the freedom to pursue dreams.

Dysfunctional scripts. Family scripts can be dysfunctional and disturbing and can do a lot of harm if they are used in a combative manner. Family scripts can be filled with disrespect and a lack of boundaries and privacy. In disrespectful communication, verbal abuse may be mistaken as a way of wielding power, for example. Sadly, this form of communication has a steep emotional price attached to it. Children who grew up in verbally abusive homes are likely to imitate this dysfunctional pattern of behavior in their own adult interactions (Fewell, 2016; Noriega, 2010).

Scripts and culture. Family scripts can also be guided by cultural norms (Krause, 2001). For instance, the respect that is shown toward elders can differ in various cultural contexts. If elders are treated with great respect, this influences how the grandparenting role will play out. Many of the patterns that we learn in our families of origin, especially when it comes to communication, will find wider application in our adult lives. Much of our working life will demand good communication (Riggio, 2017). Common wisdom states that people are hired for their skills, but they are fired for their personalities. In practice, the way we communicate may spill over in the work environment. If we grew up in a family that did not encourage or value emotional regulation, we may find it hard to maintain a respectful and negotiating stand in difficult interpersonal situations.

Very often it is not so much about the *what*, or content, of communication but about the *how*, the way in which we communicate a message. Skilled communicators manage to be respectful and avoid blaming behavior while also expressing the desire to solve a problem or address a situation (Guerrero & Ramos-Salazar, 2015). If a critique has to occur, that critical message needs to be sandwiched between two pieces of positive information. The way a family communicates will also determine turn taking within that family. In some families, members interrupt each other, which can be disrespectful. In most conversations, it is courteous to hear out the speaker, which, in itself, displays courtesy within the bidirectionality of a conversation. Still, this family script is very culturally driven. A friend of mine once attended the family dinner of her best friend in university. Here is my friend's experience:

> My first meal at Rachel's house was a special Friday evening one with her family, which was large and boisterous. At the end of the meal she asked me why I was so aloof and quiet at the dinner table. Didn't I like her mother, father, brother, and sister? Didn't I enjoy their conversation? I told her I was waiting for a break in the conversation to speak, as I had been told that interrupting was rude. She laughed and explained my dilemma to her folks, and after that one or another of them would "call me out" whenever I looked like I wanted to speak—"What do you say, Brooke? Do you agree?"

Compliments. Very few people are insensitive to an appropriate and genuine display of appreciation for good work. A compliment is only of worth if it is congruent

FOCUS POINT

The family script may define the unique way a family manages content and information. Some families have cues that act as codes, signaling to other members. Scripts in the family of origin can influence the children from that family into adulthood and set the tone for their own families of creation. Family scripts can also be guided by cultural norms. Our families can contribute to our sense of confidence in conversations.

and appropriate. If the recipient gets a sense that the compliment is false or merely used as a cheap shortcut to favors, it will probably affect all the other communication between those two persons. Unless compliments are genuine and congruent, they will come across as devalued currency, without particular value. The respectful comment by a parent can provide the child with a sense of genuine appreciation, which, in turn, adds to the formation of a good self-concept and self-efficacy.

Our families can contribute to our sense of confidence in conversations. Will our voice be heard? Are verbal contributions valued? Are we allowed to express an opinion? Are we allowed to question? All these processes allow us to explore points of view and help us form opinions about major topics (Erskine, 2018). It is helpful when a family creates a platform where this questioning can occur in a respectful manner without the questioner being prematurely cut off. Being able to question the validity of an argument, or the relevance of a fact, may prove to be a useful skill in later life, when we will be required to make a judgment call between information that is valuable and information that can be discarded.

The family is the playpen where we learn about the *process* of communication; we learn the rules of turn taking, of respect, of listening, of not interrupting, and much more. Later on, when we have perfected this process, we can add *content* of any form, and the process will still guide us toward respectful and constructive interactions and exchanges of ideas.

> **"Family concerns can invade our lives and leave an indelible fingerprint on our current and future relationships."**

The Power of Disinformation

Disinformation. When we are part of an exchange of ideas, the communicator can lead us astray by providing disinformation or incorrect facts. The motive behind providing disinformation can be various, as well as devious. In essence, disinformation has to do with power, maintaining it, regaining it, and disempowering the opponent. Whatever technique is used, the party spreading disinformation clearly feels there is a benefit involved. Disinformation can come in several guises: it can mean omitting the truth, bending the facts, leaving things unsaid so that incorrect conclusions are drawn, or intentionally lying.

The context in which the disinformation occurs is important, as that context will contribute to our understanding concerning whether the disinformation is malicious or merely a so-called white lie. Sometimes we omit information in order to spare someone's feelings, to shield a person from harm. Not all truth is constructive, and sometimes the situation may call for diplomacy or bending of the truth with good outcomes in mind. For instance, there is little positive benefit in criticizing a person's appearance, as doing so can be hurtful and demeaning. As a process, this form of criticism ignores the total person while the critic is distracted by superficial external detail.

Gaslighting

In essence, **gaslighting** is form of falsifying the truth or lying. It is correctly characterized for its manipulative quality. In extreme forms, gaslighting is an attempt to make a person question her or his own perceptions, memory, and even sanity. It is an insidious form of warfare in which the victim pays the price.

This form of disinformation can be particularly harmful because it is capable of slowly eroding a person's perception of the world. Gaslighting is intended to weaken others while strengthening the one who is spreading the misinformation. Think of the parent who creates an alternative reality for children with the motive of making them fearful of the external world and dependent; the children will be second-guessing themselves and ultimately uncertain about whether they can trust their own feelings and perceptions (Thomas, 2018). This maneuver is often found in the context of an illicit relationship; the person who fears being exposed as an adulterer feeds so much disinformation to the spouse that the latter begins to doubt his or her own perceptions.

Historic underpinnings. The term *gaslighting* was derived from an interaction depicted in the play *Gas Light*, by Patrick Hamilton (1938). Later, the 1944 movie *Gaslight*, directed by George Cukor and starring Ingrid Bergman and Charles Boyer, made the concept of gaslighting part of popular culture (Thomas, 2018; Shoos, 2017). In both dramas, the husband kept on turning down the lights. When the wife remarked that the room was slightly darker, he would deny it and accuse her of incorrect perceptions. Eventually, the wife becomes very unsure of her observations, which is exactly what the gaslighter wishes to achieve. In the movie, this manipulation drives the wife to borderline insanity and self-doubt (Thomas, 2018). By undermining his opponent, the attacker thinks he can control whether he will be caught out for his crime or not.

Victim vulnerability. Gaslighting often goes undetected, because it is a subtle form of abuse and the victim may play into it. Initially, the disinformation may come across as a misunderstanding, but if the lying is a persistent and ongoing ploy to maintain control, then it takes on pathological dimensions. Several related behaviors can occur together with gaslighting, for instance, the manipulator never compliments or provides positive support to the victim, increasing that person's vulnerability. Additionally, a victim's self-esteem is at risk if he or she is repeatedly put down and made to doubt perceptions. The abuser may also accuse the victim of being oversensitive and imagining things. In this way, the blame is displaced to the victim. It may even go so far as victims thinking that they are contributing to the situation. The line between the victim and the abuser can be blurred intentionally—another tactic of the individual using this particular weapon. In an interview, Tara Westover (2018), author of the book *Educated*, discusses her family's creation of an alternative world to keep a secret (Seamons, 2018):

> One of the reasons I wrote the book is because of the gaslighting I experienced from my parents. I think the tragedy here isn't that bad people do bad things. I think the tragedy is what good people do to keep secrets.

Whistleblowers. When the alternative world of the gaslighter is threatened by an individual about to tell the truth, the goal is to shift the blame and to pin a lie or misperception on the potential whistleblower. If the perceptions of the whistleblower are shown to be incorrect or doubtful, that evidence loses its validity. One of the situations in which gaslighting typically occurs is spousal abuse (Sarkis, 2018). The victims are led to believe that the abuse is actually their fault and that whatever they perceive is incorrect. Such gaslighting is an additional form of abuse because the dominant partner plays a cat and mouse game with a victim's perceptions, disempowering the victim mentally and physically. The less power a victim has, the more likely she or he will remain trapped in the abusive relationship.

In normal relationships, disagreements can occur. If they lead to a respectful exchange of feelings and ideas, they can take the relationship to another level of understanding. So a disagreement over perceptions can occur without it representing true gaslighting. In gaslighting, there is an intentional distortion of the victim's perceptions. The abuser manipulates the situation for personal gain and to increase her or his power.

Being Kept Out of the Loop

There is power in *not* disclosing information to everybody in a network. A person who is willfully kept out of the communication loop may not have access to all the information required to make a judgment call or exercise free choice. Withholding information can be an oversight. Depending on the outcome, it can be more benign. Still, keeping somebody out of the loop means that information does not reach that person, which, in turn, can have certain implications.

In some family situations, it may be appropriate to keep members out of the loop (Rober, Walravens, & Versteynen, 2011). For instance, during the holidays or for birthdays, it may be important not to include the children in all the planning of the gifts and the festivities, as doing so would take away some of the surprise element and could perhaps alert them to the fact that grown-ups are the ones sourcing the gifts.

In most forms of communication, being included or excluded can indicate control of power, and motives for exclusion can range from keeping a well-intended surprise secret to overt hostility. For instance, stonewalling can be seen as a way of making communication impossible or blocking it. It can be a destructive process, as it sends a number of negative messages, both intended and unintended.

Well-intended secrets. In some Western cultural contexts, the ritual of asking a person to consider marriage is supposed to contain an element of surprise. Presumably, much talk between the partners has preceded this event. As couples individualize how they want to display their commitment, these practices are changing to accommodate unique preferences. The betrothed-to-be might anticipate a

FOCUS POINT

Communication can lead us astray by providing disinformation or incorrect facts. The motives can be various, as well as devious. Disinformation has to do with power—maintaining it, regaining it, or disempowering the opponent. Gaslighting weakens one person while strengthening the one who is spreading the misinformation. This form of disinformation erodes a person's perception of the world. There is power in not disclosing information to everybody in a network. A person who is willfully kept out of the communication loop can be disempowered. Stonewalling, which is defined as blocking all communication with an individual, actually sends a number of negative messages.

proposal, but the details could be kept secret. How and where the question was asked becomes an important part of the ritual and should symbolize and reflect some of the shared values and treasured connections of the couple. A more recent ritual is the baby gender reveal. Because couples can routinely be informed of the gender of a child before its birth (if this is legal in the country where they live, and if it is their preference), a gender-reveal party may share this information with close family and friends.

Family Secrets

Family stories. Each family has its own oral history. This history consists of the stories relayed from generation to generation, and these stories can provide insight into the symbolic content of that family's life. Families will remember certain heroic stories, events that were stressful or exceptionally joyful, stories that are humorous, and those that reflect the essence of a family member's identity, for example. These stories are often retold at family reunions, and the younger generations like to hear the stories about grandparents and how different their lives may have been. In this way, the family stories connect the generations and form an important dialogue. Family stories can be prompted by shared events such as family reunions. Children may also want to hear the story of how they joined the family and of how important and loved they are within this family context (Segrin & Flora, 2011, p. 57).

Families have an important function in that they can record family history, sometimes not entirely accurately, but maybe the embellishments and selected omissions are also indicative of what matters in that particular family. Families choose to tell and share certain stories whereas other tales are omitted, possibly because they are accompanied by unwelcome emotions (Barnwell, 2018). Children are also interested in the courtship story of their parents: how did mom and dad meet? Knowing these stories can be an entry point for children into the family, as they slowly acquire details surrounding their own family history. As the stories are being told and retold, subtle alterations take place, and the stories are revised and subtly changed. In this manner, stories can be transformative while redefining reality (Segrin & Flora, 2011, p. 58). Storytelling can contribute to the family identity that is construed in social contexts. When the story is retold, even when all participants already know it, it can add to family cohesion and group identity.

Storytelling can impart values and lessons to be learned. In our parenting classes taught at the university, our students produce a book for children that addresses a particular theme or lesson to be learned. Stories become the vehicles to impart concepts such as distinguishing between right and wrong, group membership, and the cruelty of bullying. Stories can be inclusive and tell us about cultures and customs with which we are not familiar. The list is endless, as stories concerning the family appeal to many of us; after all, we can all claim families of our own even if our families might not be ideal or perfect.

Taboo topics. In certain families, there are taboo topics that cannot be discussed. There may also be family secrets that are solidified, firmly fixed, and kept quiet because the damage that the truth can inflict is perceived to outweigh the weight of the secret (Barnwell, 2018). An area that is increasingly requiring revisiting is that of DNA testing. Many of these tests warn consumers in advance that the results could be far-reaching. By that is typically meant the disclosure of hereditary traits linked to disease, but also to paternity and maternity. In the past, it may have been possible to keep an illicit liaison secret, but DNA testing has the ability to expose even the darkest secret. This exposure of hitherto private information can set off a domino effect that the family is not equipped to handle (Bell & Bennett, 2017).

Not all information is helpful to all people. We know from the many stories about the world wars that, in certain instances, lives depended on information *not* being distributed because once the information is out there, it can also reach the ears of the enemy and be used as a weapon. In most organizations, there are levels of confidentiality and privileged information that cannot be shared. For instance, in a university, the grades of adult students cannot be shared with their parents without the students' consent. Similarly, psychiatric and psychological information has strict boundaries concerning the contexts in which it can be shared.

In certain families, there are taboo topics that cannot be discussed. There may also be family secrets because the truth has the potential to inflict damage. Sharing some privileged information, including gossip, can be a way of exchanging information and strengthening alliances.

Source: © iStock.com/PORNCHAI SODA.

Privileged information. When a person discloses private information, that individual loses some control over that information. When it is shared, it can snowball outward, and then there is no telling where that information may resurface. Human nature being what it is, shared privileged information (also known as gossip) has an uncanny way of spreading like wildfire. Once the metaphorical genie has been released from the bottle, it can become impossible to contain. The workplace and the family can be similar when it comes to sharing or not sharing privileged information. Both have numerous spoken and unspoken rules concerning disclosure boundaries. For instance, it may be inappropriate to discuss personal political preferences, and it may be inadvisable to mix private life with work life by having fuzzy boundaries between the two. Even in job interviews, certain questions will be out of bound.

> **"A family without secrets is rare indeed."**
>
> Kuhn (2002, p. 2)

Secrets: Shame and Pain

Protecting secrets. The painful nature of family secrets is hinted at by the amount of effort families invest in protecting their secrets. A secret is a secret precisely because opening up the information to all parties may jeopardize an individual's position in the family system or open a Pandora's box of shame and pain. Secrets are a way of hiding and disguising information, and doing so in a deliberate way. As Galvin, Braithwaite, and Bylund (2014, p. 91) state, "Making, keeping, and revealing secrets all shape a family's interaction patterns."

Not all secrets are intentionally bad; they are often perpetuated because people are afraid of the repercussions of telling the truth. The problem, though, is that a small secret can grow and take on an overbearing dominance over the years until finally it reaches the point at which it becomes too big to contain. Family secrets can also surface because the dynamic balance of the system changes; for instance, the death of a family member who was guarding the secret may change the entire dynamic (Barnwell, 2015).

A deceased person no longer has control over the particular secret. Even when a secret is taken to the grave, circumstantial evidence may still trigger disclosure. The paper trail left by most people often contains clues about family secrets, and an unsuspecting family member tidying up the estate may stumble across these revelations (Cohen, 2013). It is obvious, then, that family secrets can change over time and that their hold over the family can relax.

> A family without secrets is rare indeed. People who live in families make every effort to keep certain things concealed from the rest of the world, and at times from each other as well. Things will be lied about, or simply never mentioned. Sometimes family secrets are so deeply buried that they elude the conscious awareness even of those most closely involved. From the involuntary amnesias of repression to the wilful forgetting of matters it might be less than convenient to recall, secrets inhabit the borderlands of memory. Secrets in fact are a necessary condition of the stories we are prompted by memory to tell about our lives. (Kuhn, 2002, p. 2)

Because families represent a form of social organization, investigating what a family keeps secret or tells, as well as the sequence of events determining these decisions, provides us with a window into the inner workings of that family's organization. Almost all families harbor truths and tales they would prefer not to share with the outside. Sometimes they feign forgetfulness because the price of letting the secret escape into the open may be too high.

> **"Making, keeping, and revealing secrets all shape a family's interaction patterns."**
>
> Galvin, Braithwaite, and Bylund (2014, p. 91)

Topic avoidance. An area related to nondisclosure within families is topic avoidance. Whereas keeping a secret can mean hiding acknowledged truthful information that is sensitive and that could have consequences if revealed, avoiding a topic is more like escapism and denial. Certain topics may be avoided or even taboo within the family context. Self-censorship can occur within the family in that certain topics are off limits (Roded & Raviv, 2017). For instance, in some families, children cannot ask about sexual matters, and, typically, sex and relationship education will not occur on the home front. According to Segrin and Flora (2011, p. 63),

> Research on family secrets and topic avoidance has largely revolved around the analysis of risks and benefits in revealing information. Common questions in these analyses ask how the keeping or revealing of information relates to relationship protection, self protection, other protection, or a lack of closeness in the relationship.

Clearly some topics can create collateral damage if they are talked about or aired in the family context, and the decision may be that avoiding these potential pitfalls is preferable to being congruent and putting the topic on the table for discussion. Sometimes, family members may have vastly opposing points of view, for instance concerning politics, religion, moral conscience, and the like. Because the family peace is being protected, parties may agree to disagree or simply avoid the potentially inflammable subject matter (Roded & Raviv, 2017).

In therapeutic interventions after extramarital affairs, the parties may agree to avoid mentioning the time before the reconciliation, when betrayal occurred, because returning to this family history would prove too destructive for the fragile new relationship to manage (Brown, 2013). When it becomes necessary to revisit these difficult facts and times, it may be necessary to do so in a formal therapeutic context so that there is professional damage control and management. If couples vent and question, demanding details that will only be hurtful, there may be a therapeutic indication for selective topic avoidance, which will serve as a form of cease-fire. The partners who are trying to put together the pieces of the marriage may be unable to deal with the entire truth, so it may not be a constructive outcome to go to that place (Romo, 2015). Clearly, the specific context and indications of each case may be different, and the therapist would follow an approach that is suitable for best outcomes. It may differ from case to case.

> **"Stories can both reveal and hide information."**
>
> Segrin and Flora (2011, p. 61)

Authentic Insight

Making the Invisible Visible

In an authentic tale of divided loyalties, a young woman discovers that virtually everything she had thought about her parent's marriage was inaccurate. She tries to unravel the fabric of the past, to get to the bottom of it, but in doing so, she also risks disturbing her present. That is one of the prices to pay as a secret moves out of the shadows and is no longer a secret. What becomes apparent can never be moved back to invisibility.

The bottom line is that she discovered she had been born out of wedlock, and there was plenty of documentation in the paper trail to prove it. This discovery led her to question her relationships with her siblings, who were both older and younger than she was. Human curiosity being what it is, she found her inner detective to track down what might have happened in her parents' marriage. It turns out the parents divorced during a time of civil war, as they felt stigmatized because of their opposing alliances and wanted to make a public statement concerning who supported whom, who sided with which party (Roded & Raviv, 2017).

As the war played out and progressed on a macrosystemic level, it also precipitated a microsystemic war on the home front. This family felt very seriously about its external allegiances, and the war became very personal to family members; it fragmented this particular family system. When that devastating war ended, the family was reunited and had two more children. The parents found a way of reconciling their differences and eventually married (they had not been legally married before but had lived together as common-law man and wife). For the child born during the war, her birth certificate was the explanation and proof of a much wider rift that had taken place in her family of origin, and between her parents.

The personal papers to which this woman gained access triggered a series of memories and connections. But talking to her siblings, especially the older ones, enabled her to piece together, from their combined memories, an image of their father as both a conflicted soldier and a family man with divided loyalties. The combined sibling memories extended beyond the personal domain to bring in cultural, social, and economic factors that were precipitated and maintained by history and even by the tragedy of a major war (Kuhn, 2002, p. 5). In this case, the public historical events intersected with intensely private family matters, which, on the one hand, fragmented the family and, on the other hand, reunited it during peaceful postwar times. Kuhn (2002, p. 6) describes this process poetically:

> **"As the veils of forgetfulness are drawn aside, layer upon layer of meaning and association peel away; revealing not ultimate truth, but greater knowledge."**

Secrets and Family Challenges

Historic underpinnings. In Victorian times, a family went to great lengths to conceal the fact that a child born outside of the family had been welcomed into the family circle. The norm at that time was never to disclose birth parents, and the process of adoption was a closely guarded secret.

Deborah Cohen (2014), in her book *Family Secrets: The Things We Tried to Hide*, describes a type of family secret that once concealed heartbreak mixed with shame: the birth of a child with special needs. The child would be hidden from view in the home, or if a family could afford it, the child did not stay at home. Instead it was fostered outside the parental home. Parents might visit once a year in a shroud of secrecy. The first home serving children with Down's syndrome was established by Dr. John Langdon Down, the physician who first described the syndrome in the 1860s. The home, located at Normansfield near Teddington, outside London, is currently a museum and headquarters of the Down's Syndrome Association (UK).

Mental illness was also considered a serious family secret. This secret had the added complication that, in years to come, family members were unaware of their possible genetic predisposition to particular illnesses, and each family unit had to take on the discovery and management of mental illness as if it were an entirely new occurrence within the family. Secrecy also meant that there was little or no support for the patient or for the extended family dealing with the situation (Cohen, 2013). As one mother of an atypical child reflected,

> **"There were people for whom it was such a blow; they just curled up inside and closed the door to the world."**
>
> Deborah Cohen (2013, p. 114)

The intent of secrets. Secrets fulfill various functions and roles in the dynamics of a family system. Secrets can range from *benevolent* to distinctly *malevolent.* On the benevolent end of the spectrum, we can find harmless surprises, such as a surprise birthday party, or creating a special treat for a family member. Malevolent secrets can range from toxic to outright life-threatening.

Galvin, Braithwaite, and Bylund (2014, pp. 93–94) consolidated some of the research on keeping secrets and identified several reasons for perpetuating secrets. Initially, a **benevolent secret** may be a form of not communicating or not keeping family members in the loop. It can be an extension of privacy, and a particular family may characteristically function in a somewhat disengaged manner, one in which sharing is not highly valued. In families that are fairly outspoken and critical of members, a secret can serve to help a member avoid these mild attacks. Family members may not share information about their dating relationships or friendships, probably fearing that they may be criticized or even ridiculed should this information be made public. In that case, secrecy serves to preserve autonomy. Clearly, this is not the best way of achieving individuation, but families find patterns according to their particular emotional resources. Once this secret is in place, it may be difficult to change the status quo, and the secret then serves to maintain the system in some form of homeostasis. But such a secret tends to lead to family disengagement and to degrees of distrust.

Secrets become more problematic when they are the preferred way of managing situations in the family, as they can polarize different subsections of the family into groups—the group that knows the secret and the group that is excluded (Roded & Ravaiv, 2017). This division also tells us something about the level of trust among different members of that family. The family members that know the secret tend to use this privileged information as a form of bonding and to strengthen their position within the family.

Difficult disclosures. Secrets can take on a toxic quality; they can harm family members. A clear example of this type of **malevolent secret** is keeping quiet about abuse in any form. Abuse can traumatize victims both emotionally and physically, and, generally, there is a duty to inform others about and to interrupt harmful victimization. Secrets in the dangerous category include those that could precipitate harming and self-harming behavior. If a threat to commit suicide or engage in self-harming behavior of any kind is held captive by the threat that opening up this secret will precipitate an even worse outcome, we are dealing with a potentially explosive situation, one best handled by authorities and trained professionals.

Secrets can be maintained for fear of judgment. Many a teen pregnancy is kept secret during the early months for fear of parental wrath. Teenagers dealing with sexual identity issues may find it difficult to disclose their sexual orientation, even to trusted and close family members. They may have already come out in their group of like-minded friends but are hesitant to disclose themselves to family and fearful of parental or sibling rejection. The Family Acceptance Project® under the auspices of San Francisco State University has been honored for its work in suicide prevention as it relates to supporting youth who identify as LGBT and the parents of these young people.

Secrets and insularity. Another difficult disclosure pertains to health and illness. A person may be aware of a life-threatening illness but be reluctant to make this knowledge public in the context of his or her family. A powerful example of this type of situation is declaring HIV status to family and to select others (Baker, 2012). As long as information is completely secret, the person concerned cannot access support, and the secret can increase that person's sense of insularity. Secrets can also touch on conventions held by the family. People may fear that not conforming to family expectations will mean being rejected or even ostracized (Fielden, Chapman, & Cadell, 2011). In that case, keeping the secret is a matter of maintaining one's place within the family system (Segrin & Flora, 2011, p. 63).

Ongoing and destructive secrets have the power of poisoning the family atmosphere, destroying any hope of cohesion between family members. Additionally, threats that demand continued secrecy are often suspect, as they may be maintaining a pathological and abusive system. Initiatives to address domestic violence may try to provide the victim with a safe opportunity to report the crime. In most routine wellness exams in hospital and medical practitioner contexts, the patient is asked whether he or she is subject to any form of abuse for which intervention is required. Ultimately, secrets can be a form of trying to maintain a position of power; for instance, the abuser demands secrecy so that the behavior can continue unreported. In therapeutic contexts, it is wise to try to understand the role and function of the family secret and, in that light, to determine the nature of an intervention.

Revealing secrets. Whether a secret will be disclosed or not may also depend on the alliances in the family system. Sometimes, the act of revelation is an attempt at gaining or maintaining power. Revealing a secret, especially when one has promised to keep it, may be an act of defiance, betrayal, or even revenge. Disclosure of a family secret will always shift the dynamics of that particular family system. There is always some level of turbulence attached to disclosure, and the family, after the initial shock, will have to explore ways of rearranging itself and, ultimately, new ways of functioning. Disclosure can have beneficial effects, as well, in that family members can be more congruent and mutually supportive once the truth is out. Nevertheless, the nature and intent of a particular secret will determine the path of the outcome of its disclosure.

Sometimes, families go through periods of severe stress and very difficult transition. At these times, a mutually supportive family would get closer and communicate more in order to help members. But not all families have these resources at hand. During difficult times, keeping a secret may seem like an easy way to avoid confrontation or the destabilization of the family system. Sometimes, then, secrets originate at these exact stress points as family members attempt to make the situation more manageable.

Betrayal. Betrayal is a multifaceted event associated with complex emotions. In essence, it means that the outcome is different from what one had anticipated and hoped for. Betrayal implies being abandoned or sold out. It is an act that does not consider the implications for the victim (Akerstrom, 2017). It is also a way of breaking trust and damaging a relationship. Betrayal carries with it the risk of having permanent effects and doing lasting damage. In committed relationships such as marriages, betrayal of the spouse or partner sends a message that something or someone outside that primary commitment was regarded as more important, so the partner was sold out or betrayed (Agllias & Gray, 2013). Betrayals can lead to distrust and divorce. They have the ability to change everything, and once the truth—or untruth, depending on how one looks at it—is revealed, a perception shift occurs (Agllias, 2016).

Betrayal has the power of shifting the balance and changing everything one has taken for granted. In many ways, betrayal is the opposite of trust (Butler et al., 2010). Trust is a quality that has to be earned. By behaving in a trustworthy manner, we display those qualities that elicit trust. If we do not work at defending that core of commitment toward truth and intimacy in a relationship, we are also expressing our lack of investment.

Authentic Insight

Family Privacy: The Decision to Disclose

Communication scholars have long studied how comfortable (or uncomfortable) people are made by uncertainty. The uncertainty reduction theory of Berger and Calabrese (1975) suggests that the experience of uncertainty generates discomfort for human beings. The theory argues that, depending on several variables connected to one's motivation to reduce uncertainty, an individual will use particular strategies to reduce or eliminate as much uncertainty as possible. However, there are exceptions to this. In some situations, individuals are actually made *less* comfortable by the thought of gaining more clarity. For example, some people would prefer not to be faced with the reality of either a partner's infidelity or a potentially life-threatening health diagnosis.

The same can be true of family disclosures. When a family member experiences discomfort because of a perception of uncertainty, that person may choose to seek out answers through direct questioning, through indirect information seeking, or through negative and circuitous methods. If an individual's level of discomfort begins to *increase* due to the information gained, that person may decide to stop or postpone actions that could continue to reduce this uncertainty.

As an example, I might decide not to pursue unsettling information about a beloved family member that would tarnish my perception of that individual, especially if we share a close relationship. Additionally, saving face may be more important than confronting information threatening to one's own sense of self (Goffman, 1955) or to the reputation, or face, of a close family member. It could also be difficult to accept information that threatens the dignity of the family as a whole. The decision of whether to reduce uncertainty comes down simply to an estimation of costs and rewards (i.e., whether the reward of gaining more certainty or the information one seeks will ultimately result in more comfort). This assessment is affected by one's personal capacity for uncertainty and also, in this context, greatly affected by one's sense of maintaining familial relationships or face negotiation.

Ashley J. George, PhD, is an assistant professor of communication studies.

Intergenerational Trauma

Survivors from World War I and II may find it exceptionally difficult to revisit their painful and traumatizing memories. One way of managing what can often be post-traumatic stress is to avoid any reference to the traumatizing topic. The offspring of war veterans are often faced with a silent generation; in fact, war and everything related to that war can become taboo subjects. This intergenerational silence is typically broken by the grandchildren, who have sufficient distance to explore difficult topics without direct painful impact. This pattern has been seen in the authorship of literature dealing with the great wars. A significant amount of research and related publications have been written by those who are two or more generations removed from the trauma caused by these wars.

Any major conflict significantly affects at least three generations. The parents (and living grandparents) of the soldiers being deployed form the oldest generation affected by war. The middle generation is formed by the soldiers themselves and their partners or spouses (Zerach et al., 2016). The youngest generation is comprised of the children of the deployed, who fear for the lives of their parents. They have to deal with the potential of an injured and traumatized parent or the possibility of losing a parent (Nagata, Kim, & Nguyen, 2015).

Similarly, families who have suffered catastrophic losses and severe extended trauma might possibly display intergenerational trauma as a result of the immense suffering and stress triggered by inhumane situations. Bowers and Yehuda (2016) explore the biological, sociological, and psychological processes that transmit this trauma between generations:

> Parental stress-mediated effects in offspring could be explained by genetics or social learning theory. Alternatively, biological variations stemming from stress exposure in parents could more directly have an impact on offspring, a concept we refer to here as "intergenerational transmission" via changes to gametes and the gestational uterine environment. We further extend this definition to include the transmission of stress to offspring via early postnatal care. (p. 232)

Bowers and Yehuda (2016) maintain that complex interactional factors are at work. **Intergenerational transmission** has been studied across situations, cultures, species, and trauma types, as well as in relation to various psychiatric disorders. Lengthy exposure to stress is thought possibly to precipitate epigenetic changes in the parental biological systems. These may affect gene expression in future offspring (Yehuda & Bierer, 2009, as cited in Bowers & Yehuda, 2016, p. 232). This area of research is on the cutting edge, and the collective findings will probably point toward several hypotheses.

Red poppies have become the memorial symbol for World War I and II—a symbol inspired by the poem "In Flanders Fields," written by Canadian John McCrae. The poem describes the soldiers' graves, covered with red poppies, and the battlefields in Flanders, a region of Belgium.

Source: © iStock.com/CraigRJD.

War of Words, War of Silence

The war of words and the war of silence can be equally damaging in the context of relationships. As much as we would like communication to facilitate good outcomes, that same powerful tool can become a weapon of hostility.

Authentic Insight

Family Secrets, Family Pain

When I found out that things are not all they appear to be, it was the beginning of the unraveling of a part of the tapestry of my life. My mother's house contained many secrets, most not disclosed to us as children. Through the years, they inadvertently became visible. But don't let me get ahead of myself.

Our house leaned into the hillside. It had a long red, waxed, polished stairway leading to the front door. On rainy days, these stairs transformed into a treacherous slide. In the garden was a willow tree that had been grown from a single branch. Over the years, it dominated the front lawn. The yard was edged by a row of pine trees in varying heights, each a remembrance of a Christmas past. There was a sheltered little courtyard behind the kitchen door. Every morning, the sun would turn this forgotten spot into a sunny retreat, even though the rest of the house was cold.

In the house there was a hidden room; and it contained shadows of the past. The room with the secrets was tucked under the house—at the end of a dark, narrow corridor, at basement level. It had been intended as a storage room, but here my family had stashed the unwanted leftovers of their lives, the things they chose not to remember. These were the objects and memories of a sacrificial period of their lives, filled with heartache and separation. They did not want the reminders intruding into their new life; yet they could not discard what had scarred them and become part of their souls.

My brother and I knew the unspoken importance of this room. On days when we knew our parents had gone to town and were definitely nowhere in sight, we would unlock the mysterious door and start our treasure hunt. I can still feel that room: the clammy dankness, the sense of dread and borrowed time. The windows were small and high to block any outside view. There was a trunk girdled with wooden slats; it had been carried onto a steamer to the New World. A disconnected oil furnace with tiny glass panes, the kind one would expect to find in a Scandinavian farmstead, filled up the center area. And then there were the boxes, containing guarded and discarded secrets of someone's past.

The old trunk drew us like moths to a flame. It was like Pandora's box; we had no idea what would fly out from underneath the creaky lid. Some of the things we found made no sense to us as 8- and 11-year-olds—we pieced them together thirty years later. With the objects also came the burden of lost innocence. We joined the circle in a family secret that we couldn't fully understand, but that we instinctively knew had great emotional weight. We lacked the narrative to unlock the clues. We were protected by our childlike worlds that would not allow us to understand the weight of the objects.

Inventory of Trunk #1:

One pair of men's leather uniform boots, black

One shoebox filled with small 2×2 inch photographs with serrated edges, black and white

One military cap, insignias unknown

One large map with red lines retracing someone's steps

One day we were discovered in the room. My father beat us with anger disproportionate to our trespass. After that, the key was nowhere to be found. My brother and I could only piece together the threads when we were much older. Surely our parents tried to shelter us from the pain they had experienced; they had tried to launch us into a new environment where our own experiences would find us over a lifetime.

In some ways, I feel as if I have lived two lives, one in childhood and one as a grown-up—two halves that didn't quite make a whole. But then again, looking at it differently, it felt like a life to the power of two, exponentially greater than I had anticipated. With maturity, we gained the compassion to understand that these were remnants of another generation's painful past, of separation over a period of years, of unthinkable sacrifices. The fragments of a family shattered by World War II.

We, as the following generation, would carry only a fraction of the original burden.

"A secret is only a secret because we cannot see or comprehend all it represents."

Clara Gerhardt

The critical positivity ratio. Research by Losada and Heaphy (2004) gained much attention initially as it focused on the so-called critical positivity ratio, but it has been questioned subsequently. Their work seemed to imply that there is a tipping point, a ratio between positive and negative feelings and communications, that distinguishes between the healthy and the unhealthy. In terms of communication, then, the ratio between kind and hurtful words needs to be about 5:1 to be thought of as positive, although being absolute about such ratios is difficult, as so many other factors may be influential, especially context. So for every crushing utterance, about five times as many favorable communications are required to neutralize communication or to balance it out (Zenger & Folkman, 2013). We have to take those ratios with a pinch of salt. Even so, the hurtful words will be remembered or, as folklore states, forgiven but not forgotten.

Hostility. Research concerning criticism and relationship satisfaction has conclusively shown that hostile criticism tends to do harm to relationships and to initiate sequences of negative relationship processes, although it does have the effect of drawing attention to a situation. In one study, women reacted more negatively to hostile communications than did men. These findings have powerful implications for marital communication (Campbell, Renshaw, & Klein, 2017).

In business environments, constructive communication and feedback are crucial in managing the labor force. Poor communication may destroy morale and lead to mismanagement and lower productivity. Good communication, on the other hand, will allow creativity, organizational effectiveness, and efficiency, which will contribute to enhanced outcomes (Bergsieker, Leslie, Constantine, & Fiske, 2012). If communication is negative or hostile, there is a tendency for the person who is receiving it to shut down. In other words, exactly the opposite of the intended outcome is achieved, and instead of exchanging and transmitting ideas in a respectful environment, breakdown of communication is likely to occur. Naturally, the art of negotiation plays into constructive communication as well, as parties participating in a discussion may have differing opinions. Communicating respectfully means finding a bridge to accommodate various opinions. Useful characteristics might include the ability to apologize, to be sensitive to feelings, and to learn the art of conveying constructive criticism in a manner that is not hurtful or damaging.

Psychologists and researchers John and Julie Gottman observed marital interactions in order to identify the sequences of communication that predicted good versus poor outcomes. Couples who negotiated respectfully could bridge their differences constructively. Those who presented with negative content faced less promising outcomes in their relationships. Gottman (1993) identified what he called "The Four Horsemen of the Apocalypse"—four corrosive behaviors that lead to marital breakdown (Olson & Donahey, 2018, p. 156). These hostilities can predict breakdown in communication and in other relationships as well. They can escalate or, in the words of Gottman, "cascade toward . . . dissolution." It seems that there can be a cumulative effect; if we signal hostile actions accompanied by less-than-friendly comments, we rack up a bill of negativity that may prove very difficult to undo (and equally hard for our communication partner to ignore or forget). The four patterns of negative communication are criticism (including complaints), contempt, defensiveness, and stonewalling. See Diagram 7.1.

Victims of hostility. If hostility is acted out as a form of verbal or even physical abuse, the alarm bells should go off. Unfounded hostility and critical communication may be forms of displaying power; they can also be the preferred choices of a very authoritarian person. In authoritarianism, we are dealing with a control issue; someone else's will is subjugated to the dominating personality. Authoritarianism is typically an expression of power, and the authoritarian may prefer to seek victims among the helpless and defenseless. This power seeking would also explain the dynamic of bullying behavior.

DIAGRAM 7.1

These four negative and destructive ways of communicating, dubbed the "Four Horsemen of the Apocalypse" by researcher John Gottman (1993), can escalate; they predict a breakdown in communications and relationships. The intensity of toxicity increases from the left of the diagram to the right.

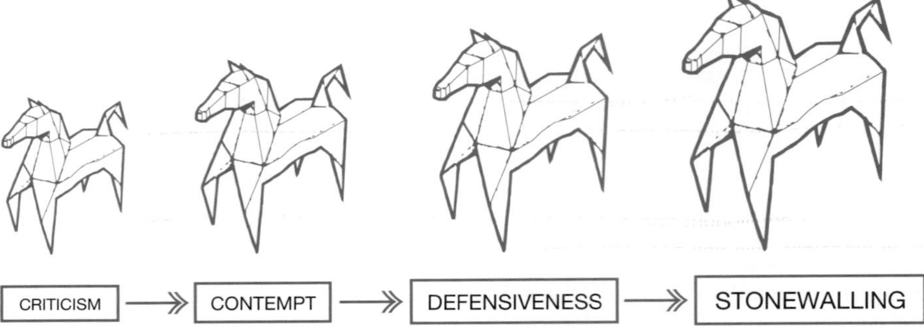

CRITICISM → CONTEMPT → DEFENSIVENESS → STONEWALLING

Sources: Based on Olson and Donahey (2018, p. 156); see Braithwaite, Suter, and Floyd (2018).

In essence, bullies are trying to establish their own power in the relationship; and to assure themselves of power, they seek out victims whom they perceive as being weaker. In that respect, bullying is a cowardly game, as it engages an opponent who is vulnerable and often defenseless (Carter, 2011; Rodkin, 2011). The specific content of the bullying behavior is subjugated to the process of the bullying. The process is rooted in seeking control and domination, often because neither can be found in relationships that are in balance as far as power is concerned (Juvonen & Graham, 2014).

Negative communication can easily fuel gossip and misinformation, and it can travel through the grapevine at alarming speed. An additional problem is that incomplete facts will be padded with hearsay, which makes information less reliable. Out-of-control emotions like anger, hostility, frustration, and disdain can create more damage, becoming wrecking balls destroying the carefully built morale of the work team or family. Nonverbal gestures and facial expressions can convey hostility as well—for example, a threatening posture or the rolling of eyes can signifying disrespect and invalidate the contents of a communication.

Reconciliation and forgiveness. Where there are secrets, rifts, and feuds, there may also come a time for family reconciliation. Whenever old wounds are allowed to heal, it improves the health of the entire family, especially intergenerationally (Hargrave & Zasowski, 2016). It may be difficult to reweave the threads of trustworthiness, but if the family as a unit is regarded as worthwhile to the individual, no effort is too great. Frequently, families may need professional help to walk this difficult path and a range of emotions may either obstruct or facilitate the process.

FOCUS POINT

Secrets fulfill various functions and play a role in the dynamics of a family system. Secrets can range from *benevolent* (beneficial) to distinctly *malevolent* (harmful). Whether a secret will be disclosed or not may depend on the alliances in the family system. The act of revelation can be an attempt to gaining or maintain power. The disclosure of secrets will shift the dynamics of that particular family system. Unfounded hostility and critical communication may be a form of displaying power. Bullying is an example of such behavior. Communicating respectfully intends to accommodate various opinions.

Authentic Insight

Does a Fish Know That It's Wet?

Most of us go through life wearing specialized goggles—a combination of rose-colored glasses and blinders. Even in my peaceful, successful middle-class life, I have managed to avoid the water surrounding me: conflict. I hate conflict. I have always taken the Rodney King approach to conflict: "Why can't we all just get along?"

The quick fix to conflict has been just that—a quick return to equilibrium and a reduction of stress. In hindsight, this has not served me well, and it won't help you in the long run either.

There are five responses to conflict, and they all have to do with how assertive and cooperative you are. I recently realized that my reaction to conflict is to seek "avoidance" or "accommodation." Is this because I value cooperation much more than assertiveness? Culturally, Americans tend to value assertiveness more than cooperation, and the favored response to conflict is a third option, "competition." But competition usually results in a win-lose proposition that isn't optimal for long-term relationships. Aside from the fact that I must have been born in the wrong country, my conflict resolution choices are classic lose-lose propositions. Even meeting another party with a fourth response, "compromising," is seen as less than optimal since both sides have to give up something of value.

At the same time, I've always considered myself a pretty assertive communicator. I've always thought I had a healthy streak of passive-aggressive Machiavellianism in me. That cunning and cleverness would win the day. So, there's more to my avoidance of conflict than a lack of assertiveness.

All five responses to conflict have their place and value. Time, pressure, and circumstances have a great bearing on which response you choose. Another determining variable is trust. The amount of trust you have in the other party will determine if you have A-type conflict (emotional) or C-type conflict (content or issue based). A lack of trust tends to turn all disagreements into emotional conflict resulting in defensiveness and anger.

The more you trust someone, the greater the chance of making the conflict constructive. The goal when you encounter conflict is a fifth response: "collaboration." Here, with equal amounts of trust, assertiveness, and cooperation, opposing parties can work together toward mutual ends, but openness and communication must keep all cards on the table through the process. Collaboration is the only approach that has a chance of resulting in a win-win for both parties.

Obviously, collaboration takes time and trust, and every issue doesn't warrant deliberative problem solving. But too often I have dismissed collaboration as an option. As a fish, I acted like the water wasn't there.

But I'm not a fish. I'm human, and that in turn reflects the idiosyncrasies of human communication.

David Shipley, PhD, is a professor of journalism and mass communication.

GLOBAL GLIMPSE

SO SORRY: APOLOGIES IN MANY VOICES

There are cultural differences in how apologetic people are and in what is regarded as appropriate in a given cultural context. Apologies also tell us something about the power balance between the participating parties. In Asian cultural contexts, it is important to respect "face," also "to save face," by not embarrassing one's family or oneself (Littlejohn, Foss, & Oetzel, 2017, p. 412). Depending on social customs, individuals can go to great lengths not to offend the person to whom they are speaking, and can take blame for situations to maintain the peace and goodwill.

In the following poem by Dale Wisely, a story is created by stringing together numerous apologies from a variety of sources that are acknowledged after the poem. It is also revealing concerning how we interact, the lengths we will go to facilitate relationships, and how vulnerable we can be in the face of the various demands of family, life, and work. An apology can

(Continued)

(Continued)

be an expression of genuine regret, an attempt to undo a hurtful statement.

The many ways to say "sorry" . . .

I owe you an apology for my behavior at work over the past few weeks. Mistakes are often made in the passive voice. I've been coming in late each day, I've been distracted during meetings, and the projects I've been turning in have been full of errors and mistakes that I should've been able to catch. Did you never call? I waited for your call. A series of very bad mistakes were made, and a tragic accident occurred. History is harsh. What is done cannot be undone. I am sorry that I used the word. And it's a shame that I did because the point I was trying to make was in the exact opposite spirit of the word itself. Even now, I find myself speechless and my heart is rent with the utmost grief. How deep is the scar? My work has been shamefully sloppy, and for that, I am very sorry. I've been letting my home life get in the way of my work. We have a new baby, and she has been keeping us busy around the clock. I don't think I can say anything that will help, but I hope through your God, you can forgive me. I'm definitely not the person now that I was then. I was sick, afraid, and looking for love in all the wrong ways. You cannot touch a person. It would be wrong to touch a person. Touching someone is not for me. Plus, our oldest has just started school, and he's having trouble making the transition. I realize that there's no excuse for letting my personal affairs impact my work like this, though. Starting Monday, I promise that things will improve. I hope that you can forgive my poor performance and allow me to prove to you, once more, that your trust is well deserved. We're so sorry if we caused you any pain. The hour of departure has arrived, and we go our ways.

Sources: "So. Central Rain," by R.E.M.; Bill Clinton on the accidental bombing of the Chinese embassy in 1999; Japan's PM Shinzo Abe's 2015 speech on the 70th anniversary of Japan's defeat in WWII; John Mayer apologizing for using an inappropriate word in an interview; "Uncle Albert/Admirable Halsey" by Paul McCartney; Kanye West apologies to Taylor Swift on Twitter; Plato quoting Socrates on his sentencing; Sample email apology from WikiHow; Final words of an executed man in Texas; Reggie Jackson apologizes for profane outburst caught on video.

Dale Wisely, PhD, is a clinical psychologist and former public-school administrator.

Source: Wisely (2016, March).

Certain professions have detailed guidelines concerning privacy boundaries and the ethics associated with privileged and confidential information. In psychotherapeutic contexts, the general rule is to respect the confidentiality between a therapist and a client, unless a situation calls for a duty to inform.

Source: © iStock.com/Cecilie_Arcurs.

Professional and Work-Related Communication

Privileged information. Family scientists and the helping professions in general follow actual as well as aspirational guidelines concerning ethical behavior in professional contexts. The intent of these ethical principles is to safeguard the professionalism surrounding the relationship by ensuring that both the client and the therapist are protected because guidelines concerning best ethical practices are in place. Additionally, these safeguard the public in general because licensed professionals are known to be guided by ethical principles and violating these principles can have dire consequences, such as suspension from the profession.

In certain contexts, privacy is respected and the disclosure of privileged information is guided by law and professional codes of ethics, and by what will ensure the well-being of the client, as well as of the professional providing the service or intervention. This private exchange of privileged information could occur in many circumstances, for example, in legal, medical, and psychotherapeutic contexts. Another example would be the confession booth in the Catholic Church, where a person can confess to wrongdoings without fear of reprisal by the legal system. We also find client privilege respected in professions we might not think of as having privacy concerns: for instance, our accountant and banker are both guided by professional rules that limit the disclosure of personal financial information. Persons concerned with the safety of citizens, law enforcement, and many related issues have professional guidelines concerning nondisclosure. Another example would be the locksmith who cannot divulge the location and code of the safe he installed. It is in the professional interests of those in trusted positions that sensitive information is safeguarded.

Boundaries and boundary violations. Certain professions have detailed guidelines concerning privacy boundaries and the ethics within that profession may be tied to whether the material is privileged or not and should be protected as confidential or not. In the psychotherapeutic professions, for instance, the general rule is toward respecting the confidentiality that is created between a therapist and a client. Clear exceptions are if some information needs to be shared with a professional team involved in the treatment process, shared appropriately with a supervisor, or disclosed to medical insurance for billing purposes.

Confidentiality can generally be provided as long as the client is informed at the outset that certain situations may fall beyond the boundaries of privacy. Most important in this category is the duty to protect and the duty to inform. When a client or someone close to the client is suspected of becoming the target of a harmful intention or if clients intend to harm themselves or others, then therapists have a duty to inform. Not only the particular authorities dealing with these types of situation need to be informed but also the intended victim.

In certain situations, privacy and even secrecy may be enforceable by the nature of the profession because it would be an ethical violation to disclose certain privileged information. In a legal context, the distribution of information can be contained by requiring parties to sign nondisclosure clauses. These documents warn the person concerned of the dire consequences attached to disclosing the information, and it becomes a legal obligation to maintain the secret.

If we look at the number of ethical complaints against psychologists that are made to supervisory professional bodies, most address boundary violation concerns or accusations related to the improper handling of confidential information. Clearly, what can and cannot be shared is an important part of many professions and is guided and specified by the ethical guidelines of those professions.

From history, it is clear that privileged information has often been used as a weapon; lives have been lost, personal fortunes destroyed, and the outcome of wars determined by who was holding the cards in terms of privileged information.

"Families hold the key to our history and ultimately to our identity."

Sea Urchin (anonymous blogger) commenting on the book *Second Lives*, by Daniel Alarcon

FOCUS POINT

In certain situations, privacy and even secrecy may be enforceable by the nature of the profession because it would be an ethical violation to disclose certain privileged information. What can and cannot be shared is guided and specified by the ethical guidelines of those professions. The abuse of access to privileged information has been used as a power-control strategy.

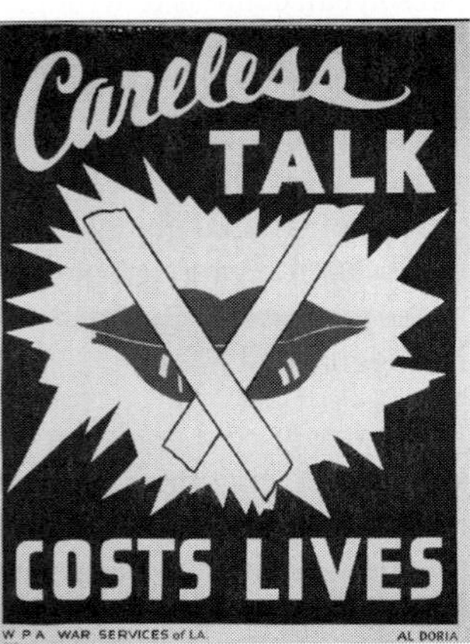

A series of World War II posters, reminding the public to be discreet. History has shown that privileged information has been used as a weapon; lives have been lost, personal fortunes destroyed, and the outcome of wars determined by who knew and shared secrets.

Source: Public domain.

SPOTLIGHT ON THEORIES

Communication Privacy Management (CPM) Theory

Privacy and boundaries lead us to the concept of emotional proximity. Intimacy as enhanced by communication sharing implies that exclusive confidences, information, or experiences are accessible to both parties in the communication relationship, for example, to both partners in a couple. Opening that relationship to outsiders removes the exclusivity of that particular relationship. The privacy boundaries that people draw for themselves and for others are based on a number of guidelines. Privacy is regarded as the antonym or opposite of publicity, but there are gradations on the scale of what should remain private and what can be made public. Communicators will have formed ideas about where these demarcations lie; these will indicate what can be revealed in which contexts and what would be appropriate to share or not to share (Petronio, 2016, 2018).

Communication privacy management (CPM) was originally known as communication boundary management. The word *boundary* reveals a space beyond which we will not trespass; it is invisible, yet it is a barrier to information. Replacing the word boundary with *privacy* gives us a clue as to how relative some of these spaces can be. They can be private because they are very personal; the information could be damaging in the wrong context. Limiting information to only privileged parties can also provide those persons with additional power (Galvin, Braithwaite, & Bylund, 2014).

The CPM theory tries to explain how people manage sensitive material that can influence the power balance or imbalance between parties. The theory is attributed to Sandra Petronio (2016, 2018). Typically, people vary in what they regard as private information, and there is a strong cultural component to this as well. What is private can also slot into the hierarchical system of the family. For instance, in the parent dyad, we may find information that pertains only to the persons sharing that relationship, to those who are included in that particular dyad. It would be inappropriate for that information to be shared with other subsystems of the family. An example would be the personal and private sex lives of the parents. That is something between them and would be inappropriate for the children to know. There is a clear boundary, one demarcated not only by the sensitivity of the material but also by the participants who may be sharing that privileged information.

The communication privacy management theory argues that when people disclose privileged or private information, they also try to control access to it. If information is regarded as having value and imparting power, it makes sense to try to align the persons who may have access to this type of information. Typically, there will be a management system directing who can access what, and it may be based on a system of rules. People may also differ in what they regard as private or not.

In general contexts, CPM can additionally be influenced by who the recipients are and what the cultural norms dictate. For instance, a teenager may freely share sensitive information concerning illicit drug use with her peers but will go to great lengths to shield her parents from that same information. In this situation, it is appropriate to confide in persons who may be participating in the same kind of behavior or who support and facilitate that behavior (Petronio & Venetis, 2017). On the other hand, any person who is perceived as an authority figure who will make demands concerning following appropriate and healthful behavior may be excluded from the inner circle of confidantes.

Boundary turbulence. To make disclosures in a safe environment may require commitment from both parties. For instance, they may promise each other not to disclose anything to any outsiders. This promise, in itself, affirms their bond, and they become partners in containing the secret. There may be clear rules in place as to what can be disclosed to whom. When there is uncertainty about whether the private material will be honored as being private, the disclosing party may feel unsure and uncomfortable about having to disclose the material. This feeling of discomfort can cause distress and is formally known as "*boundary turbulence*."

There are several rules or principles concerning the process of sharing information with the intent of exerting a protective or controlling barrier. Some of these rules are as follows (Galvin, Braithwaite, & Bylund, 2014):

- Generally, people think and believe that they have a right and are able to control information pertaining to them, information that they consider to be private.
- Persons have personal privacy rules that guide how they may control their personal and private information.
- When private information is shared with another party, it becomes the property of both the parties who share it, and secrecy may be more difficult to negotiate.
- When parties exchange private information, it may be wise to decide beforehand how this information can or cannot be used and whether privacy rules should be put in place.
- When the boundaries are unclear and it becomes tempting for one of the parties to disclose the information, boundary turbulence will probably ensue.

We know that self-disclosure is one way of fostering and developing intimacy in close relationships. The **social penetration theory** of Altman and Taylor (1973) examined to what extent self-disclosure

(Continued)

(Continued)

could be applied to manage relationships. This theory focuses on disclosing information. But after any disclosure there is an important counterpart, namely, managing *privacy*.

When we control and conceal information that is very private or personal, we may do so to protect a vulnerable party. On the other hand, disclosure of information may have several motivators. It may have to do with trying to influence the opinions of others, or what is regarded as the truth may be used to undo a wrong. Then there may be the simple psychological reason of finding relief when a burden is shared. The latter often occurs in good friendships when parties exchange fairly personal information and find relief and resonance if the other person displays either empathy or sympathy.

Interestingly, our lifespan position also influences the size of our privacy sphere. When we are young children, we may have few or no secrets, but the art of keeping things private may be perfected during adolescence. Typically, an adult has the most to keep private whereas the circle decreases with age and the elderly may have fewer areas of privacy to protect.

How privacy is managed has several other important criteria:

- *Cultural differences.* There may be strong cultural guidelines concerning privacy boundaries. For instance, Americans may be more open than Germans or Asians in disclosing personal information.
- *Gender differences.* The stereotype is that women are socialized to disclose more than men, but this generalization has to be adjusted depending on the particular context. In a social situation with other women, this may be so, but in work contexts there are probably fewer discernable differences as the boundaries of disclosure are laid down by guiding ethical principles.
- *Contextual differences.* When shared information can lead to greater social cohesion or even friendship, then appropriate self-disclosure would be acceptable. On the other hand, not getting close to persons and withholding information from them sends a clear message concerning the nature of that particular relationship.
- *Motivation for disclosure.* Self-disclosure may require reciprocal disclosure. This may ring true in informal and social relationships but may not be the case in a formal psychotherapeutic relationship.
- *Risk-benefit ratio.* Each disclosure is accompanied by a risk assessment, whether on a conscious or subconscious level. Benefits may include strengthening a relationship, and disadvantages may include losing control over sensitive information that might be used as a weapon.

This theory of communication privacy management finds strong application in family communication. It may govern the rules that parents set for their children, and it may define relationships. It also has application in work environments, in health care, and, increasingly, in the social media world where privacy concerns are coming under the magnifying glass.

Some related concepts also deal with aspects of disclosure and privacy:

- *Social penetration.* Disclosure can contribute to greater closeness and greater investment in a friendship or relationship. It may also imply that both parties involved co-own the boundaries concerning privacy.
- *Coordinated management of meaning.* When several parties decide to pool their information, they might be able to put together or decipher a greater picture and gain insight. As a group, therefore, the parties manage the meaning of what has been disclosed and discovered. This type of coordinated management of meaning would have occurred in the Enigma team, whose members collaborated during World War II in a major deciphering effort.
- *Expectancy violations.* When we work in close proximity or live in close quarters, violating privacy boundaries may be easier because the physical proximity can create a sense of familiarity that could facilitate self-disclosure. Whether constructive or destructive outcomes result depends on context. An extreme example of a destructive outcome might be an informant who creates a sense of

false intimacy in order to gain access to valuable and privileged information. Individuals display personal reactions in response to unexpected violations of social norms, especially those related to personal space and personal distance.

In the helping professions and in the family-related professions, we are bound to ethical guidelines and principles that mandate us to use sensitive material constructively. Two principles should guide us: *First of all, do no harm*, and *act in the best interest of the client*.

FOCUS POINT

Privacy and boundaries concern emotional proximity. Intimacy as enhanced by sharing implies that exclusive confidences, information, or experiences are accessible to parties participating in the communication relationship. The theory of communication privacy management (CPM) finds strong application in family communication. It may govern the rules that parents set for their children, and it may define relationships. CPM also has application in work environments, in health care, and, increasingly, in the world of social media.

In a Nutshell

- Communication privacy management (CPM) was originally known as communication boundary management.
- The CPM theory tries to explain how people manage sensitive material that can influence the power balance or imbalance between parties.
- *Boundary* denotes a border beyond which we will not trespass; it is invisible yet a barrier to information.
- Self-disclosure is one way of fostering and developing intimacy in close relationships.
- Controlling and concealing private information can be done to protect a vulnerable party.
- Persons have personal privacy rules guiding their communication.
- When private information is shared with another party, it becomes the property of both the parties who share it, and secrecy may be more difficult to negotiate.

CHAPTER FOCUS POINTS

Family Scripts

- The family script may define the unique way a family manages content and information. Some families have cues that act as codes, signaling to other members.
- Scripts in the family of origin can influence the children from that family into adulthood and set the tone for their own families of creation. Family scripts can also be guided by cultural norms.
- Our families can contribute to our sense of confidence in conversations.

The Power of Disinformation

- Communication can lead us astray by providing disinformation or incorrect facts. The motives can be various, as well as devious.

- Disinformation has to do with power—maintaining it, regaining it, or disempowering the opponent.
- Gaslighting weakens one person while strengthening the one who is spreading the misinformation. This form of disinformation erodes a person's perception of the world.
- There is power in not disclosing information to everybody in a network. A person who is willfully kept out of the communication loop can be disempowered.
- Stonewalling, which is defined as blocking all communication with an individual, actually sends a number of negative messages.

Family Secrets

- Secrets fulfill various functions and play a role in the dynamics of a family system. Secrets can range from *benevolent* (beneficial) to distinctly *malevolent* (harmful).
- Whether a secret will be disclosed or not may depend on the alliances in the family system. The act of revelation can be an attempt to gain or maintain power. The disclosure of secrets will shift the dynamics of that particular family system.
- Unfounded hostility and critical communication may be forms of displaying power. Bullying is an example of such behavior.
- Communicating respectfully intends to accommodate various opinions.

Professional and Work-Related Communication

- In certain situations, privacy and even secrecy may be enforceable by the nature of the profession because it would be an ethical violation to disclose certain privileged information.
- What can and cannot be shared is guided and specified by the ethical guidelines of those professions.
- The abuse of access to privileged information has been used as a power-control strategy.

Spotlight on Theories: Communication Privacy Management (CPM) Theory

- Privacy and boundaries concern emotional proximity. Intimacy as enhanced by sharing implies that exclusive confidences, information, or experiences are accessible to parties participating in the communication relationship.
- The theory of communication privacy management (CPM) finds strong application in family communication. It may govern the rules that parents set for their children, and it may define relationships.
- CPM also has application in work environments, in health care, and, increasingly, in the world of social media.

CHAPTER 8

Changing Communication Patterns

Learning Outcomes

After studying this chapter, you should be able to

1. Describe how the *digital world* impacts various aspects of family life and communication.
2. Summarize how screen time influences *child development*.
3. Consider the implications of digital communications for *family dynamics*.
4. Explain the *interacting factors* that influence communication.
5. Analyze *family communication pattern theory*, and identify the four family communication patterns.

Families in a Digital World

Every couple of decades, the tempo of our lives seems to speed up by a notch or two. My great-grandparents wrote diaries and long letters and looked forward to weekly social gatherings to be part of a community. Communication for this generation was predominantly face to face or possibly by way of the hand-delivered note. In my great-grandmother's day, there were no communication facilitators: no phones, no radios, no television—no entertainment channeled into their living room via a little black and white television screen. To while away the evening hours, they would play cards, read books, make music, and have earnest conversations. Today, the family that creates its own music is rare; it is more likely that one family member or another will make music happen with a telling command to a speaker-like device in the room—"I'd like to hear some relaxing music!"—and from somewhere "in the cloud," the correct selection is streamed into the home. Adrian Ward (2013), a researcher focusing on the influences exerted by a digitally connected world, poetically describes the cognitive challenges of this changing world:

> We are creatures of flesh and blood, living in a world of bits and bytes—a world shaped by the Internet. With the simple touch of a button or swipe of a finger, we can instantaneously access vast amounts of information. . . . A few more keystrokes, and we can interact with friends 10 time zones away. . . . We know there was a time when encyclopedias represented the pinnacle of information storage and communicating with faraway friends required a trip to the post office . . . but such a time feels far removed from the present moment. (p. 341)

Technology changing our communication patterns

Digitally Connected

My first email, which I received in the early nineties, was a memorable event. A colleague announced that he would contact me by email but told me that I needed an email address—at the time, universities were early adopters of this new technology. The university technician guided me; the thought of receiving communication on a computer was astonishing. To this day, I remember the contents of that very first email: it was about magnolia trees, which bloomed in the South of the United States at that time of year.

Within months, email was no longer a novelty. We accessed it via telephone lines, using a modem with a distinct ringtone. Movies featured email communication as a prominent part of the plot. *You've Got Mail* (1998) was one of them; the storyline concerned an online romance. A digital era was beginning to replace the time in which communication and lifestyle moved at a slower face-to-face pace. As the innovations took over, deadlines shortened to become immediate. The excuse of "the check is in the mail" became redundant, as most things, including payments, could be transmitted instantaneously. There was no room to decompress or to extend time. Many transactions happened in real-time; there was hardly a gap between sending and receiving.

In an interview, researcher Adrian Ward states that the iPhone has been around for a decade plus and the Internet for about three decades (Meyer, 2017). These technologies have become so integral to daily tasks that we feel deprived without our electronic crutches. They have the potential to add positive as well as negative dimensions to our lives using this technology. We pretend to be in denial that our smartphones and the Internet can exacerbate our addictive tendencies.

If the family is viewed as a social system, communication takes place between all parties looped into that particular system. When social media is being treated as an active party that shares many of these communications, it considerably changes the dynamic within the family system. By allowing social media access to the privileged communications of a family, we open a window, allowing an entire private world to be seen by prying and anonymous eyes. If those who see posts share these with their friends, and these friends in turn share them several times more, the number of persons who can have access to the communication increases exponentially. When a message is shared repeatedly and widely enough, it can potentially reach millions of viewers. This sharing blurs the lines between privileged, personal information and public information.

In the early days of the Internet, people shared very personal items on the web. As users gained greater awareness of the risks associated with this sort of sharing, information has been edited, even curated, to a level of inauthenticity that makes online communications appear hollow and mass produced, at times. Being too public, social media have compromised those aspects of personal communication that are reserved for the privacy of a particular friendship or personal relationship.

Paradoxically, the family became less as well as more connected. Importantly, the nature of communication and connections changed. Communication devices aided communication, and smartphones allowed us to reach family members instantaneously by text or by video messaging. As much as this connected us, it also meant that our face-to-face interactions, those in which we are in the same place at the same time, decreased.

Children and digital content. Children need minimal exposure to succumb to the addictive lures of electronic entertainment. Relationships require time and investment: it is the dynamic of availability that, in turn, fosters healthy family relationships and mindful engagement. There is no shortcut, as quantity time is required to provide a quality relationship. No electronic screen should substitute for ongoing parental involvement. If digital technology is used, it should be an additional way of connecting, it should occur in the appropriate context, and it should be supervised by a responsible adult.

Postmillennial children and adolescents are very familiar with using the web for entertainment as well as communication. If an entertainment website provides social interaction, it also serves as a social media site; numerous such sites are currently available, including gaming sites. Not all are desirable for children and adolescents. Ideally, parents should ensure that their children are not exposed to inappropriate content (O'Keeffe & Clarke-Pearson, 2011). The online social platforms can have an addictive quality in that they spark our curiosity concerning our friends and acquaintances, and we return repeatedly for daily or even hourly updates.

True concern is appropriate if these electronic communications become a substitute for face-to-face communication. It is like replacing bread with candy floss. Bread is nurturing and part of our staple diet; candy floss is sweet and tempting, but it does not still hunger. Teenagers who rely on social media for a social life can get pulled into group comparisons, online competition, and a fake reality where everybody posts only their photoshopped selfies and edited content. It may look like real life, but it isn't; it vanishes like candy floss on the tongue and does not fulfill the need for solid and authentic friendships and communications. The negative effects in terms of self-concept and competitiveness can lead to what has been labeled *Facebook depression* (O'Keeffe & Clarke-Pearson, 2011). This refers to the negative self-image accompanied by depression that adolescents develop when they use a social platform as a point of comparison. Sophie Elmhirst (2019) provides an apt description of a millennial's digitally connected world and how it affects the self-perceptions and expectations of this generation:

> If you grow up online, you know what it is to be watched and how it feels to be heard, and how the more you are watched and heard, the more you want and need to be. Things don't feel real until they're shared or valid until you know what other people think about them. Your self becomes something to be recorded, posted, judged and, possibly, hopefully, monetised. You can be a brand, and maybe you should be. Deep in the guts of Instagram, there's a sense of well-meaning frenzy—a race to prove that you feel and admire and suffer and love more than anyone else. And then there's the unspoken quid pro quo: you like me and I like you.

This frenzied race to create and share and perhaps monetize an image of self can be risky on its own, and it sometimes pushes people toward even more risky sharing. Other risky online behavior includes sexting and viewing websites with inappropriate content, specifically with content pertaining to violence and sexuality. Cyberbullying has deservedly gained attention as a cause of concern and has resulted in several teenage deaths. Bullies tend to hide behind masks of anonymity. Cyber trolling, which aims vicious and destructive remarks at a victim, is also a worry.

Importantly, parents need to have a relationship of trust with their child or teenager, so that they can become confidantes if their child becomes a target of something out of the ordinary or a victim of negative online behavior. Some children and teens are so fearful of admitting that they have been victimized that they continue to meet the demands of the blackmailer, too afraid to confide in anyone.

Social media have been used by immigrant families to facilitate assimilation into the new culture. If immigrant teens spend excessive time immersed in online activities, on the other hand, it can signal that they are missing out on real-life friendships (Elias & Lemish, 2008). Even families using social media in

FOCUS POINT

Postmillennial children and adolescents are very familiar with the web for entertainment as well as communication. If a website provides social interaction, it serves as a social media site; numerous such sites are currently available. True concern is appropriate if electronic communications replace face-to-face communication, precipitate self-image anxieties, or involve online bullying. Cyber trolling, which aims vicious and destructive remarks at victims, is also problematic.

constructive ways have to ensure that the digital world does not become a substitute for all those shared family events during which face-to-face time strengthens bonds between family members—the regular family meals and celebrations, family reunions, bedtime stories, or picnics in the park.

Digitally connected. There are numerous times when this outside network can work to our advantage: for example, getting help online, when the 911 dispatcher talks us through an emergency or the remote physician helps the on-site doctor find a suitable intervention; learning online, when classrooms across geographical boundaries are electronically connected; and keeping in touch with family online, when family members are scattered across the globe. Digital technology facilitates many other helpful and productive communications as well. An entire generation can work remotely, thanks to connected communication networks. Clearly, there are great advantages, as long as we are aware of the challenges and our limited ability to deal simultaneously with multiple communication channels. As one researcher succinctly states,

> When old cognitive tendencies and new technologies meet—when the world of flesh and blood collides with the world of bits and bytes—the Internet may act as a "supernormal stimulus," hijacking preexisting cognitive tendencies and creating novel outcomes. (Ward, 2013, p. 341)

The Dynamics of a Digital World

Alternating between tasks. Cell phones have a way of reaching into our minds to siphon our attention surreptitiously and stealthily. We think we can focus on our physically present conversation partner; we place our cell phone face down—we may even silence it. But if it vibrates, it beckons us, and most of us cannot resist. We will glance at it, no matter where or with whom we are. Every time we succumb to that digital temptation, we break the communication loop of our current conversation; it's as if we step outside the room for a fraction of a minute.

Students in class toggle backward and forward between listening to the professor and glancing at their cell phones. At the risk of sounding old-fashioned, this seems like trying to dance with two partners—this one, then that one. It's surprising that neither party in the system complains. Would we tolerate it if we knew that the pilot flying our plane was also playing Fortnite? How about divided attention during surgery and intricate operations? Or the person controlling a crane or driving a car with a child in the backseat—should that person be reading at the same time? We know that simultaneously driving and texting is not safe; our human brains are not wired to multitask in this manner. What happens instead is more like alternating between tasks—not doing them simultaneously. Texting while driving reduces our attention span and impairs our ability to react appropriately; yet we persist, probably because the lure of the cell phone is irresistible.

Because our brains are simply not set up to manage this type of multitasking, the quality of our conversation suffers when we try to divide our attention. Imagine having a counseling session with a therapist who repeatedly glances at her phone, or think about trying to talk with a clerk at a checkout counter who is distracted by incoming messages. Whenever we share our attention between two tasks making major cognitive demands, our brains alternate between tasks. They may do this numerous times, which gives us additional mental work and uses extra mental resources. Whatever we like to think we're doing, we pay a mental price when we divide our attention.

Daniel Oppenheimer, a psychologist, found that distraction applied to other areas beyond interaction with cell phones or technology: "Attractive objects draw attention, and it takes mental energy to keep your attention focused when a desirable distractor is nearby" (quoted in Meyer, 2017). For instance, persons on a diet might notice appetizing food, or smokers might be distracted by the availability of cigarettes. The upshot is that your smartphone can distract you even when it is turned off:

> We know that cell phones are highly desirable, and that lots of people are addicted to their phones, so in that sense it's not surprising that having one visible nearby would be a drain on mental resources . . . given the prevalence of phones in modern society, that has important implications. (Oppenheimer, quoted in Meyer, 2017)

"They spend their leisure time staring into their phones."

Snigdha Poonam, *Dreamers: How Young Indians Are Changing the World* (2018)

Brain drain. In a publication with the catchy phrase "brain drain" in the title, Ward, Duke, Gneezy, and Bos (2017) state that our online connectedness encourages and reinforces constant access to people, entertainment, and information. They tested their hypothesis of "brain drain" in two experimental situations and reported on attention span differences between two groups of students taking a memory test. One group of participants left their phones on their desks or in their backpacks, set on silent mode or vibration. The second group of students left their cell phones outside the testing room. Students whose phones were out of the room paid greater attention to the memory tests. Ward et al. (2017) concluded that the mere presence of a cell phone, even on silent mode, was subtly distracting. Students did best when their cell phones were not tempting, when they were placed outside the room. These researchers conclude that

"Cognitive costs are highest for those highest in smart phone dependence."

Ward, Duke, Gneezy, and Bos (2017)

yikes.

Being On Call for Our Smartphones

Calling our names. Smartphones are generally treated as the VIP guests in the room in that they hold our attention and we interrupt other activities to answer to their call. Ward et al. (2017, p. 3) state that certain cues capture our attention virtually immediately, as we are sensitized to them. One such cue is hearing our

Authentic Insight

Letters From the Past

Tidying up the attic at my grandparents' home, I came across a pile of letters, neatly bundled with lavender ribbon. Should I read them (after all they are private)? But as my grandparents had passed away, opening the letters beckoned me toward my own ancestry, and had an intensely personal urgency. The letters spanned the years of my grandparents' immigration to the new country; these letters told the tale of this couple going through the halls of Ellis Island, filled with expectancy and hope. What made their journey somewhat different is that my grandfather went a year ahead of my grandmother. He wanted to find a foothold before the family followed. The letters were numbered; my grandfather used even numbers and my grandmother, odd numbers to mark the sequence of the letters they sent. A letter might take as long as three to four weeks before it reached its destination, crossing the Atlantic between Europe and the New World. They managed that emotional and physical separation without an ongoing and continuous conversation, but at that time it was what it was.

My great-great-great-grandmother Angélique's cookbook from the early 1800s revealed the labor involved in producing a single meal. No electric oven with controlled temperatures was available; instead cooks relied on an open fire and guesswork or experience. One of the recipes contains instructions on how to skin a rabbit. My great-grandmother Angélique Marie, living in the early 1900s, did not have an indoor bathroom. Once a week, a washtub was dragged into the kitchen and filled with hot water, so family members could take their consecutive weekly baths—turn by turn. We take so many aspects of modern living for granted, including running water, controllable indoor temperatures, transport, an abundance of safe and healthy food, and, of course, reliable and virtually instantaneous communication.

My grandmother experienced World Wars I and II. Her life was not filled with the comforts of modern living. The attic space was reserved for storing potatoes and apples throughout the ice-cold winter. Whenever she wanted an apple, she had to pick the blemished ones first, a habit that persisted into postwar years. A fridge was unknown, and the diets were monotonous. The war years were filled with deprivation. Because everybody was in the same boat, families supported each other and shared their hardships as well as their resources.

The family in my great-grandparents' time was closely connected, and the radius of family members' daily movements was much smaller—about five miles in any direction. We easily commute 30 miles plus without blinking. As a child, I took a bus to commute seven miles and then another five city blocks to reach school. We were three youngsters travelling and walking together; my parents were not concerned about us finding our way and trusted in an environment that seemed relatively safer for unaccompanied children. As parents today, we hover and protect, sometimes knowing exactly where each child is through cell phone tracking. Times have changed, as have our concerns about safety and so many other expectations reaching all the corners of our existence.

own name or spotting our name in print. The recognition is instantaneous; we are so alert to it that it jumps out at us. Cell phones are said to have a similar hold over us; they put us on mental standby. What does that do for our ability to pay attention to other things? If our attention is limited (which it is), then it will be affected by these constant interruptions. Even the anticipation of receiving a communication or text can distract us. As Meyer (2017) states,

> If you grow dependent on your smartphone, it becomes a magical device that silently shouts your name at your brain at all times. (Now remember that this magical shouting device is the most popular consumer product ever made. In the developed world, almost everyone owns one of these magical shouting devices and carries it around with them everywhere.)

> **"We are creatures of flesh and blood, living in a world of bits and bytes—a world shaped by the Internet."**
>
> Adrian Ward (2013)

This rare image depicts wigged men drinking beverages while reading papers. Staying in the loop in the seventeenth century meant visiting coffeehouses, reading newspapers, and attending to gossip. The twenty-first-century equivalents in terms of social culture would be visiting coffeehouses (still), getting news from the Internet, and checking social websites and texted gossip.

Source: Public domain.

Dynamics of Content and Context

Much debate has focused on the interaction between quantity and quality time. Some contend that if the quality of the time we spend connecting to others is particularly good it can override deficits in the quantity of time we spend. Pressured parents like to think that even though they are away from children all day, the "quality time" they spend reading a nightly bedtime story will make up for that separation. In reality, the formula is not as simple as quantity versus quality, and there are numerous contextual factors that influence the perception of this ratio. One aspect is the age of the participants in that relationship. To a young child, both concepts, the quality of the time spent and the length of the time separated, may be too abstract to comprehend.

Digitally supporting face-to-face communication. Segrin and Flora (2011, pp. 48–49) summarize a number of studies that examine long-distance relationships and the effect of separation on the quality of those relationships. It would appear that for couples who go into this type of situation knowingly and voluntarily, or alternatively understand the necessity of it, the relationship can be managed. The ongoing thread of past and future shared activities will add to relationship cohesion. As long as there is some form of face-to-face electronic communication to link the two individuals during periods of separation, the quality of the relationship does not appear to be adversely influenced. Some examples of such relationships would be military couples, graduate students pursuing their degrees at different universities, long-distance romances, and couples with international work demands. Expats and immigrants and others who need to live away from home face separation as well.

Relationships can be kept alive and flourishing if there are opportunities for contact and conversation. Modern communication methods—for example, email, FaceTime, cell phones—can build communication bridges that are effective as long as the separation is not indefinite. Another aspect addressed by the same authors is whether shared activities will strengthen relationships. Again, the answer depends on the context. Watching a football game if one party is disinterested is not going to strengthen that relationship. The shared interest, the mutual enthusiasm creates a bond between people participating in a shared activity.

Some parents remark that driving their children to school and attending their sport activities and games are ways of bringing the family closer together. The family that celebrates successes together and offers support during crises *will* strengthen its communication and, in turn, fortify family members' emotional bonds by virtue of these activities.

Conformity. Families can create a particular family climate that demands buy-in by all members; for instance, the group expects members to be like-minded when it comes to values, attitudes, and beliefs. It is quite possible that the dominant figures within the family will influence the younger and more pliable members. Through this influence, used in a constructive manner, families impart values, ethics, and belief systems to their children and socialize them. This socialization, in turn, allows children to find their niche in society, the place where they can meet and understand the rules and demands of that particular context. Parents guide children toward appropriate self-regulation, so their children's behavior is acceptable in social contexts.

When children are exposed to authoritarian parents who demand that they conform to parental standards, including the family's belief system, these children will, in all likelihood, be shaped by these demands and conform. Seguin and Flora (2011, p. 51) summarize several research studies dealing with this topic. It would appear that children who have been in high-conformity environments tend to also conform to peer pressure. When it comes to destructive trends, such as drug use, vaping, swearing, promiscuity, and other risk-taking behavior, we hope that appropriate parental guidelines continue to be a reference point, despite peer influences.

Seguin and Flora (2011, p. 51) quote research on whether the education, employment, and social assets of parents influence the conformity or nonconformity of their children. Parents who act in an individualistic, nonconforming, and creative manner tend to work in environments valuing these qualities, and these parents may be tolerant and encouraging of similar behavior in their offspring. The type of communication patterns that are acceptable in the home environment may be generalized to other situations as well, including work. Parents generally act in the best interests of their own children, and the majority of parents try to socialize their children in ways that will lead to best outcomes.

Communication signals. Families can send signals concerning what is regarded as appropriate or inappropriate communication. Families in which parents model criticism consider this acceptable behavior in the offspring. There is not much guessing as to how these children developed in adulthood. They felt entitled to be critical and judgmental, qualities that contribute little to social contexts. Similarly, if hurtful jokes are the norm and sarcasm and biting jokes are acceptable in the family, the stage may be set for bullying behavior, especially if the potential bully is low on empathy and does not reflect on how a so-called joke at the expense of someone else's feelings may feel to the victim.

Communication and prejudice. Social psychology tells us that prejudice and stereotypes are typically modeled not only by parents but also by the close circle of friends with whom an individual interacts. Prejudice and stereotypes are learned behaviors; as the general opinions of a group of people change and evolve over time, so will the nature of the prejudices and stereotypes. It is especially disconcerting that prejudice stands between congruent and bidirectional conversation. Prejudgment is one of the toxic ways of harming a conversation or communication because the prejudiced person will neither hear nor see the entire spectrum of what is communicated. Biased people tend to foreclose connections and fill in the missing information with preconceived ideas, which may be incorrect.

To promote cultural competence, we need to be alert to what is being communicated and try to prevent prejudice from influencing the quality of communication. To display cultural competence, one has to be open to what the other has to say, willing to hear that person's side of the story. We can learn from each other. Cultural competence does not mean that we have to know everything about another culture; instead, it requires us to be open to the learning opportunity

FOCUS POINT

The world of digital media offers great advantages; computers have irrevocably changed our society and our communications. We may be limited by our inability to juggle multiple communication channels simultaneously. Cell phones put us on mental standby, diverting our attention. Our attention span is affected by constant interruptions. Parents set the tone for what is happening in the home. Digital technology and social media and related communication patterns have the ability to influence family dynamics.

represented by another cultural context. It is valuable and extends both our world and our cultural comfort zones.

It is important to remember that many aspects of communication, especially those related to peer pressure such as the drive to conform or the development of models of behavior, prejudices and stereotypes, or cultural competence, remain the same in the digital world. In fact, social media can enhance the power of one's circle of friends, making the influence of peers on communication even more significant.

Family Rituals in a Digital World

One of the key qualities of emotionally healthy families is that members celebrate and support each other. To do so, they may follow certain rituals that can be influenced by societal and cultural contexts. Jokes about ageing can lend a humorous touch, making significant birthdays easier to manage. These jokes may be acceptable rituals in North America, where roasting someone on the occasion of a 50th birthday is seen as well-intentioned fun. But they would not be in Germany or Japan, where more formality and respect for the elderly are the norms.

Nevertheless, sharing celebratory rituals and offering support during times of hardship stabilize the family unit. Being close during times of joy and sorrow adds strength and resilience to the family unit while also easing any transition, say from adolescence to adulthood or from married man to widower. Besides bringing support, shared celebrations are profoundly protective for participants. Because these gatherings are so important to the health of families, family dynamics are significantly affected if digital media replace or alter long-standing family rituals.

Escapism and distraction. As televisions entered our homes, it set off a domino effect, and other family-related activities changed. Yet another such wave is occurring as our communications and entertainments move to digital platforms and media.

Consider how a child's playtime has changed recently. Playtime with real objects and playmates stimulates and allows expression of the child's creativity while expanding and challenging motor, cognitive, interactive, and communication skills. It addresses several dimensions simultaneously: the physical, the social, the emotional, and the mental. When playtime is replaced by screen time, many of these dimensions are left out. For example, online gaming for teenagers can be a solitary pursuit even if played with online teams. Controlled and appropriate gaming can have a place in the total spectrum of entertainment, but we need to be aware that it also has addictive qualities and can lure loners, especially, into its fantasy world.

Moving into the virtual world. We all must learn to express and manage hostility and anger appropriately. Both tasks require self-regulation and social insight concerning the outcomes and implications of our behaviors. In the fantasy world, highly aggressive games can be played without actual consequence; it is easy to pull a trigger on an imaginary target. If the lines between reality and fantasy fade, the aggression of imaginary game playing can be transferred to real-life social situations. Numerous social tragedies have occurred because teens and adults have brandished guns with neither insight nor training on responsible use in supervised contexts. The real world is treated like a computer game, and the boundaries between fantasy and reality disappear.

Research has addressed major societal concerns linked to online media use and abuse (Bertot, Jaeger, & Hansen, 2012; O'Keeffe & Clarke-Pearson, 2011). One hopes that families will act responsibly and teach children about the dangers of inappropriate weapon use. Acting out hostility may seem like a powerful stance, but indiscriminate and random aggression creates devastation. For adolescents who tend to be loners and socially isolated, becoming immersed in online gaming risks exacerbating the potential of antisocial behavior.

Creativity. Playtime is a time for creativity and exploration. Teenagers and children can explore their worlds somewhat independently and in an age-appropriate manner, which supports taking age-appropriate responsibility in certain contexts. Parental involvement is crucial, as parents who display and model responsible behavior become the role models for their children. Creativity demands uninterrupted time and a place to explore. For instance, artistic creativity requires skill acquisition as well as exposure. To reach a level of proficiency that makes it fun to play an instrument, paint something, dance, write a poem, or otherwise create requires an investment in terms of time and practice.

Creativity needs to be nurtured in order to be expressed; it is difficult for creativity to grow if there is neither time nor encouragement. Excessive participation in the world of social media can draw us into a fantasy world that makes us passive and unmotivated, exactly the opposite from the proactivity required for creativity to blossom. By responding to every alert from a cell phone, we turn our day into an endless chain of interruptions, which is poison to the luxury of uninterrupted and consistent thinking time.

As much as social media has opened and expanded our worlds, allowed us to communicate across continents and cultures, we need to be aware of its addictive quality—it can consume our lives and leave us emotionally empty. It takes self-discipline to harness social media, to use its benefits without being bewitched by its darker side.

One benefit is that the digital world allows us to consolidate our knowledge base through the summation of various sources of knowledge (e.g., *Wikipedia*). According to Wegner and Ward (2013, p. 309), in an article with the catchy title "How Google Is Changing Your Brain," our memories may be affected by online sourcing in that we may find it difficult to distinguish between what we once found online and what constitutes our personal memories. A fusion of information and a blurring of boundaries between various domains may occur, which also subtly influences our personal memories. In another publication, Ward (2013) states that accessing information from the Internet can influence our personal memory banks:

> The Internet is a consistent presence in people's daily lives. As people upload, download, and offload information to and from this cloud mind, the line between people's own minds and the cloud mind of the Internet may become increasingly blurry. (Ward, 2013)

GLOBAL GLIMPSE

DIGITAL WORLDS: JUNK FOOD FOR OUR MINDS

Sitting on the porch enjoying a cup of freshly brewed Earl Grey tea, I was surprised when a bird-swarm settled in our yard: a murmuration. Not hundreds, but thousands of birds were simultaneously twittering at an overwhelming volume:

> It's called a murmuration—the bird dance, an aerial ballet with tens of thousands of starlings, grackles, cowbirds and red-wing blackbirds flying in mass but seemingly with one mind. Watching it can be mesmerizing—it's a twisting, swirling, morphing, shape-shifting living cloud. (Bob Gathany, as quoted in Flanagan, 2017)

My thought was that if just a portion of the voices on the Internet became audible, this would be the noise and attention they generated. I claim no prize for connecting with this thought the concepts of *Twitter* and *tweets,* such aptly chosen names for the electronic chattering, for our new way of voicing a thought, any thought, uncensored and impulsive, and sending it instantaneously into the universe to be retweeted and amplified.

Lured by a digital world. Journalist Snigdha Poonam interviewed dozens of millennials in her home country, India, and their stories form the core of her book *Dreamers: How Young Indians Are Changing Their World and Yours* (2018). India's population has nearly hit the billion mark, a great number accompanied by even greater challenges. The majority of the population is under the age of 25, and these youngsters are ensnared by the digital world. They are influenced by the lure of materialism and sensationalism and are making it their business to get a share of the pie. Quick rewards, no matter how achieved or which rules are broken—these end goals can supersede "nuisance" variables such as truth, morals, and ethics. Who cares that the person clicking is uninformed and curious enough to take the bait. The back cover of Poonam's book describes this phenomenon:

> In a country that is increasingly characterized by ambition and crushing limitations, this is a generation that cannot—and will not—be defined on anything but their own terms. They are wealth-chasers, hucksters, and fame-hunters, desperate to escape their narrow prospects. They are the dreamers. . . . From dubious entrepreneurs to political aspirants, from starstruck strivers to masterly swindlers, these are the clickbaiters who create viral content for Facebook and the Internet scammers who stalk you at home. (Poonam, 2018)

The battle of the click. Poonam visited the headquarters of a company churning out viral content for various media platforms. It is all about how many clicks and likes creators of content can ratchet up; they live and breathe for the split-second attention span of some global reader who is reeled in by curiosity, clicks on their stories, and swallows the half-truths they create. The game is on. Will the bait on the hook attract the indiscriminating victim? The game is aptly called "clickbait." There are some tricks to the trade. In this particular company, the content creators are all young with minimal higher education; they follow their gut feeling concerning what is sensational, what speaks to our feelings of shame, what attracts our secret curiosity, what appeals to the voyeurism of the online audience.

Reeling us in. They use words with high emotional content, words not suitable to be printed on this page. They generate lists of make-believe problem solvers, such as "Five things to melt belly fat"—all is fair game in the battle for the click. One interviewee in Poonam's book describes himself as not displaying the dedication to succeed at programming. Consequently, he turned to the Internet and began developing content, and this opened a world of possibilities for him. His interest became an obsession but also brought financial rewards. At the Delhi headquarters of some sensational content-producing site, he and other young entrepreneurs are glued to screens displaying the number of visits to their content at any given time; numbers run into the thousands, with 82 million visits monthly and 1.5 billion page views (Poonam, 2018, p. 5).

Global educational outcomes. If we translate this one site's 1.5 billion page views into time units, how many millions upon millions of hours are wasted clicking away? If these readers were using that same time to open their textbooks, go to school, study for

(Continued)

(Continued)

their tests (as spoken by a biased academic), what a significant difference it would make to global educational outcomes. But then maybe I am naïve: the textbook does not have the same allure as the potentially illicit or gossipy headlines that beckon in an irresistible manner.

Another disconcerting fact is that, according to Poonam (2018), much of this content is not written by experts in the field; rather, it is written by millennials with limited education and experience. How did it happen that we lend an ear to what is potentially disinformation? And then, going a step further, do we end up believing what is untrue and possibly rearranging our lives to accommodate it? We face an onslaught of promotional material whose primary goal is to transfer money (and its accompanying power) from our pockets into theirs.

"It is a combat zone of sorts, an electronic and digital war that crosses boundaries and cultures; and we freely let the enemy into our homes and, even scarier, into our minds."

Sources: Poonam (2018); see also Flanagan (2017).

Impressionable Minds of the Young

The thoughtful and controlled use of screen time can be enriching in select circumstances. There is a clear educational application that can be used to advantage. The flipside is that very young children (those under the age of three) should not be exposed to unsupervised and extended screen time, including television time. Early childhood is a period of very rapid and sensitive brain development; so the nature and content of the stimulation must be considered, and children should be protected from indiscriminate exposure to web-based and digital material. The American Academy of Pediatrics has published an insightful document on young children's media use and communication. It offers specific guidelines for parents, who should be the ones regulating a child's media exposure. Importantly, the document emphasizes shared media time, when parents and children watch select programming together (American Academy of Pediatrics, 2016b).

Even when children are slightly older, adults in supervising roles should mediate the timing and content of media exposure; and maintaining an interpersonal context remains crucial, while also allocating sufficient opportunities for other activities that are developmentally appropriate and healthy.

Once children go to school, they will be exposed to the appropriate use of tablets and computers in controlled settings so that technology can be a constructive tool for learning and communication. Some young children (aged one to five years) have been known to throw temper tantrums if their access to social media is limited or cut off. This can be difficult for families, and parents are hesitant to intervene, especially if the tantrum occurs in public. Parents need to be aware of the risks of ongoing and excessive screen time. It is helpful to pause screen time at a natural stopping point.

Some parents make use of a timer on their own cell phones to indicate a child's remaining minutes of screen time. When the timer rings, the parent is able to help the child transition to other activities. According to Hiniker, Suh, Cao, and Kientz (2016) technology-mediated transitions are significantly more successful than parent-mediated transitions. Parents can also help a child use technologies to set boundaries and define limits, for instance, by having the child use an electronic timer that indicates when daily screen time is almost finished. A child who self-audits screen time has learned an important lesson and benefited from good parenting techniques. Always remember, though, that screen time should not take on the role of an electronic babysitter.

According to research by Kabali et al. (2015), the age at which children first use media is becoming progressively younger, and "first use" is often in the first year of life. Parents have various reasons for letting their children play with mobile devices. Those of us who have taken care of young children can identify with many of these challenges. For instance, a parent might hand over a cell phone to keep the child calm and amused while travelling, waiting in a restaurant, or visiting a public place. Surprisingly, almost a quarter of questioned parents in another research study admitted to using a mobile device to put their children to sleep, probably by playing lullabies but not exposing them to screen time. These same authors stated that virtually all households had some form of access to cell phones, tablets, computers, or television. By age two, many children could use the swiping movement to change images on the screen of a cell phone or tablet.

The more prevalent use of these technologies by children and the growing number of hours they spend in front of a screen can damage their health. For example, screen time affects sleep patterns; devices cause interruptions, exacerbating short attention spans; and sitting in front of a computer means not moving or being physically active, which in turn encourages obesity. Exposure to inaccurate and inappropriate content is always troubling, and privacy concerns persist (American Academy of Pediatrics, 2016a).

Relevant and appropriate information is powerful, on the other hand. Because information is so freely available, both the good and the bad can enter our homes through our laptops and screens. Appropriately used, the Internet can be a helpful resource that allows us to check facts, learn a skill, and so much more. It requires some education to be able to distinguish between solid information and misinformation. A middle-schooler randomly accessing websites could be flooded with harmful misinformation. There are predators who make it their business to lure minors into compromising situations from which the children struggle to extract themselves. Ultimately, a child's uneducated and unrestricted use of the Internet can potentially precipitate significant long-term harm.

The "me" generation. In the age of the selfie, we can go down the rabbit hole of egocentric behavior; it's all about me, myself, and I. Because we can take selfies, it is easy to make ourselves the center point. We have a captive audience if we post online. This level of self-absorption is unhealthy and distracting and can certainly influence family dynamics as well as how we communicate with others. People have died chasing the unique selfie—falling off a cliff, getting hit by a train, or being mauled by a wild animal. Surely no picture is so important that it should endanger our lives.

Theories. The family communication patterns theory is appropriate to address aspects such as when and how families communicate and in what contexts. If the media are included, this adds another dimension to the communication patterns. This theory does not provide a value judgment as to whether the allocation of time is appropriate or not; instead it describes family communication within a given context (Koerner, Schrodt, & Fitzpatrick, 2018). What happens within families, the quality of their relationships, and how these affect family members will translate to the next level of societal functioning.

Although digital technologies bring clear educational benefits, families should be proactive in balancing digital and real-life experiences from birth to adulthood. For the children pictured here, who are six and older, the American Academy of Pediatrics recommends that parents "set media use limits that factor in other health-promoting activities such as physical activity, sleep, family meals, school, and friends" (American Academy of Pediatrics, 2016c).

Source: © iStock.com/monkeybusinessimages.

"The family occupies a central position in the lives of individuals and is humanity's most enduring and most fundamental social institution."

Koerner and Schrodt (2014, p. 1)

FOCUS POINT

The thoughtful and controlled use of screen time can be enriching in select circumstances. Some online communication offers clear educational advantages. The flipside is that very young children (those under the age of three) should not be exposed to unsupervised and extended screen time, including television time. Early childhood is a period of very rapid and sensitive brain development for the young; so the nature and content of a child's stimulation must be considered, and children should be protected from indiscriminate exposure to web-based and digital material.

Authentic Insight

Transition Generation

My grandfather told me how he and his eight siblings would gather around the radio to tune in to their favorite sitcoms. To an extent technology has always been an immersive experience, and for my generation (born around the Millennium) digital technology has been both a burden and a benefit.

Because my generation grew up during the transition into the digital era, we are very adept with technology. By the age of three, I could rewind a VHS tape, and at eleven I was showing my mother how to use her cell phone. Touchscreen devices took us to a whole new level. As my cohort matured, digital technology advanced with lightning speed.

Growing up in the early 2000s, change was a consistent factor. We have to process something in order to fully comprehend it. With rapidly advancing technology, few were able to stay ahead of the frequent changes. Well, no one except for the children. Kids are resilient and adaptive. Sponge-like, they absorb whatever surrounds them. As children of the early 2000s, we were immersed in constantly evolving technology. While some adults struggled to grasp the basic features of a device, as children we learned by osmosis. We were conditioned to accept the tech world's changing nature; we could navigate this transitional environment.

We adapted socially to living in a digital-based society. Extensive conversations are a thing of the past, and texting is our main form of communication. We meet people online, we talk to people online, and we spend the majority of our days online. Yes, we have adapted and learned to accept the prominence of technology in our society, but as a result, technology is consuming the majority of our day-to-day lives.

We have the whole world at our fingertips, yet we go out less frequently to physically experience things; after all, virtual reality lets us experience the world in a simpler, two-dimensional way. Sitting in a coffee shop, I am surrounded by friends and strangers all focused on their laptops and tablets.

Current society is centered on screens of all shapes and sizes. Yet we attempt to have personal connections with others. So, we incorporate socializing with the indispensable use of our electronic gadgets. We can't have our cake and eat it too, but we think we can, as we navigate our lives through a technological maze. We have withdrawal symptoms if the Wi-Fi reception lets us down; could that possibly be a sign of addiction? Personally, I'll take the bad with the good, and in the appropriate context, technology can be beneficial and powerful. I cannot imagine life without it, maybe the true sign that I am a Millennial. The genie is out of the bottle and there is no going back.

Jordan Dombrowski majored in human development and family science.

Family Communication Networks

Mediated interaction. Postmillennial communication has been heavily influenced by what has been called **mediated interaction**, or communication using media. For instance, emails, texts, posted photos, social media communications, and the like: these media interactions are instantaneous and connect a wide range of people, who are not all part of a "friend" network. By the same token, they can become public, and one has to be intentional about whom to include in communication.

Yet in spite of our choosing which circles of friends we want to include and with whom we want to communicate, we can send numerous unintended or unintentional communications. For instance, friends of friends on social platforms may be able to see the content we posted. There are ways of restricting access, but the communicator has to be very intentional and knowledgeable about putting boundaries in place.

When social connections occur through digital media, the influences on interactions and relationships are far-reaching. An advantage is that social media give us the ability to maintain acquaintances and friendships in far-flung places. Because of this extended network, we can find childhood friends, long-lost relatives, and acquaintances we barely met. Additionally, through the suggestions of the social media site itself, we can be connected to friends of friends. This technology creates a very wide network of people whom we can contact but with whom we cannot possibly maintain true friendships.

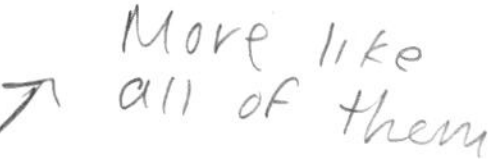

Some social media and web platforms have been overtaken by consumerist motives, making them advertising and marketing platforms more than networks of friends. Hence, one has to battle through the 90 percent of material that is irrelevant to see the 10 percent that is of interest. There are clear intergenerational differences in the use of these social media platforms. Interestingly, the older generation enjoys networking with grandchildren and discovering school friends after many years. Social media and the connectedness provided by cell phones, online chats, and the like allow family members to communicate almost instantaneously and to document moments from their lives to share, which keeps the elderly and the extended family in the loop. Forming social circles on social media sites can help an individual maintain contact with subgroups; for instance, all the cousins from one family can create their own group and remain connected.

Undoubtedly, this new electronic and web-based communication has had far-reaching implications. It has changed the dating scene, and numerous relationships begin online. It has allowed us to maintain a wide circle of acquaintances and follow their lives from a distance as onlookers—a double-edged sword, as social media users can become abusers, stalking and possibly harassing people online. Indeed, each benefit of our digitally connected world seems linked to a drawback. Our friendships may be wide, but they lack depth. Our communications may be numerous and instantaneous, but they are also ephemeral and often superficial or even commercial, lacking thought and attention to the individual.

We can see these changes in the artifacts of communication. The handwritten card or letter has largely been replaced by group emails. Holiday cards, invitations, and even wedding announcements are increasingly electronic. Of course, there will be numerous exceptions but the electronic option is alive and well. There is something charming and permanent about the old-school handwritten card, and it is more likely to be preserved, under special circumstances, than the electronic card. Of course, communicating online in real-time is very useful and instantaneous. But what if families stop having conversations, and touch base mainly via text messages? These are abbreviated communications, almost like punctuation marks. Clearly, we cannot go back in time. But we can try to take the best from both worlds and use modern technology in appropriate contexts while maintaining a place for face-to-face communication and time spent in each other's company.

Netiquette

With new communication methods come new rules. Texting in capital letters is regarded as shouting. The use of acronyms, which seem to change with each season, is a byproduct of texting. Formal forms of address fall by the wayside, and the new replacements such as *Hey* seem overly familiar to older generations.

Communicating electronically, especially through social media, creates a public "track record" of what was communicated; posts can be retrieved and quoted or misquoted in contexts not intended by the sender. It is wise to check those hastily written texts and emails to make sure that the message is professional and represents what was intended. With this ease of communication, we can be tempted to send something into the world impulsively. Once it has been sent, there is no "unsending" it. Knowing that even our most impulsive communications could become part of our public story changes how we communicate and how much detail we send via these types of communication channels.

The etiquette of dating has been influenced by digital communication as well. Persons who break up after a relationship have to figure out to what extent they will leave not only each other's lives but also each other's online personas. A whole new genre of advice has grown around these topics. One practice is unfriending someone with whom you want to split, removing that person from a list of social media contacts. Or you could simply ghost that person by keeping the connection but not responding to any of her or his communications. Doing either may seem like a convenient solution to the person initiating the breakup, as it avoids the challenging breakup conversation. The person being jilted, however, may appreciate clarification, especially if that person is still vested in the relationship. Depending on how long the relationship lasted, a face-to-face breakup would display greater integrity than disappearing without a word. A face-to-face conversation may be advisable even if this has to be done in the presence of a mediator.

Noncommunication may seem an effective way of sending a message, but it may not be the most constructive way out. Undoubtedly new rules and guidelines will develop as we go along.

Multicultural Contexts

We can anticipate that culture will influence the type of conversations we have. But we must remember that cultures are made up of individuals, so broad cultural generalizations only take us so far. Also, cultures, families, and individuals exist within changing times, so the communications of the younger generation will not exactly mirror those of older generations.

Still, culture affects communication. Intercultural research looking at family communication patterns and conflict styles in Chinese families found that Chinese family communication patterns, which were more conformity oriented than those in other cultural contexts, encouraged collaborating and accommodating behavior in children (Zhang, 2007). These children did not have to be competitive or avoidant in their relationships with their parents. As a parenting style, this approach has the same qualities or characteristics as an authoritative (or constructive and positive) parenting approach. Because children are not required to be overly conforming while there is also a warm, accepting orientation toward communication, these types of families are likely to collaborate. In terms of family functioning, these are characteristics associated with a healthy family.

Feedback loops. How we communicate is ultimately influenced by a number of interacting factors. One of them is how other people react to what we say and how we say it; responses can strengthen us in certain patterns or give us cues to avoid communicating in a particular manner. Communication patterns are also modeled and influenced by the examples of significant persons in our lives; hence, families and close peer groups may imitate aspects of each other's interactions and communications.

Communication and global concerns. The ripple effect of the digital world has left virtually no corner of interactional dynamics untouched. Here are some areas in which shifts have occurred:

- *Privilege and power.* Changes have occurred to women's education and roles, gender roles, gay rights, cultural and diversity rights, and power relations, including an increase in the imbalance between the privileged few and the underprivileged many, which is linked to diminishing economic opportunities and the challenges of poverty.
- *Societal influences.* Currently, materialistic values have swept across nations, with e-commerce fueling consumption. How sustainable is the economic growth model?
- *Family dynamics.* Families are embedded in a society that is changing dramatically: can each generation keep up with the next generation?
- *Dynamics of leisure.* How does our diminishing leisure time affect self-reflection, self-insight, and quality of life? There is no downtime, no time lapse; all is instantaneous (the dynamics of leisure).
- *Making a difference.* The reward of volunteering has been enhanced by our broader social connections, more detailed and varied social perspectives, and the social comparisons the digital world enables, which can lead to gratitude and self-reflection.

The Dynamics of Change

Social change theories propose that once major changes occur, there is no going back; one cannot undo the awareness of what that paradigm shift elicits. The digital revolution that we have experienced since the early 1990s is such a shift; it has created a world we could not have envisioned. As Rosenau (1990, pp. 4–5) states,

> If one senses that exploding technologies and expanding interdependencies are of great moment, then one must suspend normal standards of evidence long enough to consider alternative interpretations of what may be at work on the global scene.

Like Pandora opening the box, we have been confronted with all kinds of unanticipated surprises. The ripple effect has been major and has left very little untouched as it rolled our way—into our homes and into our minds.

> **"Spread out and examine the patterns of events, and you will find yourself face to face with the new scheme of being, hitherto unimaginable by the human mind."**
>
> H. G. Wells, English author, especially of science fiction (1866–1946), from *Mind at the End of Its Tether*

FOCUS POINT

We can anticipate that culture influences the type and nature of our conversations. As younger generations are exposed to digital and other social media, some of the attention has shifted away from the family unit. Millennials are becoming increasingly self-focused and peer-referenced. How we communicate is influenced by a number of interacting factors, including how other people react to what we say and how we say it. Communication patterns are also modeled and influenced by the examples of significant persons in our lives; hence, families and close peer groups may imitate aspects of each other's interactions and communications.

HISTORIC GLIMPSE

THE ART OF CONVERSATION

Here are twelve golden rules from over a century ago, published in *The Art of Conversation: Twelve Gold Rules* by Josephine Turck Baker (1907). In this little gem of a book (unearthed at a library book sale), Baker guides the reader concerning basic rules for easy and respectful conversation. It was written before the advent of the radio, the telephone, or the television. Clearly, conversation was valued as the social art of whiling away time. It was a form of entertainment that deserved cultivation and skill. Although enumerated for an earlier generation, most of these rules are equally applicable today; there is always a place for active listening, for tact, and for genuine interest—not much has changed when it comes to being respectful of the conversation partner and displaying genuine interest.

Twelve Golden Rules of Conversation

1. Avoid unnecessary details (p. 9).
2. Do not ask question number two until question number one has been answered; and, furthermore, one must be neither too curious nor too disinterested; that is, one must not ask too few nor too many questions (p. 13).
3. Do not interrupt another while he is speaking (p. 14).
4. Do not contradict another, especially when the subject under discussion is of trivial importance (p. 20).
5. Do not do all the talking; give your tired listener a chance (p. 24).
6. Be not continually the hero of your own story; and, on the other hand, do not leave your story without a hero (p 29).
7. Choose [a] subject of mutual interest (p. 33).
8. Be a good listener (p 38).
9. Make your speech in harmony with your surroundings (p. 45).
10. Do not exaggerate (p. 49).
11. Indulge occasionally in a relevant quotation, but do not garble it (p. 54).
12. Cultivate tact (p. 57).

Baker (1907/1919, p. 54) also suggests that we commit interesting passages in verse and prose to memory, which we can insert in our conversations for greater interest. Baker quotes from an article written in 1872 by Vernon Lushington titled "Learning by Heart"; the article was quite well known because it was included in *The Sixth Reader* by Lewis B. Monroe, dean of the Boston University School of Oratory. Monroe wrote a series of readers for schools, books designed to perfect the reading skills of pupils. The article reiterates the importance of memorizing "relevant quotations" and describes their usefulness in contexts other than conversation:

> They may come to us in our dull moments,
> to refresh us as with spring flowers; in our
> selfish musings, to win us by pure delight
> from the tyranny of foolish castle-building,
> self-congratulations, and mean anxiety.
> They may be with us in the workshop,
> in the crowded streets, by the fireside;
> sometimes, perhaps, on pleasant hill-sides,
> or by sounding shores;—noble friends and
> companions—our own! never intrusive, ever
> at hand, coming at our call. (Lushington,
> quoted in Monroe, 1872, p. 166)

In a more current source, namely an interview by Jolie Kerr with Terry Gross of National Public Radio (NPR), Gross summed up her guidelines for insightful interviews. Her most favored opening line in an interview is "Tell me about yourself," also known as "the only ice-breaker you'll ever need" (Kerr, 2018). After this initial invitation, it is up to the interviewee to direct the conversation toward areas that she or he finds comfortable and is willing to share. By listening very carefully, the interviewer will be able to pick up the threads that deserve further exploration. Body language, humor, and curiosity are other key ingredients for a rich conversation. Importantly, Gross prepares for interviews so that she is well informed concerning the person with whom she will be having this in-depth conversation. She displays a genuine interest and a listening ear: a winning combination.

Sources: Baker (1907/1919); Kerr (2018); and Monroe (1872).

The (Great) Tower of Babel, by Pieter Bruegel the Elder (c. 1563). In the Bible story about the Tower of Babel, people were talking in so many tongues that they could not understand each other and could not collaborate in building their tower. An estimated 6,500 languages are spoken in our modern world. Even if we speak the same language, we can still fail to communicate.

Source: Public domain.

SPOTLIGHT ON THEORIES

Family Communication Patterns Theory

Braithwaite and Baxter (2006), the editors of a book on family communication, state the following concerning family communication patterns theory, which is partly attributed to the work of Mary Anne Fitzpatrick (2004):

Family communication patterns theory takes a view of communication that is both cognitive and interpersonal. The theory grows out of mass media research, built on earlier work from

(Continued)

(Continued)

> cognitive psychology . . . it is concerned with causal explanation of why people communicate the way they do based on cognitive orientations in family relationships (p. 50)

In essence, this theory is based on the premise of the interaction between two dimensions, namely, conversation and conformity. See Diagram 8.1. These dimensions echo the general work concerning parenting styles, which fluctuate between the axes of nurture and structure (Gerhardt, in Bigner & Gerhardt, 2019, p. 47). See Diagram 8.2.

- **Conversation** refers to the verbal interaction that takes place between family members and to their willingness to discuss topics. If related to parenting, conversation would be the axis relating to the nurture or the emotional expressiveness displayed in family relationships.
- **Conformity** refers to the extent family members subscribe to the same values, attitudes, and beliefs. If related to parenting, conformity would be the axis relating to the structure (or control) displayed in family relationships.

Based on these two dimensions of conversation (nurture) and conformity (structure/control), a model of family communication patterns is created. It would appear that the processes that are described are similar in the two disciplines of psychology and communication science, but the terminology differs. The visual representation of these quadrants also allows us to consider the distance from the center as reflecting nuances in family functioning. The further a family system's functioning is from the center, the more extreme

DIAGRAM 8.1 **Note the interaction between the dimensions of "conversation" and "conformity" in family communication patterns.**

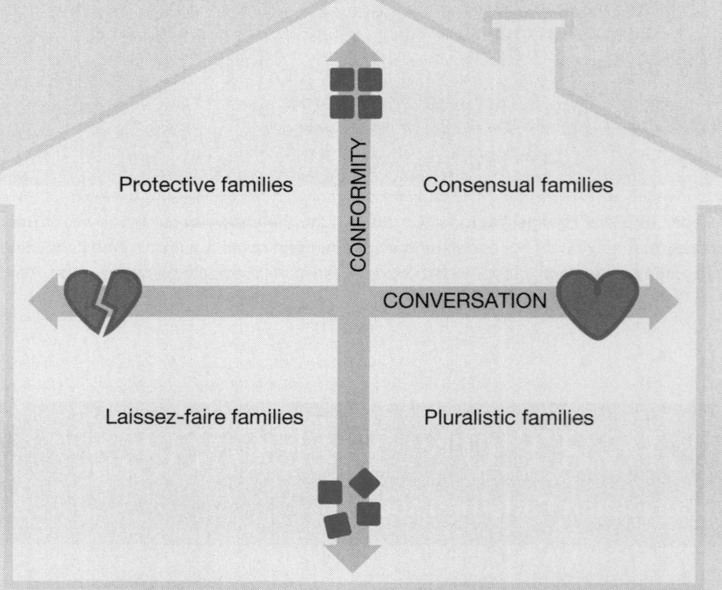

Sources: Based on Galvin, Braithwaite, and Bylund (2014, p. 176) and Le Poire (2006).

DIAGRAM 8.2

Note the interaction between the dimensions of nurture (emotional expressiveness) and structure (control, order) in parenting styles. These are similar to the axes described in the family communication styles, where the horizontal axis relating to emotional expressiveness is labeled "conversation" and the vertical axis relating to the control and order in the relationship is represented by "conformity" in family communication patterns.

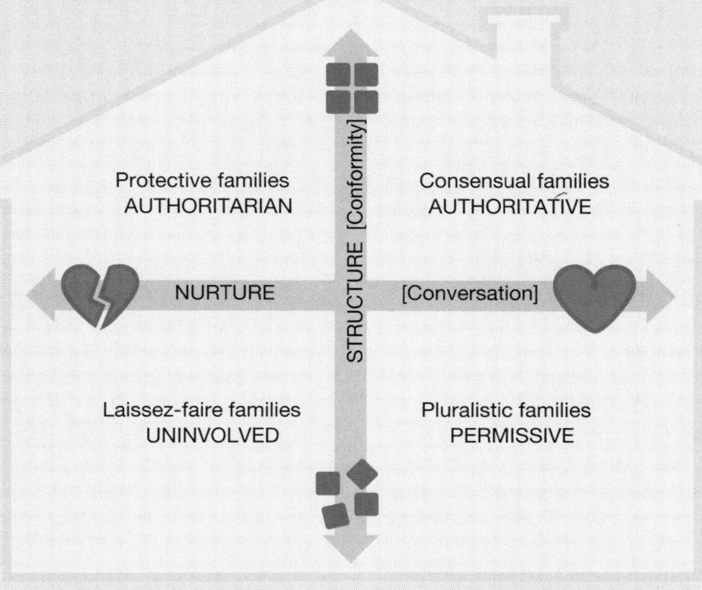

Source: Bigner and Gerhardt (2019, p. 47).

the systemic presentation of the behavioral patterns (Bigner & Gerhardt, 2019, p. 46).

Additionally, family systems are not static; rather, they are dynamic. For that reason, families may change their communication patterns and interactions depending on context. Also, the lifespan position of participants can influence the quality of interactions (Bigner & Gerhardt, 2019, p. 10).

Fitzpatrick (2004) describes the following four quadrants that result as these two axes of conversation and conformity intersect:

- *Consensual.* High engagement combined with high conformity.
- *Protective.* High conformity and low engagement (in this interactional style difficult topics will be avoided).
- *Laissez-faire.* Low engagement combined with low conformity (in this interactional style conversation can be very permissive, with low censorship).
- *Pluralistic.* Low conformity and high conversational engagement (in this interactional style participants are motivated to engage, and they are open to diverse conversations, hence the word pluralistic, as many topics can be addressed).

(Continued)

(Continued)

One can expect the greatest likelihood of conversation in consensual and the pluralistic families. These are the talkative ones, but they differ in that their motives for talking and conversation may not be the same. These families may enjoy talking with their children because they like communication, and it is a way of showing their affection; communication represents a form of emotional bonding. In these family types, relationship is paramount, and that, in turn, motivates the need for enthusiastic conversation.

One would expect to find less conversation in protective and laissez-faire families. In families that tend to be more protective of their children, communication might be limited because it is mainly about exerting control. In the laissez-faire type of family, control is low and family members are typically left to their own devices, so communication is not often necessary. There is no conscious or concerted effort to create moments of conversation.

Family communication takes place on two levels. On the one hand, it is *personal* in that we have an inner language and inner thoughts, which we may wish to share with others. On the other hand, communication has *interpersonal* components when it happens between people, in this case, between family members. Both these components play a role. For example, the individual may formulate ideas (personal) but may do so in response to the input of somebody else (interpersonal). So both interpersonal communication processes and the inner dialogue a person may have can be circular (Koerner & Fitzpatrick, 2006, pp. 51–52).

The family communication patterns theory looks at family communication from the point of view of relational cognition as well as interpersonal behavior. As Koerner and Fitzpatrick (2006) state,

> We consider the origin of family communication patterns theory as a model of how families create a shared social reality through the process of coorientation and the subsequent reformulation of the model as a theory of interpersonal behavior. (p. 51)

According to these authors, underlying cognitive processes will be revealed in the resulting communication behaviors within families. This in turn will group them into four family types (Koerner & Fitzpatrick, 2006, p. 51).

The concept that families share a social reality and that this social reality will influence how they communicate represents early elements of the theory based on the work of McLeod and Chaffee (McLeod, Atkin, & Chaffee, 1972; McLeod & Chaffee 1973) who came from the world of mass media. In the early seventies, cognitive psychology was pushing the boundaries of behaviorism and wanted to explore wider contexts and applications. Fitzpatrick (2011, pp. 167–179) was influenced by elements in various communication theories; also, her undergraduate major in political science, intercultural communication, and advertising all influenced aspects of her theory on family communication patterns.

Several research studies have looked at aspects of conversational styles within families, for instance, the work by Rueter and Koerner (2008) who study community and family patterns that affect adjustment. In this particular study, they looked at children who had joined the family through adoption. They found that a conversation orientation within the families—one that was neither too demanding of conformity nor exclusively focused on conversation—seemed to have the best outcomes in terms of parenting. This type of approach could be compared to authoritative parenting where communication is available yet appropriately structured.

Overlap with models of family functioning. The family communication patterns theory has some commonalities with the Olson circumplex model, as well as with the parenting circumplex model. In the latter, nurture and structure act as the horizontal and vertical axes, respectively, to illustrate various parenting dimensions (Bigner & Gerhardt, 2019, pp. 46–47). In the family communication patterns theory, structure as a parenting dimension is represented by the concept of conformity, and nurture as a parenting dimension is represented by the concept of conversation. This is fairly intuitive. The resulting communication styles have some similarities with parenting styles. One could deduct that laissez-faire parents are also likely to adopt laissez-faire communication styles.

In a Nutshell

Family Communication Patterns Theory

- Communication has both cognitive (personal) and interpersonal dimensions.
- In communications, an interaction occurs between two dimensions, namely, conversation and conformity.
- Based on these two dimensions of conversation and conformity, a model of family communication patterns is created.
- The four family communication patterns are consensual, protective, laissez-faire, and protective.
- One can expect the greatest likelihood of conversation in consensual and pluralistic families.
- One can expect to find less conversation in protective and laissez-faire families.
- The family communication patterns theory has some commonalities with the Olson circumplex model, as well as with the parenting circumplex model.
- Interpersonal communication processes are circular, as is a person's inner dialogue.

CHAPTER FOCUS POINTS

Families in a Digital World

- Postmillennial children and adolescents are very familiar with the web for entertainment and communication. If a website provides social interaction, it serves as a social media site; numerous such sites are currently available.
- True concern is appropriate if electronic communications replace face-to-face communications, precipitate self-image anxieties, or involve online bullying. Cyber trolling, which aims vicious and destructive remarks at victims, is also problematic.

The Dynamics of a Digital World

- The world of digital media offers great advantages; computers have irrevocably changed our society and our communications. We may be limited by our inability to juggle multiple communication channels simultaneously.
- Cell phones put us on mental standby, diverting our attention. Our attention span is affected by constant interruptions.
- Parents set the tone for what is happening in the home. Digital and social media and related communication patterns have the ability to influence family dynamics.

Family Rituals in a Digital World

- The thoughtful and controlled use of screen time can be enriching in select circumstances. Some online communication offers clear educational advantages.
- The flipside is that very young children (those under the age of three) should not be exposed to unsupervised and extended screen time, including television time.
- Early childhood is a period of very rapid and sensitive brain development for the young; so the nature and content of a child's stimulation must be considered, and children should be protected from indiscriminate exposure to web-based and digital material.

Family Communication Networks

- We can anticipate that culture influences the type and nature of our conversations. As younger generations are exposed to digital and other social media, some of the attention has shifted away from the family unit.
- Millennials are becoming increasingly self-focused and peer-referenced. How we communicate is influenced by a number of interacting factors, including how other people react to what we say and how we say it.

- Communication patterns are also modeled and influenced by the examples of significant persons in our lives; hence, families and close peer groups may imitate aspects of each other's interactions and communications.

Spotlight on Theories: Family Communication Patterns Theory

- Communication has both cognitive (personal) and interpersonal dimensions.
- In communication, an interaction occurs between two dimensions, namely, conversation and conformity.
- Based on these two dimensions of conversation and conformity, a model of family communication patterns is created.
- The four family communication patterns are consensual, protective, laissez-faire, and protective. One can expect the greatest likelihood of conversation in consensual and pluralistic families. One can expect to find less conversation in protective and laissez-faire families.
- The family communication patterns theory has some commonalities with the Olson circumplex model, as well as with the parenting circumplex model.
- Interpersonal communication processes are circular, as is a person's inner dialogue.

CHAPTER 9

Communication and Resilience

Learning Outcomes

After studying this chapter, you should be able to

1. Examine the contributory factors that facilitate the display of *resilience.*
2. Discuss the connection between resilience and *self-regulation.*
3. Explain how factors contributing to resilience act on various *systemic levels.*
4. Describe the *theory* of resilience and relational load (TRRL).

The Pillars of Resilience

Resilience is multifactorial; it includes personal, family, and societal strengths. It gains momentum under the umbrella of civic engagement and social policy. In short, it consists of a complex network of interrelated factors. Factors contributing to resilience can be found on micro, meso, and macro levels of systems, and the effects are bidirectional and multidirectional.

If a context is created that supports and invests in the potential that nurtures adaptive behavior, it cocreates the conditions that amplify resilience. The clues of resilient behavior can be found in the daily interactions between people, the sense of hope gained from civic engagement, the fulfillment of completing meaningful tasks, and the realization of making a difference. Resilience is also characterized by a level of plasticity that allows for adaptation when facing adversity.

Resilience has seemingly magical effects, but it does not surface from nowhere. Like a nurtured plant, resilience needs to be fostered through appropriate attention, responsiveness in relationships, and the provision of opportunities for growth and development. Resilience is embedded in a web of other traits and conditions, many of them based on what happens within the home and within families (Aburn, Gott, & Hoare, 2016) and then circling outward to include communities and larger social systems.

Family education concerning constructive parenting approaches, the value of mutually supportive relationships, and the importance of emotional engagement is crucial, and promoted by family scientists in their work. If we think of resilience as broadly based, we can gain access to a number of entry points, and thereby influence the systems that feed this quality.

Pillars of resilience. A balanced approach to family resilience will bring together and acknowledge a number of pillars that support it. This approach is much like the Bronfenbrenner model: it starts with the individual in the center, surrounded by her or his closest and dearest (the microsystem) and then emanates outward to include meso- through to macrosystemic supports. These include access to education, health care, employment, extended family relationships, social support, and civic engagement. It expands even wider to include environmental factors, public policy, and cultural values and the like (Bigner & Gerhardt, 2019, p. 398). These are all factors that facilitate adaptive systems in various social contexts; and adaptive capability, in turn, promises improved opportunities because families are able to alter and influence future outcomes.

Family resilience emanates from the individual outward, providing protection much in the way immunizations do; exposure to illness cannot always be entirely avoided, but responses to it will be modified through immunity or a strengthened immune system, at least. Henry, Morris, and Harrist (2015) are of the opinion that any talk about resilience represents an integration of concepts pertaining to individual resilience, general systems perspectives on families, and family stress theory. Models also interface to incorporate meaning systems, emotion systems, control systems, maintenance systems, and family stress-response systems. Theory about resilience involves the coming together of many strands and influences.

Emotional capital. In popular self-help literature, a system of credits and debits (like a bank account) is frequently used as a metaphor for conditions supporting resilience. We save and put away during the good times, so we can withdraw from some of that accrued credit during lean times, a more constructive approach than declaring bankruptcy when resources are fully depleted.

We can build up our resilience "accounts" in many family- and society-related ways. The supportive family with good communication skills, firm attachments, and constructive family dynamics will help a family member handle stress and adversity. Combined, these family characteristics and circumstances add credits that can be applied, or cashed in, later. Emulating this way of thinking, my grandfather used to guide us: "Save a little apple to quench your thirst!" Do not use all your resources when times are good; keep something for the lean times.

Self-regulation and long-term thinking help us to preserve assets until they are needed and to streamline our goals into the bigger, more permanent ones that affect quality of life and other outcomes meaningful to us. What encourages us to be resilient can be somewhat individualistic in that we do not all subscribe to the same goals and we do not all gain fulfillment from similar sources. Whereas materialistic outcomes can be a great motivator for many, others will persevere to achieve fame or to feel useful. Much psychological research has been dedicated to why money in itself is not enough. People crave recognition, acknowledgment, a sense of meaning, self-actualization, and other abstract goals.

Children who grew up in the isolation of poverty or within orphanages struggle with these early deprivations, even after they are welcomed into emotionally generous and stable homes. A good childhood, by fulfilling needs and providing physical and emotional shelter during the vulnerable years, goes a long way toward establishing adult resilience. On the other hand, the child who faced adversity at a young age may realize the value of perseverance when it comes to finding a way out of constraining circumstances (Fay-Stammbach, Hawes, & Meredith, 2014; Keating, 2017).

Research by psychologist Angela Lee Duckworth (2016), published in her book *Grit: The Power of Passion and Perseverance*, concerns the experience of and reaction to adversity. Some adversity is part of the reality of life, and it helps to encourage children and adolescents to cope with this discomfort in constructive ways. For instance, in every game of basketball, football, and the like, one team will be the victor while the other team must gracefully deal with defeat. When parents try to shield their children from all adversity, however well intentioned this shielding may be, it does not necessarily promote best outcomes. Encouraging children to persevere while facing difficult tasks, and providing appropriate emotional support, may teach them how to deal with the frustrations that life will inevitably spring on them. Importantly, though, the child should not self-identify with the failure but should instead focus on finding a way through it by learning from the situation and developing strengths and resilience, which, in turn, can be part of the formula for future success (https://angeladuckworth.com). The interacting factors are complex, and there is neither a simple nor a clear predictor as to who will react constructively to adversity.

Definition. Resilience refers to the capacity to adapt constructively to and recover from challenging or even adversarial situations; various factors interact to create this capacity.

Family Strengths

Family transitions are often mentioned in the same breath as family resilience. There is a clear overlap in that resilience contributes to how we negotiate transitions and what meaning we attach to them (Walsh, 2016a, 2016b). Resilience is not one trait abiding in the resilient person; instead, we find it at the crossroads where several conditions meet. Different family members will react very individually to stress and to transitions, even the joyful ones like moving to a roomier house or going on vacation.

Nevertheless, families can transfer attitudes toward resilience through family stories, symbols, and expectations. This process tends to tumble from the top of the family hierarchy downward. Parents can metaphorically unload self-fulfilling prophecies on their children and set the stage for future triumphs or disappointments. Sometimes, attitudes to resilience are related to an impactful intergenerational event, and the patterns of those gone before influence descendants. For example, families who faced the hardships of fleeing their home country, or who experienced extended poverty or war, may incorporate these challenges into their personal family stories, and these, in turn, subtly color the identities of the offspring. A severely traumatic period in the life of a family can affect the children, and possibly their children. Not all adversity is detrimental. Growing up with immigrant parents, children tend to understand these challenges, which can strengthen them when opportunities occur.

When these intergenerational transmissions are negative and families pass on destructive and unwanted elements to an unwitting next generation, a family can be left with few or no emotional credit, and little resilience. For instance, intergenerational poverty can severely prune the dreams of a child because growing up in a limiting environment can emphasize obstacles as opposed to opportunities. This type of environment can also foster poorly functioning or maladjusted families. Where there is distrust, members cannot rely on support, which may contribute to further emotional depletion. By and large, such a family cannot easily adapt to challenges.

Well-functioning families, on the other hand, act as a team. Members value and display cohesion. They are available when joys and sorrows need to be shared. Such a family is resilient. Family members know that they can call in favors, when difficulties arise, as there is communal cohesiveness (Afifi & Harrison, 2018). Because these are long-term relationships with a history and a future, the family's resources are self-renewing.

> **"Resilience resembles a journey: it is a way of finding the best route through a landscape, the preferred way to traverse obstacles presented by life."**

Family hardiness. Your family and circle of trusted friends are important resources. They invest in you and add to your emotional reserves. Interactions are reaffirming in overt and covert ways. Investing in the family is also an important premise of parenting; children develop strong and confident self-concepts because their closest and most significant caregivers created these circles of trust and support. Family members contribute to one another's well-being by being mutually supportive, by displaying positive affect, and by showing love through touching, nonverbal gestures, eye contact, and so much more. The unique language of the family serves an important function in strengthening and affirming family members. It is this constant interpersonal backup system that can provide strength during times of challenge. This interpersonal support, in turn, fosters personal resilience, the inner voice that pipes up and says, "Yes, I can!" Walsh (2016, p. 14) provides the following definition of **family resilience**:

> Family resilience is defined as the ability of the family, as a functional system, to withstand and rebound from adversity. Crucial family processes mediate stressful conditions and enable families and their members to surmount crises and weather prolonged hardship.

In a South African research study on resilience in teenagers, those who displayed greater resilience were less avoidant in their behavior. They tackled challenges more directly by exploring coping strategies behaviorally or cognitively. Additionally, they were strengthened by families with effective communication, families in which coping skills were modeled and supported (Mashego & Taruvinga, 2014). When crisis situations occurred, these families tried to cope and resolve the difficulties as effectively as possible, and the term *family hardiness* was used. For teenagers from divorced homes, the results were optimistic if they had at least one parent or constant mentor linked to a constructive social environment. Importantly, for all participants in the study, the way a family unit managed and coped with challenges was an important precursor of whether the teenagers would display resilient behavior.

Based on statistical analyses, the authors identified specific factors that contributed to resilience. These included the knowledge that one has the power to overcome obstacles, being able to rely on the strength of the family, not being avoidant in dealing with a challenge, and being actively involved in faith-based and civic communities (Mashego & Taruvinga, 2014, p. 25). Family communication and support are highly effective protective factors, and these ingredients are recognized as promoting family adaptation and allowing family units to remain functional during crises (Mashego & Taruvinga, 2014, p. 31).

FOCUS POINT

Resilience is multifactorial. It surfaces from a web of traits and conditions, many of them related to home and families influences, and then circles outward to include communities and larger social systems. Resilience includes personal, familial, and societal strengths merging with a complex network of interrelated factors. It gains momentum through civic engagement and social policy. Factors contributing to resilience occur on micro-, meso- and macrosystemic levels, and the effects are bidirectional and multidirectional. Models of resilience also incorporate systems of meaning, emotion, control, maintenance, and family stress response.

"Each day of our lives we make deposits in the memory banks of our children."

Charles R. Swindoll (1991, p. 38)

CULTURAL GLIMPSE

ACHILLES' HEEL

Resilience: Our Unique Strengths and Vulnerabilities

Within the family circle, cohesion imparts seemingly mythical protection, which in turn fuels resilience. Constructive parental love is powerful. In this snapshot from Greek mythology, we explore the story of Achilles, whose mother's love tried to shield him from harm.

The phrase "Achilles' heel" denotes our unique vulnerabilities. Achilles, a brave hero, fought in the Trojan War. His secret and most powerful weapon was given to him by his mother. She immersed Achilles in the river Styx, which imparted immortality to bathers. She held him by his heel to dip him into the river. As that body part was not immersed, it was not invulnerable. Achilles was killed by an arrow that targeted his only vulnerable part—*Achilles' heel*.

We may know where our unique weaknesses are located; but our families also applaud our strengths. In dysfunctional families, our vulnerabilities become target zones for dirty fighting, insults, and other negative interactional patterns—in short, this is a dynamic of destruction. In well-functioning families, on the other hand, a family member's vulnerability is protected, and strengths are celebrated. The support and guidance of our families can help us become the best we can be, despite our imperfections.

Authentic Insight

The Pearl Necklace: A Story of Resilience and Empowerment

Through my own life struggles, I discovered specific tools that empower me. These are now pearls of wisdom that I wear daily to remind me of how far I have come, while not being fearful of challenges ahead. Each pearl has been shaped and cultivated with love by people like my late mother and grandmothers. These pearls have also been placed there by my father, husband, mentors, teachers, pastors, and friends.

Figuring out how to cope with life's challenges can be the difference between living in despair and thriving in the face of adversity. For individuals tackling their hardships head on, being resilient is key to overcoming misfortune. Making the decision to live life positively doesn't occur naturally or automatically. We have to make a concerted effort to reach a place of fulfillment and to remain there.

Unfortunately, I experienced the loss of my mother at a very young age—and shortly thereafter things got progressively worse. Our family possessions were lost in a house fire, other close relatives passed away, and I was forced to assume the responsibilities of an adult, even though I was still a child. Through educational opportunities, I explored my ancestry and history. Having a sense of community shaped my character, and I realized the value of connecting to others. This inspired me to pursue my passion and purpose in life, which is to educate and encourage those experiencing their own setbacks. Having a strong educational background allowed me to leverage opportunities, which leads to my next point.

Throughout my academic journey from elementary school to doctoral studies, I fostered relationships with those who had my best interests in

(Continued)

(Continued)

mind. These persons were a source of encouragement, allowing me to see life through someone else's eyes. The most significant aspect of fostering personal relationships with others has come in the form of mentorship. Connecting with women who have lived a little longer and have experienced and learned from their own challenges gave me access to valuable insights. Generational transference of knowledge allows us to have an understanding and foresight gained from those who have traveled the road before us. Whether I am facing a simple daily task or have to make a monumental decision that could affect my entire life, I try to apply those life skills that contribute to resilience. I remember to reflect on what I have lost, gained, learned, and accomplished. I acknowledge that I am not alone.

As I move ahead, I choose to adorn myself with a pearl necklace of knowledge, experience, and wisdom that I have been gifted through my personal experiences, as well as by people who carry my best interests at heart.

Idrissa N. Snider, PhD, is an artist, writer, and womanist scholar residing in Alabama.

Resilience and Self-Regulation

Self-regulation concerns taming our inner impulses and demons, the ones wanting to be heard and acknowledged immediately. When we self-regulate, we put those urgent voices on hold; we tame them and control them, until, to an extent, they become subservient to other important and overriding guidelines. One well-known illustration of this principle is the so-called marshmallow experiment, originally devised by Mischel and colleagues in the late sixties, but subsequently questioned for its experimental design (Mischel, 1974). Children were tested to see whether they could delay gratification. Each child was left alone in a room for a few minutes with a very tempting marshmallow on a table within easy reach. All the children were told that if they waited and ate the marshmallow only when the experimenter came back into the room, they would get an additional marshmallow. Some children rose to the task; others could not resist the temptation. This difference we ascribe to self-regulation (Mischel, Shoda, & Rodriguez, 1989; Gianessi, 2012).

In a related follow-up experiment, it was shown that children who were in what they perceived to be a *reliable* environment were able to postpone and wait longer than children who were in what they perceived to be an *unreliable* environment (Kidd, Palmeri, & Aslin, 2013). This finding has implications for resilience, as it appears that unreliable environments could be less supportive of individual goals than reliable ones. For family support to be effective, it needs to be reliable.

The ability to regulate emotions, needs, and urges gets perfected throughout childhood and is a part of socialization. We cannot impulsively do or say whatever enters our mind or whatever calls us. We have to channel those urges into socially acceptable expressions. As adults, some of us are more self-regulated than others. Some of us find the telling of an inappropriate joke irresistible, even though the context indicates that it is not a wise move to do so. In a saturated society where everything is plentiful, it can be tempting to overindulge. What can be good in moderate amounts can tip to addictions in excessive proportions. The so-called seven deadly sins of early Christianity can be thought of as immoderate behaviors and feelings—excesses of self-indulgence. For instance, our *appetite* for the food that sustains us when consumed in appropriate amounts can become the sin of *gluttony*.

Self-regulation with the accompanying delay of gratification helps us in attaining long-term goals by making the seemingly urgent short-term ones subservient to the prize on the horizon. Many of our abstract planned activities require discipline and self-control. Completing an education, learning challenging subjects, sticking to our budgets or our diets, making monthly mortgage payments, not letting our feelings of anger get the better of us, controlling our sarcastic remarks—all are examples of how daily life, including our present interactions and future dreams, is made possible and influenced by the powers of self-regulation. In so many instances, we need the ability to say no, or to tell ourselves to postpone, in order to reach a long-term goal.

Much of the research points toward the fact that prosocial behaviors require significant self-control or self-regulation (Bauer & Baumeister, 2011). If people become overly stressed, or too many emotional demands are made on them, they may feel cognitively depleted and unable to muster the additional control required to self-regulate. Many of us have regained weight lost. Perhaps we find ourselves in stressful situations and the self-control required to follow a diet exceeds our capacity when several other demands require self-regulation as well. Deadlines, exams, meetings—all these endeavors can deplete us of our resources allocated to self-regulation. Goals that crash are probably the lowest on the priority list. More subtle demands are also made on our self-regulatory skills when we have to maintain our demeanor. Dealing with an irritable supervisor, being graceful during our daily commute, tolerating the annoying behavior of an untidy roommate—each can chip away at our composure until the proverbial last straw breaks the camel's back.

One suggestion for maintaining a reserve of emotional capital is to build moments of respite into our daily routine. Time for a morning cup of coffee, taking a daily lunch break as opposed to eating at one's desk, fighting for and protecting workout time: whatever it is that we need to refuel our batteries is important, and we should allocate resources to those activities.

Emotional self-regulation is influenced by our personal and unique dispositions and temperament and by the wiring of our neural networks. We are not all created equal, and the challenges of delayed gratification affect us differently. Many techniques have been developed to help us achieve greater control and to delay the impulsive component of a behavioral process, including visualization. For example, people working on anger control are taught to visualize their emotions in terms of temperature and color: when the emotions are volatile, they are cognitively coded red and hot, whereas when they cool down and become more controlled, they reenter a blue zone. Distraction can also be a useful technique in altering the focus and thereby the urgency of the surfacing need (Mischel & Ayduk, 2011).

In the opera *The Magic Flute*, by Mozart, Tamino, one of the lead characters, has to complete a hero's journey that includes several challenges, including not speaking. Only by controlling his behavior and remaining focused on his long-range goal of finding his soul mate Pamina can he traverse the many symbolic obstacles that stand between him and his goal. This opera provides an excellent example of how appropriate self-regulation allows us to align our inner feelings, needs, and urges to reach the overarching goals we regard as important. Mozart wrote this, his last opera, when he was 35 years old in 1791, the same year he died.

FOCUS POINT

The ability to regulate emotions, needs, and urges is perfected throughout childhood and is a part of socialization. We have to channel some urges into socially acceptable and prosocial expressions. Self-regulation and delaying gratification help us attain long-term goals by making the seemingly urgent short-term ones subservient to the long-range outcomes. Reliable, stable, and emotionally responsive and positive family networks seem to support self-regulation favorably. Many of our abstract planned activities require discipline and self-control. Emotional self-regulation is influenced by our personal dispositions and temperament and by the unique wiring of our neural networks.

Authentic Insight

Negotiating Vulnerability With Resilience

Like most parents, when my first child was born, I was terrified of everything. I obsessed over my age (40) and how old I would be when he graduated from high school. I fretted about every little infant ailment. I worried excessively about my own health, about my need to stay alive for him. I was concerned about my wife's health and how we would get along if something happened to her. In short, I had nightmares about everything that could go wrong. Then at four months he nearly died. On the day of his baptism, I noticed purple spots under his skin, and we came to learn that he had a serious infection, perhaps meningitis. My family waited in a hospital hallway, and I helped nurses hold him still while a doctor performed a lumbar puncture. He spent much of the next week hospitalized until it was safe for him to come home.

Our second scare came when he was three and we learned over ice cream that he had a serious peanut and tree nut allergy. This, in turn, became more and more frightening. Anyone with these allergies knows that no matter how careful you are, you are never careful enough. And every parent of a child with serious food allergies learns that you can't be with your child all of the time, that children with serious allergies have to learn how to take care of themselves earlier than most children. The ambulance rides and emergency room visits always stick with you, and you learn how fragile the entire enterprise of parenting can be. And you hear stories on the news of how quickly a child can die from an allergic reaction. You think to yourself, how will we ever manage this? How will he ever learn to cope with this?

You learn that your earliest fears of parenting can come true, but it is an egotistical exaggeration to think you can't handle adversity. It is worse to think you are so important that your wife and children couldn't manage without you. You learn just how resilient you are and, moreover, how resilient you need to be. What would I tell a younger parent? You will survive disasters, and because you are the parent, you have to survive them with grace, strength, and resilience. It isn't good enough where your children are concerned to mythologize your own frailty. To my way of thinking, giving your children the impression that you can't survive, that you can't endure, is one of the most destructive lessons you can teach.

Tolstoy famously wrote in *Anna Karenina* that "Happy families are all alike; every unhappy family is unhappy in its own way." This is true of the family crisis as well. There is no complete or satisfying preparation for every childhood illness, every childhood injury. Accepting this uncertainty is the clearest way to habituate yourself to resilience. This isn't an invitation to quietism or carelessness, but it is a means to develop the kinds of inner strengths necessary to good parenting.

Bryan Johnson, PhD, is a professor of English and the director of University Fellows & Micah Fellows, Samford University.

Resilience on Various Systemic Levels

Social Policy: Improving Family Outcomes

Significant shifts in family life. Geographically, the original extended family tended to be located in one space. Family members lived together in clusters, they worked as a team, and they supported each other in caring for the elderly, the infirm, and youngsters. If a family member faced a challenge, those closest to him or her would provide support. As is the case today, family units focused on survival and were the building blocks of the larger societal structures. One relevant difference is that current families tend to be more scattered, and older generations cannot consistently support younger generations and vice versa.

The Industrial Revolution. With the Industrial Revolution, families migrated toward employment opportunities, and those were found in and around cities. The workplace was no longer exclusively on the farm; instead, it could be in the factory or the workshop. This shift in location was most significant, as it instantly created a number of challenges for the family in terms of finding social and economic support. Family groups who had to move into urban areas often ended up in high-density and decaying housing. These frequently appalling living conditions did not support the emotional and physical health of the family. There is ample documentation of young children working in porcelain factories where they breathed in the dust of the unfired clay and the fumes of the glazes. Many of these children developed breathing related problems, as they were working in untenable surroundings.

We know from historical diaries and court documents that family violence, disease, and child abandonment escalated when living conditions were cramped and challenging. Housing conditions were appalling and tenants were frequently taken advantage of by gouging slumlords who rented out quarters that were barely livable.

> Many of these families often found themselves living in crowded tenements with more than one family living in small and rodent-infested quarters. Many individuals, including children, also found themselves working in the highly dangerous, unsafe, and exploitative conditions in the emerging factory system. Living in such marginally economic and otherwise vulnerable conditions these individuals were without the benefit of health protection and coverage for themselves and their families. (Rasheed, Rasheed, & Marley, 2010, p. 6)

The extremely challenging work environments affected an especially vulnerable population group, namely, the children. Labor was exploited, youngsters frequently had to work, and education suffered so illiteracy grew.

Displaced families. Both workplace and home conditions combined to precipitate numerous social problems. Displaced families, desperate for work and barely surviving, were at the mercy of an emerging factory system that was typically exploitative and did not serve the interests of the family. There are exceptions to these tales of oppression. Two British confectionery manufacturers, Rowntree and Cadbury, created villages for factory employees where families could live under good conditions and children could receive an education in schools supported by the factories. Similarly, in the United States, chocolatier Milton S. Hershey built a model town called Hershey, Pennsylvania, and founded numerous related philanthropic initiatives (see in this chapter the Global Glimpse titled "Chocolate and the Sweeter Life").

Political and Social Reform Movements

Historically, horrific social, housing, and work conditions were documented both in North America and Europe. As with all pressing problems, these also elicited a response from society in the form of various political and social reform movements intent on influencing social policy pertaining to the family (Rasheed et al., 2010, pp. 5–6). Groups of forward-thinking initiators petitioned governments and raised public awareness that reform was imperative. They targeted areas such as child labor, compensation (children were earning but pennies a day), health-care support, and other ways to help those in poverty.

Authentic Insight

Policy as a Protective Process

Resilience is described as a family's ability to surface from a difficult situation even stronger than before. Froma Walsh (2016), a therapist and researcher on family resilience, identified nine processes in the family resilience framework that are key to strengthening family responses to adversity: making meaning of adversity, maintaining a positive outlook, valuing transcendence and spirituality, being flexible, balancing connectedness and separateness, sharing social and economic resources, communicating with clarity, expressing emotions openly, and using collaborative problem solving.

Ecological theory suggests that families are affected by the interactions of direct and indirect environmental influences. Bogenschneider (2014), an expert in family policy, argues that policy shapes many of the environmental conditions under which families function.

For example, policy influences the following family processes:

> Who and when we marry, and who can perform the ceremony.
>
> Who can be on a parent's insurance policy, and which conditions are covered, such as prenatal care for a dependent or birth control options.
>
> Where a baby can be delivered, and who can deliver it.
>
> When and how a child can be removed from a family.
>
> How much assistance a family can receive to purchase food and under which circumstances (e.g., unemployment or addictive disorders).
>
> Where low-income families can live.
>
> Who can have release time from work to care for a family member, which family member, and under what circumstances.

Family policy, a subset of social policy, is described by Bogenschneider (2014) as

> Policy that aims to protect, promote, and strengthen families by addressing one or more of the five explicit functions families perform: family formation, partner relationships, economic support, child rearing, and caregiving. (p. 57)

Unfortunately, family policy often takes a backseat to other types of policy, particularly economic policy. The primary reason is a lack of professionals trained in evidence-based family policy (Bogenschneider, 2014). More research is needed to determine the consequences of current family policies and the need for additional family-related policies.

Family professionals are in a unique position to educate policy makers about the intended and unintended consequences of policies on families. What would happen if more family practitioners focused on social policy, specifically family policy, as the tenth protective process for family resilience? Instead of making a difference in the life of one family, policy can simultaneously impact the lives of many families.

Kristie B. Chandler, PhD, is a chair and professor in human development and family science, with a special interest in family-related policies.

Sources: Bogenschneider (2014); Walsh (2016a).

Part of the agenda was accessibility to humane employment and housing conditions. In England as well as Holland and other European countries, we can, to this day, visit historically preserved "poorhouses," which replaced the medieval almshouses and were a tribute to these early movements focused on taking responsibility for the elderly, poor, and outcast within communities.

Social policy is a crucial link in ensuring the well-being of the people. For educators, the following resource affiliated with Purdue University's Family Impact Institute is helpful: http://www.familyimpactseminars.org. This organization also publishes a detailed brochure titled *The Family Impact Rationale: An Evidence Base for the Family Impact Lens*, which presents an empirical and theoretical case for promoting family policies and programs that create the conditions for families to do their best (see Bogenschneider, Little, Ooms, Benning, & Cadigan, 2012).

Belief systems, including religion. How we create the meaning of our worlds will determine how we interpret and experience the events occurring in our lives. As Walsh (2016b, p. 39) poetically states,

> Belief systems are at the heart of all family functioning and are powerful forces in resilience. We cope with crisis and prolonged adversity by making meaning of our experience: linking it to our social world, to our cultural and spiritual beliefs, to our multigenerational past, and to our hopes and dreams for the future.

We view our lives through the lenses of our culture, our gender, our education, our socioeconomic situation, our spirituality, and our ethics and values. Our world is filtered through them, explaining why we each have such differing subjective realities. In turn, these shape our identity. Belief systems can be secular or religious, but even for persons who do not subscribe to a formal religious stance, cultural components embodied by religion are present and can be influential. For instance, if we were raised in the West in European cultural contexts, we are influenced by Judeo-Christian traditions, so an understanding of the major themes and symbols in Christianity unlock and explain so much of the fabric of society as represented by rituals and customs. A visit to a cemetery will reveal religious symbols on grave markers. Art and literature most likely contain religious symbolism. There is no clear way of separating culture and belief systems into watertight compartments.

By the same token, our belief systems can guide and support us in finding meaning, especially in the face of adversity. Belief or, indeed, the human struggle to create meaning can allow us to find significance within the challenges that face us, as Viktor Frankl, the Austrian Holocaust survivor, stated in his book *Man's Search for Meaning*. He said that people have a choice concerning the dignity and the attitude with which they face great suffering and that, absent either an actual, internal purpose or a spiritual, external purpose, humans create their own "existential" meaning. This "striving to find meaning" involves personal choice—the freedom to make one's own decision about one's own unique life task. This choice can, in itself, provide some meaning in situations that appear to be devoid of meaning or reason.

In religious and spiritual contexts, this transcendence allows an individual to find a larger purpose or meaning, with the hope that transformation takes place through growth (Walsh, 2016b, p. 44). This process of choosing life's meaning ties in with the sense of control; namely, if an individual has such a choice, that person is not completely at the mercy of adversity.

Religious organizations have a long history of helping communities. In the Middle Ages and beyond, the monasteries and convents were a refuge for travelers, scholars, destitute mothers, orphans, and others in need of shelter. The concepts of helping one's neighbor and allocating charity as part of life's obligations were emphasized by the religious doctrines at the time. Currently, most religious groups and all the major world religions are aware of the challenges some in their congregations may face and have put formal support systems in place. Treating your neighbor as you yourself would like to be treated is a recurrent theme.

Throughout their history, religious organizations and other institutions concerned with social well-being explored ways to help families. Much of this help occurred within the extended family and community and was provided by physicians, priests, respected elders in the community, and other figures identified as having the wisdom that managing challenging situations would require. For instance, a number of contemporary religious institutions run groups supporting single parents, divorced individuals, teenagers, singles, parents of young children, the elderly, and the grieving. Groups may be run by professional counselors or other health professionals, such as social workers and clergy, and these groups serve a very important role within the community. Some clients feel that if help is provided within the wider religious context, it is destigmatized and more acceptable.

Additionally, in these settings the personal religious and spiritual opinions of participants are respected. In the Catholic Church, the practice of confession also serves a special function. Apart from its religious aims, confession provides a safe and confidential way to share one's innermost turmoil. For many people, their spiritual and religious community is a valued source of support and wisdom concerning life's many transitions and challenges.

Sacred spaces anchoring community. Places of worship become witnesses to humanity's joys and sorrows, irrespective of the specific faith they represent. They are among the physical spaces where we celebrate new life and new love, and say farewell at the time of death. Faith-based organizations can house documents that provide clues to history, that tell who a congregation welcomed, married, and buried. These records often link us to our distant past. Religious organizations also serve an important role in immortalizing history. Plaques on the walls and names on the graves and crypts of churches, cathedrals, cemeteries, and other sacred spaces bear witness to generations passed, and, specifically, to individuals who served their particular faith, community, or nation.

Hindu and Buddhist temples and Islamic mosques celebrate these core faiths in culturally unique ways. They also present a sacred space in which communities can unite and reflect and individuals can renew their personal connections to core beliefs. Just as our sacred spaces reflect some of our individual belief and spiritual systems, they are also shaped by the needs of those they serve. This bidirectional relationship establishes many of the attributes we recognize from a well-functioning family (Gerhardt, 2013, p. 12). Entering most religious sanctuaries, we encounter a place where we can bring our joys and our sorrows, and they resonate with fellow worshippers.

Viscount Melbourne's tomb in St. Paul's Cathedral in London is guarded by two beautifully sculpted angels. Particularly touching are the nearby memorials to the fallen from the two world wars and other conflicts. These individuals paid the highest price by serving their country. As one enters Westminster Abbey, one sees the grave of the "Unknown Warrior" seasonally decorated with the red poppies of remembrance and other floral tributes. This memorial reminds all of us who enter that many have fought and sacrificed for the values we hold dear. Sacred spaces are where we can weep in despair and mourn our dead. In this way, architecture serves to support us in our fragile human hours, and what we consider to be holy ground shelters and sustains us so that we can regain sufficient strength and hope to continue life's journey (Kilde, 2008).

Much like the family system shelters an individual family member, the places of worship provide both the emotional and spiritual shelter to families and communities. A place of worship can become part of the fabric that connects us. Through ritual, they contribute to marking transitions in the family life cycle. Through community, they provide a wider fabric of connectedness.

Social connectedness and well-being. Lifestyle choices contribute to life outcomes. We choose and work toward wellness. It takes effort to choose healthful behaviors, but doing so can contribute to well-being and thus to resilience. The mind likes to be housed in a body that is respected. The joy we feel within the comfort of our closest and most trusted friendships and family circles radiates its own sense of well-being and contentment. This kind of connectedness obviously facilitates emotional well-being, but research among seniors suggests that it also encourages longevity and general wellness. What characterized the long-living seniors included a physical lifestyle that supported good health, appropriate daily life activity to complete chores (health and wellness), and, importantly, a social support system of long-standing friends and close relatives. Specific factors that this review study highlighted were social and psychological well-being, physical health, spirituality and transcendence, and environmental and economic security (Zanjari, Sani, Chavoshi, Rafiey, & Shahboulaghi, 2017).

This important social network may be fairly accessible for persons who spend most of their lives in the same village or region; after all, they complete the life cycle with the same group of trusted friends. Social contact and the sense of being accepted for oneself contribute to feelings of belongingness and well-being (Gupta & Sharma, 2018). Human beings are wired to be social; we need a group to support and validate us. We thrive on constant social exchange—the opportunity to belong. The group also supports us in our chances of survival.

Additionally, group connectedness can provide a sense of coherence, which can enable an individual, as a member of a social group or family system, to share a crisis event and derive meaning from it. The group will contribute to perseverance and strength, to resilience, allowing a person to tolerate ambiguity and to gather strength for those aspects of events and circumstances that are unchangeable (Walsh, 2016b, p. 44). Additionally, the group can anchor an experience and provide a sense of continuity, normalcy, and context. When attribution bias tends to occur, the family or social group can mitigate self-blame and balance perceptions with their points of view. Importantly, families can ease the process of pain, even if they are helpless in the face of its outcome (Walsh, 2016b, p. 61).

Precisely for these reasons, *civic engagement* is also important. It not only supports the life goals of a participating individual but also, in its group expressions, represents the quality and nature of our culture and society. How we create and maintain societal order, how we manage power and subservience as a group: all these dimensions find an outlet in social policy, as well as in cultural and artistic expressions.

> **The future of peace and prosperity that we seek for all the world's peoples needs a foundation of tolerance, security, equality and justice. That foundation is the family. It is only by protecting families, from famine as well as from fragmentation, that they can prosper.**
>
> Kofi Annan, seventh secretary general of the United Nations and Nobel Peace Prize recipient

Self-help organizations. Some help-giving behaviors that support resilience are offered, to this day, by lay counselors, coaches, and other nonprofessionals who seek to intervene, often because they themselves have experienced similar challenges. For instance, women with breast cancer are supported by extended networks of survivors who offer the lessons they learned from their experiences to newly diagnosed patients. This is a very powerful network because of its accessibility. It also serves the function of supporting the multi-professional team involved

FOCUS POINT

Historically, dismal social, housing, and work conditions were documented both in North American and Europe. Groups petitioned governments for change and raised public awareness that reform was imperative. They targeted areas such as child labor, compensation, education, health care, and social policy pertaining to the family. The way we derive meaning from and manage adversity is influenced by numerous factors related to resilience. We view our lives through the lenses of our culture, our gender, our education, our socioeconomic situation, our spirituality, our ethics and values, and other personal and social factors. These, in turn, allow us to find significance within challenges. Additionally, group connectedness can provide a sense of cohesiveness that supports us because, as part of a social group or family system, we can share and derive meaning from a crisis.

HISTORIC GLIMPSE

THE SUNDAY SCHOOL MOVEMENT

The early Sunday school movement in eighteenth- and nineteenth-century England addressed the needs of child laborers, who missed out on schooling because they worked long hours. Although history documents schools in England as early as the sixth century, education was considered a great privilege. School attendance from age 5 to 10 was not compulsory in England until the 1880s, schools were unregulated, and working-class children rarely benefitted from continuity in education. In the United States, a school in Boston (Boston Latin School) is regarded as the oldest public school.

Frequently education was provided in the context of a church setting, and the Sunday school did offer only religious-based training in morals and literacy, with perhaps some rudimentary mathematics thrown in. Still, a main concern of the Sunday school movement was to educate children who could not go to school during the week. They were taught on the only free day they had, namely, on Sundays.

The Sunday school movement is usually attributed to William King, who convinced his friend Robert Raikes (1736–1811) of the importance of such an initiative. Raikes seems to have garnered most of the credit, which should justly be shared with King. A statue in the Victoria Embankment Gardens in London honors Raikes. The movement's outcome was to teach working children on Sundays and empower them with literacy.

This statue in the Victoria Embankment Gardens in London honors Robert Raikes (1736–1811), who together with his friend William King founded the first Sunday school in England in 1780. These schools empowered working-class children with literacy.

Source: Public domain.

in treatment. Other examples can be found in the field of addiction disorders and weight management. Persons dealing with similar situations may be matched to a sponsor or an informal buddy who provides nonprofessional or lay support.

GLOBAL GLIMPSE

CHOCOLATE AND THE SWEETER LIFE: THE VISION FOR ENHANCED COMMUNITY LIVING

Catering for the sweet tooth has always been lucrative; not much has changed in that respect. But when some of those earnings are reinvested for the greater good of a community, it is an exemplary tale. It serves as an inspiration to our present-day economic giants and supports the notion that grassroots initiatives can make a significant difference because they add up to initiate social changes. A contemporary equivalent is the Bill and Melinda Gates Foundation.

Utopia or as close as it gets. At the turn of the twentieth century, reports concerning public and slum housing were appalling. They painted pictures of dark, unsanitary living conditions that promoted illness and of overcrowded spaces where several children shared a bed. Not surprisingly, the tragedy of infant mortality was common.

Confectionary entrepreneur Joseph Rowntree had a vision to uplift the lives of his factory workers and the local community:

> I do not want to establish communities bearing the stamp of charity but rather of rightly ordered and self-governing communities.

Following his Quaker ideals, he acquired 150 acres near Earswick in England with the purpose of creating a community that supported family values. It was planned around a generous green space planted with numerous trees. The first houses were built in the early 1900s. Because of his religious beliefs, Joseph Rowntree did not include a public house (or pub, as we now know it); he sought to minimize the use of alcohol. Rowntree's estate continues to this day, and his first village, New Earswick, has been added to by the Joseph Rowntree Housing Trust, which now maintains thirty sustainable neighborhoods that govern themselves. New Earswick is intended as mixed housing for people from different financial backgrounds. Rowntree, the company, was eventually incorporated by Nestlé (Richardson, 2002).

A similar concept was implemented by the Cadbury brothers, George and Richard, who used their skills to manage the chocolate factory they inherited from their father, John Cadbury. Bournville (the model village) was established with funds generated by the Cadbury chocolate empire. For cocoa lovers, the brand name Bournville was associated with a dark chocolate bar named after the local river Bourn. Bournville is located near Birmingham, England. The Cadbury family, which also had Quaker religious values, was vested in the health and well-being of their employees. Queen Victoria was said to have loved the brand and granted Cadbury a "Royal Warrant," meaning that the company supplied sweets to the royal household. To this day, the Cadbury brand name is internationally recognized.

Milton S. Hershey (1857–1945), the American chocolatier, instigated a similar initiative in Pennsylvania, creating the Hershey model town. Additionally this philanthropist opened a school for orphan boys, later the Milton Hershey School; a hospital; the Hershey Gardens and the Hershey Theatre; and other establishments. He also provided an endowment to Pennsylvania State University. To this day, the Hershey Trust continues to fulfill the community-centered initiatives of its founder (http://www.hersheypa.com/about-hershey/milton-hershey.php).

A present-day example of a designed village supporting family values and the family-work balance was initiated by the UK's Prince Charles. Poundbury, located near Dorchester in the county of Dorset, England, is a mixed-use community that focuses on pedestrians rather than cars and represents a fresh approach to living arrangements in the twenty-first century (https://duchyofcornwall.org/poundbury.html).

Sources: Cadbury (2010, 2019); Fitzgerald (1995); Hershey (2019); J. Martin (2018); Vernon (2005).

The Bournville village green, Bournville, Birmingham, West Midlands, UK. This common area is part of the village that chocolate built. These model villages were initiatives to create healthy communities supporting family life.

Source: Universal History Archive/Getty Images.

Authentic Insight

A Canopy of Social Reality: Sociological Understanding and Family Dynamics

Early sociological thinking included work by classical theorists who addressed human experience at both the societal and personal levels. The idea that society is a system of order that can give meaning to one's personal and interpersonal experiences is foundational to sociological thinking.

Émile Durkheim (1858–1917) provided early research that focused on societal influences as they impacted on suicide rates. He demonstrated that individuals who live within social contexts of isolation and alienation were at greater risk of taking their own lives. Durkheim borrowed the French term "anomie" from the French philosopher Jean-Marie Guyau and loosely used it to denote "without order." In such social settings, life was filled with lack of clarity and with associated feelings of detachment. In contrast, he argued that rigid social contexts could present as oppressive and restrictive, posing a higher risk to personal feelings of selfhood. The former represent contexts of *underintegration*, or lack of integration, whereas the latter are contexts of *overintegration*. Neither represents an optimal condition for individuals.

Subsequently, sociology has envisioned a dialectical relationship between the person and society. The work of Berger and Luckman (1966), titled *The Social Construction of Reality: A Treatise in the Sociology of Knowledge*, has become a benchmark of this understanding. They argue that, historically, humans have "created themselves" through the construction of institutions that form a "canopy" of social reality. It is under this canopy that lived experiences are taken for granted. Lives are lived collectively. With sufficient order and predictability, personal behavior and emotion seem to provide continuity of the self. As these elements of the canopy intersect in the same context, they define our lives.

Alfred Schütz (1899–1959), the social phenomenologist, suggested that there are multiple realities. These can be sufficiently integrated, and a context is thereby created in which individuals can navigate through their daily lives with minimal behavioral or emotional disruption. If these multiple realities are oppositional and not sufficiently interdependent, an individual's lived experience can be filled with unanticipated disruptions, and that individual is at risk of becoming a disintegrated self and of feeling an existential dread. Anthony Giddens (b. 1938), a British sociologist, argues that the ushering in of modernity and later postmodernity produced a fragmentation of the self and thus a feeling of "ontological insecurity," or, in simpler terms, an unstable mental state.

Within society, the family as an institution is a primary group that provides a lifelong social location. The family frames our experience by introducing us to the possibility of social participation. Later, this can become the family of procreation in which a parent is charged with framing the capacities and resources for the social participation of children. It is within the family that society, as a set of institutions, intersects with individuals living their lives.

Families who engage in a balanced and integrated structure of roles and processes, within a social context of rigidity or chaos, can buffer their members against extremes in the external social order. In short, they foster resilience. When families construct their own order and process, while maximizing their individual and collective resources through discourse, they can reduce the impact of outside forces on family members. Some societies offer policies and stability that maximize family processes, and these societal-level structures increase the buffering effect of the family. Poverty, war, or societies without social policies challenge families, so that even the most resilient may struggle to create healthy contexts for their members.

Importantly, sociology presents a systemic framework to enhance the examination and understanding of family processes.

Hugh Floyd, PhD, is a professor and past chair of sociology and licensed marriage and family therapist and supervisor.

SPOTLIGHT ON THEORIES

Theory of Resilience and Relational Load (TRRL)

The **theory of resilience and relational load (TRRL)** counts as a fairly recent development, but as with most theories, it has antecedents and is rooted in several other theories pertaining to communication, family stress management, attachment theory, family systems dynamics, and affectionate exchange theory, to name a few (Afifi & Harrison, 2018).

Integrating these combined underpinnings into TRRL is partly accredited to authors Afifi, Merrill, and Davis (2016). The core of this theory emphasizes the complex interactions between individuals, their families, communication patterns, family dynamics, and the physiologic processes associated with stress. The essence of this approach can be summarized as follows:

> TRRL . . . assumes that social relationships have the power to significantly alter an individual's stress trajectories—either positively or negatively—because the individual is inherently embedded within the larger relational systems that influence those trajectories. (Afifi & Harrison, 2018, p. 325)

What happens in the family, especially in terms of communication, support, and modeling, plays a role in strengthening us in our ability to handle challenges and in the manner in which we approach them. If our families demonstrate that they are trustworthy safety nets, they will thereby give us greater courage to negotiate the unknown, and, importantly, they can lessen the physiologic expressions of stress. It is as if they provide the soothing balm for life's injuries.

Regaining our balance. If our families maintain their deep-rooted positive regard for us, they neutralize the negative feedback loops elicited by

(Continued)

(Continued)

failure, rejection, and loss, and they can lessen the impact of those events by providing us with a protective shield, which is predominantly emotional in nature. As they protect our self-esteem, they also encourage us to try again, to get up and face the difficulties that initially caused us to lose our balance.

The theory of resilience and relational load illuminates that the nature of the family network affects the relationships within that family in an ongoing manner. How we communicate may be affected by how safe and valued we feel within a family context and by the tone of and the warmth contained in those communications. This, in turn, can increase our stakes in what we dare to tackle—whether we will reach for those goals that might seem a little out of reach, initially. Importantly, too, family emotional quality and tone can mitigate the frustrations experienced while facing difficulty.

These are important components of resilience:

- How we perceive the obstacle, given that we can rely on the combined efforts of the family to overcome it
- Whether we can muster the self-regulation and discipline to continue trying after setbacks
- Whether we can reach for long-range goals while relinquishing short-term pleasures and avoiding immediate distractors

Theoretical Approach

According to Afifi and Harrison (2018, pp. 325–326) several aspects characterize the theory of resilience and relational load:

- *Communication.* Generally, it is regarded as a theory anchored in communication sciences and acknowledging major influences from related disciplines. How and with whom we communicate are important elements in this theory. When facing adversity, we talk to our closest and most trusted circle about these challenges, and their response can guide as well as strengthen us. These conversations allow us to manage and mitigate the stress accompanying the adversity or challenge.
- *Relationships.* TRRL emphasizes relationships. When we seek support and encouragement from others, we can access a systemic cache of pooled resources. If emotional capital is used in an individual context, it can also be applied systemically and vice versa. TRRL focuses on the supportive components of relationships, as opposed to the threatening parts.
- *Communal orientation.* Additionally, there is a focus on who invests in whom. The term used for this is "communal orientation." In families, for instance, we might find specific dyads composed of family members that seek each other out for support, whereas other family members are kept in the dark or not accessed. Who is included may also be related to their ability and competence in providing the required support. A person who tends to catastrophize would not be an ideal choice in an adverse situation; that individual could make matters worse, or make them *seem* worse, which is hardly helpful when it comes to resilient behavior.
- *Cyclical process of calibration.* As we interact with others, we are within feedback loops where our responses receive counter responses. Depending on how those persons around us relate to and interpret the adverse or challenging situation, we may adjust our own reactions as well. Calibration is adjusting against a norm; for instance, we can calibrate scales so that they all give the same reading when weighing the same mass. In the same way, we can calibrate our responses to crises in relation to the responses of family members.
- *Physiologic stress response.* How our bodies react to stress, including the related long-term bodily outcomes, is an important factor in resilience. Increasingly, current research on many facets of cognitive, emotional, and social functioning integrate the physiological component. We may vary in what triggers our stress, and our

tipping points are individual. Factors that can influence these relate to genetic predispositions, neuroplasticity, prenatal influences, early childhood experiences related to attachment, need gratification, and more. It is a complex topic that is receiving much interest from current researchers.

Evaluation of TRRL

The central theme is relationship maintenance; the factors that strengthen versus those that weaken relationships are studied. Much of this research echoes the work that has been done in the context of marriage and family therapy. The presumption is that couples and families can improve their communication patterns. If a family chooses to do so, it may improve the overall climate within that family and its available resources.

The theory is applicable in contexts where persons are closely invested and bonded through family ties, be they marital, through shared ancestry, or otherwise. The presence of emotional *attachment* is important, as this goes hand in hand with emotional *investment*.

Afifi and Harrison (2018) maintain that "the ultimate test of the theory is the development of interventions that can foster resilience and thriving . . . [and] help couples and families learn maintenance skills" (p. 335).

Therapy fosters similar goals. Much of the training of therapists is dedicated to addressing some of these desired outcomes. For therapists, this particular framework may be helpful, especially as it pertains to resilience.

In a Nutshell

- The theory of resilience and relational load (TRRL) is a fairly recent development and is strongly reliant on insights from related fields such as communication, family stress management, attachment theory, family systems dynamics, and affectionate exchange theory.
- How and with whom we *communicate* are important elements in this theory.
- The central theme is *relationship maintenance*, and the factors that strengthen versus those that weaken relationships are studied. When we seek support and encouragement from others, we can access a systemic cache of pooled resources.
- TRRL focuses on who invests in whom, which is called *communal orientation.*
- As we interact with others, we adjust our responses in relation to those of others within our communication "feedback loop." This is referred to as *calibration*.
- Increasingly, current research on *physiologic stress responses* reveals that facets of cognitive, emotional, and social functioning have physiological components. We may vary in what triggers our stress, and our tipping points are individual.

CHAPTER FOCUS POINTS

The Pillars of Resilience

- Resilience is multifactorial. It surfaces from a web of traits and conditions, many of them related to home and family influences, and then circles outward to include communities and larger social systems.
- Resilience includes personal, familial, and societal strengths that merge into a complex network of interrelated factors. It gains momentum through civic engagement and social policy.
- Factors contributing to resilience occur on micro-, meso- and macrosystemic levels, and the effects are bidirectional and multidirectional.
- Models of resilience also incorporate systems of meaning, emotion, control, maintenance, and family stress response.

Resilience and Self-Regulation

- The ability to regulate emotions, needs, and urges is perfected throughout childhood and is part of socialization. We have to channel some urges into socially acceptable and prosocial expressions.
- Self-regulation and delayed gratification help us attain long-term goals by making the seemingly urgent short-term ones subservient to the long-range outcomes.
- Reliable, stable, and emotionally responsive and positive family networks seem to support self-regulation favorably. Many of our abstract, planned activities require discipline and self-control.
- Emotional self-regulation is influenced by our personal dispositions and temperament and by the unique wiring of our neural networks.

Resilience on Various Systemic Levels

- Historically, abysmal social, housing, and work conditions were documented in both North American and Europe. Groups petitioned governments for change and raised public awareness that reform was imperative.
- Social reformers targeted areas such as child labor, compensation, education, health care, and other social policies pertaining to the family.
- The way we derive meaning from and manage adversity is influenced by numerous factors related to resilience. We view our lives through the lenses of our culture, our gender, our education, our socioeconomic situation, our spirituality, our ethics and values, and other personal and social factors. These perspectives can allow us to find significance within challenges.
- Additionally, group connectedness can provide a sense of cohesiveness, so we can share a crisis event and derive meaning from it as part of a social group or family system.

Spotlight on Theories: Theory of Resilience and Relational Load (TRRL)

- The theory of resilience and relational load (TRRL) is a fairly recent development and is strongly reliant on insights from related fields such as communication, family stress management, attachment theory, family systems dynamics, and affectionate exchange theory.
- How and with whom we *communicate* are important elements in this theory.
- The central theme is *relationship maintenance*, and the factors that strengthen versus those that weaken relationships are studied. When we seek support and encouragement from others, we can access a systemic cache of pooled resources.
- TRRL focuses on who invests in whom, which is called *communal orientation*.
- As we interact with others, we adjust our responses in relation to those of others within our communication "feedback loop." This is referred to as *calibration*.
- Increasingly, current research on *physiologic stress responses* reveals that facets of cognitive, emotional, and social functioning have physiological components. We may vary in what triggers our stress, and our tipping points are individual.

CHAPTER 10

Communication and Life's Journey

Learning Outcomes

After studying this chapter, you should be able to

1. Illustrate the influences and growth of *intergenerational* family systems.
2. Describe the process and importance of *partner selection*.
3. Summarize the *shifts* between parents and children that occur throughout a family's lifespan.
4. Express the two lead factors that characterize *coparenting* activities.
5. Analyze *relational dialectics theory* and identify four assumptions of this theory.

Families: Constant yet Ever Changing

As a child, I was given a kaleidoscope and was fascinated by the same little pieces' ability to shift and drop to create ever-changing magical patterns. There seemed to be no end to the configurations; sometimes they were predominantly in one color while at other times they seemed overcrowded and busy. Families function like that as well. In our dynamic dance of engagement and disengagement (getting closer and moving further away from each other), we are like those kaleidoscopic pieces, forever reinventing our configurations.

The beauty of the family journey is that it is ever changing. Additionally, it is multidimensional because each one of our journeys is unique. Even so, we are all woven together in a single plait of sorts because we are connected as a family. There is that interplay between individuality and being part of a collective whole.

Family Lifespan Tracks

If we focus only on our own lives, each of us could be compared to a train speeding on a railway track, the different carriages representing different facets of life. But in this imaginary railway system, several tracks may be running parallel to each other. Each one of those trains has started its journey at a different time; each could represent a different generation. If we had three trains running on three sets of parallel tracks, and if we could climb from one train to the other across the tracks, we would be bridging generations. However, the lifespan of each of us contains or designates us to a particular life and generation, which we call our own. Still, we are significantly linked to and affected by the lives of family members in close proximity. This means that the family system becomes multidimensional because it includes not only different members but also, importantly, different generations.

Like a kaleidoscope, a family seeks and finds ever-changing configurations in its dynamic dance of engagement and disengagement. The family is forever reinventing structured patterns.

Source: Shutterstock/Tetyana Pavlovna.

Each generation is defined by and deals with challenges particular to where its members are in their lives. At each point of our lives, the major themes that preoccupy and challenge us are different, but we share them with other travellers who are at the same point in their lifespan journeys.

If we look at a family as an interrelated system, then, we can imagine each generation's lifespan as a track. We can stagger these tracks or lifespans and see where they overlap and intersect. Doing so provides us with a slice of the intergenerational family in terms of the developmental time of each member. Each generation is at a different point in its lifespan, but, chronologically, we are looking at this intergenerational family system at one particular moment in the family's history. Typically, generations are about 20 to 30 years apart, so by the time the fourth or youngest generation is born, the first or oldest generation is dealing with late adulthood and end-of-life themes (Bigner & Gerhardt, 2019, p. 122).

Intergenerational Families in Developmental Time

There are a number of ways to increase our understanding of families. One significant way is to look at families in the context of developmental time. Typical lifespan challenges tend to occur during predictable stages of a family's development. For example, newly formed families facing the task of raising young children may experience similar joys and difficulties—those associated with infancy and toddlerhood. Another typical challenge is that the new parents are solidifying their relationship with each other. Developmental challenges seldom arise in isolation. Instead there is an interaction between the generations, which highlights all the typical lifespan challenges for the generations involved.

Looking at families in a systemic manner, we observe the layers of the different generations as they stack up and influence each other. The grandmother who is dealing with recent bereavement because of the loss of her spouse (the grandfather in this family system) may be at a completely different place both emotionally and developmentally as compared to her adolescent grandchild, whose predominant challenges seem to be getting a driver's license (independence) and making decisions concerning higher education. Another example: while the baby is learning to walk, the grandfather is dealing with loss of balance. A subtle irony is that some of the challenges in early and later life display similar qualities: we struggle to gain skill in early life, and we struggle as we lose skill during later life (Bigner & Gerhardt, 2019, p. 120).

A family systems approach emphasizes the interrelatedness between components of that family system. This interrelatedness involves members of the nuclear family, but it can also stretch forward and backward to include the various generations of the extended family, typically up to four generations. In exceptional cases of longevity, it might include five generations. Typically, we assume that families add additional generations between ages 20 to 40, although there are exceptions. For that reason, we can stagger the lifespan stages in intervals of 25 years. This composite family could consist not only of various family members in the parental and child generations but also of grandparents and great-grandparents. In general, three to four generations could be interacting at any given time.

Intergenerational family systems can grow through the addition of new members, but they can also shrink as members pass away, especially members of the oldest generation. When someone from the younger generation dies, it typically affects the older generations significantly because, in an ideal world, we would hope that the oldest are the first to pass on. There can be loss in any generation, however, and the impact is always significant. As the oldest generation passes on, the next generation in line will take on the honored place of being the matriarchs and patriarchs of that particular family system. We can also compare this constant renewal of generations to the pattern we find in any school. As the highest classes graduate, new freshmen enter at the lowest levels. Every year, a class steps up one rung on the ladder until it, too, will become the graduating class. Each generation slowly matures to replace the generation ahead, ultimately. In short, new generations are added while older generations fall away (Bigner & Gerhardt, 2019, p. 120). The cyclical renewal of generations has been compared to a layered structure (Laszloffy, 2002). I tend to imagine building sand castles at the beach. We add new details on top while the bottom structures get absorbed by the beach because of the movement of the water.

If we look at this entire family structure with its different generations, it becomes easier to understand family-of-origin influences. Grandparents may influence their children because of their parenting approaches, and these children, in turn, become the parents of yet another generation. It is like an endless chain stretching over generations right back to the earliest known origins of humankind. By the same token, we hope that this intergenerational chain will also stretch forward into the future, into a time containing challenges we may not conceive of from our vantage point. We hope that we leave our children and their children with a world that displays hope and potential, but ultimately, we will not be around to witness the details.

The intergenerational layered structure, called the family, can be represented visually (see Diagram 10.1). It is possible to take a metaphorical slice out of the structure, and this slice would contain the different generations. In this way, one can see how the generations stack up and that there is a bidirectional influence between these generations.

DIAGRAM 10.1 **The family system is multidimensional and includes different members and generations. Each generation is at a different point in its lifespan, but we see where these lifespans overlap and intersect when we look at the intergenerational family system at one particular moment in the family's history.**

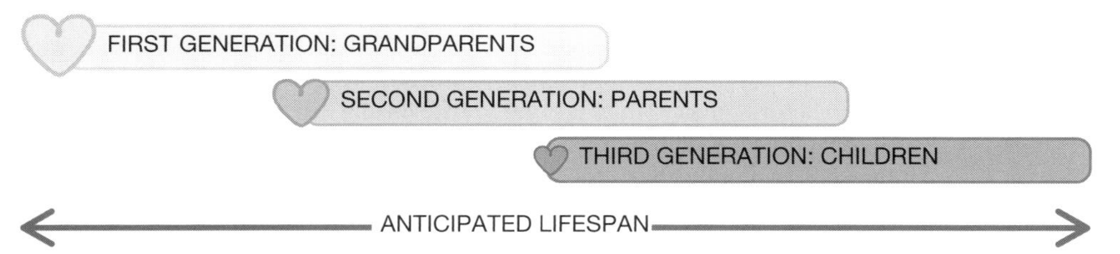

Source: Adapted from Bigner and Gerhardt (2019, p. 122).

FOCUS POINT

Family interactions and family transitions gain greater clarity when we see them against the backdrop of rituals and other significant markers. Looking at families from a systemic approach helps us see how different generations influence each other. We can best understand family-of-origin influences by looking at the entire family structure, which includes all the different generations. We can look at families in the context of developmental time and the predictable stages of family development. Intergenerational family systems grow and shrink. If we look at this entire family structure consisting of different generations, it is easier to understand family-of-origin influences. Three to four generations could be interacting at any given time. Each generation is on its own timeline determined by its members' time of birth.

Dynamics of Partner Selection

Traditionally, partner selection had much to do with the exchange of assets, especially those pertaining to possessions and power. Families searched for ways to enhance their own positions within the community, and the union of two individuals from different family groups could add to each family's position and importance within societal contexts. Because of these status and wealth considerations, matchmaking and arranged marriages were very common, even the norm. In a Chinese manuscript concerning family rituals dating back to the twelfth century, there are detailed instructions on how to negotiate a marriage, present betrothal gifts, welcome the bride, and then present her to her new in-laws. Important, too, was the presentation of the couple at the family shrine, which reinforced the symbolism of the joining of families (Hsi, 1991/2014).

Today, arranged marriages are not the norm in Western societies. But adults seeking partners do sometimes seek external help by subscribing to dating sites. Their choice of a specific site may narrow down their potential selection. For instance, the dating site may serve members of a particular religion, language group, or ethnicity. The person joining such a site knows that one of the factors he or she finds important in a mate has been preselected. Dating sites are also known to require members to fill in lengthy questionnaires; the thought is that algorithms can find appropriate choices based on the details provided (Ray, Bishop, & Dow, 2018). Persons on dating sites may narrow down the choices considerably by ranking factors that are important to them, and level of education, children from a previous marriage, or geographical location may be dealmakers or deal breakers, depending on the wish list (Jednak & Schulte, 2018).

The factors we find acceptable in acquaintances, work colleagues, or even the general public may not be the same as the stringent requirements we have for a potential partner, the individual who may be sharing some of the most intimate parts of our lives. One study that analyzed the choices of all applicants on a major dating site found that preferences concerning ethnicity, race, and cultural background play a prominent role in intimate partner choices (Hutson, Taft, Barocas, & Levy, 2018, p. 2). Generally, the applicants to the dating site were comfortable with great diversity and heterogeneity when it came to friends and acquaintances, but they showed less acceptance of diversity when it came to choosing a partner. They may also be influenced by family characteristics in their families of origin (Yu & Hertog, 2018).

Much of partner selection has to do with social exchange theory. We are willing to widen our choices considerably and to make major compromises, if we feel that exchanging assets is fair or beneficial. Partnering contains a large element of deal brokering. We negotiate in terms of what we feel we have to offer and, simultaneously, what we feel we can demand given our specific assets. Additionally, some assets may be more important than others; for instance, physical attractiveness may be equal in and equally important to both partners. People slot themselves into a category; they are looking for someone with equal or greater assets. Research on attractiveness has found that partners feel comfortable choosing someone as attractive as themselves, but that other qualities of a nonphysical nature also play a role (Nicholson, Coe, Emory, & Song, 2016).

On the other hand, McClintock (2017) states that statistical analyses of studies on so-called trophy wives do not strongly support the hypothesis that these wives exchange their looks for the social status or wealth of husbands; when studies did support this hypothesis, she found they lacked robustness, and other research simply did not support this premise. In the case of the beauty-status exchange hypothesis, there is also contrary evidence. Probably the truth can be found somewhere in the middle; for some couples, this exchange may factor in, for others, not. Heterogeneity, including the May-December couple, can be attributed to a variety of causes (Watkins, 2017). Partner selection, after all, is the culmination of predictable and unpredictable influences combined with timing; who knows what may spark mutual attraction and when that moment may occur?

A study by Bekk, Spörrle, Völckner, Spieß, and Woschée (2017) notes that, in the context of advertising, endorsers seem more convincing if their attractiveness matches that of the target viewer, or at least the viewer's perception of his or her attractiveness level. This creates a difficult situation for advertisers who target great numbers and diverse audiences. The researchers conclude, "These findings reveal attractiveness similarity as a new variable in endorser advertising" (Bekk et al., 2017, p. 509). Customers are also prone to judge a book by its cover; they are influenced by superficial appearances (Elmer & Houran, n.d.). This emphasis on the superficial may partly explain the preference for having highly attractive models and spokespersons represent beauty products and perfumes (Patel & Basil, 2017). Current research also confirms older findings: physical attractiveness can create a positive feedback loop in that those who are good looking may benefit from social and economic advantages, a variation of the halo effect. Physical attractiveness has a number of subtle and not-so-subtle advantages since appearance can influence psychological well-being as well (Gupta, Etcoff, & Jaeger, 2016).

Attractiveness does have a very subjective component to it, and what may be charming to one person may be off-putting to another. Research by Nicholson, Coe, Emory, and Song (2016) looked at subjective ratings of attractiveness in the context of political elections. It was evident that persons were rated as being less attractive if their political leanings were dissimilar to those of the raters. This confirms the subjective component of perception.

Also consider that an individual may not value appearance highly when it comes to choosing a partner. We rank the specific characteristics we value. One person is attracted to a sense of humor whereas another person is interested only in animal lovers. There is no telling what will be attractive to whom, and good matchmaking tries to match similarities. The wisdom from folklore that "opposites attract" holds much truth. Introverts and extroverts often match; we have one listener (introvert) and one talker (extrovert). Opposites can be attractive when we are assessing peripheral qualities, which creates greater diversity in relationships, but like often attracts like when it comes to central beliefs and attitudes.

Having different core value systems or dissimilar ethical, religious, or political views (e.g., conservative versus liberal) can definitely be a deal breaker in the search for a long-term partner. These differences may make it impossible for people to reach a neutral meeting point, and being too dissimilar can create dissonance or even conflict, which is not a desirable outcome for a long-term pairing.

Left: Marriage ceremonies are imbued with unique cultural and religious symbolism. Additionally, families merge and form new bonds through betrothal. *Right:* In this baby blessing ceremony, the family unites to welcome a child.

Sources: © iStock.com/triloks *(left)*; Dr. C. Adedoyin *(right)*.

Authentic Insight

Relational Development: The Unique Patterns of Family Relationship Development

In most of our relationships throughout the course of human life, we can observe patterns of development that follow one of several different developmental models. We can track romantic relationships through three models, for example: Knapp's stage model (1978), which outlines the five stages of coming together and the five stages of coming apart; the turning points model (Bolton, 1961), which lets us study relationship development through a series of meaningful turning points in dyads; and the relational dialectics model (Baxter, 1988), which lets us study the ebb and flow of relationships through an ever-fluctuating, dynamic course of interactions (dialectical tensions).

When analyzing our relationships though these models, most of the time we are considering voluntary relationships, or relationships that we sought out or chose. The inception and development of our familial relationships can look a bit different. There are, of course, exceptions to this premise, as the definition of family has expanded to include people we have chosen to be in our lives (e.g., through adoption or perhaps framing a network of friends as family). And we know that when we marry, most individuals are intentionally choosing a particular partner.

Many familial relationships develop in a more passive way; we are born into a family biologically connected. We do not have the autonomy to select our biological siblings, parents, cousins, or grandparents, and thus the course of relational development among these relationships can be quite different, as compared to those that we intentionally seek out. Interestingly, relational maintenance strategies are often presented with no distinction between these type of relationships (whether naturally placed in our lives or specifically chosen), and an argument could be made that this is an area needing further exploration in family communication scholarship.

Ashley J. George, PhD, is an assistant professor of communication studies.

Uncoupling

The reality of partnering or coupling also presents the flipside, namely, uncoupling. When we enter relationships, we hope that they will be ongoing—that, as in the fairy tales, we will be provided with the "and they lived happily ever after" option. In real life, people change and grow, and also grow apart. Relationships start with the best intentions but may flounder because they were built on what we were hoping to find instead of a foundation of reality.

In most significant relationships, there is a learning curve in which we accommodate, negotiate, and learn to anticipate each other's needs. Relationships that have a better promise of survival may be the ones in which the partners have learned to communicate well and, above all, to negotiate their way through the obstacle course of miscommunication and misunderstanding. Couples who have been together for a significant time know that it is important to pick their battles and to fight respectfully and with a sense of humor. The problem is not whether disagreements will occur; instead, it has to do with how these disagreements are handled (Curtis, 2015).

Crucially, there needs to be mutual respect and a neutral way of working through glitches, one that focuses on the process of reaching a mutually beneficial outcome. In unfair fighting, arguments from the past are dragged out and used as ammunition at inopportune times. In this type of relationship, winning seems paramount, as well as bringing one's partner down by any conceivable means—whether fair or unfair. Two people who have a successful relationship treat it as if it were a company in which both partners invest. The outcome of a disagreement should be beneficial to both, and negotiations should be respectful and uplifting to the other party (Curtis, 2015). The minute the partnership becomes the headquarters of a power battle, trouble is brewing. Individual partners will do and say things in order to gain power and position in the relationship. In essence, a true partnership is about acknowledging individual strengths and differences and using these to enhance collaboration. It is not a competition between partners with a secret blog log keeping track of who wins and who loses.

Some relationships are not meant to work out despite the labor and emotion invested in them. Relationships in which physical or verbal abuse plays a part in maintaining the power differential are ruled by fear, not respect. Ideally, partners should strengthen each other to bring out the best, not the beast, in each other. When one partner has just disinvested from the primary partnership and invested elsewhere, there may be no constructive alternative but to uncouple. This is especially relevant if a partner threatens the safety and well-being of the rest of the family. Frequently, addiction disorders can contribute to unbalanced relationships in which one partner feels that he or she cannot access the rational core of the other.

Relationship turbulence. When a relationship consists predominantly of turbulent and difficult times, it may be impossible to find that point of balance each family is seeking. External factors may contribute to the turbulence, such as addiction disorders, including gambling, substance abuse, sex addiction, or irresponsible spending. These conditions often encourage highly undesirable characteristics and behaviors, such as lying, deceit, unreliability, irresponsibility, and untrustworthiness. Relationship turbulence has a very high price tag attached to it, and that price is frequently paid by the children in the family as well as relatives and grandparents. Eventually, this type of interpersonal destruction has the ability to bankrupt the family system. In order for family members to survive, they need to extricate themselves from this tornado-like chaos, which threatens to swallow them and deplete their emotional and material resources or causes them to put everything but responding to family crises on hold (Hadfield, Amos, Ungar, Gosselin, & Ganong, 2018).

Children in unstable households may struggle with attachment as well as trust. How can one trust parents who go back on their word repeatedly? Children tend to forgive parents and, in a childlike manner, will hope against all expectation. But

FOCUS POINT

Social exchange theory is useful in explaining partner selection. Partnering contains a large element of deal brokering. We negotiate in terms of what we feel we have to offer and, simultaneously, what we feel we can demand given our specific assets. In most significant relationships, we accommodate, negotiate, and learn to anticipate each other's needs. Relationships that have a better promise of survival may be the ones in which partners have learned to communicate well and, above all, to negotiate respectfully. Uncoupling happens when a relationship is built on what participants were hoping to find instead of reality. Relationship turbulence can create partner instability, which creates a stressful family environment, especially for children. Well-functioning families require stability and an ongoing effort to seek homeostasis.

Authentic Insight

My Life in Numbers

I can sum up my life in numbers: 7 different placements in 6 years, while having attended 12 schools. But the most important number is "one," and it represents that one person who truly took an interest in me, who was the catalyst in turning my life around.

When I was eight years old, my life changed forever. I had to grow up. I could no longer be a kid. My mom needed me to protect her. My stepfather was addicted to cocaine and alcohol, and he was violent. Slowly, our household disintegrated—no water or power for two months, a can of soup for the family meal. When I look back, I see that growing up was a duty I had to fulfill. Then my mom became pregnant from a careless one-night stand, and the problems just piled up.

We settled in a small rural town, where everything was everybody's business. That also brought DHR* to our doorstep, thankfully so. I began working at age eleven, first at a haunted house then a skating rink, doing anything I could. Eventually all of this crashed, and by thirteen my will to live shimmered to almost nothing. It wasn't until I realized that hiding our miseries wasn't helping my family; maybe exposing them would help. With that in mind I confided in the social worker, and we were all removed from my mother's care.

In the right foster family things started turning around. I have been blessed to have been a part of many families. Most people look at foster care as a curse, but I have come to find that the most important people in my life are foster parents.

In high school I was president of the senior class and a drum major of the marching band. Being a drum major helped kids like me, who needed a peer group and a calling. In the welfare system, there are a few success stories, and I want to make sure that I will be an example of the best outcome rather than the worst. My life is not made up of the things that have happened to me, or the mistakes I have made, but it's made up of strength and perseverance, and of a few people who believed in me and inspired me with hope and a sense of worth.

In the midst of my despair, I was the least hopeful. But I am the story of dreams coming true. I have come so far and I will be forever grateful to those gracious donors who provided educational scholarships. Because of them I will be the first person in my family to graduate from university. The greatest lesson that I learned is that with Faith I can be in charge of my life, I can choose to make my life what it is. To put my experiences into words would be impossible. My story is a story of truth, faith, hard work, perseverance, and success. Take it from me, I am living it.

Anonymous

*In this case, DHR refers to an employee (possibly a social worker) from the Department of Human Resources, which, in some states, is charged with investigating allegations of child abuse or neglect.

this can exacerbate an unhealthy family environment and does not support the raising of emotionally resilient children. Erratic behavior that is combined with authoritarian outbursts can be exceptionally destructive for defenseless youngsters. Add to this destabilizing threats and one has a perfect recipe for major challenging situations.

Partner Instability and Union Disruptions

Relationship turbulence can be expressed in partner instability, which can be particularly stressful for children within a family. The on-again, off-again relationship leaves children as well as partners with insecurity. Well-functioning families require ongoing stability, and one of the goals of families is to seek homeostasis.

Partner instability creates an unstable platform for all those involved, and it does not contribute to healthy outcomes. Not all partnerships will be forever, and it is realistic that some will not last. For children, these scenarios of uncoupling or family disruption challenge many facets of their well-being.

> **"Any problem, big or small, within a family, always seems to start with bad communication. Someone isn't listening."**
>
> Emma Thompson (b. 1959), British actor and Oscar winner

Transitions and Turning Points

A lifespan contains many significant transitions and turning points, often marked by rituals. These transitions can be navigated more easily when they are recognized and supported by the community and its cultural context. In Hinduism, a person goes through 16 rites of passage during a lifetime; these are known as *Sanskaras*. Each one is described in detail, and there are instructions as to the appropriate way of acknowledging and celebrating these important lifespan markers. Different cultural contexts will have other rich ceremonies marking rites of passage. For participants, there is comfort in knowing that others have gone through similar rituals, and this knowledge adds a sense of cohesion and community.

Because rituals are shared within a specific cultural context, members of that cultural group understand the symbolism and can read the metaphorical shorthand of the messages that are being conveyed. Wedding and partnering ceremonies are universal, and most people choose to celebrate with a ritual promise to make an ongoing and serious commitment to a life partner. The specific way in which these ceremonies are celebrated varies tremendously from group to group, acknowledging cultural context. According to the Pew Research Center, about half the adults in the United States are married, and about 15 percent state that they met their partners through online dating services (Geiger & Livingston, 2019).

The relationship between parents and their children shifts repeatedly during a lifespan. Although we tend to view this relationship as being bidirectional, in that both parties influence one another, one of the parties may be the dominant initiator. In other words, one of the parties may be proactive, and the other may tend to be reactive. While caring for infants and toddlers, parents may seem to be predominantly in control and to initiate most of the caretaking rituals. That may be true in as much as the parent decides on the appropriate feeding and caring of the helpless infant. But as young as this infant is, she or he will communicate by means of crying, body language, and general responsiveness, providing clues to the caretaker concerning needs. For a new parent, this kind of communication can be a very intimidating process, similar to learning a new language. Initially, it may be difficult to decipher what the infant needs, but as the interaction between caretaker and child extends over time, a greater intuitive understanding grows as the bond between the adult and the infant strengthens.

Fast forward to the teenage years. During adolescence, children make an appropriate and distinct effort to assert their independence. They are becoming increasingly self-aware, extending ideas about their self-concept, reflecting on the major questions in life, and chiseling away at a personal philosophy. During this phase, we expect adolescents to try to balance out interpersonal power equally between themselves and their parents, and most of the adolescent tug of war pertains to independence and autonomy. It is for this reason that Erikson labeled this stage's life task as developing *identity* in spite of experiencing *role confusion*. According to Erikson, this stage happens when children are between 12 and 18 years old. Various coming of age rituals are associated with this stage, including the sweet-sixteen birthday party, the bar mitzvah, and the *quinceañera*.

During emerging or early adulthood, the focus shifts yet again (Arnett, 2000). Young adults are intent on partnering, and Erikson describes this phase as focusing on *intimacy* versus *isolation*. In Erikson's theory, a person has to resolve a psychosocial crisis, and if it is successfully mastered, that person moves on to face the challenges of the next stage. Many of our psychological theories incorporate life transition points and formally associate them with psychological tasks to be mastered. A major ritual of young adulthood is marriage or moving in together. Diagram 10.2 lists some of the reasons that people commit to marriage; note that establishing intimacy is related to the top three reasons.

DIAGRAM 10.2 **According to the Pew Research Center, about half the adults in the United States are married. The motivations for seeking this legal union are varied, with "love" being one of the leading factors. Four in ten new marriages involve a remarriage.**

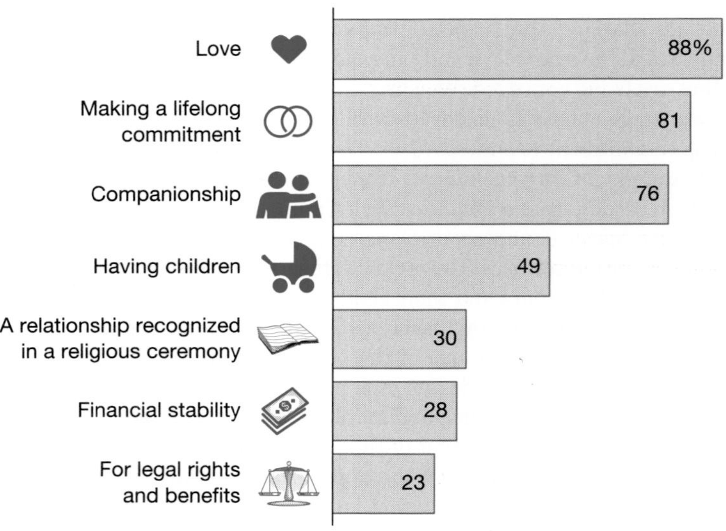

Source: Adapted from "Why get married?" Pew Research Center, Washington, D.C. (February 13, 2017), https://www.pewresearch.org/ft_17-02-09_lovemarriage_reasons.

FOCUS POINT

Rituals often mark significant transitions and turning points shared within specific cultural contexts. Children are central to many people, and rituals surrounding this life stage are particularly sacred throughout most of the world. Since antiquity, numerous rites have focused on the well-being and blessing of children.

After a young adult masters intimacy, he or she is in a position to become a parent, and the cycle starts again with the birth of a child. Because children are central to many people's lives and because they represent our future and the continuance of our species, rituals relating to children are particularly sacred. Most world religions recognize sacraments blessing infants and protecting them from harm. The high infant mortality of earlier centuries, which still exists in developing countries, made parents vulnerable because they lacked the ability to protect their children from harm. Even today we harbor fears for the safety of our children. Is it any wonder, then, that since antiquity numerous rites have focused on the well-being and blessing of children. Whether it is rubbing an infant with healing herbs mixed with red clay or the wearing of amulets, it is virtually universal to wish the vulnerable infant and young child a protected life journey.

Lifespan-Related Theories

Erik Erikson. The theory of Erik Erikson (1902–1994) focuses on lifespan development. The essence of Erikson's theory is that certain developmental crises need to be resolved and managed and that negotiating each crisis, or completing each stage, lays the foundation for continuing to the subsequent developmental stage. The one builds on the other, and the lessons learned at each stage of life will equip us for what is to follow. A good childhood is the foundation for appropriate adult development because one's lifespan is an integrated whole. At the time when Erikson formulated his theory, a lifespan approach was unusual. In this regard, he is considered a pioneer.

Erikson describes eight stages that stretch over a lifespan. Each stage acknowledges specific aspects of personality development (Erikson, 1950/1993). During the first four stages, from infancy to adulthood, parents can support and promote healthy development in their children. Parents or significant caregivers who hinder children may facilitate difficulties in subsequent stages. When parents care for children, the tasks that are mastered are bidirectional. For instance, as parents are raising a toddler who is dealing with what Erikson labeled autonomy versus shame or doubt (at age 18 months to 3 years), that child learns to bond as well as to display initiative. The task is to hold on to parents, as in achieving healthy attachment, while simultaneously displaying age-appropriate autonomy, as in taking early steps in self-care. As this process is occurring, the parents, who could be in their mid-thirties to early forties, may be dealing with themes such as taking care of others and displaying concern or learning empathy and responsibility. For the adult, this would represent stage 7, namely, generativity versus self-absorption.

The beauty of a theory such as Erikson's is that it acknowledges the mutual influence that occurs as two or even three generations intersect while also focusing on the challenges of an individual's life path. Typically, Erikson is approached by discussing the eight developmental stages in sequence, but his theory lends itself well to a more systemic interpretation, one that stacks or overlays the various intergenerational psychosocial crises. Additionally, as in this example of the parent and the preschooler, we can see how one person's resolution and management of her or his psychosocial state also facilitates similar emotional processes in the person with whom the first person is interacting. Put in another way, it is not only the child who is growing and mastering a specific psychosocial crisis but also the parent who interacts with that child. Each navigates different but related developmental growth processes that are appropriate for their own lifespan positions. As we parent, we teach and we learn; as we are being parented, we learn and some of our learning rubs off on our parents and even our grandparents. It is a bidirectional, even a multidirectional, process (Sanson, Letcher, & Havighurst, 2018).

Erikson's original theory provided the basic framework for understanding the psychosocial changes experienced by an individual. In that respect, it did not originally intend to address multigenerational concerns. We also need to be reminded that the family systems movement developed after Erikson was at the height of his career. His theory can be applied to a family system on several different developmental levels, however. The family system, for instance, can consist of parents and children and grandparents, and these family members will represent various age groups and generations, each at particular psychosocial stages (Greene & Kropf, 2009/2017).

In an intergenerational family, the parents could be dealing with general *generativity* versus *self-absorption*. Their parents, or the grandparents of the children, could be dealing with stage 8, which focuses on *ego integrity* versus *despair*. At that stage, people reflect on the meaning of life and their own imminent death; it is a time for life-end concerns, spirituality, and existential reflections. The youngsters in the same family system may be at several different developmental stages. For example, the oldest boy could be nudging adolescence, so his focus might be on *identity* versus *role confusion*. He would emphasize peer groups and friendships, individuation, and autonomy. The next child could be a preadolescent girl dealing with stage 4, *industry* versus *inferiority* (Bigner & Gerhardt, 2019, p. 105). At this stage, she would be developing competence in terms of making and mastering things, as well as expanding her social connections through individual friendships, often with children of the same gender.

Reciprocal Interaction

When parents and children, and even grandparents, are experiencing simultaneous or congruent developmental stages, Erikson refers to this as **reciprocal interaction**. Hence the parents and the children go about their daily tasks of interacting, and each participant in that particular subsystem of the family facilitates and promotes the appropriate resolution of a psychosocial focus point in the other. As parents provide appropriate parental care to their children, they are resolving their own psychosocial crisis as well as supporting the children resolving theirs. Any parent of a young child knows that it is impossible to remain self-absorbed if one takes the parenting role seriously. Parenting is one way of making us selfless and focused on another human being. Empathy, responsibility, caretaking skills, and many more desirable attributes merge as we support a young child who, in turn, is dealing with his or her own psychosocial crisis surrounding *trust* versus *mistrust*, or aspects that we find in basic attachment.

Parenting behavior is modified as we progress on the lifespan path and as both children and their parents grow older. Children's needs change as they pass through various stages of psychosocial development, and parental needs change as well (Sanson, Letcher, & Havighurst, 2018). The concept of *reciprocal interaction* and *adaptation* suggests that parents and children will seek and find a new level of balance in their relationships. Parents improve their parenting skills to meet the demands of their children at different stages of childhood development. In this way, the parent can assist or inhibit the developmental progress of the child, and the child has a reciprocal effect on the parent. Like the larger family system of which it is a part, the parent-child subsystem must adapt to changes in the individual participants to maintain stability and effective functioning (Bigner & Gerhardt, 2019, pp. 105–106).

Stages of Parenthood

Ellen Galinsky (b. 1942) has referenced ongoing lifespan stages in her work and documented these in a book titled *The Six Stages of Parenthood* (Galinsky, 1987; Fracasso, 2017). She describes six stages of parenting but emphasizes that parenting is complex and that no two parents have the same experience of this life journey. She also acknowledges the bidirectionality of parent-child interactions, as have other theorists before her. Additionally, she suggests that parental needs affect parent-child relationships, which, in itself, is a clear way of emphasizing that these relationships are never static but change and adjust in a multidirectional manner (Galinsky, 1987). Galinsky based her findings on a relatively small yet diverse sample of parents.

In brief, the stages consist of the following (Galinsky, 1987):

1. *Image-making.* This stage involves preparing for parenthood before the actual birth of the child. Parents dream about the child that will join their family, and about the transitions that will occur in their family. Parents may anticipate future events that they will share with the child, especially in terms of human developmental lifespan stages.
2. *Nurturing.* This stage is especially pertinent during infancy and early toddlerhood. It allows for attachment or bonding to occur. Parents are juggling to give parenthood its rightful place in their lives.
3. *Authority.* This stage occurs when children are between two and four. The theme of control, as countered by loss of control, enters the relationship as the child is developing and testing her or his increasing autonomy.
4. *Interpretive.* Parents focus on what they will emphasize to their children in terms of beliefs, ethics, hopes, aspirations, and other core principles and attitudes. It is a stage of actively imparting values and building the foundation for the future launching of the children.
5. *Interdependent.* The child is working on autonomy, as this stage covers the teenage years. Important concerns are providing guidance and structure, and doing this by maintaining a relationship with open communication.
6. *Departure.* Children are leaving the home, and parents second-guess their success as parents while also adjusting their levels of control and involvement with their children. Ultimately, both parents and their children reach a new level of separateness while remaining connected in a manner that suits the adult status of the children.

Galinsky has been credited with bringing a contemporary angle to the analysis of the parenting relationship and the challenges each new generation of parents face. Hence, her emphasis on the uniqueness of the parenthood experience for all involved.

Parenthood. Parenting tends to put human relationships, especially partnerships, under the magnifying glass. As parents learn to collaborate and focus on the well-being of their offspring, they often become more selfless. Memories of their own parents and the nurturing love they received from those parents tend to echo from the past. The experiences of partnering and parenting, both tests of resilience, have an uncanny way of magnifying all that has gone before. Our own childhoods tend to form the foundation on which we build our parenting skills, and our own parents inspire us to do as well as they did, or better. A good childhood gives us a built-in example of how to be a good parent and leaves us relatively unencumbered to proceed forward.

On the other hand, if we have been exposed to challenging parents as children, we have to find ways of neutralizing those experiences when we become parents, of finding the resilience and creativity to choose a different path, so we do not recreate the trauma we experienced in our own childhoods. If we are lucky enough to be partnered with someone who has good parenting skills, we can learn from this interaction and are given a second chance at a healthy family life, even if we missed that experience when we were children ourselves.

Parenting is the emotional link between generations. It is an ongoing interaction in which we selflessly wish the best for our children, and we work unceasingly to equip them with the skills they will require to launch successfully. Children who can go into the world with relative optimism and maintain a respectful relationship with their parents and siblings will bear this invisible shield of family love and concern to strengthen them in their futures, including in the creation of their own families and in parenting their own children.

Coparenthood. Those studying families professionally or who support families therapeutically know that families come in many shapes and arrangements. The healthy marriage framework can be extended and augmented by acknowledging the important role of coparenting alliances. These alliances constitute a group of relationships at the heart and soul of the supportive systems developed in the family (McHale & Irace, 2011, p. 17):

> Coparenting is an enterprise undertaken by two or more adults, who together take on the care and upbringing of children for whom they share responsibility. (McHale & Lindahl, 2011, p. 3)

Dramatic shifts and changes have affected family systems over the past decades. Family structure can become a microsystemic reflection of all the cultural, sociological, economic, and other shifts occurring in the bigger systems harboring family life. These changes have affected coparenting arrangements too; there are many various combinations of persons making the raising of children their central concern in the modern world: for example, blended families, families parenting from a distance (such as deployed military parents who bring in on-site parenting reinforcements), grandparents who consistently back up dual-career families, and couples identifying as LGBT. Caring adults who are prepared to sacrifice to create stability and nurturing environments for children can be found in numerous contexts.

In essence, then, **coparents** are persons who parent in a collaborative way, in ongoing and serious relationships within the nuclear, the extended, or the chosen family. Often, there are legal implications such as guardianship or adoptive parenting responsibilities. Coparenting should not be confused with temporary childcare arrangements, even if these relationships are ongoing and emotionally vested. Coparents can be intergenerational, and there can be more people involved than in the typical and traditional two-parent household. Coparenting activities and roles are distinguished by two lead factors:

- *Relationship:* The coparent has an ongoing, responsible, and serious involvement with the child, combined with an emotional investment in the child (McHale & Irace, 2011, p. 17).
- *Executive role:* The coparent has the ability to exert executive decision making for aspects pertaining to the child's well being, including, for instance, educational choices and medical care (Bigner & Gerhardt, 2019, p. 4).

Although the variations and arrangements of coparents are seemingly endless, the core of their roles is the same. They need to display commitment to their task, emotional investment, and be able to make decisions that serve in the best interests of the child. Two biological parents can share the parenting role from two separate households (probably because their union was disrupted for any number of reasons). Military families dealing with deployment may be parenting from multiple locations and parenting at a distance while also being supported by extended family members. Coparents can be adults who significantly support parents in the parenting role, or they may take over the parenting role for an absent or incapacitated parent. In this way, grandparents, supportive family members, friends, and foster parents could act as coparents. Adults could have a biological link to the children they coparent, but they need not have this connection. Parents and stepparents in post-divorce situations may coparent (Stolnicu & Hendrick, 2017). Same sex couples may coparent. Unmarried parents may coparent from two separate homes. Foster parents could coparent, occasionally with a biological parent (Bigner & Gerhardt, 2019). For teenage parents, the coparenting provided by their own parents (grandparents to the newborn) can be crucial in ensuring best outcomes for both the teen and the baby. It can allow the teen to complete an education and create stability for the family (Mollborn & Jacobs, 2015).

The participating persons in these coparenting roles can be diverse, and we should be careful not to define coparenting only by the people involved. Instead, coparenting is better described by the *nature* of the relationship between a coparent and child; ideally, devotion to a child and an ongoing interest in the well-being of that child are core characteristics of coparenting relationships (Drozd, Saini, & Olesen, 2016). The level of investment is parent-like, and it occurs in collaborative fashion, possibly with another parent, a partner, or relative. Coparents take on

The painting *After Swimming*, by Zimbabwean-South African artist Makiwa Mutomba, depicts the joys of childhood. Our tender years tend to inspire us as parents and form the foundation on which we build our parenting skills.

Source: After Swimming/Makiwa Mutomba.

semipermanent and permanent roles in a child's upbringing, typically with legal responsibilities and obligations.

Grandparenthood. One of the sweet and often unexpected gifts of lifespan progression is grandparenthood. There is something endearing about that magical moment of holding a baby and knowing that this child is the offspring of the generation that follows us. More sobering is the flipside of the coin, namely, that as grandparents, we have moved up a generation in the chain of life (Smith, 2017). If we embrace this role constructively, grandparenthood brings new responsibilities, new lessons to be learned, and truly unforeseen joys.

Many of us remember the almost sacred moment when people close to us became new parents and stepped out of the hospital holding a newborn in their arms. It represented the promise of fresh beginnings and widened responsibilities, and the challenge of countless journeys on the path of life. Any family that has experienced this moment can identify with its emotional significance.

With grandparenthood comes the realization that our parenting and coparenting roles continue throughout our lifespans (Henderson & Bailey, 2015). Unless we did not take on parenting tasks or those sacred family bonds were interrupted, we are likely to be parents, coparents, and grandparents "for better, for worse, for richer, for poorer, in sickness and health"—just as the marriage vows state.

As fledgling parents, some of us initially thought (with youthful ignorance and arrogance) that no person as small as a baby could change the life we were plotting for ourselves. We were going to hang on to it all: career, family, travel—whatever we dreamt up in our naiveté. Some of us were convinced that parenting was a 25-year project, give or take a year or two. You launch the kids and then give each other, as parents, the congratulatory high five for a job well done.

We had no inkling of how vulnerable we would become on this journey. We did not calculate into our formula that every family will have an individual cross to bear, that some deeply personal pain is likely to be woven into the fabric of parenthood. Dusting off the superficial fairy gloss reveals that all families face challenges and that each family deals with personal parenting obstacles. But these are counterbalanced by the rewards, the joys, and the gratitude that we feel as we experience this unique facet of the human condition.

As we enter the zone beyond the magical launch of adult children, new surprises are revealed. Most important, we learn with deep humility that the parenting role never ends, nor should it end. We learn that adult children everywhere are facing increasingly complex worlds and challenges, ones they can best handle by sharing the burdens and joys of parenting and coparenting with an extended family, namely, by accessing the valuable resources of grandparents. Grandparenthood is a life gift, an immense privilege, and yet another way to go back humbly to the drawing board of life's curriculum. As we fulfill this role, we'll remember countless persons who accompanied us on our parenthood journey—for moments or for years.

Just as many musicians collaborate to produce a symphony, children are supported by an entire team of vested persons, each running the relay race for short periods alongside or sometimes instead of the parents. As grandparents, we are part of this team. We accept the challenges and privileges that this phase of the multigenerational cycle of life presents, as have generations before us.

> **"Children see their families as a collection of individuals who love and care for them . . . who step up to take responsibility."**
>
> McHale and Irace (2011, p. 15)

FOCUS POINT

Erik Erikson theorized that certain developmental crises need to be resolved and managed in order to lay the foundation for subsequent developmental stages. In Erikson's theory, the first four stages, from infancy to adulthood, give parents the opportunity to support and promote healthy development in their children. If parents or significant caregivers hinder a child's development, that child may have difficulties in subsequent stages. Parenting is the emotional link between generations. Ideally, it is an ongoing interaction that equips children with the skills they require to launch successfully. A good childhood is the foundation of appropriate adult development. Reciprocal interaction occurs when parents or grandparents and children experience simultaneous or congruent developmental stages. Coparenting activities and roles are distinguished by two lead factors:

1. An ongoing, responsible, and serious involvement with a child, combined with an emotional investment in that child.
2. The ability to exert executive decision making for aspects pertaining to the child's well-being.

GLOBAL GLIMPSE

FOR THE WELL-BEING OF OUR CHILDREN

Rituals: Universally, parents wish their children well; they would like their children to be blessed with the best life has to offer while simultaneously avoiding life's hardships and tribulations. The major world religions and various cultures and ethnic groups have ceremonies that welcome a newborn into the world and wish both child and parents all the best for this lifelong journey. These blessings may be sought even before the child is conceived. In Hinduism, there is a moving yet very private ritual focused on the intent of having a child. In many marriage ceremonies, the desire for offspring may be incorporated into the wedding ritual. In a secular world, potential parents are encouraged to plan pregnancies and seek medical advice before conception, to strive for optimal outcomes. The reality is not as poetic; globally, unplanned pregnancies are the norm rather than the exception.

The old Sanskrit texts in Hinduism describe a number of rites and passages that occur during a typical lifespan. In particular, there are 40 so-called *Samskaras* (spelled with an "m") and 16 *Sanskaras* (spelled with an "n") that mark important points during the entire lifespan. Some of the *Sanskaras* pertain specifically to the lifespan of the child, marking developmental milestones such as being named or being taken to a Guru at age eight. Globally, childbirth is celebrated, and the naming of a child is also very significant, as that is the point at which parents give their child a unique "label" or a name, which will accompany him or her for life.

Although the act of naming is universal, the specific rites and timing surrounding this event are culturally specific. For instance, a twelfth-century Chinese manual on the performance of rituals (Hsi, 1991/2014, p. 35) mentions that the giving of an adult name for a woman only occurs once she has been pledged to someone in marriage. On that occasion, she will be capped and pinned, as in receiving a cap and a hairpin, and this ceremony will include "the giving of the adult name." Traditional Chinese custom regarded it as bad luck to name babies before they were born, but they did receive a name after birth. Present customs may not be following these twelfth-century guidelines.

In the globally connected world, some persons who work in international contexts will choose a Western name similar to their birth name, one that sounds like their birth name but is more recognizable in Western script. Korean, Chinese, Greek, Indian, Hebrew, and other nationals using a variety of scripts might bridge the cultural divide in this

(Continued)

(Continued)

manner. Alternatively, a person's name, given in his or her home language and script, may be pronounced and spelled phonetically in another language. It is a sign of respect and cultural competence to learn and pronounce names correctly, and to be cognizant of cultural naming differences.

Some of the rituals that are unique to Hinduism pertain to the baby's first outing (*Nishkramana*), the baby's first solid food (*Annaprashana*), the baby's first haircut (*Chudakarana*), and the baby's earlobe piercing rite (*Karnavedha*). Another series of rights pertain to the child's acquisition of knowledge and an education, for instance, the child's entrance into school and, ultimately, the formal graduation ceremony.

What connects us across these cultural variations is our respect and reverence for life and the eternal optimism of parents who hope their offspring will have better opportunities than they themselves have had. Cultural practices and specifically rituals serve to mark these momentous occasions in a manner that is recognizable and receives the dignified acknowledgment it deserves.

Sources: Babycentre (2017); Fuller (2004); Hsi (1991/2014).

What connects us across cultural variations is our respect and reverence for life and the eternal optimism of parents who hope that their offspring will have better opportunities than they themselves have had.

Source: © iStock.com/fishbones.

SPOTLIGHT ON THEORIES

Relational Dialectics Theory

The central premise of **relational dialectics theory (RDT)** is that relationships are not static; instead, they are constantly changing and evolving. Not all interactions or communications are tension free and straightforward. All relationships and therefore all communications go through phases in which the participating individuals experience dialectical tensions; there will be diverted ideas, and not everybody will be on the same page. This does not imply an overt conflict situation; instead it means that there will be a backward and forward negotiation as people subscribe to different opinions and points of view (Baxter & Braithwaite, 2010).

The word *dialectic* basically relates to two persons in a dialogue holding different points of view but wanting to reach a point of mutual understanding by finding the most compelling or truthful essence, which is sometimes a synthesis (Baxter & Braithwaite, 2010). Dialectic inquiry is often used in the training of lawyers and can be a characteristic of debate teams. A constructive debate encourages participants to hold differing or even opposing points of view. By communicating in a mutually respectful manner, the parties in dialogue may find the thread of truth that resides between their differing perspectives.

Many of the concepts of RDT are similar to those of family systems theory, and this subsection focuses on some of these similarities. In both theories, communications and interactions have the following characteristics:

- *Nonlinear:* Relationships are not linear; instead they can be seen as contextual. The communication may contain circular components. What has happened before has an influence in determining the response afterward. Preceding matters influence subsequent ones.
- *Evolving:* Life is viewed in terms of relationships, which are prized for their evolving and changing nature. Families, too, constantly evolve as they progress on the lifespan path, and opinions evolve in tandem. These changes can co-opt entire family systems. Communication contributes to relationships and the social context in which these communications occur (Suter & Seurer, 2018).
- *Progressive:* Relationships can contain tension and contradiction, and this can validate the ongoing progression or growth of a shared dialogue. Systems thinking posits that there are attempts to regain homeostasis or balance.
- *Negotiable:* Communication is crucial in establishing points of agreement and in finding negotiable platforms that will bridge the contradictions that can occur in some of these relationships. In systems thinking, the concept of equifinality posits that there are multiple paths to a goal or an end state, which supports the idea that negotiation through communication is key.

Central to the theory of relational dialectics are four core concepts, all of which fit well with the basic premises of a family systems approach. These are contradiction, totality, process, and praxis (or practical behavior). When we relate the same concepts to family systems theory, we can make the following connections:

- *Contradiction.* Opposite opinions and positions can meet, and there is a dynamic interplay. The parties involved can negotiate to find the calm midpoint, and in a relationship, there is an interaction between closeness and distance. In family systems theory, we acknowledge that communication is bidirectional and that both parties

(Continued)

(Continued)

influence each other. Persons can hold different points of view, and through conversations, they can negotiate a new perspective or agree to disagree. Being respectful and empathic means that we can understand the other person's position without necessarily feeling the same. If we think of a family's lifespan, we know that merely being at a specific point in one's lifespan can alter what is seen as important. For instance, a dialogue between an adult and an adolescent may reveal two individuals who come from different perspectives, yet they are able to converse respectfully.

- *Totality.* Totality can be represented as being part of a greater whole, and this can be unifying. Communication is embedded in a context; namely, it does not occur in isolation. Additionally, there are components such as openness versus privacy or dependence versus interdependence that can color a dialogue. In family systems theory, this totality is frequently referred to as the *context* or the larger whole or the system. In a systemic approach, we look at how that communication fits into the bigger whole or system. Other terms used in systems therapy would be engaged versus disengaged.
- *Process.* Social processes present the context for some interpersonal or relational dialectics. Communicating participants may position themselves between open (disclosure) and closed (secretive) forms of communication. Likewise, in systemic family therapy, the *process* is demarcated by the boundaries within which an interaction occurs, whereas *content* describes the specifics. Hence the process may be ongoing, but the content may change from situation to situation. For instance, being respectful toward another person may represent the process occurring between two individuals. Opening the door or helping with a task could exemplify the content or details of this interaction, which, in turn, is part of the greater process of courtesy or respect.
- *Praxis.* This term denotes the practical situation in which simply having a relationship with another exposes one to another's needs and values. The participation and the interaction can produce tension. If we are engaged in interpersonal relationships, we will also be exposed to the needs, feelings, values, and the preferences of the other person. By engaging, we become part of the bidirectional communication process.

One of the strengths of this theory is that the focus is shifted from the individual to the systemic in that groups of people can cocreate meaning (Suter & Seurer, 2018). Contexts such as different cultures, varying communication styles, the nature of the particular relationship, and the like can influence how the dialectics or the conversations play out. We are also likely to compare the reality of our relationships with the idealized versions in our minds.

The dialectics of communication are influenced by the personalities and communication skills of the communicators. For instance, a person on the continuum of autism spectrum disorder may find it challenging to interpret nonverbal emotional content and could take some of aspects of the conversation literally. This would influence the quality of verbal relationships. Additionally, various tensions within relationships can be expressed, and these are seen as contradictions or struggles in the discourse (Baxter & Scharp, 2015).

The length of the relationship between participating partners may also influence the nature of communication; for instance, a long-married couple may appear to be sitting silently at the dinner table, but these individuals can communicate nonverbally and may not have the need for constant conversation.

In short, communication is influenced by numerous aspects, including the greater context in which it takes place as well as the participants themselves. Tension within these conversations exists by definition and can vary depending on the goal and context of a particular conversation or exchange.

In a Nutshell

Relational Dialectics Theory

- The word *dialectic* relates to persons in a dialogue holding different points of view but communicating to reach a point of mutual understanding.
- Dialogues typically occur between two or more people and are influenced by the personalities and communication skills of the communicators.
- Relationships change and evolve and can display tension. Both the relationship between the participating parties and the context within which the dialogue occurs determine the nature and extent of the tension.
- Dialogues can contain contradictions, and participating parties may find ways of negotiating toward a point of agreement or of maintaining mutual respect for the other person's values and opinions.
- It is important to look at how this conversational negotiation process is played out in practical contexts.
- Every dialogue contains as well as reflects a social process occurring between the participating parties.
- The four core concepts of relational dialectics theory are contradiction, totality, process, and praxis.
- Relational dialectics theory is relatively young and was described in the late 1980s, initially by theorists Lesley Baxter and Barbara Montgomery. Baxter's work focused predominantly on relationships in family contexts, hence the word *relational* in the theory's name.

CHAPTER FOCUS POINTS

Families: Constant yet Ever Changing

- Family interactions and family transitions gain greater clarity when we see them against the backdrop of rituals and other significant markers.
- Looking at families from a systemic approach helps us see how different generations influence each other.
- We can best understand family of origin influences by looking at the entire family structure, which includes all the different generations.
- We can look at families in the context of developmental time and the predictable stages of family development. Intergenerational family systems grow and shrink. If we look at this entire family structure consisting of different generations, it is easier to understand family-of-origin influences.
- Three to four generations could be interacting at any given time. Each generation is on its own timeline determined by its members' time of birth.

Dynamics of Partner Selection

- Social exchange theory is useful in explaining partner selection. Partnering contains a large element of the deal brokering. We negotiate in terms of what we feel we have to offer and, simultaneously, what we feel we can demand given our specific assets. In most significant relationships, we accommodate, negotiate, and learn to anticipate each other's needs.
- Relationships that have a better promise of survival may be the ones in which partners have learned to communicate well and, above all, to negotiate respectfully.
- Uncoupling happens when a relationship is built on what participants were hoping to find instead of reality.
- Relationship turbulence can create partner instability, which creates a stressful family environment, especially for children.
- Well-functioning families require stability and an ongoing effort to seek homeostasis.

Transitions and Turning Points

- Rituals often mark significant transitions and turning points shared within specific cultural contexts.
- Children are central to many people, and rituals surrounding this life stage are particularly sacred throughout most of the world.
- Since antiquity, numerous rites have focused on the well-being and blessing of children.

Lifespan-Related Theories

- Erik Erikson theorized that certain developmental crises need to be resolved and managed in order to lay the foundation for subsequent developmental stages. In Erikson's theory, the first four stages, from infancy to adulthood, give parents the opportunity to support and promote healthy development in their children.
- If parents or significant caregivers hinder a child's development, that child may have difficulties in subsequent stages. Parenting is the emotional link between generations. Ideally, it is an ongoing interaction that equips children with the skills they require to launch successfully.
- A good childhood is the foundation of appropriate adult development.
- Reciprocal interaction occurs when parents or grandparents and children experience simultaneous or congruent developmental stages.
- Coparenting activities and roles are distinguished by two lead factors:
    - An ongoing, responsible, and serious involvement with a child, combined with an emotional investment in that child.
    - The ability to exert executive decision making for aspects pertaining to a child's well-being.

Spotlight on Theories: Relational Dialectics Theory

- The word *dialectic* relates to persons in a dialogue holding different points of view but communicating to reach a point of mutual understanding.
- Dialogues typically occur between two or more people and are influenced by the personalities and communication skills of the communicators.
- Relationships change and evolve and can display tension. Both the relationship between the participating parties and the context within which the dialogue occurs determine the nature and extent of the tension.
- Dialogues can contain contradictions, and participating parties may find ways of negotiating toward a point of agreement or of maintaining mutual respect for the other person's values and opinions.
- It is important to look at how this conversational negotiation process is played out in practical contexts.
- Every dialogue contains as well as reflects a social process occurring between the participating parties.
- The four core concepts of relational dialectics theory are contradiction, totality, process, and praxis.
- Relational dialectics theory is relatively young and was described in the late 1980s, initially by theorists Lesley Baxter and Barbara Montgomery. Baxter's work focused predominantly on relationships in family contexts, hence the word *relational* in the theory's name.

Dynamics in Diverse Contexts

PART

III

Family stories have numerous beginnings and a multitude of endings. Families meander through time, exposed to diverse influences. Raising children successfully and maintaining rewarding relationships require a thousand skills and attributes, among them responsibility, dedication, patience, foresight, and a sense of humor. If families are dynamic systems and the members of each system influence and are influenced by each other, it follows that understanding and supporting these unique kinship groupings enables us to be more effective in our family-focused relationships.

A number of dynamic systems interact to beckon favorable family outcomes. Parental love and structure may be starting points, but we require family-friendly policies to face the larger challenges. Families are culturally anchored. In some ways, they are alike while also differing dramatically. Various facets of the future of humankind lie within these sacred bonds of kinship. The tentacles of what promotes family life reach deep and far.

Well-intentioned families nurture their members. They give them layers of experiences, which become memories, and like the washes of color in a watercolor painting, these layers are not overworked but translucent. Layer upon layer, they build to the depth of meaningful lifelong relationships. Love is never lost. It is given from parent to child in that long chain of little events: the daily hugs, the support, the acceptance. Love grows and love links us—generation to generation. An Irish proverb reminds us that we live in the protective shelter (or shadow) of one another. And it is within this dynamic of the family that we find a harbor, and hope.

The greatest gift we can give the world is creating a continuous, uninterrupted, loving family structure. ”

Aldona Laita

(cited in Tenneson, 2002)

CHAPTER 11

Dynamics of Loss

Learning Outcomes

After studying this chapter, you should be able to

1. Describe the *process* of loss.
2. Summarize *constructivist* psychotherapy.
3. Explain *ambiguous loss* and how it affects the family system.
4. Describe the therapeutic goals of *narrative therapy*.
5. Discuss the *stage-*, *task-*, and *process-based models* of coping with grief, and explain how these connect to family dynamics.

Grief and Mourning

Loss can touch all dimensions and aspects of life, affecting us in numerous anticipated and unanticipated ways. Each loss can be profound in its own way and affects our quality of life, mental stability, security, and so much more. We tend to think of loss as the death or absence of a beloved person. This is a most painful and permanent form of loss. But the spectrum of loss and its associated pain and grief stretches wide and far; it is part of the human condition and crops up in mythology and world religions. In Christian doctrine, we find the "Tree of Knowledge of Good and Evil." It is a profound metaphor of the human condition; life on earth means that confronting good and evil, and the related dimensions of joy and pain, is inevitable. It also serves to describe the "up" and "down" facets of attachment. From a Buddhist and Hindu perspective, both pain and pleasure bind us to suffering. "Joy"—or the "peace of God, which passeth all understanding" (Philippians 4:7, King James Version)—is a product of nonattachment, of embracing life's pleasures and sorrows with equanimity, living for the good of all, and living a life centered in that which is unchanging. A nearly insurmountable goal for any human being!

Loss has many faces and many guises. The common denominator of life's gifts is that they can slip through our fingers; there is no guarantee of permanence. There can be loss of good health (physical and mental), of mobility, youth, memory, employment, housing, possessions, good fortune, good name, honor, opportunity, innocence . . . the list is endless. The many blessings life bestows on us can all be taken away. We are not immune to the possibility of tragedy striking. If we draw back the curtain from the stage of life, we will see that every family bears its own cross and experiences pain—often a very private pain hidden from the eyes of the world. One way of thinking about love is to see it as being free of expectation—care is rendered without the need for reciprocation. However, most expressions of love contain disguised expressions of attachment. So loss can mean an attachment broken.

It is tempting to think of happiness as the antithesis of grief. At second glance, this is too simplistic. It is doubtful that they are opposites, as they seem interrelated and entwined. Each one is complex and multifaceted; the one seems to have the other in tow. Grief reflects the realization that nothing is as it was before, when we might have been happy; we have crossed the threshold and cannot reconstruct the world we once knew. In the case of coping with a death, we have to rebuild our universe without the beloved person.

"Joy and woe are woven fine, a clothing for the soul divine.

Under every grief and pine, runs a joy with silken twine."

William Blake (1757–1827)

The Dual Process of Mourning

Loss survivors oscillate between two natural rhythms of survivorship: *evade* and *encounter*, or *avoidance* and *approach* (Wolfelt, 2010). Survivors partly heal through gradual exposure to that which is painful. So although it is important to embrace our grief, it is likewise efficacious to balance our exposures to it by "pacing" or "dosing" our mourning—by securing respite from it. The Dutch bereavement researchers Margaret Stroebe and Henk Schut (1999) have likewise postulated that survivors oscillate between two forms of grief work, which unfold simultaneously and concurrently: a "loss" orientation that focuses on the inner (psychological) experience of bereavement and a "restoration" orientation that focuses on the rebuilding of one's life. This is referred to as the **dual process model** of mourning (Humphrey, 2009).

Part of the process of loss and of coming to terms with a shattered inner world happens during mourning, which requires us to reach a different and new destination. Maybe we have to do this without the companion we loved and valued. Grief can give us a visceral feeling, a punch in the solar plexus. We feel we have to rearrange ourselves in our altered personhood; we have to create a new map of our world, and at first it is a place that feels incomplete and different, even unfamiliar and frightening. Grieving is a journey. It is personal and individual, and there is no way around it, no bridge over it. We have to traverse it, swim through it, temper it, tame it, look it in the eye.

At the core of the therapeutic process remains the fact that clients must examine their grief and the emotional pain they are experiencing. There is no single prescription for something as personal and far reaching as facing the agony of loss, and our own mortality.

In a park bordering the Thames River in London is a statue depicting grief. A woman in a semi-draped robe bows her head. With the crook of her arm, she tries to shield herself from further pain. Her eyes are closed to keep out the onslaught of the world. Most telling are her hands: ballerina-like, they seem to have given up on all of life's tasks—the holding, touching, reaching, and doing. The hands seem exceptionally still, as if she is begging time to stop: she needs to absorb the loss. The statue is a tribute to Sir Arthur Sullivan (1842–1900), who died from a heart attack at age 58. He was the composer of the famed Gilbert & Sullivan duo, writers and producers of musicals. The statue is by Sir William Goscombe (London Remembers, 2019). Inscribed on the pedestal are these words by W. S. Gilbert (1836–1911): "Is life a boon? If so, it must befall that Death, whene'er he call, must call too soon."

"When you lose someone you were close to, you have to reassess your picture of the world and your place in it. The more your identity was wrapped up with the deceased, the more difficult the mental loss."

Meghan O'Rourke (b. 1976), American author and journalist, from *The Long Goodbye*

The psychoanalytic and psychodynamic approach. In the psychoanalytic approach by Freud, he used the term **object cathexis**. In Greek, *cathexis* means "I occupy." In essence, then, the term refers to an investment of emotion, mental energy, or life force in an object, person, or idea. (In classical psychoanalytic theory, object cathexis is the investment of psychic energy or life force, which Freud referred to as "libido," in objects outside the self.) By vesting some of our feelings in another, by falling in love or loving in general, we also become vulnerable to loss. The Freudian psychodynamic grief-work concept of "working through" has been replaced by the gentler behavioral concept of "habituation," gradual exposure and acclimation to that which is painful. Even so, the Freudian view of decathexis (the process of disinvestment) with the death of a loved one has been severely critiqued (Neimeyer, 1999, p. 65).

When Queen Victoria lost her husband Albert when he was 42, she was overcome by grief and remained in mourning for many years. The couple had nine children. The Albert Memorial in Kensington, London, was erected in his honor.

Source: © iStock.com/fotolupa.

We can use a simplistic example from real life that does not sound as formidable as Freud's concept of object cathexis (emotional investment), which can sound like Greek, as in being unintelligible. If we lend something we cherish and value dearly to another person, then we have less control over it. We have to trust that person to take good care of it. If the person loses or rejects that object, then we in turn feel that loss and that rejection. If our investment is lost, it is as if our emotional stock crashes, and it will take a while, if ever, before we can rebuild our world.

We can explain love and emotional investment in that way. Imagine you love another person and invest a bit of yourself in that person. It is as if that person now owns some of your heart. The poet e. e. cummings (1894–1962), who incidentally did not capitalize words, not even his own name, poetically described this emotional transfer and the bonds we share with others:

"i carry your heart with me(i carry it in

my heart)i am never without it(anywhere

i go you go,my dear; . . .)"

e. e. cummings (1991)

FOCUS POINT

Loss has many faces and many guises. Life's gifts can slip through our fingers; there is no guarantee of permanence. The process of loss requires exploration of ways of coming to terms with a shattered world. During mourning, a new emotional destination has to be negotiated. Several theoretical models seek to explain dimensions of the grieving process, including the dual process model and psychoanalytic and psychodynamic approaches.

GLOBAL GLIMPSE

ON JOY AND SORROW

Kahlil Gibran (1883–1931) was a Lebanese-American poet and philosopher who was best known for *The Prophet* (1923), a book of prose fables on the dimensions of human life. He commented on being a parent, on joy, loss, and death, and on many other topics that we can all relate to. Here are three sections of his poem "On Joy and Sorrow" from *The Prophet*:

> Your joy is your sorrow unmasked.
> And the selfsame well from which your laughter
> rises was oftentimes filled with your tears.
> And how else can it be?
> The deeper that sorrow carves into your being,
> the more joy you can contain.
> . . .
> When you are joyous, look deep into your heart
> and you shall find it is only that which has given you
> sorrow that is giving you joy.
> When you are sorrowful look again in your heart,
> and you shall see that in truth you are weeping for
> that which has been your delight.
> . . .
> Verily you are suspended like scales between your
> sorrow and your joy. (Gibran, 1923/2019, p. 37)

Authentic Insight

The Loss of a Child

The loss of a child is also the loss of a family's dreams, hopes, desires, and expectations. As a bereavement specialist, I accompany families week after week, as they start navigating a lifelong pain that not only affects the mom and dad but the family system as a whole. How a mother and father learned to respond to grief, death, and dying in their own childhoods will weigh heavily on their perceptions of finding their own and authentic ways to grieve. Some families were taught to lay their feelings on the table and show each heartfelt stirring as it arises, while other families hold each emotion under lock and key, hiding it deep inside. Men and women on the whole may grieve in unique ways, and are rarely simultaneously on the same emotional page (Doka, 2016).

The dynamics of grief are exponentially complex, and a family trying to navigate this process typically feels overwhelmed. Although loss is most intense for parents, it also draws in grandparents, who are hurting for their children's loss and the loss of a grandchild. Siblings usually begin to fear their own mortality and, depending on the age, have minimal understanding of the finality of death. Young children can be very literal and therefore talk to their parents in uniquely blunt ways about the death of their sibling. Child, spousal, sibling, and parental loss can each bear its own signature. In dealing with grief, we need to respect these differences and honor the authenticity of each individual mourner (Doka, 2016).

Grief is a lifelong process that tends not to happen in an orderly fashion. When grieving parents are trying to connect, there can be a lot of "misses" as they are not at the same places at the same time. Communication is key. Sharing where you are that day and how you are feeling is vital in maintaining a healthy relationship. When couples don't share their thoughts and feelings directly, misperception, bitterness, and frustration toward the other person can emerge. This is why family therapy can be so useful in facilitating mourning, loss adaptation, and bonding among family members: a counselor can assist survivors in developing sensitivity to divergent mourning and coping styles, lifespan development factors that impact mourning and coping, and family roles (functional or nonfunctional) that impact acclimation to the loss. The goal of such therapy is to assist family members in more effectively supporting one another and to heighten their capacity to work together to move the family forward.

Grief that does not have the ability to be shared directly tends to come out "sideways" and can cause extra pain and confusion. It is important that we allow those we love to express their grief in the way that enables healing and health. It is natural for grieving to look a little differently for everyone. Attempting to fix the grieving process for others usually contributes additional stress and resentment. Such behavior impedes rather than promotes healing. If we feel the need to hurry others through the pain of loss, we may need to examine our own losses and how and if we've dealt with those feelings. The way we transfer our own feelings of impatience, fear, concern, or other feelings related to loss can impact how we relate to grieving persons.

When I am working with a family right after the loss of a child, I am touched by how the extended family system thinks it knows what is best for the parents. Research tells us that, in most cases, it is better for the grieving process of the parents if they are granted ample time to spend with their deceased child; they find closure in holding, dressing, or bathing their baby. But families are quick to discourage the parents from spending time with the child they have lost. If family members discourage this, even though it is well meaning, they may be putting undue pressure on the parents.

This is new territory for all involved, and nobody can nor should be rushed. Parents have a need to find the courage for that moment of the last farewell. They may draw out this process as it is so final and so heartbreaking.

Marisa S. Dempsey, BA in human development and family science, is a certified childbirth educator and certified doula.

Interventions: Constructivist Psychotherapy

Constructivist psychotherapy (CPT) is a therapeutic approach frequently applied in the context of grief therapy. Its key distinguishing feature is that it accompanies clients in their search to *construct meaning* within the greater context of their world (Corey, 2012, p. 291). Although it is closely aligned with cognitive behavioral therapy, it has distinguishing features, predominantly in that it is anchored in constructivism, to put it simply, in the context of the "construction of reality." There is an emphasis on emotion but also on meaning and action (Neimeyer, 2009, pp. viii–ix). Constructivist psychotherapy draws from several underpinnings, including humanistic and systemic approaches especially.

A central tenet is that the way clients see and interpret their worlds and how they talk about these worlds are worthy and important themes of therapy. The *validity* of these worlds, whether clients' perceptions are "true" or realistic, is not as significant as how the clients feel they experience them—their subjective realities are all important. In this way, the *viability* or utility of a client's story is of central importance (Neimeyer & Neimeyer, 1993). This seeking for and finding meaning is part of the process of adaptation in bereavement. The three activities that support this reconstruction of meaning during the grief journey are sense making, benefit finding, and identity change (Gillies & Neimeyer, 2006).

As the circle of impact widens to include individual grievers, so the dynamic of this group changes; there is reciprocal influence and a shared reality, which combines to create a greater whole than the individual component parts (Neimeyer, 1999, p. 67). This sense of communal or shared grief can be observed when a much-loved public figure dies. Those who knew about this celebrity only through the media have a quasi-familial investment and feel a personal sense of loss. Examples would be the assassination of Mahatma Gandhi, the death of Elvis Presley (surmised to be linked to an overdose), or the unanticipated loss of Princess Diana. These public figures became so revered that their deaths touch us deeply.

The Narrative Arc

Survivors can cope more effectively with loss if they can place their painful, disjointed life experiences within contexts of understanding (Neimeyer, 2001a). A story or narrative is one such context, and telling the story of surviving a loss has the potential to restore meaning, internal cohesion, purpose, and hopefulness. The story of a character in a novel, for instance, takes on greater meaning if readers know both the prelude and postlude to the painful "middle chapter" of the heroine's unexpected ordeal or traumatic loss. The "hero's journey," a format frequently employed in storytelling, follows the central character as his perfect world shatters and he embarks on the obstacle-strewn journey of saving himself or finding that "happily ever after" ending. For the reader, such stories give a sense of closure and satisfaction, and the feeling of having learned a lesson if the outcome is constructive and hopeful. The narrative arc allows the teller of the narrative to reconstruct meaning, and to find new possibility in each retelling of the story (Neimeyer, 2014, p. 27).

In telling their stories, Neimeyer (2014) states that survivors focus in evolving fashion on the external, the internal, and the reflexive:

- **External** matters are the facts as survivors perceive them.
- **Internal** matters are impacts, the emotional and other effects of the facts.
- **Reflexive** matters are the meanings they create, the narratives of their survivorship experiences.

Neimeyer (2014) borrows this concept of **restorying**, in part, from the work of Rynearson (2001) who utilizes *restorative retelling* in his work with survivors. With each retelling of the pain-laden story to a responsive, understanding, and empathic witness (the counselor), the survivor (one hopes) discerns meanings, patterns, and relationships that she or he had not recognized previously.

The cognitive therapy roots of constructivist therapy can be recognized in this process, namely, the reframing of the "tragic" story of loss into a narrative that engenders hopefulness. Such interventions can be helpful if they are targeted to specific survivor needs: for example, the need to process a loss, the need for marital therapy to lessen the distress of a wife who is not feeling supported by her unresponsive husband, the need to address a wound suffered through interaction with a parent who was alternately loving and hurtful, or the need to appropriate instrumental forms of coping (Neimeyer, 2001b).

"No one ever told me that grief felt so like fear. . . . There is a sort of invisible blanket between the world and me."

C. S. Lewis (1898–1963), British writer and lay theologian, from *A Grief Observed* (1961)

FOCUS POINT

The constructivist angle supports grief support interventions. Its key feature is that clients are encouraged to construct meaning within the greater context of their worlds. Survivors can cope more effectively with loss if they can place their painful, disjointed life experiences within contexts of understanding. One such context, a story, has the potential to restore meaning and internal cohesion and provide purpose and hopefulness.

Authentic Insight

Behind the Mask: The Tragedy of Unresolved Loss

Psychotherapists are frequently presented with a family crisis that obscures deeper issues of betrayal, destructive family games, troubling relationships, or the painful dynamics of unresolved loss. This crisis intends to guard and camouflage the underlying pain of the family. The therapist's task is to create a context in which these rigidly constructed protective crises may be deconstructed and opened up to deal with the pain behind the family mask. The following supervision session illustrates a context of complex family dynamics involving loss.

From behind a one-way mirror, a supervisor and trainees observed a session with a small nuclear family with a trainee as the therapist. The father, in his sixties and dressed in a black suit, displayed a corpse-like lack of emotion. A younger man of 25 pretended to read a newspaper, but it served more as a shield for his scowling face. His sister, in her late twenties, giggled inappropriately and made meaningless, quasi-philosophical statements. The trainee was asking lots of questions to which he received no answers. He was leaning forward in his chair while attempting to look into the elusive eyes of the three family members. The therapist's intrusive questions and body position were followed by an escalation in the young woman's comments, and agitated movements by the brother. The father withdrew further in response to his children's behavior, which prompted louder questions and rapid speech by the therapist.

The supervisor suspected that this family behavior was a decoy for a more sensitive and primary family theme. The disorganized behavior served as a metaphor for an as yet unknown ecology of relationships. The therapist was instructed to light a single candle in the center of the therapy room, to dim the overhead lights, and to sit quietly without talking. As silence settled, the girl talked more intently; the men became very quiet. The therapist dimmed the lights further. The silences became more prolonged; then the girl fell into silence. Suddenly the father started sobbing; the son tore up his newspaper and stormed out of the room. Eventually the others left the room—tears streaming down their faces. The context of stoic defensiveness had yielded to grief.

These family members acquired the masks concealing unresolved family pain after the death of the mother, several years prior. It became the topic no one dared to address or even reference. Altering a family's rigid organization around painful issues might require creative and at times novel interventions that exceed the intensity of the family's defensive mask. For this family, the space, safety, and trusting environment allowed them to take tentative steps in their grief-related journey.

Rick Snyders, DLitt et Phil, is a clinical psychologist specializing in systemic family therapy and a professor emeritus in psychology.

Loss in Limbo: Ambiguous Loss

When loss presents with no clear road toward closure, **ambiguous loss** may ensue. Examples of this type of loss occur when a person's body is not found or a loved one disappears. Imagine the vessel lost at sea with no chance of recovery or the soldiers who sacrificed their lives during war, especially major wars such as World Wars I and II when bodies could not be identified and returned. Their loved ones had no idea of the events surrounding their deaths (Boss, 2016).

The tomb of the unknown soldier in Westminster Abbey in London is a symbolic resting place for all those whose bodies remained in far-flung lands, whose families could only guess at what their circumstances may have been. Numerous churches and diverse places of worship, public monuments, and cemeteries worldwide testify to the greatest sacrifices made by those who laid down their lives for their countries. Countless plaques mark the names of soldiers who never returned from their deployment. The families were left nursing the pain of ambiguous loss; there was no closure to these unfinished life stories. The cemeteries in Normandy became the lasting resting place of soldiers from numerous countries. In Europe, in North America, and elsewhere in the world, public monuments honor the fallen—"lest we forget." The families concerned will never forget: there is no peace, no closure; theirs is ambiguous loss (Boss, 2019, pp. 91–92).

Ambiguous loss can also be extended to situations such as adoption, divorce, and various forms of migration, including refugee situations and legal immigration. A mother who made the difficult sacrifice to opt for adoption as part of her baby's birth plan may second-guess this decision as she deals with ambiguous loss. She remembers and celebrates the birth date of the child she could not raise, and it is etched deeply into her mind as she carries that child forever in her heart.

Partially losing a loved one also occurs in the case of the elderly suffering from dementia or Alzheimer's. The father who raised a family no longer recognizes his own children and retreats to his own distant world, inaccessible to the family. Every time family members interact with a loved one afflicted with one of these debilitating conditions, there is less of that person's former self. The body may be present, but the mind is elsewhere. These situations can exist in the context of traumatic brain injury, autism, various forms of mental illness, coma, drug-induced coma, stroke, and the like. Additionally, persons can be psychological absent because they are caught up in their own world of addiction disorders, gambling, computer games, and other forms of mental preoccupation. A more subtle absence can occur when a person is present in body but is clearly not sharing all dimensions of her or his emotional life; such is the case when someone is involved in an extramarital affair or has other preoccupations (Boss, 2019, p. 92).

This sense of being held in limbo is described by Boss in the following manner:

> In the absence of clarity about a family member's absence or presence, people are immobilized, holding on to hope that the missing person will return or a person psychologically absent will go into remission and come back as before. . . . The culprit here . . . is not death but the traumatizing context of ambiguity. (Boss, 2019, pp. 91–92)

The types of ambiguous loss described, fall into two major groups:

- Physical absence with psychological presence
- Physical presence with psychological absence

As is clear from this discussion of ambiguous loss, death can mean more than physical death, and various types of death cause grief. A historical work by Sudnow

(1967) examines four kinds of death: the social, psychological, biological, and physiological:

- **Social death** is defined as the symbolic death of the person within the world that he or she knew and inhabited socially. For example, the bereaved survivor's social world may shrink because of the gradual loss of contact with friends of the deceased.
- **Psychological death** may occur when aspects of the person's personality are no longer accessible or are altered, for instance, because of an illness process or a debilitating traumatic injury.
- **Biological death** is death of the biological organism as a functioning entity. It occurs when a human being can no longer exist without artificial life support. For example, if on a ventilator, the body of a person who is brain dead may be maintained for organ donations, but that person is biologically dead (Freeman, 2005, p. 4).
- **Physiological death** means the cessation of the functioning of the vital organs. It is possible for biological death to precede physiological death, which can have legal and ethical implications (Freeman, 2005, pp. 4–5).

How Loss Affects the Family System

Although the concepts of social, psychological, biological, and physiological death have a lot to offer researchers and therapists, let us consider the two broader categories of death enumerated earlier: death as physical absence with psychological presence and death as physical presence with psychological absence. There can be difficulties with the grieving process when families experience the first type of death (physical absence with psychological presence). Lack of information can be linked to incomplete processing. Loved ones may obsessively wonder about the factors surrounding the death: was their loved one in pain, did she suffer, how long did he know that death was imminent? Additionally, threads of guilt may be interwoven with grief. There can be repeated questions that have no answers. "Could I have prevented the death?" "Could this have been avoided?"

Cultural and religious traditions and rituals provide ways to maintain emotional connections with the deceased. In this Guatemalan kite festival, the dead are honored. It takes place on the first and second of November each year and is part of All Saints' Day celebrations. The festival is called Barriletes Gigantes, meaning "giant kites."

Source: © iStock.com/Lucy Brown—loca4motion.

When death means physical presence with psychological absence, family caretaking roles have to be negotiated. The stress of the changing situation shifts the former balances and subsystems of the family. There may be financial concerns and questions surrounding who is best appointed the guardian, especially if the absent person did not designate these roles when he or she could.

However the loss occurred, it will always affect family dynamics. It has to affect dynamics because the place occupied by that particular family member will have to be redefined in concrete as well as symbolic manner (Boss, 2019, p. 92). It alters family rituals, decision making, and the complexity of subsystems within the family. There is ambiguity each step of the way. Part of the grief journey is to develop greater tolerance in dealing with this ambiguity. Finding meaning and adjusting and mastering the challenges of these situations are aspects that can be explored during grief support. Having the freedom to be able to talk about or otherwise express these ambiguous feelings is of utmost importance, as sharing validates that the person grieving is not alone in her or his perceptions; the individual's reality is echoed in the grief of other family members.

Grief as a personal journey. Individuals may present differing styles of grieving, ones as unique as the people presenting them (Gillies & Neimeyer, 2005). Divergent mourning and coping styles dependent upon temperament, personality, and family history may be observed. Survivors may utilize "feeling-expressive," "instrumental," or "blended" styles. As Wolfelt (2010, p. 8) states,

> The bereaved individual's and family's response to the death, even when complicated, must be respected as the family's best response given the backdrop of family history . . . and [the] supportive resources available to the family. . . . Family members are grieving and mourning in the only way they know.

As for family dynamics and coping, in the context of the dynamics of "closed" versus "open" family systems, the following can be noted (Wolfelt, 2010, p. 9):

- Open family systems may present as psychologically healthy and accept support while coping with situations of loss.
- They have the capacity to acknowledge and process honestly the changes that death may bring to their family system.
- They present with flexibility concerning roles and rules within the family, while also maintaining appropriate autonomy and individuation.
- Communication is open and honest within a caring and supportive environment.
- All of the above contribute to and facilitate the enhancement of growth.

FOCUS POINT

Grieving styles can be as unique as the people presenting them. Ambiguous loss refers to loss with no clear road toward closure, such as if a person disappears or the body of someone presumed dead cannot be located. Lack of information can be linked to incomplete processing. However the loss occurred, it will always affect dynamics. The place occupied by that particular family member will have to be redefined in a concrete and symbolic manner. Being able to talk about or otherwise express ambiguous feelings validates that the grieving person is not alone in her or his perceptions; that person's reality is echoed in the grief of other family members.

Authentic Insight

Narratives of Loss

The helping professions accompany persons on journeys of pain and loss. In the following paragraph, physician Paige Luneburg (2019, p. 546) describes some events that are etched in her mind:

> All patients bring their stories . . . and we physicians are called upon to examine patients, not only with our eyes but also with our hearts. Let us be truthful with ourselves—do we really see? Do we see our patients, their journeys, their narratives?

She remembers the detail of her patients' turning points, especially those points of grief after which life will never be the same:

> I carry the narratives of my patients—the stories, their victories, their losses. . . . The stance of the parents, holding vigil at the bedside of their newborn child, his lungs driven by the rhythmic shaking of the oscillator. The . . . blanket donned by a child lost too soon. The tears of a mother who mourned her adult son, dead by suicide—her firstborn child, born on her birthday. . . . These stories and people I will never forget. Their triumphs were my triumphs, their tears were my tears. Their narratives have written my narrative. (Luneburg, 2019, p. 546)

These are sacred moments, when we are close to life and close to death.

"There is a land of the living and a land of the dead and the bridge is love, the only survival, the only meaning."

Thornton Wilder (1897–1975), American novelist, closing lines of *The Bridge of San Luis Rey* (1927)

Source: Luneburg (2019).

Narrative Therapy

"Speaking isn't neutral or passive. Every time we speak, we bring forth a reality. Each time we share words we give legitimacy to the distinctions that those words bring forth."

Freedman and Combs (1996, p. 29)

Narrative therapy, which is especially relevant in grief and trauma counseling, counts among the leading interventions for situations relating to traumatic transitions and loss. Michael White and his colleague David Epston are predominantly associated with the initial narrative therapy movement. In the early nineties, I attended several workshops by Michael White (1948–2008), the Australian social worker and family therapist. He presented the workshops at two major events in South Africa: the first was in the Valley of a Thousand Hills, near Durban, KwaZulu, South Africa, at the 6th International Conference of the South African Association of Marital and Family Therapy; and the second was at the same association's seventh international conference (Gerhardt, 2003, p. 169). White's approach came at the precise historical moment when it was needed; narrative therapy gave a voice to people, a means to be heard authentically. White's nonjudgmental and profoundly compassionate attitude was clearly apparent. In a transitional nation such as South Africa at that time, his message was healing and collaborative; it provided a platform to build connections, to grow mutual respect, and to find extended understanding. Here is one description of these events:

> Bridges were built, creating a different ethos to the "problem saturated" history. . . There was talk of a spirit of hope, the healing and affirming nature of the experience, the openness and sharing, the sense of inclusiveness and togetherness. All these qualities . . . represent the essence of family [and] contributed to a feeling of unity and a sense of growth along the progress path. (Tarboton as cited in Gerhardt, 2003, p. 169)

In essence, narrative therapy incorporates an emphasis on the greater context, and this context can include any number of dimensions, including the social, cultural, political. Each person embedded in these various overlapping contexts may give individual meaning to his or her own situation and challenges. In this way, each person creates a unique narrative that tells a personal story against the backdrop of that individual's unique world. This emphasis on context (on all of the greater picture) makes narrative therapy a derivative of systemic therapy (Vetere & Dowling, 2005, p. xv). It is also a powerful way in which to include a child's perspective in the conversation because each child is embedded in a family, which fosters the social customs, the cultural nuances, and even the prejudices and misconceptions that can be passed on within a family system. Children learn an endless range of reactions and skills from those closest to them; as adults, we influence children's beliefs more than we would like to admit. The problems and anxieties of families spill over to their youngest members, so children can offer useful insights concerning a family's narrative. Although each family member may have a different take on that narrative, a view from a personal perspective, the family's story is usually influential.

When a therapist is added to this dialogue, he or she may facilitate the client's discovery of personal strengths and competencies. In this way, clients can modify their own stories or narratives and describe themselves in new ways that can also be empowering. These altered stories can provide the client with new insights and possibilities concerning the family's situation or his or her own circumstances (Monk, Winslade, Crocket, & Epston, 1997). Importantly, this approach lends itself to use in a variety of cultural contexts addressing the entire lifespan; it is useful in therapies involving children and equally useful in end-of-life and severe-trauma situations. Therapists do well to remember that a client's experience is privileged—the client has ownership over her or his story. The therapist needs to find a way of understanding that story fully. Therapists can also point out contradictions in family stories, which will help family members explore the meaning of narratives, so they can be used for therapeutic gain.

Language of Possibilities

In the dynamic of family interactions, it can sometimes be difficult to tease out the leading voice or narrative. Whose story should we be listening to, that of the parent about the teenaged boy or the adolescent's narrative about himself? Probably both. We know that the story of the index patient is never the only story, and the account of the person struggling with addiction disorders may have to be bookended by the stories of possible enablers. It is a complicated network, crisscrossing a system.

Another example of multiple narratives could be the stories told after a divorce. The partners dissolving the union may be emphasizing different themes to the children in that household. It may be important to develop new narratives as the system undergoes changes, so the narratives can keep pace with current realities. This process of creative involvement in narrative construction is also labeled the "language of becoming" (Wachtel, 2001). Children may find it especially helpful to use puppets or dolls to retell the family's emerging story, and play has a distinct place in communications.

The concept of the *narrative* has become mainstream, and there is widespread acknowledgment of the importance of stories in helping us elicit meaning from our relationships, our communities, and our lives in general. Even so, narrative therapy should not be underestimated—neither in its power nor in the amount of skill and training required to apply this technique as a legitimate therapeutic domain.

Narrative therapists are more than listeners. They need to be able to observe social and family narratives and interactions and, importantly, to identify resilience and resources that can be accessed in creating growing *possibilities* for the client (Vetere & Dowling, 2005). There is great complexity in these interwoven strands of narrative. Burck makes the following statement:

> Working with narrative always raises questions about what we are able to do in language and what we do in silence. Becoming attuned to when silence is resistance and when it is lack of voice is particularly pertinent in our work with children. Although our use of language can be very powerful, language on its own is never sufficient. (Vetere & Dowling, 2005, p. xiv)

One of the key insights White (as cited in Gerhardt, 2003) emphasized concerned the relevance and validity of the subjective reality of the patient. The story as told by the client is real to that person: it is consequently valid, and it elicits unique emotions because it tells how an individual experienced these emotions and the events that occasioned them. We as bystanders will not experience the same event in the same manner. In therapeutic situations, it is important that we listen to clients' authentic tales with deep respect and reverence (White, 2007). These narratives will be the picture of the client's world as perceived by that person. As clients progress on their journeys, they may shift the emphasis of their stories, which is potentially part of the healing and resolution processes taking place.

The words *authoring* and *coauthoring* are used in connection with narrative therapy. Clients retelling their stories are much like authors creating, or authoring, their tales. Therapists can help this process and can even contribute to coauthoring by collaborating with clients to create a richer, expanded narrative. In this way, the approach is constructive and hopeful; there are novel avenues to be found and explored, fresh ways of looking at things.

Importantly, narrative therapy has distinct elements that bring the approach to another level of professionalism and makes it a discipline that requires training and experience. Some of the elements of narrative therapy highlight the following (Corey, 2012, pp. 374–382):

- The storyteller can identify a dominant or lead story. Particularly if this story is traumatic, it can shape how a person sees himself or herself, that is, that person's identity.
- Acknowledging that there can be novel outcomes that are not anticipated is key; every situation carries a uniqueness within it, and outcomes could be surprising (Polkinghorne, 2004, p. 55).

- There is an effort to externalize. For example, instead of thinking "I have a problem, so I am a person who is problematic," the individual shifts the focus back to the problem and to matters inherent in the problem itself. This is a step away from stories of personal failure, or misery myths.
- The person gains new perspectives by taking a step back and separating personal identity from the problem at hand. This "externalizing" approach "puts the problem in its place," namely, outside the self. Preventing the problem from taking ownership of the person concerned protects that individual's self-concept (Payne, 2006, p. 12).

"The problem is the problem, the person is not the problem."

Michael White and David Epston (1990)

Authentic Insight

When Pink Clouds Are More Than Clouds

A family gathered in the north Georgia mountains last weekend, and at dawn on a Southern Sunday scattered the remains of its matriarch at a secret place she loved.

The clouds above were pink as morning broke. They seemed to come from her.

Tears came next, of course. And smiles. And hugs.

And memories. Because that's what becomes of us, if we're lucky. We leave pink clouds and stories. Smiles and tears and legends.

Some of those who gathered came with their own added pain, burdened with the heavy weight of accumulated grief. Others worried for the living, and hoped only to prevent more sorrow. At times that anguish, etched on faces and heard in words, seemed almost too much for them to bear. Others came almost guiltily, still awash in their good fortune, with new loves or the little triumphs of their own lives.

All that is family, and humanity, and how our stories are written. They are easier to see in the shadow of death.

They're not just what becomes of us. They're what we are, what life is. Joy and sorrow and pain and loss and celebration and a desperate hope that what we leave will somehow be remembered, and appreciated, and maybe even understood.

Like those pink clouds. Which spoke more powerfully than any of those who saw them and were struck silent by them.

They spoke of good will and kind thoughts from the matriarch, for she sent pink clouds to her four children throughout their lives, in times of suffering and in times of success.

She told them so when they were children facing stress or travel or uncertainty.

I'll send you pink clouds.

She told them when they became adults and moved far away, with life's health questions and job worries and marriages and pregnancies and loss.

I'm sending pink clouds.

And somehow, remarkably, it helped. It soothed pain and steeled the will and gave them strength to rise. It told them they were loved. It reminded them they shared a bond life's storms could not shake.

When darkness fell, pink clouds would come in the morning.

Pink clouds were her prayers and her insistence and her sheer force of will. They were her words and her example and her assurance that those children had the strength and character and ability to stand up after life's inevitable knockouts.

If they couldn't she would be there to soothe them until they could stand on their own.

That, I think, is what I dreaded most about losing my Mom. With her death, I feared there would be no more pink clouds.

With her death, after all, my siblings and I would become the oldest generation of our family. With her death, as my sister put it, we would be orphans. Aging, aged orphans.

And I would be on my own. We—the full-grown children—would be on our own to face a world that is frightening no matter your age. A world that, like always, is full or sadness and sorrow and conflict and fears and slips and slopes and traps.

But on Sunday morning ashes went to ashes and Mom to her secret place. And pink clouds rolled across the sky.

So tears came. And hugs and memories and smiles.

We stood together in the cold—in the warmth of each other and the tangle of emotions that make us feel the preciousness of life—and knew the bond could not be broken.

Not even by death.

John Archibald, a Pulitzer Prize winner, is a columnist for Reckon by AL.com. His columns are syndicated in various newspapers.

Used with permission of the author and the Alabama Media Group.

Grief Support*

Journeys of Transformation and Healing

When it comes to grief and bereavement in this age of evidence-based practice, we need to explore the helpful and healing approaches. What can the behavioral sciences and common sense teach us? Our clues can be found in our shared human history, in folklore and primordial legend.

In my lengthy career as a health-care chaplain, I noticed a curious phenomenon that often occurred when I called on families who had suffered sudden, traumatic loss. Members of these grief-stricken clans had a tendency to tell and retell their stories of loss to each family member, friend, nurse, or attendant who entered the emergency department conference room to render care. Each retelling seemed to bring about (for both speaker and listener, however brief or incremental) heightened acceptance, release from the pain, insight into the meaning of the loss and actions to be taken in the service of self-care, and increased bonding with others.

Storytelling is as old as humanity itself. As children, we huddled together during an autumn night's chill, enraptured and spellbound by a campfire's rich luminosity and the larger-than-life ghost stories that we told. We enjoyed the proverbial bedtime fables that brought us relief and rest after the rigors of a difficult day. In these narrative retellings, threats were contained and the villainous aspects of life were subdued. There is something very foundational and primitive—indeed very human and reassuring—about the need to tell and hear a story. One can imagine our ancestors huddling together on similar nights thousands of years ago, their only light and warmth emanating from the shimmering stars above, the glowing embers before them, and the stories that were woven and rewoven with each retelling. Somehow, the majestic and frightening phenomena of nature, the utter mystery of their own existences and mortality, and the inexplicable grief of their bitterly hard, circumscribed lives were rendered more understandable and manageable when put into words or ritualized.

If we look at this "re-storying" process—one as old as time yet timely as today's breaking news—as a defining metaphor *for* and a primary method *of* mourning and coping, what can we learn? Human beings tell or enact stories in order to gain *mastery*

**Note:* The section entitled "Grief Support" was authored by Steve Sweatt, LPC, LMFT. He is the clinical and agency director of Community Grief Support Services. Previously published in *CFLE Network*, an NCFR publication, Fall 2013, pp. 16 and 20. Used with permission.

over that which is challenging, frightening, and overwhelming. In ancient cultures the world over, the power to *name* or define something or someone allowed a human being some degree of control over the feared phenomenon of nature. Mastery was therefore attained through efforts at meaning or sense making and through bonding with others who could help hold and contain the difficult experience.

As we tell and retell our stories within the empathic presences of professional caregivers or peers, the afflictive emotions that constitute our grief become more manageable. A capable and understanding counselor or a group of committed peers can assist us in holding and carrying our pain as we do the work of mourning. They provide a safe container of presence that will not abandon, leave, or forsake us in the hour of our vulnerability. The containing space they create will not fracture under the pressure of emotional intensity (a quality referred to in the professional literature as "object constancy"). The turmoil that threatens to overwhelm us is tempered and harmonized into our being through the calm, compassionate acceptance assimilated from others. I experienced the power of "the therapeutic hold" in my own life some sixteen years after the loss of my father when, with the help of a collegial support group, I was able to reengage the mourning that had lain dormant for some time.

Observe people who are retelling their stories and you'll discover that the narratives often change over time in much the same way that plots shift in a highly absorbing novel. New insights, perspectives, and information become available that weren't accessible earlier. These hard-won understandings often lead to more hopeful, expansive interpretations of oneself and of life's possibilities—movements that facilitate healing. Sometimes, self-discovery emerges through introspection and contemplation and, at other times, by way of the offerings of others. Meaning for human beings is socially constructed in a manner not unlike that of our ancestors who told or enacted stories around the campfire. Storytelling helps survivors heal through a reworking of the intrinsic meaning of our life stories, with the ensuing constructs providing continuity and context where none had been present before. Rips and tears in the delicate narratives of our lives wrought by loss are thus woven together, but in new, different, and oftentimes unintended ways.

What kinds of themes do survivors address in their narrative retellings or enactments? Sometimes, survivors focus on the impacts of the losses—emotional and otherwise—what Neimeyer refers to as the "internal narrative." At other times, survivors may fathom the "reflexive narrative" (Neimeyer, 2001a, 2001b, 2012) or the meaning of the loss. Stories are also told in an effort to "problem solve"—secure practical solutions to the exigencies of living, the post-loss "adaptive challenges" of mourning brought about by changes in role and responsibility after the death of a loved one. There are other occasions when stories are told to solidify or rework the bonds between survivors and those who have died or to affirm or modify one's life philosophy or value system in much the same way that narratives and rituals were utilized by our ancestors to contextualize their losses within the wisdom and lived experiences of earlier generations.

Stories may be verbalized sparingly, if at all, by some survivors, who may prefer various forms of enactment in giving expression to their mourning. Verbalization of stories—at least in public—is often eschewed by survivors who express their grief "instrumentally" (Doka & Martin, 2010) through quiet reflection and directed activity: writing, various other artistic expressions, and memorializations. As bereavement researchers Fraley and Bonanno (2004) pointed out, not everyone profits from prolonged, intensive "processing" of grief experiences. The forms that grief work takes are exquisitely diversified, dependent as they are on a multitude of factors such as the nature of the loss; the survivor's temperament, personality, and social history; the nature of the bond with the person who has died; and the presence or absence of other stressors. The caregiver's role is to honor the diversity of grief experience and expression.

FOCUS POINT

Stories help us elicit meaning from our relationships, our communities, and our lives in general. Narrative therapy incorporates this greater context. The words *authoring* and *coauthoring* are used. Clients retell their stories much like authors create their tales. Therapists can help this process and facilitate the creation of an expanded narrative, one in which novel avenues are found and explored. Narrative therapy has distinct elements: the storyteller can identify a dominant or lead story, especially in traumatic circumstances, and the narrative can shape the identity of the storyteller by acknowledging novel and unanticipated outcomes. By externalizing, the person gains new perspectives.

It has been said that science fiction and fantasy are the mythologies of our time. No mythology speaks more eloquently to the sustaining and healing power of companionship amid grief than does J. R. R. Tolkien's epic, *The Lord of the Rings* (1954–1955/2001). In this masterpiece, we read the story of young Frodo Baggins, called out of his sheltered, nurturing existence into an unexpected encounter with the brutalities of life—one that he neither wanted nor sought: the challenge of grief came into his life quite unbidden. His discovery of a ring of great and terrible power launches him on a quest to subdue that selfsame power by returning the talisman to its source. In doing so, he will transform his own life and that of his world. Knowing that the power of the ring is much too great for one person to bear alone, a wise wizard commissions a fellowship of friends who will comfort, challenge, support, and guide the ring bearer in his quest. The group itself, in a very real sense, functions as ring bearer and assists Frodo in holding and carrying the burden.

The Angel of Grief Weeping over the Dismantled Altar of Life, by American sculptor William Wetmore Story (1819–1895). This statue marks the graves of the artist and his wife Emelyn Story in the Protestant Cemetery, Rome, Italy. William Story graduated from Harvard Law School but dedicated his life to being a sculptor.

Source: © iStock.com/akisling.

Each comrade offers a different gift toward that end. Gandalf the Grey, a wizard, encourages Frodo to believe in himself—in his capacity to "bear the ring"—and facilitates a substantial expansion of Frodo's view of himself by helping him to envision his mortal life as part of an epic adventure, one that brings hope and a priceless gift to all humanity. Gimli the Dwarf offers dogged determination—the will to persevere when the going gets rough (how many loss survivors have had the experience of having to push themselves out of bed in the mornings?). Merry and Pippin, fellow Hobbits, offer diversion and amusement—distraction—from the rigors of the journey (what grief counselors call "avoidant coping," which can be useful if utilized strategically). Legolas the Elf and his Elvish kin provide spiritual transcendence—entry into oases of beauty and splendor where the rigors of grief are suspended for a time and the survivor is revived and reoriented via reconnection with, and grounding in, a higher order of reality (spiritual practice is an indispensable ally for many loss survivors). Samwise Gamgee, Frodo's closest and most practical companion, encourages self-care—to rest, to eat well, to be easy on oneself, to place a priority on putting one's need for care first, and in so doing, to be discerning about which companions to trust while on the journey.

In this manner healing is activated via the power of presence—the conscious, steadfast presences of ourselves and those of others. In the dark night of grief when the light of the sun and the warmth of love are but distant points upon an ever-receding horizon, a sad, fearful, and weary pilgrim can find light, love, and transcendence in the empathic presences of self and others. These fellow pilgrims who are committed to a survivor's care will need little else but "eyes to see" and "ears to hear" the heartache and travail presented in myriad forms, and "a heart of flesh" that beats and resonates with those selfsame sufferings. In the magic and mystery of such joining, the possibilities for healing and transformation are greatly magnified.

> **"All that is family, and humanity, and how our stories are written. They are easier to see in the shadow of death."**
>
> John Archibald, American journalist and Pulitzer Prize winner

Grief: The Real Story**

Grief does not discriminate. It does not care what color you are, how much money you make, or your social status. It affects people at all ages and, at some point, will affect every person in some way. The work that I do is specifically with people who have experienced the death of a significant person in their lives.

Many times, when I meet with the bereaved for the first time, they begin by telling me which stage of grief they believe they are currently in, have just completed, or are afraid of going through. These stages have painted our picture of grief for decades through the integration of the stage model into popular culture. However, many times these individuals find themselves at a loss when intense emotions resurface. The stage they thought they had completed comes rushing back like a tidal wave, challenging their sense of emotional stability.

Elizabeth Kübler-Ross presented the model for the five stages of grief in her book *Death and Dying* in 1969. This model was derived from observations made by Kübler-Ross while she worked with terminally ill individuals facing their own imminent death. However, this model, when applied to individuals grieving the death of a significant person in their life, does not adequately encapsulate all the chaotic, intense emotions and thoughts they experience.

Task-Oriented Model

Several other models of bereavement have been postulated throughout the years, but J. William Worden (2018) introduced a model that changed the way we think about the process of grief and mourning. This model is task oriented and, from my experience, relatable to individuals experiencing grief associated with a significant death. Unlike the stage model, the task model is action oriented and is targeted at the individual regaining some control over his or her life.

** *Note:* The section entitled "Grief: The Real Story" was authored by Matthew Bunt, MEd, LPC-S. Bunt is a licensed counselor with The Amelia Center, a comprehensive grief counseling center of Children's of Alabama.

The four tasks of mourning include the following:

To accept the reality of the loss. This task emphasizes overcoming denial and disbelief and understanding the death is irreversible.

Acceptance is both cognitive and emotional. Cognitively, this task involves the understanding that the deceased is dead and permanently separated from the bereaved in this life. Young children may ask the same questions multiple times trying to understand the concept of finality in death. This is why it is important for caregivers to use words such as "died" and "dead" to help children grasp an understanding of this new concept they are experiencing. Often euphemisms such as "lost" or "asleep" can confuse young children and hinder their ability to work through this task fully. For older children and adults, this task involves realizing the finality of death and that the deceased will not be seen or heard from again in this life.

Gaining an emotional acceptance is something that happens over time for both children and adults. Emotional acceptance involves experiences or activities in which the bereaved is currently engaged where the deceased would have had some anticipated involvement. For example, a child who has been picked up from school every day by his mother might revisit the emotions associated with the loss at the end of each school day when she is not there. Emotional acceptance of the reality of the loss can be experienced for quite a while after the death and often includes activities associated with holidays, birthdays, and even everyday events.

To process the pain of grief. This task focuses on finding a way to experience the emotional pain related to the loss without becoming overwhelmed.

Frequently, the families I work with have preconceived ideas of what this task should look like in their spouses, children, and themselves. They often believe that they are not crying enough, or maybe they think they are crying too much. Society in general also places some expectations on how different genders should manage themselves through this task. Personality has a profound impact on the way a person works through the pain of grief. There are many ways to work through the pain of grief, which can include crying, thinking, talking, writing, or artistic expression.

Ken Doka and Terry Martin, in their book *Grieving Beyond Gender: Understanding Ways Men and Women Mourn* (2010), explained that there are intuitive grievers, whose behavior is driven more by feelings, and instrumental grievers, whose behavior is driven more by thoughts. These terms better define a griever's preferred method of processing the pain of grief rather than placing stereotypical ideas of how men or women should express their emotional pain. An intuitive griever may experience this task through talking and crying. An instrumental griever still experiences the feelings related to grief but perhaps not as overtly as an intuitive griever, so these feelings may not be easily observed by others. For example, a middle-aged male whose son died may choose to experience his emotional pain while running, which allows him to maintain a sense of internal control while cognitively processing his grief (Doka, 2016).

To adjust to a world without the deceased. This task expands the understanding of loss to more than just a relationship. It includes all the roles the deceased individual fulfilled within a relationship and the bereaved person's work to find a way to have these needs met without the individual.

This is what I describe as the "nuts and bolts" task, which often involves everyday activities. For example, an elderly man whose spouse of fifty years dies might find it difficult to complete all of the daily tasks that his spouse performed. These tasks may have included things such as grocery shopping, cooking dinner every night, and cleaning the house. Finding a new way to have these roles fulfilled, either by learning them himself or asking someone new to complete them, can be a frustrating and exhausting part of the grief experience (Doka, 2016).

To find a way to remember the deceased while embarking on the rest of one's journey through life. This task involves finding a way to maintain an emotional connection with the deceased while also investing emotional energy in one's own life and identity after the death.

After the death of a significant person, the bereaved naturally focuses much of his or her emotional energy on the death event or related circumstances. The focus of this emotional energy should expand over time to include memories of the life of the person who died, as well as investing in current relationships. Well-meaning family members or friends may inadvertently send the message that the bereaved individual must forget about the deceased to move on with life. When a bereaved person hears statements such as "You need to move on" or "You need to get over it," he or she usually feels like others do not understand the impact of the death.

In reality, the bereaved individual will never forget the person who died. Fully understanding this task gives the bereaved permission to remember the person who died while also investing in current relationships and activities. Public and personal rituals, such as memorial services or visiting the grave of the deceased, are often used to help the bereaved work through this task. For example, parents who experienced the death of a child may attend a monthly support group to allow them a specific time to talk about and remember their child. Designated activities such as this give the bereaved a safe, structured way to focus emotional energy on the deceased while living life in the present.

The task model is nonlinear and fluid in nature and can be experienced in different ways as time passes. When people understand that the experience described through the task model is a normal and natural process, it allows them to engage fully in the work that must be completed to work through grief (Meagher & Balk, 2013).

FOCUS POINT

The four tasks of mourning are

- *To accept the reality of the loss.* This task emphasizes overcoming denial and disbelief and understanding that the death is irreversible.
- *To process the pain of grief.* This task focuses on finding a way to experience the emotional pain related to the loss without becoming overwhelmed.
- *To adjust to a world without the deceased.* This task expands the understanding of loss to more than just a relationship. It requires acknowledging all the roles the deceased individual fulfilled within a relationship and working to find a way to have these needs met without the individual.
- *To find a way to remember the deceased while embarking on the rest of one's journey through life.* This task involves finding a way to maintain an emotional connection with the deceased while also investing emotional energy in one's own life and identity after the death.

When people understand that the experience described through the task model is a normal and natural process, they can engage fully in the labor that must be completed to work through the pain of grief (Doka, 2016).

SPOTLIGHT ON THEORIES

Stages, Tasks, and Processes: Various Models

Although stage-based approaches have gained much publicity, there are numerous other valuable contributors to grief therapy, some highlighting the tasks to be completed during the grief journey and others its overall process (see "Grief: The Real Story"). The stage-based approach used to be a frequently referenced framework in discussions of the grieving process and the end of life, and one that entered popular culture, but in terms of therapeutic approaches, it has been overshadowed by more recent contributions. These look beyond the potentially linear stages toward context, and they are associated with emotional growth that facilitates dynamic and systemic outcomes.

Historic background. Elisabeth Kübler-Ross (1926–2004) was a Swiss-American psychiatrist who dedicated her career to working with the incurably ill and addressing issues concerning life's end. Kübler-Ross volunteered as a nurses' aide during World War II, and after war's end she went to medical school. One of the touching and significant moments in her life was her visit to a concentration camp in Poland after the war. On some of the walls, inmates had carved hundreds of butterflies. Kübler-Ross said that these poignant images stayed with her for years and inspired her work. Even in the final moments, during excruciatingly difficult circumstances, these artists had found a way to express their immortality and spirituality (Dugan, 2004).

At the time of her research there was not much material focusing on the process of accompanying terminally ill patients on their journey toward death, and Kübler-Ross filled this void with seminars and a book titled *On Death and Dying* (1969). As with most theorists, she was inspired by various authors and topics, which contributed to the underpinnings of her theory and fueled the interests of other clinicians and researchers.

Theoretical influences. Kübler-Ross was influenced by earlier clinician's thinking about loss and bereavement. John Bowlby (1907–1990) was known for his work on attachment and for first proposing attachment theory, much of which arose out of the postwar years when many children had lost a parent, were orphaned, or were displaced. Other clinicians who developed structural frameworks surrounding the topic of bereavement were Colin Murray Parkes (1972) and Erich Lindemann. Lindemann (1944) was a psychiatrist with an interest in traumatic grief and associated responses (p. 145).

Bowlby is also remembered for the insightful report that he wrote for the World Health Organization (WHO) in 1950, titled *Maternal Care and Mental Health*, which emphasized the long-range implications of early childhood care in terms of attachment and subsequent development and well-being (Bowlby, 1951). Because of Bowlby's work with attachment and loss, he knew that it could be difficult to free oneself from the trauma of bereavement or abandonment; some of its aftereffects may remain in hidden corners of our brains, to influence future patterns of attachment (Bigner & Gerhardt, 2019, p. 100).

Bowlby and Parkes (1970) copublished work on separation and loss within the family and described four stages of grief. We recognize much of the thinking for which Kübler-Ross won accolades when we consider the following stages outlined by Bowlby and Parkes:

- Shock and numbness (Kübler-Ross labeled it *denial*, saying it was a defense mechanism).
- Yearning and searching (Kübler-Ross incorporated some of these aspects in *bargaining*).
- Despair and disorganization (Kübler-Ross points to *depression*).
- Reorganization and recovery (Kübler-Ross calls this *acceptance*).

In essence, these stages represent the crisis, the disorganization following the crisis, and the subsequent reorganization. The latter may lead the client to greater insight and acceptance, but it need not have such a constructive outcome. Clients find their own level of adaptation depending on various interacting factors, including their own emotional resources and the support they receive.

(Continued)

(Continued)

The ABC-X model first described by Reuben Hill in 1947 also tackled these concerns of reorganization under duress (Rosino, 2016). This model and the expanded versions are still relevant in family-related research (Bigner & Gerhardt, 2019, p. 341).

The work of Viktor Frankl (1905–1997) also hones in on the process that allows some persons to find meaning in their suffering and to do so with dignity, maintaining their self-worth. Frankl's book *Man's Search for Meaning* (1959) elaborated on this process.

Kübler-Ross's extensive work with the terminally ill allowed her to observe that patients tried to find individual ways of coping with the end of life, as well as with facing terminal illness (Kübler-Ross, 1969, 1998). Kübler-Ross's approach has been helpful in creating an explanatory model that can also guide health-care workers and support teams. The model should not be taken too literally; the suggested stages need not be present in every person in this particular sequence. It is also possible that various cultural contexts allow for different approaches to end-of-life concerns. Her descriptions are helpful in gaining an understanding of the path to be traveled by the person facing illness and death and can provide a useful frame of reference if we interpret and apply it flexibly.

Ethics. Ultimately Kübler-Ross's work added several dimensions to the study and ethical management of end-of-life care and decision making, which affected the hospice movement and supported professionals dealing with end-of-life scenarios (Dugan, 2004):

- Hospice and palliative care benefited from the scholarly framework of her work, and, importantly, it provided an ethical context.
- It opened up discussions about end-of-life options and discussions pertaining to informed consent, whereby the patient was involved in this decision-making process. In a sense, this changed the end-of-life journey of patients as they could express their concerns and participate in management choices.
- The process of end-of-life journeys could be managed ethically, in ways that were more supportive and comforting and that respected the needs, wishes, and concerns of patients and their loved ones and addressed the needs of the team of caring and support professionals.
- Persons working in end-of-life helping professions required support to prevent burnout and to be empowered in providing the appropriate ethical and respectful accompaniment for patients and their loved ones. Formal end-of-life education is an important component of training in these helping professions (Zimmerman, 2017).

Five stages of grief. Kübler-Ross described five stages or phases in the process of coming to terms with loss. It is important for those wishing to understand grief and mourning to be aware of this model, which has historical value. It represents an earlier approach to thinking about the end of life. Since the model's inception, many additions and variations to it have been proposed. Importantly, it should not be taken too literally because the stages do not consistently occur in set patterns or in a linear sequence, and stages are not necessarily fully resolved at any given time.

The Kübler-Ross model is typically remembered with the acronym DABDA, which uses the first letters of the **five stages of grief**:

- *Denial.* The initial reaction, when faced with the almost unbelievable reality of the catastrophic illness or death of a loved one, may be to question the truth and realness of this information. The defense mechanism of denial, initially described by Sigmund Freud as well as his daughter Anna Freud, plays a role in helping people cope with tragedy (Freud, 1936/1992). This defense seeks to distort the truth in order to make the anxiety surrounding it more manageable. Denial of a medical diagnosis, or of any major catastrophic disclosure, may be an initial attempt at dealing with reality and the flooding of emotions.

  The *denial* or pushback process attendant upon survivorship, as survivors attempt to insulate themselves from excessive exposure to that which is painful, is described by Wolfelt (2010) as an "evade and encounter" response.

- *Anger.* After the initial disbelief, feelings of anger and aggression may set in. This is also a way of mobilizing emotions that try to protect the individual. In other situations in daily life, anger and displays of aggression may signal power and could possibly scare away an opponent. Anger is also a means of venting emotion in a somewhat uncontrolled manner.

  Wolfelt (2010) describes the adaptive functions of anger and guilt in the survivorship process. These are "protest emotions" (attempts to assign culpability for the loss to someone else or to oneself) and are oftentimes experienced within days, weeks, or months following the onset of loss. These ways of delaying or suspending acceptance are associated with a bereavement that is very difficult to bear.

- *Bargaining.* This behavior emulates something that might work in day-to-day interaction, namely, trying to barter or exchange one thing for another. By doing this, the subject is trying to regain control, giving up something in exchange for a greater cause. Typical examples are of terminally ill persons promising to improve their lives and to make sacrifices in order to delay death. Bargaining may also be a way of mental reasoning, much in the line of "If I had done this, then that would not have happened."

- *Depression.* During this fourth stage, feelings of sadness and loss are frequently combined with a sense of helplessness and hopelessness. People feel empty, withdrawn, and overwhelmed, as if they cannot go on. Depression may be one way of moving closer to acknowledging the reality of the impending passing.

- *Acceptance.* This last stage ideally leads to an integration of feelings as well as adding meaning, but it does not necessarily occur in all subjects. It is typically associated with the mature and stable reassessment of values and life in general. In essence, it also represents a reintegration of the psyche; the person accepts and engages in knowing the boundaries of the inevitable.

Some of the literature proposes that these stages could be useful in forming a loose theoretical framework that helps us anticipate some of the emotions felt by a person faced with catastrophic events or learning about the diagnosis of a terminal illness (Nathoo & Ellis, 2019). People in other situations seem to go through these or similar stages: for example, the parents of children with severe disabilities and congenital challenges or of infants requiring congenital heart surgery (Nakazuru, Sato, & Nakamura, 2017). Those reacting to natural disasters, such as earthquakes and tsunamis, can go through similar stages, as can individuals involved in other challenging situations, such as partnership breakups (Finkelstein, 2014). The work of Kübler-Ross has had an enduring influence and reappears in numerous textbooks (Corr, 2018).

Most grief counselors could reference this model in conjunction with other approaches, which include therapies related to meaning, transformation, and empowerment. In clinical studies of bereavement survivorship, models have evolved from those emphasizing *stages* or *phases* (Kübler-Ross, 1969; Bowlby & Parkes, 1970), *tasks* (Worden, 2008; Wolfelt, 2010), and *processes* (Rando, 1993; Stroebe & Schut, 1999). Clinical psychologist Bonanno (2009) highlighted the role of resiliency and advocated rethinking the supposedly vital part played by emotional processing in loss survivorship.

The knowledge that our lives on earth are finite is a reality humankind shares. Thus, death can be interpreted as part of the life story or life journey, and a life well lived as contributing to a meaningful ending. Bluck and Mroz (2018) express this sentiment: "The fact that humans know that their story will one day end may affect what they do and the stories they tell about their lives well beforehand." Knowing that there is a finish line adds to the urgency of valuing life and enables us to recognize that death is an integral and unavoidable part of the life story.

> **"Learn to get in touch with the silence within yourself, and know that everything in life has purpose."**
>
> Elisabeth Kübler-Ross (1926–2004)

FOCUS POINT

Although stage-based approaches have gained much publicity, there are numerous other valuable contributors to grief therapy, some highlighting the *tasks* to be completed during the grief journey and others its overall *process*. Theoretical models such as the one by Kübler-Ross are stage based. Since this model's inception, many additions and variations to it have been proposed. It should not be taken too literally, as stages do not occur in set patterns consistently or in a linear sequence, and stages are not necessarily fully resolved at any given time. The narrative approaches to grief therapy have supported important interventions that help people contextualize events and find renewed hope and meaning while traveling the journey associated with loss.

In a Nutshell

- Besides stage-based approaches, valuable alternatives highlight tasks as well as process during the grief journey.
- One stage-based framework was provided by Elisabeth Kübler-Ross who was influenced by earlier theorists. Her work influenced ethical end-of-life care and hospice practices.
- She described five stages or phases in the process of coming to terms with loss, remembered with the acronym DABDA.
- The stages are denial, anger, bargaining, depression, and acceptance.
- Importantly, stages need not follow the suggested sequence in a predictable linear manner.
- The narrative approaches to grief therapy have supported important interventions that help people contextualize events and find renewed hope and meaning while traveling the journey associated with loss.

CHAPTER FOCUS POINTS

Grief and Mourning

- Loss has many faces and many guises. Life's gifts can slip through our fingers; there is no guarantee of permanence.
- The process of loss requires exploration of ways of coming to terms with a shattered world. During mourning, a new emotional destination has to be negotiated.
- Several theoretical models seek to explain dimensions of the grieving process, including the dual process model and psychoanalytic and psychodynamic approaches.

Interventions: Constructivist Psychotherapy

- The constructivist angle supports grief support interventions. Its key feature is that clients are encouraged to construct meaning within the greater context of their worlds.
- Survivors can cope more effectively with loss if they can place their painful, disjointed life experiences within contexts of understanding.
- One such context, a story, has the potential to restore meaning and internal cohesion and provide purpose and hopefulness.

Loss in Limbo: Ambiguous Loss

- Grieving styles can be as unique as the people presenting them.
- Ambiguous loss refers to loss with no clear road toward closure, such as if a person disappears or the body of someone presumed dead cannot be located. Lack of information can be linked to incomplete processing.
- However the loss occurred, it will always affect family dynamics. The place occupied by that particular family member will have to be

redefined in a concrete and symbolic manner.

- Being able to talk about and express ambiguous feelings validates that the grieving person is not alone in her or his perceptions; that person's reality is echoed in the grief of other family members.

Narrative Therapy

- Stories help us elicit meaning from our relationships, our communities, and our lives in general. Narrative therapy incorporates this greater context.
- The words *authoring* and *coauthoring* are used. Clients retell their stories much like authors create their tales.
- Therapists can help this process and facilitate the creation of an expanded narrative, one in which novel avenues are found and explored.
- Narrative therapy has distinct elements: the storyteller can identify a dominant or lead story, especially in traumatic circumstances, and the narrative can shape the identity of the storyteller by acknowledging novel and unanticipated outcomes.
- By externalizing, the person gains new perspectives.

Grief Support and Grief: The Real Story

- The four tasks of mourning are
  - *To accept the reality of the loss.* This task emphasizes overcoming denial and disbelief and understanding that the death is irreversible.
  - *To process the pain of grief.* This task focuses on finding a way to experience the emotional pain related to the loss without becoming overwhelmed.
  - *To adjust to a world without the deceased.* This task expands the understanding of loss to more than just a relationship. It requires acknowledging all the roles the deceased individual fulfilled within a relationship and working to find a way to have these needs met without the individual.
  - *To find a way to remember the deceased while embarking on the rest of one's journey through life.* This task involves finding a way to maintain an emotional connection with the deceased while also investing emotional energy in one's own life and identity after the death.
- When people understand that the experience described through the task model is a normal and natural process, they can engage fully in the labor that must be completed to work through the pain of grief (Doka, 2016).

Spotlight on Theories: Stages, Tasks, and Processes—Various Models

- Although stage-based approaches have gained much publicity, there are numerous other valuable contributors to grief therapy, some highlighting the *tasks* to be completed during the grief journey and others its overall *process*.
- Theoretical models such as the one by Kübler-Ross are stage based. Since the model's inception, many additions and variations to it have been proposed.
- It should not be taken too literally, as stages do not occur in set patterns consistently or in a linear sequence, and stages are not fully resolved at any given time.
- The narrative approaches to grief therapy have supported important interventions that help people contextualize events and find renewed hope and meaning while traveling the journey associated with loss.

CHAPTER

12 Dynamics of Power and Excess

Learning Outcomes

After studying this chapter, you should be able to

1. Summarize the dimensions of *power* and how they present in family systems.
2. Discuss the dynamics of *excess*.
3. Analyze the dynamics of *collecting*, and describe how it presents.
4. Identify the characteristics of *hoarding*, and express how collecting can transition to hoarding.
5. Recognize the influence of *addictive behaviors* on the family system.
6. Define *cognitive behavioral therapy*, and explore its therapeutic focus.

The Dynamics of Power

Children spend many a happy playground hour on the seesaw—those wonderful up and down balancing activities in children's parks. Seesawing is based on shifting weight, pushing up from the ground and propelling one side of the balanced board upward and then reversing the action, so what goes up, must come down. The best partnerships are those in which the children's weights are about equal. When partners are balanced, the interplay between the up and the down of the seesaw is fair and at regular intervals. That optimum balance of power is similarly desirable in everyday life.

Power has two faces depending on context and motive. It can be good and benevolent, as is the case when we use our skills or access to resources to the general advantage of all those in our dynamic system. The teacher with intellectual expertise in an area of specialization can share that in the classroom; she can be an educator of worth. In amplified form, power can change social systems. Major philanthropies demonstrate how position and privilege can be applied for the greater good and in support of worthwhile causes worldwide. This type of power works as a catalyst. It changes a system to set off a domino effect that, one hopes, generates positive change.

Constructive power does not have to occur on a world platform to be effective. Each one of us has some degree of social power; we can influence the relationships closest to us, and we can make a difference in our daily tasks and with our attitudes. In the family unit, this interpersonal power is exceptionally important as it feeds the hierarchy of parenting, sibling relationships, and intergenerational ties. It gives the parents who are responsible for the family (usually the parental dyad) the appropriate power to act in ways that are best for their children, with ripple effects spreading into the extended family.

Additionally, our position in the life cycle may define part of our power. Children typically are in a balanced relationship with their parents, but, in terms of taking responsibility for family outcomes, the children are subservient to the parents. Minuchin talked about the parental dyad as a hierarchy, or a level on its own (Minuchin & Fishman, 1981; Wood, 1985). This separateness denotes responsibilities and boundaries. For instance, sexual matters pertaining to the parents should be contained within the parental dyad; these should not spill over to the level of the children. Children should not be involved in the details of what goes on sexually between grownups. It would be a transgression or a breaking of the boundaries if that intimate knowledge were to spill over, and if the information was not age inappropriate, it could also do harm.

Parental power that is constructively applied can do wonders; it can transform the worlds of children, supporting the formation of confidence, skills, and positive self-concepts. The strong and positive investment of parents will allow children to grow and develop to their potential. Children, in turn, can feel the positive investment of the parents and incorporate it into their lives, giving them a sense of worth. In this way, appropriately applied parental power and attention can unleash the promise of children becoming the best they can be, because they have a parental fan club.

Appropriate social power. Appropriate social power is a gift to be shared; it leads to constructive team efforts, and the collaborative work ethic it fosters facilitates outcomes that increase exponentially. We find the metaphor of the caregiver or the caretaker in many guises and forms. It is also part of the hero myth (Campbell, 1990/2003; Campbell, 2008) in which good vanquishes evil. The emotional light displaces the metaphorical dark. The protector can be the proverbial shepherd or the figurehead. We invest our collective trust in a worthy power figure with the hope that this hero will lead us toward best outcomes. The superheroes remind us that with great power comes great responsibility. The power dynamic should protect the vulnerable because in many of these relationships, vulnerability causes the power imbalance.

Consider the client-therapist relationship. The therapist or other professional holds great power over a client, a patient, a subject, or a minor; those professional roles are defined by the fact that the power should not be misapplied. Consequently, many professions have detailed codes of ethics to add an extra layer of safety. In the helping professions, this power imbalance is an almost sacred tool. It can be used ethically to bring about change, to serve the best interests of the client, with the proviso that, first of all, the help provider does no harm. We seek out persons who are exceptionally skilled in their professions so that they can guide and help us, typically for a professional fee. But even though the power dynamic of the client-professional relationship is not balanced, the participants start out by building rapport, and the relationship is continued largely by building trust. That is the hope and the intention of any number of relationships containing varying degrees of power imbalances.

Two faces of power. In some ways, power has two faces. It can represent the positive force eliciting good and demonstrating the qualities we expect in the hero. By the same token, power can be negative if abused and misdirected. The Roman god Janus was depicted as having a head with two faces, one facing forward and one backward. The month January is named after this god, as Janus has the ability to look back into the previous year and forward into the coming year. Power used for good and power used for evil can also be likened to the yin

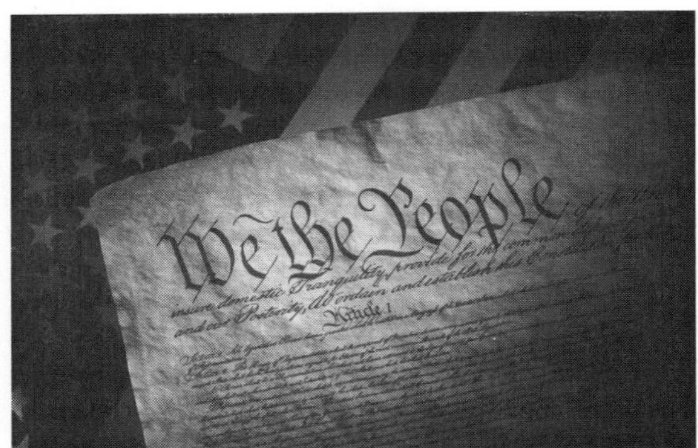

Appropriate social power is a gift to be shared; it leads to constructive team efforts, and the collaborative work ethic it fosters facilitates outcomes that increase exponentially.

Source: Public domain.

and the yang in that boundaries can be very fragile and, really, these seemingly opposite forces are interconnected parts of a whole; good can morph into evil, especially taking context into consideration.

Our history and especially the history of major wars demonstrate how power can be used and abused—and take on a life of its own. Seeking power can be a great controlling and motivating force. The powerful persons align all those who are subservient to them, to serve the needs of the powerful ones, often at the expense of the underlings. It is a complicated battle as old as humankind.

When I was in training as a young psychologist, my mentor and professor gave me this abbreviated piece of advice concerning psychotherapy. Always ask in whose interests a specific action is taken or a specific statement is made. If it serves the best interests of the client, it was probably the right therapeutic intervention. If it seems to be in the self-focused interest of the therapist, it probably requires a second and closer look to determine true underlying motives. If, as a therapist, I say things because I have a personal emotional need to

GLOBAL GLIMPSE

JANUS: THE MYTHICAL GOD OF TRANSITIONS

The Roman god Janus was depicted on numerous Roman coins. He is regarded as the god of beginnings and also of transitions. The month January is named after him as it marks the beginning of a new year. He is characterized as having two faces, one looking forward and one looking backward, which gives him the unique capability of seeing what is ahead and behind at the same time, a great bonus if one wants to be vigilant and safe. In the Roman context, his symbol often appeared on doorways and arches, as well as above other points of transition, such as gates and passageways. Being able to glance in both directions also means that Janus can look forward into the future and back into the past. The thought is that the past can be a warning for the future.

We find this symbolism in psychology as well; if we learn from where we have been, it can influence where we are going. It is thought that we can metaphorically meet our own past in our future. Reworded more simply, we carry our baggage and our history with us, and these exert an influence in the days to come. In insight-based therapy we access our past and create a more constructive and insightful relationship with what has happened; we can learn from it, and we can reframe it. In that way, when we reconnect to our past in our own future lives, it will provide us with a more meaningful context.

As opposed to holding us back or traumatizing us, the past can provide us with insights we can build on. Insight-based psychotherapy has to do with putting things into a constructive perspective to gain understanding, so that this content cannot continue to have a hold on us. We aim to create a more positive and hopeful future for ourselves, living the best lives possible despite the negatives and trauma of earlier years. With our gained insight (our vision into the past), we can create or follow a safer, more informed, productive and harmonious path going forward.

Just like Janus guarding the doorways and looking in both directions, we can look back to enhance our vision into the future. In this way, our past can support us as we transition toward optimal outcomes.

"it takes courage to grow up and become who you really are."

e. e. cummings (1894–1962),
American poet

be heard or because my boundaries are permeable, I may be hurting my client. So ask about motives. Am I showing off, disinterested, or was this a power display? Whatever the motive was, I recommended taking a second look at these interactions. If an interaction truly was in the best interests of the client, as the professional codes of ethics remind us it must be, then it was probably serving a therapeutic goal toward a constructive outcome. If it became a power play, it might very well camouflage personal feelings of need—to feel in control, to be admired, to own the situation . . . there are many variations. But, more important, that particular interaction may not serve the needs of the client, may not be helping. Proceed with caution, and consult your supervisor.

"Power is more addictive than money."

Taken from folklore

Janus.

Janus, the Roman god of beginnings and also of transitions, is characterized as having two faces, one looking forward and one looking backward. A consideration of both the past and the future is significant when individuals are making transitions through transformative therapies.

Source: © iStock.com/ZU_09.

The Power That Gives Us Courage

Power can be a driving force. We need to be careful how we use it, and we need to direct it so that it produces positive and constructive outcomes. We can summarize this more poetically:

> Almost all the things that turned me into a more complex and multidimensional person, I did not ask for. It wasn't a choice. The challenge appeared in my life, and I had to wade through it. It added many layers to the watercolor painting that is my life. That depth is what sharpens all the other senses and grows the heart. It is called the journey of life.

The Power That Disables

Disabling power seems to be a contradiction in terms. It is the kind of power that is characterized by gross inequality between the participating parties. Persons who truly are in command can do so because they are respected, they display leadership qualities, and they know how to facilitate group cohesion. Bringing out the best in each individual within that group may be the outcome of appropriate leadership (Simpson, Farrell, Oriña, & Rothman, 2015). Some leaders rule by example, and some leaders encourage: they unravel the knots that prevent optimal functioning. But then there are the toxic leaders who display their power by force and thrust it onto others through intimidation, threats, and other undemocratic means. This power may seem strong because victims try to avoid such situations of confrontation. Ultimately, however, this kind of power may reflect the deficits within the person exerting it in unfair ways to scare, intimidate, and overrule people.

An example of power abuse is bullying. **Intimate partner violence (IPV)** is a form of bullying as well, but one from which victims may find it difficult to shield themselves, as it transgresses within relationships of intimacy and shared vulnerability (Overall, 2019). For children who have been sexually molested by adults, there is a boundary violation and a physical transgression that damages the child in far-reaching ways. The adult survivors of childhood abuse and sexual molestation require extended treatment as adults (Anguelova, 2018). In the wake of every abuse case, the adult survivor has to deal with denial, crippling shame, self-blaming behavior, depression, and anxiety. All these obstacles can stand in the path toward appropriate adult intimate-partner relationships. Therapists who venture into this challenging field need specialized training, so they can identify the stages of abuse and the various effects on the victim, creating a profile of the abused and the abuser and identifying and providing appropriate interventions (Anguelova, 2018).

Bullies appear to hold the power because they overrule their victims. In doing so, they show an intimidating and negative side of themselves, one that often has to do with personal insecurity and the need to display power in a convincing and overruling manner.

Intimate partner violence may be particularly insidious, as the abuser also sets about isolating the victim. The fewer support systems and resources a victim has, the more vice like the control can be (Goodman, Fauci, Hailes, & Gonzalez, 2019). If the options to escape from such a powerful grip are systematically undermined by the abuser, the victim may feel trapped and helpless. One of the pillars of these pathological interactions is to force the victim into secrecy and confidentiality. The threats revolve around the abusive behavior being something intimate that cannot be disclosed to the world, as doing so would precipitate catastrophic outcomes. Child abuse, both emotional and physical (including sexual abuse), can also enforce this secrecy and associated shame. It becomes a closely guarded secret because the abused do not know their rights and start attributing the negative outcomes to their own behavior. Many victims have been crippled by shame because they falsely attribute these toxic relationships to some fault of their own. Clearly, this shame only solidifies the terms of entrapment. The effects can stretch forward affecting and tainting all future attempts at forming healthy, respectful partnerships.

IPV can occur in any relationship where intimacy and pathological control are intertwined. It can occur between opposite sexes but just as easily between those in same sex relationships and in a variety of family contexts (Anderson, 2010; Gaman, McAfee, Homel, & Jacob, 2017; Trotman, 2017). According to Gaman et al. (2017), IPV is a major social condition but it also has distinct mental health implications. Although their sample size was modest, they found support for the idea that female-to-female abuse patterns were linked to females having experiencing increased levels of abuse in their families of origin and before age 18. Parents and relatives could be implicated. These findings seem to support what we have already surmised, and the findings of many other literature studies, namely, that exposure to abusive parenting may pave the way to later abusive behavior by the victims (Kopystynska & Beck, 2018). Having experienced abuse was also linked to aggressive parenting interactions, such as spanking children or being verbally and physically abusive in a wide range of ways (Taylor et al., 2016).

Well-adjusted couples tend to use negotiation as a form of conflict resolution and extended communication. In the cases of IPV, physical aggression and control are overriding themes, combined with psychologically damaging behavior (Gilchrist, Radcliffe, Noto, & Lucas d'Oliveira, 2017). Abuse need not be limited to physically aggressive behavior. The range of psychological damage that can be done by abusive comments and behavior is extensive.

The cycle of abuse. In 1969, after interviewing women who had been subjected to IPV, Lenore Walker described a repeated pattern of behavior that she called "the cycle of abuse" (Walker, 1979; Walker, 2016). Initially, the cycle starts when tensions between the partners build sufficiently to trigger an incident by the abuser. The victim can sense that the buildup is occurring and is walking on eggshells to avoid an attack. But any pretense can be used by the aggressor to display acute violence and attack the victim. Once this explosive event is over, it is followed by a reconciliatory phase filled with promises and fueled by remorse. Because of its temporarily hopeful overtures, this phase is named the "honeymoon" phase. Typically, the happy ending does not occur; instead, the honeymoon phase is followed initially by a period of calm and soon after by a renewed buildup of tensions, which will lead to an outburst. These cycles are taxing, especially for the victim.

This model has limitations if it is interpreted too literally or simplistically. Phases are not as predictably sequential, and a variety of subtleties can characterize each stage. A host of contributory factors can influence behavioral intensities at different times. Some can be external while others can be very individually tailored to the background and experiences of the perpetrator. Many factors affect the abuser-victim interaction, such as the specific situations that trigger the aggressor, the reactions and feelings of the victim, the secret desire for revenge felt by both parties, and, importantly, the unique destructive dynamic between this pair.

Behind closed doors. "What happens behind closed doors stays behind closed doors" is a common saying that acknowledges the importance of privacy to intimacy. A portion of that phrase is contained in the title of a book on violence in the American family, *Behind Closed Doors*, by Straus, Gelles, and Steinmetz (2006). The title highlights the irony that violent practices, shrouded in secrecy and shame, assume the cloak of respectability or even of love by claiming the privacy of intimate relationships. Women who have been victims of IPV have reported stalking behavior by former partners (McEwan et al., 2017). Dynamically, the display of obsessive behavior—namely, being preoccupied with the other person, wanting to control that person's actions and whereabouts, and in essence intruding into her or his autonomous personal space—can be expressions of boundary transgressions. In the study by these authors, the stalking behavior was significantly associated with other mental health concerns, including physical violence to victims. Stalking may be less noticeable than other forms of abuse because it is often a secret act; even so, it can represent a highly damaging form of behavior, implying dynamics of control. Because many individuals have a media presence these days, electronic stalking has become worrisome, and the victim may not be aware of this behavior.

Additionally, persons in abusive relationships need to be proactive in defending their digital privacy (Consolvo, 2017). Use of social media and cell phones can be traceable, and the abuser may check the victim's phone for contacts and related information that might signal independent and support-seeking behaviors. Victims of intimate partner violence may need to plan complex exit strategies from these relationships and keep them secret, as their personal movements can be tracked by those closest to them.

Bullying. Teenage bullying underlies a number of adolescent suicides, as vulnerable victims feel intensely humiliated, belittled, and defenseless. Schools and youth groups are working at creating safe and respectful environments where empathy is encouraged and mutual respect is the lead theme (Smith & Thompson, 1991/2017). Parents and educators have important roles to play in spreading the awareness that bullying represents antisocial and essentially cowardly behavior. Taking advantage of a younger and more vulnerable victim is nothing to be proud of. Parents are typically quick to react when they know that their child is the victim.

More often than not, they are not aware when their own child is the perpetrator, as the child concerned will participate in these acts secretively. Bullying dynamics are also described in terms of systematic abuse of power (Wolke & Lereya, 2015).

Cyberbullying. This form of power play has an added dimension—it is difficult to escape. Social media platforms and smartphones are accessible from anywhere, so a cyberbully can even target children in their own homes. The dynamic of bullying is strongly intertwined with the bully's need to be powerful, but this need can sprout from insecurity (Waasdorp & Bradshaw, 2015). It is a seemingly paradoxical dynamic. Importantly, in all interventions, we need to address supportive environments, fostering good relationships between students and teachers, and emphasizing an environment of respect. The culture of respect for differences is an important cornerstone in this process. Positive support networks in schools and social circles can provide strength and force the secretive abusive behavior from its hiding place. The outcome of these destructive practices is that they deeply affect self-esteem in the targeted children, which in turn can exacerbate loneliness (Brewer & Kerslake, 2015).

Self-Centered Power

Power has to do with personal confidence and a sense of being fulfilled. For that same reason, lack of emotional power can reflect an inner void that causes an individual to seek to be comforted, acknowledged, and admired.

The motivation for seeking power in unorthodox ways partly has to do with the selfhood of the leading person in a family or relationship. For example, a narcissistic personality may need to be center stage with an admiring audience and so seeks power to fulfill this need; the admiration is required to prop up the ego of the narcissist (Macenczak et al., 2016). A narcissist is typically somewhat unconcerned about the other persons in that relationship, except when it comes to needing their admiration and approval, or needing them as an audience. The audience is used to provide the applause while narcissists are focused on their own needs. This narcissistic pattern of behavior can be displayed in a negative and aggressive manner and has been associated with an increase in lawsuits initiated by persons demanding to exert their control (O'Reilly, Doerr, & Chatman, 2018).

The problem is determining how much power or admiration or control is enough. In many of these scenarios, the central person seems to be motivated by a bottomless need—nothing is ever enough. Fill that void with admiration or power and fame, and these will quickly dissipate. Because the void is bottomless, it cannot be filled on a permanent basis. Part of this dynamic also underlies excessive collecting and addictive disorders.

An individual can become obsessed or addicted, in part, because of his or her attempts to assuage emptiness, to fill the void. Because the need can never be truly fulfilled, the rewarding behavior—whether it is attention seeking or controlling another—is repeated again and again. Ultimately, the individual is trapped in a cycle of seeking the reward because of tension buildup, obtaining the reward and the accompanying feeling of pleasure or relief, and, as that feeling dissipates, initiating the cycle all over again.

Power on Many Platforms

An ecological theory of interrelatedness between systems tells us that each part of a system is interlinked to another part. Just like a pebble falling into water, change in one area of this interlinked whole can have ripple effects reaching outward across systems. As individuals, we are embedded in families. Those families are nested in extended support groups, circles of friends and acquaintances, and general social networks. These large clustered communities, in turn, find their place in society as a whole. In other words, group dynamics, including those related to power, play out in many social contexts, ranging from micro- to macrosystems (Forsyth, 2018), as well as in teams (Levi, 2013). Power can be found and acted out on all these levels, and groups can display a very unique psychological functioning or dynamic associated with power differences (Thibaut, 1959/2017).

Thus, a **power dynamic** can be represented by one person or party *having a problem exerting greater control* over another party. It follows that the seesaw of power will not be consistently balanced, and the interplay between power forces will be significant (Dunbar, Lane, & Abra, 2016). Power inequalities can be created because of gender, age, socioeconomic status, education, partnership status, health, ability or disability, race, political affiliations, and many other circumstances.

Power can be used for control, and leadership struggles have been the key factor in wars worldwide. Power and control act like conjoined twins; the one enables the other, but they have somewhat separate identities. In practice, however, the one goes with the other. If the outcome is intended to be constructive, power can mobilize change. But then again, what is seen as being constructive can be subjective.

Power dynamics are forceful and key components in the motion within a family. There can be the power of the parent and the countering power of the child. Certain illnesses, conditions, and behaviors can be used to express helplessness or the lack of power, but in enacting these situations individuals can become very powerful. Think of the family with a severely disabled child. The child cannot participate fully in many of the day-to-day activities of that family but, at the same time, exerts a powerful influence on how that family operates, and not only on how it will have to work with and around this challenge. Similarly, addiction disorders can take their toll: the mother who struggles with alcohol dependence cannot be the same mother that she would have been if not shackled by her addiction to the substance and by all the concomitant behavioral patterns and outcomes that surround this addiction.

"Power and control act like conjoined twins; the one enables the other."

Not reacting. Not only the display of power but also not reacting to power from a position of powerlessness influences family dynamics. In communication science, we are taught that the message we communicate is powerful but that the message we do *not* communicate can be equally if not more powerful. In the same way, not responding to power with displays of power can affect the power dynamic. Think of Gandhi's nonviolent resistance and its effects on British rule in India.

Now consider bullying. The school bully's attempts at humiliating and crushing a fellow schoolmate become less intrusive when these overtures get minimal acknowledgment, not only from the victim but, importantly, from the friends and support systems surrounding the victim. Bullying can never be condoned, but students can be taught not to laugh at bullying behavior, and teachers can avoid attending to the bully in front of the whole class, after ensuring everyone's safety, of course. In this way, the reward of receiving attention is removed, even if this attention is merely negative in nature.

Here is another example. As parents and caregivers, we are familiar with children avoiding authority by not responding or by assuming a position of powerlessness to resist parental rules and exert control. Think of the attention-seeking child who calls us back to the bedroom three times in a row on the pretext of needing water, needing the curtains drawn, needing the blanket adjusted . . . whatever excuse can be found.

Dyadic Power Theory

When people interact, they define that interaction and that relationship through the manner of their interaction. This occurs in addition to whatever else may be occuring in that relationship (Watzlavic, Beavin, & Jackson, 1967, pp. 120–121). Consequently, relationships have a systemic quality that builds over time, influencing how those relationships are formed and maintained (Littlejohn, Foss, & Oetzel, 2017, p. 229).

In other words, because it is a relationship, it is something that occurs *between* people. That also explains why some relationships are more strained while others are more easygoing. In the relationship I have with one of my close friends, a lot of joking and laughing characterizes the interaction, whereas this is not the case in my other relationships. Each interaction has a unique interpersonal quality. The nature of the interactions may also determine what can be expected from that particular relationship or interaction (Dunbar, Lane, & Abra, 2016).

Norah Dunbar, a communications scholar, is credited with the **dyadic power theory**, an extension of the social exchange theory (Dunbar, 2004). She sums up an aspect of communication in the following manner:

> Power is a fundamental part of all human relationships. Dyadic power theory assumes that when you are in a power-equal relationship, you are more free to express dominance than when you are constrained by power differences in an unequal relationship. The resources you each have access to and your level of dependence create boundaries through which you must interact. (Dunbar, quoted by Littlejohn, Foss, & Oetzel, 2017, pp. 230–231)

Power equality and inequality. Power equality or, by the same token, power inequality counts among the core attributes of relationships and will define those interactions (Dunbar, 2017). According to Dunbar (2015), several theories address aspects of the power dynamic:

- Social exchange theory
- Interdependence theory
- Normative resource theory
- Equity theory
- Dyadic power theory
- Necessary convergence communication theory
- Bilateral deterrence theory
- The chilling effect
- Relational control approaches
- Sex role theories

In short power (or who is in control of what and of whom), social roles and attribution, power inequities, and so much more, all influence the dynamic of interpersonal communication.

Authentic Insight

The Dynamics of Gatekeeping

Scholars use the word *gatekeeping* to describe many functions, but all reflect the basic concept that defines the gatekeeper as being in charge of a gate. Though this definition appears simplistic, the phrase "in charge" implies authority: both power and responsibility. The idea of a gate implies decision making, screening, and evaluation experienced from different perspectives. Gatekeeping also may be viewed with a different emotional valence depending on the perspective: one who is shut out will likely view gatekeeping differently from one who is allowed in, and differently still from those who control the gate.

Gatekeeping has different functions in different contexts. The role of physicians as gatekeepers of medical services is known to most. Other professions describe information gatekeeping as screening testimony for admission in a court of law or screening articles for publication. There is also the type of gatekeeping that regulates membership in a profession.

Psychotherapy professions use the word *gatekeeping* to describe a way of regulating membership. Teachers, accreditation boards, ethics investigation boards, state licensure examination boards, and peers may serve as gatekeepers. They fulfill this function by assessing the potential of practicing clinicians. These varied gatekeepers may use exams, academic tests, interviews, departmental policies, judicial proceedings, rulings, legislation, and recommendations to prevent impaired clinicians from practicing.

Gatekeeping, as a form of self-regulation, provides credibility for the profession. This function protects the public by enforcing the minimum criteria for practitioners of therapy. Gatekeeping at this level prevents or minimizes harm to clients. Effective gatekeeping in training promotes the reputation of a profession in terms of quality care and qualifications of practitioners. Identification of serious problems at an early stage allows trainees to make alternative choices and direct their aspirations into areas better befitting their talents.

Jonathan Davis, PhD, is a professor of human development and family science and a licensed marriage and family therapist. This excerpt was adapted from his doctoral dissertation.

Source: Davis, J. C. (2004). *Gatekeeping in family therapy supervision: An exploratory qualitative study* (Unpublished Doctoral Dissertation). Purdue University. West Lafayette, IN.

FOCUS POINT

A power dynamic can be represented by one person or party having and probably exerting greater control over another party. Examples of power abuse are bullying and intimate partner violence (IPV). Power can be found and acted out on all levels of a system, from the micro- to macrosystemic level. The opportunities an individual has to display power occur at all levels of interpersonal relations, including the family and larger societal systems, and those opportunities are affected by gender, age, socioeconomic status, education, partnership status, health, ability or disability, race, political affiliations, and many other circumstances. In amplified form, power can change social systems.

The Dynamics of Excess

The dynamic influences of excess are insidious and affect us individually and as families. Every social media page is a potential onslaught; consumerism is trying to set up shop inside our minds—sneak into our worlds. Ads for items we viewed once online and decided against follow us indefinitely whether we like them or not.

We think we are immune to all the advertising images, but even if we do not buy the wares, they steal milliseconds of our time, as we have to skim over them, ignore them, neutralize their powers, push back. When we think about all the things in our lives, the clutter, the stuff, we can ask ourselves a question similar to the one we posed earlier about control in interpersonal relationships: When it comes to my relationship with consumer goods and consumption, who has power over whom?

If we allow all these influences into our mental worlds, they chip away at our resistance. We become a nation ridden with credit card debt, all in the name of the endless purchase of possessions that promise to provide us with blissful perceptions of our "new" selves, reaffirm our worth, solve a marketing-created problem, or deliver on happiness ever after.

Most of our grandparents recall their frugal possessions, especially if they lived during years of economic depression or recession. My own grandmother owned three pairs of shoes and six dresses. All her possessions easily fit into one suitcase. And look at us now, how our "needs" have grown. In westernized and affluent countries, we are renting storage units to swallow the excesses that we can no longer store in homes, which are also larger than the dwellings of previous generations. Television shows reveal the secrets of hoarders who are being throttled by their possessions, most of which support neither their lifestyles nor their dreams. All these possessions become hollow objects trying to fill emotional voids, and the need to add ever more takes on addictive qualities.

Overconsumption and Waste

Raising awareness. The first step in altering situations involving excess is awareness that they exist. If we become aware of the incessant pressure of marketing, we may become more competent at pushing back, at developing those defenses that shield us from the song of the sirens. In Greek mythology, the sirens were female and partly human creatures who sang achingly beautiful songs and lured the sailors and their ships onto the rocks toward shipwreck. The same metaphor fits our current materialistic consumerist world, except the sirens' song leads to the mall.

Many of us have seen images of overwhelming amounts of plastic debris, accumulating on remote Pacific islands through the movements of ocean currents. Our recycling centers are bursting at the seams, unable to manage the avalanches of one-time-use articles. This evidence of our excessive, throwaway lifestyle leaves us with a degree of shame. Is it possible to raise our environmental awareness and push back? We underestimate how each one of us contributes to the problem: a few dozen disposable water bottles, daily coffee cups from takeaway vendors, all those Styrofoam plates, plastic cutlery, straws, and so much more. Multiply that by the world's population, and we have a major problem that requires a systemic, and a global, rethink. We will have to reevaluate our consumption and pay more attention to the adage "Reduce, Reuse, Recycle."

The dynamic involved is that each one of us tends to think that excessive consumption is not our problem, or does not involve us directly. The illusion is that waste will be handled on a macrosystemic level, on a greater scale. But if we each cut off our contributions or at least significantly reduced our input to that stream of waste, it would have a major effect. Clearly, we have to revisit how things are packaged, how our lifestyle promotes excess, the situations that create the waste, and, importantly, how we can intervene.

Another factor in the dynamics of excessive consumption is that our culture validates it. Through the voyeurism of television reality shows, we can have a secret peek at someone's closet, housing 80 plus mostly unworn hats. How did we get to this place? Clearly, mass production and the relentless push of marketers have

FOCUS POINT

The dynamics of excess are complicated and affect more than the solitary victim; they have systemic effects. The first step in altering situations involving excess is awareness of their existence. Excesses occur in a wide range of conditions and situations, ranging from the relatively innocuous to the life threatening. In the case of overconsumption, we need to raise our awareness concerning the incessant pressure of marketing. We may become more competent at pushing back and developing defenses that allow us to disengage from the signals that nudge us to consume excessively, to the point at which consumption becomes an addiction.

led us down a garden path that confuses inner fulfillment with consumption. We are told that these activities trigger pleasure centers in the brain, that shopping can become an addiction, like drug use or overeating (other forms of "consumption"). Or, alternatively, we are told that our purchases speak to our deepest fears concerning the fulfillment of needs and, in this way, reinforce destructive behavior.

Still the addictive component of excessive consumption sets in when the action no longer satisfies, or the satisfaction is shorter; we escalate the behavior, increase the dose. We have to shop more, eat more, binge view more, fill our closets with more things that almost instantly lose their allure. Clothes with price tags still attached, shoes in their boxes—all are wasted capital while the credit card bills with hefty interest shackle us into a recurring debt cycle. It is not a pretty picture, but it is one we can tame and keep in its place with awareness of the dynamic and how this behavior affects so many aspects of our lives.

The Bergen Shopping Addiction Scale is a tool that screens for and assesses the condition of obsessive acquisition, which can potentially lead to hoarding (Andreassen et al., 2015). A similar scale assesses online shopping compulsions (Manchiraju, Sadachar, & Ridgway, 2017). Several popular self-help books have also addressed the topic.

Summer (1572), by Giuseppe Arcimboldo (1527–1593), an Italian painter best known for forming images out of objects. His work can also depict a sense of excess. What if we were consumed by edibles, would this be the outcome—our preoccupations becoming visible?

Source: Public domain.

The Dynamics of Collecting

Collecting has some commonalities with human interactions, as there is a power game and a dynamic at play. Consider people involved in collecting; who has more power? Who possesses what, and in making a collection, what attributes does a collector add? Do we add to our power, our prestige, whether we are envied or desired? Is the object adding something to our persona, and if so, what?

Collecting usually starts innocently. The man who accumulates 160 pairs of athletic shoes (mostly unworn, labels still attached) may have memories of a childhood without shoes. It is perfectly understandable that being able to access such a commodity initially seems like a newfound freedom, a sign of success that signaled a journey away from the insecurity of poverty and need. And so the initial need is met, until strangely, at some point, collecting takes on a life of its own; it crosses a line and it owns the collector. Just as squirrels collect nuts for the winter and display the seemingly insatiable urge to do so, we may be collecting to deal with a metaphorical emotional winter.

But collecting does not necessarily need to become a compulsion. In their book focused on collecting, Karch and Robertson (2014) display a very tolerant joyous approach to the pursuit:

> [Collecting] is not about celebrating who owns the biggest, rarest, or most expensive objects. Collecting is not inherently an elite pursuit. Rather, it is universal, accessible, and all-inclusive. Yes, there are those who chase obscure museum-caliber finds, but there is equal nobility and novelty in a collection of bottle caps salvaged from the recycling bin. You don't have to be a person of extraordinary means to be considered a collector. You just need to have a hunger for the pursuit, a thrill for the chase, and an openness to objects around you—and to welcoming joy into your life. (p. 11)

Collections come in all sorts, shapes, and sizes; there is no telling what will connect with our personal history or, even more important, with our secret longings and desires. If an object features in our lives and has a very personal meaning to us, it is collectible. Antique dealers often buy collections sold by grandchildren, who no longer find the same meaning in those objects that their grandparents did. Because a collection is intensely personal and echoes some of our deepest needs and longings, we can find it difficult to fulfill those longings. That is when a collection keeps on growing; there is an ongoing quest to find that seemingly perfect object that will fulfill our needs and still our metaphorical hunger.

To complete a collection, an individual needs a sense of arrival; the journey has been completed, and no extra object is required. If the collection comes to this natural sense of closure, it is as if every need has been satiated. People are also willing to dissolve and dispose of their collections once the meaning underlying that collection process has changed. The need is no longer beckoning; the wish has been fulfilled.

A fairly common form of collecting is associated with supporting a particular sports team. By collecting the team's T-shirts, posters, and other paraphernalia, we show that we are fans, which provides us with a sense of belonging. We get a group identity that we share with other fans. Displaying our collection can be a shorthand to identify like-minded enthusiasts.

Collecting has many facets. Initially, it requires a combination of interest and the availability of the collectible. Here are some other factors influencing the process:

- Interests of the collector
- Availability or scarcity of the collectible
- Financial implications, for example, cost, value, rarity, provenance or history
- Practical considerations, for example, space to house the collection

- Acquisition motivations, for example, the hunt and the joy of hunting and finding the objects
- Intellectual considerations, for example, knowledge and expertise about the collectibles
- Emotional considerations, for example, prestige, rarity of collectible
- Emotional needs of collector, for example, insecurity, emotional hunger, anxiety, admiration, power

The list is extensive.

Collecting seems to be common irrespective of resources. In a very natural environment, humans have been known to collect rare feathers, shells, unique rocks, and other artifacts, and they have even used these to barter or as a form of money. The headdresses, clothing, or body coverings of chiefs or other important persons in a tribe can contain some of these rare objects to denote status, power, or position within the group. Additionally, Kossenjans and Buttle (2016) identify four forms of value in the collection process:

- the value of self discovery,
- the value of recognition and distinction,
- the value of immortality, and
- the value of group acceptance.

Treasure hunt. The actual rare object imparts its own thrill, especially if no one else has spotted it. It is a little like winning the lottery. Just like the hunter looking for his prey, a collector gets a strange satisfaction in spotting a seemingly rare object. Collecting of this sort becomes a treasure hunt that is all the more enjoyable if we require special skills to identify our collectible objects. The more we collect, the more discerning we may become. Rarer, stranger, more precious! The challenge is to raise the bar and meet that higher standard continually.

Artifacts. Historical and archeological artifacts are the metaphorical letters from the past allowing us to eavesdrop on a bygone era. In her book on the cultural study of museums and collections, Susan Pearce (1992/2017) makes the statement that artifacts can give us clues about the persons who created (or collected) those artifacts. She mentions a piece of moon rock in the National Air and Space Museum in Washington, DC, which is displayed on an altar-like construction and is guarded. Surprisingly, visitors are encouraged to touch it—an irresistible invitation. This object is so much more than a 4-million-year-old rock; it represents a journey, a context, a dream, and an aspiration. It tells us about the pursuits of humankind, or, as Pearce puts it, "it has become part of the world of human values" (Pearce, 1992/2017, Chapter 1).

The brain is wired to seek patterns and meanings, and there is comfort in both repetition and creating a whole. So our brains like it when we find and collect like things, say potsherds from the fourteenth century, and piece them together to make a whole; we experience the same sense of relief when we find that missing piece and complete a jigsaw puzzle. Looking for variety can be an additional motive for collecting; variations on a theme are stimulating and fulfill our needs for novelty. And novel artifacts can give us new historical and scientific insights.

Amulets. Other objects may be collected because certain attributes are associated with them. On an elite level, a priceless crown can embody the status of the royal personage who once wore it. Other objects such as amulets protect the wearer against threat or evil influences and thus take on a very special meaning. The Victoria and Albert Museum in London, dedicated to art and design, houses a very large collection of jewelry spanning hundreds of years and reaching back to ancient Greek and Roman adornments (https://www.vam.ac.uk/). Interestingly, these objects cover the entire lifespan. Before conception, the would-be mother may wear an amulet that will facilitate parenthood. There are pieces of jewelry commemorating the birth of an infant and amulets to protect the baby and the child from evil influences.

Symbols. We collect some objects because they are significant symbols or mementos. Engagement and wedding rings have personal significance and, as public displays of betrothal, have become a virtually universal symbol denoting a committed couple, especially in westernized cultural contexts (L. Davis, 2018). We might collect locks of our child's hair, cut at different stages of life. In Victorian times, mourning jewelry, created by weaving strands of the deceased's hair into decorative knots or using that hair to create imagery such as the weeping willow tree, commemorated the departed loved one. Or collected hair was incorporated into a locket and worn by the bereaved.

The important aspect about these amulets, rare objects, and pieces of jewelry worn in various contexts is that an emotional meaning is associated to an otherwise neutral object. These objects are infused with sentimental feelings and are cherished by the owner.

The meaning attached to an amulet is what makes it powerful in the eyes of the beholder. One could also collect and wear lucky charms believing that they will bring good fortune. Sometimes assigning luck to an object occurs at random; for instance, if something good happened while I was wearing particular socks, I might feel that wearing the socks again will open the door for lady luck to revisit me—these are now my lucky socks. Keeping or collecting these lucky objects may be regarded as superstition by some, but the person subscribing to the belief truly thinks that his or her collection could make a difference. As psychologists, we know that the power of association and reinforcement contribute to this process of assigning meaning to objects.

The Obsessive Collector

Is the obsessive collector the hunter or the hunted? In this scenario the hunt has taken over entirely. Who was the collector, and what was being collected? Who was in control, and who or what was being controlled? The positions in the power dynamic have been exchanged. This reversal opened the door to an insatiability, an emotional hunger that could not be stilled.

Extreme and obsessive collecting is accompanied by its own problems. Expeditions to acquire the desired objects are costly, on top of the actual price of the cherished item. Not only do collectibles cost money but also, unless they are rare and unique objects with potential buyers, the acquired objects seldom have much resale value. Persons trapped in the cycle of consumption may run up debt, which can bring them to ruin.

By virtue of association, neutral objects can be infused with special meaning. The nature and specifics of that meaning can often be found by examining the lives and childhoods of the person collecting the object. One serious and very affluent collector filled a special building with various models of an expensive

Authentic Insight

Collecting: Who Owns Whom?

Roses Are Red, and Violets Are Blue . . .

As I was tidying up my late mother's treasures, a dust-covered saucer with an African violet caught my eye. The limp violet appeared to be in mourning too. I drenched the parched plant in water and washed the saucer. Out of the coagulated dust appeared a luminous image of a hand-painted violet with a jewel-colored background. I gave the saucer a special place in my home, but not before I had associated it with saying farewell to my mom. In doing so, I had inadvertently set the dynamic of collecting in motion.

A couple of months later, I spotted a vase with the same pattern in an antique store. It piqued my interest but still not sufficiently to buy it. Weeks passed and some connection in my brain prompted me that by buying another piece similar to my mother's saucer, I could magically bring back a memory of my mom; at the same time, I could acquire a little of what she had liked. The vase ended up in my home, marking the beginning of my journey into collecting art deco porcelain. I researched who the painters were, namely, a group of women in a studio in the 1930s. Here and there a piece was added to my collection, but still I denied that I was a little hooked.

On a visit to the Isle of Wight, I stopped at a little antique fair in the church hall. It was pouring outside. On the last table, I spotted a bowl similar to my saucer. More important, I met Jenny, the lady selling it, and found that we shared an enthusiasm for that particular style of porcelain. We became firm friends. Fast forward: when Jenny passed away, her porcelain children found a permanent place in my home.

It was at this point that I decided "enough is enough," my porcelain family was complete, so I stopped collecting. I still love and cherish the pieces that I have, but the hunt for more has been called off. My relationship with beautiful hand-painted porcelain has changed. It no longer represents an effort to bring back a piece of my mother; now it also reminds me of Jenny.

On the other hand, it simply is what it is, a collection of beautiful objects asking to be used. So I put flowers in the vases and incorporate them into my daily life. In this way, they become both more and less precious—and that is liberating.

Clara Gerhardt, in memory of Jenny Wray

sports car. A company manufacturing a specific type of aircraft documented its history with a collection of airplanes and built a special hangar, and later several hangars, to accommodate this collection (see https://www.beechcraftheritagemuseum.org/). Often, significant collections are put to good use and become incorporated into a museum, as did the corporate aircraft collection eventually. In London, Sir John Soane's collection of architectural objects continues to fascinate visitors from near and far (https://www.soane.org/). His house became a museum and has remained virtually untouched for over 180 years, apart from appropriate maintenance. Further afield is the Wellcome Collection (https://wellcomecollection.org/), which is much more eclectic. It started with collector Sir Henry Wellcome (1853–1936), a pharmacist and entrepreneur who amassed a collection of medical antiquities and other objects related to health. Although specialized, clearly all his acquisitions resonate with some members of the public. Many serious collectors, such as Soane and Wellcome, collect around themes, and the dynamics concern the themes that speak to them. These are so personal and meaningful to them that their collections continue to grow in an irresistible manner.

At other times, the collections are so personal, obscure, and esoteric that they do not speak to the imagination of the general public. But they do represent something intensely personal and meaningful to the collector. Some collections depict challenging aspects of life, for instance, a series of miniature carvings made by prisoners and carved from chicken bones or objects decorated with shells made by the waiting wives of fishermen at sea. Some collections are the product of ample time but no money, for instance, a collection of miniature furniture pieces made from matches, even burnt matches.

One person's rubbish is another person's treasure. Discarded objects also make excellent collectibles. In developing countries, bottle tops may be an exotic reminder of the sheer variety of beverages seldom available to the collector. Because these objects have no value to most, they bring collecting within reach of all. Stubs of boarding passes, tickets to events, free hotel pens, free matchbooks from bars, discarded hub caps from wheels, license plates from cars: there is seemingly no end to the ingenuity of collectors.

There are no boundaries to speak of in this sort of collecting, and the original motivator may have become blurred. We collect because it soothes us in some strange way, and the process of collecting seems to reduce anxiety. I once visited a house that was being offered for sale; the homeowner collected fridge magnets. Needless to say, it was almost more magnets than home; the correct relationship had been lost along the way, and the behavior repeated itself endlessly until, eventually, it virtually pushed the homeowner out of the by-now limited living space.

Another had all the garage walls covered with narrow shelves where mugs from all over the world were lined up. Somewhere on these journeys of collection, the original goal and joy of making a collection had been lost, and the process of collecting had taken on a life of its own. The need to collect had become a bottomless pit; nothing was enough to fill it. There could be no closure because closure had to be found in another emotional dimension.

Personal journeys. The dynamics of these collector's journeys tell us that each choice of collectible is highly personal. It may represent something meaningful from childhood, it can symbolize a turning point, or it can express a need, a void to be filled. The little girl who fled under wartime conditions and had to leave her favorite doll behind may, as an adult, fill a room with rare porcelain dolls. Often the collection is an attempt to ease the pain of its origins. If it succeeds, that is good. It becomes more challenging if the collection takes on a life of its own and seemingly knows no boundaries. At that point, the collection will overtake the collector; it will assume unintended powers over the collector, and it probably is unable to fulfill the original need or desire that gave birth to the somewhat obsessive pastime, bearing in mind that an obsession can be intrusive in that it tends to be associated with preoccupation and a single-minded interest that can exclude other things and activities.

FOCUS POINT

Collecting has some commonalities with human interactions in that there is a power game and a dynamic at play. Appropriate collecting can be a pleasurable and constructive activity. Extreme and obsessive collecting is accompanied by its own problems, as these collections take up resources in terms of time, money, space, and the energies of collectors.

From Collecting to Hoarding

Collections can be a product of context. Stamp collections have lost some of their popularity in a digital world. People collect objects that are meaningful to them, yet there may be no discernible reason when it comes to determining who collects what and why.

Source: Public domain.

The line between collecting and **hoarding** can become fuzzy. One of the differences is that collecting tends to be focused, and collectors discriminate between objects. The collector has a plan and seeks variety within the same genre of object. The hoarder expands the acquisition of objects beyond any organized plan and has lost the ability to discriminate in the selection process. The element of *uncontrolled* enters the formula. It is particularly distressing when the hoarding is so indiscriminate that it becomes destructive. Then, acquiring objects has neither clear constructive psychological meaning nor boundaries (Vilaverde, Gonçalves, & Morgado, 2017). The person who fills room after room with old newspapers, dirty food containers, empty bottles, or whatever other objects that might fall into the trash category has crossed a threshold of mental health and is heading toward instability. Hoarding, then, is a disorder in its own right as well as a symptom of other conditions, including obsessive-compulsive disorders (Albert et al., 2015; de la Cruz & Mataix-Cols, 2019). It has been associated with an older population and so could be linked to conditions such as dementia and Alzheimer's (Thew & Salkovskis, 2016). In the *DSM-5*, hoarding disorder has been defined in the following manner: "Persistent difficulty discarding or parting with possessions, regardless of their actual value" (American Psychiatric Association, 2013).

Hoarders may be trapped in such a disorganized and dysfunctional lifestyle that they cannot hold down a job with a steady income. They become increasingly isolated, as they do not let visitors into their homes out of sheer embarrassment, and those who pass the threshold feel uncomfortable, even fearful and overwhelmed. The lack of systematization is evident as their possessions spread everywhere, which adds to an already dysfunctional environment. Additionally, hoarders may subscribe to their own belief systems. Here are some of the typical beliefs and characteristics of hoarders:

- They see a possible use for many things and will keep them for some future application.
- They may feel that what they have collected is truly unique and that only they have the gift to recognize its true function. This is sometimes the case for persons who are technically handy and who save and collect odd parts of engines and the like, thinking they will repurpose them.
- Because they have difficulty throwing things away, they may consider the collection of trash a valuable behavior. They may even feel that they will make the environment worse by throwing away items and think they can recycle or upcycle collected trash, which never happens.
- Being surrounded by all the objects adds to their sense of comfort and safety, almost as if they were nesting.
- They may worry about not having something that they need, yet, as possessions pile up, they struggle to find things, losing bills or papers

that require urgent attention. Both this worry and the disorganized state of their hoards lead to duplication of possessions; new items are bought because the ones already owned cannot be located.

- Areas such as the kitchen, that should be used for prepping food, or the bathrooms that should serve the occupant's sanitary requirements, become random storage space and therefore dysfunctional.
- They experience difficulties in moving in their own home. In an emergency, they could not easily escape, or, alternatively, help would not be able to reach them quickly.

The urge to collect. The downside of the urge to collect is that it is never satisfied, and the cycle has to be repeated. There is the hunt when the anticipation of finding the desired object raises the spirits, the elation of finding the object, the conquering stage when the object is acquired, and then the stage of bringing the trophy home. All the while, the emotional rush is ebbing until the same low spot is reached. The cycle has to be repeated to experience another rush. Briefly the cycle looks like this:

- *Anticipation.* Thinking about the desirable object or activity.
- *Action.* Setting about making acquiring the object a reality: researching, locating, and engaging in getting it.
- *Acquisition.* Owning the object.
- *Anticlimax.* Experiencing a shift in power and emotion; because the object is owned, it loses luster.
- *Acceleration.* Heading toward depression and emptiness.

The urge to collect takes on pathological proportions and destroys relationships and family life, as well as bank balances. For the hoarder, there is no off switch, no endpoint. Hoarders are controlled by the need to fill spaces, even if in doing so they pose a threat to their own and their families' health. Increasingly, they isolate themselves; nobody can visit them. Their homes become a secret fortress of possessions, and they are trapped within.

Hoarding as a vulnerability. In the popular media, we have seen images of hoarders being evicted from their homes; the top floor might crash in because it is overloaded with years of random trash. The hoarder may not know what she or he possesses. It is hardly about the ownership or the intrinsic meaning of these out-of-control collections.

Hoarders face an illness that robs them of insight concerning their condition, and they are in denial concerning the proportions their hoarding has taken on. All attempts at intervening are rebuffed, and hoarders feel upset if the piles around them are discarded or removed.

Hoarding can be a symptom of psychopathology and has a range of associated underlying conditions. It may be a sign of early dementia, of the individual gradually losing the ability to discriminate between the useful and that which should be discarded. With age progression, some persons lose self-censorship abilities or are unable to distinguish between appropriate and inappropriate behavior. The elderly may make jokes that are too risqué, display inappropriately flirtatious behavior, or generally make uncensored statements that can be hurtful and unsuitable.

This same gradual inability to discriminate between what is appropriate or not may apply to their physical surroundings. It may be difficult for them to judge what to keep and what to discard, so they keep everything. By accumulating so much random stuff, hoarders lose control of their environment; the hoarder's house is typically unclean and unsanitary and can present a health hazard. Extreme depression has also been associated with hoarding behavior.

Hoarding can be a symptom of underlying brain pathology as well as psychopathological conditions (Albert et al., 2015; de la Cruz & Mataix-Cols, 2019). It is associated with a destructive and unproductive approach to managing life's various challenges. Besides the physical hoarding and excessive accumulation of random objects, hoarders may neglect their own health and well-being. They have crowded their personal space to such an extent that there is no room to sleep, prepare healthy meals, sit at a table to do paperwork, or shower or keep clean, as even the bathrooms get swamped. All the chores of the day are made impossible by the overwhelming destruction of the random and mostly useless objects that are being collected.

An overwhelming world. Years ago, I accompanied social workers on a house call to a person who was to be evicted because of her dangerous living conditions. Every inch of the home was filled, the rooms were stacked floor to ceiling, and there were person-high piles of newspapers forming little corridors between all the chaos. The bathtub and the sink had been filled with clutter, and the kitchen was unusable. The bed had only a small corner for sleeping; the rest was piled sky-high with clothing and various unidentifiable objects. It was a very physical reflection of the overwhelming and oppressing mental world that person was occupying.

Because hoarding is frequently part of a cycle that includes loneliness, anxiety, and depression, the latter two may require a psychiatric approach and medication. Once these conditions are brought under control, it becomes more feasible to deal with the hoarding behavior.

Emotional Hoarding

Emotional hoarding means holding on to resentments, anger, and a host of other emotions. The emotional hoarder cannot let go, and this becomes the basis for family feuds, emotional cutoffs, and other destructive interpersonal patterns. By holding on to a bitter past, the emotional hoarder finds it increasingly difficult to move forward into the future. Another factor may be at play, namely, the sense of psychological ownership (Dawkins, Tian, Newman, & Martin, 2015).

In the Freudian or psychoanalytic approach to therapy, it was thought that revisiting the past could be liberating if it provided greater understanding. From there one could move forward with renewed insight. There is a point at which looking back into the past can become debilitating, though, and that point is when it prevents psychological growth and change behavior in the future. We can mourn and complain about our pasts, and doing so may be legitimately therapeutic up to a point. But we do have to move forward and find more competent ways of managing our lives. This exploration of constructive alternatives leads us away from the original heartaches and allows us to turn over a fresh emotional page.

By moving forward, change in the process can occur. By remaining fixated on the past, we risk being immobilized by it. Blaming excessively is another form of emotional hoarding. We go back to the past and pin responsibility on whomever is co-responsible for a circumstance or happening. In certain situations, this blaming may be an important exploratory phase. Emotionally, however, we need to be aware that by blaming we are also blocking ourselves from moving forward,

FOCUS POINT

Hoarding exceeds all boundaries of appropriate collecting. Hoarding can be a symptom of psychopathology and of a range of associated underlying conditions (e.g., loneliness, anxiety, and depression) that may require psychiatric intervention. From a psychodynamic point of view, hoarding can be interpreted as an act motivated by a sense of emptiness and by the need to fill that void. Emotional hoarding means holding on to resentments, anger, grief, and a host of other emotions. Emotional hoarders cannot let go, and this form of hoarding becomes the basis for family feuds, emotional cutoffs, and other destructive interpersonal patterns.

from setting up a different system that could empower us and allow us to choose new ways of handling challenges. To an extent blaming is the opposite of taking responsibility. By taking responsibility, we are empowering ourselves and opening up various avenues of choice.

An underlying dynamic to the process of forgiveness is coming to terms with what has been and neutralizing it with the act of pardon that lets go of hoarded emotions such as anger and resentment. Forgiving has an important function in freeing us up to move in a new direction. This forward movement can be healing and empowering. We know from grief counseling that part of the grieving and mourning process entails a slow reemerging. The bereaved explores a new self who has to face life without the loved one who was lost. Both letting go of grief and forgiving ourselves and others are ways of restructuring.

Obviously a bereaved spouse can become an emotional hoarder as well. There is a fine balance between constructive remembrance and immobilizing emotional hoarding. By maintaining feelings of resentment and anger or grief and excessive nostalgia, feelings that are anchored in the past, we are making it difficult for ourselves to move forward. One metaphor of this process is the act of refurnishing a room. As long as we keep all the old furniture in place, we cannot renew the decorations. In order to refurbish, we need to remove the old appropriately, so we can make a place for the new. Emotions have a similar function in our complex inner lives. Our emotional scenery keeps changing in response to and in interaction with our lifespan challenges and where we find ourselves emotionally at any given point. The feelings we had a year ago may not be the feelings we have today.

Life is a bidirectional journey in which we are influenced by all the wondrous things we experience, and they shape us into the persons we are. Simultaneously, our personalities and our previous experiences may contribute to how we react to what life is offering us. As much as we may try to keep our lives static, the essence of life itself is that it changes and is dynamic.

"Blaming immobilizes the system." 

The Addicted System

For every family member who struggles with an addiction disorder, there is a family that has to cope with the disruption that follows in the wake of that addiction. These disorders are as destructive as a tornado ripping up everything in its path. The victim seems to undergo a personality change, often becoming secretive, manipulative, untruthful, unpredictable, and out of control. These are not qualities that support stable relationships, and marriages become vulnerable as a partner lies and evades in an effort to manage an ever more powerful addiction.

Physiological and Related Factors

In the addictive and related disorders, the brain gets a sense of reward every time the addictive behavior is repeated. Brain scans have shown that the areas in the brain housing the pleasure centers light up when this behavior occurs. The behavior becomes self-reinforcing (Koob & Volkow, 2016). The person wants and needs to repeat the behavior in order to obtain that same high feeling. One of the major problems with addictive disorders is **habituation**. The body gets used to either the substance or the experience, so its intensity or frequency has to be increased in order for the addict to achieve the same effect. Habituation explains why stopping is such a challenge. The person needs to go beyond what would satisfy most other people in most other circumstances.

The addiction cycle starts with craving; then the addict seeks the substance that will reduce the craving and finds temporary satisfaction and an accompanying high feeling. That will be followed by a wearing off of the exuberant emotional state, which possibly dips lower than before. In order to feel a sense of equilibrium or to cope (if it is a physiological addiction), the cycle has to be repeated. The person suffering from the addictive behavior will repeat the addiction cycle over and over again despite its self-destructive nature.

Substance and Other Addictive Disorders

In substance disorders, the addiction centers on a substance that has to be ingested in order for the addict to experience the physiological as well as psychological effect. Examples of these disorders are alcohol, drug, and other substance abuse. There is a physiological withdrawal effect if the habituated body does not receive another dose of the particular substance. The addiction holds the user hostage. It may be exceptionally difficult to break an addiction without professional help because the cravings can be strong and overrule the willpower of the victim (Van Wormer & Davis, 2017). Addictive disorders are consequently very serious.

Research has shown that the younger a person is when she or he is first exposed to the potentially addictive substance, the greater the possible damage (Jensen, 2015). The metaphor has been used that addiction is almost like flipping a switch, and once that change has occurred in the brain, it is sensitized in a way that cannot be undone. For these reasons, it is crucial to protect young bodies and minds from addictive substances.

Gateways. Additionally, one addiction can pave the way for another, hence the concept of gateway drugs. Nicotine is highly addictive and can pave the way to the abuse of other substances. The current trend of teenage vaping is particularly concerning as it targets young and vulnerable brains that have not fully matured and are more susceptible to the damaging effects of some of the ingredients.

Possibly habit-forming substances have a greater addictive potential for the younger user (Jensen, 2015). Adolescents may want to identify with their peers and participate in risky behavior in order to gain group acceptance, but sadly these teens may discount the risks of exposure to addictive substances at this young age. Education is part of prevention, and teens need to be informed. Just as pregnant mothers receive support from their environments to abstain from caffeine, alcohol, and nicotine during pregnancy, young people should receive the same level of support to encourage abstinence from alcohol and other addictive substances.

Our current opioid crisis is increasingly claiming lives—literally and metaphorically (Vestal, 2018). Many factors have contributed to this crisis. Some of the blame has been allocated to drug manufacturers producing substances that are exceedingly powerful, especially in the wrong hands. Legitimate exposure to opioids as painkillers has triggered unanticipated addictive and drug-seeking behavior in patients (Blendon & Benson, 2018). Persons seeking drugs become devious and self-destructive as they are gripped by the control the drug exerts over them.

There is no single magic bullet to manage complexity of this nature. Managing the opioid crisis will require a multipronged approach, whereby the drugs become unavailable on the street, prescriptions are limited, and patients as well as prescribing doctors are educated concerning the dangers. Intervention teams require training, and rehabilitation facilities will need multi-professional input. Many of these interventions have already been put into place, but the opioid crisis is widespread and unintended overdosing is frequent. Every time this happens, it not only claims the life of an individual but also brings tragedy into families. Family members are guilt-ridden and question what they could have done to prevent these events.

FOCUS POINT

For every family member who struggles with an addiction disorder, there is a family that has to cope with the disruption that follows in the wake of that addiction. One addiction can pave the way for another, hence the concept of gateway drugs. Persons seeking drugs can become devious and self-destructive as they are gripped by the control the drug exerts over them. Every time an addiction claims an individual, it not only claims the life of that individual but also brings tragedy into families. It precipitates an extended dynamic.

Authentic Insight

Addiction Disorders: There Is Freedom in Letting Go of the Past

The word *addiction* seems very distant and brings to mind sensationalized movie images of drug abuse. It is very difficult for me to say that my dad was addicted, or even an alcoholic. Yet his behavior ticked all those boxes.

My dad was a heavy drinker. Despite his excesses, I thought we were a pretty "normal" family. Both my parents worked full time, rarely missed work, and provided financially. I attended private school, we went on family vacations, and I don't remember feeling that we missed out on anything. I was very active in extracurricular activities and excelled academically. I was voted "Most Likely to Succeed" in my senior year of high school.

Now that I am an adult, those same childhood memories are not as positive. I can no longer fool myself. Memories of our yearly beach vacations include my father being drunk and falling or acting inappropriately, my parents fighting, and my dad threatening to leave us. I rarely had school friends spend the night and avoided close friendships: what if the shameful secrets of our home life were discovered? I stayed very busy to avoid home as much as possible. I struggled with self-confidence, avoided conflict, and changed according to my environment in order to fit in or please others.

Characteristics of adult children of alcoholics include a fear of losing control, caution with emotions, and a targeted manner of avoiding conflict. Low self-esteem and an oversized dose of self-criticism fuel our inability to relax and have fun. I was constantly negotiating my way around this person who was unpredictable while under the influence. Because of my dad's erratic behavior, I had perfected the art of being invisible, unless I could excel. The fear of triggering an outburst was always looming in the background, like an unexploded landmine.

A dozen years later, I recognize that the impact of my father's addiction to alcohol colored several facets of my life, although its hold on me has weakened considerably. My dad's history and how that upended our family prompted me to choose an alcohol-free life and partner. It freed me from some of the residual issues that I had experienced. Those decisions were wise ones; I am now happily married and have a career that I love. I have an especially strong desire to build a different home environment for my family, and so far it is working.

Each day I implement self-care into my schedule. Instead of blaming my issues on my dad or his alcoholism, I strive to overcome my inner critic and focus on the people and things that matter. My experiences have given me a path and a wisdom that I would not have had otherwise.

There is freedom in letting go of the past, forgiving others, and focusing on life's many joys.

Anonymous

SPOTLIGHT ON THEORIES

Cognitive Behavioral Therapy

Theories frequently form the foundation for interventions, as they provide a structure or model to support the treatment modalities. **Cognitive behavioral therapy (CBT)** is one of the approaches most frequently used in a variety of settings, and it is helpful for treating addictions and other excessive behaviors as well (Dobson & Dozois, 2019). *Cognitive* refers to the thinking component, and *behavioral* references what we do, our actions. In order to change our behavior, we may have to start thinking about it differently. To put this idea another way, as our thinking shifts, our behavior follows suit. In order to achieve change, then, CBT combines elements from both behavioral and cognitive psychology.

In this approach, the central tenet is to find solutions to problems. For this reason, CBT focuses on actions (behavioral) and problem-solving capabilities (cognitive). By changing how I do things, I may change how I think about them and vice versa. In a simple form, we have all treated ourselves using some of these approaches. Here are examples. I do not feel wonderful, but I know that if I go and work out, I'll probably see my world differently afterward. Or I feel despondent after a romantic breakup, so my friends encourage me to spend some extra time on self-grooming and establishing healthy lifestyle habits. The change of behavior contributes to an overall improved feeling.

Because CBT does not require people to spend extended time on trying to unravel underlying motivations and delving into the past, it tends to offer quicker and more targeted results. These approaches can also be very helpful in targeting distracting behaviors, such as mild phobias (fears relating to specific situations and things) or disrupting and destructive behaviors. For the treatment of addiction disorders, they have held a steadfast place in the tried and trusted therapies. People suffering from weight management problems, mood disorders, or anxiety-related conditions have all found benefit from CBT. It can be used in addition to possible medication, making it a flexible and trusted option for therapists. Clearly, to be effective, therapists need to be trained and skilled in its use.

The terms *cognitive* and *behavioral* are applied to a number of therapeutic approaches. Here is a brief selection of some approaches containing cognitive and/or behavioral components. Note that the intended outcome of the therapy is often included in its name:

(Continued)

(Continued)

- Cognitive therapy
- Behavior therapy
- Cognitive behavior modification
- Cognitive emotional behavioral therapy
- Compassion-focused therapy
- Mindfulness-based cognitive therapy
- Multimodal therapy

In CBT treatments, the emphasis is on psychoeducation, which can be used to change how we think about things, how we manage our emotions (emotion regulation), and, importantly, how we behave. In practice, most approaches contain these phases:

- *Assessment.* Finding out what the problem is.
- *Reconceptualization.* Thinking differently about things (cognitive), and acquiring skill sets (behavioral) to manage the situation.
- *Application.* Applying these new skills in practical and possibly problem situations. This phase requires training and a strengthening of the new behavior patterns.
- *Maintaining.* Continuing with the new skills.
- *Reassessment.* Checking to see if the intervention was appropriate and effective.

Cognitive behavioral therapy has so many contributors and applications that it is a field of study in its own right. Current research is exploring computerized and cell phone apps to reinforce desired behaviors. Many of us have used wearable fitness trackers. Besides keeping track of certain parameters such as movement, planned work out sessions, and standing, these may send us messages to "nudge" our behaviors in the right direction (Mirsch, Lehrer, & Jung, 2017). Encouraging messages are thought to remind us in a positive way to complete our exercise and movement goals for a specific day. Nudges gently push us toward behavior with suggestions we do not have to question extensively or think much about. In those decisions that require intense reasoning, people find it easier to default to old behaviors or to procrastinate, so approaches that seem easy are effective (Gronchi, Ciangherotti, Parri, Pampaloni, & Brand, 2018). This positive and gentle approach of reminding individuals of goals or actions they want to take is useful in encouraging other behaviors as well. Health care apps may help a patient with medication compliance or support other wellness-directed behavior. The ethical appropriateness and long-term effectiveness of these CBT applications require further investigation (Marchiori, Adriaanse, & De Ridder, 2017).

Clearly, CBT is found outside clinical settings. We apply the principles in education, in learning, as well as in potentially darker areas such as marketing or propaganda. Every time that image of an item you researched reappears in an online ad, it is intended to nudge you toward purchase, to remind you to take action. It takes some willpower as well as proactive computer interventions to steer clear of what the marketers would like us to do. We are living in an era of digital pushback; too many outsiders are trying to get inside our heads (as cognitive influences) to change our behavior.

The basic principles of combining thinking and thinking about behavior (metacognition) with actions eliciting altered behavior also form the basis for wellness interventions. Here we encourage desirable behavior and reward it with digital badges or other symbolic or concrete rewards. In that generalized format, thousands if not millions of us have been exposed to some of the principles of cognitive behavioral intervention.

In clinical contexts, therapists are guided by ethical and professional codes, so their interventions do no harm and serve the best interests of clients. Therapists are held accountable for their actions. The same cannot be said for the thousands of messages that bombard our world daily, trying to influence not only our actions but also our thinking. Add to this sophisticated and often secretive digital behavior tracking, and we realize that the playing field has forever changed. We can no longer fool ourselves that the digital world is consistently serving our best interests.

In a Nutshell

Cognitive Behavioral Therapy

- Theories frequently form the foundation for interventions, as they provide a structure or model to support the treatment modalities.
- Cognitive behavioral therapy (CBT) is one of the most frequently used therapeutic approaches and is particularly useful in treating addiction and other excessive behaviors.
- *Cognitive* refers to the thinking component, and *behavioral* references what we do, our actions.
- Because CBT does not require people to spend extended time on trying to unravel underlying motivations and delving into the past, it tends to offer quicker and more targeted results.
- Cognitive behavioral therapy has so many contributors and applications that it is a field of study in its own right.

CHAPTER FOCUS POINTS

The Dynamics of Power

- A power dynamic can be represented by one person or party having and probably exerting greater control over another party.
- Examples of power abuse are bullying and intimate partner violence (IPV).
- Power can be found and acted out on all levels of a system, from the micro- to macrosystemic level.
- The opportunities an individual has to display power occur at all levels of interpersonal relations, including the family and larger societal systems, and those opportunities are affected by gender, age, socioeconomic status, education, partnership status, health, ability or disability, race, political affiliations, and many other circumstances.
- In amplified form, power can change social systems.

The Dynamics of Excess

- The dynamics of excess are complicated and affect more than the solitary victim; they have systemic effects.
- The first step in altering situations involving excess is awareness of their existence.
- Excesses occur in a wide range of conditions and situations, ranging from the relatively innocuous to the life threatening.
- In the case of overconsumption, we need to raise our awareness concerning the incessant pressure of marketing. We may become more competent at pushing back and developing defenses that allow us to disengage from the signals that nudge us to consume excessively, to the point at which consumption becomes an addiction.

The Dynamics of Collecting

- Collecting has some commonalities with human interactions in that there is a power game and a dynamic at play.
- Appropriate collecting can be a pleasurable and constructive activity.
- Extreme and obsessive collecting is accompanied by its own problems, as these collections take up resources in terms of time, money, space, and the energies of collectors.

From Collecting to Hoarding

- Hoarding exceeds all boundaries of appropriate collecting. Hoarding can be a symptom of psychopathology and of a range of associated underlying conditions (e.g., loneliness, anxiety, and depression) that may require psychiatric intervention.
- From a psychodynamic point of view, hoarding can be interpreted as an act motivated by a sense of emptiness and by the need to fill that void.

- Emotional hoarding means holding on to resentments, anger, grief, and a host of other emotions. Emotional hoarders cannot let go, and this form of hoarding becomes the basis for family feuds, emotional cutoffs, and other destructive interpersonal patterns.

The Addicted System

- For every family member who struggles with an addiction disorder, there is a family that has to cope with the disruption that follows in the wake of that addiction.
- One addiction can pave the way for another, hence the concept of gateway drugs.
- Persons seeking drugs can become devious and self-destructive as they are gripped by the control the drug exerts over them.
- Every time an addiction claims an individual, it not only claims the life of that individual but also brings tragedy into families. It precipitates an extended dynamic.

Spotlight on Theories: Cognitive Behavioral Therapy

- Theories frequently form the foundation for interventions, as they provide a structure or model to support the treatment modalities.
- Cognitive behavioral therapy (CBT) is one of the most frequently used therapeutic approaches and is particularly useful in treating addiction and other excessive behaviors.
- *Cognitive* refers to the thinking component, and *behavioral* references what we do, our actions.
- Because CBT does not require people to spend extended time on trying to unravel underlying motivations and delving into the past, it tends to offer quicker and more targeted results.
- Cognitive behavioral therapy has so many contributors and applications that it is a field of study in its own right.

CHAPTER

13

Dynamics of Family Structure and Transitions

Learning Outcomes

After studying this chapter, you should be able to

1. Discuss how adverse influences affect and present in *individual families.*
2. Explain why the dynamics of *intergenerational relationships* are best understood in a systemic context.
3. Describe the unique challenges of the *single-child family system.*
4. Reflect on how variations in *family structure* influence family functioning and dynamics.
5. Assess the strengths of *blended families*, while also considering their challenges.
6. Consider how and why *family transitions* can lead to varying outcomes, ranging from destructive to constructive and improved functioning.

Individual Families

Because families are as individual as snowflakes, no two families will provide the same context to their members. A number of factors contribute to this heterogeneity, including size, composition, age, gender, social context, and, of course, the unique psychological climate within the family bubble. Research on family lifespans indicates that another important variable is what psychological tasks the various generations within a particular family face at a given time.

Imagine family members being connected to each other by invisible threads. A small family has few connections, but as the size of the family increases, the connections increase exponentially. If we include the extended family, the number of intersecting points can be plentiful. It does not require the insight of a family scientist to know that the small starter family of a couple and their firstborn will function differently from the midlife partnership with children from two previous relationships. One of the themes that connects this diversity is the particular style of family functioning, by which is meant whether the family supports its members constructively or struggles with this task.

If we consider how adverse childhood experiences influence health and well-being throughout a lifespan, we note that each sequential set of contributing factors tends to build on its antecedent. This process can be represented in a pyramid to show how the accumulation of stressors from various sources can negatively affect longevity (see Diagram 13.1). Contributing factors are interrelated and include events and circumstances in existence before a child's birth. For example, a parents' historical trauma influences the conditions into which a child is born, which affects the likelihood of that child experiencing neglect or abuse. An adverse childhood experience can contribute to a child's disrupted neurological development, which can cause social, emotional, and cognitive impairment and the adoption of risky behaviors. These risky behaviors can bring health and social problems that can affect longevity negatively. This mechanism by which childhood trauma and household dysfunction influence health and well-being was a major finding of the ACE Study, research undertaken by the Centers for Disease Control and Prevention and Kaiser-Permanente, a group involved in health care (Centers for Disease Control and Prevention, 2019).

Obviously, the family provides the context in which adverse childhood experiences occur, but it is also an important conduit or catalyst for a number of social, emotional, and cognitive factors that have the potential to influence and alter ultimate outcomes. We know from research, for example, that a significant mitigating factor in self-harming behaviors can be ascribed to the acceptance and support received in the family of origin. The Family Acceptance Project has been singled out for its exemplary work in suicide prevention and in supporting families, especially in the context of LGBT youth (San Francisco State University, n.d.).

As far as family climate in general and parenting in particular are concerned, we know that positive relations feature in everything that is built upon that foundation. Safe, stable, and nurturing relationships are the foundation for constructive family outcomes (Walsh, 2016). The Search Institute has focused on these positive contributing factors in greater detail and grouped them into two major categories, namely, internal as well as external assets (Search Institute, n.d.). Internal

DIAGRAM 13.1 **Mechanisms by which adverse childhood experiences influence health and well-being throughout the lifespan.**

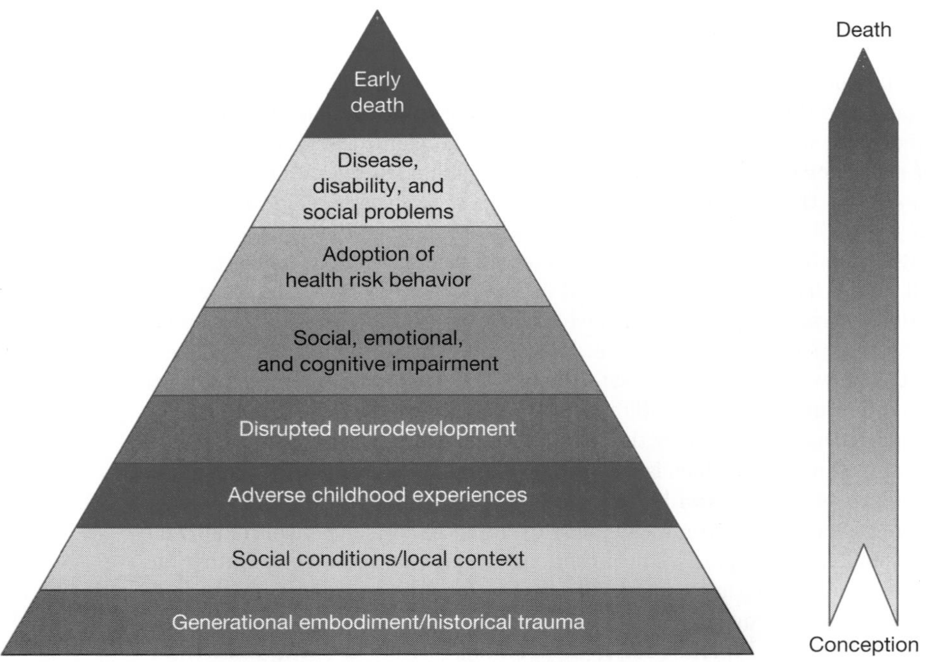

Source: Centers for Disease Control and Prevention/CDC-Kaiser Permanente Adverse Childhood Experiences (ACE) Study.

assets describe numerous characteristics, but of special importance for the family are those that support social competencies and positive identity. When it comes to external assets, the family can reach out to the social support systems provided by civic initiatives, educational services, and spiritual and religious communities (Roehlkepartain, 2013; Search Institute, 2016).

Changes on a macrosystemic level will trickle down to families. Large-scale studies reveal the sociocultural factors contribute to variations in the contact and support between the different generations comprising a family system. Larger sociocultural systems have a direct impact on the smaller units of a society, namely, on individual families (Garbarino, 2017; Ungar, 2014). Generally, the countries with less pronounced social welfare place greater emphasis on the family network to provide care for those requiring support, irrespective of whether that support involves disability, illness, or aging. Corporate social responsibility is also a concern in these various contexts (Tilt, 2016).

Increasingly, families are becoming smaller, many choosing one-child family structures or no children as the preferred family form. In these families, the intergenerational relationships are also affected. An only child may experience a greater burden being sandwiched between a younger and an older generation. On the other hand, for dual career families, the backup systems that one or two sets of grandparents can provide may be invaluable.

Additionally, divorce rates have climbed since the mid-twentieth century, and, increasingly, couples partner and commit later. After a divorce, the formation of a blended family is a possibility, and again the oldest generation may have to adjust to the choices their children make. Once a blended family is formed after a divorce, loyalties may be divided. The grandparents may feel loyalties toward all the grandchildren, but the time that they can interact with each grandchild may be limited by the custodial parent, especially if this person was an in-law. They may have to negotiate the new relationships and family additions brought about by subsequent marriages (Kumar, 2017). Variables that may have an impact on the effects of divorce on grandchildren and grandparents include proximity, family structure, and the pressures derived from need.

Family Systems and Structures

Family systems can harbor so much more than meets the eye. Ideally, the family represents our safest and most intimate space, the place where we can be vulnerable, where we can show our true colors, and where we will find authentic support. The level of trust brought on by the safety and intimacy of the family makes it possible for each of us to receive the constructive feedback that will guide us toward being the best we can be.

Several theorists, including Salvador Minuchin and Murray Bowen, have described subsystems of the family and emphasized the roles these can play. Kerig (2019) clarifies many of the major concepts related to family functioning in a chapter on parenting and family systems in the *Handbook on Parenting* (Bornstein, 2019). Here are some of those family structures and substructures:

Dyads. Dyads consist of two people who interact in some manner or other. Typical dyads are parental dyads and grandparental dyads. The setup of the family naturally allocates certain roles and responsibilities to these partnerships. Members within family groups can also form dyads; for instance, two siblings who feel particularly close to each other may connect.

Triangles or triads. In a triangle, three people are in some form of interaction with each other. Triangles run the risk of leaving one person in the group on

FOCUS POINT

Each family provides a unique context for its members. A number of factors contribute to this heterogeneity, including size, composition, age, gender, social context, and the psychological climate within a particular family. Another important variable relates to the family's lifespan—to the psychological tasks of that family at a given time.

the periphery while the other two form a subsystem in the form of a dyad. Triangles have also been described on a larger scale, for example, those occurring within societal systems (Titelman, 2008).

Hierarchies. In family systems, some members can form their own domain of responsibility. For instance, in a parental hierarchy, the two parents are given responsibility for and power over their children.

Sibling subsystem. Siblings within the family can form their own bonds, which are separate and different from the relationships they form with their parents. A sibling relationship can be similar to a peer relationship, with the addition that the members of that sibling system share the same family culture. They are all aware of the unique climate within their family of origin, and they are in the unique situation of witnessing most family events that include their siblings.

Intergenerational Relationships*

Several generations living together are typically known as an intergenerational or multigenerational family. This family form was more prevalent in rural and farming communities, especially before the Industrial Revolution. With industrialization, single-family units moved to cities to find employment, which meant the breakdown of the extended family system. To an extent, these same motivators are still operational, as today's families follow the lure of career and economic opportunities, even if the sacrifice occurs in the form of family separation.

In our not too distant past, extended family living arrangements allowed for a natural and daily intergenerational interaction. This family form is still prevalent in developing countries. In some parts of Africa, where the AIDS epidemic has been severe and has claimed many lives, children are raised by grandparents (Short & Goldberg, 2015). Several factors are contributing to changing demographics in the developing and the developed world.

As a family form, the multigenerational family is regaining prevalence, especially in some cultural subgroups within the United States. Longer lifespan expectancy, later partnership formation and parenthood, and teen pregnancy are some of the scenarios that encourage intergenerational collaborations. Extended families display economic advantages. Grandparents can help raise their grandchildren while the middle generation becomes the lead breadwinners. Strong and healthy family relationships contribute to family well-being and resilience (Thomas, Liu, & Umberson, 2017).

* *Acknowledgment:* Sections of "Intergenerational Relationships" have been previously published in a slightly different format. See Gerhardt, C. (2016). Intergenerational relationships. In C. L. Shehan (Ed.), *The Wiley Blackwell Encyclopedia of Family Studies* (Vol. 3, pp. 1159–1166). Chichester, UK: Wiley Blackwell. Used with permission of the publishers, John Wiley & Sons, Inc.

The dynamics of intergenerational families are best understood when approached in a systemic manner. The three generations that are interdependent form a larger system and have mutual influence on each other. As in all other family relationships, the influences are bidirectional, as participating parties receive and provide input. As the family's lifespan progresses, the needs of the family members will change to reflect their particular life stage.

Multigenerational family systems are more complex than a single nuclear family unit because they comprise the needs, challenges, strengths, and individual personalities of persons representing different generations. With these generational differences come cultural differences (Campbell et al., 2014). Every cohort that was subjected to similar societal and cultural influences will share experiences because its members lived during the same era. For this reason, different cohorts are described with unique identifiers such as the baby boomers, the millennials, or Generation X, to name but a few.

Intergenerational systems exert power over their members, and the members in turn influence the family systems in a bidirectional manner. Any change in a multigenerational family system can influence the nuclear family system that is embedded within this greater intergenerational constellation. This system functions also as an emotional system that influences family roles.

An intergenerational family system fulfills a number of important functions for its members. As a system, it offers exchanges that can represent emotional, social, and financial support. It also offers caregiving exchanges, whereby any member in need of care can be sheltered by the umbrella of family cohesion. The youngest generation may display the greatest need for caretaker support, but the oldest generation will require care as well as its members move into positions of physical, emotional, or cognitive frailty. Many grandparents live in close proximity to their children and grandchildren, providing support when necessary. In the reverse situation, children keep an eye on their own elderly and frail parents. The middle generation, with responsibilities for both an older and a younger generation, is sandwiched by caretaking responsibilities.

It can be difficult sharing limited space with several generations, but advantages are found when different generations form friendships and are willing to learn from each other (Hatzifilalithis & Grenier, 2018). Matching the oldest and youngest generations can be beneficial to both. A number of initiatives make sense in a social context and because all participants benefit. In several studies from the Netherlands (Jansen, 2015), where communities have co-housed students and seniors, a number of positive outcomes have been observed, as each generation learns from and widens its social experiences through exposure to the other (Bouma & Voorbij, 2009; Newman & Hatton-Yeo, 2008).

Intergenerational learning is important as it increases the "social capital" of individuals or a family, which is related to the outcomes of extending learning and financial opportunities—a result that can ultimately have global implications. Universities are well positioned for initiating and maintaining such intergenerational teaching and learning opportunities. These can become part of coursework and provide practical experiences that are of a pedagogical nature. Newman and Hatton-Yeo (2008) state that, historically and in a variety of cultural contexts, intergenerational teaching and learning has proven itself to be ideally suited to transferring knowledge, skills, and competencies in a systematic manner. Additionally, it also provides fertile opportunities for sharing norms, ethics, and values. In short, these intergenerational teaching and learning exchanges are as old as humankind (Newman & Hatton-Yeo, 2008, p. 31).

Current research emphasizes the influence of multigenerational family dynamics on the participating parties, the sociological and psychological implications of this intergenerational interaction, and optimal intergenerational parenting outcomes. In a decade review of articles on aging and family life, Silverstein and Giarrusso (2010) identified several overarching themes. These pertain to the complexity of emotions, relationships, roles, and functions within the multigenerational family system, which are interdependent, as well as to the patterns and outcomes related to providing care within this system. These interdependent dynamics, in turn, contribute to and influence the quality of the relationships within the intergenerational family system and, importantly, add to the diversity that is found within these systems.

The frequency of intergenerational contacts will be mediated by factors such as cultural and ethnic value systems, gender and social class, and the dimension of expression of closeness between the generations, which can be culturally specific. The age of parents can also influence the parent-child relationship; for example, older parents may display a different dynamic than younger ones (Silverstein, Gans, Lowenstein, Giarrusso, & Bengston, 2010). Research indicates that grandmothers tend to initiate and maintain greater frequency of contact than grandfathers. Of all the dyads, grandmothers and granddaughters report the closest bonds, and this finding has been referred to as the *matrifocal tilt* (Sheehan & Petrovic, 2008, p. 108). A gender-based role definition in this older generation may shape its members' perception of the demands of the grandparent role.

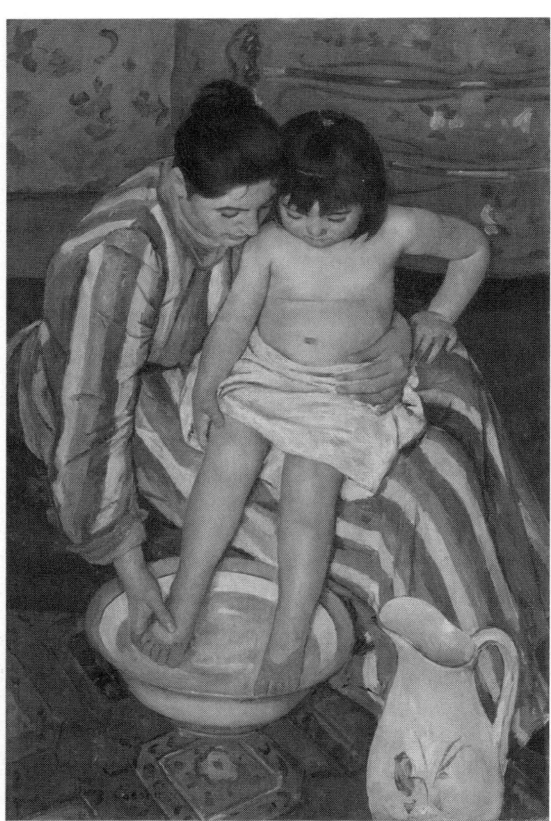

American artist Mary Cassatt (1844–1926) observed and painted the tender relationships between generations. She is an important artist from her era and studied in France as a contemporary of Degas. She stopped painting after 1914, due to visual impairment.

Source: Public domain.

Geographic proximity also influences the frequency of contact between generations with an extended family, although electronic communication can make frequent long-distance communication possible if the oldest generation is able and willing to be technologically engaged. The frequency of contact is more important than proximity in determining the emotional closeness between the oldest and the youngest generations. The wise adage concerning parenting also applies to grandparenting: "If you don't spend a certain quantity of time, you won't be spending quality time." Sustaining a meaningful and rewarding intergenerational relationship requires an investment—especially of time—which is reflected by frequency of contact. Admittedly, geographical closeness may facilitate frequency of contact and support mutual assistance.

Perhaps to the surprise of their own children, members of the older generation are creating families of choice in which the elderly from various original family groups live together. Sometimes, this cohabitation is occurring because people have been widowed and do not want to enter another marriage later in life, as doing so may affect financial assets unless clear legal provisions are put in place. Members of the oldest generation in the intergenerational system may be more concerned with societal opinion and judgment if they cohabit, but generalizations are difficult as cultural and socioeconomic factors play a strong role in these choices.

GLOBAL GLIMPSE

"ONE COMMUNITY, MANY EYES"

Aboriginal Culture Acts as a Protective Force

Aboriginal family life and child-rearing practices contain unique strengths that can be applied in other cross-cultural settings. Aboriginal people engage in traditional cultural practices that foster cohesion, not only in their families but also in their extended communities.

Aboriginal people, as a group, value social relationships, are proud of the physical and emotional bonds they have to their country, and, importantly, respect their connection to the spirit of their ancestors. As compared to other mainstream definitions, the Aboriginal definition of "family" is broader and encompasses a wider range of social connections. In traditional Aboriginal communities, the social structures are defined and delineated by kinship systems. When Aboriginal people who do not know each other meet in new contexts, they explore these wider connections as demarcated by sense of place, geographic location, extended family, and kinship circles.

Especially in remote areas, households of Aboriginal people tend to be complex and fluid in their composition, with kinship networks overlapping and adults and children often moving between households (Lohoar, Butera, & Kennedy, 2014, p. 3).

In the Aboriginal context, families are what the people choose them to be. They can consist of those living together under a roof or people who are related; but these characteristics need not be the determining ones. Importantly, families can also include those people sharing emotional bonds or having other shared connections.

Here are some key characteristics of Aboriginal kinship relationships:

- *"One community, many eyes"*: This Aboriginal idiom means that an entire collective community is involved in raising and protecting the children, which adds to child safety and well-being, as each community member has an obligation and a responsibility to look out for all members of that community.
- *"We let the kids go . . . as long as it's safe"*: Appropriate autonomy is provided to children to explore and experience their world, but children know their community is keeping watch. This responsibility and support empowers children.
- *Respect the wisdom of the elders*: The elders fulfill an important communal role in supporting family functioning. Elders are respected for their wisdom and are valued members of the community.
- *"Dreaming is impossible to relay in words"*: The spiritual practice of "dreaming" is uniquely Aboriginal and is regarded as an abstract and an experiential concept. Family challenges are eased by emphasizing spiritual strengths and values (SNAICC, 2011, p. 49).
- *Share and care*: At the core of Aboriginal culture and spirituality is an emphasis on sharing and caring. These are the values that bring cohesion and strength and nurture the children (Lohoar, Butera, & Kennedy, 2014, pp. 14–16).

The kinship system, which embodies the spiritual essence of the *dreaming*, helps Aboriginal people to understand their relationship to one another and the roles and responsibilities they have in raising children. The importance of harmonious social relationships and the spirit of the culture continue to be a feature of traditional Aboriginal family and community life.

Sources: Lohoar, Butera, and Kennedy (2014); SNAICC (2011); see also Carter and King (2018).

In short, there is no blueprint for the intergenerational family structure, as these families are also defined and characterized by their diversity, which, in turn, is influenced by cultural factors and processes that morph and change from generation to generation. In their review of research on aging and the family, Silverstein and Giarrusso (2010, pp. 1039–1040) summarize a decade of findings into four overarching themes:

- Emotional relationships of varying complexity,
- Diversity between and within intergenerational systems,
- Interdependence between the roles fulfilled by various members of this system, and
- Outcomes and patterns in caregiving and nurturing relationships.

Skipped-Generation Households

Grandparents. Grandparents can be the stabilizers of systems in flux, the bridge over troubled water. In the case of the temporary or permanent absence of the middle generation, grandparents may fill the void with their own resources, providing parenting to grandchildren or a financial safety net. Doing so can impact their own economic viability and retirement plans. Past and current relationship quality determines the willingness of grandparents to invest in their children's families, either emotionally or economically.

Grandparents may be raising grandchildren for a number of compelling reasons, including absence of the middle generation through incarceration, addictive disorders, deployment, mental health concerns, physical challenges, and other situations making that generation incapable of shouldering the responsibilities of parenthood. The youngest generation makes its own unique and valuable contributions to the grandparent-grandchild relationship. Grandchildren keep the grandparents who raise them in the proverbial loop, familiarizing the older generation with technological advances and current expressions, such as verbal slang, fashion, and other trends marking societal changes. Each generation learns from each other, and a mutual socialization occurs.

Ambivalence can occur in intergenerational relationships as well, especially those in which a generation is skipped. Seemingly conflicting emotions may surface depending on the context and persons involved. Silverstein and Giarrusso (2010), in their important decade-long review of the family life of an aging generation, challenge the notion that relationships in intergenerational families are predominantly harmonious. Ambivalence and ambiguity, role strain, divided loyalties, emotional discordance, and stressful outcomes can characterize these particular family systems. Participants juggle roles and demands, often involuntarily and driven by necessity.

They may express ambiguity if not outright resentment. Generations may experience **structural ambivalence**, which refers to the competing forces making demands on resources, especially financial resources but also time and space management. **Collective ambivalence** describes disruptions that extend into larger and more complex social systems (Silverstein & Giarrusso, 2010). Typically, society does not expect grandparents to

Aboriginal decorative arts. In the Aboriginal context, families are what the people choose them to be. They can consist of people who are related by blood; but these characteristics need not be the determining ones. Importantly, families can include those people sharing emotional bonds or having other shared connections.

Source: © iStock.com/lore.

raise their grandchildren or assume financial responsibility for them. So participants in a skipped-generation family may feel the ambivalence brought on by the difference between the structure of their own family versus society's stereotypes and expectations of family structure.

Grandparents in these situations may feel that all dimensions of their lives have been affected. The grandparent raising a grandchild in the absence of the middle or parental generation is a family form that is becoming increasingly prevalent. The U.S. Census of 2016 revealed that most of the children in the United States permanently living with grandparents were under the age of six. When an aging generation takes responsibility for a younger generation, the stressors can be burdensome, as this responsibility alters the entire trajectory of the grandparents' lives—all that they had planned for their own retirement.

Silverstein and Giarrusso (2010) state that an intergenerational family structure is directly linked to diversity in family composition, complexity in relationships, interdependence of roles, and outcomes of caregiving.

Attribution bias. Grandparents can provide grandchildren with a priceless legacy in terms of family history and personal identity. They can also teach certain skills and activities, family rituals, and possibly religious rites, which contributes to intergenerational learning and enhances the feelings of belonging and connectedness within the family. In the United States, older generations are also likely to support the younger ones financially. That support can range from small monetary gifts to large sums that pay for tuition or help offspring buy a first home.

But how much support is actually given and received? Members of the oldest generation typically overreport the help and support they give to those in generations below them, while also underreporting the help and support they receive. An **attribution bias**, or self-serving bias, is at play; perceptions are colored to benefit the image of the person doing the reporting

This attribution bias occurs in the reports of each generation. Adult children focus more strongly on the amount of support they give aging parents and tend to overreport their own contributions. On the other hand, they underreport and may underestimate the help they receive.

Members of each of the adult generations (parents or grandparents) may see themselves as providing the most support while receiving the least support. Similarly, perceptions regarding the emotional closeness and cohesion of the relationships between the generations will shift and change. The middle generation often feels less invested emotionally, whereas the oldest generation feels that it contributes greatly to family closeness. In this manner, there is a discrepancy in how each generation views its contributions within the intergenerational system (Giarrusso, Feng, & Bengtson, 2005). Often, these discrepant views are the result of each generation contributing differently: the middle generation may take care

FOCUS POINT

An intergenerational family system fulfills a number of important functions for its members, irrespective of their generation. As a system, it offers exchanges in terms of emotional, social, and financial support. Skipped-generation families may experience structured ambivalence because generational expectations regarding roles, responsibilities, and resources compete with actual family circumstances. Competing forces may also make demands on resources in these families. Grandparents may be raising grandchildren for a number of compelling reasons, and, in this circumstance, each generation learns from the other.

Authentic Insight

Building Intergenerational Bridges

Bridging the generation gap between two generations, namely seniors (baby boomers) and students (millennials), leads to unexpected benefits for both parties. Computer literacy classes, including some that license "Cyber Seniors," build these intergenerational bridges. Seniors and students participate in shared interactions during which the younger group takes on teaching roles by sharing and encouraging computer literacy in the older group.

For the past several years, the Family Life Education and Gerontology classes have been involved in this intergenerational teaching-learning project. It is meaningful to all involved because it encourages friendships across generations, and this in turn has positive social implications. As the seniors are encouraged to develop and expand their computer skills on any electronic device of their choosing, they are also socializing and being cognitively challenged.

They are encouraged to explore and navigate computers in a nonthreatening environment, and this helps them connect and communicate with their own families, especially if they live far apart. The project called "Cyber Seniors" is maintained under the auspices of several charitable organizations. Students familiarized seniors with computers and expanded the seniors' skill base by sharing their own literacy and expertise. Additionally, the students could perfect their teaching skills by accessing scholarly sources and networking with persons who had particular computer-related expertise.

In addition to being involved in the actual class project focusing on computer literacy and Internet safety for seniors, this group of students learned valuable lessons by working as a team and collaborating. At the end of the computer literacy course, students presented a formal Family Life Education project, focusing on Internet safety and privacy. This encouraged students to build their skills in providing education in family-related contexts, an expertise that is important in later work environments.

A number of anticipated and unanticipated outcomes occurred. The project primarily concentrated on teaching computer-related skills to seniors, but the metacognitive learning that took place in both parties was most rewarding. Students gained respect, empathy, and greater understanding for the seniors. Their gerontology coursework found practical application. Most importantly, they formed friendships, some extending long after the course was over.

Celeste Hill, PhD, is an associate professor of human development and family science.

of day-to-day work and the chores related to economic survival, while the elders may contribute to the wisdom and education of grandchildren, a most valuable task indeed as it provides continuity in oral history, cultural heritage, and so much more.

> **"The 'Four Rs' of respect, responsibility, reciprocity, and resiliency . . . generally characterize intergenerational relationships."**
>
> Timothy Brubaker and Ellie Brubaker (1999), family scientists

The Single-Child Family System**

In sibling systems of two or more, the children grow up with a peer group consisting of family members sharing the same household. For an only child, this type of social interaction is to be found only within a peer system outside the home: social

** *Acknowledgment:* Sections of "The Single-Child Family System" have been previously published in a slightly different format: See Gerhardt, C. (2016). Only children. In C. L. Shehan (Ed.), *The Wiley Blackwell Encyclopedia of Family Studies* (Vol. 3, pp. 1533–1536). Chichester, UK: Wiley Blackwell. Used with permission of the publishers, John Wiley & Sons, Inc.

interactions with children of the only child's age group are predominantly with friends and occur in school, sport, and other social contexts.

Much of the research on only children was done in China where, until recently, the predominant family form was that of the single-child family (Zhang, 2017). This demographic situation has allowed a number of meta-analyses of data, providing a wealth of information concerning this particular family form. At the same time, the cultural context is different to that of North America, and not all findings can be generalized.

The number sequence "4-2-1" denotes the ratio of participants in the typical intergenerational single-child family: there are four grandparents, two parents, and one child. The attention focused on a single child, then, can be represented in the form of an inverse pyramid: four grandparents and two parents all focus on the one youngster. In reverse, this structure can also be particularly daunting. When elderly grandparents require care or a parent is incapacitated or dies, then the sole child has to carry an enormous responsibility while having no sibling resources for support. The dynamics of both receiving overly focused and possibly excessive attention and shouldering great responsibility for older generations can be overwhelming for the only child. Parents and grandparents are also affected by this dynamic. There are fewer young family members with whom to relate, for example, and any calamities affecting the only child can be devastating for older family members. The loss of a child is always tragic, whatever the circumstance, but losing an only child can be excruciating for grandparents and parents, who may have pinned their hopes and dreams on their only offspring (Fong, 2016; Liu & Sun, 2015).

In the traditional one-child family in China, there was a preference for male children. Cultural and religious norms make the male heir responsible for carrying on the name of the family and respecting the wishes of elders, including those departed. In contemporary China, this gender selection has caused major imbalances, and men have difficulty in finding life partners among their peers due to a shortage of women (Du, Wang, & Zhang, 2015). Clearly this type of inequity on a macro scale influences the dynamics of dating and partnering. It has presented in unanticipated dynamic shifts.

In some Western European countries, the single-child family form has also gained prominence, especially in dual career and dual income families. Declining birth rates have been persistent in countries where mothers have attained postsecondary, or tertiary education, as this education influences women's career options. The postwar baby boom has not been repeated. Countries with intense growth rates tend to be developing countries, where the future of children is somewhat uncertain, as they face economic and health challenges, and where women's education may not be freely accessible.

The advantage of being an only child is that much of the attention of parents and grandparents is exclusively focused on you. Only children, who receive quality attention from a number of adults, may have more advanced language than their peers because it is influenced by being in the world of grown-ups. If they are seen as more diligent and responsible, this may be ascribed also to the focused attention they receive from several adults (Fong, 2016). But all this attention could become excessive, and these children have been described as "little emperors" in their native China. In reality, if parents apply balanced and constructive parenting techniques, this drawback need not occur.

Studies with large samples, and meta-analyses of combined research studies, have indicated what seems intuitive, namely, that the one-child situation, in itself, is not the cause of major differences in outcomes for these children; instead, these children are as heterogeneous as any found in a large cohort. For that same reason, the research on only children has not confirmed that they are consistently overindulged. Instead, the outcomes vary depending on the parenting styles only children experienced. Overprotective or helicopter parenting is more prevalent in general and not only in families with only children. The reasons are several, including the immense investment that parents currently make in their children, both emotionally and financially. In the developed world, children usually require many years of schooling and support before they become financially independent, for example. Additionally, modern society appears to harbor greater threats, especially if one considers school shootings and other forms of violence that put children at risk. Parents cannot realistically protect their children from all potential harm, but it is natural that parents would become hypervigilant if they sensed that potential risks to their children were increasing.

The Only Child: Historical Insights

Alfred Adler. Alfred Adler (1870–1937), one of the early psychoanalysts and a contemporary of Sigmund Freud's, sensed the importance of these unique relationships and focused on birth order. He thought that siblings could contribute valuable social support and exert educational influences on each other. In his mind, an only child missed out on these valuable learning and bonding opportunities provided within the security of the family. Siblings are a ready-made peer group, teaching and learning each other while also having to be responsible and looking out for each other's safety and well-being. In this sense, having brothers and sisters could mean being part of a very prosocial learning school, teaching one to share, be considerate, negotiate, and so much more (Lundin, 1989/2015).

G. Stanley Hall. G. Stanley Hall (1844–1924) was eminent in the history of American psychology and the first president of the American Psychological Association. He was of the opinion, albeit a very controversial one, that being an only child could have severe negative outcomes; in 1898, he stated that being an only child was a disease unto itself. Needless to say, his opinion was not particularly well received. One can understand the concern with family size somewhat better if the greater societal and cultural contexts of nineteenth-century thinking are considered. With limited medical interventions, childbirth was risky, and safe and trustworthy family planning was nonexistent. Consequently, childhood mortality was very high. Also, gender roles favored males, so most families wanted at least one child who was masculine. One-child families were not the norm, therefore; instead they were viewed with intolerance and possibly some suspicion.

> **"I suppose since I was an only child that we might've been a little closer than—I mean everyone loves their mother, but I was an only child, and Mother was always right with me all my life."**
>
> Elvis Presley (1935–1977), American singer and actor,
> from an interview in Brooklyn, New York, September 22, 1958

FOCUS POINT

In some Western European countries, the single-child family form has gained prominence, especially in dual career and dual income families. Only children, and children in general, are shaped by varied inputs, ranging from micro- to macrosystemic influences. Outcomes for only children vary and depend on the parenting styles they experience.

Variations in Family Structure

Children who grew up with siblings maintain that sense of a cohort throughout their lifespans, even if they grow apart. Siblings are blood ties and the only persons who have true insight into the family of origin. Additionally, children are part of several systems ranging from micro- to macro levels, as referenced by the ecological family systems theory. These systems include all the relevant persons, organizations, policies, and the like that may influence a child at various points of that child's lifespan. For siblings growing up in one household, these influences may be similar.

Of the parties participating in the intergenerational relationships within a family, siblings at any generational level may vie for attention and position. Siblings who are adults may remember favoritism in their nuclear family and carry these competitive feelings into adult relationships. Siblings on one generational level may also feel that they compete with nieces and nephews in terms of dominance and esteem within a given generation. Clearly, family of origin issues can influence later intergenerational relationships (Widmer, 2010).

Authentic Insight

The Dynamic of Connectedness: When Two Are One

Since the moment I came into this world, I have only communicated from one point of view: that of an identical twin. I have always had a counterpart and have always lived in a way that has expressed the equality of our lives.

The dynamics of this relationship and how we interact within our family unit completely changed in August of 2016 when my twin sister, Megan, was diagnosed with osteosarcoma. She shaved her head on our 24th birthday and started chemotherapy 2 days later. We spent Halloween, Thanksgiving, and Christmas Eve in the hospital. She was sick on New Year's. It was the most exhausting and emotionally draining year.

My sister went from independent 20-something young professional to having to move home. My mom went from an empty nester who had freedom to work and socialize on her own schedule, to full-time caretaking parent. I went from a full-time graduate student who was also working part time, to juggling school and work while traveling home on the weekends so that my mom could work on the weekends in order to keep her job.

Not only were our schedules altered but the way we communicated shifted radically. Megan and I were used to having unique but equal roles within our family unit, but when the diagnosis happened, we could no longer maintain equal places within our system. She became the "patient" or child again, my mom the main caregiver/parent, and I had a mixed role of supporter, second caregiver, and communicator to the other systems within the larger family unit.

These role changes were quickly settled into for necessity's sake. But as recovery happened and Megan began to heal and return to a more intact life, we struggled as a family unit to fall back into communicating and interacting as equal parties. I no longer felt like I had experienced everything in the same way that my twin sister had, and that made it a lot more difficult for me to reconnect to my role as her counterpart.

Cancer happened to Megan. She was the one who had to physically go through every excruciating chemotherapy treatment, every emergency trip to the hospital, every terrible emotion that came with having such an undesired diagnosis. I experienced cancer from the role of caretaker, communicator, and twin sister. I didn't have to experience the physical or emotional repercussions of actual treatment. But I had to see my twin sister, the one person that I have experienced 100% of my life, be pumped with necessary poison, become sick and weak and angry and sad. I had become sick and weak and angry and sad too . . . but in a completely different way.

There's an extent of understood pain that comes with witnessing a once extremely strong and vivacious young woman become weak and helpless, dependent on the people around her.

(Continued)

(Continued)

But unless Megan and I emotionally reversed roles, neither of us would be able to understand exactly what the other was experiencing.

I don't understand what having cancer was like for her. And she doesn't understand what seeing her have cancer was like for me.

For two people who are so used to not having to explain every detail of a situation to understand completely, this has been a new experience for us. The connection of still being there for each other exists, and will always do. But now it looks different. We get to be "the Smith Twins" in most every other area of our lives, but this will always be one thing that cannot be fully understood or experienced deeply together because of the drastically different sides of the experience we both inhabited. There's beauty in the brutal road of those couple of years, as we've been able to look back and care more deeply for each other. We have found a renewed connection because of the time we couldn't fully understand each other and because we traveled to such foreign ground.

Nicole Smith has an MA in counseling and is both an associate licensed counselor (ALC) and a national certified counselor (NCC).

The Cholmondeley Ladies (c. 1600–1610), painted by an unknown artist, is a charming historical document of the synchronicity of life events. An inscription on the painting provides us with these clues: "Two Ladies of the Cholmondeley Family, Who were born the same day, Married the same day, And brought to Bed [gave birth] the same day." (Cholmondeley is pronounced "Chumley.")

Source: Tate, image released under Creative Commons CC-BY-NC-ND (3.0 Unported).

Twins and Other Multiples

Being part of a twin pair shapes the life experiences of both twins. The stakes are raised further in the case of other multiples, for example, triplets. Having an identical twin is like having a mirrored version of oneself, and often someone with similarities in many areas other than appearance. A unique subsystem with its own dynamic characteristics is formed between multiples, which can be particularly strong in identical twins. Additionally, there is the dynamic between the parents and the multiples. Many parents report finding it stressful raising multiples (Wenze, Battle, & Texanos, 2015).

Renesting Children

Children who return to their parental home after having been launched create another variation of intergenerational family life. These emerging adults may be forced by financial reasons, such as unemployment, a job market without prospects, or increasingly high student debt, to rejoin their family of origin in order to survive economically. This move has far-reaching effects on dating patterns and the ability of these emerging adults to form families of their own and become gainfully employed.

The generation they return to, typically the middle generation, may have some resentments as its parental responsibilities seem to have become never ending. Frequently, parents resume overprotective and controlling roles when dealing with their returning children, which can be an added stressor and requires skillful negotiation and balance across generations.

FOCUS POINT

Children with siblings maintain a cohort throughout their lifespans, even if brothers and sisters grow apart. Siblings may vie for attention and position. Being part of a twin pair, or of multiples, shapes the life experiences and dynamic of the participating children and their parents. Children who return to their parental home after having been launched may have to subscribe to implicit and explicit rules. Being single can be a conscious choice or an involuntary circumstance. Being single can mean that the duties of family management rest on the shoulders of one person.

The complexities of relationships that bridge several generations are intricate, and there may be a number of implicit and explicit rules that have to be respected by all participants. Participants in intergenerational relationships typically wear several hats. They fulfill several roles, some within their own generation and others across generations (Steinbach, Kopp, & Lazarevic, 2017). Imagine the roles filled by a young married woman with a child having to move back home because her husband is ill. She may face all the responsibilities and privileges of a spouse, a mother, a sibling, and an adult child of aging parents. At one stage, young adults who moved home were referred to as **boomerang kids** (Mitchell, 2007).

Singledom. Being single can be a conscious choice, or it can be attributed to the death of a spouse or partner, partnership breakup, or partnership instability, which can cause long spells of singledom. From a systemic angle, being single means that the duties of family management rest on the shoulders of one person. If that person is also a parent or a grandparent, then her or his roles, responsibilities, and duties increase accordingly.

Singles follow different journeys. People who are single by choice may make a conscious decision for this lifestyle, which allows them to focus on professional and career aspirations. It is becoming an increasingly common choice as gender equality in developed countries has brought with it the ability to earn an independent living regardless of gender (Henriksson, 2019). If children are involved, then these singles form single-parent households, which are very common in developed countries. Single-parent families also tend to favor mothers in custody arrangements, although dual custody or custody sharing is a preferable option if both parental parties are able to shoulder parenting tasks responsibly.

If singlehood is caused by the loss of a partner, the dynamics include all the tasks related to the bereavement journey (Fried et al., 2015). When singledom occurs because a previous partnership that produced children was dissolved, the way in which both parties can continue to collaborate for the sake of the children is one of the cornerstones of a successful post-partnership arrangement.

Blended Families

Subsequent partnerships imply that families are joined even though each has its own previous partnership and family history. An individual in a blended family may have all the past connections and influences that accompany his or her family of origin, fused with the various painful experiences that culminated in partnership dissolution (Kumar, 2017). This is a much more complex storyline than the one in which two persons fall in love and live happily ever after. Refer to the Authentic Insight titled "Perfecting the Family Dance: Choreography for Blended Families," which highlights some of these challenges.

As far as dynamics for blended families are concerned, several strands tend to vie for attention. Dynamics concern the following:

- Dynamics accompanying the partnership dissolution.
- How the children from the blended families interpret the events.
- Resentments, grief, anger, and other emotions and memories concerning previous partnerships.
- Family-of-origin concerns of all parties uniting in the blended family.
- Cultural pressures concerning repartnering.
- Dealing with ex partners and ex in-laws.
- Grandparental rights and roles.

Authentic Insight

Perfecting the Family Dance: Choreography for Blended Families

When the therapist maps the multigenerational history of a young couple celebrating their first marriage, the cultural differences between their respective families of origin may be clear to see. Even though the couple might belong to the same overarching cultural group, their individual family cultures can differ greatly.

As they share this new bond of commitment, many facets will intersect. There are the vertical vectors and legacies meeting with the brittle horizontal connections between the two people. Each partner brings different family epistemologies to the table, meaning that they are introducing their own beliefs and opinions into this new shared emotional space. This background music, as it were, consists of money matters, professions, children, in-laws, and a host of other influences. They can be depicted in an ecomap (or ecogram), in which the interrelationships between significant relationships, life events, resources, needs, and the like are depicted visually, by connecting them. The result looks a little like an interconnected planetary system, or a star sign, in which the connections have been made visible.

Couples can easily get derailed if they focus excessively on their personal ecology, as opposed to their shared ecology. Not seeing the connections or the time spent in shared activities means that the cohesion between them gets lost. The couple, as the executive subsystem of a nuclear family, might run the risk of neglecting their relationship in order to manage other challenges and provocations in their daily contexts of living. Entropy describes the order or organization of a system. This order (or lack thereof) can be recognized when a gradual rundown of connection, affection, communication, and intimacy occurs. This may lead to stale marriages, divorce, violence, and a host of symptomatic presentations.

In the case of the blended or reconstituted family, the ecology of the couple and their family system is even more complicated. It can be helpful to map this complexity with a family ecomap (or ecogram). It is the classical case of his, hers, and theirs, and the stressors on the couple relationship can push it to a fracture point. The couple is exposed to the different legacies and conventions from their individual families of origin, the failed or disbanded marital systems they had been part of before the latest marital union, and probably four sets of in-law systems!

In therapy, it is wise to work toward strengthening the permeable boundary enveloping the new partners, so they can deal with their complex ecology as an executive system. It would be senseless to work toward premature compression of the new relationship, which may already be a few years old. Premature compression, or overly keen efforts to solidify the relationship, may precipitate years of bickering, conflict, symptoms, and the repeated and painful fighting of the "weary wranglers," as partners who argue endlessly are referred to in couple's literature.

It is advisable to rotate the family subsystems attending specific therapeutic sessions. This allows detection of unfinished business in the history of the older subsystems and provides an opportunity to address these concerns. These unfinished themes can create structural blockages in the formation of the new blended family. For example, the mother in the "new" couple could be included in a session, with her children and without the "new" husband or partner. Similarly, the husband and his children could be seen in another session. Important themes that may present themselves concern mourning the loss of the previous nuclear family and children's questions and observations about the new family structure.

It is tempting for a therapist to set reductionistic goals in an attempt to find or restore a new balance. But avoid the pull; it will not lead the family to the metaphorical promised land. Instead, playing the ecological detective and intervening in the different subsystems disrupts the interactional stalemate in the blended system, and clients find their own solutions and positions in the system.

Invite various combinations and subsystems of the blended family into the therapy sessions, use circular questioning, structural techniques, or provocative interventions with the new couple, the couple plus his children, the couple plus her offspring, the couple and his parents, the couple and her parents, and so on.

The therapist should be the choreographer of a rotating therapeutic system rather than a social controller specializing in instructive interaction. This generally leads to new alliances, family games, and fresh sets of interactions.

Family members will discover their authentic movements within this new choreography, and then it is up to them to perfect their dance.

Rick Snyders, DLitt et Phil, is a clinical psychologist specialized in systemic family therapy and a professor emeritus in psychology.

Family Transitions

As a person who loves to travel, I have been puzzled about why I still get agitated before a trip. Why do I do this to myself if I love the stimulation of novelty and experiencing new contexts and cultures? Many of us experience transitional anxiety when we have to change from one situation to the next. There is an upheaval in routine, apprehension about the unknown, and worry about the impetus required to disrupt the balance or homeostasis of the known and the familiar. Even good situations that fill us with a positive version of stress (eustress) have the ability to increase our sense of being disrupted. Situations causing positive stress include things like getting married, the prospect of having a child, changing jobs, or, indeed, going on vacation. Many other transitions, ranging from the mundane to the life altering, cause stress as well (Szabo, 2016).

On an individual level, transitional anxiety can be managed by the person experiencing it. When it occurs on the family level, all the members of that family can be implicated. Researchers have discussed the variable impact of stress-causing life events and which various dimensions of function these events affect (Cohen, Gianaros, & Manuck, 2016). How these events are experienced and interpreted will vary greatly depending on a number of factors. External and internal factors intersect. The resources and resilience of the family form one part of the formula, but the other part pertains to the context of the stressor and the meanings that the family can attach to that event.

In stressful situations, reorganization takes place as we access our emotional, interpersonal, and other resources, while also having to deal with our vulnerabilities. This period of reorganization can feel uncomfortable and disrupting. We rearrange, while also accessing our resources. This process can culminate in one of several scenarios: a new configuration that maintains a balance or homeostasis (remaining the same) or a worse situation. Ideally, we like to reach option three, namely, a better outcome than before. This would represent growth, adaptation, and learning. In the accompanying diagram this process is depicted, flowing from the original situation through a period of adaptation to a resolution or outcome (see Diagram 13.2).

DIAGRAM 13.2

When faced with adversity or other life challenges, individuals regroup emotionally. This process can feel turbulent and uncomfortable. The outcomes vary, ranging from less to more desirable. This inevitable journey of adaptation is worthwhile if it leads to constructive adaptation implying improved outcomes.

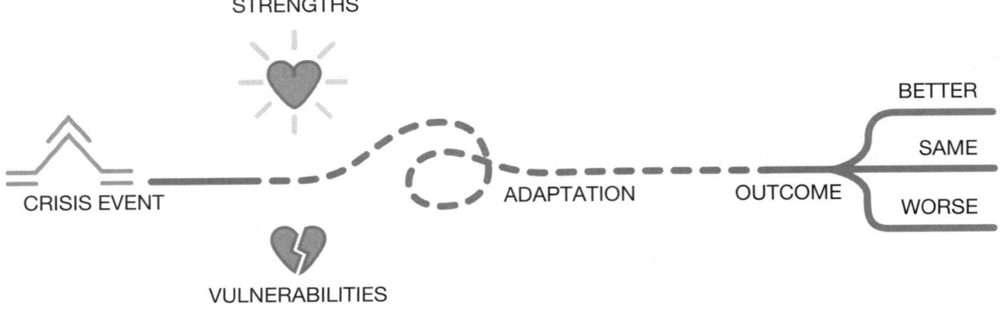

HISTORICAL GLOBAL GLIMPSE

HISTORIC FAMILY RITUALS IN A CHINESE CULTURAL CONTEXT

Chu Hsi's Family Rituals, compiled by the great neo-Confucian philosopher Chu Hsi (1130–1200), is a historic manual for the private performance of the standard Chinese family rituals: initiations, weddings, funerals, and sacrifices to ancestral spirits. It was among the best-known books of late imperial China. And copies of it could be found in almost every home in China. Both this book and the family rituals it describes went through many transformations. Initially, the book was regarded as a convenient manual for encouraging proper rituals among the people, but from the sixteenth century on, it became a controversial book and was at times found to be unsuitable. Nevertheless, it describes the importance of these rituals to the family and culture:

> These rituals expressed and reproduced the key principles underlying the family system: the relationships between ancestors and descendants, men and women, parents and children, and families linked through marriage. (Hsi, 1991/2014, p. xiv)

In this unique historical volume, translator Patricia Buckley Ebrey brings several family rituals to life. In this paragraph the rituals surrounding a special event such as a birthday are described:

> Whenever there is a seasonal celebration, a special family banquet, or the birthday of the family head, all the younger members of the family, in full attire, line up in order of rank, as in the ceremony used on the new and full moons of every month. First they bow twice. Then, the oldest of the sons or brothers advances to the front of the family head. . . . The eldest then sticks his official plaque in his belt, kneels down, pours the wine and prays. . . . After the seniors have all taken a drink, he gives the decanter and the cup back to the two younger ones, who return to where they were. (Hsi, 1991/2014, pp. 30–31)

These specially choreographed family rituals have accompanied social groups for centuries, and they provide guidance and social decorum to festive events. Another description concerning the feeding and raising of infants is also charming and somewhat quaint when read in the twenty-first century:

If a wetnurse is sought for a newborn son, a woman from a respectable family of a gentle and modest nature should be chosen. (Not only would a bad wet nurse violate family regulations, but she would also influence the temperament and behavior of the child in her care.) Children old enough to eat should be given food and taught to use their right hands in eating. Those old enough to talk should be taught their names and greetings such as "at your service," "bless you," and "sleep well." As they gain some understanding, they should be taught to respect their seniors. Any time they fail to behave properly toward them, they must be scolded and warned not to act that way again. (Hsi, 1991/2014, p. 31)

Even as far back as the twelfth century, then, people have been coping through rituals with the transitional anxiety occasioned by birth, birthdays, and the passing of time. Also, parents and others have sought guidance regarding the proper way to organize and celebrate these transitions.

Source: Hsi (1991/2014).

Healthy Families

Whatever constitutes a *healthy* family may also reflect some of the generally held beliefs based on norms within given contexts. Therefore, it may *not* be a useful exercise to delineate one set of characteristics regarding what is meant by well-functioning families, as this may be influenced by historical, social, and cultural contexts.

Well-functioning or emotionally healthy families do have several typical characteristics and roles (Bai & Repetti, 2015). As research has shown, families that function well, or can be labeled as healthy, display common characteristics, but these work in unique ways in each particular family to support that family's functioning in a constructive manner.

Well-functioning families tend to be characterized by the following:

- Healthy families are loyal to each other and invest in their families. It is a lifelong commitment, as we cannot choose or change our families.
- They celebrate achievements and joyous occasions together. When a family member does something well, the family unit acknowledges that event. They share a sense of humor and laughter.
- They have shared rituals and family customs. They create meaningful traditions that they pass from generation to generation, and these provide strength as well as an identity to the family.
- Healthy families like to spend time together, not all the time, but some time. They share some meals, and they make time to visit and connect. These times become valuable opportunities to strengthen family bonds and to keep family members up to date. They communicate well and support each other.
- They respect both the cohesiveness of the family, as well as the autonomy of family members; there is a context-appropriate balance between the individualistic functioning of members and the collectivist or combined

outcomes required by the family unit. Family members can pool their resources to display greater resilience.

- They focus on the positive and constructive processes that will increase their emotional resources as a family. To do this, they let go of resentments and do not practice the art of futile and hurtful guilt-tripping.
- Through civic engagement, they invest in the greater social system that houses and sustains them. Parents display moral and ethical values as an example to their children and guide the moral development of their offspring. Civic and other social engagement increases the family's resilience (Friesen & Brennan, 2005, p. 295).

Importantly, these principles apply across cultures and in various contexts, although the particular challenges may vary as determined by individually cultural situations. One set of characteristics facilitates the expression of other strength-promoting behaviors. For that reason, the qualities that promote strength and resilience can hardly be seen in isolation; they tend to come in clusters in a systemic manner. Families who communicate well, for instance, will also find it easy to express encouragement and appreciation. By the same token, if the qualities of being encouraging and supportive are acknowledged within the family, they indicate and help create a pattern of good communication. Garbarino (2005), in his foreword for a textbook pertaining to resilience in cross-cultural contexts, makes the following remark: "Human beings

Historic Research on Healthy Families

In 1990 the U.S. Department of Health and Human Services produced an extensive report on what constituted healthy families (Krysan, Moore, & Zill, 1990). The dimensions they chose to research, based on an extensive literature study, reflect the important facets that tend to strengthen family life. They studied and took measure of the following dimensions, all thought to be relevant in contributing to family health:

- Communication
- Encouragement, appreciation, and commitment
- Religious orientation
- Adaptability
- Social connectedness
- Clear roles
- Time together

The authors of this study concluded that these factors are correlated and interact. As one positive quality increases, it tends to correlate with other aspects that facilitate good outcomes. This may not seem like a major "aha" moment looking back, but, importantly, it solidified the notion that, within a system, a climate can be created to facilitate the development of all those qualities that combine to contribute to good outcomes.

Another analogy: if one creates a garden in which the conditions are optimal, for example, with fertile soil and adequate water and sunlight, it will be possible to grow a variety of healthy plants, and they will produce diverse flowers. To create a good emotional climate within the family—one that promotes individual as well as group wellness—requires a variety of qualities and characteristics. Families differ in the resources that they bring to the table; parents create families with varying skill sets and expectations. If a climate is created that fosters mutual respect and the willingness to be truly concerned about the others' well-being, then there is hope.

"Love is true concern for the others' wellbeing."

Clara Gerhardt
(Bigner & Gerhardt, 2019)

are indeed generally adaptive and resourceful but that resilience is not unlimited, automatic, or universal" (Ungar, 2005, p. xi). Instead, healthy resilience requires careful nurturing, and the family unit and society in general can be crucial links in strengthening the expression of this almost magical resource, which Garbarino describes as "a many splendored thing" (p. xiii).

Consider this insight by Ungar (2005), which draws our attention to the importance of the family and the community as we raise children. It truly "takes a village" as the African proverb reminds us:

> To say "I" am resilient is to be mistaken. The *I* of which we speak is a cultural artifact, a perspective that is social and historical, relational and constructed. Instead, we might better say, "There is resilience in this child and his or her community, family, and culture." Resilience is simultaneously a quality of the individual and the individual's environment. (p. xxiv)

In a nutshell, healthy families create an environment that fosters good family functioning across several platforms. There is no single magic bullet that will guarantee success. Instead, a climate is created and maintained that fosters the expression and maintenance of all those factors that promote good family outcomes and make individuals feel supported and welcomed.

Folk wisdom states that if we are far from our possessions, we are close to our losses. Rephrased, that means that if we are not around to keep an eye on things that matter to us, if we neglect our affairs, we are opening the door to misfortune.

To be a member of a healthy family (or a profitable company), we need to do work, make an investment. Families represent our support networks of choice. Being part of a family, we often have to make minute-by-minute choices: Is this for *me*, or is this for *us*? An understanding and mutually supportive family will ensure space for the fulfillment of both the individual family member (the *me*) and the collective family unit (the *us*). And if the individual does well, the group of the family will celebrate for and with that family member. If times are hard, the family as a whole shares the burden, and its members comfort each other while extending hope.

Families do not just happen out of thin air. Families are built, gesture by gesture and moment by moment, by the actions and experiences of individuals woven together into a rich tapestry of family life.

"What greater blessing to give thanks for than the family."

Engraved on an antique silver platter seen in the
Birmingham Museum of Art

FOCUS POINT

Subsequent partnerships imply that families are joined even though each has its own previous partnership and family history. Transitional anxiety occurs when we change from one situation to the next. Apprehension about the unknown and the desire to maintain homeostasis may imply that different family members will react differently to stress and to transitions. Resilience is embedded in a web of other traits and conditions, many of them based on what happens within the home and within families. Healthy families create an environment that fosters good family functioning across several platforms.

SPOTLIGHT ON THEORIES

Approaches Addressing Family Transitions

As we study families in transition and, in particular, the family structures reflecting those transitions, it becomes apparent that a number of theoretical approaches are useful in providing a lens through which to view these changes and their rippling effects.

Frequently, family theorists reference theories such as the following:

- Attachment theory
- Family systems perspective
- Ecological model (Bronfenbrenner)

These succeed in clarifying aspects of the greater whole. Shannon, Baumwell, and Tamis-LeMonda (2013, p. 256) state that the changing demographics in various cultural contexts create the need for theories that can address the larger entity of these contexts, while also being able to integrate and extend the diverse approaches we currently have at our disposal. We have been served well by theories that address the parental dyad (attachment theory), the traditional family subsystems (the family systems perspective), and the interrelatedness of families and society at large on several levels, ranging from the most innermost and intimate to the large and macrosystemic (ecological theory). According to Shannon, Baumwell, and Tamis-LeMonda our current approaches tend to have originated from cultural contexts associated with developed countries (p. 257). Parenthood and family life can have very different expressions across the diversity of global cultural contexts, and additional research is required to address the insider's, or emic, perspective.

Family stress theory. Some theories address major transition and crisis points in families and societies. The **family stress theory** is such an approach. According to Smith and Hamon (2017, p. 110), it focuses on a particular challenge or task within a family that requires further contextualization and intervention. These authors describe various models that deal with stress-related situations (pp. 112–118). Additionally, these authors summarize the basic assumptions concerning theories that address family stress, and they highlight the essential criteria that co-influence how a family will perceive stress and the degree to which a family will be affected by a stressor (Smith & Hamon, 2017, p. 115):

- *Internal or external.* Is the stressor internal or external to the family?
- *Focus.* Does the stressor focus on one family member or all family members?
- *Onset.* Is the stressor's onset gradual or sudden?
- *Severity.* How severe is the stressor, on a scale from life threatening to mundane?
- *Duration.* How long does the family have to deal with this situation? Is it acute or chronic?
- *Impact.* How will it change the family and its members? Is the change permanent?
- *Natural or intentional.* Is the disaster a natural phenomenon or a willful act (e.g., Hurricane Katrina versus a school shooting)?
- *Locus of control.* Is this a crisis the family can influence by how its members manage it, or is it beyond their control?

Diagram 13.3 illustrates this process of contextualization over time, which in turn influences adaptation.

ABC-X model. Another theoretical approach to studying transitions is the by now historical **ABC-X model** created by Reuben Hill (1949), which focuses on how recovery and family reorganization will proceed. Contributing factors include the nature of the crisis, the period of disorganization that the crisis precipitates, and the recovery process that has to take place (Smith & Hamon, 2017, p. 111).

Double ABC-X model. This approach is a refinement of the initial ABC-X model. The **double ABC-X model** adds the post-crisis period of adjustment. It is attributed to McCubbin and Patterson (1982). They determined that, in a

DIAGRAM 13.3 **In the adaptation process, family resources can strengthen and support a family member by providing a context and influencing how we perceive the challenging events. Combined, these factors contribute to resilience.**

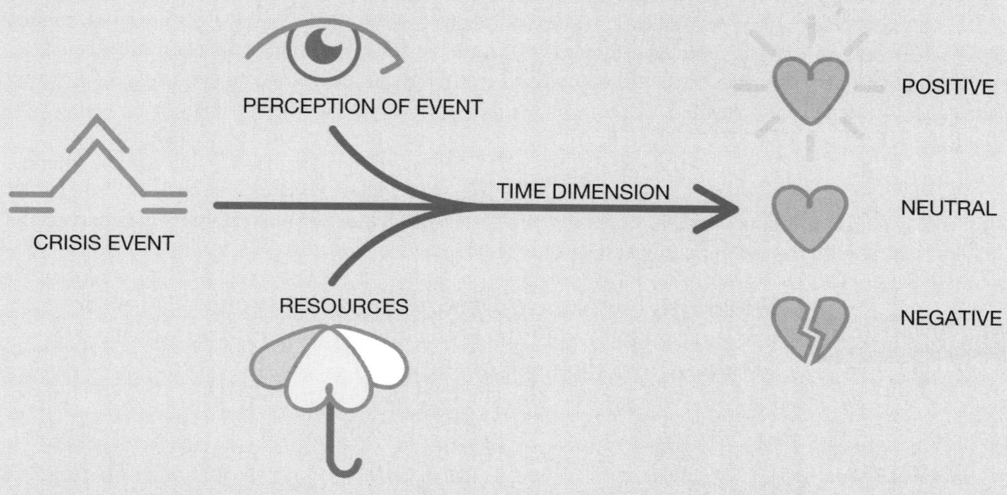

family's attempts to cope with the first precipitating stressor, other secondary stressors may arise. These authors succeeded in pointing out how each antecedent event can influence the subsequent outcomes. In a sense, they posit a circular model as opposed to a linear model in understanding stress and transitions. The journey is seldom easy, as additional challenges arise throughout the journey itself, and sometimes caused by this journey. Transitions can beget more transitions. Stress can beget more stress.

Extreme environmental stress model. Certain life situations such as poverty have intrinsic stressors built into them. Researchers have tried to examine whether racism (overt or covert), social isolation, prejudice, stereotypes, and other societal and cultural factors can co-construct stressful environments that have the potential of influencing psychophysiological responses, which could be transmitted intergenerationally (Bowers & Yehuda, 2016). One study focused on the offspring of Holocaust survivors (Yehuda et al., 2016). Other research, for example the work of Barker and his colleagues (2002), pointed in the direction of environmental stress affecting childhood development. Barker studied the influences on developmental plasticity precipitated by interactions between various prenatal conditions. His initial studies focused predominantly on whether the chronic malnourishment of mothers affected later health outcomes for their offspring.

FAAR model: Family adjustment and adaptation response. Patterson (1988) took the individual stress models a step further by contextualizing them in relation to family circumstances. Families will try to manage stress according to their capacity to deal with these challenges, and they will include their perceptions and interpretations of the situation to help them find the appropriate response. When the crisis exceeds the resources of the family, it precipitates a crisis (Smith & Hamon, 2017, p. 114). The family will actively seek a way of restoring and finding balance by using a variety of resources in various systems, for example, the local system of the family's friends and community.

Patterson (2004) extended her research to point out that resilience is not a specific character trait but rather a combination of factors that include components of capacity and capability in dealing with stress. The resiliency journey is complex and includes a number of dimensions, including protective processes. Aspects

(Continued)

(Continued)

to be considered are the meanings or definitions attached to the risk exposure (normative or not for that particular family) and the protective processes the family can access. For instance, if partners experience severe marital discord, and they are unable to access protective factors to shield them from these stressors, the outcome can lead to marital breakdown. This process is depicted in Diagram 13.4.

Contextual model. This model assesses both internal and external stressors. Internal contributors to stress allow for a degree of control and include changes in such things as family values, beliefs, or structure. For example, an adult family member's decision to go back to school would be considered an internal stressor. External stressors or transitions involve things beyond our reach of control, such as genetics, culture, position in the life cycle, or the major sociocultural, economic, and related events facing our cohort. This is an adaptation of the family stress theory by Boss (2002).

Research on families and how they handle stress has also been closely linked to studies on resilience. Clearly, resilience facilitates the optimal handling of stress.

DIAGRAM 13.4 **When risk factors are overwhelming and protective factors are limited or inadequate, the situation could culminate in a breakdown of the relationship.**

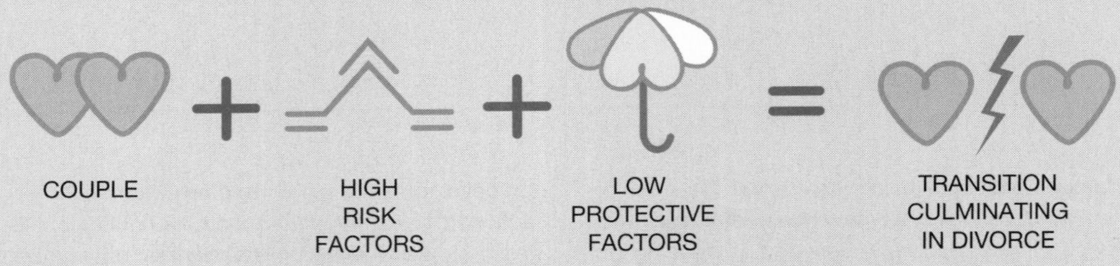

FOCUS POINT

A number of theoretical approaches can be useful in providing a lens with which to view the changes and their rippling effects experienced by families in transition. Various frames of reference are provided by theories that address the parental dyad (attachment theory), the traditional family subsystems (family systems perspective), and the family's interrelatedness with society at large on several levels (ecological theory). Research on resilience has focused on how families manage and recover from stress in challenging circumstances.

In a Nutshell

Approaches Addressing Family Transitions

- Research on families and how they handle stress has also been closely linked to studies on resilience. Clearly, resilience facilitates the optimal handling of stress.
- A number of different theories provide various views regarding how families attempt to handle stress.
- The changing demographics in various cultural contexts create a need for theories that can

address the larger entity of these contexts, while also being able to integrate and extend the diverse approaches we currently have at our disposal.

- Theories that address family stress highlight the essential criteria that co-influence how a family will perceive stress and the degree to which a family will be affected by a stressor. These criteria include whether a stressor is internal or external; its focus, onset, severity, duration, and impact; whether the stressful event is a natural occurrence or an intentional act; and the stressor's locus of control.
- These particular theories, models, and approaches are useful in studying and helping families undergoing transitions:
    - Family stress therapy, which focuses on a particular challenge or task within a family that requires further contextualization and intervention;
    - The ABC-X and double ABC-A models, which focus on how families recover from and reorganize after an initial stressor and the subsequent transitions and challenges that initial stressor creates; and
    - Models such as the extreme environmental stress model, the FAAR model, and the contextual model, which consider multiple stressors and the various contexts affecting their impact and the family's ability to cope, including socioeconomic and cultural factors, family resources, and other internal and external circumstances affecting degree of control.

CHAPTER FOCUS POINTS

Individual Families

- Each family provides a unique context for its members.
- A number of factors contribute to this heterogeneity, including size, composition, age, gender, social context, and the unique psychological climate within a particular family.
- Another important variable relates to the family's lifespan—to the psychological tasks of that family at a given time.

Intergenerational Relationships

- An intergenerational family system fulfills a number of important functions for its members, irrespective of their generation.
- As a system, it offers exchanges in terms of emotional, social, and financial support. Skipped-generation families may experience structured ambivalence because generational expectations regarding roles, responsibilities, and resources compete with actual family circumstances. Competing forces may also make demands on resources in these families.
- Grandparents may be raising grandchildren for a number of compelling reasons, and, in this circumstance, each generation learns from the other.

The Single-Child Family System

- In some Western European countries, the single-child family form has gained prominence, especially in dual career and dual income families.
- Only children, and children in general, are shaped by varied inputs, ranging from micro- to macrosystemic influences.
- Outcomes for only children vary and depend on the parenting styles they experience.

Variations in Family Structure

- Children with siblings maintain a cohort throughout their lifespans, even if brothers and sisters grow apart. Siblings may vie for attention and position.
- Being part of a twin pair, or of multiples, shapes the life experiences and dynamic of the participating children and their parents.
- Children who return to their parental home after having been launched may have to subscribe to implicit and explicit rules.
- Being single can be a conscious choice or an involuntary circumstance. Being single can mean that the duties of family management rest on the shoulders of one person.

Blended Families, Family Transitions, and Healthy Families

- Subsequent partnerships imply that two families are joined even though each has its own previous partnership and family history.
- Transitional anxiety occurs when we change from one situation to the next. Apprehension about the unknown and the desire to maintain homeostasis may imply that different family members will react differently to stress and to transitions.
- Resilience is embedded in a web of other traits and conditions, many of them based on what happens within the home and within families.
- Healthy families create an environment that fosters good family functioning across several platforms.

Spotlight on Theories: Approaches Addressing Family Transitions

- A number of theoretical approaches can be useful in providing a lens with which to view the changes and their rippling effects as experienced by families in transition.
- Various frames of reference are provided by theories that address
    - the parental dyad (attachment theory),
    - the traditional family subsystems (family systems perspective), and
    - the family's interrelatedness with society at large on several levels (ecological theory).
- Research on resilience has focused on how families manage and recover from stress in challenging circumstances.

CHAPTER

14

Dynamics of Culture and Change

Learning Outcomes

After studying this chapter, you should be able to

1. Consider the *dynamics of change* and how these dynamics affect cultural expression.
2. Describe the unique dynamics and challenges faced by *international families*.
3. Analyze the process of *assimilation* by describing how it occurs and the implications of being exposed to the cultural content of the host culture.
4. Examine why *communication* is an essential part of cultural identity, and reflect on the implications of learning languages in addition to one's mother tongue.
5. Distinguish between *enculturation* and *acculturation* by highlighting the differences and similarities of these processes.

Culture and Change

Dynamics of change. Change is the essence of dynamics. Life is characterized by change. We are constantly evolving, growing, changing, maturing, aging. Change also occurs in our surroundings—the day-night cycles, the rhythm of the seasons. Some of us seek change; we want novelty or adventure, perhaps. These impulses may lead us to change our surroundings. We exchange the landscapes of familiarity with those of novelty.

The demographics of families in the twenty-first century are changing rapidly and dramatically; often these changes are driven by the direct and indirect effects of globalization. Family forms that were the norm until recently are under threat. Families relocate and are fragmented through voluntary or involuntary migratory patterns, for example, because they are lured to other countries by better opportunities or because war, famine, and other disasters mean they have to move to survive.

In immigrant families, cultural uprooting and the demands to assimilate affect parenting and place parents in different cultural contexts from their own offspring. High-pressure and ruthless economic demands are stealing parent-child time and facilitate child exploitation. There is a multilevel disinvestment in the family as an institution—some of it intentional and some unintended. This disinvestment is changing the cultural fabric of our society and the futures of families. Serious efforts are required to contain the destructive effects of globalization, while also nurturing those initiatives that carve out better futures for the world's children and their families (Steger, 2017; Trask, 2010).

Restless feet. The U.S. Federal Interagency Forum on Child and Family Statistics reported in 2011 that about one fifth of children living in the United States can claim one foreign-born parent. For each of these children—one in five—there is a story. Each child probably has a second language other than English, a culture of origin, and challenges adapting, assimilating, and, ultimately, integrating into the mainstream or host culture. These immigrant families may try to juggle both cultural and ethnic value systems, the old and the new. They become bicultural being exposed to cultural forces from two or more contexts.

Additionally, 3 percent of children are foreign-born themselves, with one foreign-born parent. These figures have been steadily and undeniably swelling: from about 15 percent of the population claiming one foreign-born parent in 1994, the numbers have risen to 23 percent in 2010. In the United States, as per the 2010 U.S. Census, approximately 9 million individuals (or 2.9 percent of the population) described themselves as multiracial. Even though many of these persons may not have translocated during their own lifetimes, they represent a blending and meeting of ethnicities and cultures. They are also a tangible sign that the demographic face of the United States is transforming. Clearly, the transformations spurred by globalization will affect family dynamics.

Any study of globalization and families must consider worldwide mobility—the various voluntary and involuntary migratory patterns—and the concomitant effects of this mobility on families. Some families have the choice to be mobile; they leave their countries of origin to permanently emigrate, to seek educational opportunities, or to live and work temporarily in other countries. Others undergo these transitions involuntarily because they are in war zones and have to flee or the poverty is crippling and the conditions do not support family survival. The overall picture of families on the move addresses both the brightest and darkest prospects (Lazaridis, 2011).

Delving back into our own roots as a species, we know that many families adopted a nomadic lifestyle. Humans followed the lure of food, and as hunter-gatherers, they uprooted regularly for survival (Manning, 2013; Marsella & Ring, 2003). Once agriculture and livestock provided more predictable sustenance, families could afford to be vested in their land. Permanence versus mobility seems ultimately to pivot on the instinct for survival. Those who went before us had restless feet. Over the span of about 200+ generations, large groups of people migrated across continents, walking step by step. To paraphrase the first astronaut to walk on the moon, this migration may have been a small step for each individual, but added up it represented a giant leap for humankind. Historically, movements by groups of people have shaped nations. The current DNA-based research confirms extended migrations of various population groups.

Some more recent examples are the emigrants who left Ireland during the potato blight, pinning their hopes on foreign shores. Religious persecution has been the motive for seeking greener pastures also. The Huguenots left France to seek religious freedom. After the partition of India in 1947, countless families relocated. The United States has strong immigrant underpinnings. When the relocations are initiated by political unrest, persecution, war, or major threats to survival, they are accompanied by much pain and suffering, and an entire generation may be scarred by the emotional trauma these events elicit.

Families undergo this upheaval for many reasons. They can move temporarily so that a family member can study or find employment, or they can move to be reunited with other family members and loved ones. An individual could have been adopted internationally, or the family's breadwinner might work as an expat in a foreign country, for instance, for a large international company, the military, or in international relations. Immigrants have various legal standings, too. They can be legal immigrants or illegal or legal refugees. Academics can work in a variety of international educational contexts and contribute to the transformations occurring through higher learning (Altbach & Yudkevich, 2017). Underlying these demographic shifts are economic and social pressures and prospects—the grass is perceived as greener on the other side, even though a popular idiom also attributes this phenomenon to the prevalence of manure.

As family scientists, we are concerned with the effects of these transitions on families and, specifically, on the children in these families. Every move is accompanied by various degrees of expected and unexpected disorientation, even trauma. The involuntary moves may be of greater concern; many families on the move have little or no choice in the matter. Global movement may separate and split families (Mavroudi & Nagel, 2016).

For most of these families, poverty is also part of the packet of challenges. Immigrant parents and their offspring may find it harder to get a grip on the economic ladder and to secure appropriate living conditions and employment opportunities because of language barriers, educational limitations, and acculturation problems. The Federal Interagency Forum on Child and Family Statistics reported in 2011 that one third of the foreign-born children living in the United States lived in poverty, and living conditions were characterized by overcrowding. For a child growing up in this milieu, the simplest tasks, such as doing homework, may represent an obstacle. Add English as a second language and the scholastic challenges escalate further. On the positive side, immigrant parents are well aware of the doors of opportunity opened through education, and they can go to the other extreme of pressuring their children to achieve and excel. With youth on their side, the younger generation has the distinct advantage of being able to master English more easily than their parents. These children become the literal and cultural translators for their families and represent a bilingual and bicultural segment of the American society. This adds yet another layer of diversity to an already heterogeneous nation.

Globalization, international work opportunities, and social mobility entice families into venturing beyond cultural familiarity, toward what promises to be a "greener pasture on the other side of the fence." But immigrant families, or those hoping to become immigrant families, face many obstacles. Tighter border control and immigration regulations result in physical boundaries and bureaucratic thresholds, serving as barriers to manage the influx of migrants and to control their access to employment and other benefits of citizenship. When the pressures are great enough, refugees and illegal immigrants may sacrifice their closest and dearest in the pursuit of a better quality of life or survival. Sometimes family units are fragmented, lives are lost, and the hope for a better future remains elusive or becomes the prize for an arduous journey.

On the other hand, globalization has created opportunities in countless contexts. There is a constant exchange of goods and ideas, and international work opportunities have encouraged some social mobility. The flipside of the coin reveals a darker and more shameful truth. According to Polakoff (2007), free trade and the international collaborations that have been sanctioned through economic globalization have also left large segments of the population in developing countries, and in countries delivering labor in manufacturing plants and other production facilities, vulnerable to abject poverty and exploitation. These conditions draw in children as well. Although there is a strong movement to abolish child labor and to regulate labor practices stringently, the risk remains, and there is tangible evidence that the exploitation of illegal child labor has yet to see its last day. When it comes to underage labor, the entire family is involved because the family may not see any other opportunities for survival but to sacrifice the children. Additionally, the children producing the work are precluded from educational opportunities and exposed to dangerous environments and practices, precipitating human rights violations with lifelong effects for the children concerned.

"A people without the knowledge of their past history, origin and culture, is like a tree without roots."

Marcus Garvey

Globalization and poverty. There are clear and definite links between globalization, world poverty, and child labor. These practices foreclose on the childhood of individual children and on their educational opportunities and therefore their future employability (Polakoff, 2007). This condition, in turn, affects both their families of procreation and their families of origin, and fixes an intergenerational cycle of poverty. It is crucial that international as well as domestic laws prohibit the practices involving child labor and child exploitation. These abominable practices extend beyond the factory floor; children are exploited for warfare and for the sex trade. Their childhood is stolen from them, and their families and their societies feel the effects and pay for the outcomes of these social injustices.

UNICEF confirms that more children are involved in child labor than we dare imagine. The organization estimates that, in the least developed countries, approximately one in four children aged 5 to 17 were "engaged in labour that is considered detrimental to their health and development" (UNICEF, 2017). And the number of victimized children worldwide runs into the millions. Children are used and exploited in dangerous situations, such as in wars and in mines. In the sex trade, they get groomed for roles that rob them of their innocence and their health, and they are forced to enter a seedy world that children should not even know about. Irresponsible, greedy, and unethical adults sanction these practices, and it will take many more adults backed by legislation and public policy to intervene and abolish these child-focused violations once and for all.

Child labor is a manifestation of societal and economic problems that are linked to economic globalization. Work environments may expose laborers, including children, to harmful pollutants including teratogens, which can affect the unborn children of pregnant laborers. According to Polakoff (2007), these forces have penetrated deep into the international society; they have crossed boundaries, reaching virtually the most inaccessible parts of our world and leaving in their wake misery, social exclusion, diminished hope, fewer opportunities, and, of course, the huge elephant in the room: global poverty.

Tree of Life at Night, a work by ceramic artist Anton Bosch, depicts the interrelatedness and interconnectedness of systems. Our rootedness in our cultural past influences the present and the future.

Source: Tree of Life at Night/Anton Bosch.

Cultural identity. Children who reach adolescence are not out of the emotional danger zone. An important developmental task of adolescence is the formation of a personal and cultural identity. Adolescents have to take positions toward values, beliefs, notions about relationships, spirituality and religion, politics, social constructs, and more; these add up, shaping and contributing to their personal

FOCUS POINT

Change is the essence of dynamics. The demographics of families in the twenty-first century are changing dramatically, fueled by globalization. Frequently, in modern society, there is a multilevel disinvestment in the family as an institution, which changes the cultural fabric of our society and the futures of families. Poverty forces families to relocate. Political dynamics underlie the refugee crisis. As globalization spreads, emerging adults grow up in a hyperconnected context through media exposure and advertising, which, in turn, affects cultural identity and fuels consumerism.

identity (Bigner & Gerhardt, 2019, p. 88). Clearly, adolescents and emerging adults have to find their way through a variety of cultural contexts to integrate these into their personal self-concepts, and a formal process of **cultural integration** will occur in which they choose and integrate the components of various cultural inputs. This process goes beyond immigration; it is a *cultural identity path* that adolescents have to carve out for themselves (Jensen & Arnett, 2012, p. 477).

Globalization affects the world, so few adolescents or emerging adults grow up in an isolated monocultural context that can escape the effects of media culture (Jensen & Arnett, 2012). If they live in developed countries, chances are that they are connected via social media and various Internet-based sites, as well as through cultural products such as television and cinema. Consequently, they see and are exposed to the knowledge that their own culture is not the only culture (Gunkel, Schlaegel, & Taras, 2016). Increasingly, their world may also contain interactions with persons from other cultures, and through advertising, they may be made aware of a material world that includes all the beckoning brand labels of consumerism. Be it for better or for worse, these multicultural influences exist and tend to reach, even target, adolescents. In developing countries, there is a chance that the tentacles of the media have not quite reached the very rural and isolated areas, but even that presumption is changing.

> **"Give me your tired, your poor, / Your huddled masses yearning to breathe free."**
>
> Emma Lazarus (1849–1887), from the poem "The New Colossus," which was inscribed on a plaque and placed on the inner wall of the pedestal of the Statue of Liberty, New York

Dynamics of International Families

Culture and family dynamics. The cultural dimension is a cornerstone in the context of family life. It is of utmost importance because it reflects, among other things, the values, beliefs, and attitudes of persons sharing a culture, and these, in turn, influence rituals, family life transitions, parenting, and more. Religious values and beliefs incorporate dimensions of cultural values and beliefs and vice versa. Culture's visible and invisible tentacles reach into the furthest corners of family life, to the extent that the dominant cultural values within a family will become a virtual instruction manual as to how things are done in that particular family or group.

Psychologically based definitions of culture typically point to a shared information base that contains values, attitudes, and beliefs; these dimensions are said to be transmitted intergenerationally and between members through a sophisticated process of teaching, learning, and imitation. Change is possible—the tempo of the change being dictated by several interacting factors. This information base enhances a family's chances for survival and can contribute to perceptions regarding quality of life because it defines what is regarded as important in the family's culture and, hence, links to the family's experience of well-being. It provides a platform for stability, as the shared content becomes a shorthand and a code for participating members. Subscribing to the same culture imparts a sense of belonging and understanding because members of a cultural group become insiders and are privy to understanding the code of that specific culture (Bigner & Gerhardt, 2019). When a family makes a global move, when it relocates, it is immersed in change, much of it cultural change, and this can be bewildering and challenging.

Changing cultural contexts creates the cultural disorientation felt by transitioning persons. As we change the country or region where we live, there is a good chance that we also change the cultural context. Regular travelers, expats, and so-called citizens of the world may find it easier to negotiate these changes, as they have experienced them so often that they may subscribe to a **third culture**, the product of blending *cultures of origin* with the *host cultures*. For others, however, changing cultures may be as disorienting as changing the music mid-dance. When one is still anticipating the rhythm of a familiar tango, the sudden change to a waltz requires a whole new angle of attack. It is one thing if a person knows and anticipates this change but another if the individual is facing the unknown. Parents and their children are in different cultural places emotionally, as each generation's formative years contain a different mix of cultural input.

For refugees and persons seeking opportunities for economic survival, the luxury of *cultural acclimatization* is out of reach, and it may take an entire generation for a family system to slowly conform to the beat of a different cultural drum.

Parents are usually selfless when it comes to their family's well-being. They make unthinkable sacrifices to reach for improved outcomes. Whatever is asked of them, they will try to oblige if it is in the best interest of their offspring. They may even separate as a family to make important goals possible. Extended educations, apprenticeships, work demands: if these are part of the entry fee to the promised land, grandparents are pulled on board to bridge childcare gaps and offer general support, even if they do so in their countries of origin while their adult children are trying to find a foothold in the host country. If they have higher education, immigrant parents may have to re-qualify professionally to establish credentials in the country they are migrating to. Alternatively, they may wish to take work of any kind immediately in order to establish themselves financially and set up a home with the infrastructure that can support a family. In other cases, immigrants ask their parents to follow them once they have established themselves and their offspring. The possibilities are strongly dependent on immigration legislation.

Sometimes, young children left behind in the "home country" are reunited with their immigrant parents only when it is time for those children to enter the formal education system; these children can face major challenges in emotional attachment to parents because the critical window for attachment has passed. Negotiating the new host culture and language is an arduous process. Under favorable circumstances, these children may reap the benefits of having two or more cultures at their fingertips, making them a good fit for jobs on the international stage. The long-term and more pervasive effects relating to attachment and family loyalties can vary greatly, however, and are influenced by the quality of care and emotional support offered by the grandparents.

If the lead breadwinner works internationally while the rest of the family remains in another location, that parent is coparenting from a distance. The lead parent is the constant point of reference for the children and provides the dominant influence. In other situations, the family members live as expats, and to facilitate educational continuity, older children may attend boarding schools in the country of origin. In terms of a cultural identity, they embrace what is lovingly referred to as a "third culture," a hybrid of the two cultures to which they have been exposed.

Cultural globalization has implications for parenting practices as well. For families migrating from rural to urban contexts, from developing to developed countries, from agricultural to industrialized environments, from collective to individualistic societies, there are giant leaps to be made to cross the geographical and cultural divides. Much of the global movement is from developing to developed countries, as families are seeking to improve their living conditions. What these families seek may include the wish for better educational opportunities for their children, a higher standard of living, improved medical care, or a peaceful environment away from the ravages of war and economic instability.

The immigrant family may have distinct cultural and ethnic values related to intergenerational families, perhaps accepting such families as the norm rather than being wary of this family form. Shared resources may ease the threats of poverty and enhance the lives of all the family's participating members. Latino families, for example, are more likely to have three generations living under one roof, which makes economic sense and is in line with the cultural values of this group. African American families may reveal strong intergenerational cohesion as well. Across ethnicities, higher levels of education in the older generation may support the expression and appreciation of the value of intergenerational relationships. Even so, the results from various ethnic groups need to be controlled for socioeconomic status, specifically poverty (Edin & Kassane, 2010), to place these relationships within their larger context. Clearly, a number of factors interact in the expression of closeness between generations.

> **"Globalization is not only something that will concern and threaten us in the future, but something that is taking place in the present and to which we must first open our eyes."**
>
> Ulrich Beck (1944– 2015), German sociologist who studied modernization and globalization

FOCUS POINT

The cultural dimension is a cornerstone in the context of family life. It is of utmost importance because it reflects, among other things, the values, beliefs, and attitudes of persons sharing a culture, and these, in turn, influence rituals, family life transitions, parenting, and more. Culture reaches into the furthest corners of family life. The larger cultural context within which the family's culture is embedded is also significant, and there is a bidirectional influence. Psychologically based definitions of culture describe a shared information base that contains values, attitudes, and beliefs; these dimensions are transmitted intergenerationally and between members through learning. Changing cultural contexts create the cultural disorientation felt by transitioning persons. A *third culture* is the product of blending a *culture of origin* with a *host culture*.

Authentic Insight

The Family Quilt

In a sheltered corner of our home hangs our wedding photo. We smile with the innocence of youth, the joy of anticipation. Shiny hair, peachy faces—virtually unscarred by life's experiences and the accompanying lessons. That was several decades ago. There are other treasured photos. A double window frame has been filled with images of generations back: the families of origin. There they stand, little groups of people. Great grandmother, my namesake, is pictured in a blurry haze of Victorian lace and a stern expression. Great grandfather is in military uniform, a ceremonial sword by his side. My maternal grandfather has a pointed beard, round glasses, and the same heart-shaped lips as my mom.

The pictures move forward through the generations. An image of my parents shows them surrounded by at least two dozen bouquets of flowers, my mother wearing a formal dark suit. Childhood pictures of my own generation are also present, including one of my brother as a cuddly toddler. My sister's children are here: my niece, inquisitive and engaged, at the tender age of four. Move forward in time. My children join the crowd, and then, as the youngest representatives of this generational line-up, so do my own granddaughters, with the expectancy of youth in their faces.

The visual recordings span a good century and then some. Six generations were represented, I counted them . . . and then I wondered whose genes went where? Who was responsible for that creative genetic material that made some of us artistic? Who loved music, and who had a fragile constitution? Who was the thrill seeker? Who was secretive? Virtues and vices are shaken up, surfacing again in new combinations. Who were these people, really?

A few photos are missing. There is only one wedding photograph, a solitary memento marking the beginning of my own marital journey. There could be no other wedding photographs. The person who had captured these moments had lost his life prematurely in a cruel accident involving a gas explosion. He had given us a few proofs, but his recordings of family events had stopped midway through his short life. I wondered about the lost images. Had the negatives been destroyed in a major cleanup? Were they silently and patiently waiting in an attic somewhere as people moved houses, celebrated birthdays, and simply moved on?

Sometimes in life, we simply cannot complete the cycles we had wanted or intended. We cannot record every event. We cannot reach across time. The quality of our wedding and ensuing marriage was not influenced by whether we did or did not have photos. Life swells and ebbs in its own way. Members of each generation live within the boundaries and confines of their personal lives, firmly anchored in the here and now. With a little bonus, lives overlap and continue forward.

Recently I traveled across continents for a major family reunion. From the oldest to the youngest, all generations were represented—four generations linked by name, by tradition, and by visible and invisible family connections. The metaphoric mantle of love was placed around my shoulders, and the family ties were knotted more firmly as we revisited and rediscovered places and relationships. We moved forward and backward in time. I discovered important family truths. But as one of the older members of the family, I was asked many things as well. What was Great-Grandma really like? Could she possibly be the genetic culprit for the idiosyncrasies of some of the offspring? We pieced it together like a complex mosaic, trying to see an intergenerational picture.

As I tried to unlock some of the family secrets for the younger members, someone in my circle reciprocated. In that big group of people collectively called "family," someone was giving me hope for the future while completing a segment of my past. Unknown to me, the missing puzzle pieces were being filled in. The family was lovingly completing what needed completion—while I was blissfully unaware of what was being done for me, the treasure given to me.

After almost thirty years of wandering from one storage space to another, a forgotten box had found its way home. My niece was reunited with all the negatives of photos taken by her late father. My niece, no longer the four-year-old youngster on my wall of family photographs, was now the mother of grown offspring. And so she had done what only the dearest and closest of kin can do: she had captured the soap bubbles of my youth, her youth, our family by putting together the many images her father had captured of us over the decades—images of promise, of love, of childhoods lost and refound, of threads of connection over years and over continents. And in the process, she also reunited me with my wedding photographs.

She offered more than images capturing treasured moments; she had succeeded in filling in the blanks of personal stories, and, importantly, she had reintroduced her late father to our family circle. She had kept his memory alive and completed tasks he was not able to complete. Through his photos, he rejoined us; his presence was felt. Printed, cherished, and eternalized, the photos remind us not only of special rituals and transitions in our lives but also of the love of families, from one generation to the next. The way that families can step in for one another, can carry us when we need carrying, and can nurture us when we thought we were forsaken. Mementos such as these teach us that we stand on the foundations of those who went before us and that we reach forward to guide those who will succeed us.

We cannot truly reach across and beyond the boundaries of each personal life, except through oral and recorded history—through remembrances, keepsakes, and photographs. That is why reunions are so important. We pass on the baton of collective memory; we piece together the patches of the family quilt.

Family ties bind us for better or for worse from one generation to the next. Over time, they knit us together in desired and undesired moments, in awareness and in blissful ignorance—but definitely for the long haul. Together, as a family, we are more; the sum is greater than the parts. Together we form an endless chain, linked from one generation to the next.

Clara Gerhardt, in honor of my namesake Clara Wiehahn

Dynamics of Assimilation

Frequently the destination culture is idealized until the family settles in it. After a traumatic landing in the host culture, the culture of origin may be idealized. In the old country, the ways were familiar and the social exchanges understandable. How do parents raise their children in this new environment, and to what cultural values will they subscribe? Assimilation also depends on how different the culture of origin is from the new hosting culture. Ultimately, a hybrid style develops. A point of contention between parents and their offspring is frequently the degree to which each culture can play a role in personal lives.

Parents and children who have immigrated come from two different cultural places; the children can never be enculturated in exactly the same way as the parents were, as they have to find their feet and acculturate to the new host culture. The disappointments may be many, and families may feel disillusioned by not finding the anticipated greener pasture in the new country. A saying attributed to the early Italian immigrants that passed through Ellis Island into the United States reflects the often unrealistic expectations of immigrants: "In America, the streets are paved with gold." The new arrivals would find that there was no gold, and what was even more sobering, the roads had to be constructed by the newcomers.

As much as the immigrant parents in the parental dyad may feel proud that their offspring are absorbing the language of the host culture by virtual osmosis and can act as literal and cultural translators, these parents may add even more demands on their offspring because of the bicultural situation. Children can explain the nuances of the new culture to the rest of the family, and, because of their bilingualism, they feel at home in both cultural contexts. In this instance, it is the youngest generation in the intergenerational triad that may have the greatest chance of becoming competent in the new environment, and members of this generation may be asked to offer support to the generations above them.

Cultural demands. Parents may place visible and invisible cultural demands on their children. A visible and tangible demand could be complying with a dress code, and a less tangible demand might be acting in accordance with cultural values. The family may continue to follow dietary preferences from its culture of origin, seek out these foods, and expect children to fall into the same patterns. Food preferences are remarkably consistent, even in families exposed to globalization, and food can become the connecting factor that binds the family, especially during celebrations and days of religious significance. The parents, or the immigrating dyad, may have made the physical move to a new cultural context, but they maintain their *separateness* as they hold onto some expressions from their culture of origin, and they are cautious concerning the ways of the host culture (Ward & Geeraert, 2016).

Parents may demand various degrees of conformity to old-country traditions, going as far as insisting on having a say in their child's choice of a life partner. In some cultures, the pressures are high to marry from the same cultural, racial, and religious background. Parents may go as far as matching their child to a future spouse from their country of origin. When these marriages occur, partners often experience a dissonance in terms of their level of cultural adaptation. The newly "imported" spouse may experience *culture shock*, while the spouse who has been partly assimilated into the host culture may not fully understand the challenges his or her partner is facing. Marrying from the same cultural background has both advantages and disadvantages. The interpersonal demands that contribute to the success of a partnership remain the same, and a mere cultural match cannot ensure a successful pairing. Mutual understanding of the partner's cultural background may be a facilitator in that the couple can understand and access shared cultural codes. Going beyond the shared cultural heritage, the individual challenges of acculturation remain. Being part of a supportive community and engaging in procivic behaviors that are vested in the host country contribute to a successful transition. Parents also have to realize that their children can never share the cultural content of the country of origin totally because the children are being raised in a different cultural context and their acculturation to the host culture demands bicultural values and experiences.

> **"Acculturation is an unfolding process of change arising from intercultural contact."**
>
> Ward and Geeraert (2016)

Cultural appropriation and cultural plagiarism. In scholarly and intellectual property contexts, the word *plagiarism* denotes forms of appropriation, which strongly resemble stealing. Importantly, it means that intellectual property (including cultural expressions in various forms) is used and appropriated without permission or acknowledgment. Plagiarism disguises the original context of the creation, so the craftspersons, artists, designers, innovators, and creators do not gain recognition or benefit from the appropriated material, which, in essence, is their intellectual property. In select cases, the fashion and design industries have been called out for appropriating cultural expressions, often without acknowledging sources, while passing appropriation off as inspiration. The "excuse" that is often offered when the appropriator is caught out is to say that the appropriation was done respectfully, that the end product was created with aesthetic intent. But this does not condone the fact that a creative work was appropriated without acknowledgment or permission or that the original creators probably do not benefit from that use or appropriation.

The rules for sharing intellectual property are complex, but ignoring the source and original context of something one borrows is problematic, as is using that borrowed and non-referenced material for personal gain. Folk and ethnic expressions of artistry have deep-rooted cultural connections and contexts. These roots should be respected, acknowledged, and honored.

Cultural misappropriation. Cultural misappropriation, at times also referred to as cultural appropriation, can occur when a cultural outsider lays claim to cultural products, symbols, and expressions that are typical of another cultural context. An important element in determining whether cultural misappropriation has occurred is assessing the underlying *meaning* and *intent* when cultural content is used outside its original context. If the appropriated symbol or content is used in any way that is insulting, demeaning, incorrect, or culturally insensitive, or if its use references a painful historic or social reality or injustice, then that use is misappropriation and amounts to a lack of cultural sensitivity displayed through acts of cultural disrespect. In escalated situations, the cultural group whose cultural symbols have been misappropriated can feel violated and alienated. From a social dynamic standpoint, cultural misappropriation alters the dynamic relationships between the parties. Misappropriating symbols that are emotionally laden with significance, for example, religious symbols, can amount to disrespect.

Assimilation. Inappropriate cultural appropriation should not be confused with a genuine and respectful meeting of cultures, during which fruitful cultural exchanges are bound to occur and learning about other cultures can be a way of reaching out and connecting. Assimilation, acculturation, and other cultural exchanges can occur in constructive and voluntary contexts. They evolve as a result of individuals or groups fusing and blending various cultural components in an evolutionary process.

Typical expressions of constructive cultural fusion have occurred in music and in the culinary arts (food and cooking). Children in bicultural families or growing up in multicultural contexts will fuse and blend various cultural threads as well. This blending of cultures is part of the process of assimilation in which people from one culture adopt customs from a different culture while constructing and identifying with a new hybrid cultural context.

On the other hand, uneven assimilation can cause major difficulties between the generations in an immigrant family. Culture shock refers to the disorientation experienced by some persons trying to acclimatize to cultural content that is unfamiliar and overwhelming.

Cultural competence. An important influence on family dynamics is whether differences in culture are respected, both inside the family itself and in the family's external environment. Helping professionals and family scientists should display cultural competence by respecting and trying to understand the unique cultural contexts of their clients. Cultural competence represents a willingness to learn about another person's culture, without accessing preconceived ideas, even stereotypes.

Historical underpinnings. The history of humankind is also a history of migration; it is filled with the meetings of different cultures that have expanded and influenced each others' shared cultural heritage, for better or for worse.

Here are some of the processes and cautionary concerns that occur when cultures meet and blend in our present age of globalization:

- *Assimilation:* Constructive mutual influence and the blending of cultures will occur as part of the assimilation process; these should not be confused with cultural plagiarism, appropriation, and misappropriation.

- *Acknowledgment of sources:* The original sources, cultural contexts, and creators of intellectual and/or cultural property should be acknowledged and respected.
- *Intellectual property:* This material, especially if it is culturally sensitive, should not be appropriated for personal gain while ignoring the original creators. Doing so amounts to a form of intellectual theft.
- *Misappropriation:* Be cautious. When an original cultural symbol or context is distorted and changed to mean something new or even negative, it amounts to misappropriation. Additionally, misappropriation contaminates the symbol for the original creators and users of that symbolic content.

Authentic Insight

Not so Different: Cultural Similarities

Recently, I worked with a group of internationally trained physical therapists preparing to sit for their licensing exams. They had been in the United States for only a short time. During our interactions, it became clear that they had the same desires and aspirations that I had (and still have) when I arrived in this country over two decades ago. They want to do well as practicing therapists, use their skills to rehabilitate those entrusted to them, improve their patients' and their own lives, and be embraced as colleagues within the field. We may have arrived in the United States at different times, under varying circumstances, and express our dreams in unique ways, but there is a common thread—the desire to serve professionally and to assimilate with the people in our new home and adopted country.

In my conversations with this group, I recognized the same challenges I had faced. One is lack of knowledge about the backgrounds and cultures of internationally trained therapists—among both employers and the general public. Assimilation is a two-way process; we must put forth the effort to learn and adapt to this new culture, and we hope our efforts are supported. It is quite challenging to shed some of our cultural norms, and to translate our thoughts into English. I recall instructing a patient to put her hands on the mat, lift her body off the mat by straightening her elbows, and then swing her hips to the left, only to learn I could have said, "Scoot over to your left." I wasn't dumb; I was thinking how I would instruct this patient in my native language, and I translated the instructions word for word. I could tell my coworkers at that time thought otherwise. Wouldn't it have been helpful if they had simply taught me the current terminology, the right words to use? Maybe I should have asked; after all it's a shared responsibility.

In our efforts to do well, we develop a fear of making errors, and we become overly sensitive to criticism. Consequently, we become cautious and guarded. I believe this is when a support system for acculturation can be valuable.

As an educator, when I ask my graduating American students what they hope to accomplish in the field, their responses are familiar and echo all those desires the internationally trained students were expressing as well. The main difference is internationally trained therapists face additional barriers and challenges. This makes me wonder what would happen if we incorporated acculturation into the orientation process of internationally trained therapists in the context of patient care, while also stepping up our own cultural competence levels? Could this level the playing field?

You may ask, "Why bother?" The answer is simple: Like their peers, they are therapists who interact with clients, and first and foremost we should do no harm—not to our clients, and not to each other.

Nelson Marquez, EdD, is a licensed physical therapist and vice president for institutional effectiveness and research for Webber International University.

FOCUS POINT

Frequently, the destination culture is idealized until the family settles in its new surroundings. The degree to which social exchanges are understandable depends on how different the culture of origin is from the new hosting culture. Ultimately, a hybrid cultural style develops. Parents may place visible and invisible cultural demands on their children and require various degrees of conformity, especially to cultural heritage. Individual challenges of acculturation remain. Being part of a supportive community and engaging in procivic behaviors that are vested in the host country contribute to a successful transition. Parents need to acknowledge that their children can never totally share the cultural content of the country of origin because the children are being raised in a different cultural context and their acculturation to the host culture demands bicultural values and experiences.

Adolescence and assimilation. Adolescents may find it remarkably difficult to emigrate and relocate, despite their emotional willingness to explore the world of adults. They have formed peer groups, and they attach utmost value to this social system that extends beyond the family. If traumatic circumstances force them to relocate, as in the case of being refugees, additional trauma occurs.

Identity formation, which is also anchored in cultural identity, extends well into emerging adulthood (Jensen & Arnett, 2012). The risk of being flung across cultures like jetsam is that it may invite antisocial and anti-civic behavior patterns.

These potential outcomes occur because the identity with and loyalty for the new culture of the host country have not yet been crystallized, and there is a void where the culture of origin had been. Adolescents may feel *marginalized* as they are crossing the bridge between cultures. They have left behind one familiar cultural context, but they have not yet been fully acculturated into the host culture. The need for a peer group and the urgency to feel included can lead to poor choices, especially if the host culture's cultural codes remain elusive. This sense of isolation opens the door to falling in with the wrong crowd and to behaving in ways that may have undesirable outcomes. At this time, parental guidance is crucial, but if parents are both working long hours to secure the family's survival, parental supervision may be at its lowest. Frequently, the adolescents have to be substitute parents as they babysit younger siblings, which places additional strain on the system and leaves the adolescents little time to dedicate to scholastic pursuits.

On the positive side is that adolescence is also characterized by plasticity and adaptability. These youngsters can absorb the new accent and make it their own, integrate with the host culture in ways that elude their parent, and truly use the opportunities offered by the host culture, which will probably soon feel like their own cultural reference point (Ward & Geeraert, 2016).

> **"It is impossible to live outside the culture we're born into. Our communities claim us from the start, extending a thousand tentacles of possession."**
>
> Carol Shields (1935–2003), American-born Canadian author, from her novel *The Republic of Love* (1992)

Culture and Communication

Language is an admission ticket to a culture (Hayakawa). Language development occurs at lightning speed, and within the first three years of birth, a complete, though simple language system is in place. Other languages can be added, preferably one by one and linked to either a person or place so that the child has a way of separating the languages. Mixing them all in one conversation is not a good idea. Until early adolescence, appropriate pronunciation will also fall into place unwittingly. Due to their age, immigrant parents can hardly ever attain a native speaker's accent, and often fluency in the language of their adopted country is hampered.

The kids have it made, and for parents struggling with language difficulties, children act as interpreters. This in itself shifts the power balance between parents and their offspring because perfect language mastery opens an invisible cultural door for the children, a door that provides entry into the community and familiarity with the cultural components of the new country. It allows them to join the dominant cultural group—at least in terms of language and communication.

> **"The fact is that immigrants come here from every part of the world, and, in a generation or so, have all kinds of successful careers . . . But for these opportunities to open up immigrants and their descendants must learn English as quickly as possible, that's the admission ticket to the culture."**
>
> Samuel Ichiye Hayakawa (1906–1992), Canadian-born American of Japanese ancestry, linguist, semanticist, and English professor who served as a U.S. senator for California

Culture and Socialization

Culture is like an invisible veil that enfolds us. We look at the world through it; it colors our perceptions. Culture is also a blueprint of the mind. It represents the preplanned ways we can think about things, the rituals we engage in, and the nuances of our connections with our fellow beings. It's a blueprint in the way that the architect's blueprint can guide the builder to make the architect's vision a reality. Subtly, it provides a structure within which we can place meaning, and it gives meaning in short cuts and abbreviated ways, so that we can understand and connect socially in a predictable manner that is instantly understood by our fellow cultural travelers.

Culture is also like a computer operating system; it is always working in the background, and all the other programs run on top of this system and use it as a launching platform. There are a number of formal definitions of culture, and over time, they have changed as our insights have shifted. A streamlined and simple definition is this: "Culture involves shared attitudes, beliefs, norms, roles, and self-definitions" (Triandis, 1996). Here is another definition: "Culture is a set of attitudes, behaviors, and symbols shared by a group of people and usually communicated from one generation to the next" (Shiraev & Levy, 2016, p. 25).

We know that this mental material is collective because we identify with a group that shares these ideations with us. For that reason, it is an easy jump forward to think that all people from one place or country who are of the same race, ethnicity, or language group may share cultural values because they share other components of the formula as well. Yes and no: they *can* share cultural values, but they need not.

There is so much diversity within ethnic groups and even within nations that seemingly homogeneous groups can have different cultural nuances. We could all come from Switzerland, but culturally we would be separated by language and regional characteristics. (Note that three major languages are spoken in

Switzerland.) Also we could all share a language (we could all speak English), but we could be culturally and geographically separated by our histories and continents: we could be Europeans from the United Kingdom, Northern Americans from Canada or the United States, or Australians, for instance. People can share ethnicity or race and not share culture too. We might be Chinese, but depending on where we were raised—on mainland China, in Hong Kong, or in Canada—we could be culturally different.

Culture is learned: our parents and closest significant others metaphorically bathe us in the meanings and the rituals that will comprise our culture. If an American family adopts a girl in infancy from mainland China, and she is raised in the United States, she will have a North American cultural identity, or an Asian American cultural identity, even though her ethnic identifier and racial characteristics are Asian. Culture changes over time as well. Our grandparents subscribed to cultural values that, to an extent, may seem somewhat out of date today, proving that culture is not carved in stone and that it grows and adapts like a living organism.

The usual conflicts between parents and their children over socialization, which occur, in part, because of societal and cultural changes taking place over time, are exacerbated when two cultures—the culture of origin and the acquired culture—come into play. Parents would like their children to maintain the cultural identity of the "old land" and respect its traditions and belief systems. The children bridge into a new cultural system, and if they want to belong, they have to cross that cultural bridge, eventually becoming bicultural. In other words, children have to understand the belief systems and attitudes of their parents but also belong to a new world (Moore & Whelan, 2016). Culturally, the children are the go-betweens, bridging cultures and allowing their parents to reap the benefit of this cultural understanding (Raj, 2016). By the third generation, the language of the "old country" has usually been lost, and children are fluent in the language of their new homeland.

Statue of Annie Moore (1874–1924) and her brothers, Cobh, Ireland. At age 15, Annie was the first immigrant to the United States to pass through the Ellis Island facility in the year 1892. Ellis Island was the location for major transitions. Apart from welcoming immigrants, the facility recorded about 350 babies born, but about ten times that number of persons died there.

Source: Alamy Stock Photo/travelbild.com.

Migration and language. In learning a second language, we need to remember that this language is learned "in addition to the mother tongue" (UNESCO). The English of an immigrant may not be fluent or of native-speaker quality, but we should guard against being judgmental or implying that one language is better than another. Whatever the first tongue of the native speaker, it should be honored. Bilingualism has allowed translators to build bridges and act as go-betweens in ways that would have been impossible otherwise.

In reality each next generation will become more fully absorbed by the host culture, and greater portions of the culture of origin will fade into obscurity. Typically, the language of the country of origin is lost within about three generations, unless there are special efforts to maintain it and the host country values the bilingualism. The immigrating generation still speaks the language of origin and learns the language of the host country; albeit this generation's speech is accented as the music of its original language colors every subsequent language. The offspring of the immigrant parents, the first generation growing up in a new context, will be bilingual if the parents make efforts to maintain the language of origin (Raj, 2016). If not, the children typically understand more than they speak, or they start using hybrid languages such as "Spanglish" (Spanish and English) or "Hinglish" (Hindi and English).

Each generation gets further removed from the original cultural reference points, and unless there is frequent contact with the culture of origin, those values will gradually fade and a new hybrid identity is formed. This process has many merits as it allows individuals to assimilate into the host culture. They eventually need to feel truly rooted and at home in this culture, so they can become part of the heterogeneous fabric of the nation and perceive it as *home,* a place of well-being and emotional shelter. The United States prides itself on having formed a mosaic-like mixture of cultures and ethnicities in which each group shares mainstream American culture while simultaneously expressing some unique cultural characteristics that it shares (Heinze, 2017; Jones-Correa, Marrow, Okamoto, & Tropp, 2018).

Education and social dynamics. Another issue that affects family dynamics and communication in the cross-cultural family is gender equality. In the postmillennial United States, more women are reaching for higher education than at any previous time in history. Professions are less likely to be stereotypically associated with one

Authentic Insight

The Language of Winter and Love

The Inuit dialect,
spoken in Canada's
Nunavik region,
has at least 53 words
for snow,
including "matsaauti,"
for wet snow
that can be used
to ice a sleigh's runners.

A tutorial on how to say
"I love you" in French
requires five steps,
the fourth of which
instructs the reader
on the addition of
"ma chérie" or "mon chéri"
for "my darling."

Men and women in regions
of Indiana and Ohio
have at least nine
words or phrases
to refer to the remote control
for a fireplace. One of those
is "InfraLog Igniter 3000."

But, informally, and
addressed to an intimate,
one might hear an American say,
"Hey, how about handing me
the fireclicker, Girl-Baby?"

Dale Wisely, PhD, is a clinical psychologist specializing in work with children and adolescents.

Source: Reprinted with permission from the online poetry journal *Truck*. See Wisely (2016, February).

FOCUS POINT

Language can be an entry point into a culture, an admission ticket of sorts. Language mastery opens the invisible cultural door that provides access to both the community and the cultural components of the new cultural home. It allows assimilation with the dominant cultural group—at least in terms of language and communication. Immigrant parents and their children often clash over issues arising from differences between culture of origin and acquired culture. Each subsequent generation gets further removed from the original cultural reference points. Unless there is frequent and intentional contact with the culture of origin, those values will gradually fade and a hybrid identity will be formed. The United States prides itself on being home to a variety of cultures and ethnicities. Americans share mainstream American culture while simultaneously expressing some unique cultural characteristics.

gender, as both men and women seek out employment of their choice, irrespective of former gender barriers. As people from non-Western cultures seek their fortune in Western contexts, some families hold higher aspirations for their own daughters (Sanagavarapu, 2010). They want their female offspring to be protected from the inequality and bias experienced in the countries they left.

Family structure and family roles are changing dramatically. Education is the equalizer in the competitive arena of work (Banks, 2015). In seeking tertiary education and better career opportunities, women have less time to devote to seeking a life partner and building a family. In the leading developed countries, adults are less likely to be in long-term stable partnerships than half a century ago, and family size has shrunk, often to lower than replacement value for a nation. Slowly but surely, the population size in these countries is shrinking unless it makes gains through immigration. At the same time, population growth in developing countries is exploding, and these countries typically lack the economic, educational, medical, nutritional, and other resources to sustain that growth or to offer hopeful futures to families. Many of these factors play out on a macrosystemic level, but they are powerful in influencing individual families and family members.

> **"Education is simply the soul of a society as it passes from one generation to another."**
>
> Gilbert K. Chesterton (1874–1936),
> English writer, from "What Is Called Education?"
> *The Illustrated London News*, May 7, 1924

Enculturation and Acculturation

The very first cultural wash that we absorb with our mother's milk is significant; we are enculturated in this culture. It sits deepest. It is part of the cultural loom on which the fabric will be woven.

What about immigrants? What happens to their cultural identity when they move countries and contexts? A next cultural influence can be washed over the first. Depending on the age of the child or the parent, the assimilation of the family, and individual personality characteristics, degrees of **acculturation** will occur (Shiraev & Levy, 2016). Here is a little memorization trick: *acculturation* begins with the letter *a*, the same letter as the word *acquire*. So *a*cculturation represents the *a*cquired cultural identity, acquired after the first **enculturation**.

On a plaque placed in 1903 on the pedestal of the Statue of Liberty in New York appear these words by Emma Lazarus: "Give me your tired, your poor, / Your huddled masses yearning to breathe free." Among other things, the statue represents the friendship between nations and freedom from oppression.

Source: Photo via Good Free Photos.

It follows that members of the next generation, the offspring of the original immigrants, cannot possibly share the exact same cultural influences as their parents. Whatever culture of origin the parents subscribe to, the children will be in the environment of the adopted country as well. This is how we have cultural blends that form unique expression within groups.

Etic and emic. When we become culturally competent, we aim to understand and bridge cultural differences by showing respect and empathy for cultures different from our own. There are two useful terms in this context as well. When we share values with virtually all cultures, and they become universal values, beliefs, or feelings, we talk about *etic* components (rhyming with *pathetic*). The short description of *etic* is *culturally universal*. For instance, if we all laugh when we are happy, irrespective of culture, then that would be an etic quality.

We usually trip up over culturally specific qualities, things that are culturally unique to a group. This too has a term: *emic* (rhyming with *scenic*). These are the components of culture that are specific to a group. They can be unique and represent the qualities the original immigrants want to cherish as a heritage. Because these emic characteristics often represent differences, things that distinguish one cultural group from others, they can be misunderstood or elicit intolerance. We know that cultural values are learned, usually from those closest to us. By the same token, prejudice and hatred can be learned from undesirable role models.

But culture is fluid. Even though it is transmitted by learning from one generation to the next, other influences in the greater social system of the child mean that a child's culture is never a copy of its parents'. Culture changes with time and from generation to generation, so that the cultural world of our grandparents cannot possibly be the cultural world of our grandchildren.

In some ways, the forces of globalization, once extant, cannot be contained, and we find ourselves in a situation similar to that of Goethe's "Sorcerer's Apprentice"; once activated, the system gains momentum exponentially. Initially the sorcerer's apprentice thought it was an innovative labor-saving device to cast a magic spell on the broom so it would carry water. Once his needs had been fulfilled, he hacked the broom apart; yet each fragment of the broom took on a life of its own.

Organizations such as UNESCO are raising awareness concerning the global state of our fragile families. As developed nations, we have a responsibility to initiate family-friendly policies and workplaces and accessible education and health care, while also taking a stance against child- and gender-based exploitation and discrimination. Serious efforts are called for to contain the destructive effects of globalization on families while also nurturing those initiatives that carve out better futures for the world's families and their children.

"The negative side to globalization is that it wipes out entire economic systems and in doing so wipes out the accompanying culture."

Peter L. Berger (b. 1929), Austrian sociologist

Acknowledgment: Sections of this chapter were reworked and adapted from previously published material. See Gerhardt, C. (2016c). Globalization and families. In

C. L. Shehan (Ed.), *The Wiley Blackwell Encyclopedia of Family Studies* (Vol. 2, pp. 979–986. Chichester, UK: John Wiley & Sons, Inc. Used with permission of the publishers John Wiley & Sons, Inc.

FOCUS POINT

The very first cultural wash that we absorb is significant; we are *enculturated* in this culture. It sits deepest. It is part of our core identity. A next cultural influence can be washed over the first, and this process is called *acculturation*. Acculturation frequently occurs with immigration or ongoing exposure to another cultural context. Culture is fluid. Even though culture is transmitted by learning from one generation to the next, other influences in the greater social system of the child mean that a child's culture is never a copy of its parents'. Culture changes with time and from generation to generation, influenced by historical and sociocultural events. The cultural world of our grandparents cannot possibly be the cultural world of our grandchildren.

GLOBAL GLIMPSE

ACCULTURATION: FROM MELTING POT TO MOSAIC

To understand and respect other cultural contexts, we need to be exposed to them. Joining a dynamic cultural system requires immersion. Children from bicultural backgrounds, expats, and international workers are juggling two or more cultural contexts and learning from the challenges. The early insights about acculturation proposed an exchange of cultures, like putting on a new suit to change one's cultural identity. Out with the old and in with the new (Chiou & Mercado, 2016). This might have been an influencing factor in trying to assimilate immigrants to the United States at the turn of the previous century. They became part of the melting pot, and were encouraged to leave their mother tongue, special rituals, and cultural "baggage" outside the gates of Ellis Island. We have done a 180-degree turn, as we now celebrate diversity and acknowledge the mosaic of uniqueness and strength that accompanies variations in cultural heritage.

How we speak about cultural contexts can also carry intended and unintended messages. Persons who juggle two cultures may refer to their *heritage* or *home* culture as the one in which they were enculturated: the first cultural context to which they were exposed. The second layer of the acculturation process can occur for immigrants, refugees, international workers, and travelers and is referred to as the *host* culture. It may be more neutral to refer to these two cultural contexts as the *culture of origin* and the *new culture* (Matsudaira, 2006).

Part of the problem in trying to measure levels of psychological acculturation or adaptation to another culture is that it can occur on two levels. It can be an outwardly visible process, as in adapting to local dietary, dress, and etiquette guidelines. But this is counterbalanced by more private feelings toward that culture. On the surface, a person may seem very accepting of another cultural and ethnic context while being secretive about attitudes that would be perceived as politically incorrect. The guarded and critical components may be hidden and very personal. These aspects are the ones that could create tension between cultural and ethnic groups.

Clearly, there is a strong dynamic contained in transcultural meetings. By adapting, socializing, and communicating, we enhance mutual understanding and respect. Acknowledging cultural differences respectfully allows us to find a meeting ground and explore points of connection. When it comes to long-term cultural connections, it is seldom either/or; instead, it is merging and evolving as we learn from each other, increasing the cultural competence of all participants in the dialogue.

Source: Based on Matsudaira (2006).

Authentic Insight

A Letter to Hope

Hope, you really are beautiful aren't you? You strengthen and make people soar. You're there in the depths of human despair, not flinching from pain and sorrows. Some places seem to have you more abundantly. Where wealth eliminates the starkest realities, it seems there's a cheap copy of you that recalls something closer to wishing.

Where I am right now, you also seem distant in the eyes of the people around me. Where is the fire you bring to people's bellies and light in their eyes? Where are the sounds of laughter and warm embraces between families? Where are the children's dreams and the elder's stories? It seems they've died or gone to a very faraway land, almost forgotten.

Can the sand whipping across the desert blow you away? Is there not a chink in the armor of hearts jaded by death and disease? Does starvation and thirst squash your seed? Does the inescapable cycle of birth, child marriage, too many children to feed, hard labor on a harder ground, and the inevitable early deaths of friends, children, and themselves not have a season for you?

Where have you gone hope? You're needed desperately here in this weary place.

Where a malnourished 15-year-old—soon to be a mother—must walk miles under the sun to get a portion of food that will feed her family, but was meant only to strengthen her. Where I try to console a mother for the loss of her child, and she blankly asks me why she would need comforting. Where children's dreams aren't of fantasy and adventure, but of haunting and fear. Where families are broken beyond repair for generations, due to poverty. Where women and men are too twisted and crooked to see straight. Where disease stalks and spares no one.

Why are you gone hope? You're needed here, but would you be known?

Although my heart is being broken for those without you, you still reside in my heart.

Kathleen Nolin Needham, MA (International Human Relations), wrote this "Letter to Hope" in 2015 while she was working in sub-Saharan Africa. An extract is reproduced here.

SPOTLIGHT ON THEORIES

Anxiety-Uncertainty Management Theory

Anxiety relates to feelings of discomfort and worry in response to a perceived threat. This threat may be realistic or not, concrete or abstract. Importantly, it feels real to the person experiencing it, so subjectively, it is real. Uncertainty refers to the ambiguity of a situation; something is ambiguous because it is not immediately clear what it entails. When an individual is confronted by new and unknown cultural contexts and content, this unknown entity may be perceived with some trepidation.

In the context of cultural confrontation, the initial theory by Charles Berger on uncertainty reduction was expanded by William Gudykunst and his colleagues to include intercultural situations (Littlejohn, Foss, & Oetzel, 2017, p. 396). In this theory, Gudykunst describes that there are parameters within which intercultural communications will occur with relative comfort and effectiveness. These are bracketed by a lower and an upper threshold of uncertainty, as they are referred to in this theory, within which effective communication between cultures is impaired. So good cross-cultural communication can be compared to being on a certain bandwidth at which communication will be optimal. Gudykunst argues that if an individual is below his or her minimum threshold of uncertainty, communication will be hampered because that person will not be interested or motivated enough to engage in cross-cultural communication. But the other scenario, being too uncertain and anxious, is frequently more dangerous.

The level of comfort one feels during cross-cultural communication may relate to how much familiarity can be recognized in the communication process and, related to that, how much meaning can be inferred from it. If the communication elicits anxiety and exceeds the threshold of what is comfortable for a particular person, intercultural anxiety may set in: "If our anxiety is above our maximum thresholds, we are so uneasy that we do not want to communicate with host nationals [or we] tend to process information about host nationals in a simplistic fashion" (Gudykunst, 2005, p. 422).

Some of the simplistic ways in which we could respond may be negative, such as relying on stereotypes, preconceived ideas, and heuristics to ascribe meaning. By doing this, we are adding presumed content that may or may not be accurate. Different people have varying thresholds, meaning that they may differ regarding what will tip their comfort toward discomfort and elicit uncertainty and accompanying anxiety.

Two additional concepts are valuable in understanding this theory:

Effective communication. By this is meant the extent to which the communicators can convey their intent and be understood. We know from our experiences with trying to learn another language that our communication in this new language may be dictated by what we *can* say rather than by what we *want* to say. For instance, we may weave our conversation around the phrases we have learned, and trying to express our core life philosophy may be totally out of reach.

Cultural variability. This phrase relates to how comfortable we feel interacting and connecting with strangers, especially strangers whose cultural cues may be somewhat unclear and ambiguous to us. Additionally, our group identity may influence us in our perceptions, in that we bring cultural heritage and background with us as we enter new intercultural exchanges.

Intercultural Communication Competence

Intercultural communication competence is also referred to by the currently preferred term of *cultural competence*. Other terms that are used in similar contexts are intercultural sensitivity, cultural humility, cultural safety, and cultural effectiveness (Littlejohn et al., 2017, p. 396).

How we communicate is filtered and modified by the cultural context within which communication occurs. What we are conveying is shaped by the specific language we use, our cultural background, our social customs, and more. Here is one definition of culture and its influence on communication:

> Culture is any group of social significance in which members share elements of identity and communication patterns to varying degrees; people have different subjective experiences of these elements. (Littlejohn et al., 2017, p. 87)

Gudykunst's theory regarding the influence of anxiety in intercultural communication is underpinned by this definition of culture. Communication apprehension occurs in relation to how closely cultural identity and communication patterns are shared, or not, by communicators, but it is also influenced by their subjective experiences. Communication uncertainty, therefore, will play out in an interpersonal and systemic context.

Communication Accommodation Theory

The communication accommodation theory (CAT) was proposed by Howard Giles and his colleagues (Littlejohn et al., 2017, p. 401). In essence, it describes the process of how communicators adjust to accommodate each other. We change our communication style subtly, depending on the cues we receive from our communication partner. For instance, observations have shown that if we communicate with persons whom we know are not fluent in the language we are using, we tend to simplify our grammar and word choice, and often we also increase the volume, as if that will enhance comprehension (Bentz, Verkerk, Kiela, Hill, & Buttery, 2015). Additionally, we may increase our use of hand signals and facial expressions to add a nonverbal component to the interaction.

Two concepts are of importance in this theory, namely convergence and divergence. Convergence refers to an adjustment that is made to facilitate communication, and typically, it is a reaction to the cues we receive from the communication partner. Divergence, on the other hand, describes the opposite process when distancing or moving apart occurs. In extreme form, divergence can be observed in an argument or a

(Continued)

(Continued)

miscommunication. It is as if the two communication channels are on different bandwidths and do not connect. Convergence and divergence can be mutual or nonmutual. Mutual means that the parties agree about the direction of their interaction; they both come together, or they both part. It does not refer to the degree of understanding; rather, the agreement is about the direction of the communication. When we think of communication processes such as disdain and criticism, as described by Gottman (1993) in his classic work on marital communication, we can note that the movement that occurs is divergence. This is what makes these types of communications risky and predictors of other conflicts and disagreements (Littlejohn et al., 2017, p. 401).

These interpersonal patterns are complicated because another factor is added to them—the goal of the communication. For instance, if a person needs information or to be affirmed as a person, then the communication process can take on a different tone. Many factors and aims influence how we communicate; we do not always enter these interactions solely for the purpose of exchanging information, for example. Any communication interaction takes place against a complex background of culture and cultural social identity and is influenced by personal needs, goals, power games, and more. We can only guess at its complexity.

Theories Concerning Cultural Adaptation and Change

Several theories have focused on the adaptations that occur in intercultural communications. Similar to the stages approach that we met in theories dealing with grief, for instance, in the work of Elizabeth Kübler-Ross, we find theories that take a stages approach to the cultural adaptation process. The work on cultural adaptation by Milton Bennett (2004) tends to fall in this group. In the approaches to dealing with grief, the stages approaches were overtaken by focusing on tasks to be completed in the journey of dealing with grief. Cultural adaptation and ultimately aspects of cultural assimilation are meaningfully described in terms of tasks as well. Numerous smaller theories and angles have evolved to describe aspects of the transcultural and intercultural journey; interestingly, many of the theorists in this field come from bicultural and multicultural backgrounds and rely on their personal experiences to provide meaning to their journeys.

In moving toward the goal of increased cultural competence, we see that attitudes are important. A willingness to explore fresh cultural content is key. Each individual will negotiate his or her terms of assimilation or adaptation, what is acceptable and what not. Often the values that are close to our hearts, such as religious beliefs, standards of behavior, and ethics, are resistant to superficial cultural influence. Those cultural expressions that are more superficial and external, as it were, such as food and clothing preferences, may be more easily shared. Hence, immigrant groups tend to hold on to their religion longer than they maintain the language of their country of origin. Food preferences can become the symbol of the culture, with different groups prizing their unique cuisines; yet this is also an area that can be shared easily and pave the way to cross-cultural respect and understanding. Breaking bread together is a good starting point for an intercultural conversation.

In a Nutshell

Anxiety-Uncertainty Management Theory and Communication Accommodation Theory

- Anxiety-uncertainty management theory addresses the uncertainty and ambiguity of a situation that is unclear. This anxiety can occur when an individual is confronted by new and unknown cultural content and contexts.
- We may respond to unfamiliar cultural content in negative ways, such as by relying on stereotypes, preconceived ideas, and heuristics to ascribe meaning. This process can occur at the risk of relying on inaccurate information.
- Intercultural communication competence requires an openness toward new cultural content and a willingness to learn in an unbiased manner.

- The communication accommodation theory (CAT) describes how communicators adjust to and accommodate each other. We subtly change our communication style, depending on the cues we receive from our communication partner.
- Several theories have focused on the adaptations that occur in intercultural communications. Some theorists take a stage approach to the cultural adaptation process.
- Cultural adaptation and, ultimately, aspects of cultural assimilation are meaningfully described in terms of tasks as well.
- Cultural adaptation requires a willingness and an openness to explore fresh cultural content. An individual will negotiate what is acceptable in terms of assimilation and what would present a challenge in terms of extending her or his cultural comfort zone.

CHAPTER FOCUS POINTS

Culture and Change

- Change is the essence of dynamics.
- The demographics of families in the twenty-first century are changing dramatically, fueled by globalization.
- Frequently, in modern society, there is a multilevel disinvestment in the family as an institution, which changes the cultural fabric of our society and the futures of families.
- Poverty forces families to relocate. Political dynamics underlie the refugee crisis.
- As globalization spreads, emerging adults grow up in a hyperconnected context through media exposure and advertising, which, in turn, affects cultural identity and fuels consumerism.

Dynamics of International Families

- The cultural dimension is a cornerstone in the context of family life. It is of utmost importance because it reflects, among other things, the values, the beliefs, and attitudes of persons sharing a culture, and these, in turn, influence rituals, family life transitions, parenting, and more.
- Culture reaches into the furthest corners of family life. The larger cultural context within which the family's culture is embedded is also significant, and there is a bidirectional influence.
- Psychologically based definitions of culture describe a shared information base that contains values, attitudes, and beliefs; these dimensions are transmitted intergenerationally and between members through learning.
- Changing cultural contexts create the cultural disorientation felt by transitioning persons. A *third culture* is the product of blending a *culture of origin* with a *host culture*.

Dynamics of Assimilation

- Frequently, the destination culture is idealized until the family settles in its new surroundings. The degree to which social exchanges are understandable depends on how different the culture of origin is from the new hosting culture. Ultimately, a hybrid cultural style develops.
- Parents may place visible and invisible cultural demands on their children and require various degrees of conformity, especially to cultural heritage. Individual challenges of acculturation remain.
- Being part of a supportive community and engaging in procivic behaviors that are vested in the host country contribute to a successful transition.
- Parents need to acknowledge that their children can never totally share the cultural content of the country of origin because the children are being raised in a different cultural context and their acculturation to the host culture demands bicultural values and experiences.

Culture and Communication

- Language can be an entry point into a culture, an admission ticket of sorts. Language mastery opens the invisible cultural door that provides access to both the community and the cultural components of the new cultural home. It allows assimilation with the dominant cultural group—at least in terms of language and communication.

- Immigrant parents and their children often clash over issues arising from differences between culture of origin and acquired culture. Each subsequent generation gets further removed from the original cultural reference points. Unless there is frequent and intentional contact with the culture of origin, those values will gradually fade and a hybrid identity will be formed.
- The United States prides itself on being home to a variety of cultures and ethnicities. Americans share mainstream American culture while simultaneously expressing some unique cultural characteristics.

Enculturation and Acculturation

- The very first cultural wash that we absorb is significant; we are *enculturated* in this culture. It sits deepest. It is part of our core identity.
- A next cultural influence can be washed over the first, and this process is called *acculturation*. Acculturation frequently occurs with immigration or ongoing exposure to another cultural context.
- Culture is fluid. Even though culture is transmitted by learning from one generation to the next, other influences in the greater social system of the child mean that a child's culture is never an exact copy of its parents'.
- Culture changes with time and from generation to generation, influenced by historical and sociocultural events. The cultural world of our grandparents cannot possibly be the cultural world of our grandchildren.

Spotlight on Theories: Anxiety-Uncertainty Management Theory and Communication Accommodation Theory

- Anxiety-uncertainty management theory addresses the uncertainty and ambiguity of a situation that is unclear. This anxiety can occur when an individual is confronted by new and unknown cultural content and contexts.
- We may respond to unfamiliar cultural content in negative ways, such as by relying on stereotypes, preconceived ideas, and heuristics to ascribe meaning. This process can occur at the risk of relying on inaccurate information.
- Intercultural communication competence requires an openness toward new cultural content and a willingness to learn in an unbiased manner.
- The communication accommodation theory (CAT) describes how communicators adjust to and accommodate each other. We subtly change our communication style, depending on the cues we receive from our communication partner.
- Several theories have focused on the adaptations that occur in intercultural communications. Some theorists take a stage approach to the cultural adaptation process.
- Cultural adaptation and, ultimately, aspects of cultural assimilation are meaningfully described in terms of tasks as well.
- Cultural adaptation requires a willingness and an openness to explore fresh cultural content. An individual will negotiate what is acceptable in terms of assimilation and what would present a challenge in terms of extending her or his cultural comfort zone.

CHAPTER 15

Dynamics of Happiness

Learning Outcomes

After studying this chapter, you should be able to

1. Describe some of the challenges current theoretical approaches have in describing *happiness*, and comment on the role of *intentionality*.
2. Explain how the dynamics of *spiritual development* can contribute to meaning and favorable outcomes.
3. Discuss how both *education* and *public policy* have the potential to influence well-being.
4. Explain how family *connections* and *rituals* support the well-being of the family system.
5. Consider the major contributions of the *positive psychology* movement.

The Intentionality of Happiness

In eras gone by, **happiness** was regarded as a fragile gift. The daily struggles of survival reminded our ancestors of life's fleeting nature and inescapable hardship. Life was harsh with the realities of illness and death and hunger and poverty looming large over most of earth's inhabitants. As standards of living increased in the developed countries and medical science made rapid advances in health care, the luxury of thinking about happiness as an additional dimension of life became more pronounced. In many developed societies, we currently tend to think of happiness as a definite aspect to strive for; it seems attainable—albeit in limited quantities (McMahon, 2006).

Before and around the new millennium, psychological researchers focused particularly strongly on the dimensions related to happiness and well-being, calling this focus **positive psychology**. Much of the pioneering work is ascribed to Martin Seligman, a prolific writer and inspiring psychologist whose book, *Authentic Happiness* (2002), contributed to spreading the word.

Possibly the post–World War II years, which were accompanied by economic upturns, also contributed to the change in perspective. The millennial context of entering the next thousand years and looking back at the previous three thousand recorded ones was also an impetus to reflect on our state of mind. Still, thinking about happiness and how to achieve it is not new. The ancient Greek philosophers, as well as the major world religions, have all grappled with what contributes to a life well lived—a meaningful and constructive life in a societal context (Compton & Hoffman, 2019).

Happiness has a subjective quality. It is not necessarily linked to possessions, and, typically, it is not something that we acquire by handing over gold coins. Rather, it reflects a state of mind, a conscious awareness and experience of satisfaction and joy, without the excessive pressure of desiring more and better (McMahon, 2006). Happiness is difficult to define because of the exceptions. Some definitions identify the so-called four pillars of a good life: meaning, virtue, resilience, and well-being (Wong, 2011). Wong also emphasizes the cross-cultural perspective, in that cultures near and far seek well-being in their various and unique contexts. Other descriptors related to happiness are found in positive psychology: flourishing, being prosperous, having positive experiences, being well, being virtuous, being positively oriented, and the like (Hefferson & Boniwell, 2011).

Our sense of well-being can be improved as we reflect on privileges, joys, opportunities, experiences, and the like, while seeing these in a positive light accompanied by a healthy dose of gratitude (Schueller, 2010). In other words, consciously reflecting on that which adds positively to our lives can enhance our well-being. If we attribute meaning to our lives and find meaning in our tasks, we also add considerably to our well-being and satisfaction. Some psychological approaches have encouraged those seeking to improve their level of perceived happiness to reflect on and verbalize this sense of thankfulness, making it a daily practice incorporated into spirituality. These moments and opportunities that create the potential for joy and gratitude are blessings in a spiritual context.

If we can observe and study happiness and its manifestations, then we can seek to become happier, perhaps by discovering that elusive key to happiness. We definitely wish for our children to experience the benefits of joy. Importantly, though, happiness is not only a destination but also a process that manifests in many forms and intensities. What we do know is that it can be identified as a physiological response: certain areas in the brain light up when we experience it. For that reason, happiness seems to be an experiential occurrence, one that triggers certain neurons in brain functioning. What triggers happiness, and how can we maintain it? Several biological and genetic factors are involved (Farhud, Malmir, & Khanahmadi, 2014).

Happiness on a continuum. Happiness can mean feeling mildly optimistic all the way through to experiencing blinding exhilaration. We cannot maintain happiness at its highest levels of intensity, as we have to get on with all the normal demands of life. Individuals seem capable of consciously focusing on and experiencing happiness, and this varies from person to person and over time. It ebbs and flows, and we have to pause and acknowledge its presence to feel how it envelops us in positivity (Keyes, 2014).

Happiness as a process. Happiness is much more like a journey than an end destination. It requires (like fitness) repeated moments of awareness and associated feelings of gratitude to make its presence known. When we reflect on our strengths and our fortunate opportunities with gratitude, on what is good in our lives, we elicit contentment. The mindfulness movement pursues this aspect; we can become happier by being more fully aware or mindful, especially of the small things that can contribute to feelings of joy. Happiness, then, includes the process; it is not exclusively defined by the end product. The things we trade and acquire might create moments of fulfillment; they may contribute to positive experiences and create a sustaining lifestyle or appeal to our aesthetic senses. They provide shelter and contribute to our survival. They certainly can add to our quality of life. But they do not ensure happiness.

Happy by nature. Some people seem to be happy by nature. They have the luck of the draw and appear to be born with sunny dispositions; their genetic configurations have given them an advantage. At the other end of the spectrum are those suffering from mood disorders, which may have very real genetic underpinnings. The body's own endorphins can contribute to an elated mood. They are intended to contribute to the body's own pain management system, but they also have the power to bring about feelings of well-being. Runners and intense athletes will persevere beyond their comfort zones to experience the flood of the body's own feel-good medication. Current research has focused on what constitutes a so-called "happy brain" with contributory factors including the role of neurotransmitters, neuroplasticity, and pleasure centers in the brain (Compton & Hoffman, 2019; Farhud, Malmir, & Khanahmadi, 2014).

Pursuit of happiness. Benjamin Franklin and Thomas Jefferson were members of the American Enlightenment (generally the 1700s). It is thought that the general *Zeitgeist,* or spirit of the age, at this particular time in history is reflected in the American Declaration of Independence, adopted by Congress on July 4, 1776. At the time, this document was groundbreaking in all ways, and it was the first ever to address the happiness of individuals: "We hold these truths to be self-evident, that all men are created equal, that they are endowed by their Creator with certain unalienable Rights, that among these are Life, Liberty *and the pursuit of Happiness*" (italics added). Note that happiness is not considered a right; but it is considered a human right to pursue happiness. And that raises the question of equity, of whether certain individuals are given a leg up in this pursuit.

Happiness may be considered more likely in an environment where individuals have moments and possibilities of worth. Can they find meaning in their own labors and their friendships? Are there people to share the joys? Is there a meaningful context for the happiness? This last question points to philosophies of life, being able to enjoy the fruits of one's labor, and the specific outcomes one is striving for, among other things.

Research shows that wealth and material possessions are not necessarily an indicator of happiness. In self-evaluations, rich and poor people from countries across the globe have expressed their personal perceptions regarding their levels of happiness. Their sense of joy comes from various sources, but definitely it is not exclusively linked to money and wealth. Wealth can provide opportunities and privilege, but unless an individual adds a personal meaning to life's experiences, they can remain hollow, and happiness can remain elusive (Veenhoven, 2015). This finding leads us to believe that happiness may have more to do with an attitude and with the ability to be consciously cognizant of things that create happiness. We can immerse ourselves in delight, but if we do not perceive it as such, it will not impart joy.

Psychological research into the effects of support has shown that the perception of being supported is just as valuable as receiving concrete help. Those friends who show concern during loss, who express caring feelings, make a tangible difference to the person who is experiencing the loss. Similarly, a person who feels supported by family, friends, and community is more likely to be in a position to pursue happiness successfully.

Lost in the moment. An entire body of research is dedicated to the process described as *flow*. The concept is attributed to Mihaly Csikszentmihalyi, who published extensively examining the dimensions of this process (Seligman & Csikszentmihalyi, 2014). In essence, **flow** is the feeling of being lost within the moment, within an activity that absorbs us so fully we become part of it. The boundary between ourselves and what we are doing fades, and time seems to stand still. So powerful is this process that it can impart feelings of well-being and a sense of emotional reward. It is tempting to draw examples from illustrious persons with extraordinary skills. The pianist who performs an intricate piece of music will certainly be lost within that moment and activity, and will reconnect with the "outside" world at the finale as if emerging from a trancelike state. The surgeon who is concentrating on a complex intervention may be totally absorbed by the task and experiencing "flow" (Csikszentmihalyi, Abuhamdeh, & Nakamura, 2014).

Importantly, feeling flow is not the monopoly of geniuses. You and I, we as ordinary persons, can experience our own periods of flow when we are absorbed by the moment. The gardener, the flower designer, the auto mechanic, the woodworker, the tailor, the craftsperson: all can experience the magic of being absorbed by something that has claimed their proficiency and their emotional investment. It is not a reserved domain favoring certain activities (Csikszentmihalyi, 2017).

Do we need a high level of proficiency to experience this feeling? Not necessarily. But proficiency is often an expression of interest in and engagement with an activity or specialty. The more we do something, the more likely we are to improve that skill, given a certain ability and potential for development. Education is the steppingstone toward that proficiency. Luckily for all of us, we can and we do find joy in the ordinary. The happiness implied and elicited by flow can be accessible to us all.

Self-actualization can be found in the solitary pursuit of acquiring a wider network of cognitive skills, pursuing higher learning, solving a complex problem, or finding a novel solution to a vexing situation. These target predominantly the cognitive domain. The dancer who endures hours of training and discipline so that his body can transcend the limitations of the untrained physique, and who at that point can almost forget the "how" of achieving artistic expression, makes these sacrifices because of the fulfillment he experiences. The audience at the Super Bowl certainly experiences a sense of heightened alertness and excitement and a true love for the game, all of which impart feelings of well-being. Whether spectator or participant, we feel happiness when these complex physical expressions draw us into the circle of action, when we share these peak performances for that lingering moment. For the physically gifted, the creation of joy lies within the movement. Certainly, the perception of happiness interacts with our personalities (Cloninger & Zohar, 2011).

Not taking the environment for granted but mining it for its richness and for the treasure it holds in terms of possibilities for observation is one of many ways to enhance quality of life. Parental guidance is powerful in showing us the world that the parent thinks is important for the child to see, for widening horizons and creating opportunities. Beauty and the happiness that comes from appreciating it can be found in many situations.

> **"A joyful life is an individual creation that cannot be copied from a recipe."**
>
> Mihaly Csikszentmihalyi

Perception of happiness. Sometimes we need an education or repeated exposure to truly appreciate what a certain situation or activity can yield. Playing a musical instrument may not always reward the player with instant gratification, as there is a discipline attached to it. Similarly, education does not yield its gifts readily; an apprenticeship may be required. Education has a way of expanding both our skills and our minds, and this in itself creates a wider array of opportunities that we may find pleasurable or interpret as being pleasurable. Additionally, education provides the ability to attach meaning to experiences and observations, which in turns provides a quality that contributes to the perception of happiness. The following quotation by British author Iris Murdoch touches on this particular aspect of education:

FOCUS POINT

Around the new millennium, psychological researchers focused on the dimensions of happiness, calling it *positive psychology*. Happiness has a subjective quality and reflects a state of mind, a conscious awareness and experience of satisfaction and joy—one without the excessive pressure of desiring more and better. Happiness is difficult to define. *Flow* describes being lost in the moment, becoming part of an activity that absorbs us. This process imparts feelings of well-being and a sense of emotional reward. Civic engagement supports the life goals of a participating individual, and, as a group expression, it reflects the quality of our cultural expressions and societal engagement.

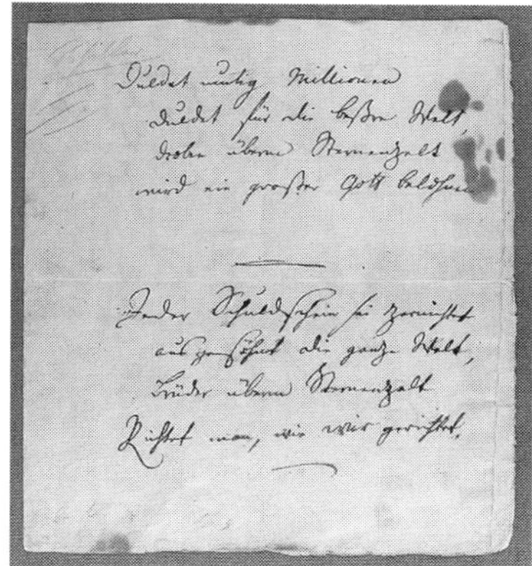

The German poet and philosopher Friedrich von Schiller (1759–1805) wrote the words to the "Ode to Joy," which Beethoven (1770–1827) incorporated in his Ninth Symphony. The original manuscript by Schiller sold at auction in 2011 for over half a million U.S. dollars. On the left is Beethoven's sketch of the opening bars of his Piano Sonata in E minor, Op. 90.

Source: Public domain.

> Education doesn't make you happy. Nor does freedom. We don't become happy just because we're free—if we are. Or because we've been educated—if we have. But because education may be the means by which we realize we are happy. It opens our eyes, our ears, tells us where delights are lurking, convinces us that there is only one freedom of any importance whatsoever, that of the mind, and gives us the assurance—the confidence—to walk the path our mind, our educated mind, offers.
>
> Attributed to Dame Iris Murdoch (1919–1999),
> Irish-born British author

Dynamics of Spiritual Development

The psychological interpretations we attach to things, our belief systems, spirituality and faith—all these are powerful components in adding meaning and support to our existence. There are tremendous cultural variations in these dimensions, but we are unified in that humankind acknowledges that appropriate and constructive belief systems can contribute to our conscious experience of joy.

Viktor Emil Frankl (1905–1997), the Austrian psychiatrist and Holocaust survivor, emphasized repeatedly that if a person has found meaning in life, she or he will also find the will to survive. His illuminating insights based on his personal hardships affirmed that when people seem to have lost everything, they still have a choice concerning the dignity and courage with which they will face that loss. His book *Man's Search for Meaning* (1946) was written post–World War II and elaborates these ideas. *The Will to Meaning* (1969) is a later book containing a compilation of speeches on logotherapy.

As a young therapist in training, I had the privilege of hearing Viktor Frankl speak about some of these experiences in a public lecture. It has remained a highlight experience. He was slight in stature but great in presence. Frankl's personal story attests to his philosophy, which ultimately carried him through and beyond the atrocities of war. He sacrificed possessions and the products of his labor: the manuscript of his book was burned. He made the tragic and inconceivable personal sacrifice—the loss of his loved ones. Despite the seemingly unbearable trauma in his life, he found the courage to move forward and beyond, to remain engaged, and to leave a legacy of hope in his writings.

> **"If you have your *why?* for life, then you can get along with almost any *how?*"**
>
> Friedrich Nietzsche, from *Twilight of the Gods*

Contributing and Receiving

By fulfilling obligations, we contribute to a system, which gives meaning and purpose to our lives. These interlocking components—of contributing to and receiving from something beyond self—have bidirectional influence. The one fuels the other in a circular manner. These are also essential components of those complex contexts that foster resilience and facilitate happiness.

Religion or spirituality is one context that enables an individual to find meaning through this kind of giving and getting. Yet, according to Roehlkepartain (2013, p. 83), spirituality and spiritual development are frequently seen as aspects of religious development, and, for that reason, family-life professionals do not address these factors. Roehlkepartain thinks they should and suggests that spiritual development can be seen as a normative developmental process that stretches widely into many areas of living:

> Spiritual development is a normative developmental process involving critical developmental tasks such as connectedness, belongingness, purpose, and contribution. All persons in all societies "do" spiritual development, though culture plays a major role in its process and content. Spiritual development does not require divinity or belief in a supernatural power, though a lot of people include these in their stories. . . . Spiritual development is a normative developmental process that, like cognitive or social development, is informed and shaped by family, kinship, peers, school, culture, social norms, and programmes. (Roehlkepartain, 2013, p. 83)

See Diagram 15.1 for a graphic representation of what informs and shapes spiritual development. These factors interact throughout a person's lifespan, within the dimension of time.

DIAGRAM 15.1 **The elements in a comprehensive theory of spiritual development include several dimensions such as culture, social contexts, and interpretive frameworks. These interact on the dimension of time.**

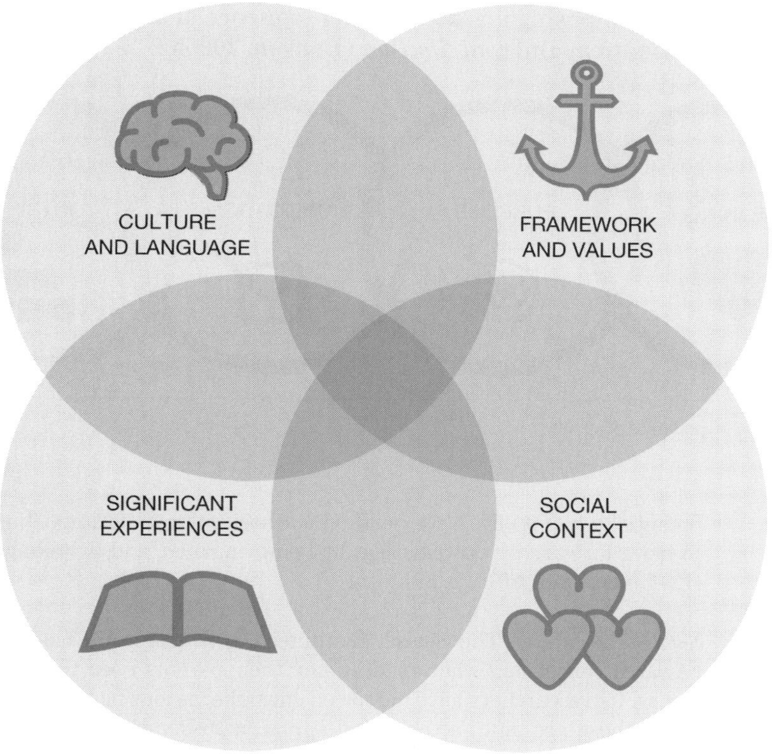

Sources: Based on Benson (2006b) and Roehlkepartain (2013, p. 85).

Several aspects support the dynamics of spiritual development, including

- Awareness of the self and metacognition,
- Seeking meaning and a connection between inward and outward journeys in a coherent and harmonious manner, and
- Living a life that exemplifies spiritual values. (Roehlkepartain, 2013, p. 85)

Intriguingly, the work of Benson (2006a) deals with religion and spiritual development in children. This model that references spiritual development is complex and acknowledges the interplay between cultural and social contexts. These occur on a time scale and facilitate the individual and significant life experiences of the person. This approach toward spiritual development superimposes an interlocking sequence of *meaning, purpose, obligation*, and *contribution* (Benson, 2006b).

A two-pronged approach, consisting of components of *contributing to* and *receiving from* the varied contexts, explains the complexity within which personhood is embedded. See Diagram 15.2. This model also refers to what we inherit and what we create. There is a give and take. When it comes to living meaningful (and

DIAGRAM 15.2

When it comes to living meaningful lives, there is bidirectional responsibility. We build on our sociocultural heritage, but we also need to move forward by contributing, by being engaged, and by taking responsibility. Spiritual development aids in this task by superimposing an interlocking sequence of *meaning, purpose, obligation*, and *contribution* (Benson, 2006b).

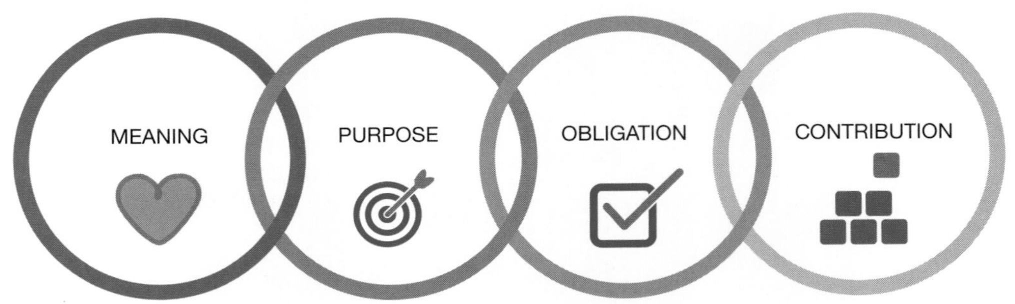

Source: Based on Roehlkepartain (2013, p. 89).

potentially happy) lives, we build on our sociocultural heritage, but we also need to move forward by contributing, by being engaged, and by taking responsibility (Roehlkepartain, 2013, p. 89).

Search Institute. The Search Institute, a U.S. nonprofit, has been involved in research concerning what children and their parents need to promote good outcomes. Its researchers have narrowed down the various factors that promote resilience; these are multifactorial and spread across various systems including the family, the community, educational institutions, and more. In particular, researchers identified developmental assets consisting of positive supports and strengths that will pave the way toward successful outcomes. These assets are grouped into two major areas: the *internal* and the *external.* Internal assets include the skills, commitments, and values that people need to make good choices. External assets are the supports, opportunities, and relationships people need across all aspects of their lives to achieve well-being. See the text box titled "Search Institute: Developmental Assets" for more information.

The outlines offered by the Search Institute, which cover developmental assets and developmental relationships, are reader friendly and are available in numerous languages that address groups globally and in a variety of sociocultural contexts. Much like the United Nations' recommendations concerning the universal rights of children, the Search Institute's accessible guidelines can support families nationally as well as internationally (http://www.search-institute.org/).

"It is the client who knows what hurts, what directions to go, what problems are crucial, what experiences have been deeply buried."

Carl Rogers, American psychotherapist,
from *On Becoming a Person* (1961)

Historic research on moral development. Whether one speaks of external assets such as expectations and opportunities to serve others, spiritual development, or being able to live a purposeful life by giving back to a nurturing community, it is clear that the ethic of charity, of treating others with benevolent goodwill, is a

Search Institute: Developmental Assets

Internal assets

- *Commitment to learning*
- *Positive values* such as caring, honesty, responsibility, restraint
- *Social competencies* such as cultural competence, peaceful conflict resolution, planning and decision making
- *Positive identity*, which is related to personal power, self-esteem, sense of purpose and optimism

External assets

- *Support* from the family and other adult relationships, caring neighborhoods and schools, and positive communication and involvement
- *Empowerment* by a community that values youth, sees youth as an asset, and provides a safe environment and opportunities to serve others
- *Boundaries* and expectations that imply adult role models, positive peer influences, and high standards, rules, consequences, and responsibilities
- Constructive use of time invested in creative activities, youth programs, religious activities, and time at home

significant contributor to well-being. Approaches to understanding this spiritual dimension of life, an aspect of happiness that can contain ethical and moral components, owe much to the historic work of Kohlberg (Colby, 1987/2011). Lawrence Kohlberg (1927–1987) is best remembered for his research pertaining to morality. He maintained that we move through stages of moral development, ranging from concrete stages, at which we make choices based on the fear of punishment or self-interest, to more abstract stages, at which we recognize social norms, experience the pressure to conform to society's rules, and, eventually, are guided by universal ethical principles. He was not optimistic that most people would reach the highest level of internally guided moral guidelines. These would present as an inner moral compass of sorts, and an individual could find a moral code in unique situations by relying on factors such as empathy, the context, the principles of doing no harm, and acting in the best interests of those involved. In developing his theory, he studied the work of great civic leaders, such as Martin Luther King Jr., philosophers such as Socrates, and the writings of Abraham Lincoln. He tried to follow their line of reasoning in reaching the outcomes they did, which could not have been dictated by existing moral guidelines; instead, they were generated in response to pressing social needs or intellectual reflections concerning humankind.

Predisposing, Precipitating, and Sustaining Factors

The acorn and the oak tree. Will we be able to raise happy children, or is there a genetic influence that determines their well-being? The simple and also complex answer to that is, "Both." For an acorn to grown into an oak tree, there needs to be water, good soil, and sunlight. These are environmental factors. But even with ample environmental ingredients to support the growth process, nothing will happen unless we start off with an acorn. In psychology, we refer to *predisposing*, *precipitating*, and *sustaining* factors. Here the predisposing factor is that we need to have an acorn. It can lie dormant for a long time, but it will only germinate once the precipitating factors, the environmental triggers, are introduced. Once the acorn has germinated, it still requires a long and arduous path of sustaining factors, so it can reach maturity.

In many ways, human children are subject to the same principles. There is the genetic potential of a specific child. Environmental factors interact. We add the concept of epigenesis, namely, the potential to shape or guide development according to the specific input. And then life itself needs to provide the ongoing environment to sustain the person.

Grandparents may be in the fortunate position to rerun mentally the images of their grown children and replay the film in reverse and in slow motion. There may be flashbulb memories, events that stand out, frozen in time for their significance.

FOCUS POINT

One model referencing spiritual development acknowledges the interplay between cultural and social contexts. This approach toward spiritual development superimposes an interlocking sequence of *meaning, purpose, obligation*, and *contribution.* Components of *contributing to* and *receiving from* the varied contexts explain the complexity within which personhood is embedded. When it comes to living meaningful lives, we build on our sociocultural heritage, but we also need to move forward by contributing, by being engaged, and by taking responsibility. Predisposing, precipitating, and maintaining factors can interact to influence outcomes.

Authentic Insight

On Considering the Family Dynamics of Loss (and of Resilience and Happiness . . .)

"Joy & Woe are woven fine." –William Blake

In considering the family dynamics of loss, one must think also on the dynamics of resilience and happiness, as strange as it may sound. I have had the great privilege of caring for young patients and their families over the decades, and I have been witness to times of loss, some small but many great. It remains amazing to me to see the resilience of young patients in the face of life-changing—and often life-threatening and even life-ending—disease. That same spirit of resilience is embodied in the respective families of these children, adolescents, and young adults. Just as a child does not develop and thrive apart from a nurturing family, so too must a sick child find from within the family the resilience to adjust and compensate. So, also must each member of the family find her or his own way through the loss and grief.

It's a phenomenally inspiring circumstance for a physician to be in when individuals a fraction of my age display a courage and equanimity in the face of disease and death that I could only hope to muster if I were to find myself a patient in similar straits. Not all loss involves death, but we grieve nonetheless for the things we have lost. Whether it be the young athlete with a once-promising sports career now unable to play because of a heart condition (made even more cruel by being outwardly invisible) or a young family grieving at the loss of a "normal" future for their infant just diagnosed with a genetic disorder, the loss is just as palpable, and the despair just as thick as death, if not more so. Somehow, the mystery of the family and the human spirit plays out, much in some unseen realm, but loss is coped with and resilience and even happiness tend to replace despair and grief.

Of course, there are scars. Just as heart surgery leaves a visible and outward scar, as well as considerable internal scars, so does loss leave its marks on the family and its members even after painful memories fade.

When an occasional person, upon finding out what I do, asks how I can face such things, the question always takes me by surprise, and I find myself answering in a simplistic and offhand way. I must remember next time to tell them of the small miracles I am witness to almost daily, and that for these I am thankful, and for these I continue to do what I do.

Walter H. Johnson Jr., MD, pediatric cardiologist, Children's of Alabama

Moments we return to alter with the realization that we had a little glimpse of things to come. With hindsight, we might recognize the characteristics that were already forming while our adult children were little. When children are little, we do not have the benefit of hindsight. We only have the promise of hope; we cross our fingers that the outcomes will be optimal. We say a little prayer that as parents we can contribute whatever it takes to create those good circumstances that will allow for good potential to develop and blossom into a fulfilled and meaningful adulthood.

Typically the genetic part is what it is. We make choices as to the partner with whom we choose to have offspring, and that influences the genetic parameters. The sustaining family environment can contribute to good or poor outcomes. It is good that these core mysteries of life remain hidden from us most of the time; how else would we find the courage to venture forth into that unchartered territory of life.

Education and Public Policy

Education could be classified as both a precipitating and a sustaining principle when it comes to well-being. Therefore, educational policy has a role in creating equitable access to schooling. Unfortunately, according to a UNICEF global estimate, about 63 million adolescents aged 12 to 15 are not receiving the benefits of an education (UNESCO & UNICEF, 2015). Additionally, about 58 million children of primary school age are deprived of an education because they cannot attend school. The numbers are growing, revealing an alarming trend. A 2015 initiative aimed at dramatically raising school attendance focused its efforts especially on areas in Africa, Central Asia, and the Arab States, where the numbers of children never expected to attend school were highest. The gender inequality in education is also particularly alarming. Girls face societal as well as cultural and traditional barriers keeping them out of the classroom. In sub-Saharan Africa, three quarters of out-of-school girls will in all likelihood never have access to an education. This in turn affects their resources for parenting and economic survival while making them vulnerable to violence and human trafficking.

As mothers become better educated, even minimally so, the infant mortality rate decreases. Mothers who have a broader education have greater access to employment opportunities that can raise their families' standard of living. This, is turn, tends to lead to smaller family size, as the parents are no longer fully dependent on the number of offspring to sustain them in advancing years.

The return of an education lies in rewards and outcomes for future generations. Even though the rates for boys missing out on schooling are also unreasonably high, gender inequality as it plays out in education tips the scale very negatively for girls. Education opens a variety of opportunities, including entry into those professions that were traditionally seen as male dominated. By the same token, men enter professions that were traditionally female dominated, for instance, nursing, when educational and professional opportunities become gender neutral. Having gender-balanced ratios within schools and professions creates an environment in which self-concept can be formed around notions of equal opportunities.

Children and Schools

Education is indisputably an important buffer that equips children with social skills and promotes resilience. But for children to benefit from education, educational opportunities need to exist. The infrastructure of schooling needs to be in place, which links educational policy to public policy and social concerns on a macrosystemic level. Schooling needs to be safeguarded from the interruption of strikes and unrest. Schools need to provide a safe environment. Schools also play an important role in communities; they can become magnets for parental involvement and help sustain community cohesion. At a school parents get to know each other and work together in supporting their mutual concern, namely, the outcomes of an appropriate educational initiative.

The Indian Schoolgirls, by Makiwa Mutomba, a Zimbabwean–South African artist, depicts girls in their school uniforms. Education is indisputably an important buffer that equips children with social skills, promotes resilience, and opens doors to opportunity. But for children to benefit from education, appropriate educational opportunities need to be accessible.

Source: The Indian Schoolgirls/Makiwa Mutomba.

Individual families can find an entry point by doing everything in their power to encourage children going to school. Teachers, mentors, and schools can contribute by providing a network that fosters resilience. If a child feels supported and education is seen as an achievement of merit, the benefits will spread to the community, as opportunities for meaningful contributions are increased. Children need parental involvement to do their daily homework and to find a place to rest, sleep, and play. They need clean clothing and meals. Grassroots initiatives have sprung up to provide encouragement at this level. Family life educators can play a valuable role in educating parents concerning the power of education.

Education is like a pebble dropping into water; the ever-widening circles of change that it causes have the power to raise societal standards and aspirational goals. Education is also about character building. It is a system to impart moral and ethical values, assets that will strengthen the fabric of society. The key to change lies predominantly with education, as this capstone piece of the interrelated global challenges has the power to influence virtually all other areas of concern (Bigner & Gerhardt, 2019, p. 402).

Civic Engagement Versus Social Isolation

Social isolation can be a warning sign. It can be the silent withdrawal by a person who is depressed and does not feel connected. During these phases of isolation, the disconnected person may not feel the same level of empathy that would normally guide his or her behavior. The individual no longer engages with or supports fellow human beings. If others are seen as the enemy, tragedy is more likely to ensue. Because society is a system, we can explore how it provides entry points for various persons to find a social point of connection, a place of belonging.

Vandalism and gang behavior is thought to indicate that perpetrators feel that they are functioning at the fringes of society. To show that they are a force to be reckoned with or to make their own identities more visible, they get involved in activities whose outcomes or effects cannot be ignored. Splashing their graffiti on walls creates images the passersby have to acknowledge—it's in one's face. They or their parents may feel marginalized; they may have moved from rural to urban neighborhoods; they may have lost their connection to civic engagement. The cultural connection has eluded them. Parents may be battling their own demons, as in addiction disorders and poverty. Constructive civic engagement creates an atmosphere in which young people can invest in their own community and feel connected with it. It is buying into that which nurtures and shelters us as community members. This connection translates into ownership and empowerment, which improve well-being.

Social isolation is one of the characteristics that seems to have defined a number of perpetrators involved in mass shootings. A recurring theme has been the social isolation of the aggressor. This isolation can be a cause as well as a symptom; the one influences the other. The phenomenon's complexity does not allow it to be reduced to a simplistic formula.

On the other hand, there are many examples of engagement encouraging positive social outcomes. The system of micro loans in developing countries is based on engaging the borrower in the project. There is personal pride in the outcome of a very personal investment. The results have been remarkable. In the creation of a park and communal playground in a shantytown in Southern Africa, the gardeners were sourced from the local community. They also became the guardians of the park and were rewarded for good outcomes. Being local, they knew where to find support in their own community, and they had a sense of belonging and ownership that went beyond what a pay slip could impart.

Illustration for the first edition of *Utopia*, by Thomas More. Over 500 years ago, in 1516, author Thomas More described an imaginary island, which he named Utopia. This is the first historical reference to the word. It is based on the Greek meaning "no place" or "nowhere," which in Greek sounds similar to "good place." It referred to an imaginary location where things were perfect. We use the word *utopia* to this day in reference to a place of perfection, one that is unlikely to be found or created.

Source: Public domain.

Gardening projects in the United States have started vegetable gardens in underserved communities and in schools; these gardens are used to combat food insecurity and as learning opportunities. An example of such an initiative is Big Green started by Kimball Musk and Hugo Matheson in 2011. Big Green says that its "learning gardens" or "dynamic outdoor classrooms" are "building a national school food culture that promotes youth wellness" (https://biggreen.org/). The persons responsible for the maintenance and care of these gardens are typically sourced locally from the community benefiting from the project. Only by people belonging, and participating, can the further maintenance and the future of these projects be ensured.

Other policies encourage connection and combat isolation. In a study of immigrant communities from North Africa, social assimilation improved when families were matched to host families who had been in the area longer. Being and feeling connected counteracted the forces of anonymity and isolation, and proved to be valuable tools in creating better outcomes.

Two popular and very touching documentaries shows us this path toward belonging. The films focus on the predicament of nearly 25,000 boys who were orphaned or became homeless during civil wars in the Sudan. About 3,600 of these youngsters were offered resettlement opportunities in the United States. In the documentary films *The Lost Boys of the Sudan* and the more commercial venture *God Grew Tired of Us* (2006), the filmmakers trace the boys' path from their initial excitement at the prospect of a more promising life to their experience of the challenges and obstacles that a new and unfamiliar community provided. Their journey included culture shock, alienation, and disorientation. The boys who revealed the best outcomes were those who were incorporated into civic and religious groups, who found meaningful work, and who found renewed social belongingness and civic engagement. The title of the documentary *God Grew Tired of Us* was a quotation from one of the Sudanese participants—his effort to explain the despair he felt.

> **"The greatest gifts you can give your children are the roots of responsibility and the wings of independence."**
>
> Denis Waitley

Avenues of Tomorrow

Parents in developed countries ideally have the power of public policy to back them in practices that benefit the entire family. The universal desire of virtually all parents is to prioritize the well-being of their own children. Usually, the good in parents prevails when it comes to their own offspring. Parents in developed countries can call in help from the various systems in which families are embedded, such as extended families, religious groups, social services, and humanitarian organizations. In a responsible and democratic society, there are systems in place to alleviate need. Seek them out and connect to them.

Public policy. If juggling family and work in dual-career homes is easier, it may be as a result of support from the public sector, specifically public policy. Some of these helpful policies have instituted better quality childcare settings, good educational systems, and flexible work and leave schedules to accommodate family and work needs, job sharing, pregnancy leave, family leave, and adaptable job reentry. The wish list may be longer than is realistically feasible, as these family-friendly practices require a sustainable tax base. In cash-strapped economies, good intentions may not be translated into reality.

Sociocultural changes. Sociocultural changes, such as the increasing number of divorced or separated couples, have the potential to affect family well-being. The important thing is to preserve a stable family life in balance with work demands despite these societal pressures. The percentage of couples committing to legal marriages is steadily declining, while blended families and single-parent families are becoming more numerous. These trends can be counteracted by societal and family-friendly support systems, including those provided by religious organizations. Information is becoming increasingly accessible and retrievable, and support groups can connect in cyberspace or in real time, providing information as well as a sense of belonging. Policies supporting family health are significant contributors to personal and societal well-being.

> **"Families are symbols of stability in a changing world. We need to understand the impact [of social change] . . . to help families adapt and thrive."**
>
> Bahira Sherif Trask,
> American family scientist and author

FOCUS POINT

Education provides the reward of meaningful life stories leading to various opportunities. Education is one of the most powerful mechanisms to empower future generations and promote best outcomes for all involved. Civic engagement allows access to valuable resources supported by public policy. It provides a social network that can cushion individuals and foster resilience.

"The very essence of the creative is its novelty, and hence we have no standard by which to judge it."

Carl Rogers, American psychotherapist,
from *On Becoming a Person* (1961)

Family Connections and Rituals

Family rituals typically mark the transition points in the family life cycle and are closely intertwined with cultural practices. Rituals are typically rich in symbolism and meaning, and they can facilitate going from one lifespan event to another. Major rituals throughout the family lifespan are, for instance, ceremonies and rituals surrounding birth, birthdays, stages of parenthood, school entry, adolescence, leaving school, getting engaged, marriage, retirement, and, of course, death and dying. Rituals and celebrations can be religious, secular, or a combination of both.

Family rituals support closer relationships between family members and create significance and meaning surrounding these important life events (Shiraev & Levy, 2016). There are numerous cultural differences between major ceremonies and rituals, but there is also much that connects us with other cultures, quite a bit that is familiar. Rituals may also express feelings and customs that have developed between family members. Rituals are also attached to special days in the calendar, marking religious and other holidays.

Rituals can be a kind of cultural shorthand or symbol; members from the same cultural context understand quickly the overt and covert symbolism attached to the event. It can be very comforting to recognize rituals because they link the individual to the larger cultural context. Consider how certain religious holidays are celebrated, whether Hanukkah, Diwali, Ramadan, or Christmas; these special days ask for family togetherness, goodwill, and a continuity that may become a family tradition that extends across generations.

Rituals and celebrations are also vehicles for transmitting values and other cultural content, and they often publicly mark a major life transition. Most nations in the world celebrate marriages in elaborate ways, and these are public events inasmuch as all the friends and family of the couple may be invited. The marriage ceremony is also a symbol shared by a group of witnesses who will support the newly joined partners in their new status as a separate family. By committing to each other, they are also typically leaving their parental homes and aspiring to create their own family unit. A marriage ceremony makes the commitment of the two visible to their social context, which, in turn, can provide the support to strengthen this commitment, even during difficult and challenging times.

Family and societal rituals offer opportunities for support. During these times, families and friends gather closely, and there is a certain sacredness attached to these events as they mark milestone transitional points. Rituals comfort through predictability because there is a social script that can guide families as to how these events should be celebrated. For instance, there can be detailed guidelines for families when a loved one passes away, and this predictability and the rituals surrounding death and dying can be comforting when there is so much uncertainty in other areas. These rituals can also provide some cushioning during painful and challenging times. They enable members of a community to acknowledge that the family concerned requires societal support and compassion.

Closely linked to rituals are traditions and routines. Both are repetitive events or processes that add predictability and order to daily life (Segrin & Flora, 2011, p. 54). The family meal can be example of a routine that supports healthy family communication and interaction.

Family rituals can show weak spots within a family's functioning. The stress of togetherness may reveal family feuds and family cutoffs. When family members enact these difficult situations during a public ritual, it can draw additional attention to difficulties within a family system. According to Segrin and Flora (2011, p. 56), family rituals can also characterize the following problematic situations:

- *Under ritualized.* These families ignore or play down the social and cultural symbolism attached to family life transition points. Healthy families tend to celebrate together, and ignoring rituals can be a symptom of family-related difficulties.
- *Rigidly ritualized.* Similar to authoritarian parenting, rigidly ritualized processes are ways of maintaining control and sameness. Culture typically changes over time, but if rituals are very rigid, this change can be minimal. Some orthodox or very conservative religious communities may tend toward inflexible ritualization.
- *Skewed ritualization.* One particular cultural context may dominate over another in family rituals, or one particular behavior may be ritualized at the expense of a fair and balanced expression. The marginalized ritual could also be mocked and devalued in this scenario.
- *Hollow ritualization.* Family members may be going through the motions of the ritual, but, for them, it is devoid of personal meaning. For instance, the eloping couples who exchange their wedding vows in five-minute drive-through ceremonies in Las Vegas, without family or friends, may have opted for minimal ritual and not sharing the event with family and friends because the marriage ceremony itself has little significance for them.
- *Interrupted ritualization.* Certain events, such as war, death, and illness, can prevent a ritual from being completed in the anticipated manner. For instance, the soldier who does not return from a war and whose body is not repatriated cannot be prepared for burial or taken leave of physically—the funeral ritual is interrupted, leaving the family with incompleteness, which can be most painful. During World Wars I and II, plaques and memorials were erected to provide anchor points of mourning and remembrance.
- *Adaptable ritualization.* Sometimes rituals are adapted and personalized to accommodate the unique characteristics of the person or family. Currently, there is a tendency for marriage and funerals to be personalized, which makes these events meaningful for those concerned. Graduation ceremonies are adapted to reveal the particular character of a university or school.

Many of the difficulties families have with ritualization occur because they lack an understanding concerning the intent of the ritualized behavior. Because comprehending cultural, religious, secular, and family rituals requires an understanding of the symbols involved and an appreciation for the process of the ceremony, outsiders, people not acculturated to these rituals, may find them devoid of meaning. Rituals can be particularly meaningless to a cultural outsider. When the ritual is meaningless, it also loses its ability to comfort, to celebrate, to mark an occasion, to support, to wish well—to convey whatever other emotional content that particular ritual was meant to express. Rituals can be very important in providing emotional closure and in signaling to bystanders that this occasion requires expression of emotional support.

It will be a sad day when cultures and societies become devoid of some of their meaningful and constructive customs and rituals, as that will mean that they have severed the links to their own past.

For the human family to weather life's many provocations, it has to be connected to the larger social system and, importantly, to its immediate system of the family.

Families provide the unifying threads in life's intricate tapestry. They provide us with continuity by welcoming us at birth, celebrating our major rites of passage, and ultimately bidding us a loving farewell at death. We are vested in each other's lives in a family; we care deeply about the outcomes of those lives. This connection and caring can foster well-being. The commitment of the family is usually unquestionably loyal and transcends boundaries and barriers. Families are the constant anchoring point whatever the level of turbulence around us.

Tree of Life, by South African artist and ceramicist Anton Bosch. This work explores the life-giving force of trees. "Like the branches on a tree, we all grow in different directions, but our roots remain the same" (Unknown). This is especially true of families.

Source: Tree of Life/Anton Bosch.

Family scientist Michael E. Kerr (2019) wrote a book about Bowen theory with the subtitle *Revealing the Hidden Life of Families.* In the introduction to his book, he mentions that he was inspired by a book on trees, which contained a similar phrase ("the hidden life of trees"), and Wohlleben (2015) offered this description of the intricate connections found in forests, ones Kerr likes to compare to a social network:

> [T]rees are like human families: tree parents live together with their children, communicate with them, support them as they grow, share nutrients with those who are sick or struggling, and even warn each other of impending dangers. (Wohlleben, 2015)

FOCUS POINT

Family connections are strengthened by family rituals, togetherness, and mutual support. Rituals mark transition points in the family life cycle and are closely intertwined with cultural practices. Rituals are rich in symbolism and meaning and can facilitate movement from one lifespan event to another. Family rituals can reveal weak spots of family functioning, such as family feuds and cutoffs. Culture is, among other things, a set of symbols, values, and beliefs that can be understood by persons sharing that same culture. This understanding ascribes meaning and context to rituals.

We become family through biological, social, legal, and emotional ties. Socially, we are grouped in distinct yet also fluid ways; we may choose families of creation, but ultimately the families that welcome and nurture us, and that do the heavy lifting of the daily family routine, are the ones etched into our minds and our hearts.

Families provide the unifying threads in life's intricate tapestry.

Authentic Insight

The Bouquet of Parental Love

My mom used to gather small bunches of flowers and dot them all over our home. Not the bold carnations or the confident roses. Her bouquets of wild gatherings consisted of a sprig of heather, a dash of marigold, a little branch that would only reveal its beauty on close inspection. This was my mom's gift: she could find and appreciate beauty in the most ordinary.

My mom held onto life and onto happiness. She wanted to live fully; she did not want to be reminded of the passing of time. When my mother's last year on earth arrived, she changed slowly and almost imperceptibly. A brain tumor was robbing her of her old self. The last time she visited me, she again gathered miniature bouquets and sprinkled them in all our favorite places. I did not want to discard them. As they dried up, faded, and shriveled, I held on to them, as if I could hold on to my mother.

One sunny morning, after her death, I replaced them with fresh flowers. I looked for the humble varieties. I looked for small forgotten daisies, a curl of jasmine, a yellow bloom posing as a weed, a dark brown prunus leaf. I grouped this unlikely collection of God's flora together in little vases, and knew that it was right. My mom was no longer with us, but she had given me the skills to live my life fully and constructively. The ability to find and appreciate little flowers anywhere was now within my repertoire.

And so parents give to children. They give them layers of experiences, which become memories, like the color washes in a watercolor painting, not overworked but translucent. Layer upon layer, memories build to deepen the parent-child relationship. Often it feels as if I lost my mom too early in my life. And then again, when I am reminded how to be the best parent I can be for my own children, it all comes together. Love is never lost. It is given from parent to child in that long chain of little events: the daily hugs, the support, the acceptance.

Love grows and love links us, generation to generation.

Clara Gerhardt, Tribute to Anna Alida

In many ways these hand-knotted bridges remind us of the power of united relationships. They were built strand by strand by communities to benefit all. The bridges make the formidable approachable and navigable. By being embedded in a supportive family and community, we can cross those emotional canyons thought to be impassable.

Source: © iStock.com/Joerg Steber.

"Children are the living messages we send to a time we will not see."

Neil Postman, from *The Disappearance of Childhood* (1982)

GLOBAL GLIMPSE

OF HUMAN CONNECTIONS AND PERUVIAN ROPE BRIDGES

The Incas perfected the art of the rope bridge. It is a structure made of grass that is skillfully knotted into ropes, which, combined, form a suspension bridge. Without these bridges, the many canyons would have remained impassable. For centuries, these bridges formed the artery of connections across Peru and the wider South American landscape. One such bridge, the Q'eswachaka Bridge, thought to be the last of its kind, is the only contemporary example of a handwoven bridge made by the Inca people. It precariously crosses the Apurímac River, in a gorge high in the Peruvian Andes. The bridge itself is 118 feet and towers 60 feet above the dangerous precipice below.

In 2013, the bridge was allocated special status by UNESCO because it was part of the "intangible cultural heritage of humanity"; it is also still important to the locals. Despite a nearby bridge that can deal with more mundane travel options, such as motor vehicles, the pedestrian grass bridge remains a beloved symbol that the locals love to use and honor. They also take part in a yearly ceremony in which the bridge is painstakingly renewed. Entire communities collaborate to make this a reality. Barreiro, a source interviewed by the National Geographic, made this comment: "As the political empire of the Incas was destroyed, what was left behind was the culture of the people at the village level."

In times gone by, the bridges were part of a communication network and were used by special runners known as *chasquis,* who were messengers. More than just carrying the information, they were literate and could read and translate the messages they carried to higher authorities. They were extremely fit, being able to cross these significant distances at high altitudes.

According to the *Atlas Obscura* the geographic coordinates of this bridge are −14.3811214, −71.484012.

Sources: Foehr and Thuras (2016); Sewell (n.d.).

SPOTLIGHT ON THEORIES

Positive Psychology

Three traditional theories are predominantly associated with positivity and happiness. They preceded the current emergence of the positivity movement considerably. Theorists and philosophers dating back to before the common era have been interested in explaining this desirable yet semi-elusive fairy-tale promise: ". . . and they lived happily ever after." Part of the challenge is that the word "happily" can mean different things to different people, and once we start dissecting what contributes to happiness, the situation gains in complexity.

The positive psychology movement looks at what is associated with positive emotions and at what behaviors seek out the ways and means to attain and maintain that positive state. Although attaining happiness can be a highly individual path, commonalities can be recognized. A positive outlook and hope facing the future are significant. According to Compton and Hoffman (2019), the word "flourishing" is often associated with the behavior that promotes well-being, fortitude, and resilience. These same authors highlight some factors that contribute to promising outcomes in

(Continued)

(Continued)

terms of well-being (Compton & Hoffman, 2019, pp. 7–9):

> *Social relationships.* A recurrent theme and important in providing support, social relationships give individuals the opportunity to feel heard and acknowledged, to feel connected and purposeful.
>
> *Virtues and strengths.* These contribute to our fortitude, our ability to face life; some of these qualities can include courage, loyalty, and honesty.
>
> *Compassion and empathy.* If we feel with and for our fellow humans, we are connected socially and emotionally—we can relate to the landscape of human emotion. Also, we expect to be treated with compassion and empathy when we are in a relationship of significance, as this gives us a sense of being understood.
>
> *Positive and negative.* Both emotions have a role in promoting well-being, but they can occur relatively independently from one another. Although challenging life situations can precipitate negative feelings, the opposite is not necessarily true. Just because we are experiencing good fortune does not necessarily provide us with the outcome of positivity. Eliminating the negative does not automatically strengthen the positive (p. 9):

> The good life, then, is found in the total context of a person's life. It is not just a transitory state or even one specific emotion. (p. 14)

Even earlier theories relate to the pursuit of happiness. The ancient Greek philosophers theorized that pleasure is the chief good in life, a philosophy called "hedonism." As far back as the fourth century BCE, Aristippus referred to the hedonic moments of life. Plato and Socrates and Aristotle each contributed insights about happiness that guide us to this day. These philosophers agreed that we need to distinguish between happiness as a state of mind and happiness associated with good outcomes for the person concerned, in other words, the happiness of a life that is relatively rewarding emotionally and otherwise.

According to Compton and Hoffman (2019, p. 12), the ancient Hebrews contributed to a concept of social identity that incorporated a relationship with a personal God and provided wisdom and guidelines to support living meaningful and constructive lives. These authors trace various philosophical approaches to the happiness question right through to the twenty-first century and provide a succinct overview of historic events leading up to the current approaches to positive psychology.

- *Hedonism theory.* This theory acknowledges the subjectivity attached to how we interpret our lives and therefore what level of joy we attach to it.
- *Desire theory.* Are our desires fulfilled? This theory of happiness focuses on meeting our goals or reaching our destination, be it material, spiritual, or otherwise.
- *Objective list theory.* Certain things are objectively supposed to be associated with happiness, such as success, satisfactory relationships, educational goals, and good health; some things are more elusive than others.

Authors Seligman and Royzman (2003) suggest a three-pronged approach to happiness. They distinguish between

- *The pleasant life* focused on enjoyable experiences, which can include positive subjective states;
- *The good life* focused on engagement and involvement, which can include positive traits; and
- *The meaningful life* focused on the sense of meaning and its interpretation, which can include positive institutions.

If we combine this approach with that of Compton and Hoffman (2019, p. 27), we note the implication that there are different kinds of happiness; one size does not fit all. Several happiness scales have sought to explore these various dimensions of happiness; such scales rely heavily on the subjective statements of the participants.

In a Nutshell

- Happiness cannot be pinned down to one emotion or state. It is complex and contextual and involves several contributory and interacting components.
- Three traditional theories are predominantly associated with happiness: hedonism theory, desire theory, and objective list theory.
- Positive psychology, which is associated with Martin Seligman, focuses on what makes humans well and happy rather than on psychic ailments and how to treat them; it has a positive rather than a negative orientation.
- Generally, several dimensions are acknowledged as contributing to human well-being, including the neurophysiological and genetic; traits, virtues, and attitudes; and meaning, interpretations, and goals—to mention but a few.
- Distinctions have been made between
    - the pleasant life, focused on enjoyable experiences;
    - the good life, focused on engagement and involvement; and
    - the meaningful life, focused on a sense of meaning and its interpretation.

CHAPTER FOCUS POINTS

The Intentionality of Happiness

- Around the new millennium, psychological researchers focused on the dimensions of happiness, calling this study *positive psychology*.
- Happiness has a subjective quality and reflects a state of mind, a conscious awareness and experience of satisfaction and joy—one without the excessive pressure of desiring more and better. Happiness is difficult to define.
- *Flow* describes being lost in the moment, becoming a part of an activity that absorbs us fully. This process imparts feelings of well-being and a sense of emotional reward.
- Civic engagement supports the life goals of a participating individual, and, as a group expression, it reflects the quality of our cultural expressions and societal engagement.

Dynamics of Spiritual Development

- One model referencing spiritual development acknowledges the interplay between cultural and social contexts.
- This approach toward spiritual development superimposes an interlocking sequence of *meaning, purpose, obligation*, and *contribution.*
- Components of *contributing to* and *receiving from* the varied contexts explain the complexity within which personhood is embedded.
- When it comes to living meaningful lives, we build on our sociocultural heritage, but we also need to move forward by contributing, by being engaged, and by taking responsibility.
- Predisposing, precipitating, and maintaining factors can interact to influence outcomes.

Education and Public Policy

- Education provides the reward of meaningful life stories leading to various opportunities. Education is one of the most powerful mechanisms to empower future generations and promote best outcomes for all involved.
- Civic engagement allows us access to valuable resources supported by public policy. It provides a social network that can cushion individuals and foster resilience.

Family Connections and Rituals

- Family connections are strengthened by family rituals, togetherness, and mutual support. Rituals mark transition points in the family life cycle and are closely intertwined with cultural practices.

- Rituals are rich in symbolism and meaning and can facilitate movement from one lifespan event to another.
- Family rituals can reveal weak spots of family functioning, such as family feuds and cutoffs.
- Culture is, among other things, a set of symbols, values, and beliefs that can be understood by persons sharing that same culture. This understanding ascribes meaning and context to rituals.

Spotlight on Theories: Positive Psychology

- Happiness cannot be pinned down to one emotion or state. It is complex and contextual and involves several contributory and interacting components. Three traditional theories are predominantly associated with happiness: hedonism theory, desire theory, and objective list theory.
- Positive psychology, which is associated with Martin Seligman, focuses on what makes humans well and happy rather than on psychic ailments and how to treat them; it has a positive rather than a negative orientation.
- Generally, several dimensions are acknowledged as contributing to human well-being, including the neurophysiological and genetic; traits, virtues, and attitudes; and meaning, interpretations, and goals—to mention but a few.
- Distinctions have been made between
  - *the pleasant life*, focused on enjoyable experiences;
  - *the good life*, focused on engagement and involvement; and
  - *the meaningful life*, focused on a sense of meaning and its interpretation.

Glossary

ABC-X model: Historic model that focuses on recovery and reorganization within families. It considers contributing factors such as the nature of the crisis, how long the crisis causes disorganization, and the recovery process.

Acculturation: Acquired cultural identity. This term is most often used in the context of assimilating into a host culture.

Active listening: The full allocation of attention to concentrate, understand, respond, and remember what another person is saying.

Ambiguous loss: Loss with no clarity of outcome and no accompanying closure. An example of this phenomenon occurs when a person disappears and there is no information regarding whether that person is dead or alive, leaving loved ones in a state of limbo.

Attribution bias: Self-serving bias, slanting or altering one's value judgments usually to favor oneself.

Beneficence: The quality or state of producing good or acting in a way that is for the good of the individual, family, and society. The phrase used in this context is "In the best interests of . . ."

Benevolent secret: A secret intended to provide a good or favorable outcome. These secrets also relate to not communicating or not keeping family members in the loop.

Bidirectional: The flow of influence that goes both ways, or in both directions, for instance individuals and culture influencing each other.

Boomerang kids: Individuals who had launched by leaving for college, or for work, and then return home because of various factors, which can include economic and emotional concerns.

Boundaries: Natural borderlines that indicate levels of privacy and space a family member may require. Professional boundaries denote appropriate professional distance between, for instance, clients and therapists.

Bowen theory: A theory based on the work of Murray Bowen that views the family as a unit interacting in a multigenerational manner. Also known as natural systems theory, Bowen theory emphasizes the individuation process. The core of Bowen theory describes eight interlocking concepts. See also *family systems theory*.

Causal attribution theory: A theory concerned with how ordinary people explain the causes of behavior and events. When we explain someone's behavior, we add our own biases, tending to favor what pertains to ourselves and being more critical of others. See also *attribution bias*.

Chronosystem: The time dimension within the ecological systems model (Bronfenbrenner), which encompasses the entire network of other systems. This time dimension can involve the organization of events and changes at a particular historical time.

Circular questioning: Repeated questioning used within systemic family therapy to expand the client's own insight and generate multiple explanations and stories of a family situation.

Cognitive behavioral therapy (CBT): A theory focusing on actions (behavioral) and problem-solving capabilities (cognitive) to find solutions to problems. This type of therapy has proven to be a powerful and frequently used form of intervention.

Collective ambivalence: Disruptions or unclear situations that extend into larger and more complex social systems.

Communication accommodation theory (CAT): A theory that explores how we adjust our interactions to accommodate others and facilitate progress. CAT emphasizes the interpersonal dimensions of the communication process, which can occur in one-on-one communication, in group conversations, and in intergroup contexts.

Conformity: The extent to which family members subscribe to the same values, attitudes, and beliefs.

Constructivist psychotherapy (CPT): Therapeutic approach that encourages clients in their search to *construct meaning* within the context of the greater world.

Content: The specific techniques and/or details within a given situation or process. See also *process*.

Context: The greater background, which provides additional information to understand and interpret situations.

Convergence: Getting closer to the communication partner by adapting to and, to an extent, modeling that individual.

Conversation: Verbal interaction that takes place between family members. To be a fully realized interaction, the conversation must involve individuals willing to discuss topics.

Coparents: Persons who parent in a collaborative manner and in an ongoing, responsible, and committed manner. Typically, the parents can make decisions for and on behalf of the child and fulfill their executive function, while sustaining a healthy emotional investment.

Covert: The quality of being secret or hidden from view.

Cultural echo: The cultural thread woven into communication. Within the fabric of each individual language comes a cultural echo, as words convey not only meaning but also cultural context.

Cultural humility: A quality of respect and openness to learn from cultures or contexts other than one's own.

Cultural integration: Choosing and integrating the components of various cultural influences in a respectful manner.

***Declaration of the Rights of the Child*:** A set of aspirational goals and guidelines pertaining to the well-being of children universally. First formulated in 1959 by UNESCO.

Defense mechanisms: Ways of disguising and/or distorting certain material because it is too threatening or elicits anxiety. The term was first used by psychoanalysts.

Disabling power: Inequality between participating parties, often placing one of the participants in a submissive position. Disabling power often leads to destructive patterns of communication.

Disengaged: Growing distance between members in a family system. Characteristics of disengagement include decreased connection, sharing, and intimacy among family members.

Divergence: When the communicator moves away from the communication partner.

Double ABC-X model: An extension of the initial ABC-X model. By trying to cope with initial crises and stressors, secondary stressors arise. This model is a circular understanding of stress and transitions and how preceding events can influence later outcomes.

Dual process model: A model that describes oscillating between two forms of grief work. For survivors, this includes grieving "loss" while also seeking restoration by rebuilding one's life. These forms of grief unfold simultaneously and concurrently.

Dyadic power theory: A theory emphasizing the relative perceived power of partners in a relationship. When people interact, they define that interaction and that relationship through the manner of their interaction. An extension of social exchange theory, dyadic power theory has a systemic quality that builds over time, influencing how those relationships are formed and maintained.

Dynamics: Those aspects that change or progress within a system or process; the study of where movement and growth occur.

Dysfunctional family: Family system that relates in counter-constructive ways by exerting direct or indirect pressures on its members.

Ecological systems theory: The theory, proposed by Urie Bronfenbrenner, that different environments affect individual and family functioning. The family is represented as a part of many interrelated nested systems that have bidirectional influence.

Ecology: The interrelatedness between systems; considering that influence can be bidirectional.

Emotional cutoff: Disconnecting from emotional contact with other family members.

Emotional disinvestment: When one person in a relationship no longer invests in or holds positive regard for the other person. This detachment often signals a break in the relationship.

Emotional fusion: Excessive closeness to and being overly involved with other family members. Emotional fusion hinders individuation.

Emotional hoarding: Holding onto resentments, anger, and a host of other emotions.

Emotional intimacy: Mutual investment, between two people, to create and sustain emotional closeness. Both parties need to display their feelings and emotionally invest in the relationship in order to foster intimacy.

Emotional regulation: A person's ability to react and respond effectively to an emotional situation and/or experience by managing emotional expressiveness in context-appropriate ways.

Enculturation: The first cultural identity to which a child is exposed, typically the culture of origin.

Engage: To become a participant or take part in an interaction.

Enmeshed: A family system that is excessively intertwined and close, hampering individuation.

Exosystem: The systemic level above the mesosystem. The exosystem may be comprised of government agencies or community programs that are distant but still influence a child indirectly.

Extended family: Individuals beyond the nuclear or immediate family who are related through blood or marriage.

Face-negotiation theory (FNT): A theory that focuses on tokens and expressions of respect to honor the communication partner. These gestures allow alignment or loyalty to develop, which defines aspects of the relationship.

Family board: Technique of placing family members in relationship contexts to each other. Felt boards onto which Velcro images of people are attached can be used to illustrate connections.

Family communication patterns theory: A theory based on the premise of the interaction between two dimensions: conversation and conformity.

Family dynamics: Patterns of relating, or interactions, between family members. In social contexts such as family systems, the word *dynamics* is used to denote those aspects that change or progress—where movement and growth occur. See also *dynamics*.

Family life course development: Changes—predictable and unpredictable—that occur within the family over the lifespan of the family unit.

Family of choice: A group of people who have kinship-like bonds but are not necessarily related through marriage or genetics.

Family power: A complex power that extends beyond the individual member roles and represents the power of the collective family unit. This power structure can be influenced by social positions and resources.

Family resilience: The ability of the family, as a functional system, to withstand and rebound from adversity. See also *resilience*.

Family rituals: Ceremonies surrounding transitional lifespan stages, including birth and death. These rituals can be religious, secular, or a combination of both.

Family scientists: Helping professionals directly concerned with the family and family well-being.

Family script: The unique way a family manages content and information.

Family sculpting: A therapeutic technique that asks a family member to place other members of the family in a scene or sculpture. This placement of family members can reveal the perspective of a central family member. Sculpting is a subjective experience in which one individual depicts his or her own specific connections within the family.

Family stress theory: A theory that focuses on a particular challenge or task that requires further contextualization and intervention.

Family systems theory: This theory perceives of the family as a unit or system. The relationship between parents and children is seen as a subsystem of the larger social system, and family functioning is described in ways that resemble descriptions of other systems in nature. See *Bowen theory*.

Five stages of grief: Elisabeth Kübler-Ross (1926–2004) outlined the following five stages of coming to terms with loss, remembered by the acronym DABDA: denial, anger, bargaining, depression, and acceptance.

Flow: The feeling of being lost within the moment, which we experience when an activity absorbs us so fully that we become part of it. The boundary between ourselves and what we are doing fades, and time seems to stand still. Flow imparts feelings of well-being and a sense of emotional reward. The concept is attributed to Mihaly Csikszentmihalyi.

Gaslighting: Psychological manipulation that seeks to plant doubt in the mind of a targeted individual. Victims of gaslighting question their own memories, perceptions, or sanity.

Genogram: A form of family notation similar to a traditional family tree documenting ancestors. The genogram contains more information than a traditional family tree; it can categorize hereditary patterns as well as psychological factors within specific ancestral branches. One can adapt this technique to focus on a variety of topics.

Habituation: Getting used to either a substance or an experience. Over time, the stimulants one becomes habituated to must be increased or escalated to achieve the same effect.

Happiness: A conscious awareness and experience of satisfaction, contentment and joy—without the excessive pressure of desiring more and better. Being in a state of happiness has a subjective quality and is difficult to define.

Hierarchies: Systems in which some people or groups of people are ranked higher than others according to their status or power. Parental units in the family, for example, take on responsibilities, provide for children, and have authority, which places them higher in the family hierarchy. This definition pertains to the family context proposed by therapist Salvador Minuchin.

Hoarding: According to the *DSM-5*, hoarding is "persistent difficulty discarding or parting with possessions, regardless of their actual values" (American Psychiatry Association, 2013).

Human lifespan development: How individuals change over the course of their lives.

Humor: Used as an approach to ease the relationships within the therapeutic context and facilitate insight in a positive manner.

Immediate family: The smallest family unit consisting of a parental subunit and children.

Individuation: The development of a sense of self and autonomy through self-differentiation. In common language, individuation means finding one's own unique personality as a separate person or individual.

Integrative therapeutic approach: An approach that combines and integrates other therapeutic approaches in a systematic and organized manner to support best practices and outcomes.

Intergenerational transmission: Lengthy exposure to stress, or other conditions, that may precipitate epigenetic changes that might subsequently influence offspring.

Intergroup distinctiveness theory: A theory that proposes that people adjust their behavior and speech to support group membership and group identity.

Interpsychic approaches: Therapeutic approaches that focus on what happens between people.

Intimate partner violence (IPV): A type of dominance, even bullying, that takes place within the context of partner intimacy and vulnerability. IPV can involve physical, sexual, emotional, and psychological abuse.

Intrapsychic approaches: Therapeutic approaches that predominantly focus on the inner life of individuals.

Macrosystem: The largest context of the nested layers that affect an individual. The influence is often indirect. This environment involves the larger culture, values, and policies on a national scale. Because of their breadth, macrosystems often influence in indirect ways, and they encompass all the other systems.

Malevolent secret: Guarded information with negative or destructive content.

Mediated interaction: An interaction in which a third party or process can intervene in communication. For example, a mediator can facilitate discussions between divorcing partners.

Mesosystem: The mesosystem consists of connections or interactions between microsystems. Bronfenbrenner labeled this dimension to refer to the connections children make between their close environments, typically family, community, and school.

Metacognition: The ability to reflect on the inner landscape of our feelings. In layperson's terms, metacognition is referred to as "thinking about thinking."

Metacommunication: A second layer of communication hidden behind verbal communication. Often, metacommunication is not formally expressed; instead, it is implied contextually.

Microclimate: An atmosphere defined and created by a group of people.

Microsystem: The innermost and smallest setting in which a child (for example) is embedded. This setting is comprised of the very personal influences and environments provided by the immediate family and related social contexts.

Multigenerational: Relationships and related influences across several generations.

Narrative approaches: Approaches that emphasize the story, or narrative, that clients convey. These acknowledge both objective and subjective realities.

Narrative therapy: One of the leading interventions for situations related to traumatic transitions and loss; incorporates the emphasis on a greater context. Narrative therapy allows clients to retell their stories: in each therapeutic retelling, the client is encouraged to find greater meaning or additional perspectives.

Negative suggestions: Defeating suggestions that do not support the targeted person.

Neuroscience: The study of the brain and nervous system, including neurological development, structure, and function. Neuropsychology studies the brain and nervous system in the quest to understand the interrelationship between physical, psychological, and neurological components.

Non-maleficence: The quality or action of avoiding that which causes harm. The phrase used in this context is "First of all, do no harm."

Nuclear family: The core family unit. An example of a nuclear family could be a parental dyad and children.

Object cathexis: An investment of emotion, mental energy, or life force in an object, person, or idea. This concept was first attributed to Freud and used in psychoanalysis.

Observer effect: The change that occurs in a family system when a family is being watched or when an outsider joins the system.

Overt: The quality of being obvious or out in the open.

Parental unit: Typically composed of one to two adults who take responsibility and provide for the family.

Play therapy: A technique focusing on the expressiveness of therapeutic play, which allows children to share aspects of their family and social functioning.

Positive psychology: The branch of psychology that focuses on the dimensions related to happiness and well-being. Positive psychology came to prominence around the new millennium.

Positive suggestions: Encouraging suggestions that reinforce and support the targeted person.

Power dynamic: One person or party tries to exert control over another party or person, ranging from subtle to extreme.

Process: The broader boundaries within which the content can be contained; the bigger picture. See also *content*.

Psychoanalysis: Approach that acknowledges a subconscious dimension and is based on the theoretical concepts of the psychoanalytic movement. The therapeutic process aims to facilitate insight into that dimension through psychoanalysis.

Psychodynamics: Approach that attempts to explain the reasons, motivations, and meanings of behavior. In the original psychoanalytic context, it included subconscious motivations; currently, the term is used more generally.

Psychoeducation: Providing facts, insights, and contributions to the educational process. Examples of psychoeducation are character, sexual, and social/emotional education, as well as college and career readiness.

Psychotherapy: A talk-based psychological intervention aiming to increase insight. Psychotherapy emerged around the turn of the twentieth century to treat mental vulnerabilities. Freud is associated with its early beginnings.

Reciprocal interaction: Interactions that influence the participating parties. For example, when different generations interact, an outcome could be bidirectional influence.

Relational dialectics theory (RDT): An interpersonal communications theory that examines dialectical tensions and accommodations.

Resilience: Various interacting factors contributing to constructive adaptability and outcomes in the face of challenging and even adversarial situations. See also *family resilience*.

Responsible parenting: Awareness and application of appropriate and acceptable childcare practices.

Responsive parenting: Parents actively react to the needs displayed by a child.

Restorying: Retelling of a pain-laden story in a therapeutic setting to help the storyteller reconstruct meaning and explore new possibilities.

Self-disclosure: Displaying vulnerability by revealing information about oneself. This vulnerability can contribute to interpersonal cohesion, emotional trust, and intimacy.

Self-regulation: The ability to balance, contain, constructively redirect, or regulate one's emotions, needs, and urges.

Similarity-attraction theory: We are likely to be attracted to those people who hold similar attitudes and beliefs.

Social exchange process theory: Persons exchange perceived rewards to meet their own goals.

Social isolation: The silent withdrawal by a person from opportunities of family and civic engagement. This type of isolation can signal being depressed and not feeling connected.

Social penetration theory: Theory examining the extent that self-disclosure can be applied to manage relationships.

Social systems: Integrated family units that demonstrate complex interactions.

Stonewalling: To place a metaphorical barrier between oneself and another, one that prevents further dialogue. This barrier cuts off interaction by using noncommunication as a tactic.

Structural ambivalence: The uncertainty that arises when competing forces make demands on resources, including financial, time, and space-related resources.

Subsystems: Smaller sections within a unit, for example, the parents or children within a family.

Theory: A way of organizing information to facilitate understanding, research, and treatment. A theory is typically based on observations, and it can change over time as new insights are gained.

Theory of resilience and rational load (TRRL): A theoretical approach to understanding how and why resilience is created and maintained in relationships. Social relationships have the power to alter an individual's stress trajectories significantly—either positively or negatively. Because the individual is embedded within the larger relational systems, these social relationships can influence trajectories.

Third culture: A cultural identity that incorporates aspects of the two cultures to which an individual has been exposed extensively. For example, expatriates living in international contexts for extended periods of time can create a third culture.

Wholeness: The quality of not being divided into parts. An undivided group that makes up a complete or whole unit is said to have wholeness. A family unit is greater than the sum of its parts, that is, of the individuals making up that unit.

References

Abercrombie, S. H., & Hastings, S. L. (2016). Feminization of poverty. In *The Wiley Blackwell Encyclopedia of Gender and Sexuality Studies*. Retrieved from https://doi.org/10.1002/9781118663219.wbegss550

Aburn, G., Gott, M., & Hoare, K. (2016). What is resilience? An integrative review of the empirical literature. *Journal of Advanced Nursing, 72*(5), 980–1000. https://doi.org/10.1111/jan.12888

Afifi, T. D., & Harrison, K. (2018). Theory of resilience and relational load (TRRL): Understanding families as systems of stress and calibration. In D. O. Braithwaite, E. A. Suter, & K. Floyd (Eds.). *Engaging theories in family communication: Multiple perspectives* (2nd ed., pp. 324–336). New York, NY: Routledge.

Afifi, T. D., Merrill, A. F., & Davis, S. (2016). The theory of resilience and relational load. *Personal Relationships, 23*(4), 663–683. Retrieved from https://doi.org/10.1111/pere.12159

Agllias, K. (2016). *Family estrangement: A matter of perspective*. New York, NY: Routledge.

Agllias, K., & Gray, M. (2013). *Secrets and lies: the ethical implications of family estrangement*. Retrieved from https://www.researchgate.net/publication/273455620_Secrets_and_lies_The_ethical_implications_of_family_estrangement

Akamatsu, T. J., Crowther, J. H., Hobfoll, S. E., & Stephens, A. P. (Eds.). (2016). *Family health psychology*. Washington, DC: Taylor & Francis. (Original work published in 1992)

Akerstrom, M. (2017). *Betrayal and betrayers: The sociology of treachery*. New York, NY: Routledge.

Al Udaidi, B. A. (2017). Cost of growing up in dysfunctional family. *Journal of Family Medicine and Disease Prevention, 3*(3). Retrieved from https://clinmedjournals.org/articles/jfmdp/journal-of-family-medicine-and-disease-prevention-jfmdp-3-059.php?jid=jfmdp

Albert, U., De Cori, D., Barbaro, E., Fernández de la Cruz, L., Nordsletten, A. E., & Mataix-Cols, D. (2015). Hoarding disorder: A new obsessive-compulsive related disorder in DSM–5. *Journal of Psychopathology, 21*, 354–364. Retrieved from https://www.researchgate.net/publication/285883585_Hoarding_disorder_A_new_obsessive-compulsive_related_disorder_in_DSM-5

Alford, C. F. (2016). Mirror neurons, psychoanalysis, and the age of empathy. *International Journal of Applied Psychoanalytic Studies, 13*(1), 7–23. https://doi.org/10.1002/aps.1411

Altbach, P. G., & Yudkevich, M. (2017). Twenty-first century mobility: The role of international faculty. *International Higher Education, 90*, 8–10. https://doi.org/10.6017/ihe.2017.90.9995

Altman, I., & Taylor, D. A. (1973). *Social penetration: The development of interpersonal relationships*. New York, NY: Rinehart & Winston.

Amato, P. R. (2014). Who is family? *NCFR Report*, 3–4. Retrieved from https://www.ncfr.org/ncfr-report/past-issues/summer-2014/what-family

American Academy of Pediatrics. (2016a). Children and adolescents and digital media. *Pediatrics, 138*(5). https://doi.org/10.1542/peds.2016-2593

American Academy of Pediatrics. (2016b). Media and young minds. *Pediatrics, 138*(5). https://doi.org/10.1542/peds.2016-2591

American Academy of Pediatrics. (2016c, October 21). Media use for 5- to 8-year-olds should reflect personalization, balance. *AAP News*. Retrieved from https://www.aappublications.org/news/2016/10/21/MediaSchool102116

American Counseling Association [ACA]. (2014). *ACA Code of Ethics*. Alexandria, VA.

American Psychiatric Association. (2013). *Diagnostic and statistical manual of mental disorders* (5th ed.). Arlington, VA: American Psychiatric Publishing.

American Psychological Association. (n.d.). *Stress effects on the body*. Retrieved from http://www.apa.org/helpcenter/stress-body.aspx

Anderson, H. E., & Larsen, K. V. (2015). Sculpting with people: An experimental learning technique. *Nurse Education in Practice, 15*(6), 556–560. https://doi.org/10.1016/j.nepr.2015.07.014

Anderson, K. L. (2010). Conflict, power, and violence in families. *Journal of Marriage and Family, 72*(3), 726–742. https://doi.org/10.1111/j.1741-3737.2010.00727.x

Andreassen, C. S., Griffiths, M. D., Pallesen, S., Bilder, R. M., Torsheim, T., & Aboujaoude, E. (2015). The Bergen shopping addiction scale: Reliability and validity of a brief screening test. *Frontier of Psychology*. https://doi.org/10.3389/fpsyg.2015.01374

Anguelova, L. (2018). *Working with adult survivors of childhood sexual abuse*. New York, NY: Routledge.

Arnett, J. J. (2000). Emerging adulthood: A theory of development from the late teens through the twenties. *American Psychologist, 55*(5), 469–480. https://doi.org/10.1037/0003-066X.55.5.469

Arnold, L. B., & Basden, L. (2008). *Family communication: Theory and research.* Upper River Saddle, NJ: Pearson.

Babycentre. (2017, August). *Baby-naming practices from around the world.* Retrieved from https://www.babycentre.co.uk/a568884/baby-naming-practices-from-around-the-world

Bai, S., & Repetti, R. L. (2015). Short-term resilience processes in the family. *Family Relations, 64*(1), 109–119. https://doi.org/10.1111/fare.12101

Baker, J. M. (2012). *Family secrets: Gay sons. A mother's story.* New York, NY: Routledge.

Baker, J. T. (1919). *The art of conversation: Twelve gold rules.* Evanston, IL: Correct English Publishing Company. (Originally published in 1907)

Ballard, M. B., Fazio-Griffith, L., & Marino, R. (2016). Transgenerational family therapy: A case study of a couple in crisis. *The Family Journal, 24*(2), 109–113. https://doi.org/10.1177/1066480716628564

Banks, J. A. (2015). *Cultural diversity and education* (6th ed.). New York, NY: Routledge.

Barcai, A., & Rabkin, L. Y. (1972). Excommunication as a family therapy technique. *Archives of General Psychiatry, 27*(6), 804–808. https://doi.org/10.1001/archpsyc.1972.01750300066011

Barker, D. P. (2004). The developmental origins of chronic adult disease. *Acta Paediatrica. Supplement, 93*(s446), 26–33.

Barker, D., Eriksson, J., Forsén, T., & Osmond, C. (2002). Fetal origins of adult disease: Strength of effects and biological basis. *International Journal of Epidemiology, 31*(6), 1235–1239.

Barnwell, A. (2018). Hidden heirlooms: Keeping family secrets across generations. *Journal of Sociology, 54*(3). https://doi.org/10.1177/1440783317727878

Bauer, I. M., & Baumeister, R. F. (2011). Self-regulatory strength. In K. D. Vohs & R. F. Baumeister (Eds.). *Handbook of self-regulation: Research, theory, and application* (2nd ed., pp. 64–82). New York, NY: The Guildford Press.

Baumrind, D. (1966). Effects of authoritative parental control on child behavior. *Child Development, 37*(4), 887–907.

Baumrind, D. (1967). Child care practices anteceding three patterns of preschool behavior. *Genetic Psychology Monographs, 75*(1), 43–88.

Baxter, L. A. (1988). A dialectical perspective on communication strategies in relationship development. In S. Duck (Ed.), *Handbook of personal relationships: Theory, research, and interventions* (pp. 257–273). Chichester, UK: Wiley.

Baxter, L. A. (2004). Relationships as dialogues. *Journal of the International Association for Relationship Research, 11*(1), 1–22. https://doi.org/10.1111/j.1475-6811.2004.00068.x

Baxter, L. A., & Braithwaite, D. O. (2010). Relational dialectics theory, applied. In *New Directions in Interpersonal Communication Research* (pp. 48–68). SAGE Publications Inc.. https://doi.org/10.4135/9781483349619.n3

Baxter, L. A., & Scharp, K. M. (2015). Dialectical tensions in relationships. *The International Encyclopedia of Interpersonal Communication,* 1–5. https://doi.org/10.1002/9781118540190.wbeic017

Becvar, D., & Becvar. R. (2013). *Family therapy: A systemic integration* (8th ed.). Upper Saddle River, NJ: Pearson.

Bekk, M., Spörrle, M., Völckner, F., Spieß, & Woschée, R. (2017). What is not beautiful should match: How attractiveness similarity affects consumer responses to advertising. *Marketing Letters, 28*(4), 509–522. https://doi.org/10.1007/s11002-017-9428-3

Bell, D., & Bennett. (2005). Genetic secrets and the family. In S. A. M. McLean (Ed.), *Genetics and the gene therapy* (pp. 209–240).

Bell, G. (2000). *Somewhere over the rainbow: Travels in South Africa.* Great Britain: Little, Brown and Company.

Bennett, J. (2015). Narrating family histories: Negotiating identity and belonging through tropes of nostalgia and authenticity. *Current Sociology.* https://doi.org/10.1177/0011392115578984

Bennett, M. J. (2004). Becoming interculturally competent. In J. S. Wurzel (Ed.), *Towards multiculturalism: A reader in multicultural education.* Newton, MA: Intercultural Resource Corporation. Retrieved from https://www.idrinstitute.org/wp-content/uploads/2018/02/becoming_ic_competent.pdf

Benson, P. L. (2006a). *All kids are our kids: What communities must do to raise caring and responsible children and adolescents* (2nd ed.). San Francisco, CA: Josef-Bass.

Benson, P. L. (2006b). The science of children and adolescent spiritual development: Definitional, theoretical, and field-building challenges. In E. C. Roehlkepartain, P. E. King, L. Wagener, & P. L. Benson (Eds.). *The Handbook of Spiritual Development in Childhood and Adolescence* (pp. 484–497). Thousand Oaks, CA: SAGE Publications, Inc.

Bentz, C., Verkerk, A., Kiela, D., Hill, F., & Buttery, P. (2015). Adaptive communication: Languages with more non-native speakers tend to have fewer word forms. *PLOS One.* https://doi.org/10.1371/journal.pone.0128254

Berger, A. A. (2018). Sigmund Freud on psychopathology in everyday life. In A. A. Berger *Perspectives on everyday life: A cross disciplinary cultural analysis* (pp. 39–43). New York, NY: Springer.

Berger, C. R., & Calabrese, R. J. (1975). Some explorations in initial interaction and beyond: Toward a developmental theory of interpersonal communication. *Human Communication Theory, 1*, 99–112.

Berger, J. (1972). *Ways of seeing*. Harmondsworth, UK: Penguin.

Berger, M. M., & Rosenbaum, M. (2015). Notes on help-rejecting complainers. *International Journal of Group Psychotherapy, 17*(3), 357–370. https://doi.org/10.1080/00207284.1967.11643035. (Original work published in 1967)

Berger, P. L., & Luckmann, T. (1966). *The social construction of reality: The treatise in the sociology of knowledge*. Garden City, NY: Doubleday.

Bergsieker, H. B., Leslie, L. M., Constantine, V. S., & Fiske, S. T. (2012). Stereotyping by omission: Eliminate the negative, accentuate the positive. *Journal of Personality and Social Psychology, 102*(6), 1214–1238.

Bertot, J. C., Jaeger, P. T., & Hansen, D. (2012). The impact of policies on government social media usage: Issues, challenges, and recommendations. *Government Information Quarterly. 29*, 30–40. Retrieved from https://www.academia.edu/2292394/The_impact_of_polices_on_government_social_media_usage_Issues_challenges_and_recommendations

Biermann, G., & Biermann, R. (1998). [The Sceno Game in the course of time]. *Praxis Der Kinderpsychologie Und Kinderpsychiatrie, 47*(3), 186–202.

Bigner, J. J,. & Gerhardt, C. (2019). *Parent-child relations: An introduction to parenting* (10th ed.). Upper Saddle River, NJ: Pearson.

Bitter, J. R., & Carlson, J. (2017). Adlerian thought and process in systems of family therapy. *Journal of Individual Psychology, 73*(4), 307–327. https://doi.org/10.1353/jip.2017.0026

Bjornestad, A. G., & Mims, G. A. (2017). Paradoxes and paradoxical intervention. In J. Carlson & S. B. Dermer (Eds.), *The SAGE encyclopedia of marriage, family, and couples counseling* (pp. 1191–1194) Thousand Oaks, CA: SAGE Publications, Inc.

Black, J., & Green, A. (1992). *Gods, demons, and symbols of ancient Mesopotamia: An illustrated dictionary*. London, England: The British Museum Press.

Blendon, R. J., & Benson, J. M. (2018). The public and the opioid-abuse epidemic. *The New England Journal of Medicine*, 378, 407–411. https://doi.org/10.1056/NEJMp1714529

Blieszner, R., & Artale, L. M. (2001). Benefits of intergenerational service-learning to human service majors. *Educational Gerontology, 27*(1), 71–87.

Bluck, S., & Mroz, E. L. (2018). The end: Death as part of the life story. *The International Journal of Reminiscence and Life Review, 5*(1), 6–14. Retrieved from http://journals.radford.edu/index.php/IJRLR/article/view/105/47

Bogenschneider, K. (2014). *Family policy matters: How policymaking affects families and what professionals can do* (3rd ed.). New York, NY: Routledge.

Bogenschneider, K., Little, O., Ooms, T., Benning, S., & Cadigan, K. (2012). *The family impact rationale: An evidence base for the family impact lens*. Madison, WI: Family Impact Institute.

Bolton, C. D. (1961). Mate selection as the development of a relationship. *Marriage and Family Living, 23*, 234–240.

Bonanno, G. (2009). *The other side of sadness: What the new science of bereavement tells us about life after loss*. New York, NY: Basic Books.

Bondi, L. (2013). Between Christianity and secularity: Counselling and psychotherapy provision in Scotland. *Social & Cultural Geography, 14*(6), 668–688. https://doi.org/10.1080/14649365.2013.802369

Bornstein, M. H. (2019). *Handbook of parenting. Volume 3: Being and becoming a parent* (3rd ed.). New York, NY: Routledge.

Boss, P. (2002). *Family stress management: A contextual approach* (2nd ed.). Thousand Oaks, CA: SAGE Publications, Inc.

Boss, P. (2016). The context and process of theory development: The story of ambiguous loss. *Journal of Family Theory and Review, 8*(3), 269–286. https://doi.org/10.1111/jftr.12152

Boss, P. (2019). Building resilience: The example of ambiguous loss. In B. Huppertz (Ed.), *Approaches to psychic trauma: Theory and practice* (pp. 91–105). Lanham, MD: Rowman & Littlefield.

Boss, P., Dahl, C., & Kaplan, L. (1996). The use of phenomenology for family therapy research: The search for meaning. In D. Sprenkle & S. Moon (Eds.), *Research methods in family therapy*. (pp. 83–106). New York, NY: Guilford.

Bostwick, E. N., & Johnson, A. J. (2017). Family secrets: The roles of family communication patterns and conflict styles between parents and young adult children. *Communication Reports, 31*(2), 91–102. https://doi.org/10.1080/08934215.2017.1380209

Bottero, W. (2015). Practising family history: "Identity" as a category of social practice. *The British Journal of Sociology, 66*(3). https://doi.org/10.1111/1468-4446.12133

Bouma, J., & Voorbij, L. (2009). *Factors in social interaction in cohousing communities*. Retrieved from https://research.hanze.nl/ws/portalfiles/portal/15924123/119.FactorsInSocialInteractionInCohousingCommunities_1_.pdf

Bowen, M. (1976). Theory in the practice of psychotherapy. In P. Guerin (Eds.). *Family therapy: Theory and practice* (pp. 42–90). New York, NY: Halsted Press.

Bowers, M. E., & Yehuda, R. (2016). Intergenerational transmission of stress in humans. *Neuropsychopharmacology REVIEWS, 41*, 232–244. Retrieved from https://www.ncbi.nlm.nih.gov/pmc/articles/PMC4677138/pdf/npp2015247a.pdf

Bowlby, J. (1951). Maternal care and mental health: A report prepared on behalf of the World Health Organization as a contribution to the United Nations programme for the welfare of homeless children. *Geneva: World Health Organization*, 179.

Bowlby, J., & Parkes, C. M. (1970). Separation and loss within the family. In E. J. Anthony (Ed.), *The child in his family* (pp. 197–216). New York, NY: Wiley.

Boyd, C. (Ed.). (2007). Postlude—one last principle. In *Commitment to principles: The letters of Murray Bowen, MD* (pp. 237–238). Retrieved from http://murraybowenarchives.org/files/Commitment-To-Principles.pdf

Brady, P., Kangas, M., & McGill, K. (2016). "Family matters": A systematic review of the evidence for the family psychoeducation for major depressive disorder. *Journal of Marital and Family, 43*(2), 245–263. https://doi.org/10.1111/jmft.12204

Braithwaite, D. O., & Baxter, L. A. (Eds.). (2006). *Engaging theories in family communication: Multiple perspectives* (1st ed.). Thousand Oaks, CA: Sage Publications.

Branigan, T. (2014, September 3). It's good to talk: China opens up to psychotherapy. *The Guardian*. Retrieved from https://www.theguardian.com/world/2014/sep/03/china-psychiatrists-talking-therapy-counselling

Brewer, G., & Kerslake, J. (2015). Cyberbullying, self-esteem, empathy and loneliness. *Computers in Human Behaviors, 48*, 255–260. https://doi.org/10.1016/j.chb.2015.01.073

Britton, R. (2016). Re-enactment as an unwitting professional response to family dynamics. In S. J. Box, B. Copley, J. Magagna, & E. Moustaki (Eds.), *Psychotherapy with families: An analytic approach* (pp. 48–58). New York, NY: Routledge.

Bronfenbrenner, U. (1973). *Two worlds of childhood: U.S. and U.S.S.R.* New York: Pocket Books.

Bronfenbrenner, U. (1978). Who needs parent education? *Teachers College Record, 79*, 767–787.

Bronfenbrenner, U. (1979). *The ecology of human development*. Cambridge, MA: Harvard University Press.

Bronfenbrenner, U. (1994). Who cares for the children? In H. Nuba, M. Searson, & D. L. Sheiman (Eds.), *Resources for early childhood: A handbook* (pp. 112–129). New York: Garland. (Edited paper from an individual address to UNESCO, Paris, September 7, 1989)

Bronfenbrenner, U. (Ed.). (2005). *Making human beings human: Bioecological perspectives on human development*. Thousand Oaks, CA: Sage Publications, Inc.

Brown, E. M. (2013). *Patterns of infidelity and their treatment* (2nd ed.). New York, NY: Routledge.

Brown, J. (1997). Circular questioning: An introductory guide. *A.N.Z.J. Family Therapy, 18*(2), 109–114. Retrieved from http://ift-malta.com/wp-content/uploads/2013/06/Circular-Questioining-an-introductory-guide.pdf

Brown, L. H., & Roodin, P. A. (2001). Service-learning in gerontology: An out-of-classroom experience. *Educational Gerontology, 27*(1), 89–103.

Brown, W., & Ling, A. (Eds.). (2002). *Imagining America: Stories from the promised land*. New York, NY: Persea Books.

Bruun, E. L., & Michael, L. (2014). *Not on speaking terms: Clinical strategies to resolve family and friendship cutoffs*. New York, NY: W. W. Norton & Company.

Burr, V. (1995). *An introduction to social constructionism*. New York, NY: Routledge.

Butler, M. H., Rodriguez, M-K. A., Roper, S. O., & Feinauer, L. L. (2010). Infidelity secrets in couple therapy: Therapists' views on the collision of competing ethics around relationship-relevant secrets. *Sexual Addiction & Compulsivity, 17*(2), 82–105. https://doi.org/10.1080/10720161003772041

Bütz, M. R. (1997). *Chaos and complexity: Implications for psychological theory and practice*. Philadelphia, PA: Taylor & Francis.

Bütz, M. R., Chamberlain, L. L., & McCown, W. G. (1997). *Strange attractors: Chaos, complexity, and the art of family therapy*. New York, NY: John Wiley & Sons, Inc.

Cadbury. (2019). The story of Cadbury. *About Cadbury*. Retrieved from https://www.cadbury.com.au/about-cadbury/the-story-of-cadbury.aspx

Cadbury, D. (2010). *Chocolate wars: The 150-year rivalry between the world's greatest chocolate makers*. New York: Perseus Books. (Excerpt available at https://www.npr.org/templates/story/story.php?storyId=130558647)

Campbell, F., Conti, G., Heckman, J. J., Moon, S. H., Pinto, R., Pungello, E., & Pan, Y. (2014). Early childhood investments substantially boost adult health. *Science, 343*(6178), 1478–1485. https://doi.org/10.1126/science.1248429

Campbell, J. (1990/2003). *The hero's journey: Joseph Campbell on his life and work*. Novato, CA: New World Library.

Campbell, J. (2008). *The hero with a thousand faces* (3rd ed.). Novato, CA: New World Library.

Campbell, S. B., Renshaw, K. D., & Klein, S. R. (2017). Sex differences in associations of hostile and non-hostile criticism with relationship quality. *The Journal of Psychology, 151*(4), 416–430.

Canary, D. J., & Yum, Y-O. (2016). Relationship maintenance strategies. *The International Encyclopedia of Interpersonal Communication*, 1–9. https://doi.org/10.1002/9781118540190.wbeic248

Carnes, P. J. (2018). *The betrayal bond: Breaking free of exploitive relationships* (Revised Ed.). Deerfield Beach, FL: Health Communications, Inc.

Carr, A. (2012). *Family therapy: Concepts, process, and practice* (3rd ed.). New York, NY: John Wiley & Sons, Inc.

Carter, S. (2011). Bullies and power: A look at the research. *Issues in comprehensive pediatric nursing, 34*(2), 97–102.

Carter, W., & King, J. (2018, July). [*Personal communication to the author*]. Dr. J. King (clinical psychologist) and W. Carter (social worker) communicated from NW Australia.

Center on the Developing Child. (n.d.). Serve and return. Retrieved from https://developingchild.harvard.edu/science/key-concepts/serve-and-return

Centers for Disease Control and Prevention. (2019). *About the CDC-Kaiser ACE Study*. Retrieved from https://www.cdc.gov/violenceprevention/childabuseandneglect/acestudy/about.html

Child Welfare Information Gateway. (n.d.). Adoption. Retrieved from https://www.childwelfare.gov/topics/adoption

Child Welfare Information Gateway. (2011). *How many children were adopted in 2007 and 2008?* Washington, DC: U.S. Department of Health and Human Services, Children's Bureau. Retrieved from https://www.childwelfare.gov/pubPDFs/adopted0708.pdf

Child Welfare Information Gateway. (2016). *Trends in the U.S. adoptions: 2008–2012*. Washington, DC: U.S. Department of Health and Human Services, Children's Bureau. Retrieved from https://www.childwelfare.gov/pubPDFs/adopted0812.pdf

Chiou, A. Y., & Mercado, B. K. (2016). Flexible loyalties: How malleable are bicultural loyalties. *Frontiers in Psychology*. https://doi.org/10.3389/fpsyg.2016.01985

Chiu, Y.-C. (2010). What drives patients to sue doctors? The role of cultural factors in the pursuit of malpractice claims in Taiwan. *Social Science & Medicine, 71*(4), 702–707. https://doi.org/10.1016/j.socscimed.2010.04.040

Clark, D., & Layard, R. (2014). *Thrive: The power of evidence-based psychological therapies*. London, England: Penguin Books.

Cloninger, C. R., & Zohar, A. H. (2011). Personality and the perception of health and happiness. *Journal of Affective Disorder, 128*(1-2), 24–32. https://doi.org/10.1016/j.jad.2010.06.012

Cohen, D. (2013). *Family secrets: Things we try to hide*. London, UK: Oxford University Press.

Cohen, S., Gianaros, P. J., & Manuck, S. B. (2016). A stage model of stress and disease. *Perspectives on Psychological Science, 11*(4), 456–463. https://doi.org/10.1177/1745691616646305

Colby, A. (1987/2011). *The measurement of moral judgment* (Vol. 1). Cambridge, UK: Cambridge University Press.

Compton, W. C., & Hoffman, E. (2019). *Positive psychology: The science of happiness and flourishing*. Thousand Oaks, CA: SAGE Publications, Inc.

Consolvo, S. (2017, Feb. 1). *Privacy and security practices of individuals coping with intimate partner violence*. Enigma 2017, Oakland, CA.

Conti, R. P. (2015). Family estrangement: Establishing a prevalence rate. *Journal of Psychology and Behavioral Science, 3*(2), 28–55. Retrieved from http://jpbsnet.com/journals/jpbs/Vol_3_No_2_December_2015/4.pdf

Conti, R. P., & Ryan, W. J. (2013). Defining and measuring estrangement. *International Journal of Research and Social Sciences, 3*(4), 57–67.

Coontz, S. (2000). Historical perspectives on family studies. *Journal of Marriage and Family, 62*(2), 283–297. Retrieved from https://pdfs.semanticscholar.org/83ab/ba5b222f591ce47ee9f43b0858a566f696c7.pdf

Corey, G. (2012). *Theory and practice of counseling and psychotherapy* (9th ed.). Belmont, CA: Cengage Learning.

Corr, C. A. (2018). Elisabeth Kübler-Ross and the "Five Stages" Model in a sampling of recent American textbooks. *OMEGA–Journal of Death and Dying*. https://doi.org/10.1177/0030222818809766

Council on Communications and Media. (2016). Media and young minds. *American Academy of Pediatrics, 138*(5). https://doi.org/10.1542/peds.2016-2591

Craig, R. T. (2016). Metacommunication. *The International Encyclopedia of Communication Theory and Philosophy*. https://doi.org/10.1002/9781118766804.wbiect232

Cramer, P. (2015). Understanding defense mechanism. *Psychodynamic Psychiatry, 43*(4), 523–552. https://doi.org/10.1521/pdps.2015.43.4.523

Csikszentmihalyi, M. (2017). Finding flow. *Psychology Today*. Retrieved from http://wiki.idux.com/uploads/Main/FindingFlow.pdf

Csikszentmihalyi, M., Abuhamdeh, S., & Nakamura, J. (2014). Flow. *Flow and the Foundations of Positive Psychology*, 227–238. https://doi.org/10.1007/978-94-017-9088-8_15

cummings, e. e. (1991). *Complete poems: 1904–1962*. Liveright Publishing Corporation.

Curtis, G. (2015). Civilized uncoupling: A non-adversarial approach to divorce. *Interdisciplinary Journal of Partnership Studies, 2*(1). https://doi.org/10.24926/ijps.v2i1.106

Damon, W., & Lerner, R. M. (1998). Handbook of child psychology: Theoretical models of human development (5th ed.). In U. Bronfenbrenner (Ed.), *Making human beings human* (pp. ix). Thousand Oaks, CA: SAGE Publications, Inc.

Dance, L. (2015). *Nora Ephron: Everything is copy*. Jefferson, North Carolina: McFarland & Company, Inc.

Davis, J. C. (2004). *Gatekeeping in family therapy supervision: An exploratory qualitative study*. (Unpublished Dissertation). Purdue University. West Lafayette, IN.

Davis, J. C. (2018). Personal communication, 13 September, 2018, between author and Jonathan Davis, PhD, LMFT, Samford University.

Davis, L. (2018). *The diamond elephant in the room: A phenomenological analysis of the meaning couples make of engagement rings* (Dissertation). Alliant International University. Sacramento, CA.

Dawkins, S., Tian, A. W., Newman, A., & Martin, A. (2017). Psychological ownership: A review and research agenda. *Journal of organizational behavior, 38*(2), 163–183. https://doi.org/10.1002/job.2057

de la Cruz, L. F., & Mataix-Cols, D. (2019). Hoarding disorder. In L. F. Fontenelle, & M. Yücel (Eds.), *A transdiagnostic approach to obsessions, compulsions and related phenomena* (pp. 331–344). United Kingdom: United Printing House.

Dobson, K. S., & Dozois, D. J. (Eds.). (2019). *Handbook of cognitive-behavioral therapies* (4th ed.). New York, NY: Guildford Press.

Doh, H-S., & Falbo, T. (1999). Social competence, maternal attentiveness, and overprotectiveness: Only children in Korea. *International Journal of Behavioral Development, 23*(1), 149–162. https://doi.org/10.1080/016502599384044

Doherty, W. (1990, October 6). Postlude—one last principle [from an interview with Murray Bowen]. Retrieved from http://murraybowenarchives.org/files/49_Postlude - One Last Principle.pdf

Doka, K. J. (2016). *Grief is a journey: Finding your path through loss.* New York, NY: Simon & Schuster, Inc.

Doka, K. J., & Martin, T. L. (2010). *Grieving beyond gender: Understanding the ways men and women mourn* (2nd ed.). New York, NY: Taylor & Francis Group.

Downey, D. B., & Condron, D. J. (2004). Playing well with others in Kindergarten: The benefits of siblings at home. *Journal of Marriage and Family, 66*, 333–350. https://doi.org/10.1111/j.1741-3737.2004.00024.x

Drozd, L., & Saini, M., & Olesen, N. (2016). *Parenting plan evaluations: Applied research for the family court* (2nd ed.). Oxford, UK: Oxford University Press.

Du, J., Wang, Y., & Zhang, Y. (2015). Sex imbalance, marital matching and intra-household bargaining: Evidence from China. *China Economic Review, 35*, 197–218. https://doi.org/10.1016/j.chieco.2014.11.002

Duckworth, A. L. (2016). *Grit: The power of passion and perseverance.* New York, NY: Scribner.

Dugan, D. O. (2004). Appreciating the legacy of Kübler-Ross: One clinical ethicist's perspective. *The American Journal of Bioethics, 4*(4), 24–28. https://doi.org/10.1080/15265160490908112

Dunbar, N. E. (2004). Theory in progress: Dyadic power theory: Constructing a communication-based theory of relational power. *Journal of Family Communication, 4*(3), 235–248. Retrieved from https://www.tandfonline.com/doi/abs/10.1080/15267431.2004.9670133

Dunbar, N. E. (2015). A review of theoretical approach to interpersonal power. *Review of Communication, 15*(1), 1–18. https://doi.org/10.1080/15358593.2015.1016310

Dunbar, N. E. (2017). Dominance and submission in family dynamics. In J. Lebow, A. Chambers, & D. Breulin (Eds.), *Encyclopedia of couple and family therapy* (p. 12). Cham, Switzerland: Springer. https://doi.org/10.1007/978-3-319-15877-8

Dunbar, N. E., Lane, B. L., & Abra, G. (2016). Power in close relationships: A dyadic power theory perspective. In J. A. Samp (Ed.), *Communicating interpersonal conflict in close relationships: Contexts, challenges, and opportunities* (pp. 75–92). New York, NY: Routledge.

Dykeman, C. (2016). Family theory. In D. Capuzzi, & D. R. Gross (Eds.), *Counseling and psychotherapy: Theories and interventions* (pp. 339–366). Hoboken, NJ: John Wiley & Sons.

Dynamics. (n.d.). In *Merriam-Webster online.* Retrieved from https://www.merriam-webster.com/dictionary/dynamics

Edin, K., & Kissane, R. J. (2010). Poverty and the American family: A decade in review. *Journal of Marriage and Family, 72*(3). https://doi.org/10.1111/j.1741-3737.2010.00713.x

Ellas, N., & Lemish, D. (2008). Media uses in immigrant families: Torn between inward and outward paths of integration. *International Communication Gazette, 70*(1), 21–40. https://doi.org/10.1177/1748048507084576

Elmer, E. M., & Houran, J. (n.d.). Physical attractiveness in the workplace: Customers do judge books by their covers. *2020 Skills.* Retrieved from https://www.researchgate.net/publication/228378322_Physical_Attractiveness_in_the_Workplace_Customers_Do_Judge_Books_by_Their_Covers

Elmhirst, S. (2019, December/January). Meet Alexa: Inside the mind of a digital native. *The Economist, 1843.* Retrieved from https://www.1843magazine.com/features/meet-alexa-inside-the-mind-of-a-digital-native

Erford, B. T., & Bardhoshi, G. (2018). Becoming a professional counselor: Philosophical, historical, and future considerations. In B. T. Erford, *Orientation to the counseling profession* (3rd ed., pp. 3–34). New York, NY: Pearson.

Erford, B. T., & Veron, A. (2018). Theories of counseling. In B. T. Erford, *Orientation to the counseling profession* (3rd ed., pp. 115–159). New York, NY: Pearson.

Erikson, E. (1993). *Childhood and society.* New York, NY: W.W. Norton & Company, Inc. (Original work published 1950)

Erskine, R. G. (2018). *Relational patterns, therapeutic presence: Concepts an practice of integrative psychotherapy.* New York, NY: Routledge.

Evans, N., & Whitcombe, S. (2016). Using circular questions as a tool in qualitative research. *Nurse Researcher, 23*(3), 26–29. https://doi.org/10.7748/nr.23.3.26.s6

Falbo, T. (2012). Only children: An updated review. *Journal of Individual Psychology, 68*(1), 38–49.

Farhud, D. D., Malmir, M., & Khanahmadi, M. (2014). Happiness and health: The biological factors-systematic review article. *Iranian Journal of Public Health, 43*(11), 1468–1477.

Fay-Stammbach, T., Hawes, D. J., & Meredith, P. (2014). Parenting influences on executive function in early childhood: A review. *Child Development Perspectives, 8*(4), 258–264. https://doi.org/10.1111/cdep.12095

Federal Interagency Forum on Child and Family Statistics. (2011). *America's children: Key national indicators of well-being, 2011*. Washington, DC: US Government Printing Office.

Ferrari, P. F., & Rizzolatti, G. (2015). *New Frontiers in Mirror Neurons Research*. Oxford, United Kingdom: Oxford University Press.

Fewell, J. (2016). Tattered scripts: Stories about transmission of trauma across generations. *Emotion, Space and Society, 19*, 81–86. https://doi.org/10.1016/j.emospa.2015.11.002

Fielden, S. J., & Chapman, G. E. & Cadell, S. (2011). Managing stigma in adolescent HIV: Silence, secrets and sanctioned spaces. *Culture, Health & Sexuality, 13*(3), 267–281. https://doi.org/10.1080/13691058.2010.525665

Finkelstein, L. P. (2014). *Breaking your own heart: A qualitative study of grief after initiating a breakup* (Doctoral dissertation, University of Denver). Retrieved from https://digitalcommons.du.edu/cgi/viewcontent.cgi?article=1197&context=etd

Fisher-Borne, M., Cain, J. M., & Martin, S. L. (2014). From mastery to accountability: cultural humility as an alternative to cultural competence. *The International Journal of Social Work Education, 34*(2), 165–181. https://doi.org/10.1080/02615479.2014.977244

Fitzgerald, R. (1995). *Rowntree and the marketing revolution, 1862–1969*. Cambridge, UK: University of Cambridge Press.

Fitzpatrick, M. A. (2004). Family communication patterns theory: Observations on its development and application. *Journal of Family Communication, 4*(3-4), 167–179. https://doi.org/10.1080/15267431.2004.9670129

Flanagan, B. (2017, February 10). Blackbird murmurations explained: Why you see thousands swirling together at dusk. *AL.com*. Retrieved from https://www.al.com/living/index.ssf/2017/02/blackbird_murmurations_explain.html

Foehr, J., & Thuras, D. (2016). *Atlas obscura: An explorer's guide to the world's hidden wonders*. Retrieved from https://www.atlasobscura.com/places/last-handwoven-bridge

Fong, M. (2016). *One child: The story of China's most radical experiment*. New York, NY: Houghton Mifflin Harcourt.

Foronda, C., Baptiste, D-L., Reinholdt, M. M., & Ousman, K. (2015). Cultural history: A concept analysis. *Journal of Transcultural Nursing, 27*(3), 210–217. https://doi.org/10.1177/1043659615592677

Forsyth, D. R. (2019). *Group dynamics* (7th ed.). Boston, MA: Cengage.

Fracasso, M. P. (2017). The concurrent paths of parental identity and child development. In J. D. Sinnott (Ed.), *Identity flexibility during adulthood: Perspectives in adult development* (pp. 151–162). Cham, Switzerland: Springer.

Fraiberg, S., Adelson, E., & Shapiro, V. (1975). Ghosts in the nursery: A psychoanalytic approach to the problems of impaired infant-mother relationships. *Journal of American Academy of Child Psychiatry, 14*(3), 387–421. Retrieved from http://www.dvrcv.org.au/sites/default/files/Fraiberg-Ghosts-in-Nursery.pdf

Fraley, R. C., & Bonanno, G. A. (2004). Attachment and loss: A test of three competing models on the association between attachment-related avoidance and adaptation to bereavement. *Personality and Social Psychology Bulletin, 30*(7), 878–890. https://doi.org/10.1177/0146167204264289

Frankl, V. E. (1959). *Man's search for meaning: An introduction to logotherapy*. Boston, MA: Beacon Press.

Frankl, V. E. (1969). *The will to meaning: Foundations and applications of logotherapy*. New York, NY: Plume Printing.

Freedman, J. & Combs, G. (1996). *Narrative therapy: The social construction of preferred realities*. New York, NY: W.W. Norton & Company.

Freeman, S. J. (2005). *Grief and Loss: Understanding the journey*. Belmont, CA: Cengage Learning.

Freud, A. (1992). *The ego and the mechanisms of defence*. London, England: Karnac Books. (Original work published in 1936)

Freud, S. (1990). *The interpretation of dreams: The standard edition of the complete psychological works of Sigmund Freud* (vol. 4-5). London: Hogarth and the Institute of Psycho-Analysis, 1955–1964.

Fried, E. I., Arjadi, R., Amshoff, M., Tuerlinchx, F., Bockting, C., Borsboom, D., & Carr, D. (2015). From loss to loneliness: The relationship between bereavement and depressive symptoms. *Journal of Abnormal Psychology, 124*(2), 256–265. Retrieved from https://pdfs.semanticscholar.org/1264/edbe97f1f1332fda8c8130566df91d592139.pdf

Friesen, B. J., & Brennan, E. (2005). Strengthen families and communities: System building for resilience.

In M. Ungar (Ed.), *Handbook for working with children and youth: Pathways to resilience across cultures and contexts* (pp. 295–313). Thousand Oaks, CA: Sage Publications.

Fulford. R. (Ed.). (1964). *Dearest child: Letters between Queen Victoria and the Princess Royal, 1858–61*. London, England: Evans Brothers.

Fuller, C. J. (2004). *The camphor flame: Popular Hinduism and society in India* (revised and expanded ed.). Princeton, NJ: Princeton University Press.

Gabbard, G. O. (2017). *Long-term psychodynamic psychotherapy: A basic text* (3rd ed.). Arlington, VA: American Psychiatric Association Publishing.

Gade, C. B. N. (2011). The historical development of the written discourses on ubuntu. *South African Journal of Philosophy, 30*(3), 303–329. Retrieved from https://pure.au.dk/ws/files/40165256/The_Historical_Development_of_the_Written_Discourses_on_Ubuntu.pdf

Galinsky, E. (1987). The six stages of parenthood. In R. L. Newman (Ed.), *Building relationships with parents and families in school age programs* (pp. 56–69). Reading, MA: Perseus Books.

Galvin, K. M., Braithwaite, D. O., & Bylund, C. L. (2014). *Family communication: Cohesion and change* (9th ed.). New York, NY: Routledge.

Galvin, K. M., Bylund, C. L., & Brommel, B. J. (2012). *Family communication: Cohesion and change* (8th ed.). Boston, MA: Allyn & Bacon.

Garbarino, J. (2005). Foreword. In M. Ungar (Ed.), *Handbook for working with children and youth: Pathways to resilience across cultures and contexts* (pp. xi–viii). Thousand Oaks, CA: SAGE Publications, Inc.

Garbarino, J. (2017). *Children and families in the social environment: Modern applications of social work* (2nd ed.). New York, NY: Routledge.

Garbarino, J., & Abramowitz, R. H. (1992). The family as a social system. In J. Garbarino. *Children and families in the social environment* (2nd ed.). New York, NY: Routledge.

Garman, A., McAfee, S., Homel, P., & Jacob, T. (2017). Understanding patterns of intimate partner abuse in male-male, male-female, and female-female couples. *Psychiatric Quarterly, 88*(2), 335–347. https://doi.org/10.1007/s11126-016-9450-2

Geiger, A., & Livingston, G. (2019, February 13). 8 facts about love and marriage in America. Retrieved from http://www.pewresearch.org/fact-tank/2018/02/13/8-facts-about-love-and-marriage

Gerhardt, C. (2003). Finding our own voice: The development of family therapy in South Africa. In K. S. Ng (Ed.), *Global perspectives in family therapy: Development, practice, trends* (pp. 161–172). New York, NY: Brunner-Routledge.

Gerhardt, C. (2013). Sacred spaces and community involvement. *Network: CFLE Perspectives, NCFR, Winter edition*, 12.

Gerhardt, C. (2016a). The facilitating charms of humor. *CFLE Network*, Summer, 12–15.

Gerhardt, C. (2016b). Family of procreation. In C. L. Shehan (Ed.), *Encyclopedia of family studies, 2*, 755–757. John Wiley & Sons, Inc. Retrieved from http://onlinelibrary.wiley.com/doi/ 10.1002/9781119085621.wbefs223/abstract

Gerhardt, C. (2016c). Globalization and families. In C. L. Shehan, (Ed.), *The Wiley Blackwell encyclopedia of family studies* (Vol. 2, pp. 979–986).

Gerhardt, C. (2016d). Only children. In C. L. Shehan, *The Wiley Blackwell encyclopedia of family studies*. (Vol. 3, pp. 1533–1536). Chichester, UK: Wiley Blackwell.

Gerhardt, C. (2018). South Africa: Family life as the mirror of a society. In M. Robila & A. Taylor (Eds.). *Global perspectives of Family Life Education*. New York, NY: Springer.

Gerhardt, C., & Rundell, F. (2004). *Children's stories*. Closing Plenary. Unpublished conference proceedings: Ninth International Conference of the South African Association for Marriage and Family Therapy (SAAMFT). Durban, South Africa.

Gianessi, C. A. (2012). From habits to self-regulation: How do we change? *The Yale Journal of Biology and Medicine, 85*(2), 293–299.

Giarrusso, R., Feng, D., & Bengtson, V. L. (2005). The intergenerational-stake phenomenon over 20 years. In M. Silverstein & K. W. Schaie (Eds.), *Annual review of gerontology and geriatrics: Vol. 24. Annual review of gerontology and geriatrics, 2004: Focus on intergenerational relations across time and place* (pp. 55–76). New York, NY, US: Springer Publishing Co.

Gibran, K. (2019). *The Prophet*. Mineola, NY: Ixia Press. (Republication of the work originally published in 1923 by Alfred A. Knopf, Inc. New York)

Gibson, K. R., & Peterson, A. C. (Eds.). (1991/2017). *Brain maturation and cognitive development: Comparative and cross-cultural perspectives*. New York, NY: Routledge.

Gil, E., & Drewes, A. A. (Eds.). (2004). *Cultural issues in play therapy*. New York, NY: The Guilford Press.

Gilchrist, G., Radcliffe, P., Noto, A. R. & Lucas d'Oliveira, A. F. P. (2017). The prevalence and factors associated with ever perpetrating intimate partner violence by men receiving substance use treatment in Brazil and England: A cross-cultural comparison, *36*(1), 34–51.

Gillies, J., & Neimeyer, R. A. (2006). Loss, grief, and the search for significance: Toward a model of meaning reconstruction in bereavement. *Journal of Constructivist Psychology, 19*(1), 31–65. https://doi.org/10.1080/10720530500311182

Goffman, E. (1955). On face-work: An analysis of ritual elements in social interaction. *Psychiatry: Journal for the*

Study of Interpersonal Processes, 18, 213–231. https://doi.org/10.1080/00332747.1955.11023008

Goldenberg, H., & Goldbern, I. (2013). *Family therapy: An overview* (8th ed.). Belmont, CA: Brooks/Cole, Cengage Learning.

Goodman, L. A., Fauci, J. E., Hailes, H. P., & Gonzalez, L. (2019). Power with and power over: How domestic violence advocates manage their roles as mandated reporters. *Journal of Family Violence, 34*(193), 1–15. https://doi.org/10.1007/s10896-019-00040-8

Gooso, Y., & Carvalho, A.M. (2013). Play and cultural context. *Encyclopedia on Early Childhood Development* Retrieved from: http://www.child-encyclopedia.com/play/according-experts/play-and-cultural-context

Gottman, J. M. (1994). *What predicts divorce?: The relationship between marital processes and marital outcomes.* New York, NY: Psychology Press.

Gottman, J. M., & Silver, N. (1999). *The seven principles for making marriage work.* New York, NY: Three Rivers Press.

Graesser, A. C., & Black, J. B. (Eds.). (2017/1985). *The psychology of questions.* New York, NY: Routledge.

Greene, R. R., & Kropf, N. P. (2017/2009). Erikson's eight stages of development: Different lenses. In R. R. Green, *Human Behavior Theory* (pp. 77–100). New York, NY: Routledge.

Gronchi, G., Cianferotti, L., Parri, S., Pampaloni, B., & Brand, M. L., (2018). Nudging healthier behavior: Psychological basis and potential solutions for enhancing adherence. *Clinical Cases in Mineral & Bone Metabolism, 15*(2), 158–162. Retrieved from https://www.ccmbm.com/common/php/portiere.php?ID=1cd2b503aba161ace2b6587ef385bbf4

Gudykunst, W. B. (Ed.). (2003). *Cross-cultural and intercultural communication.* Thousand Oaks, CA: SAGE Publications, Inc.

Gudykunst, W. B. (2005). *Theorizing about intercultural communication.* Thousand Oaks, CA: SAGE publications, Inc.

Gudykunst, W. B., & Lee, C. M. (2003). Cross-cultural communication theories. In W. B. Gudykunst (Ed.), *Cross-cultural and intercultural communication* (pp. 7–34). Thousand Oaks, CA: SAGE Publications, Inc.

Guerrero, L., & Ramos-Salazar, L. (2015). Nonverbal skills in emotional communication. In A. F. Hannawa & B. H. Spitzberg (Eds.), *Communication competence* (pp. 131–153). Berlin, Germany: CPI Books GmbH, Leck.

Gunkel, M., Schlaegel, C., & Taras, V. (2016). Cultural values, emotional intelligence, and conflict handling styles: A global study. *Journal of World Business, 51*(4), 568–585. https://doi.org/10.1016/j.jwb.2016.02.001

Gupta, G., & Sharma, D. L. (2018). Aging, quality of life, and social support. In B. Prasad, & S. Akbar (Eds.), *Handbook of research on geriatric health, treatment, and care* (pp. 68–80). Hershey, PA: IGI Global. https://doi.org/10.4018/978-1-5225-3480-8.ch004

Gupta, N. D., Etcoff, N. L., & Jaeger, M. M. (2016). Beauty in mind: The effects of physical attractiveness on psychological well-being and distress. *Journal of Happiness Studies, 17*(3), 1313–1325. https://doi.org/10.1007/s10902-015-9644-6

Gurman, A. S., & Kniskern, D. P (2014/1981). *Handbook of family therapy.* New York, NY: Routledge.

Hadfield, K, Amos, M., Ungar, M., Gosselin, J., & Ganong, L. (2018). Do changes to family structure affect child and family outcomes? A systematic review of the instability hypothesis. *Journal of Family Therapy & Review, 10*, 87–110. https://doi.org/10.1111/jftr.12243

Hardy, K. V., & Laszloffy, T. A. (1995). The cultural genogram: Key to training culturally competent family therapists. *Journal of Marital and Family Therapy, 21*(3), 227–237. http://dx.doi.org/10.1111/j.1752-0606.1995.tb00158.x

Hareven, T. K. (1999). *Families, history and social change: Life course and cross-cultural perspectives.* New York, NY: Routledge.

Hargrave, T. D., & Zasowski, N. E. (2016). *Families and forgiveness: Healing wounds in the intergenerational family* (2nd ed.). New York, NY: Routledge.

Hatzifilalithis, S., & Grenier, A. M. (2018). Critical perspective on current models of intergenerational learning. *Innovation in Aging, 2*(1), 374. https://doi.org/10.1093/geroni/igy023.1388

Hefferson, K., & Boniwell, I. (2011). *Positive psychology: Theory, research and applications.* New York, NY: Open University Press.

Heinze, R. (2017). *Melting pots & mosaics: Children of immigrants in US-American literature.* Veriag, Bielefld: Deutsche Nationalbibliothek.

Henderson, T. L., & Bailey, S. (2015). A culturally variant perspective: Grandparents rearing grandchildren. In K. Pasley & S. Browning (Eds.), *Understanding and treating contemporary families: Translating research into practice* (pp. 230–247). New York, NY: Routledge.

Henry, C. S., Morris, A. S., & Harrist, A. W. (2015). Family resilience: Moving into the third wave. *Family Relations: Interdisciplinary Journal of Applied Family Science, 64*(1), 22–43. https://doi.org/10.1111/fare.12106

Hershey. (2019). Milton S. Hershey. Retrieved from http://www.hersheypa.com/about-hershey/milton-hershey.php

Hess, R. D., & Handel, g. (2016). *A psychosocial approach to family life.* New York, NY: Routledge.

Hill, C., & Gerhardt, C. (2019). *Bridging the generation gap. When cyber seniors and millennials meet.* Unpublished paper and presentation at SECFR Conference, Arkansas.

Hill, R. (1949). *Families under stress: Adjustment to the crises of war separation and reunion.* New York, NY: Harper & Brothers.

Hiniker, A., Suh, H., Cao, S., & Kientz, J. A. (2016). Screen time tantrums: How families manage screen media experiences for toddlers and preschoolers. *CHI '16 Proceedings of the 2016 CHI Conference on Human Factors in Computing Systems* (pp. 648–660),San Jose, CA, May 7–12.

Holden, E. S. (1904). Copernicus. *Popular Science Monthly*, *65*, 109–113.

Hsi, C. (2014). *Chu Hsi's family rituals: A twelfth-century manual for the performance of capping, weddings, funerals, and ancestral rites* (P. B. Ebrey, Trans.). Princeton, NJ: Princeton University Press. (Original work published 1991)

Humphrey, K. M. (2009). *Counseling strategies for loss and grief.* Alexandria, VA: American Counseling Association. Retrieved from https://www.counseling.org/publications/frontmatter/72887-fm.pdf

Humpolicek, P. (2013). The Scenotest: A special type of play therapy in the projective diagnostic context. In S. K. Srivastava, N. Singh, & S. Kant (Eds.), *Psychological interventions of mental disorders* (pp. 315–331). New Delhi, India: Sarup Book Publishers PVT.

Hutson, J., Taft, J. G., Barocas, S., & Levy, K. (2018). Debiasing desire: Addressing bias & discrimination on intimate platforms. *Proceedings of the ACM on Human-Computer Interaction 2*, 1–18. https://doi.org/10.1145/3274342

Jackson, P. (Director). (2001). *Lord of the rings* [Motion Picture]. New Zealand; United States: WingNut Films.

Jansen, T. R. (2015, Oct 2). *The nursing home that's also a dorm room.* Retrieved from https://www.citylab.com/equity/2015/10/the-nursing-home-thats-also-a-dorm/408424

Jednak, S., & Schulte, E. (2018). Who gets what and why: The new economics of matchmaking and market design by Alvin E. Roth [review]. *Journal of Sustainable Business and Management Solutions in Emerging Economies*, 72–73. Retrieved from http://management.fon.bg.ac.rs/index.php/mng/article/view/225

Jensen, F. E. (2016). *The teenage brain: A neuroscientist's survival guide to raising adolescents and young adults.* New York, NY: HarperCollins Publishers.

Jensen, L. A., & Arnett, J. J. (2012). Going global: New pathways for adolescents and emerging adults in a changing world. *Journal of Social Issues*, *68*(3), 473–492. Retrieved from http://lenearnettjensen.com/wp-content/uploads/2018/10/2012-JSI-Jensen-Arnett-Going-Global-Final.pdf

Johnson, A. H., Brock, C. D., & Zacarias, A. (2014). The legacy of Michael Balint. *International Journal of Psychiatry in Medicine*, *47*(3), 175–192. https://doi.org/10.2190/PM.47.3.a

Jones, N. A., & Bullock, J. (2012). Two or more races population: 2010. *2010 Census Briefs*. Retrieved from https://www.census.gov/prod/cen2010/briefs/c2010br-13.pdf

Jones-Correa, M., Marrow, H. B., Okamoto, D. G., & Tropp, L. R. (2018). Immigrant perceptions of US-born receptivity and the shaping of American identity. *The Russell Sage Foundation of the Social Sciences*, *4*(5), 47–80. https://doi.org/10.7758/RSF.2018.4.5.03

Juvonen, J., & Graham, S. (2014). Bullying in schools: The power of bullies and the plight of victims. *Annual Review of Psychology*, *65*(1), 159–185.

Kabali, H. K., Irigoyen, M. M., Nunez-Davis, R., Budacki, J. G., Mohanty, S. H., Leister, K. P., & Bonner Jr., R. L. (2015). Exposure and use of mobile media devices by young children. *American Academy of Pediatrics, 136*(6). https://doi.org/10.1542/peds.2015-2151

Kao, T-S., & Caldwell, C. (2017). Family efficacy within ethnically diverse families: A qualitative study. *Family Process*, *56*(1), 217–233. http://dx.doi.org/10.1111/famp.12149

Karch, F., & Robertson, R. (2014). *Collected: Living with the things you love.* Abrams, New York: Abrams Publishers.

Kaslow, F. W. (1981). A South African odyssey: Family style. *Journal of Marital and Family Therapy*, *7*, 89–92.

Keating, D. P. (2017). *Born anxious: The lifelong impact early life adversity—and how to break the cycle.* New York, NY: St. Martin's Press.

Kelley, D. L., Waldron, V. R., & Kloeber, D. N. (2018). *A communicative approach to conflict, forgiveness, and reconciliation: Reimagining our relationships.* New York, NY: Routledge.

Kenriksson, A. (2019). Singles' activities: Sociability and the ambiguities of singledom. *Families and Relationships and Societies*, *8*(1), 37–52. https://doi.org/10.1332/204674317X15015138368221

Kerig, P. K. (2019). Parenting and family systems. In M. H. Bornstein (Ed.), *Handbook of parenting. Volume 3: Being and becoming a parent* (3rd ed., pp. 3–35). New York, NY: Routledge.

Kerr, J. (2018, November 18). How to talk to people, according to Terry Gross. *The New York Times*. Retrieved from https://www.nytimes.com/2018/11/17/style/self-care/terry-gross-conversation-advice.html

Kerr, M. E. (2000). One family's story: A primer on Bowen Theory. *The Bowen Center for the Study of the Family.* Retrieved from http://www.thebowencenter.org

Kerr, M. E. (2019). *Bowen theory's secrets: Revealing the hidden life of families.* New York, NY: W. W. Norton & Company.

Kerr, M. E., & Bowen, M. (1988). *Family evaluation: An approach based on Bowen Theory.* New York, NY: W. W. Norton & Company.

Keyes, C. L. M. (2014). Happiness, flourishing, and life satisfaction. *The Wiley Blackwell Encyclopedia of Health, Illness, Behavior, and Society.* https://doi.org/10.1002/9781118410868.wbehibs454

Kidd, C., Palmeri, H., & Aslin, R. N. (2013). Rational snacking: Young children's decision-making on the marshmallow task is moderated by beliefs about environmental reliability. *Cognition, 126*(1), 109–114. https://doi.org/10.1016/j.cognition.2012.08.004

Kilde, J. H. (2008). *Sacred power, sacred space: An introduction to Christian architecture and worship*. New York, NY: Oxford University Press.

King, K. A., & Fogle, L. W. (2013). Family language policy and bilingual parenting. *Language Teaching, 46*(2), 172–194. https://doi.org/10.1017/S0261444812000493

Knapp, M. L. (1978). *Social intercourse: From greeting to goodbye*. Boston, MY: Allyn and Bacon.

Koerner, A. F., & Fitzpatrick, M. A. (2006). Family communication patterns theory: A social cognitive approach. In D. O. Braithwaite, & L. A. Baxter (Eds.), *Engaging theories in family communication: Multiple perspectives* (1st ed., pp. 50–65). Thousand Oaks, CA: SAGE Publications, Inc.

Koerner, A. F., & Schrodt, P. (2014). An introduction to the special issue on family communication patterns theory. *Journal of Family Communication, 14*, 1–15. https://doi.org/10.1080/15267431.2013.857328

Koerner, A. F., Schrodt, P., & Fitzpatrick, M. A. (2018). Family communication patterns theory. In. D. O. Braithwaite, E. A. Suter, & K. Floyd (Eds.), *Engaging theories in family communication: Multiple perspectives* (2nd ed., pp. 142–153). New York, NY: Routledge.

Koob, G. F., & Volkow, N. D. (2016). Neurobiology of addiction: A neurocircuitry analysis. *Lancet Psychiatry, 3*(8), 760–773. https://doi.org/10.1016/S2215-0366(16)00104-8

Kopystynska, O., & Beck, C. J. (2018). Considering destructive interparental conflict and intimate partner abuse: Is there a difference? *Family Court Review, 56*(2), 209–218. https://doi.org/10.1111/fcre.12335

Kossenjans, J., & Buttle, F. (2016). Why I collect contemporary art: Collector motivations as value articulations. *Journal of Customer Behaviour, 15*(2), 193–212(20). https://doi.org/10.1362/147539216X14594362873811

Kottman,T. (2011). *Play therapy: Basics and beyond* (2nd ed.). Alexandria, VA: American Counseling Association.

Krause, I-B. (2001). *Culture and system in family therapy*. London, England: Routledge.

Krcmar, M., Ewoldsen, D., & Koerner, A. (2016). *Communication science theory and research*. New York, NY: Routledge.

Kruse, K. (2012, October 16). 100 best quotes on leadership. *Forbes*. Retrieved from https://www.forbes.com/sites/kevinkruse/2012/10/16/quotes-on-leadership/#136a2a942feb

Krysan, M., Moore, K. A., & Zill, N. (1990). *Identifying successful families: An overview of constructs and selected measures*. Washington, DC: Child Trends, Inc.

Kübler-Ross, E. (1969). *On death and dying*. London, UK: MacMillan.

Kübler-Ross, E. (1998). *The wheel of life: A memoir of living and dying*. New York, NY: Touchstone.

Kuhn, A. (2002). *Family secrets: Acts of memory and imagination* (2nd ed.). New York, NY: Verso.

Kumar, K. (2017). The blended family life cycle. *Journal of Divorce & Remarriage, 58*(2), 110–125. https://doi.org/10.1080/10502556.2016.1268019

Lahiri, J. (1999). *Interpreter of maladies: Stories*. Boston: Houghton Mifflin Harcourt.

Lamm, C., & Majdandžić, J. (2015). The role of shared neural activations, mirror neurons, and morality in empathy—A critical comment. *Neuroscience Research, 90*, 15–24. https://doi.org/10.1016/j.neures.2014.10.008

Lang, S. S. (2005, September 26). Urie Bronfenbrenner, father of Head Start program and pre-eminent "human ecologist," dies at age 88. *Cornell Chronicle*. Retrieved from https://news.cornell.edu/stories/2005/09/head-start-founder-urie-bronfenbrenner-dies-88

Lararidis, G. (Ed.). (2011). *Security, insecurity and migration in Europe*. Farnham, United Kingdom: Ashgate Publishing.

Laszloffy, T. A. (2002). Rethinking family development theory: Teaching with the systemic family development (SFD) model. *Family Relations, 51*(3), 206–214.

Lawson, D. W., & M. R. (2010). Siblings and childhood mental health: Evidence for a later-born advantage. *Social Science & Medicine, 70*, 2061–2069. https://doi.org/10.1016/j.socscimed.2010.03.009

Lazarevic, V. (2017). Effects of cultural brokering on individual wellbeing and family dynamics among immigrant youth. *Journal of Adolescence, 55*, 77–87. https://doi.org/10.1016/j.adolescence.2016.12.010

Le Poire, B. A. (2006). *Family communication: Nurturing and control in a changing world*. Thousand Oaks, CA: SAGE Publications, Inc.

Lerner, R. M. (2005). Urie Bronfenbrenner: Career contributions of the consummate developmental scientist. In U. Bronfenbrenner (Ed.), *Making human beings human* (pp. ix–xxvi). Thousand Oaks, CA: SAGE Publications, Inc.

Levi, D. (2013). *Group dynamics for teams* (4th ed.). Thousand Oaks, CA: SAGE Publications, Inc.

Lewis, R. A., & Sussman, M. B. (1986). *Men's changing roles in the family*. New York, NY: Routledge.

Li, Y. (2013). A perspective on health care for elderly who lose their only child in china. *Scandinavian Journal of Public Health, 41*, 550–552. https://doi.org/10.1177/1403494813490252

Lindemann, E. (1944). Symptomatology and management of acute grief. *The American Journal of Psychiatry, 101*(2), 141–148. https://doi.org/10.1176/ajp.101.2.141

Littlejohn, S. W., & Foss, K. A. (2011). *Theories of human communication* (10th ed.). Long Grove, IL: Waveland Press, Inc.

Littlejohn, S. W., Foss, K. A., & Oetzel, J. G. (2017). *Theories of human connection* (11th ed.). Long Grove, IL: Waveland Press, Inc.

Liu, F. (2006). Boys as only-children and girls as only-children: Parental gendered expectations of the only-child in the nuclear family in present day China. *Gender and Education, 18*(5), 491–505. https://doi.org/10.1080/09540250600881626

Liu, T., & Sun, L. (2015). An apocalyptic vision of ageing in China. *Zeitschrift für Gerontologie und Geriatrie, 48*(4), 354–364. Retrieved from https://link.springer.com/article/10.1007/s00391-014-0816-5

Livingston, G. (2018, April 27). About one-third of US children are living with an unmarried parent. *Pew Center Research*. Retrieved from https://www.pewresearch.org/fact-tank/2018/04/27/about-one-third-of-u-s-children-are-living-with-an-unmarried-parent

Livingston, G. (2018, September 24). Stay-at-home moms and dads account for about one-in-five U.S. parents. *Factank*. Retrieved from https://www.pewresearch.org/fact-tank/2018/09/24/stay-at-home-moms-and-dads-account-for-about-one-in-five-u-s-parents

Lohoar, S., Butera, N., & Kennedy, E. (2014). Strengths of Australian aboriginal cultural practices in family life and child rearing. *Child Family Community Australia (CFCA): Information Exchange*, 25. Retrieved from https://aifs.gov.au/cfca/sites/default/files/publication-documents/cfca25.pdf

London Remembers. (2019). Monument: Sir Arthur Sullivan. Retrieved from https://www.londonremembers.com/memorials/sir-arthur-sullivan

Losada, M., & Heaphy, E. (2004). The role of positivity and connectivity in the performance of business teams: A nonlinear dynamics model. *American Behavioral Scientist, 47*(6), 740–765.

Lu, Y., & Winter, S. (2011). Gender atypical behavior in Chinese school-aged children: Its prevalence and relation to sex, age, and only child status. *Journal of Sex Research, 48*(4), 334–348. https://doi.org/10.1080/00224491003774867

Lundin, R. W. (1989). *Alfred Adler's basic concepts and implications*. New York, NY: Routledge.

Luneburg, P. (2019). Permanent ink. *JAMA, 321*(6), 545–546. https://doi.org/10.1001/jama.2019.0242

Lyons, K. (2019, April 19). 'Here is a story! Story it is': How fairy tales are told in other tongues. *The Guardian*. Retrieved from https://www.theguardian.com/books/2019/apr/19/here-is-a-story-story-it-is-how-fairytales-are-told-in-other-tongues

Macenczak, L. A., Campbell, S. M., Henley, A. B., & Campbell, W. K. (2016). Direct and interactive effects of narcissism and power on overconfidence. *Personality and Individual Differences, 91*, 113–122. https://doi.org/10.1016/j.paid.2015.11.053

Makiwane, M., Nduna, M., & Khalema, N. E. (Eds.). (2016). *Children in South African families: Lives and times*. Newcastle upon Tyne, UK: Cambridge Scholars Publishing. https://www.cambridgescholars.com/download/sample/63326

Malamud, B. (2002). The German refugee. In W. Brown & A. Ling (Eds.), *Imagining America: Stories from the promised land*. New York, NY: Persea Books. (Originally published in 1963)

Manchiraju, S., Sadachar, A., & Ridgway, J. L. (2017). The compulsive online shopping scale (COSS): Development and validation using panel data. *International Journal of Mental Health and Addiction, 15*(1), 209–223. https://doi.org/10.1007/s11469-016-9662-6

Mancillas, A. (2006). Challenging the stereotypes about only children: A review of literature and implications for practice. *Journal of Counseling & Development, 84*, 268–275. https://doi.org/10.1002/j.1556-6678.2006.tb00405.x

Mandela, N. (1994). *Long walk to freedom: The autobiography of Nelson Mandela*. New York, NY: Little, Brown & Co.

Manning, P. (2013). *Migration in world history* (2nd ed.). New York, NY: Routledge.

Manusov, V. (2018). Attribution theory: Who's at fault in families? In D. O. Braithwaite, E. A. Suter, & K. Floyd (Eds.), *Engaging theories in family communication: Multiple perspectives* (2nd ed., pp. 51–61). New York, NY: Routledge.

Marchiori, D. R., Adriaanse, M. A., & De Ridder, D. T. D. (2017). Unsolved questions in nudging research: Putting psychology back in nudging. *Social and Personality Psychology Compass, 11*(1). https://doi.org/10.1111/spc3.12297

Marsella, A. J., & Ring, E. (2003). Human migration and immigration: An overview. In L. L. Adler & U. P. Gielen (Eds.), *Migration: Immigration and emigration in international perspective* (pp. 3–50). Westport, CT: Greenwood Publishing Group, Inc.

Marsten, D., Epston, D., & Markham, L. (2016). *Narrative therapy in wonderland: Connecting with children's imaginative know-how*. New York, NY: W.W. Norton & Company.

Martin, E. J. (2019). Bearing witness and finding meaning. *JAMA, 321*(11), 1051–1052.

Martin, J. (2018, March 29). A quick history of chocolate and Quakerism. *Quakers in Britain* [blog]. Retrieved from https://www.quaker.org.uk/blog/quakers-and-chocolate

Martin, K. (2018). Transcultural histories of psychotherapy. *European Journal of Psychotherapy & Counseling, 20*(1), 104–119. https://doi.org/10.1080/13642537.2017.1421988

Mashego, T-A. B., & Taruvinga, P. (2014). Family resilience factors influencing teenagers adaptation following parental divorce in Limpopo Province South Africa. *Journal of Psychology, 5*(1), 19–34. https://doi.org/10.1080/09764224.2014.11885502

Matsudaira, T. (2006). Measures of psychological acculturation: A review. *Transcultural Psychiatry, 43*(3), 462–487. https://doi.org/10.1177/1363461506066989

Mavroudi, E., & Nagel, C. (2016). *Global migration: Patterns, processes, and politics.* London, England: Routledge.

McAlister, A. R., & Peterson, P. P. (2013). Siblings, theory of mind, and executive functioning in children aged 3-6 years: New longitudinal evidence. *Child Development, 84*(4), 1442–58. https://doi.org/10.1111/cdev.12043

McClintock, E. A. (2017). Support for beauty-status exchange remains illusory. *American Sociological Review, 82*(5), 1100–1110.

McCubbin, H. I., & Patterson, J. M. (1982). Family adaptation to crisis. In H. I. McCubbin, A. E. Cauble, & J. M. Patterson (Eds.), *Family stress, coping, and social support.* Springfield, IL: Charles C. Thomas.

McEwan, T. E., Daffern, M., MacKenzie, R. D., & Ogloff, J. R. P. (2017). Risk factors for stalking violence, persistence, and recurrence. *The Journal of Forensic Psychiatry & Psychology, 28*(1), 38–56. https://doi.org/10.1080/14789949.2016.1247188

McGoldrick, M., & Gerson, R. (1985). *Genograms in family assessment.* New York, NY: W. W. Norton & Company.

McHale, J. P., & Irace, K. (2011). Coparenting in diverse family systems. In McHale, J. P. & K. M. Lindahl (Eds.), *Coparenting: A conceptual and clinical examination of family systems* (pp. 15–37). Washington, DC: American Psychological Association.

McLeod, J. M., Atkin, C. K., & Chaffee, S. H. (1972). Adolescents, parents, and television use: Self-report and other-report measures from the Wisconsin sample. *Television and Social Behavior, 3*, 239–313.

McLeod, J. M., & Chaffee, S. H. (1973). Interpersonal approaches to communication research. *American Behavioral Scientist, 16*(4), 469–499.

McMahon, D. M. (2006). *Happiness: A history.* New York, NY: Atlantic Monthly Press.

McPhail, T. L. (2010). *Global communication: Theories, stakeholders, and trends* (3rd ed.). New York, NY: John Wiley & Sons, Inc.

McVittie, C., & McKinlay, A. (2017). The self. In B. Gough (Ed.), *The Palgrave handbook of critical social psychology* (pp. 389–408). London, England: Palgrave MacMillan. https://doi.org/10.1057/978-1-137-51018-1_19

Meagher, D. K., & Balk, D. E. (Eds.). (2013). *Handbook of thanatology: The essential body of knowledge for the study of death, dying, and bereavement* (2nd ed.). New York, NY: Routledge.

Meca, A., Schwartz, S. J., Martinez, C. R., & McClure, H. H. (2018). Longitudinal effects of acculturation and enculturation on mental health: Does the measure of matter? *Development and Psychopathology, 30*(5), 1849–1866. https://doi.org/10.1017/S0954579418001165

Meichenbaum, D. (2017). *The evolution of cognitive behavior therapy.* New York, NY: Routledge.

Meyer, R. (2017, August 2). Your smartphone reduces your brainpower, even if it's just sitting there. *The Atlantic.* Retrieved from https://www.theatlantic.com/technology/archive/2017/08/a-sitting-phone-gathers-brain-dross/535476

Mintz, S., & Kellogg, S. (1989). *Domestic revolutions: A social history of American family life.* New York, NY: Simon & Schuster.

Minuchin, S. (1999). Retelling, reimagining, and researching: A continuing conversation. *Journal of Marital and Family Therapy, 25*(1), 9–14. https://doi.org/10.1111/j.1752-0606.1999.tb01106.x

Minuchin, S., & Fisherman, H. (1981). *Family therapy techniques.* Cambridge, MA: Harvard University Press.

Mirsch, T., Lehrer, C., & Jung, R. (2017). Digital nudging: Altering user behavior in digital environments. *Internationale Tagung Wirtschaftsinformatik*, 634–648. Retrieved from https://www.alexandria.unisg.ch/250315

Mischel, W. (1974). Processes in delay of gratification. In L. Berkowitz (Ed.), *Advances in experimental social psychology* (Vol. 7, pp. 249–292). https://doi.org/10.1016/S0065-2601(08)60039-8

Mischel, W., & Ayduk, O. (2011). Willpower in a cognitive affective processing system: The dynamics of delay of gratification. In K. D. Vohs & R. F. Baumeister (Eds.), *Handbook of self-regulation: Research, theory, and application* (2nd ed., pp. 83–105). New York, NY: The Guildford Press.

Mischel, W., Shoda, Y., & Rodriguez, M. I. (1989). Delay of gratification in children. *Science, 244*(4907), 933–938. https://doi.org/10.1126/science.2658056

Mitchell, B. A. (2007). *The boomerang age: Transitions to adulthood in families.* New York, NY: Transaction Publishers.

Mokyr, J. (Ed.). (2011). *The economics of the industrial revolution.* New York, NY: Routledge.

Mollborn, S., & Jacobs, J. (2015). "I'll be here for you": Teen parents' coparenting relationships. *Journal of Marriage and Family, 77*(2), 373–387. https://doi.org/10.1111/jomf.12175

Monk, G., Winslade, J., Crocket, K., & Epston, D. (Eds.). (1997). *The Jossey-Bass psychology series. Narrative therapy in practice: The archaeology of hope.* San Francisco, CA, US: Jossey-Bass.

Monroe, L. B. (1872). *The sixth reader.* Philadelphia, PA: Cowperthwait & Co.

Moore, N., & Whelan, Y. (Eds.). (2016). *Heritage, memory, and the politics of identity: New perspectives on the cultural landscape.* New York, NY: Routledge.

Nagata, D. K, Kim J. H. J., & Nguyen T. U. (2015). Processing cultural trauma: Intergenerational effects of the Japanese American incarceration. *Journal of Social Issues, 71*, 356–370.

Nakazuru, A., Sato, N., & Nakamura, N. (2017). Stress and coping in Japanese mothers whose infants required congenital heart disease surgery. *International Journal of Nursing Practice, 23*(S1). https://doi.org/10.1111/ijn.12550

Napier, A. (1988). *The fragile bond: In search of an equal, intimate and enduring marriage*. New York, NY: Harper & Row.

Napier, A., & Whitaker, C. (1978). *The family crucible*. New York, NY: Bantam Books.

Nathoo, D., & Ellis, J. (2019). Theories of loss and grief experienced by the patient, family, and healthcare professional: A personal account of a critical event. *Journal of Cancer Education*, 1–5. https://doi.org/10.1007/s13187-018-1462-1

National Geographic. (n.d.). Milestones in photography. Retrieved from https://www.nationalgeographic.com/photography/photos/milestones-photography

National Organization for Human Services. (2015). Responsibility to clients. *Ethical Standards for Human Services Professionals*. Retrieved from https://www.nationalhumanservices.org/ethical-standards-for-hs-professionals#clients

Neimeyer, G. J., & Neimeyer, R. A. (1993). Defining the boundaries of constructivist assessment. In *Constructivist assessment: A casebook* (pp. 1–30). Thousand Oaks, CA: SAGE Publications, Inc.

Neimeyer, R. A. (Ed.). (1994). *Death anxiety handbook: Research, instrumentation, and application*. New York, NY: Taylor and Francis Group.

Neimeyer, R. A. (1999). Narrative strategies in grief therapy. *Journal of Constructivist Psychology*, 12, 65–85. Retrieved from http://public.amie.sent.com/narrative%20strategies%20in%20grief%20therapy.pdf

Neimeyer, R. A. (2001a). The language of loss: Grief therapy as a process of meaning reconstruction. In R. A. Neimeyer (Ed.), *Meaning reconstruction and the experience of loss* (pp. 261–292). Washington, DC, US: American Psychological Association. http://dx.doi.org/10.1037/10397-014

Neimeyer, R. A. (Ed.) (2001b). *Meaning reconstruction and the experience of loss*. Washington, DC: American Psychological Association.

Neimeyer, R. A. (2009). *Constructivist psychotherapy: Distinctive features*. New York, NY: Routledge.

Neimeyer, R. A. (Ed.). (2012). *Techniques of grief therapy: Creative practices for counseling the bereaved*. New York, NY: Routledge.

Neimeyer, R. A. (2014). The narrative arc of tragic loss: Grief and the reconstruction of meaning. *International Journal of Existential Psychology & Psychotherapy, 5*(1), 27–32. Retrieved from http://journal.existentialpsychology.org/index.php/ExPsy/article/view/199/164

Newman, S., & Hatton-Yeo, A. (2008). Intergenerational Learning and the Contributions of Older People. *Ageing Horizons, 8*, 31–39.

Ng, K. S. (2003). *Global perspectives in family therapy*. New York, NY: Routledge.

Nichols, M. P., & Davis, S. (2017). *Family therapy: Concepts and methods* (11th ed.). Upper Saddle River, NJ: Pearson.

Nicholson, S. P., Coe, C. M., Emory, J., & Song, A. V. (2016). The politics of beauty: The effects of partisan bias on physical attractiveness. *Political Behavior, 38*(4), 883–898. https://doi.org/10.1007/s11109-016-9339-7

Nieuwboer, M., Perry, M., Sande, R. van der, Maassen, I., Rikkert, M., & Marck, M. V. der. (2017). It all comes down to trust; determinants for miscommunication in Primary Healthcare. *International Journal of Integrated Care, 17*(5), A127. https://doi.org/10.5334/ijic.3435

Nolte, L., Brown, R., Ferguson, S., & Sole, J. (2016). Creating ripples: Towards practice based evidence for narrative therapy within NHS contexts. *Clinical Psychology Forum, 284*, 48–52. Retrieved from http://uhra.herts.ac.uk/handle/2299/17452

Noriega, G. (2010). Transgenerational scripts: The unknown knowledge. In R. G. Erskine (Ed.), *Life scripts: A transactional analysis of unconscious relational patterns* (pp. 269–291). Finchley Road, London: Karnac Books Ltd.

O'Keeffe, G. S., & Clarke-Pearson, K. (2011). The impact of social media on children, adolescents, and families. *American Academy of Pediatrics, 127*(4). Retrieved from http://pediatrics.aappublications.org/content/pediatrics/127/4/800.full.pdf

O'Reilly, C. A., Doerr, B., & Chatman, J. A. (2018). "See You in Court": How CEO narcissism increases firms' vulnerability to lawsuits. *The Leadership Quarterly, 29*(3), 365–378.

Odum, E. P., & Barrett, G. W. (2005). *Fundamentals of ecology* (5th ed.). Belmont, CA: Thomson Brooks/Cole.

Olson, D. H. (2000). Circumplex model of marital and family systems. *Journal of Family Therapy, 22*, 144–167. Retrieved from https://onlinelibrary.wiley.com/doi/pdf/10.1111/1467-6427.00144

Olson, L. N., & Donahey, A (2018). Four horsemen of the apocalypse: A framework for the understanding of family conflict. In D. O. Braithwaite, E. A. Suter, & K. Floyd (Eds.), *Engaging theories in family communication: Multiple perspectives* (2nd ed., pp. 154–163). New York, NY: Routledge.

Overall, N. C. (2018). Attachment insecurity and power regulation in intimate relationships. *Current Opinion in Psychology, 25*, 53–58. https://doi.org/10.1016/j.copsyc.2018.03.004

Parkes, C. M. (1972). *Bereavement: studies of grief in adult life*. New York, NY: International Universities Press.

Patel, P., & Bail, M. (2017). The effects of celebrity attractiveness and identification on advertising interest. *Back to the future: Using marketing basics to provide customer value*, pp. 579–589. Retrieved from https://link.springer.com/chapter/10.1007/978-3-319-66023-3_193

Patterson, C. H. (1984). Empathy, warmth, and genuineness in psychotherapy: A review of reviews. *Psychotherapy: Theory, Research, Practice, Training, 21*(4), 431–438. http://dx.doi.org/10.1037/h0085985

Patterson, J. M. (1988). Families experiencing stress: I. The Family Adjustment and Adaptation Response Model: II. Applying the FAAR Model to health-related issues for intervention and research. *Family Systems Medicine, 6*(2), 202–237. http://dx.doi.org/10.1037/h0089739

Patterson, J. M. (2004). Integrating family resilience and family stress theory. *Journal of Marriage and Family, 64*(2). https://doi.org/10.1111/j.1741-3737.2002.00349.x

Patterson, J., Williams, L., Edwards, T. M., Charmow, L., & Grauf-Grounds, C. (2018). *Essential skills in family therapy: From the first interview to termination* (3rd ed.). New York, NY: The Guilford Press.

Patton, W., & McMahon, M. (2006). The systems theory framework of career development and counseling: Connecting theory and practice. *International Journal for the Advancement of Counseling, 28*(2), 153–166. Retrieved from https://eprints.qut.edu.au/2621/1/2621_1.pdf

Payne, M. (2006). *Narrative therapy: An introduction for counselors* (2nd ed.). Thousand Oaks, CA: SAGE Publications, Inc.

Pearce, S. M. (2017). *Museums, objects, and collections: A cultural study*. Great Britain: Leicester University Press. (Originally published 1992)

Pemberton, D. (2015, January 28). *Statistical definition of 'family' unchanged since 1930*. United States Census Bureau. Retrieved from https://www.census.gov/newsroom/blogs/random-samplings/2015/01/statistical-definition-of-family-unchanged-since-1930.html

Penn, P. (1982). Circular Questioning. *Family Process, 21*(3), 267–280. https://doi.org/10.1111/j.1545-5300.1982.00267.x

Perry, J. C. (2016). Maternal defense mechanisms influence infant development. *The American Journal of Psychiatry, 173*(2), 99–100. https://doi.org/10.1176/appi.ajp.2015.15111501

Petronio, S. (2016). Communication privacy management theory. In K. B. Jensen & R. Craig (Eds.), *The international encyclopedia of communication theory and philosophy* (pp. 1–9). London, UK: Wiley-Blackwell.

Petronio, S. (2018). Communication privacy management theory: Understanding families. In D. O. Braithwaite, E. A. Suter, & K. Floyd (Eds.), *Engaging theories in family communication: Multiple perspectives* (2nd ed., pp. 87–97). New York, NY: Routledge.

Petronio, S., & Venetis, M. K. (2017). Communication privacy management theory and health and risk messaging. *Oxford Research Encyclopedia of Communication*. https://dx.doi.org/10.1093/acrefore/9780190228613.013.513

Pew Research Center. (2015, December 17). *The American family today*. Retrieved from http://www.pewsocialtrends.org/2015/12/17/1-the-american-family-today

Piha, J., & Schmitt, F. (2016). Blind and mute family sculpting in the training of family therapists. In M. Borsca & P. Stratton (Eds.), *Origins and originality in family therapy and systemic practice* (pp. 169–186). Switzerland: Springer International Publishing. https://doi.org/10.1007/978-3-319-39061-1_11

Pipher, M. (1996). *The shelter of each other*. New York, NY: Ballantine Books.

Pogrebin, L. C. (1983). *Family politics: Love and power on an intimate frontier*. New York, NY: McGraw-Hill.

Polakoff, E. G. (2007). Globalization and child labor: Review of the issues. *Journal of Developing Societies, 23*(1-2), 259–283. https://doi.org/10.1177/0169796X0602300215

Polkinghorne, D. E. (2004). Narrative therapy and Postmodernism. In L. E. Angus & J. McLeod (Eds.), *The handbook of narrative and psychotherapy: Practice, theory, and research* (pp. 53–68). Thousand Oaks, CA: SAGE Publications, Inc.

Poonam, S. (2018). *Dreamers: How young Indians are changing the world*. Cambridge, MA: Harvard University Press.

Raj, K. (2016). Go-betweens, travelers, and cultural translators. In B. Lightman (Ed.), *A companion to the history of science* (pp. 39–57). Hoboken, NJ: John Wiley & Sons.

Rando, T. A. (1993). *Treatment of complicated mourning*. Champaign, IL: Research Press.

Rasheed, J. M., Rasheed, M. N., & Marley, J. A. (2010). *Family therapy: Models and techniques*. Thousand Oaks, CA: SAGE Publications, Inc.

Ray, C., Bishop, S. E., & Dow, A. W. (2018). Rethinking the match: A proposal for modern matchmaking. *Academic Medicine, 93*(1), 45–47. https://doi.org/10.1097/ACM.0000000000001781

Reese, C. (2018). *Attachment: 60 trauma-informed assessment and treatment interventions across the lifespan*. Eau Claire, WI: PESI, Inc.

Rice, T. R., & Hoffman, L. (2014). Defense mechanisms and implicit emotion regulation: A comparison of a psychodynamic construct with one from contemporary neuroscience, *Journal of the American Psychoanalytic Association, 62*(4), 693–708. https://doi.org/10.1177/0003065114546746

Richardson, T. (2002). *Sweets: A history of temptation.* Great Britain: Bantam Press.

Riggio, H. R. (2017). Emotional Expressiveness. In. V. Zeigler-Hill & T. Shackelford (Eds.), *Encyclopedia of personality and individual differences.* Cham, Switzerland: Springer.

Rizzolatti, G., & Sinigaglia, C. (2016). The mirror mechanism: A basic principle of brain function. *Nature Reviews Neuroscience, 17*(12), 757–765. https://doi.org/10.1038/nrn.2016.135

Rober, P., Walravens, G., & Versteynen, L. (2011). "In search of a tale they can live with": About loss, family secrets, and selective disclosure. *Journal of Marital and Family Therapy, 38*(3), 529–541. https://doi.org/10.1111/j.1752-0606.2011.00237.x

Roded, A. D., & Raviv, A. (2017). Self-censorship in the family: The double-edged sword of family secrets. In D. Bar-Tal, R. Nets-Zehngut, & K. Sharvit (Eds.), *Self-censorship in contexts of conflict: Theory and research* (pp. 19–40). Cham, Switzerland: Springer.

Rodkin, P. C. (2011). White House report: Bullying—and the power of peers. *Educational Leadership, 69*, 10–16.

Roehlkepartain, E. C. (2013). Children, religion, and spiritual development: Reframing a research agenda. In G. B. Melton, A. Ben-Arieh, J. Cashmore, G. S. Goodman, & N. K. Worley (Eds.), *The SAGE handbook of child research* (pp. 81–99). Thousand Oaks, CA: SAGE Publications, Inc.

Rogers, C. (1962). The interpersonal relationship: The core of guidance. *Harvard Educational Review, 32*(4). Retrieved from http://www.centerfortheperson.org/pdf/the-interpersonal-relationship.pdf

Romo, L. K. (2015). Family secrets. *The international encyclopedia of interpersonal communication.* https://doi.org/10.1002/9781118540190.wbeic218

Rosenau, J. N. (1990). *Turbulence in world politics: A theory of change and continuity.* Princeton, NJ: Princeton University Press.

Rosino, M. (2016). ABC-X model of family stress and coping. In *encyclopedia of family studies.* Hoboken, NJ: John Wiley & Sons. https://doi.org/10.1002/9781119085621.wbefs313

Rosman, B. L., Minuchin, S., & Liebman, R. (1975). Family lunch session: An introduction to family therapy in anorexia nervosa. *American Journal of Orthopsychiatry, 45*(5), 846–853. http://dx.doi.org/10.1111/j.1939-0025.1975.tb01212.x

Rueter, M. A., & Koerner, A. F. (2008). The effect of family communication patterns on adopted adolescent adjustment. *Journal of Marriage and the Family, 70*(3), 715–27. https://doi.org/10.1111/j.1741-3737.2008.00516.x

Rynearson, E. K. (2001). *Retelling violent death.* New York, NY: Routledge.

Samford University (2018). Things to know about: Jonathan Davis. *Inside Samford,* 14. Retrieved from https://www.samford.edu/departments/files/Marketing/winter-2018-inside-samford.pdf

San Francisco State University. (n.d.). *The family acceptance project.* Retrieved from https://familyproject.sfsu.edu

Sanagavarapu, P. (2010). What does cultural globalization mean for parenting in immigrant families in the 21st Century? *Australasian Journal of Early Childhood, 35*(2), 36–42.

Sanson, A. V., Letcher, P. L. C., & Havighurst, S. S. (2018). Child characteristics and their reciprocal effects on parenting. In M. R. Sanders & A. Morawska (Eds.), *Handbook of parenting and child development across the lifespan* (pp. 337–370). New York, NY: Springer.

Sarkis, S. M. (2018). *Gaslighting: Recognize manipulative and emotionally abusive people and break free.* New York, NY: Da Capo Press.

Schmidt, H., & Kunnig, K. (2015). Family Board: A new means for people with visual impairment to communicate inner pictures of social relations. *British Journal of Visual Impairment, 34*(1), 5–14. https://doi.org/10.1177%2F0264619615610157

Schofield, G. (1998). Inner and outer worlds: A psychosocial framework for child and family social work. *Child & Family Social Work, 3*(1), 57–67. https://doi.org/10.1046/j.1365-2206.1998.00062.x

Schueller, S. M. (2010). Preferences for positive psychology exercises. *The Journal of Positive Psychology, 5*(3), 193–203. https://doi.org/10.1080/17439761003790948

Sconfield, D. J., & Quackenbush, M. (2009). *After a loved one dies: How children grieve.* New York, NY: New York Life Foundation. https://www.aap.org/en-us/advocacy-and-policy/aap-health-initiatives/Children-and-Disasters/Documents/After-a-Loved-One-Dies-English.pdf

Seamons, N. P. (2018 Feb. 23). 'Educated' should be read with a grain of salt, says family's attorney. *The Preston Citizen.* Retrieved from https://www.hjnews.com/preston/news/educated-should-be-read-with-grain-of-salt-says-family/article_0583f217-6fd2-51de-a891-9ca32adb589c.html

Search Institute. (n.d.). *The developmental assets framework.* Retrieved from https://www.search-institute.org/our-research/development-assets/developmental-assets-framework

Search Institute. (2016). *The developmental relationships framework.* Retrieved from https://www.search-institute.org/dev-relationships-framework

SNAICC (Secretariat of National Aboriginal and Islander Child Care). (2011, December 15). *Growing up our way: Aboriginal and Torres Strait Islander child rearing practices matrix.* Retrieved from https://www.snaicc

.org.au/growing-up-our-way-aboriginal-and-torres-strait-islander-child-rearing-practices-matrix-2011-snaicc

Segrin, C., & Flora, J. (2011). *Family communication* (2nd ed.). New York, NY: Routledge.

Seligman, M. (2002). *Authentic happiness*. New York, NY: The Free Press.

Seligman, M., & Csikszentmihalyi, M. (2014). Positive psychology: An introduction. *Flow and the foundation of positive psychology*. https://doi.org/10.1007/978-94-017-9088-8_18

Seligman, M., & Royzman, E. (2003, July). Happiness. The three traditional theories. *Authentic Happiness* [newsletter]. Retrieved from https://www.authentichappiness.sas.upenn.edu/newsletters/authentichappiness/happiness

Settersten, R. A. (2018a). *Invitation to the life course: Toward new understandings of later life*. New York, NY: Routledge.

Settersten, R. A. (2018b). Nine ways that social relationships matter for the life course. In D. F. Alwin, D. H. Felmee, & D. A. Kreager (Eds.), *Social networks and the life course: Integrating the development of human lives and social relational network* (pp. 27–40). Cham, Switzerland: Springer International Publishing.

Sewell, A. (n.d.). This suspension bridge is made from grass. *National Geographic Travel*. Retrieved from https://www.nationalgeographic.com/travel/destinations/south-america/peru/inca-grass-rope-bridge-qeswachaka-unesco

Shamdasani, S. (2018). Towards transcultural histories of psychotherapies. *European Journal of Psychotherapy & Counselling*, *20*(1), 4–9. https://doi.org/10.1080/13642537.2018.1425111

Shannon, J. D., Baumwell, L. B., & Tamis-LeMonda, C. S. (2013). Transition to parenting within context. In M. A. Fine & F. D. Fincham (Eds.), *Handbook of family theories: A content-based approach* (pp. 249–262). New York, NY: Routledge.

Shapiro, D. A. (1969). Empathy, warmth, and genuineness in psychotherapy. *British Journal of Social and Clinical Psychology*, *8*(4), 350–361. https://doi.org/10.1111/j.2044-8260.1969.tb00627.x

Shariatmadari, D. (2019, May 22). Politeness costs nothing, but it may stop people understanding you. *The Guardian*. Retrieved from https://www.theguardian.com/lifeandstyle/2019/may/22/politeness-costs-nothing-but-it-may-stop-people-understanding-you?CMP=Share_iOSApp_Other

Shearman, S. M., & Dumleo, R. (2008). A cross-cultural comparison of family communication patterns and conflict between young adults and parents. *Journal of Family Communication*, *8*(3), 186–211. https://doi.org/10.1080/15267430802182456

Sheehan, N. W., & Petrovic, K. (2008). Grandparents and their adult grandchildren: Recurring themes from the literature. *Marriage and Family Review*, *44*, 99–124.

Shiraev, E. B., & Levy, D. A. (2016). *Cross-cultural psychology: Critical thinking and contemporary applications* (6th ed.). New York: Routledge.

Shoos, D. L. (2017). *Domestic violence in Hollywood film: Gaslighting*. Cham, Switzerland: Springer.

Short, S. E., & Goldberg, R. E. (2015). Children living with HIV-infected adults: Estimated for 23 countries in sub-Saharan Africa. *PLos One*. https://doi.org/10.1371/journal.pone.0142580

Silverstein, M., & Giarrusso, R. (2010). Aging and family life: A decade review. *Journal of Marriage and Family*, *72*(5), 1039–1058. https://doi.org/10.1111/j.1741-3737.2010.00749.x

Silverstein, M., Gans, G., Lowenstein, A., Giarrusso, R., & Bengston, V. L. (2010). Older parent-child relationships in six developed nations: Comparisons at the intersection of affection and conflict, *72*(4), 1006–1021. https://doi.org/10.1111/j.1741-3737.2010.00745.x

Simon, R. (2007, March–April). Ten most influential therapists of the past quarter-century. *Psychotherapy Networker*. Retrieved from https://www.psychotherapynetworker.org/magazine/article/661/the-top-10

Simpson, B. (2014). George Herbert Mead (1863–1931). In J. Helin, T. Hernes, D. Hjorth, & R. Holt (Eds.), *The Oxford handbook of process philosophy and organization studies* (pp. 272–287). Oxford, United Kingdom: Oxford University Press.

Simpson, J. A., Farrell, A. K., Oriña, M. M., & Rothman, A. J. (2015). Power and social influence in relationships. In M. Mikulincer, P. R. Shaver, J. A. Simpson, & J. F. Dovidio (Eds.), *APA handbook of personality and social psychology*, Vol. *3 Interpersonal relations* (pp. 393–420). Washington, DC, US: American Psychological Association. http://dx.doi.org/10.1037/14344-015

Smith, P. K. (2017). Introduction: The study of grandparenthood. In P. K. Smith (Ed.), *The psychology of grandparenthood: An international perspective*. Florence, KY: Taylor & Francis.

Smith, P. K., & Thompson, D. (2017). *Practical approaches to bullying*. New York, NY: Routledge. (Original work published 1991)

Smith, S. R., & Hamon, R. R. (2017). *Exploring family theories* (4th ed.). Oxford, UK: Oxford University Press.

Social Security Administration (n.d.). *Popular baby names in 2017* [Data file]. Retrieved from https://www.ssa.gov/cgi-bin/popularnames.cgi

Sorrels, J. P., & Myers, B. (1983). Comparison of group and family dynamics. *Human Relations*, *36*, 477–492. doi:10.1177/001872678303600505

Stearns, P. N. (2013). *The industrial revolution in world history* (4th ed.). Boulder, CO: Westview Press.

Steger, M. B. (2017). *Globalization: A very short introduction* (4th ed.). Oxford, UK: Oxford University Press.

Steinbach, A., Kopp, J., & Lazarevic, P. (2017). Divergent perceptions of intergenerational relationships: What implications, if any? *Journal of Family Studies*. https://doi.org/10.1080/13229400.2016.1269659

Stolnicu, A., & Hendrick, S. (2017). Toward satisfactory co-parenting after a marital breakdown. *Thérapie Familiale, 38*, 415–435. https://doi.org/10.3917/tf.174.0415

Straus, M. A., Gelles, R. J., & Steinmetz, S. K. (2006). *Behind closed doors: Violence in the American family*. New York, NY: Transaction Publishers.

Stroebe, M., & Schut, H. (1999). The dual process model of coping with bereavement: Rationale and description. *Death Studies, 23*(3), 197–224. https://doi.org/10.1080/074811899201046

Sullivan, H. S. (2011). *The interpersonal theory of psychiatry*. International behavioural and social sciences library. Abingdon, UK: Routledge. (Reprint of original work published 1955)

Sundow, D. (1967). *Passing on: The social organization of dying*. Upper Saddle River, NJ: Pearson.

Suter, E. A., & Seurer, L. M. (2018). Relational dialectics theory: Realizing the dialogic potential of family communication. In D. O. Braithwaite, E. A. Suter, & K. Floyd (Eds.), *Engaging theories in family communication: Multiple perspectives* (2nd ed., pp. 244–254). New York, NY: Routledge.

Swindoll, C. R. (1991). *The strong family: Growing wise in family life*. Portland, OR: Multnomah Press.

Szabo, S. (2016, June. 13). *Stress is 80 years old: Distress vs. eustress*. Summer School on Stress. Osijek, Croatia.

Szokolszky, A. (2016). Hungarian psychology in context. Reclaiming the past. *Hungarian Studies, 30*(1), 17–56.

Tardy, C. H., & Smithson, J. (2018). Self-disclosure: Strategic revelation of information in personal and professional relationships. In O. Hargie (Ed.), *The handbook of communication skills* (4th ed.). London, England: Routledge.

Taylor, C. A., Al-Hiyari, R., Lee, S. J., Priebe, A., Guerrero, L. W., & Bales, A. (2016). Beliefs and ideologies linked with approval of corporal punishment: A content analysis of online comments. *Health Education Research, 31*(4), 563–575. https://doi.org/10.1093/her/cyw029

Tenneson, J. (2002). *Wise women: A celebration of their insights, courage, and beauty*. Boston, MA: Little, Brown, and Co.

Thew, G. R., & Salkovskis, P. M. (2016). Hoarding among older people: An evaluative review. *The Cognitive Behaviour Therapist, 9*(e32). https://doi.org/10.1017/S1754470X16000180

Thibaut, J. W. (1959). *The social psychology of groups*. London, England: Forgotten Books.

Thomas, L. (2018). "Gaslight" and gaslighting. *The Lancet Psychiatry, 5*(2), 117–118. https://doi.org/10.1016/S2215-0366(18)30024-5

Thomas, P. A., Lui, H., & Umberson, D. (2017). Family relationships and well-being. *Innovation in Aging, 1*(3). https://doi.org/10.1093/geroni/igx025

Tilt, C. A. (2016). Corporate social responsibility research: The importance of context. *International Journal of Corporate Social Responsibility, 1*(2). Retrieved from https://link.springer.com/article/10.1186/s40991-016-0003-7

Titelman, P. (Ed.). (1998). *Clinical applications of Bowen family systems theory*. New York, NY: The Haworth Press.

Titelman, P. (Ed.). (2008). *Triangles: Bowen family systems theory perspectives*. New York, NY: The Haworth Press.

Tolstoy, L. (1877). *Anna Karenina*. Russia: The Russian Publisher.

Trask, B. S. (2010). *Globalization and families: Accelerated systemic social change* (pp. 21–38). New York, NY: Springer.

Trent, K., & Spitze, G. D. (2011). Growing up without siblings and adult sociability behaviors. *Journal of Family Issues, 32*(9), 1178–1204, https://doi.org/10.1177/0192513X11398945

Triandis, H. C. (1996). The psychological measurement of cultural syndromes. *American Psychologist, 51*(4), 407–415.

Trotman, A. D. (2017). *Relationship and power dynamics in women's same sex abusive couples*. (Dissertation). University of Rhode Island. South Kingstown, RI.

Tudge, J. R. H., Payir, A., Mercon-Vargas, E., Cao, H., Liang, Y., Li, J., & O'Brien, L. (2016). Still misused after all these years? A reevaluation of the uses of Bronfenbrenner's bioecological theory of human development. *Journal of Family Theory & Review, 8*(4). https://doi.org/10.1111/jftr.12165

Turner, R. H. (1970). *Family interaction*. New York, NY: John Wiley & Sons, Inc.

Tutu, D. M. (1999). *No future without forgiveness*. New York, NY: Random House, Inc.

UNESCO & UNICEF. (2015). *Fixing the broken promise of education for all: Findings from the global initiative on out-of-school children*. Retrieved from http://allinschool.org/wp-content/uploads/2015/05/oosci-global-report-en.pdf

Ungar, M. (Ed.). (2005). *Handbook for working with children and youth: Pathways to resilience across cultures and contexts*. Thousand Oaks, CA: Sage Publications.

Ungar, M. (2014). Practitioner review: Diagnosing childhood resilience—a systemic approach to the diagnosis of adaptation in adverse social and physical ecologies. *The*

Journal of Child Psychology and Psychiatry, 56(1), 4–17. https://doi.org/10.1111/jcpp.12306

UNICEF. (2017, December). *Child labour*. Retrieved from https://data.unicef.org/topic/child-protection/child-labour

United Nations General Assembly. (1959, November 20). *Declaration of the Rights of the Child*, A/RES/1386(XIV). Retrieved from https://www.ohchr.org/EN/Issues/Education/Training/Compilation/Pages/1DeclarationoftheRightsoftheChild(1959).aspx

United Nations General Assembly. (1989). *Convention on the Rights of the Child*. Retrieved from https://www.ohchr.org/en/professionalinterest/pages/crc.aspx

United States Census Bureau. (2015). Subject definitions. Retrieved from https://www.census.gov/programs-surveys/cps/technical-documentation/subject-definitions.html#family

United States Census Bureau. (2016). *Grandchildren under 18 years living with a grandparent householder by age of grandchild*. [Data file]. Retrieved from factfinder.census.gov/bkmk/table/1.0/en/ACS/16_1YR/B10001/0100000US

United States Census Bureau. (2017). *Median age at first marriage: 1890 to present* [Data file]. Retrieved from https://www.census.gov/content/dam/Census/library/visualizations/time-series/demo/families-and-households/ms-2.pdf

United States Census Bureau. (2019, February 11). *Current population survey (CPS)*. Retrieved from https://www.census.gov/programs-surveys/cps/technical-documentation/subject-definitions.html

Van der Kolk, B. (2014). *The body keeps the score*. New York, NY: Penguin Books.

van Wormer, K., & Davis, D. R. (2017). *Addiction treatment: A strengths perspective* (4th ed.). Boston, MA: Cengage Learning.

Veenhoven, R. (2015). Social conditions for human happiness: A review of research. *International Journal of Psychology, 50*(5), 379–391. https://doi.org/10.1002/ijop.12161

Vernon, A. (2005). *Quaker businessman: The life of Joseph Rowntree*. New York, NY: Taylor & Francis Group.

Vestal, C. (2018, August 16). Opioid overdose deaths rose in 2017 driven by Fentanyl. *Pew Stateline*. Retrieved from https://www.pewtrusts.org/en/research-and-analysis/blogs/stateline/2018/08/16/opioid-overdose-deaths-rose-in-2017-driven-by-fentanyl

Vetere, A., & Dowling, E. (Eds.). (2005). *Narrative therapies with children and their families: A practitioner's guide to concepts and approaches*. New York, NY: Routledge.

Vilaverde, D., Goncalves, J., & Morgado, P. (2017). Hoarding disorder: A case report. *Frontier in Psychiatry, 8*. https://doi.org/10.3389/fpsyt.2017.00112

Vincent, C., Young, M., & Phillips, A. (1994). Why do people sue doctors? A study of patients and relatives taking legal action. *Lancet, 343*(8913), 1609–1613.

von Ehrenfels, C. (1890). Über "Gestaltqualitäten". *Vierteljahrsschrift für wissenschaftliche Philosophie, 14*, 224–292. [Translated as "On 'Gestalt qualities.'" In B. Smith (Ed. & Trans.), (1988). *Foundations of Gestalt theory* (pp. 82–117). Munich, Germany/Vienna, Austria: Philosophia Verlag.]

Waasdrop, T. E., & Bradshaw, C. P. (2015). The overlap between cyberbullying and traditional bullying. *Journal of Adolescent Health, 56*, 483–488. http://dx.doi.org/10.1016/j.jadohealth.2014.12.002

Wachtel, E. F. (2001). The language of becoming: Helping children change how they think about themselves. *Family Process, 40*(4), 369–384. https://doi.org/10.1111/j.1545-5300.2001.4040100369.x

Walker, L. E. A. (1979). *The battered woman*. New York, NY: Harper & Row, Publishers, Inc.

Walker, L. E. A. (2016). *The battered woman syndrome* (4th ed.). New York, NY: Springer.

Walsh, F. (2016a). Family resilience: A developmental systems framework. *European Journal of Developmental Psychology, 13*(3), 1–12..

Walsh, F. (2016b). *Strengthening family resilience* (3rd ed.). New York, NY: The Guilford Press.

Ward, A. F. (2013). *One with the cloud: Why people mistake the internet's knowledge for their own* (Doctoral dissertation). Retrieved from https://dash.harvard.edu/handle/1/11004901

Ward, A. F. (2013). Supernormal: How the internet is changing our memories and our minds. *Psychological Inquiry, 24*(4), 341–48. https://doi.org/10.1080/1047840X.2013.850148

Ward, A. F., Duke, K., Gneezy, A., & Bos, M. W. (2017). Brain drain: The mere presence of one's own smartphone reduces available cognitive capacity. *Journal of the Association for Consumer Research, 2*(3), 140–54. https://doi.org/10.1086/691462

Ward, C., & Geeraert, N. (2016). Advancing acculturation theory and research: The acculturation process in its ecological context. *Current Opinion in Psychology, 8*, 98–104. https://doi.org/10.1016/j.copsyc.2015.09.021

Watkins, C. D. (2017). Creating beauty: Creativity compensates for low physical attractiveness when individuals assess the attractiveness of social and romantic partners. *Royal Society Open Science, 4*(4). https://doi.org/10.1098/rsos.160955

Watzlawick, P., Beavin, J. H., & Jackson, D. D. (1967). *Pragmatics of human communication: A study of interactional patterns, pathologies, and paradoxes*. New York, NY: W. W. Norton & Company.

We Are Family Science. (n.d.). Retrieved from http://family.science/where-we-work

Wedemeyer, N. V., & Grotevant, H. D. (1982). Mapping the family system: A technique for teaching Family Systems

Theory concepts. *Family Relations, 31*(2), 185–193. https://doi.org/10.2307/584396

Wegner, D. M., & Ward, A. F. (2013). How Google is changing your brain. *Scientific American, 309*(6), 58–61. Retrieved from https://www.scientificamerican.com/article/the-internet-has-become-the-external-hard-drive-for-our-memories

Weiser, J. (2018). *Phototherapy techniques: Exploring the secrets of personal snapshots and family albums.* New York, NY: Routledge.

Wenze, S. J., Battle, C. J., & Tezanos, K. M. (2015). Raising multiples: Mental health of mothers and fathers in early parenthood. *Archives of Women's Mental Health, 18*(2), 163–176. https://doi.org/10.1007/s00737-014-0484-x

Wertheimer, M. (1912). Experimentelle Studien über das Sehen von Bewegung. *Zeitschrift für Psychologie, 61,* 161–265. [Translated as "Experimental studies on seeing motion." In L. Spillmann (Ed.), (2012). *On motion and figure-ground organization* (pp. 1-91). Cambridge, MA: M.I.T. Press.]

White, J., Klein, J., & Todd, M. (2014). *Family theories* (4th ed.). Thousand Oaks, CA: SAGE Publications.

White, M. (2007). *Maps of narrative practice.* New York, NY:: W. W. Norton & Company.

White, M., & Epston, D. (1990). *Narrative means to therapeutic ends.* New York, NY: W. W. Norton & Company.

Whitebook, J. (2017). *Freud: An intellectual biography.* Cambridge, United Kingdom: Cambridge University Press.

Widmer, E. D. (2010). *Family configurations.* London, England: Routledge.

Willis, A., Bondi, L., Burgess, M., Miller, G., & Fergusson, D. (2014). Engaging with a history of counselling, spirituality and faith in Scotland: A readers' theatre script. *British Journal of Guidance & Counselling, 42*(5), 525–543. https://doi.org/10.1080/03069885.2014.928667

Willison, G. (1969). *Schizophrenia: Seven approaches.* New York, NY: Routledge.

Wisely, D. (2016, March). The many ways to say "sorry" in Japanese. *Drunk Monkeys, 1*(1). Retrieved from http://www.drunkmonkeys.us/poetry/the-many-ways-to-say-sorry-dale-wisely

Wisely, D. (2016, February 11) The language of winter and love, *Truck.* Retrieved from https://halvard-johnson.blogspot.com/2016/02/dale-wisely.html

Wohlleben, P. *The hidden life of trees.* Vancouver, BC: Greystone Books.

Wolfelt, A. (2010). *Understanding and responding to complicated mourning.* (Unpublished outline and handout). Community Grief Support Conference, Birmingham, AL.

Wolke, D., & Lereya, S. T. (2015). Long-term effects of bullying. *Archives of Disease in Childhood, 100*(9), 879–885. http://dx.doi.org/10.1136/archdischild-2014-306667

Wong, P. T. P. (2011). Positive psychology 2.0: Towards a balanced interactive model of the good life. *Canadian Psychology/Psychologie canadienne, 52*(2), 69–81. http://dx.doi.org/10.1037/a0022511

Wood, B. (1985). Proximity and hierarchy: Orthogonal dimensions of family interconnectedness. *Family Process, 24*(4), 487–507. https://doi.org/10.1111/j.1545-5300.1985.00487.x

Worden, J. W. (2008). *Grief counseling and grief therapy: A handbook for the mental health practitioner.* (4th ed.). New York, NY: Springer Publishing Company.

Yamamoto, H. (1998). Seventeen syllables. In *Seventeen syllables and other stories* (pp. 8–19). New Brunswick, NJ: Rutgers University Press. (Original work published in 1988)

Yehuda, R., & Bierer, L. M. (2009). The relevance of epigenetics to PTSD: implications for the DSM-V. *Journal of Trauma Stress, 22,* 427–434.

Yehuda, R., Daskalakis, N. P., Bierer, L. M., Bader, H. N., Klengel, T., Holsboer, F., & Binder, E. B. (2016). Holocaust exposure induced intergenerational effects on FKBP5 Methylation. *Biological Psychiatry, 80*(1), 372–380. https://doi.org/10.1016/j.biopsych.2015.08.005

Yu, W-H., & Hertog, E. (2018). Family characteristics and mate selection: Evidence from computer-assisted dating in Japan. *Journal of Marriage and Family, 80,* 589–606. https://doi.org/10.1111/jomf.12473

Zanjari, N., Sani, M. S., Chavoshi, M. H., Rafiey, H., & Shahboulaghi, F. M. (2017). Successful aging as a multidimensional concept: An integrative review. *Medical Journal of the Islamic Republic of Iran, 31*(100). https://doi.org/10.14196/mjiri.31.100

Zenger, J., & Folkman, J. (2013, March 15). The ideal praise-to-criticism ratio. *Harvard Business Review.* Retrieved from https://hbr.org/2013/03/the-ideal-praise-to-criticism.

Zerach, G., Kanat-Maymon, Y., Aloni, R., & Solomon, Z. (2016). The role of fathers' psychopathology in the intergenerational transmission of captivity trauma: A twenty three-year longitudinal study. *Journal of Affective Disorders, 190*(15), 84–92. https://doi.org/10.1016/j.jad.2015.09.072

Zhang, J. (2017). The evolution of China's one-child policy and its effects on family outcomes. *Journal of Economic Perspectives, 31*(1), 141–160. Retrieved from https://pubs.aeaweb.org/doi/pdfplus/10.1257/jep.31.1.141

Zhang, Q. (2007). Family communication patterns and conflict styles in Chinese parent-child relationships. *Communication Quarterly, 55*(1), 113–28. https://doi.org/10.1080/01463370600998681

Zimmerman, R. D. (2017). *End-of-life education: Experiences of respiratory therapists: Implications for university leadership* (Doctoral dissertation, Tift College of Education at Mercer University, Atlanta, Georgia). Retrieved from https://pdfs.semanticscholar.org/3bff/3a1dd93e035ece20221218ae226d750f4549.pdf

Index